CLYMER® MANUALS

YAMAHA

RAPTOR 700R • 2006-2016

More information available at Clymer.com
Phone: 805-498-6703

Haynes Publishing Group
Sparkford Nr Yeovil
Somerset BA22 7JJ England

Haynes North America, Inc
859 Lawrence Drive
Newbury Park
California 91320 USA

ISBN-10: 1-62092-273-8
ISBN-13: 978-1-62092-273-6
Library of Congress: 2016955151

Author: *2010 through 2016 information by Ed Scott*
Technical Illustrations: *Mitzi McCarthy*
Cover: *Mark Clifford Photography at www.markclifford.com*

Printed in Malaysia

M290, 11U1, 16-344 **ABCDEFGHIJKLMNOPQRS**

Chapter One
General Information

1

Chapter Two
Troubleshooting

2

Chapter Three
Lubrication, Maintenance and Tune-up

3

Chapter Four
Engine Top End

4

Chapter Five
Engine Lower End

5

Chapter Six
Clutch and External Shift Mechanism

6

Chapter Seven
Transmission and Internal Shift Mechanism

7

Chapter Eight
Fuel Injection System

8

Chapter Nine
Electrical System

9

Chapter Ten
Cooling System

10

Chapter Eleven
Wheels,Tires and Drive Chain

11

Chapter Twelve
Front Suspension and Steering

12

Chapter Thirteen
Rear Axle and Suspension

13

Chapter Fourteen
Brakes

14

Chapter Fifteen
Body

15

Index

16

Wiring Diagrams

17

Common spark plug conditions

NORMAL

Symptoms: Brown to grayish-tan color and slight electrode wear. Correct heat range for engine and operating conditions.
Recommendation: When new spark plugs are installed, replace with plugs of the same heat range.

WORN

Symptoms: Rounded electrodes with a small amount of deposits on the firing end. Normal color. Causes hard starting in damp or cold weather and poor fuel economy.
Recommendation: Plugs have been left in the engine too long. Replace with new plugs of the same heat range. Follow the recommended maintenance schedule.

CARBON DEPOSITS

Symptoms: Dry sooty deposits indicate a rich mixture or weak ignition. Causes misfiring, hard starting and hesitation.
Recommendation: Make sure the plug has the correct heat range. Check for a clogged air filter or problem in the fuel system or engine management system. Also check for ignition system problems.

ASH DEPOSITS

Symptoms: Light brown deposits encrusted on the side or center electrodes or both. Derived from oil and/ or fuel additives. Excessive amounts may mask the spark, causing misfiring and hesitation during acceleration.
Recommendation: If excessive deposits accumulate over a short time or low mileage, install new valve guide seals to prevent seepage of oil into the combustion chambers. Also try changing gasoline brands.

OIL DEPOSITS

Symptoms: Oily coating caused by poor oil control. Oil is leaking past worn valve guides or piston rings into the combustion chamber. Causes hard starting, misfiring and hesitation.
Recommendation: Correct the mechanical condition with necessary repairs and install new plugs.

GAP BRIDGING

Symptoms: Combustion deposits lodge between the electrodes. Heavy deposits accumulate and bridge the electrode gap. The plug ceases to fire, resulting in a dead cylinder.
Recommendation: Locate the faulty plug and remove the deposits from between the electrodes.

TOO HOT

Symptoms: Blistered, white insulator, eroded electrode and absence of deposits. Results in shortened plug life.
Recommendation: Check for the correct plug heat range, over-advanced ignition timing, lean fuel mixture, intake manifold vacuum leaks, sticking valves and insufficient engine cooling.

PREIGNITION

Symptoms: Melted electrodes. Insulators are white, but may be dirty due to misfiring or flying debris in the combustion chamber. Can lead to engine damage.
Recommendation: Check for the correct plug heat range, over-advanced ignition timing, lean fuel mixture, insufficient engine cooling and lack of lubrication.

HIGH SPEED GLAZING

Symptoms: Insulator has yellowish, glazed appearance. Indicates that combustion chamber temperatures have risen suddenly during hard acceleration. Normal deposits melt to form a conductive coating. Causes misfiring at high speeds.
Recommendation: Install new plugs. Consider using a colder plug if driving habits warrant.

DETONATION

Symptoms: Insulators may be cracked or chipped. Improper gap setting techniques can also result in a fractured insulator tip. Can lead to piston damage.
Recommendation: Make sure the fuel anti-knock values meet engine requirements. Use care when setting the gaps on new plugs. Avoid lugging the engine.

MECHANICAL DAMAGE

Symptoms: May be caused by a foreign object in the combustion chamber or the piston striking an incorrect reach (too long) plug. Causes a dead cylinder and could result in piston damage.
Recommendation: Repair the mechanical damage. Remove the foreign object from the engine and/or install the correct reach plug.

CONTENTS

QUICK REFERENCE DATA IX

CHAPTER ONE
GENERAL INFORMATION 1

Manual organization
Warnings, cautions and notes
Safety
Serial numbers and information labels
Fasteners
Shop supplies
Tools
Measuring tools
Electrical system fundamentals
Service methods
Storage
Specifications

CHAPTER TWO
TROUBLESHOOTING 29

Starting the engine
Engine does not start
Engine performance
Electronic diagnostic system
Engine noise
Engine leakdown test
Clutch
Transmission
External shift mechanism
Electrical testing
Engine starting system
Brakes
Steering and handling
Specifications

CHAPTER THREE
LUBRICATION, MAINTENANCE AND TUNE-UP 54

Pre-ride inspection
Tune-up
Engine oil
Air filter
Control cable inspection and lubrication
Throttle cable and speed limiter adjustment
Clutch lever
Reverse cable
Brakes
Drive chain
Tires and wheels
Front wheel bearing inspection
Steering system
Front suspension
Rear suspension
Battery
Cooling system
Fuel injection
Crankcase breather hoses
Spark plug
Ignition timing
Compression test
Valve clearance adjustment
Exhaust system
Fasteners
Specifications

CHAPTER FOUR
ENGINE TOP END 89

Exhaust system
Air induction system (2015-on models)
Cylinder head
Camshaft and rocker arms
Cam chain and guide
Valves
Cylinder
Piston and piston rings
Specifications

CHAPTER FIVE
ENGINE LOWER END 122

Servicing engine in frame
Engine
Left crankcase cover
Torque limiter
Starter idle gear
Flywheel (alternator rotor) and starter clutch
Camshaft chain and guides
Right crankcase cover
Oil pump
Crankshaft and balancer drive gears
Crankcase
Crankcase seal and bearing replacement
Crankshaft
Engine break-in
Specifications

CHAPTER SIX
CLUTCH AND EXTERNAL SHIFT MECHANISM 149

Clutch
Clutch release lever assembly
External shift mechanism
Reverse shift lever
Clutch cable
Reverse cable
Specifications

CHAPTER SEVEN
TRANSMISSION AND INTERNAL SHIFT MECHANISM 164

Transmission service
Transmission and internal shift mechanism
Mainshaft
Countershaft
Reverse countershaft
Transmission inspection
Shift drum and forks
Specifications

CHAPTER EIGHT
FUEL INJECTION SYSTEM 178

Fuel injection (FI)
Fuel delivery system tests
Fuel tank
Fuel tank plate
Fuel pump
Fuel pump relay
Throttle body
Fuel injector
ECU
Throttle position sensor
Intake air pressure sensor
Intake air temperature sensor
Coolant temperature sensor
Crankshaft position sensor
Speed sensor
Lean-angle sensor
Air box
Throttle cable replacement
Specifications

CHAPTER NINE
ELECTRICAL SYSTEM. 197

Electrical component replacement
Continuity testing
Electrical connectors
Negative battery terminal
Battery
Charging system
Alternator
Ignition system
Starter
Starting circuit cutoff system
Starter relay
Lights
Cooling system
Crankshaft position sensor
Switches
Fuses
Fuse box
Wiring diagrams
Specifications

CHAPTER TEN
COOLING SYSTEM. 221

Cooling system precautions/inspection
Cooling system pressure test
Hoses and hose clamps
Thermostat
Radiator
Coolant reservoir
Radiator fan
Coolant temperature sensor
Water pump
Specifications

CHAPTER ELEVEN
WHEELS, TIRES AND DRIVE CHAIN 231

Wheel
Tires
Sprockets
Drive chain
Specifications

CHAPTER TWELVE
FRONT SUSPENSION AND STEERING. 240

Handlebar
Shock absorbers
Front wheel hub
Tie rods
Steering knuckle
Control arms
Steering shaft
Specifications

CHAPTER THIRTEEN
REAR AXLE AND SUSPENSION 257

Wheel hub
Rear axle
Rear axle hub
Shock absorber
Shock linkage
Swing arm
Specifications

CHAPTER FOURTEEN
BRAKES 273

Brake fluid selection
Brake service
Front brake pads
Front brake caliper
Front master cylinder
Rear brake pads
Rear brake caliper
Rear master cylinder
Rear brake pedal
Brake disc
Front brake hose/line replacement
Rear brake hose replacement
Brake system draining
Brake bleeding
Specifications

CHAPTER FIFTEEN
BODY 309

Plastic screw fasteners
Retaining tabs
Seat
Front fender panel
Fuel tank cover
Front fender
Front grille
Handlebar cover
Rear lower cover
Rear fender
Rear guard
Oil tank
Foot protectors
Right footrest
Left footrest
Engine skidplate
Swing arm skidplate
Specifications

INDEX 317

WIRING DIAGRAMS 323

QUICK REFERENCE DATA

ATV INFORMATION

MODEL:______________________________ YEAR: ______________
VIN NUMBER:____
ENGINE SERIAL NUMBER:____________________________________

TIRE INFLATION PRESSURE

	psi (kPa)
Maximum	
Front	4.0 (27.5)
Rear	4.0 (27.5)
Minimum	
Front	3.6 (24.5)
Rear	3.6 (24.5)

RECOMMENDED LUBRICANTS, FLUIDS AND CAPACITIES

Brake fluid	DOT 4
Cooling system	
Coolant type	High quality ethylene-glycol*
Coolant capacity (2006-2012 models)	
Radiator and engine	1.61 L (1.70 US qt.)
Reservoir	0.25 L (0.26 US qt.)
Coolant capacity (2013-on models)	
Radiator and engine	1.68 L (1.78 US qt.)
Reservoir	0.25 L (0.26 US qt.)
Drive chain	Chain lubricant suitable for O-ring type chains or engine oil
Engine oil	
Grade	Yamalube 4, API SG (non-friction modified)
Viscosity	Refer to text
Capacity	
Oil change only	1.75 L (1.85 US qt.)
Oil and filter change	1.85 L (1.96 US qt.)
After disassembly (engine dry)	2.30 L (2.43 US qt.)
Fuel	
Type	Unleaded
Octane	Pump octane of 86 or higher
Fuel tank	
Capacity, including reserve	11.0 L (2.9 U.S. gal.)
Reserve only	
2006-2012 models	2.6 L (0.70 U.S. gal.)
2013-on models	2.9 L (0.77 U.S. gal.)

*Coolant must not contain silicate inhibitors as they can cause premature wear to the water pump seals. See text for further information

MAINTENANCE AND TUNE-UP SPECIFICATIONS

Brake pad wear limit	1.0 mm (0.04 in.)
Brake pedal height (below footrest)	15.3 mm (0.60 in.)
Clutch lever free play	5-10 mm (0.98-1.38 in.)
Drive chain free play	25-35 mm (0.98-1.38 in.)
Idle Speed	1500-1700 rpm
Parking brake cable length	
2006-2012 models	58-60 mm (2.28-2.36 in.)
2013-on models	47-51 mm (1.85-2.01 in.)
Reverse cable length	33 mm (1.30 in.)
Radiator cap pressure relief	93.3-122.7 kPa (13.3-17.4 psi)
Spark plug	
Type	CR8E (NGK)
Plug gap	0.7-0.8 mm (0.028-0.031 in.)
Throttle lever free play	2-4 mm (0.08-0.16 in.)
Throttle speed limiter	Less than 12 mm(0.47 in.)
Tire inflation pressure	4.0 psi (27.5 kPa)
Tire tread knob height (min.)	3 mm (0.12 in.)
Valve clearance (cold)	
Intake	0.09-0.13 mm (0.0035-0.0051 in.)
Exhaust	0.16-0.20 mm (0.0063-0.0079 in.)

DRIVE CHAIN SPECIFICATIONS

Drive chain	
Manufacturer	Daido
Type	
2006-2014 models	520MXV
2015-on models	520VP2-T
Number of link	98
Drive chain slack	25-35 mm (0.98-1.38 in.)
Drive chain 15 link length limit	239.3 mm (9.42 in.)
Sprocket sizes	
Drive (front)	14 teeth
Driven (rear)	38 teeth

MAINTENANCE TORQUE SPECIFICATIONS

Item	N•m	in.-lb.	ft.-lb.
Air bleed bolt	10	89	–
Axle hub pinch bolts	21	186	–
Camshaft sprocket cover bolts	10	88	–
Coolant drain bolt	10	88	–
Crankcase oil drain bolt	23	–	17
Drive sprocket nut	85	–	61
Driven sprocket nuts	72	–	53
Exhaust purge bolt	27	–	20
Flywheel nut plug			
2006-2012 models	10	89	–
2013-on models	2	1.4	–
Front shock absorber spring locknut	42	–	31
Oil filter cover bolts	10	89	–
Oil filter drain bolt	10	89	–
Oil gallery bolt	10	89	–
Oil tank drain bolt	19	168	–
Rear shock absorber spring locknut	42	–	30
Rocker cover bolts	10	89	–
Spark arrester bolt	8	71	–
Spark plug	13	115	–
Valve adjuster locknut	14	124	–
Wheel lug nuts	45	–	33

NOTES

NOTES

MAINTENANCE LOG

Date	Miles	Type of Service

MAINTENANCE LOG

Date	Miles	Type of Service

CHAPTER ONE

GENERAL INFORMATION

This detailed and comprehensive manual covers all 2006-on Yamaha Raptor 700R models. There are slight variations on the different models and years relating to the graphic designs on the body panels. All other variations are covered in the respective chapters.

The text provides complete information on maintenance, tune-up, repair and overhaul. Hundreds of photos and drawings guide the reader through every job. All procedures are in a step-by-step format and designed for the reader who may be working on the ATV for the first time.

MANUAL ORGANIZATION

A shop manual is a reference tool and, as in all Clymer manuals, the chapters are thumb-tabbed for easy reference. Important items are indexed at the end of the manual. Frequently-used specifications and capacities from individual chapters are summarized in the *Quick Reference Data* at the front of the manual.

During some of the procedures there will be references to headings in other chapters or sections of the manual. When a specific heading is called out in a step, it is *italicized* as it appears in the manual. If a sub-heading is indicated as being "in this section", it is located within the same main heading. For example, the sub-heading *Handling Gasoline Safely* is located within the main heading *SAFETY*.

This chapter provides general information on shop safety, tool use, service fundamentals and shop supplies. **Tables 1-7** at the end of the chapter provide general vehicle, mechanical and shop information.

Chapter Two provides methods for quick and accurate diagnoses of problems. Troubleshooting procedures present typical symptoms and logical methods to pinpoint and repair a problem.

Chapter Three explains all routine maintenance.

Subsequent chapters describe specific systems, such as engine, clutch, transmission, fuel system, electrical system, wheels, tires, drive chain, suspension, brakes and body components.

Specifications, when applicable, are located at the end of each chapter.

WARNINGS, CAUTIONS AND NOTES

WARNING, CAUTION and NOTE have specific meanings in this manual.

A WARNING emphasizes areas where injury or even death could result from negligence. Mechanical damage may also occur. WARNINGS *are to be taken seriously*.

A CAUTION emphasizes areas where equipment damage could result. Disregarding a CAUTION could cause permanent mechanical damage, though injury is unlikely.

A NOTE provides additional information to make a step or procedure easier or clearer. Disregarding a NOTE could cause inconvenience, but would not cause equipment damage or injury.

SAFETY

Follow these guidelines and practice common sense to safely service the ATV:

1. Do not operate the ATV in an enclosed area. The exhaust gases contain carbon monoxide, an odorless, colorless and tasteless poisonous gas. Carbon monoxide levels build quickly in small enclosed areas and can cause unconsciousness and death in a short time. Make sure the work area is properly ventilated, or operate the ATV outside.
2. *Never* use gasoline or any flammable liquid to clean parts. Refer to *Handling Gasoline Safely* and *Cleaning Parts* in this section.
3. *Never* smoke or use a torch in the vicinity of flammable liquids, such as gasoline or cleaning solvent.
4. Do not remove the radiator cap or any cooling system hose(s) while the engine is hot. The cooling system is pressurized and the high temperature coolant may cause injury.
5. Dispose of and store coolant in a safe manner. Do not allow children or pets access to open containers of coolant. Animals are attracted to antifreeze.
6. Avoid contact with engine oil and other chemicals. Most are known carcinogens. Wash your hands thoroughly after coming in contact with engine oil. If possible, wear a pair of disposable gloves.
7. If welding or brazing on the ATV, remove the fuel tank and shocks to a safe distance at least 15 m (50 ft.) away.
8. Use the correct types and sizes of tools to avoid damaging fasteners.
9. Keep tools clean and in good condition. Replace or repair worn or damaged equipment.
10. When loosening a tight fastener, be guided by what would happen if the tool slips.
11. When replacing fasteners, make sure the new fasteners are the same size and strength as the originals.
12. Keep the work area clean and organized.
13. Wear eye protection *any time* the safety of your eyes is in question. This includes procedures involving drilling, grinding, hammering, compressed air and chemicals.
14. Wear the correct clothing for the job. Tie up or cover long hair so it can not catch in moving equipment.
15. Do not carry sharp tools in clothing pockets.
16. Always have an approved fire extinguisher available. Make sure it is rated for gasoline (Class B) and electrical (Class C) fires.
17. Do not use compressed air to clean clothes, the ATV or the work area. Debris may be blown into the eyes or skin. *Never* point compressed air at someone. Do not allow children to use or play with any compressed air equipment.
18. When using compressed air to dry rotating parts, hold the part so it cannot rotate. Do not allow the force of the air to spin the part. The air jet is capable of rotating parts at extreme speeds. The part may be damaged or disintegrate, causing serious injury.
19. Do not inhale the dust created by brake pad and clutch wear. These particles may contain asbestos. In addition, some types of insulating materials and gaskets may contain asbestos. Inhaling asbestos particles is hazardous to health.
20. Never work on the ATV while someone is working under it.
21. When placing the ATV on a stand or overhead lift, make sure it is secure before walking away.

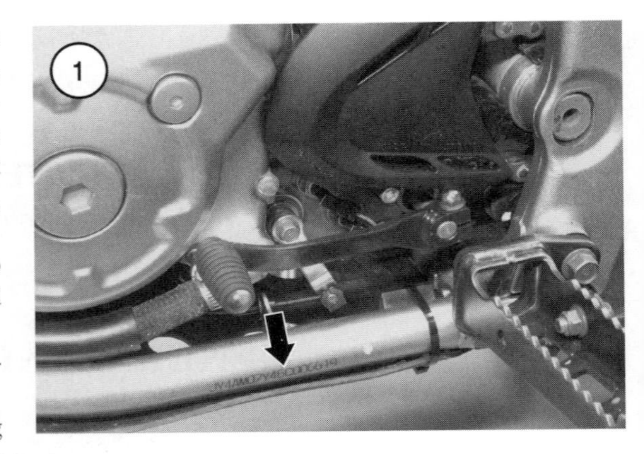

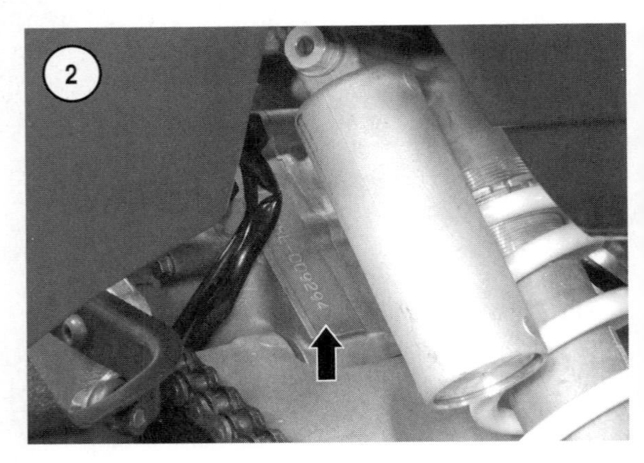

Handling Gasoline Safely

Gasoline is a volatile, flammable liquid and is one of the most dangerous items in the shop. Because gasoline is used so often, many people forget that it is hazardous. Only use gasoline as fuel for internal combustion gas engines. Keep in mind when working on an ATV, gasoline is always present in the fuel tank, fuel line and fuel body. To avoid an accident when working around the fuel system, carefully observe the following precautions:
1. *Never* use gasoline to clean parts. Refer to *Cleaning Parts* in this section.
2. When working on the fuel system, work outside or in a well-ventilated area.

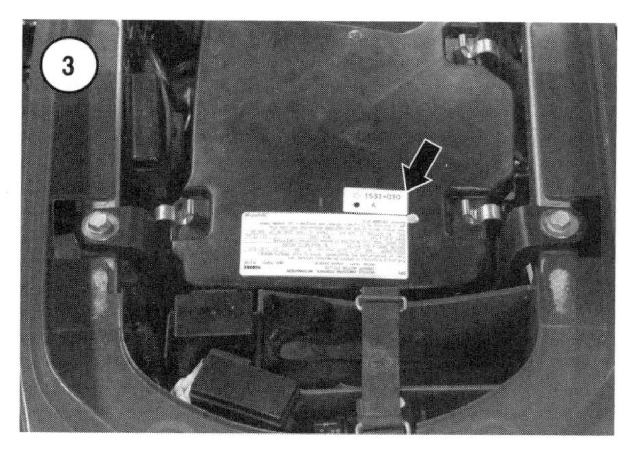

3. Do not add fuel to the fuel tank or service the fuel system while the ATV is near open flames, sparks or where someone is smoking. Gasoline vapor is heavier than air, collects in low areas and is more easily ignited than liquid gasoline.
4. Allow the engine to cool completely before working on any fuel system component.
5. Do not store gasoline in glass containers. If the glass breaks, an explosion or fire may occur.
6. Immediately wipe up spilled gasoline with rags. Store the rags in a metal container with a lid until they can be properly disposed, or place them outside in a safe place for the fuel to evaporate.
7. Do not pour water onto a gasoline fire. Water spreads the fire and makes it difficult to put out. Use a class B, BC or ABC fire extinguisher to extinguish the fire.
8. Always turn off the engine before refueling. Do not spill fuel onto the engine or exhaust system. Do not overfill the fuel tank. Leave an air space at the top of the tank to allow room for the fuel to expand due to temperature fluctuations.

Cleaning Parts

Many types of chemical cleaners and solvents are available for shop use. Most are poisonous and extremely flammable. Note the following:

1. Read and observe the entire product label before using any chemical. Always know what type of chemical is being used and whether it is poisonous and/or flammable.
2. Do not use more than one type of cleaning solvent at a time. If mixing chemicals is required, measure the proper amounts according to the manufacturer.
3. Work in a well-ventilated area.
4. Wear chemical-resistant gloves.
5. Wear safety glasses.
6. Wear a vapor respirator if necessary.
7. Wash hands and arms thoroughly after cleaning parts.
8. Keep chemicals away from children and pets, especially coolant. Animals are attracted to antifreeze.
9. Thoroughly clean all oil, grease and cleaner residue from any part that must be heated.
10. Use a nylon brush when cleaning parts. Metal brushes may cause a spark.
11. When using a parts washer, only use the solvent recommended by the manufacturer. Make sure the parts washer is equipped with a metal lid that will lower in case of fire.

Warning Labels

Most manufacturers attach information and warning labels to the ATV. These labels contain instructions that are important to safety when operating, servicing, transporting and storing the ATV Refer to the owner's manual for the description and location of labels. Order replacement labels from the manufacturer if they are missing or damaged.

SERIAL NUMBERS AND INFORMATION LABELS

Serial numbers are stamped at various locations on the frame, engine and carburetor. Record these numbers in the *Quick Reference Data* section in the front of this manual. Have these numbers available when ordering parts.

The VIN number (**Figure 1**) is located on the left side of the frame, beneath the engine.

The engine serial number (**Figure 2**) is stamped on a pad at the rear of the engine.

The vehicle model designation is noted on a label (**Figure 3**) attached to the air box.

A label (**Figure 4**) specifying tire pressure is affixed to the rear fender.

Record the key number (**Figure 5**) so it can be replaced if lost.

FASTENERS

WARNING
Do not install fasteners with a strength classification lower than what was originally installed by the manufacturer. Doing so may cause equipment failure and/or damage.

Proper fastener selection and installation is important to ensure the ATV operates as designed and can be serviced efficiently. The choice of original equipment fasteners is carefully calculated. Make sure all replacement fasteners meet the same requirements.

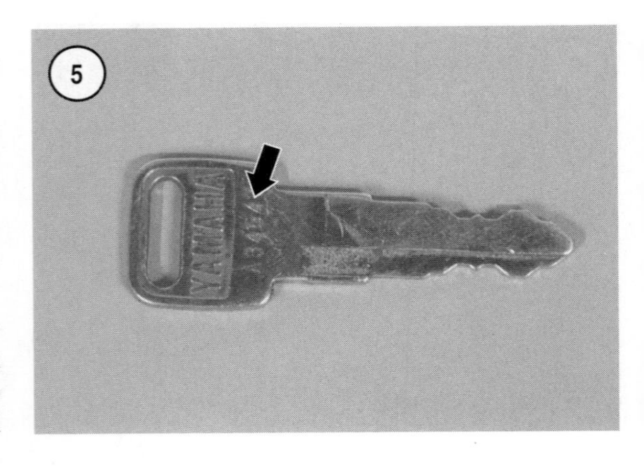

Threaded Fasteners

Threaded fasteners secure most of the components on the ATV. Most are tightened by turning them clockwise (right-hand threads). If the normal rotation of the component being tightened would loosen the fastener, it may have left-hand threads. If a left-hand threaded fastener is used, it is noted in the text.

Two dimensions are required to match the thread size of the fastener: the number of threads in a given distance and the outside diameter of the threads.

Identify threaded fastener dimensions by either the U.S. Standard system or the metric system (**Figure 6**). Pay particular attention when working with unidentified fasteners; mismatching thread types can damage threads.

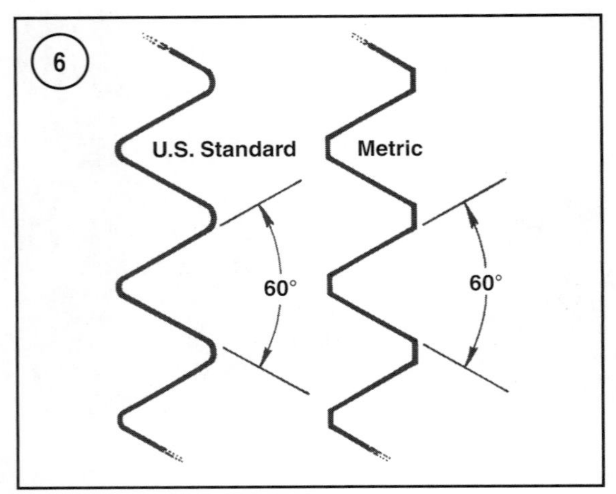

To ensure the fastener threads are not mismatched or cross-threaded, start all fasteners by hand. If a fastener is difficult to start or turn, determine the cause before tightening with a wrench.

Match fasteners by their length (L, **Figure 7**), diameter (D) and pitch (T), or the distance between thread crests. A typical metric bolt may be identified by the numbers, 8—1.25 × 130. This indicates the bolt has a diameter of 8 mm, the distance between thread crests is 1.25 mm and the length is 130 mm. Always measure bolt length as shown in L, **Figure 7** to avoid installing replacements of the wrong lengths.

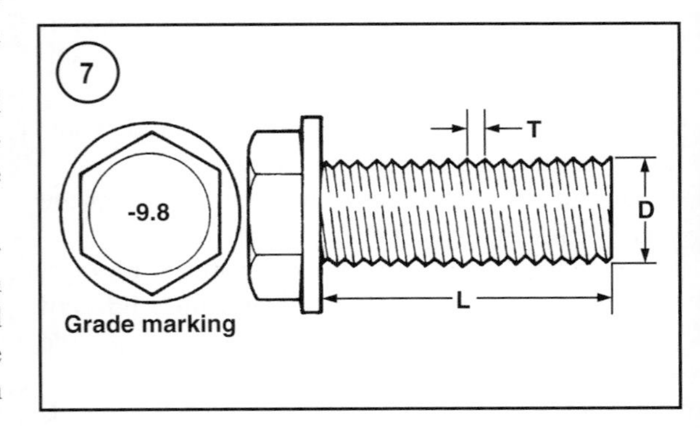

If a number is located on the top of a metric fastener (**Figure 7**), this indicates the strength. Higher numbered fasteners are stronger. Typically, unnumbered fasteners are the weakest.

Many screws, bolts and studs are combined with nuts to secure particular components. To indicate the size of a nut, manufacturers specify the internal diameter and thread pitch.

The measurement across two flats on a nut or bolt indicates the wrench size.

Torque Specifications

The materials used in the manufacture of the ATV may be subjected to uneven stresses if fasteners are not installed and tightened correctly. Improperly installed fasteners or ones that worked loose can cause extensive damage. It is essential to use an accurate torque wrench, as described in this chapter, with the torque specifications in this manual.

Specifications for torque are provided in Newton-meters (N•m), foot-pounds (ft.-lb.) and inch-pounds (in.-lb.). Refer to **Table 4** for general torque recommendations for fasteners without a specification. To

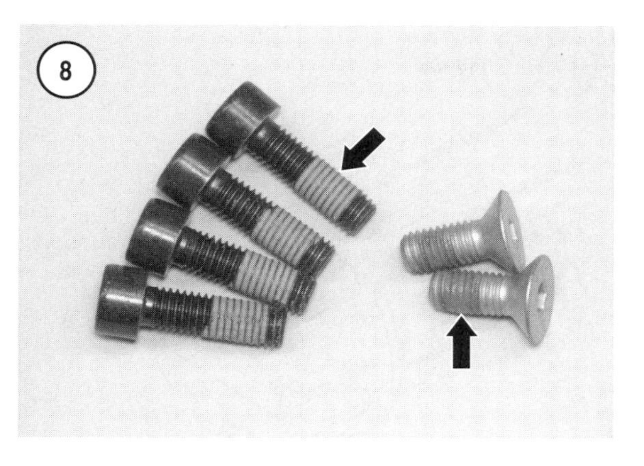

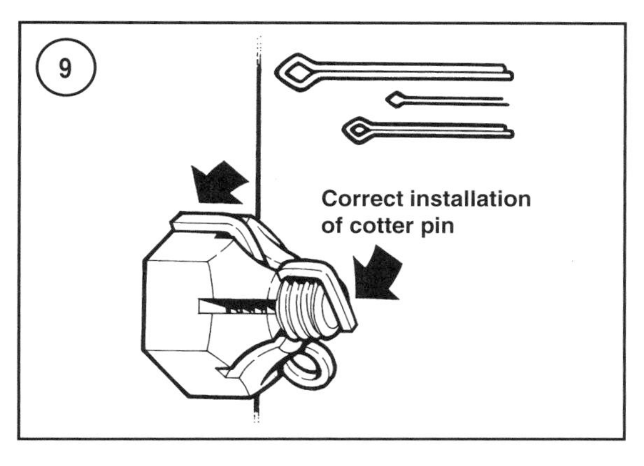

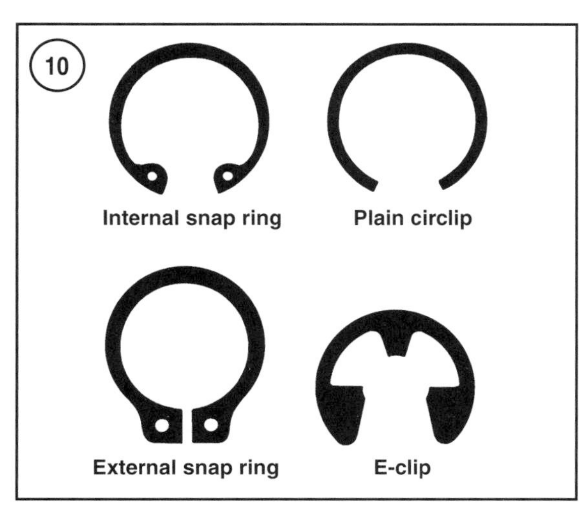

use **Table 4**, first determine the size of the fastener as described in *Threaded Fasteners* (this section). Torque specifications for specific components are listed at the end of the appropriate chapters. Torque wrenches are covered in *Tools* (this chapter).

Self-Locking Fasteners

Several types of bolts, screws and nuts incorporate a system that creates interference between the two fasteners. Interference is achieved in various ways. The most common types used are the nylon insert nut and a dry adhesive coating on the threads of a bolt.

Self-locking fasteners offer greater holding strength than standard fasteners, which improves their resistance to vibration. Self-locking fasteners cannot be reused. The materials used to form the lock become distorted after the initial installation and removal. Do not replace self-locking fasteners with standard fasteners.

Some fasteners are equipped with a threadlock (**Figure 8**) preapplied to the fastener threads. When replacing these fasteners, do not apply a separate threadlock. When it is necessary to reuse one of these fasteners, remove the threadlock residue from the threads. Then apply the threadlock specified in the text.

Washers

The two basic types of washers are flat washers and lockwashers. Flat washers are simple discs with a hole to fit a screw or bolt. Lockwashers are used to prevent a fastener from working loose. Washers can be used as spacers and seals or to help distribute fastener load and prevent the fastener from damaging the component.

As with fasteners, when replacing washers make sure the replacements meet the original specifications.

Cotter Pins

A cotter pin is a split metal pin inserted into a hole or slot to prevent a fastener from loosening. In certain applications, such as the rear axle, the fastener must be secured in this way. For these applications, a cotter pin and castellated (slotted) nut is used.

To use a cotter pin, first make sure the diameter is correct for the hole in the fastener. After correctly tightening the fastener and aligning the holes, insert the cotter pin through the hole and bend the ends (**Figure 9**) over the fastener. Unless instructed to do so, never loosen a tightened fastener to align the holes. If the holes do not align, tighten the fastener just enough to achieve alignment.

Cotter pins are available in various diameters and lengths. Measure the cotter pin length from the bottom of the head to the tip of the shortest pin.

Snap Rings and E-clips

Snap rings (**Figure 10**) are circular-shaped metal retaining clips. They are required to secure parts and gears in place on parts such as shafts, pins or rods. External type snap rings are used to retain items on shafts. Internal type snap rings secure parts within housing bores. In some applications, in addition to securing the component(s), snap rings of varying thicknesses also determine endplay. These are usually called selective snap rings.

The two basic types of snap rings are machined and stamped snap rings. Machined snap rings (**Figure 11**) can be installed in either direction because both faces have sharp edges. Stamped snap rings (**Figure 12**) are manufactured with a sharp edge and round edge. When installing a stamped snap ring in a thrust application, install the sharp edge facing away from the part producing the thrust.

E-clips are used when it is not practical to use a snap ring. Remove E-clips with a flat blade screwdriver by prying between the shaft and E-clip. To install an E-clip, center it over the shaft groove and push or tap it into place.

Observe the following when installing snap rings:

1. Remove and install snap rings with snap ring pliers. Refer to *Tools* in this chapter.
2. In some applications, it may be necessary to replace snap rings after removing them.
3. Compress or expand snap rings just enough to install them. If overly expanded, they lose their retaining ability.
4. After installing a snap ring, make sure it seats completely.
5. Wear eye protection when removing and installing snap rings.

SHOP SUPPLIES

Lubricants and Fluids

Periodic lubrication helps ensure a long service life for the equipment. The following section describes the types of lubricants most often required. Make sure to follow the manufacturer's recommendations.

Engine oils

Engine oil for use in four-stroke ATV engines is classified by three standards: the American Petroleum Institute (API) service classification, the Society of Automotive Engineers (SAE) viscosity rating and the Japanese Automobile Standards Organization (JASO) T 903 certification standard.

The API and SAE information is located on all oil container labels. The API service classification and the SAE viscosity index are not indications of oil quality. The JASO information is found on all oil manufacturers' containers that are sold specifically for ATV use.

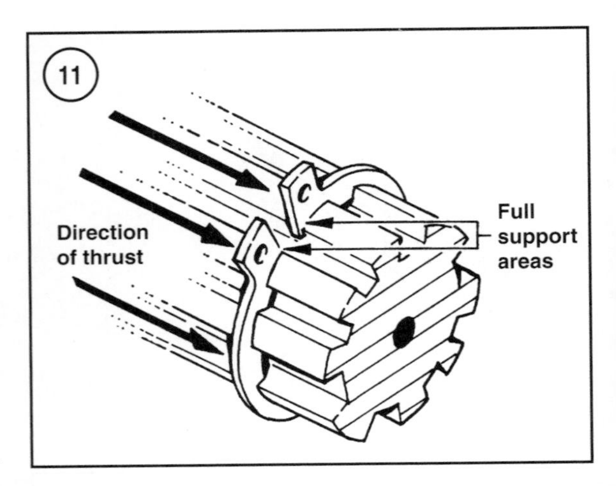

The API service classification indicates that the oil meets specific lubrication standards. Two letters indicate the API service classification. The first letter in the classification, S, indicates that the oil is for gasoline engines. The second letter indicates the standard that the oil satisfies.

The number or sequence of numbers and letter (10W-40, for example) is the SAE oil viscosity index. Viscosity is an indication of the oil's thickness. Thin oils have a lower number while thick oils have a higher number. Engine oils fall into the 5-to-50 weight range for single-grade oils.

The JASO certification label identifies two separate oil classifications and includes a registration number to ensure the oil has pass all JASO certification standards set by Japanese ATV manufacturers for use in four-stroke ATV engines. The two classifications are MA (high-friction applications) and MB (low-friction applications).

Most manufacturers recommend multi-grade oil. These oils perform efficiently across a wide range of operating conditions. Multi-grade oils are identified by a W after the first number, which indicates the low-temperature viscosity.

Engine oils are most commonly mineral (petroleum) based; however, synthetic and semi-synthetic types are being used more frequently. Always use oil with a classification recommended by the manufacturer (Chapter Three). Using oil with a different classification can cause engine damage.

Greases

Grease is lubricating oil with thickening agents added to it. The National Lubricating Grease Institute (NLGI) grades grease. Grades range from No. 000 to No. 6, with No. 6 being the thickest. Typical multipurpose grease is NLGI No. 2. For specific applications, manufacturers may recommend a

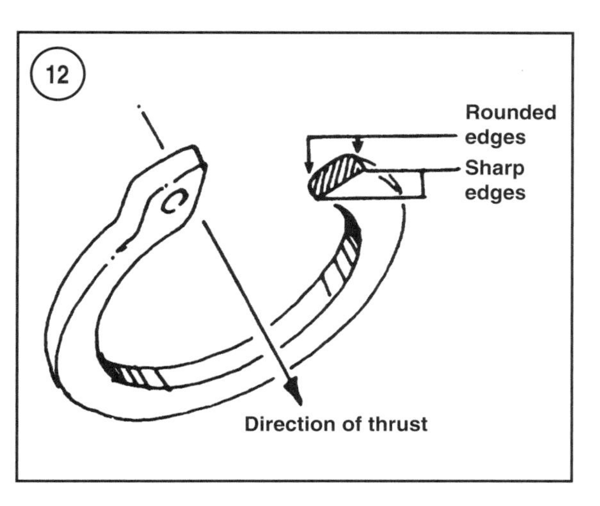

water-resistant type grease or one with an additive, such as molybdenum disulfide (MoS_2).

Brake fluid

WARNING
Never put mineral-based (petroleum) oil into the brake system. Mineral oil causes rubber parts in the system to swell and break apart, resulting in complete brake failure.

Brake fluid is the hydraulic fluid used to transmit hydraulic pressure (force) to the wheel brakes. Brake fluid is classified by the Department of Transportation (DOT). Current designations for brake fluid are DOT 3, DOT 4 and DOT 5. This classification appears on the fluid container. The models covered in this manual require DOT 4 brake fluid.

Each type of brake fluid has its own definite characteristics. Do not intermix different types of brake fluid; this may cause brake system failure. DOT 5 brake fluid is silicone based. DOT 5 is not compatible with other brake fluids or in systems for which it was not designed. Mixing DOT 5 fluid with other fluids may cause brake system failure. When adding brake fluid, *only* use DOT 4 brake fluid.

Brake fluid damages any plastic, painted or plated surface it contacts. Use extreme care when working with brake fluid, and remove any spills immediately with soap and water.

Hydraulic brake systems require clean and moisture-free brake fluid. Never reuse brake fluid. Keep containers and reservoirs properly sealed.

Cleaners, Degreasers and Solvents

Many chemicals are available to remove oil, grease and other residue from the ATV. Before using cleaning solvents, consider their uses and disposal methods, particularly if they are not water-soluble. Local ordinances may require special procedures for the disposal of many types of cleaning chemicals. Refer to *Safety* and *Cleaning Parts* in this chapter for more information on their uses.

Use brake parts cleaner to clean brake system components when contact with petroleum-based products will damage seals. Brake parts cleaner leaves no residue. Use electrical contact cleaner to clean electrical connections and components without leaving any residue. Carburetor cleaner is a powerful solvent used to remove fuel deposits and varnish from fuel system components. Use this cleaner carefully; it may damage finishes.

Generally, degreasers are strong cleaners used to remove heavy accumulations of grease from engine and frame components.

Most solvents are designed to be used with a parts washing cabinet for individual component cleaning. For safety, use only nonflammable or high flash point solvents.

Gasket Sealant

Sealants are used in combination with a gasket or seal or occasionally are used alone. Use extreme care when choosing a sealant different from the type originally recommended. Choose sealants based on their resistance to heat, various fluids and their sealing capabilities.

One of the most common sealants is RTV, or room temperature vulcanizing, sealant. This sealant cures at room temperature over a specific time period. This allows the repositioning of components without damaging gaskets.

Moisture in the air causes the RTV sealant to cure. Always install the tube cap as soon as possible after applying RTV sealant. RTV sealant has a limited shelf life and will not cure properly if the shelf life has expired. Keep partial tubes sealed and discard them if they have surpassed the expiration date. If there is no expiration date on a sealant tube, use a permanent marker and write the date on the tube when it is first opened. Manufacturers usually specify a shelf life of one year after a container is opened, though it is recommended to contact the sealant manufacturer to confirm shelf life.

Removing RTV sealant

Silicone sealant is used on many engine gasket surfaces. When cleaning parts after disassembly, a razor blade or gasket scraper is required to remove the silicone residue that cannot be pulled off by hand from the gasket surfaces. To avoid damaging gasket surfaces, use Permatex Silicone Stripper (part No. 80647) to help soften the residue before scraping.

Applying RTV sealant

Clean all old sealer residue from the mating surfaces. Then inspect the mating surfaces for damage. Remove all sealer material from blind threaded holes; it can cause inaccurate bolt torque. Spray the mating surfaces with aerosol parts cleaner, and then wipe with a lint-free cloth. Because gasket surfaces must be dry and oil-free for the sealant to adhere, be thorough when cleaning and drying the parts.

Apply RTV sealant in a continuous bead 2-3 mm (0.08-0.12 in.) thick. Circle all the fastener holes unless otherwise specified. Do not allow any sealant to enter these holes. Drawings in specific chapters show how to apply the sealer to specific gasket surfaces. Assemble and tighten the fasteners to the specified torque within the time frame recommended by the RTV sealant manufacturer.

Gasket Remover

Aerosol gasket remover can help remove stubborn gaskets. This product can speed up the removal process and prevent damage to the mating surface that may be caused by using a scraping tool. Most of these types of products are very caustic. Follow the gasket remover manufacturer's instructions for use.

Threadlock

CAUTION
Threadlock is anaerobic and damages most plastic parts and surfaces. Use caution when using these products in areas where plastic components are located.

Threadlock is a fluid applied to the threads of fasteners. After tightening the fastener, the fluid dries and becomes a solid filler between the threads. This makes it difficult for the fastener to work loose from vibration or heat expansion and contraction. Some threadlock formulas also provide a seal against fluid leaks.

Before applying threadlock, remove any residue from both thread areas and clean them with aerosol parts cleaner. Use the compound sparingly. Excess fluid can run into adjoining parts.

Threadlock is available in various strengths, temperatures and repair applications.

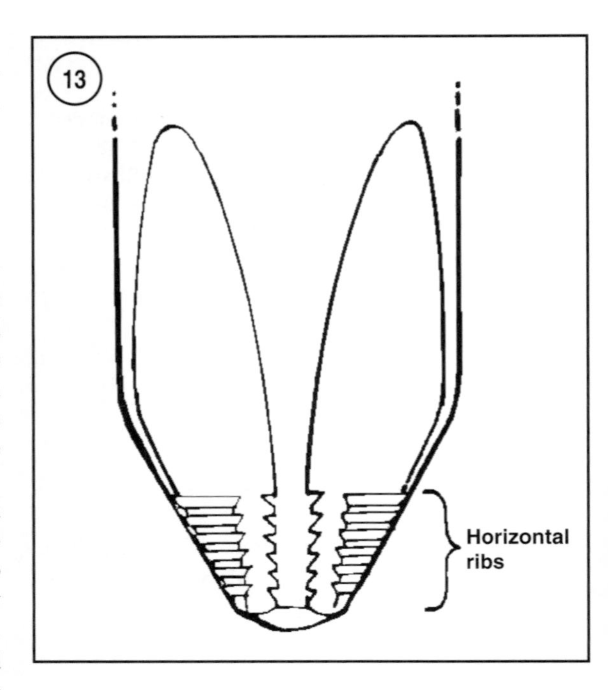

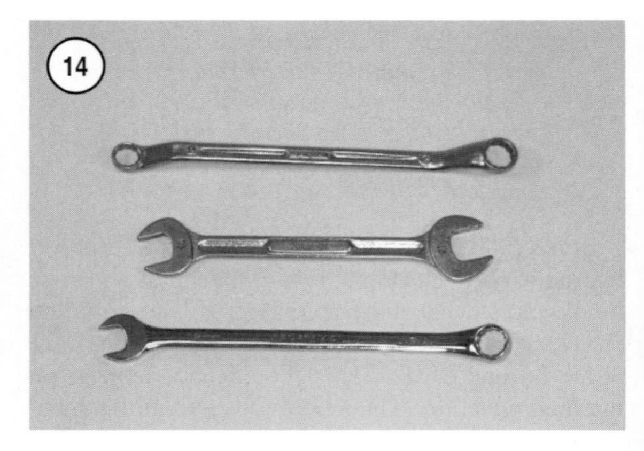

TOOLS

Most of the procedures in this manual can be carried out with hand tools and test equipment familiar to the home mechanic. Always use the correct tools for the job. Keep tools organized and clean and store them in a tool chest with related tools organized together.

Quality tools are essential. The best are constructed of high-strength alloy steel. These tools are light, easy-to-use and resistant to wear. Their working surfaces are devoid of sharp edges and the tools are carefully polished. They have an easy-to-clean finish and are comfortable to use. Quality tools are a good investment.

If you are purchasing tools to perform the procedures covered in this manual, consider the tool's potential frequency of use. If a tool kit is just now being started, consider a tool set. Sets are available

in many tool combinations and offer substantial savings when compared to individually purchased tools. As work experience grows and tasks become more complicated, specialized tools can be added.

Some of the procedures in this manual specify special tools. In most cases, the tool is illustrated in use. In some cases it may be possible to substitute similar tools or fabricate a suitable replacement. However, at times, the specialized equipment or expertise may make it impractical for the home mechanic to perform the procedure. When necessary, such operations are identified in the text with the recommendation to have a dealership or specialist perform the task.

Special tools identified in this manual are those that were available at the time of publication. The publisher cannot guarantee in the future that those tools or their part numbers will still be applicable.

Screwdrivers

The two basic types of screwdrivers are the slotted tip (flat blade) and the Phillips tip. These are available in sets that often include an assortment of tip sizes and shaft lengths.

As with all tools, use the correct screwdriver. Make sure the size of the tip conforms to the size and shape of the fastener. Use them only for driving screws. Never use a screwdriver for prying or chiseling. Repair or replace worn or damaged screwdrivers. A worn tip may damage the fastener, making it difficult to remove.

Phillips-head screws are often damaged by incorrectly fitting screwdrivers. Quality Phillips screwdrivers are manufactured with their crosshead tip machined to Phillips Screw Company specifications. Poor quality or damaged Phillips screwdrivers can back out and round over the screw head (camout). Compounding the problem of using poor quality screwdrivers are Phillips-head screws made from weak or soft materials and screws initially installed with air tools.

An effective screwdriver for Phillips screws is the ACR Phillips II screwdriver. Horizontal anti-camout ribs (ACR) on the driving faces or flutes of the screwdrivers tip (**Figure 13**) improve the driver to fastener grip. While designed for ACR Phillips II screws, the screwdriver also works well on common Phillips screws. A number of tool companies offer ACR Phillips II screwdrivers in different tip sizes and interchangeable bits to fit screwdriver bit holders.

Another way to prevent camout and increase the grip of a Phillips screwdriver is to apply valve grinding compound or Permatex Screw & Socket Gripper to the screwdriver tip. After loosening/tightening the screw, clean the screw recess to prevent possible contamination.

Wrenches

Box-end, open-end and combination wrenches (**Figure 14**) are available in a variety of types and sizes.

The number stamped on the wrench refers to the distance between the work areas. This size must match the size of the fastener head.

The box-end wrench is an excellent tool because it grips the fastener on all sides. This reduces the chance of the tool slipping. The box-end wrench is designed with either a 6- or 12-point opening. For stubborn or damaged fasteners, the 6-point provides superior holding ability by contacting the fastener across a wider area at all six edges. For general use, the 12-point works well. It allows the wrench to be removed and reinstalled without moving the handle over such a wide arc.

An open-end wrench is fast and works best in areas with limited overhead access. It contacts the fastener at only two points, and is subject to slipping under heavy force or if the tool or fastener is worn. A box-end wrench is preferred in most instances, especially when breaking loose and applying the final tightness to a fastener.

The combination wrench has a box-end on one end, and an open-end on the other. This combination makes it a convenient tool.

Adjustable Wrenches

An adjustable wrench (**Figure 15**) can fit nearly any nut or bolt head that has clear access around its entire perimeter.

However, adjustable wrenches contact the fastener at only two points, which makes them more subject to slipping off the fastener. One jaw is adjustable and may loosen, which increases this possibility.

Make certain the solid jaw is the one transmitting the force.

Adjustable wrenches are typically used to prevent a large nut or bolt from turning while the other end is being loosened or tightened with a box-end or socket wrench.

Socket Wrenches, Ratchets and Handles

WARNING
Do not use hand sockets with air or impact tools; they may shatter and cause injury. Always wear eye protection when using impact or air tools.

Sockets (**Figure 16**) that attach to a ratchet handle are available with 6-point (A, **Figure 17**) or 12-point (B) openings and different drive sizes. The drive size indicates the size of the square hole that accepts the ratchet handle. The number stamped on the socket is the size of the work area and must match the fastener head.

As with wrenches, a 6-point socket provides superior-holding ability, while a 12-point socket needs to be moved only half as far to reposition it on the fastener.

Sockets are designated for either hand or impact use. Impact sockets are made of a thicker material for more durability. Compare the size and wall thickness of a 19-mm hand socket (A, **Figure 18**) and the 19-mm impact socket (B). Use impact sockets when using an impact driver or air tool. Use hand sockets with hand-driven attachments.

Various handles are available for sockets. The ratchet is the most versatile. It allows the user to install or remove the nut without removing the socket. The speed handle is used for fast operation. Flexible ratchet heads in varying lengths allow the socket to be turned with varying force and at odd angles. Extension bars allow the socket setup to reach difficult areas.

Sockets combined with any number of drivers make them undoubtedly the fastest, safest and most convenient tool for fastener removal and installation.

Impact Driver

WARNING
Do not use hand sockets with air or impact tools; they may shatter and cause injury. Always wear eye protection when using impact or air tools.

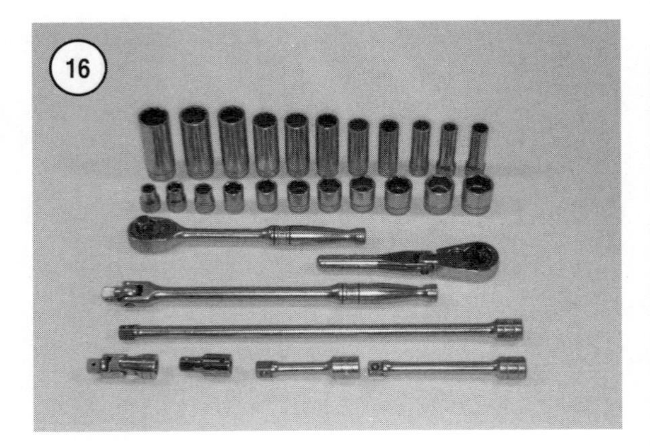

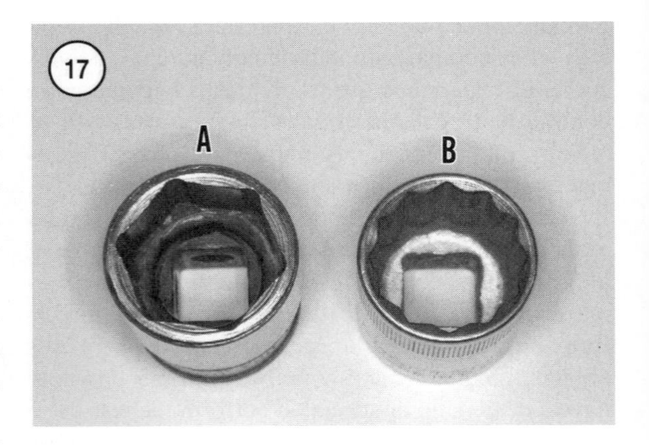

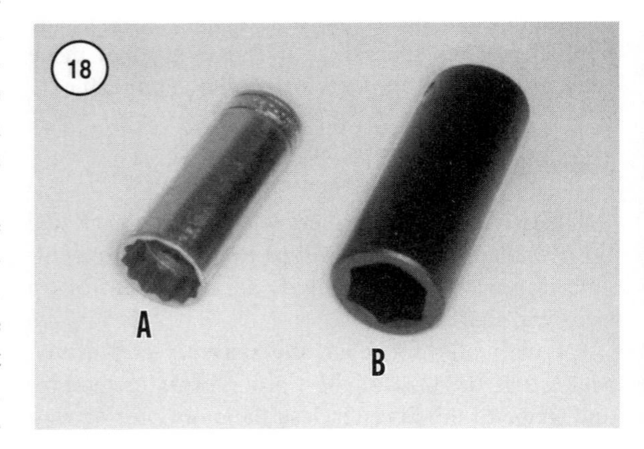

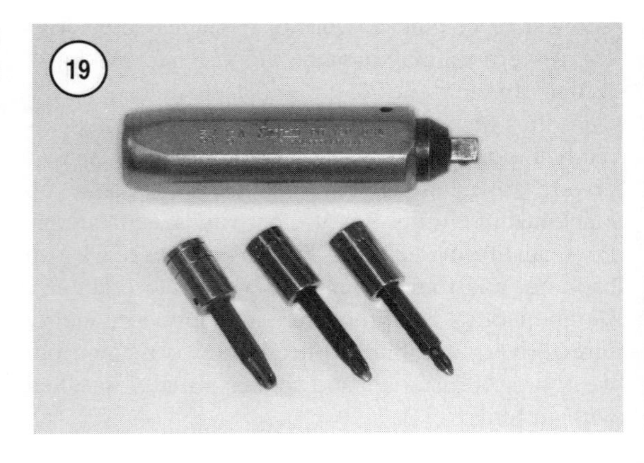

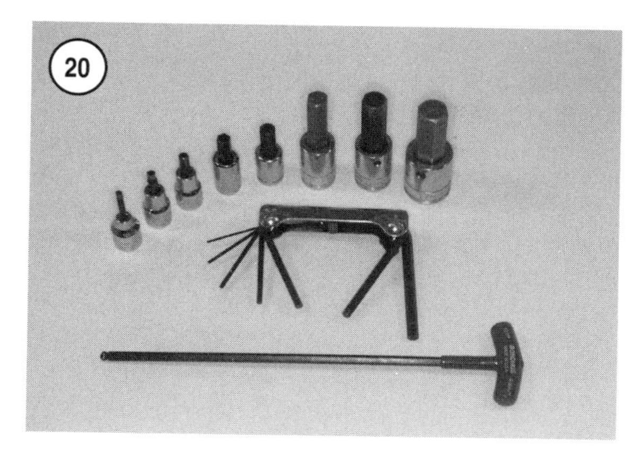
20

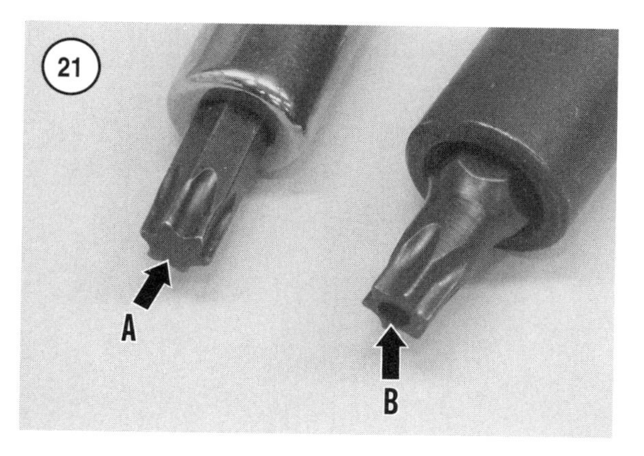

21

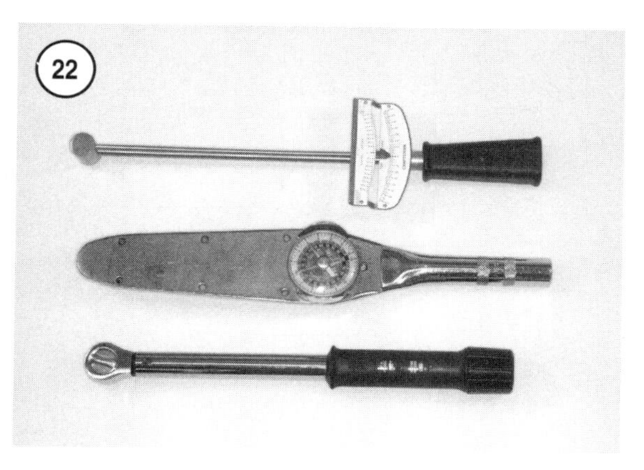
22

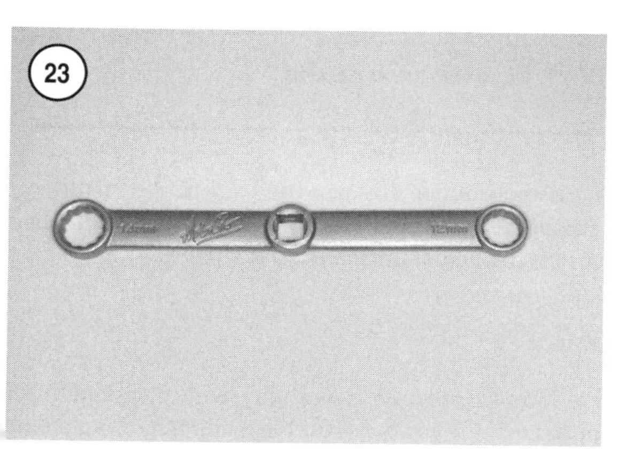
23

An impact driver provides extra force for removing fasteners by converting the impact of a hammer into a turning motion. This makes it possible to remove stubborn fasteners without damaging them. Impact drivers and interchangeable bits (**Figure 19**) are available from most tool suppliers. When using a socket with an impact driver make sure the socket is designed for impact use. Refer to *Socket Wrenches, Ratchets and Handles* in this section.

Allen Wrenches

Allen, or setscrew wrenches (**Figure 20**), are used on fasteners with hexagonal recesses in the fastener head. These wrenches are available in a L-shaped bar, socket and T-handle types. Allen bolts are sometimes called socket bolts.

Torx Fasteners

A Torx fastener head is a 6-point star-shaped pattern (A, **Figure 21**). Torx fasteners are identified with a T and a number indicating their drive size: for example, T25. Torx drivers are available in L-shaped bars, sockets and T-handles. Tamper-resistant Torx fasteners are also used and have a round shaft in the center of the fastener head. Tamper-resistant Torx fasteners require a Torx bit with a hole in the center of the bit (B, **Figure 21**).

Torque Wrenches

A torque wrench (**Figure 22**) is used with a socket, torque adapter or similar extension to tighten a fastener to a measured torque. Torque wrenches come in several drive sizes (1/4, 3/8, 1/2 and 3/4) and use various methods to display the torque value. The drive size indicates the size of the square drive that accepts the socket, adapter or extension. Common methods of displaying the torque value are the reflecting beam, the dial indicator and the audible click. When choosing a torque wrench, consider the torque range, drive size and accuracy. The torque specifications in this manual provide an indication of the range required. A torque wrench is a precision tool that must be properly cared for to remain accurate. Store torque wrenches in cases or separate padded drawers within a toolbox. Follow the manufacturer's instructions for their care and calibration.

Torque Adapters

Torque adapters (**Figure 23**), or extensions, extend or reduce the reach of a torque wrench. Specific adapters are required to perform some of the proce-

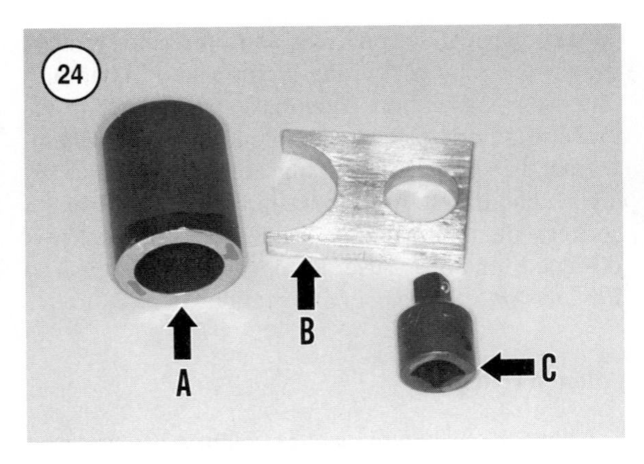

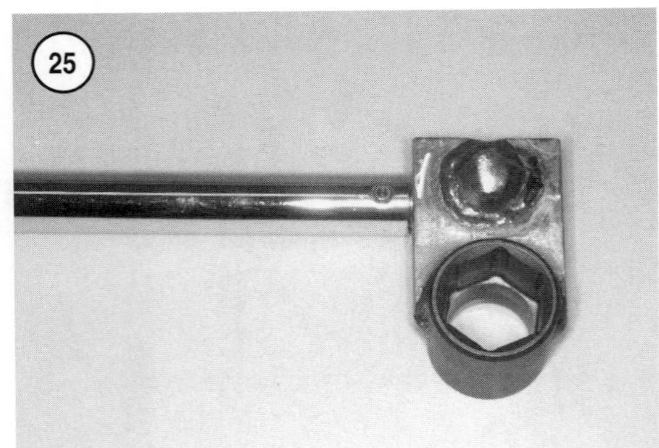

dures in this manual. These are available from the ATV manufacturer or can be fabricated by welding a socket (A, **Figure 24**) that matches the fastener onto a metal plate (B). Use another socket or extension (C, **Figure 24**) welded to the plate to attach the adapter to the torque wrench drive (**Figure 25**). The adapter shown (**Figure 26**) is used to tighten a fastener while preventing another fastener on the same shaft from turning.

If a torque adapter changes the effective lever length, the torque reading on the wrench will not equal the actual torque applied to the fastener. It is necessary to recalibrate the torque setting on the wrench to compensate for the change of lever length. When a torque adapter is used at a right angle to the drive head, calibration is not required because the lever length has not changed.

To recalculate a torque reading when using a torque adapter, use the following formula, and refer to **Figure 27**.

$$TW = \frac{TA \times L}{L + A}$$

TW is the torque setting or dial reading on the wrench.

TA is the torque specification and the actual amount of torque that will be applied to the fastener.

A is the amount the adapter increases (or in some cases reduces) the effective lever length as measured along the centerline of the torque wrench.

L is the lever length of the wrench as measured from the center of the drive to the center of the grip.

The effective lever length is the sum of *L* and *A*.

Example:

TA = 20 ft.-lb.

A = 3 in.

L = 14 in.

$$TW = \frac{20 \times 14}{14 + 3} = \frac{280}{17} = 16.5 \text{ ft.-lb.}$$

In this example, the torque wrench would be set to the recalculated torque value (TW = 16.5 ft.-lb.). When using a beam-type wrench, tighten the fastener until the pointer aligns with 16.5 ft.-lb. In this example, although the torque wrench is preset to 16.5 ft.-lb., the actual torque is 20 ft.-lb.

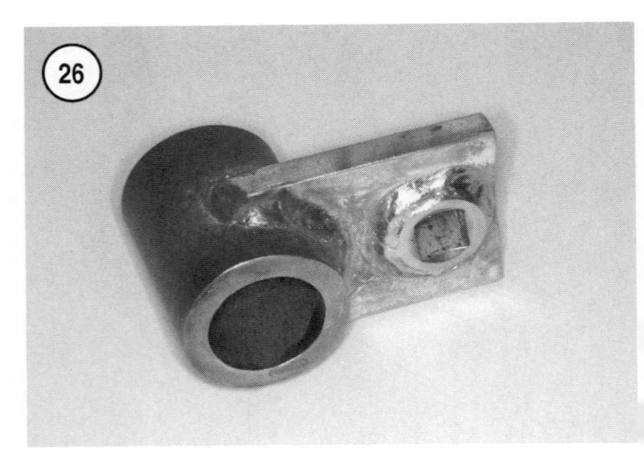

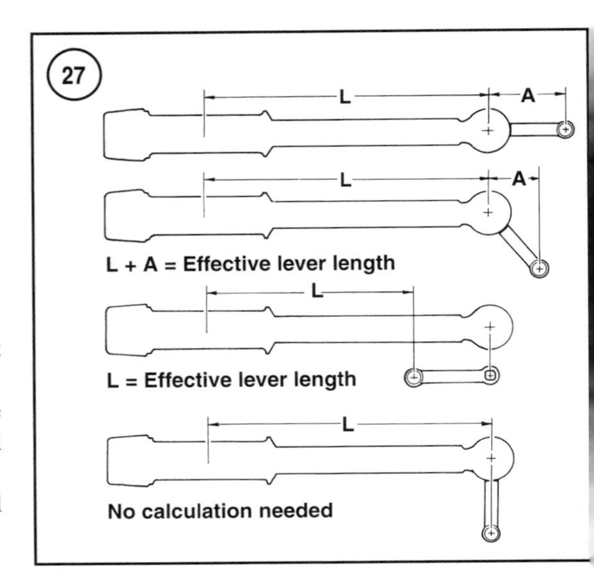

Pliers

Pliers (**Figure 28**) come in a wide range of types and sizes. Pliers are useful for holding, cutting, bend-

28

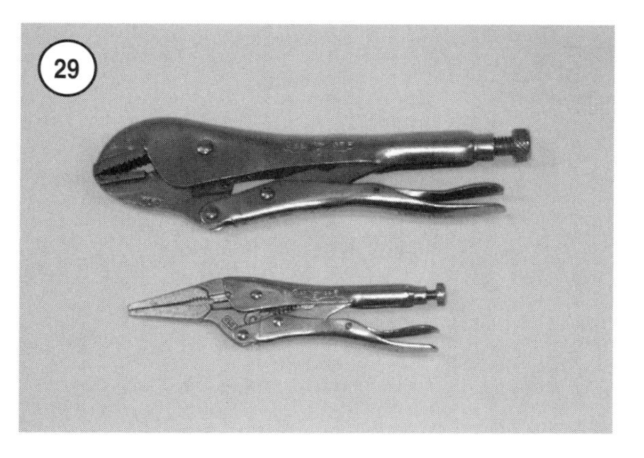

ing, and crimping. Do not use them to turn fasteners unless they are designed to do so. Each design has a specialized function. Slip-joint pliers are general-purpose pliers used for gripping and bending. Diagonal cutting pliers are needed to cut wire and can be used to remove cotter pins. Needlenose pliers are used to hold or bend small objects. Locking pliers (**Figure 29**), sometimes called Vise Grips, hold objects tightly. They have many uses ranging from holding two parts together, to gripping the end of a broken stud. Use caution when using locking pliers; the sharp jaws will damage the objects they hold.

Snap Ring Pliers

WARNING
Snap rings can slip and fly off when removing and installing them. In addition, the snap ring pliers tips may break. Always wear eye protection when using snap ring pliers.

Snap ring pliers are specialized pliers with tips that fit into the ends of snap rings to remove and install them.

Snap ring pliers (**Figure 30**) are available with a fixed action (either internal or external) or are con-

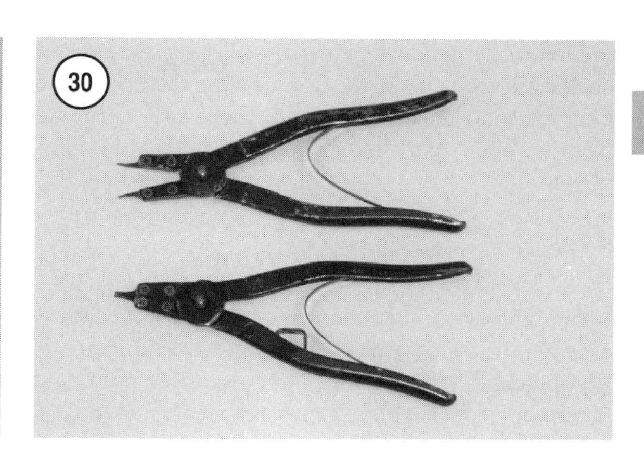

vertible (one tool works on both internal and external snap rings). They may have fixed tips or interchangeable ones of various sizes and angles. For general use, select convertible type pliers with interchangeable tips.

Hammers

WARNING
Always wear eye protection when using hammers. Make sure the hammer face is in good condition and the handle is not cracked. Select the correct hammer for the job and make sure to strike the object squarely. Do not use the handle or the side of the hammer to strike an object.

Various types of hammers are available to fit a number of applications. A ball-peen hammer is used to strike another tool, such as a punch or chisel. Soft-faced hammers are required when a metal object must be struck without damaging it. Never use a metal-faced hammer on engine and suspension components; damage will occur in most cases.

Ignition Grounding Tool

Some test procedures in this manual require turning the engine over without starting it. Do not remove the spark plug cap(s) and crank the engine without grounding the plug cap(s). Doing so will damage the ignition system.

An effective way to ground the system is to fabricate the tool shown in **Figure 31** from a No. 6 screw, two washers and a length of wire with an alligator clip soldered on one end. To use the tool, insert it into the spark plug cap and attach the alligator clip to a known engine ground. A separate grounding tool is required for each spark plug cap.

This tool is safer than a spark plug or spark tester because there is no spark firing across the end of the plug/tester to potentially ignite fuel vapor spraying from an open spark plug hole or leaking fuel component.

MEASURING TOOLS

The ability to accurately measure components is essential to successfully service many components. Equipment is manufactured to close tolerances, and obtaining consistently accurate measurements is critical.

Each type of measuring instrument is designed to measure a dimension with a certain degree of accuracy and within a specific range. When selecting the measuring tool, make sure it is applicable to the task.

As with all tools, measuring tools provide the best results if cared for properly. Improper use can damage the tool and cause inaccurate results. If any measurement is questionable, verify the measurement using another tool. A standard gauge is usually provided with measuring tools to check accuracy and calibrate the tool if necessary.

Accurate measurements are only possible if the mechanic possesses a feel for using the tool. Heavy-handed use of measuring tools produces less accurate results. Hold the tool gently by the fingertips so the point at which the tool contacts the object is easily felt. This feel for the equipment will produce more accurate measurements and reduce the risk of damaging the tool or component.

Feeler Gauge

The feeler, or thickness gauge (**Figure 32**), is used for measuring the distance between two surfaces. A feeler gauge set consists of an assortment of steel strips of graduated thicknesses. Each blade is marked with its thickness. Blades can be of various lengths and angles for different procedures. A common use for a feeler gauge is to measure valve clearance. Wire (round) type gauges are used to measure spark plug gap.

Calipers

Calipers (**Figure 33**) are excellent tools for obtaining inside, outside and depth measurements. Although not as precise as a micrometer, they allow reasonable precision, typically to within 0.05 mm (0.001 in.). Most calipers have a range up to 150 mm (6 in.).

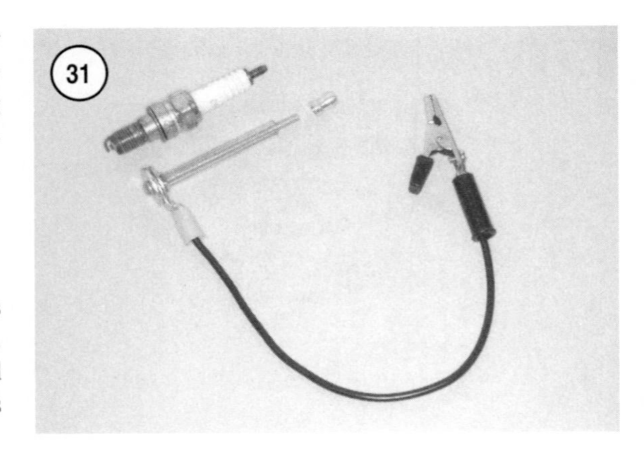
31

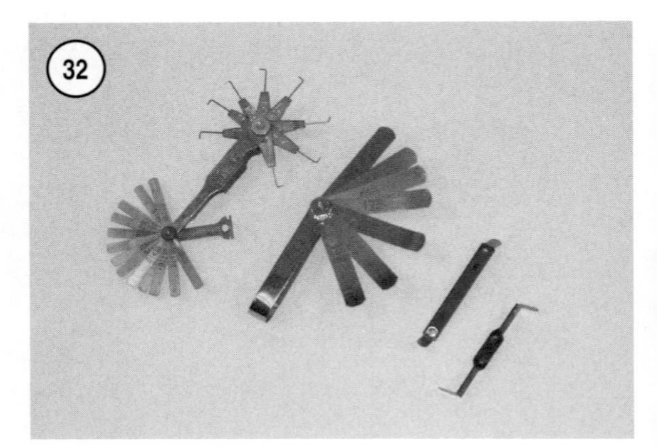
32

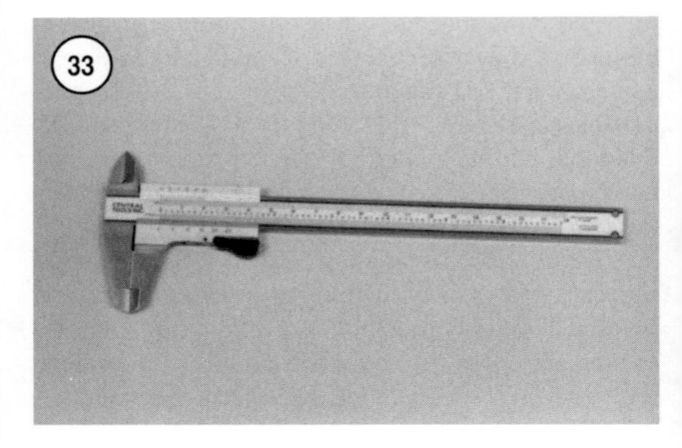
33

Calipers are available in dial, vernier or digital versions. Dial calipers have a dial readout that provides convenient reading. Vernier calipers have marked scales that must be compared to determine the measurement. The digital caliper uses a LCD to show the measurement.

Properly maintain the measuring surfaces of the caliper. There must not be any dirt or burrs between the tool and the object being measured. Never force the caliper closed around an object; close the caliper around the highest point so it can be removed with a slight drag. Some calipers require calibration. Always refer to the manufacturer's instructions when using a new or unfamiliar caliper.

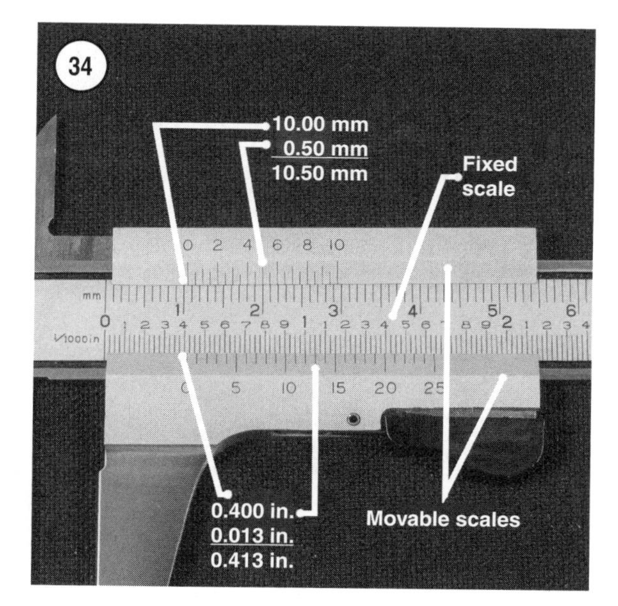

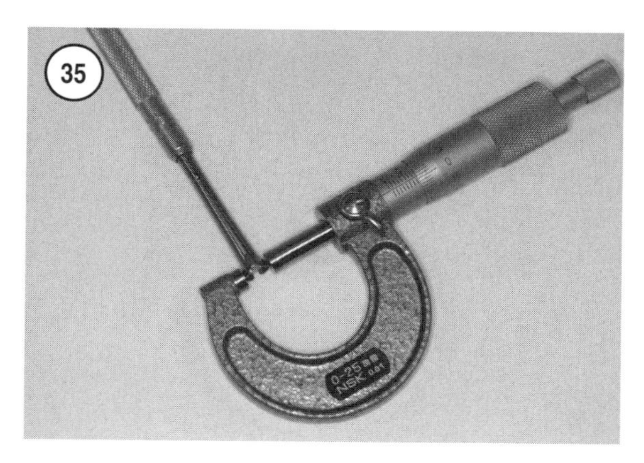

To read a vernier caliper, refer to **Figure 34**. The fixed scale is marked in 1 mm increments. Ten individual lines on the fixed scale equal 1 cm. The moveable scale is marked in 0.05 mm increments. To obtain a reading, establish the first number by the location of the 0 line on the moveable scale in relation to the first line to the left on the fixed scale. In this example, the number is 10 mm. To determine the next number, note which of the lines on the movable scale aligns with a mark on the fixed scale. A number of lines will seem close, but only one will align exactly. In this case, 0.50 mm is the reading to add to the first number. The result of adding 10 mm and 0.50 mm is a measurement of 10.50 mm.

Micrometers

A micrometer (**Figure 35**) is an instrument designed for linear measurement using the decimal divisions of the inch or meter. While there are many types and styles of micrometers, most of the procedures in this manual call for an outside micrometer. The outside micrometer is used to measure the outside diameter of cylindrical forms and the thicknesses of materials.

A micrometer's size indicates the minimum and maximum size of a part that it can measure. The usual sizes are 0-25 mm (0-1 in.), 25-50 mm (1-2 in.), 50-75 mm (2-3 in.) and 75-100 mm (3-4 in.).

Micrometers that cover a wider range of measurements are available. These use a large frame with interchangeable anvils of various lengths. This type of micrometer offers a cost savings; however, its overall size may make it less convenient to use.

Adjustment

Before using a micrometer, check its adjustment as follows.

1. Clean the anvil and spindle faces.

2A. To check a 0-1 in. or 0-25 mm micrometer:

   a. Turn the thimble until the spindle contacts the anvil. If the micrometer has a ratchet stop, use it to ensure the proper amount of pressure is applied.
   b. If the adjustment is correct, the 0 mark on the thimble will align exactly with the 0 mark on the sleeve line. If the marks do not align, the micrometer is out of adjustment.
   c. Follow the manufacturer's instructions to adjust the micrometer.

2B. To check a micrometer larger than 1 in. or 25 mm, use the standard gauge supplied by the manufacturer. A standard gauge is a steel block, disc or rod that is machined to an exact size.

   a. Place the standard gauge between the spindle and anvil and measure its outside diameter or length. If the micrometer has a ratchet stop, use it to ensure the proper amount of pressure is applied.
   b. If the adjustment is correct, the 0 mark on the thimble will align exactly with the 0 mark on the sleeve line. If the marks do not align, the micrometer is out of adjustment.
   c. Follow the manufacturer's instructions to adjust the micrometer.

Care

Micrometers are precision instruments. They must be used and maintained with great care. Note the following:

1. Store micrometers in protective cases or separate padded drawers in a toolbox.
2. When in storage, make sure the spindle and anvil faces do not contact each other or another object.

If they do, temperature changes and corrosion may damage the contact faces.
3. Do not clean a micrometer with compressed air. Dirt forced into the tool causes wear.
4. Lubricate micrometers to prevent corrosion.

Reading

When reading a micrometer, numbers are taken from different scales and added together.

For accurate results, properly maintain the measuring surfaces of the micrometer. There cannot be any dirt or burrs between the tool and the measured object. Never force the micrometer closed around an object. Close the micrometer around the highest point so it can be removed with a slight drag.

The standard metric micrometer is accurate to one one-hundredth of a millimeter (0.01 mm). The sleeve line is graduated in millimeter and half millimeter increments. The marks on the upper half of the sleeve line equal 1.00 mm. Each fifth mark above the sleeve line is identified with a number. The number sequence depends on the size of the micrometer. A 0-25 mm micrometer, for example, will have sleeve marks numbered 0 through 25 in 5 mm increments. This numbering sequence continues with larger micrometers. On all metric micrometers, each mark on the lower half of the sleeve equals 0.50 mm.

The tapered end of the thimble has 50 lines marked around it. Each mark equals 0.01 mm. One complete turn of the thimble aligns its 0 mark with the first line on the lower half of the sleeve line, or 0.50 mm.

When reading a metric micrometer, add the number of millimeters and half-millimeters on the sleeve line to the number of one one-hundredth millimeters on the thimble. Perform the following steps while referring to **Figure 36**.

1. Read the upper half of the sleeve line and count the number of lines visible. Each upper line equals 1 mm.
2. See if the half-millimeter line is visible on the lower sleeve line. If so, add 0.50 mm to the reading in Step 1.
3. Read the thimble mark that aligns with the sleeve line. Each thimble mark equals 0.01 mm.
4. If a thimble mark does not align exactly with the sleeve line, estimate the amount between the lines. For accurate readings in two-thousandths of a millimeter (0.002 mm), use a metric vernier micrometer.
5. Add the readings from Steps 1-4.

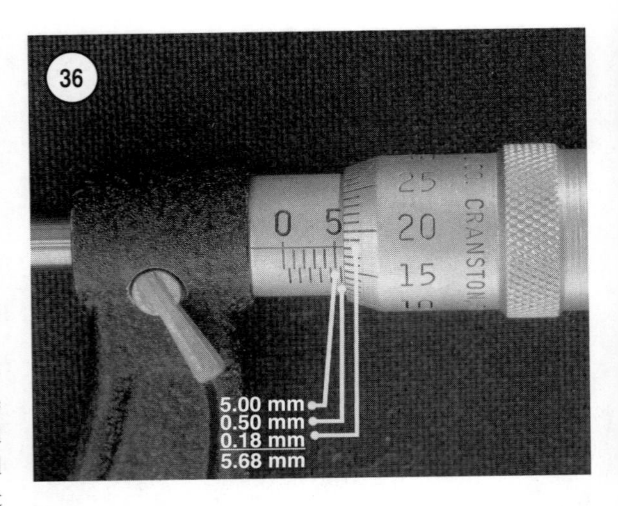

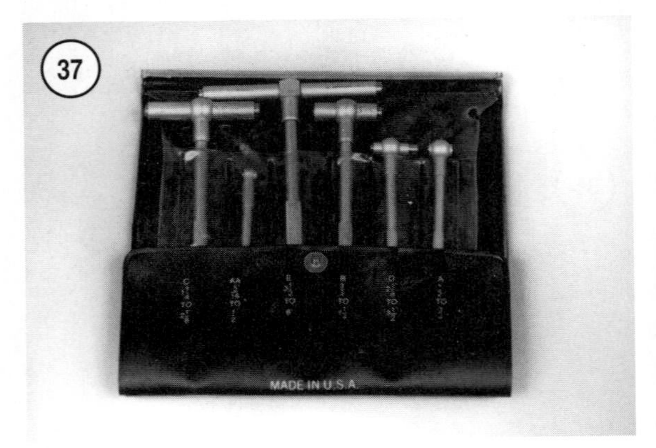

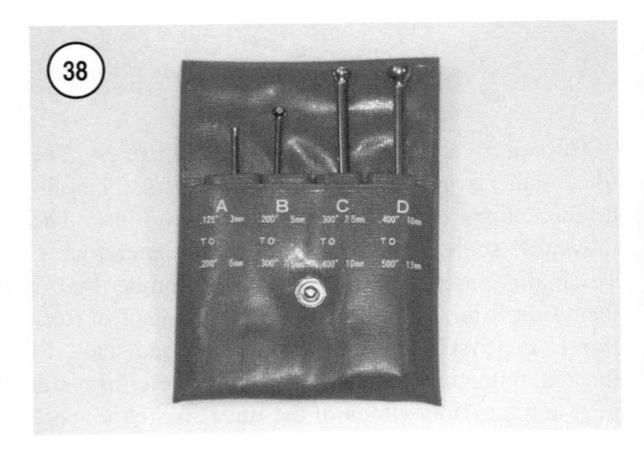

Telescoping and Small Hole Gauges

Use telescoping gauges (**Figure 37**) and small hole gauges (**Figure 38**) to measure bores. Neither gauge has a scale for direct readings. An outside micrometer must be used to determine the reading.

To use a telescoping gauge, select the correct size gauge for the bore. Compress the moveable post and carefully insert the gauge into the bore. Carefully move the gauge in the bore to make sure it is centered. Tighten the knurled end of the gauge to hold

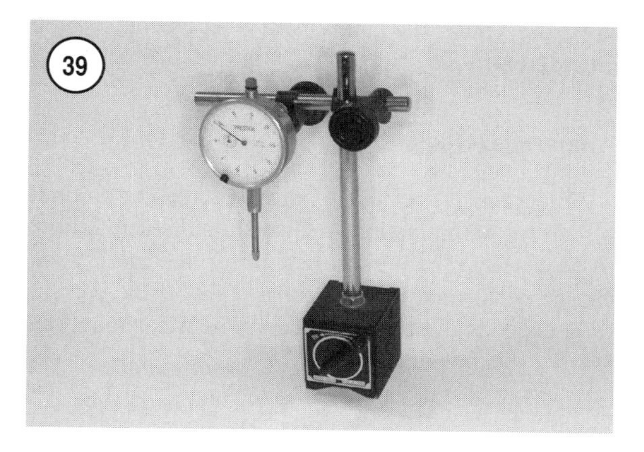

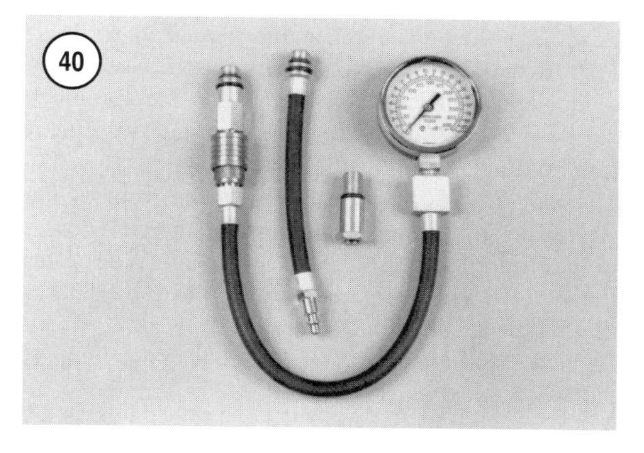

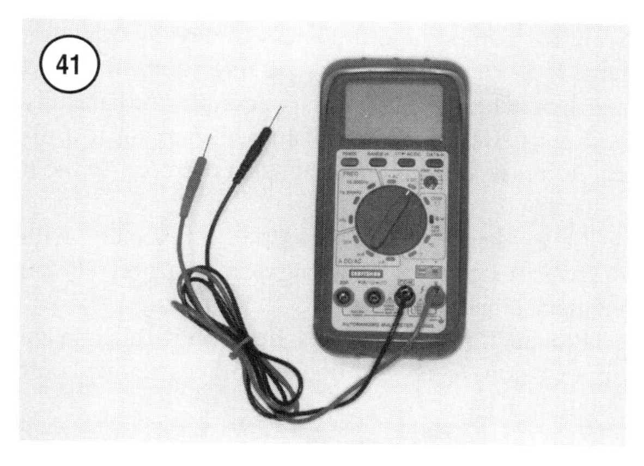

the moveable post in position. Remove the gauge and measure the length of the posts. Telescoping gauges are typically used to measure cylinder bores.

To use a small hole gauge, select the correct size gauge for the bore. Carefully insert the gauge into the bore. Tighten the knurled end of the gauge to carefully expand the gauge fingers to the limit within the bore. Do not overtighten the gauge; there is no built-in release. Excessive tightening can damage the bore surface and tool. Remove the gauge and measure the outside dimension with a micrometer (**Figure 35**). Small hole gauges are typically used to measure valve guides.

Dial Indicator

A dial indicator (**Figure 39**) is a gauge with a dial face and needle used to measure variations in dimensions and movements. Measuring brake rotor runout is a typical use for a dial indicator.

Dial indicators are available in various ranges and graduations and use three types of mounting bases: magnetic, clamp or screw-in stud.

Cylinder Bore Gauge

A cylinder bore gauge is similar to a dial indicator. These typically consist of a dial indicator, handle and different length adapters (anvils) to fit the gauge to various bore sizes. The bore gauge is used to measure bore size, taper and out-of-round. When using a bore gauge, follow the manufacturer's instructions.

Compression Gauge

A compression gauge (**Figure 40**) measures combustion chamber (cylinder) pressure, usually in psi, kg/cm^2 or kilopascals (kPa).

The gauge adapter is either inserted and held in place or screwed into the spark plug hole to obtain the reading. Disable the engine so it will not start and hold the throttle in the wide-open position when performing a compression test. An engine that does not have adequate compression cannot be properly tuned. Refer to Chapter Three to perform a compression test.

Multimeter

A multimeter (**Figure 41**) is an essential tool for electrical system diagnosis. The voltage function indicates the voltage applied or available to various electrical components. The ohmmeter function tests circuits for continuity, or lack of continuity, and measures the resistance of a circuit.

Some manufacturers' specifications for electrical components are based on results using a specific test meter. Results may vary if using a meter not recommend by the manufacturer. Such requirements are noted when applicable.

Ohmmeter (analog) calibration

Each time an analog ohmmeter is used or the scale is changed, the ohmmeter must be calibrated.

Digital ohmmeters do not require calibration.

To calibrate an analog ohmmeter, perform the following:

1. Make sure the meter battery is in good condition.
2. Make sure the meter probes are in good condition.

3. Touch the two probes together and observe the needle location on the ohms scale. The needle must align with the 0 mark to obtain accurate measurements.
4. If necessary, rotate the meter ohms adjust knob until the needle and 0 mark align.

ELECTRICAL SYSTEM FUNDAMENTALS

A thorough study of the many types of electrical systems used in today's ATVs is beyond the scope of this manual. However, a basic understanding of voltage, resistance and amperage is necessary to perform diagnostic tests.

Refer to Chapter Two for basic electrical troubleshooting.

Voltage

Voltage is the electrical potential or pressure in an electrical circuit and is expressed in volts. The more pressure (voltage) in a circuit, the more work can be performed.

Direct current (DC) voltage means the electricity flows in one direction. All circuits powered by a battery are DC circuits.

Alternating current (AC) means the electricity flows in one direction momentarily and then switches to the opposite direction. Alternator output is an example of AC voltage. This voltage must be changed or rectified to direct current to operate in a battery-powered system.

Resistance

Resistance is the opposition to the flow of electricity within a circuit or component and is measured in ohms. Resistance causes a reduction in available current and voltage.

Resistance is measured in an inactive circuit with an ohmmeter. The ohmmeter sends a small amount of current into the circuit and measures how difficult it is to push the current through the circuit.

An ohmmeter, although useful, is not always a good indicator of a circuit's actual ability under operating conditions. This is due to the low voltage (6-9 volts) that the meter uses to test the circuit. The voltage in an ignition coil secondary winding can be several thousand volts. Such high voltage can cause the coil to malfunction, even though it tests acceptable during a resistance test.

Resistance generally increases with temperature. Perform all testing with the component or circuit at room temperature. Resistance tests performed at high temperatures may indicate false resistance readings and cause the unnecessary replacement of a component.

Amperage

Amperage is the unit of measure for the amount of current within a circuit. Current is the actual flow of electricity. The higher the current, the more work can be performed up to a given point. If the current flow exceeds the circuit or component capacity, the system will be damaged.

SERVICE METHODS

Many of the procedures in this manual are straightforward and can be performed by anyone reasonably competent with tools. However, consider previous experience carefully before performing any operation involving complicated procedures.

1. Front, in this manual, refers to the front of the ATV. The front of any component is the end closest to the front of the ATV. The left and right sides refer to the position of the parts as viewed by the rider sitting on the seat facing forward.
2. When servicing the ATV, secure it in a safe manner.
3. Label all similar parts for location and mark all mating parts for position. If possible, photograph or draw the number and thickness of any shim as it is removed. Identify parts by placing them in sealed and labeled plastic bags. It is possible for carefully laid out parts to become disturbed, making it difficult to reassemble the components correctly without a diagram.
4. Label disconnected wires and connectors with masking tape and a marking pen. Do not rely on memory alone.
5. Protect finished surfaces from physical damage or corrosion. Keep gasoline and other chemicals off painted surfaces.
6. Use penetrating oil on frozen or tight bolts. Avoid using heat where possible. Heat can warp, melt or affect the temper of parts. Heat also damages the finish of paint and plastics. Refer to *Heating Components* in this section.
7. When a part is a press fit or requires a special tool for removal, the information or type of tool is identified in the text. Otherwise, if a part is difficult to remove or install, determine the cause before proceeding.
8. To prevent objects or debris from falling into the engine, cover all openings.
9. Read each procedure thoroughly and compare the figures to the actual components before starting the procedure. Perform the procedure in sequence.

10. Recommendations are occasionally made to refer service to a dealership or specialist. In these cases, the work can be performed more economically by the specialist than by the home mechanic.
11. The term *replace* means to discard a defective part and replace it with a new part. *Overhaul* means to remove, disassemble, inspect, measure, repair and/or replace parts as required to recondition an assembly.
12. Some operations require the use of a hydraulic press. If a press is not available, have these operations performed by a shop equipped with the necessary equipment. Do not use makeshift equipment that may damage the ATV. Do not direct high-pressure water at steering bearings, fuel body hoses, wheel bearings, suspension and electrical components. The water forces the grease out of the bearings and could damage the seals.
13. Repairs are much faster and easier if the ATV is clean before starting work. Degrease the ATV with a commercial degreaser; follow the directions on the container for the best results. Clean all parts with a solvent formulated for that purpose.
14. If special tools are required, have them available before starting the procedure. When special tools are required, they will be described at the beginning of the procedure.
15. Make sure all shims and washers are reinstalled in the same location and position.
16. Whenever rotating parts contact a stationary part, look for a shim or washer.
17. Use new gaskets if there is any doubt about the condition of old ones.
18. If self-locking fasteners are used, replace them. Do not install standard fasteners in place of self-locking ones.
19. Use grease to hold small parts in place if they tend to fall out during assembly. Do not apply grease to electrical or brake components.

Heating Components

WARNING
Wear protective gloves to prevent burns and injury when heating parts.

CAUTION
Do not use a welding torch when heating parts. A welding torch applies excessive heat to a small area very quickly, which can damage parts.

A heat gun or propane torch is required to disassemble, assemble, remove and install many parts and components in this manual. Read the safety and operating information supplied by the manufacturer of the heat gun or propane torch while also noting the following:
1. The work area should be clean and dry. Remove all combustible components and materials from the work area. Wipe up all grease, oil and other fluids from parts. Check for leaking or damaged fuel system components. Repair or remove these parts before beginning work.
2. Never use a flame near the battery, fuel tank, fuel lines or other flammable materials.
3. When using a heat gun, remember that the temperature can be in excess of 540° C (1000° F).
4. Have a fire extinguisher near the job.
5. Always wear protective goggles and gloves when heating parts.
6. Before heating a part installed on the ATV, check areas around the part and those *hidden* that could be damaged or possibly ignite. Do not heat surfaces than can be damaged by heat. Shield materials such as cables and wiring harnesses near the part or area to be heated.
7. Before heating a part, read the entire procedure to make sure the required tools are available. This allows quick work while the part is at its optimum temperature.
8. The amount of heat recommended to remove or install a part is typically listed in the procedure. However, before heating parts without a specific recommendation, consider the possible effects. To avoid damaging a part, monitor the temperature with heat sticks or an infrared thermometer, if possible. Another way, though not as accurate, is to place tiny drops of water on the part. When the water starts to sizzle, the part is hot enough. Keep the heat in motion to prevent overheating.

Removing Frozen Fasteners

If a fastener cannot be removed, several methods may be used to loosen it. First, liberally apply penetrating oil, and let it penetrate for 10-15 minutes. Rap the fastener several times with a small hammer. Do not hit it hard enough to cause damage. Reapply the penetrating oil if necessary.

For frozen screws, apply penetrating oil as described, and then insert a screwdriver in the slot and rap the top of the screwdriver with a hammer. This loosens the rust so the screw can be removed in the normal way. If the screw head is too damaged to use this method, grip the head with locking pliers and twist it out.

If heat is required, refer to *Heating Components* in this section.

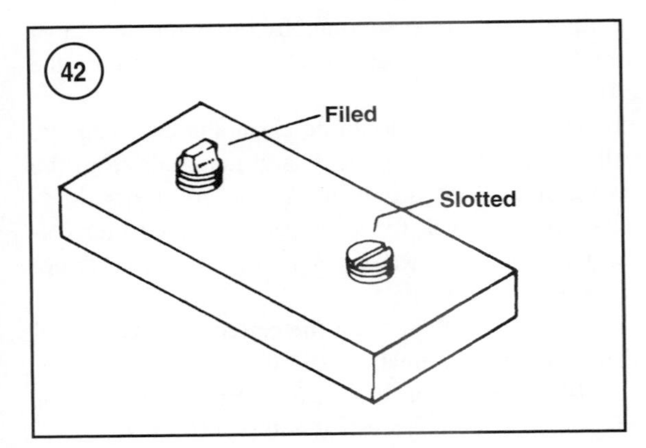

Removing Broken Fasteners

If the head breaks off a screw or bolt, several methods are available for removing the remaining portion. If a large portion of the remainder projects out, try gripping it with locking pliers. If the projecting portion is too small, file it to fit a wrench or cut a slot in it to fit a screwdriver (**Figure 42**).

If the head breaks off flush, use a screw extractor. To do this, center punch the exact center of the screw or bolt (A, **Figure 43**), and then drill a small hole in the screw (B) and tap the extractor into the hole (C). Back the screw out with a wrench on the extractor (D, **Figure 43**).

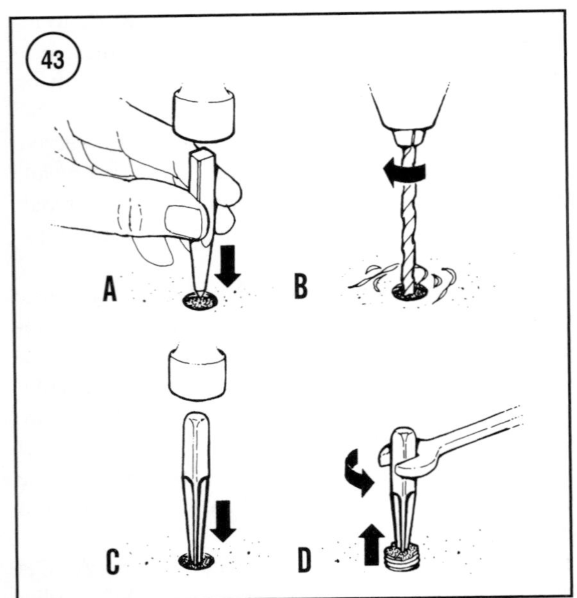

Repairing Damaged Threads

Occasionally, threads are stripped through carelessness or impact damage. Often the threads can be repaired by running a tap (for internal threads on nuts) or die (for external threads on bolts) through the threads (**Figure 44**). To clean or repair spark plug threads, use a spark plug tap.

If an internal thread is damaged, it may be necessary to install a Helicoil or some other type of thread insert. Follow the manufacturer's instructions when installing an insert.

If it is necessary to drill and tap a hole, refer to **Table 6** for metric tap and drill sizes.

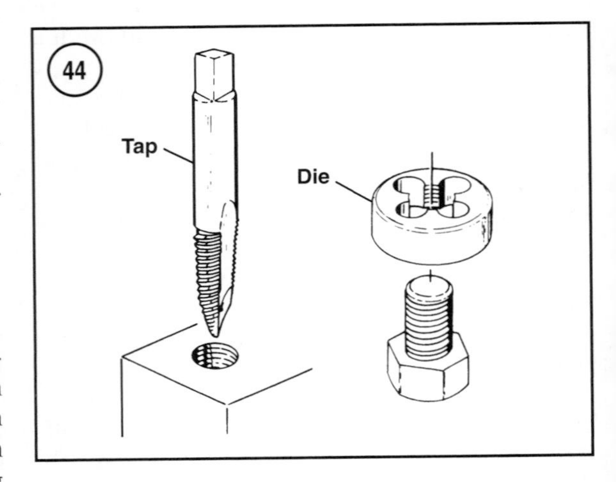

Stud Removal/Installation

A stud removal tool (**Figure 45**) is available from most tool suppliers. This tool makes the removal and installation of studs easier. If one is not available and the threads on the stud are not damaged, thread two nuts onto the stud and tighten them against each other. Remove the stud by turning the lower nut.

1. Measure the height of the stud above the surface.
2. Thread the stud removal tool onto the stud and tighten it, or thread two nuts onto the stud.
3. Remove the stud by turning the stud remover or the lower nut.
4. Remove any threadlock residue from the threaded hole. Clean the threads with an aerosol parts cleaner.
5. Install the stud removal tool onto the new stud, or thread two nuts onto the stud.
6. Apply threadlock to the threads of the stud.
7. Install the stud and tighten it with the stud removal tool or the top nut.
8. Install the stud to the height noted in Step 1 or its torque specification.
9. Remove the stud removal tool or the two nuts.

Removing Hoses

When removing stubborn hoses, do not exert excessive force on the hose or fitting. Remove the hose clamp and carefully insert a small screwdriver or similar blunt nose tool between the fitting and hose.

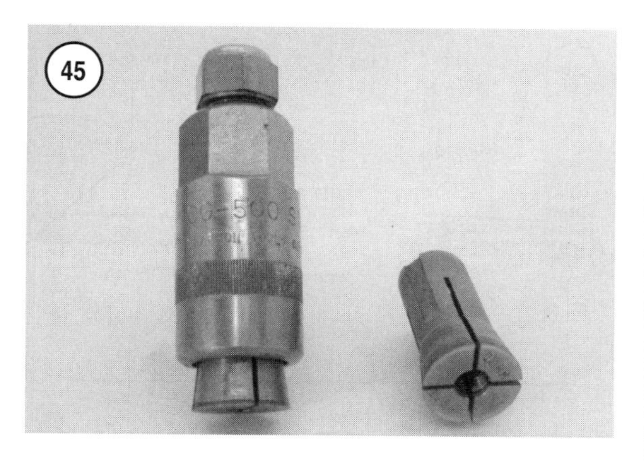
45

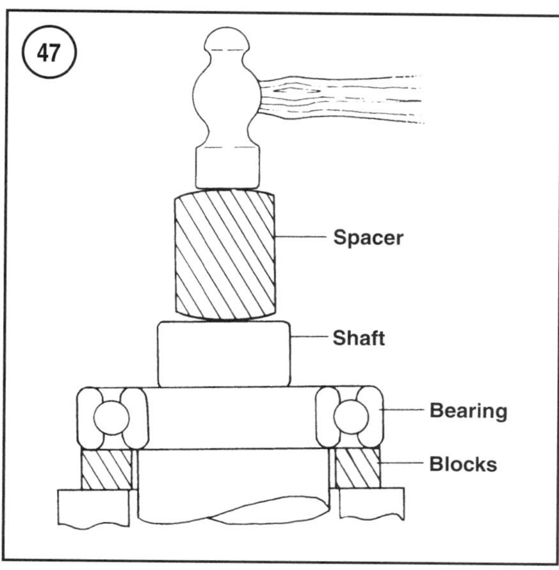

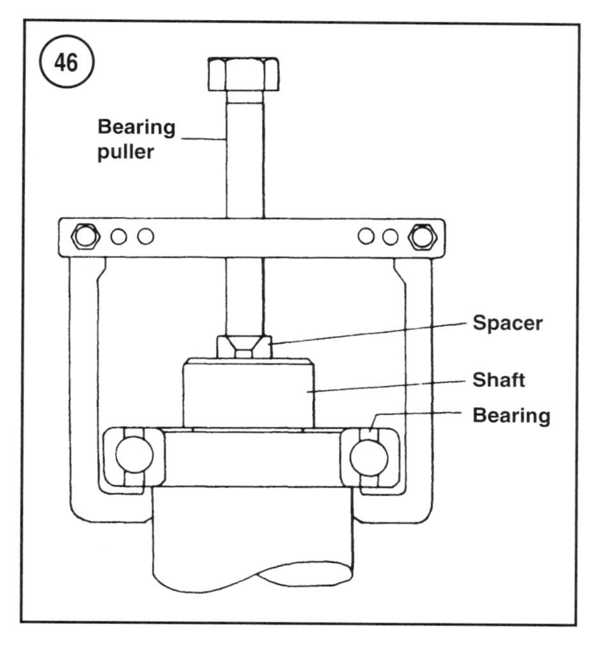

Apply a spray lubricant under the hose and carefully twist the hose off the fitting. Clean the fitting of any corrosion or rubber hose material with a wire brush. Clean the inside of the hose thoroughly. Do not use any lubricant when installing the hose (new or old). The lubricant may allow the hose to come off the fitting, even with the clamp secure.

Bearings

Bearings are precision parts; they must be maintained with proper lubrication and periodic inspection. If a bearing is damaged, replace it immediately. When installing a new bearing, make sure to prevent damaging it. Bearing replacement procedures are included in the individual chapters where applicable; however, use the procedures given here as a guideline.

Unless otherwise specified, install bearings with the manufacturer's mark or number facing outward.

Removal

While bearings are normally removed only when damaged, there may be times when it is necessary to remove a bearing that is in good condition. However, improper bearing removal will damage the bearing and maybe the shaft or case half. Note the following when removing bearings:

1. Before removing the bearings, note the following:
   a. Refer to the bearing replacement procedure in the appropriate chapter for any special instructions.
   b. Remove any seals that interfere with bearing removal. Refer to *Seal Replacement* in this section.
   c. When removing more than one bearing, identify the bearings before removing them. Refer to the bearing manufacturer's numbers on the bearing.
   d. Note and record the direction in which the bearing numbers face for proper installation.
   e. Remove any set plates or bearing retainers before removing the bearings.
2. When using a puller to remove a bearing from a shaft, make sure the shaft is not damaged. Always place a piece of metal between the end of the shaft and the puller screw. In addition, place the puller arms next to the inner bearing race. Refer to **Figure 46**.
3. When using a hammer to remove a bearing from a shaft, do not strike the hammer directly against the shaft. Instead, use a brass or aluminum rod as a spacer (**Figure 47**) between the hammer and shaft. Make sure to support both bearing races with wooden blocks as shown.

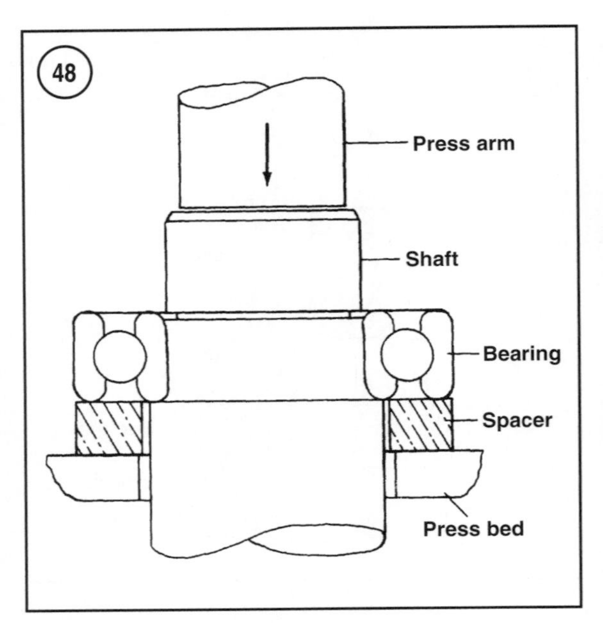

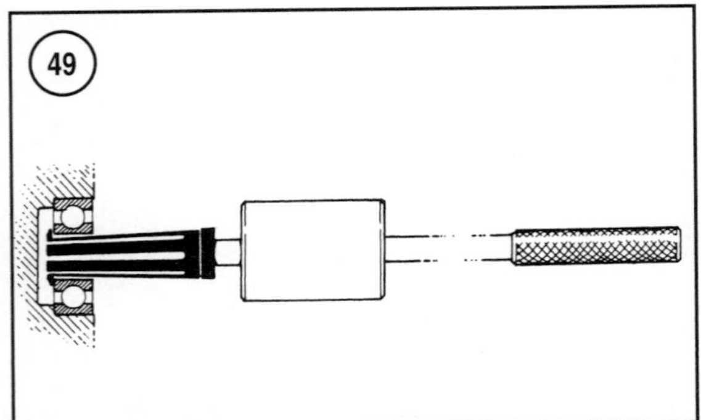

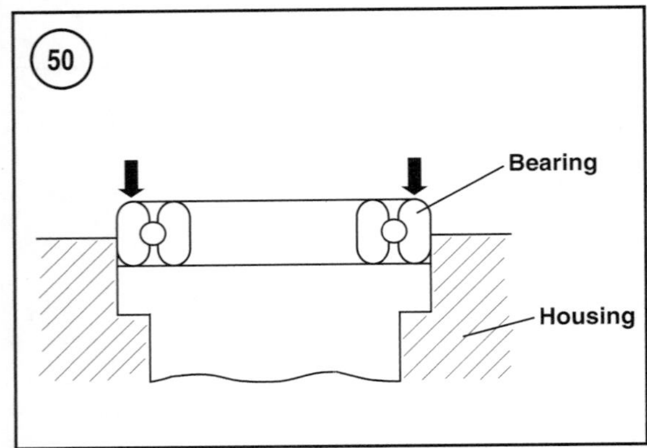

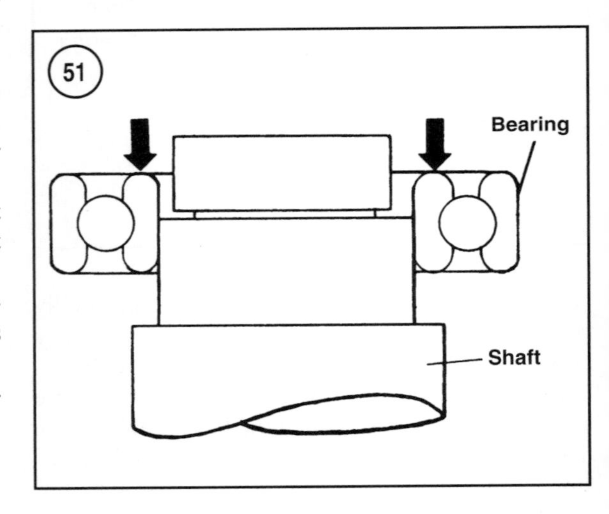

4. The ideal method of bearing removal is with a hydraulic press. Note the following when using a press:

  a. Always support the inner and outer bearing races with a suitable size wooden or aluminum ring as a spacer (**Figure 48**). If only the outer race is supported, pressure applied against the balls and/or the inner race will damage them.
  b. Always make sure the press arm (**Figure 48**) aligns with the center of the shaft. If the arm is not centered, it may damage the bearing and/or shaft.
  c. The moment the shaft is free of the bearing, it will drop to the floor. Secure or hold the shaft to prevent it from falling.
  d. When removing bearings from a housing, support the housing with 4 × 4 in. wooden blocks to prevent damage to gasket surfaces.

5. Use a blind bearing puller to remove bearings installed in blind holes (**Figure 49**).

Installation

1. When installing a bearing in a housing, apply pressure to the *outer* bearing race (**Figure 50**). When installing a bearing on a shaft, apply pressure to the *inner* bearing race (**Figure 51**).
2. When installing a bearing, a driver is required. Never strike the bearing directly with a hammer or the bearing will be damaged. Use a piece of pipe or a driver with a diameter that matches the proper bearing race. **Figure 52** shows the correct way to use a driver and hammer to install a bearing on a shaft.
3. When installing a bearing over a shaft and into the housing at the *same time*, a tight fit will be required for both outer and inner bearing races. In this situation, install a spacer underneath the driver tool so pressure is applied evenly across both races. Refer to **Figure 53**. If the outer race is not supported, the balls push against the outer bearing race and damage it.

Interference Fit

1. Follow this procedure when installing a bearing over a shaft. When a tight fit is required, the bearing inside diameter will be smaller than the shaft. In this case, driving the bearing on the shaft using normal

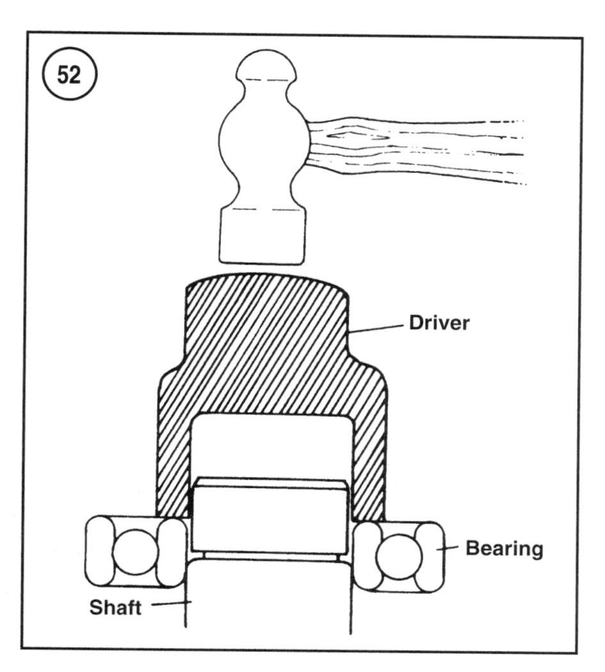

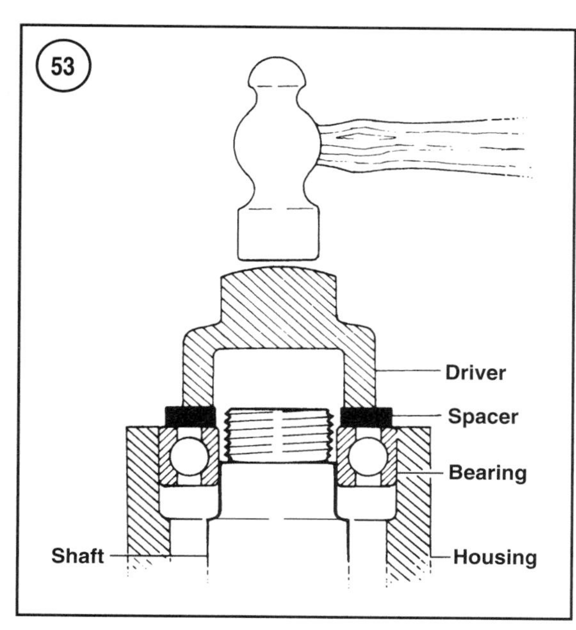

methods may cause bearing damage. Instead, heat the bearing before installation. Note the following:

a. Secure the shaft so it is ready for bearing installation.
b. Clean all residue from the bearing surface of the shaft. Remove burrs with a file.
c. Fill a suitable pot or beaker with clean mineral oil. Place a thermometer rated above 120° C (248° F) in the oil. Support the thermometer so it does not rest on the bottom or side of the pot.
d. Remove the bearing from its wrapper and secure it with a piece of heavy wire bent to hold it in the pot. Hang the bearing in the pot so it does not touch the bottom or sides of the pot.
e. Turn the heat on and monitor the thermometer. When the oil temperature rises to approximately 120° C (248° F), remove the bearing from the pot and quickly install it. If necessary, place a socket on the inner bearing race and tap the bearing into place. As the bearing chills, it tightens on the shaft, so installation must be done quickly. Make sure the bearing is installed completely.

2. Follow this step when installing a bearing in a housing. Bearings are generally installed in a housing with a slight interference fit. Driving the bearing into the housing using normal methods may damage the housing or cause bearing damage. Instead, heat the housing before the bearing is installed. Note the following:

a. Before heating the housing in this procedure, wash the housing thoroughly with detergent and water. Rinse and rewash the housing as required to remove all oil and chemicals.
b. Heat the housing to approximately 100° C (212° F) with a heat gun or on a hot plate. Monitor temperature with an infrared thermometer, heat sticks or place tiny drops of water on the housing; if they sizzle and evaporate immediately, the temperature is correct. Heat only one housing at a time.
c. If a hot plate is used, remove the housing and place it on wooden blocks.
d. Hold the housing with the bearing side down and tap the bearing out with a suitable size socket and extension. Repeat for all bearings in the housing.
e. Before heating the bearing housing, place the new bearing in a freezer, if possible. Chilling a bearing slightly reduces its outside diameter while the heated bearing housing assembly is slightly larger due to heat expansion. This makes bearing installation easier.
f. While the housing is still hot, install the new bearing(s) into the housing. Install the bearings by hand, if possible. If necessary, lightly tap the bearing(s) into the housing with a socket placed on the outer bearing race (**Figure 50**). Do not install bearings by driving on the inner-bearing race. Install the bearing(s) until it seats completely.

Seal Replacement

Seals are used to contain oil, water, grease or combustion gases in a housing or shaft. Improper removal of a seal can damage the housing or shaft. Improper installation can damage the seal.

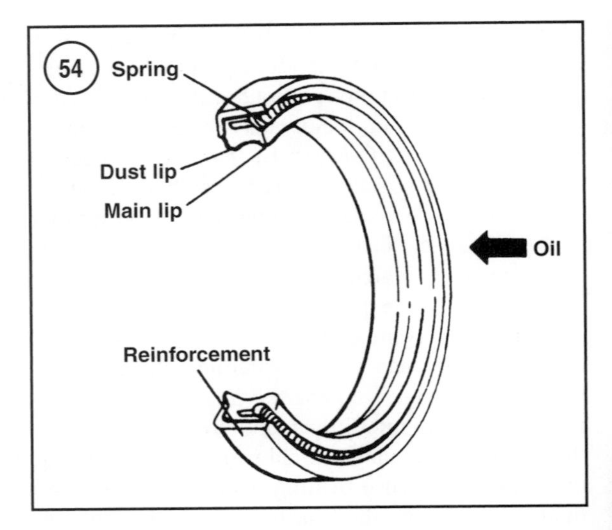

Before replacing a seal, identify it as a rubber or Teflon seal. Both types are used on the models covered in this manual. On a rubber seal (**Figure 54**), the body and sealing element will be made of the same material. The seal lip (element) will also be equipped with a garter spring. On a Teflon seal, the body and seal lip will be noticeably different. The outer part is normally made of rubber and the sealing lip, placed in the middle of the seal, is Teflon. A garter spring is not used.

Rubber seals

1. Prying is generally the easiest and most effective method of removing a seal from the housing. However, always place a rag under the pry tool (**Figure 55**) to prevent damage to the housing.
2. Before installing a typical rubber seal, pack waterproof grease in the seal lips.
3. In most cases, install seals with the manufacturer's numbers or marks face out.
4. Install seals either by hand or with tools. Center the seal in its bore and attempt to install it by hand. If necessary, install the seal with a socket or bearing driver placed on the outside of the seal as shown in **Figure 56**. Drive the seal squarely into the housing until it is flush with its mounting bore. Never install a seal by hitting against the top of the seal with a hammer.

STORAGE

Several months of non-use can cause a general deterioration of the ATV. This is especially true in areas of extreme temperature variations. This deterioration can be minimized with careful preparation for storage. A properly stored ATV is much easier to return to service.

Storage Area Selection

When selecting a storage area, consider the following:

1. The storage area must be dry. A heated area is best, but not necessary. It should be insulated to minimize extreme temperature variations.
2. If the building has large window areas, mask them to keep sunlight off the ATV.
3. Avoid storage areas close to saltwater.
4. Consider the area's risk of fire, theft or vandalism. Check with your insurer regarding ATV coverage while in storage.

Preparing the ATV for Storage

The amount of preparation a ATV should undergo before storage depends on the expected length of non-use, storage area conditions and personal preference. Consider the following list the minimum requirement:

1. Wash the ATV thoroughly. Make sure all dirt, mud and road debris are removed.
2. Start the engine and allow it to reach operating temperature. Drain the engine oil regardless of the riding time since the last service. Fill the engine with the recommended type and quantity of oil.
3. Fill the fuel tank completely.
4. Remove the spark plug from the cylinder head. Ground the spark plug cap to the engine. Refer to

Ignition Grounding Tool in this chapter. Pour a teaspoon of engine oil into the cylinder. Place a rag over the openings and slowly turn the engine over to distribute the oil. Reinstall the spark plug.
5. Remove the battery. Store it in a cool, dry location. Charge the battery once a month. Refer to *Battery* in Chapter Nine for service.
6. Cover the exhaust and intake openings.
7. Apply a protective substance to the plastic and rubber components, including the tires. Make sure to follow the manufacturer's instructions for each type of product being used.
8. Rotate the tires periodically to prevent a flat spot from developing and damaging the tire.
9. Cover the ATV with old bed sheets or something similar. Do not cover it with any plastic material that will trap moisture.

Returning the ATV to Service

The amount of service required when returning a ATV to service after storage depends on the length of non-use and storage conditions. In addition to performing the reverse of the storage procedures, make sure the brakes, clutch, throttle and engine stop switch all work properly before operating the ATV. Refer to Chapter Three and evaluate the maintenance schedule to determine which areas require service.

Table 1 GENERAL DIMENSIONS AND WEIGHT

	mm	in.
Ground clearance	240	9.45
Overall height	1130	44.5
Overall length	1845	72.6
Overall width	1170	46.1
Seat height	815	32.1
Turning radius (min.)	3500	137.8
Wheelbase	1280	50.4
Weight (with oil and fuel)	192 kg	423 lb.

Table 2 FUEL TANK CAPACITY

Total (including reserve)	11.0 L (2.9 U.S. gal.)
Reserve only	
2006-2012 models	2.6 L (0.70 U.S. gal.)
2013-on models	2.9 L (0.77 U.S. gal.)

Table 3 TECHNICAL ABBREVIATIONS

ABDC	After bottom dead center
ATDC	After top dead center
BBDC	Before bottom dead center
BDC	Bottom dead center
BTDC	Before top dead center
BARO	Barometric pressure sensor
C	Celsius (centigrade)
cc	Cubic centimeters
cid	Cubic inch displacement
CDI	Capacitor discharge ignition
CMP	Camshaft position sensor
CKP	Crankshaft position sensor
cu. in.	Cubic inches
DLC	Data link connector
DTC	Diagnostic trouble code
ECM	Engine control module
ECT	Engine coolant temperature sensor
EFI	Electronic fuel injection

(continued)

Table 3 TECHNICAL ABBREVIATIONS (continued)

EVAP	Evaporative emission
F	Fahrenheit
ft.	Feet
ft.-lb.	Foot-pounds
gal.	Gallons
H/A	High altitude
hp	Horsepower
IAC	Idle air control valve
IAT	Intake air temperature sensor
ICM	Ignition control module
in.	Inches
in.-lb.	inch-pounds
I.D.	Inside diameter
kg	Kilograms
kgm	Kilogram meters
km	kilometer
kPa	Kilopascals
L	Liter
m	meter
MIL	Malfunction indicator lamp
MAP	Manifold absolute pressure sensor
MAG	Magneto
ml	Milliliter
mm	millimeter
N•m	Newton-meters
O_2	Oxygen sensor
O.D.	Outside diameter
oz.	Ounces
PAIR	Pulsed secondary air injection system
PGM-FI	Programmed fuel injection
psi	Pounds per square inch
pt.	Pint
qt.	Quart
RPM	Revolutions per minute
RTV	Room temperature vulcanization
TPS	Throttle position sensor
VSS	Vehicle speed sensor

Table 4 GENERAL TORQUE RECOMMENDATIONS

	N•m	ft.-lb.
10 mm nut or 6 mm bolt	6	4.3
12 mm nut or 8 mm bolt	15	11
14 mm nut or 10 mm bolt	30	22
17 mm nut or 12 mm bolt	55	40
19 mm nut or 14 mm bolt	85	61
22 mm nut or 16 mm bolt	130	94

Table 5 CONVERSION FORMULAS

Multiply:	By:	To get the equivalent of:
Length		
Inches	25.4	Millimeter
Inches	2.54	Centimeter
Miles	1.609	Kilometer
Feet	0.3048	Meter
Millimeter	0.03937	Inches
Centimeter	0.3937	Inches
Kilometer	0.6214	Mile
Meter	3.281	Feet

(continued)

1

Table 5 CONVERSION FORMULAS (continued)

Multiply:	By:	To get the equivalent of:
Fluid volume		
U.S. quarts	0.9463	Liters
U.S. gallons	3.785	Liters
U.S. ounces	29.573529	Milliliters
Liters	0.2641721	U.S. gallons
Liters	1.0566882	U.S. quarts
Liters	33.814023	U.S. ounces
Milliliters	0.033814	U.S. ounces
Milliliters	1.0	Cubic centimeters
Milliliters	0.001	Liters
Torque		
Foot-pounds	1.3558	Newton-meters
Foot-pounds	0.138255	Meters-kilograms
Inch-pounds	0.11299	Newton-meters
Newton-meters	0.7375622	Foot-pounds
Newton-meters	8.8507	Inch-pounds
Meters-kilograms	7.2330139	Foot-pounds
Volume		
Cubic inches	16.387064	Cubic centimeters
Cubic centimeters	0.0610237	Cubic inches
Temperature		
Fahrenheit	(°F – 32) × 0.556	Centigrade
Centigrade	(°C × 1.8) + 32	Fahrenheit
Weight		
Ounces	28.3495	Grams
Pounds	0.4535924	Kilograms
Grams	0.035274	Ounces
Kilograms	2.2046224	Pounds
Pressure		
Pounds per square inch	0.070307	Kilograms per square centimeter
Kilograms per square centimeter	14.223343	Pounds per square inch
Kilopascals	0.1450	Pounds per square inch
Pounds per square inch	6.895	Kilopascals
Speed		
Miles per hour	1.609344	Kilometers per hour
Kilometers per hour	0.6213712	Miles per hour

Table 6 METRIC TAP DRILL SIZES

Metric size	Drill equivalent	Decimal fraction	Nearest fraction
3 × 0.50	No. 39	0.0995	3/32
3 × 0.60	3/32	0.0937	3/32
4 × 0.70	No. 30	0.1285	1/8
4 × 0.75	1/8	0.125	1/8
5 × 0.80	No. 19	0.166	11/64
5 × 0.90	No. 20	0.161	5/32
6 × 1.00	No. 9	0.196	13/64
7 × 1.00	16/64	0.234	15/64
8 × 1.00	J	0.277	9/32
8 × 1.25	17/64	0.265	17/64
9 × 1.00	5/16	0.3125	5/16
9 × 1.25	5/16	0.3125	5/16
10 × 1.25	11/32	0.3437	11/32
10 × 1.50	R	0.339	11/32
11 × 1.50	3/8	0.375	3/8
12 × 1.50	13/32	0.406	13/32
12 × 1.75	13/32	0.406	13/32

Table 7 METRIC, INCH AND FRACTIONAL EQUIVALENTS

mm	in.	Nearest fraction	mm	in.	Nearest fraction
1	0.0394	1/32	26	1.0236	1 1/32
2	0.0787	3/32	27	1.0630	1 1/16
3	0.1181	1/8	28	1.1024	1 3/32
4	0.1575	5/32	29	1.1417	1 5/32
5	0.1969	3/16	30	1.1811	1 3/16
6	0.2362	1/4	31	1.2205	1 7/32
7	0.2756	9/32	32	1.2598	1 1/4
8	0.3150	5/16	33	1.2992	1 5/16
9	0.3543	11/32	34	1.3386	1 11/32
10	0.3937	13/32	35	1.3780	1 3/8
11	0.4331	7/16	36	1.4173	1 13/32
12	0.4724	15/32	37	1.4567	1 15/32
13	0.5118	1/2	38	1.4961	1 1/2
14	0.5512	9/16	39	1.5354	1 17/32
15	0.5906	19/32	40	1.5748	1 9/16
16	0.6299	5/8	41	1.6142	1 5/8
17	0.6693	21/32	42	1.6535	1 21/32
18	0.7087	23/32	43	1.6929	1 11/16
19	0.7480	3/4	44	1.7323	1 23/32
20	0.7874	25/32	45	1.7717	1 25/32
21	0.8268	13/16	46	1.8110	1 13/16
22	0.8661	7/8	47	1.8504	1 27/32
23	0.9055	29/32	48	1.8898	1 7/8
24	0.9449	15/16	49	1.9291	1 15/16
25	0.9843	31/32	50	1.9685	1 31/32

CHAPTER TWO

TROUBLESHOOTING

The troubleshooting procedures described in this chapter provide typical symptoms and logical methods for isolating the cause(s). There may be several ways to solve a problem, but only a systematic approach will be successful in avoiding wasted time and possibly unnecessary parts replacement. Gather as much information as possible to aid in diagnosis. Never assume anything and do not overlook the obvious. Make sure the engine stop switch is in the run position and there is fuel in the tank.

An engine needs three basics to run properly: the correct air/ fuel mixture, compression and a spark at the correct time. If one of these is missing, the engine will not run.

Learning to recognize symptoms makes troubleshooting easier. In most cases, expensive and complicated test equipment is not needed. On the other hand, be realistic and do not start procedures that are beyond your experience and available equipment. If the ATV requires the attention of a professional, describe symptoms and conditions accurately and fully. The more information a technician has available, the easier it is to diagnose the problem.

STARTING THE ENGINE

The engine is equipped with a fuel-injection system that is controlled by the electronic control unit (ECU). The ECU adjusts the fuel and ignition systems as needed to start the engine in varying conditions.

Before starting the engine, always perform a pre-ride inspection of the machine (Chapter Three).

1. The machine is equipped with the following safety switches that prevent the engine from starting or running if certain conditions occur.
   a. Neutral switch. With the transmission in any position except neutral, with the clutch engaged (clutch lever out), the engine will not start.
   b. Clutch switch. With the transmission in gear, the engine will not start if the clutch is engaged (clutch lever out). If the clutch is disengaged with the transmission in gear, the engine will start.
   c. Engine stop switch (A, **Figure 1**). When moved to the off position (left), the switch will prevent the engine from starting, or, will stop the engine when it is running. The engine will start and run only when the switch is in the run position.
2. Shift the transmission into neutral.
3. Move the engine stop switch to the run position.

CAUTION
If a warning light stays on, determine the cause before operating the ATV.

4. Turn the ignition switch on. The fuel level warning light (A, **Figure 2**) and engine trouble warning light (B) should illuminate, then go out.
5. Check that the neutral light (C, **Figure 2**) comes on.

6. Press the starter button (B, **Figure 1**) while keeping the throttle closed.

CAUTION
Keep the starter button depressed until the engine is definitely started. Releasing the button too soon can cause engine kick back, potentially damaging the starter clutch assembly.

CAUTION
Do not race the engine during the warm-up period. Excessive wear and potential engine damage can occur when the engine is not up to operating temperature.

7. When the engine starts, allow the engine to warm up at an idle for one minute, or until the engine responds smoothly.

ENGINE DOES NOT START

If the engine does not start, perform the following procedure in sequence. If the engine fails to start after performing these inspections, refer to the troubleshooting procedures indicated in the steps.

All models are equipped with a self-diagnostic engine management system. Refer to *Electronic Diagnostic System* (this chapter).

1. Refer to *Starting the Engine* in this chapter to make sure all switches and starting procedures are correct.
2. If the starter does not operate, refer to *Engine Starting System* in this chapter.
3. Verify that there is fuel in the fuel tank.
4. If there is sufficient fuel in the fuel tank, remove the spark plug immediately after attempting to start the engine. The spark plug insulator should be wet, indicating that fuel is reaching the engine. If the plug tip is dry, fuel is not reaching the engine. A faulty fuel pump or a clogged fuel filter can cause this condition. If there is fuel on the spark plug and the engine will not start, the engine may not have adequate spark.
5. Make sure each spark plug cap is securely attached to the spark plug.
6. Perform the *Spark Test* described in this section.

7A. If there is a strong spark, perform a compression test as described in Chapter Three.

7B. If there is no spark or if the spark is very weak, refer to *Electronic Diagnostic System* in this chapter.

Spark Test

Perform a spark test to determine if the ignition system is producing adequate spark. This test can be performed with a spark plug or a spark tester. A spark tester (Motion Pro part No. 08-0122 or an equivalent) may be used as a substitute for the spark plug and allows the spark to be more easily observed between the adjustable air gap. If a spark tester is not available, always use a new spark plug.

1. Make sure the battery is fully charged (Chapter Nine).
2. Connect a spark plug wire and connector to a new spark plug or to a spark tester. Touch the spark plug

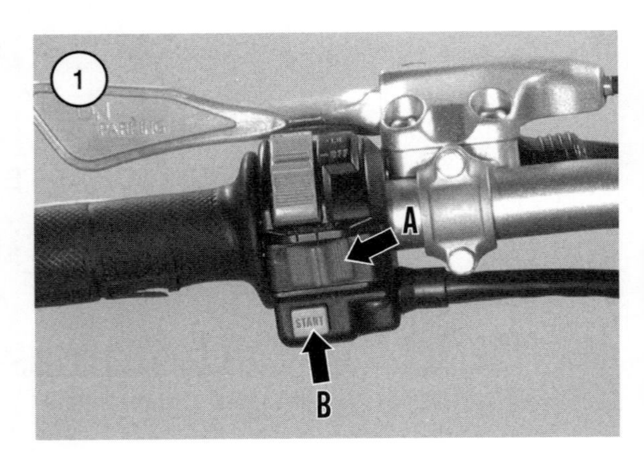

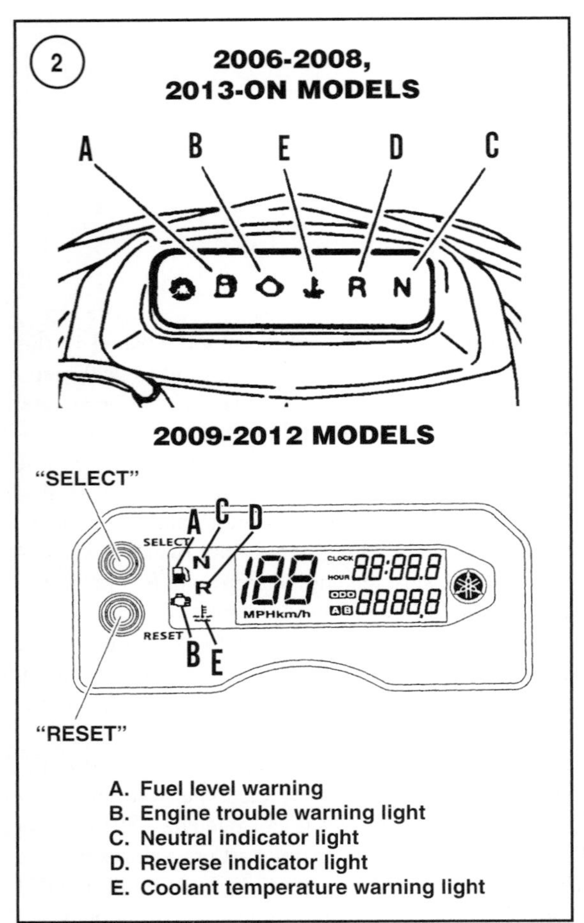

A. Fuel level warning
B. Engine trouble warning light
C. Neutral indicator light
D. Reverse indicator light
E. Coolant temperature warning light

base or the tester (**Figure 3**) to a good engine ground. Position the spark plug or tester so the electrodes are visible.

WARNING
If the spark plug has been removed, place the spark plug or spark tester away from the spark plug hole in the cylinder head so the spark plug or tester cannot ignite gasoline vapors emitted from the cylinder. If the engine is flooded, do not perform this test with the spark plug removed.

WARNING
Disable the fuel system before cranking the engine. Otherwise, fuel will enter the cylinder when the engine is turned over during the spark test, possibly flooding the cylinder and creating explosive fuel vapors.

3. If the spark plug was removed, disconnect the fuel pump electrical connector as described in fuel tank removal (Chapter Eight). Do not remove the fuel tank.
4. Shift the transmission to neutral, turn the ignition switch on and turn the engine stop switch to run.

WARNING
Do not hold the spark plug, tester, wire or connector during cranking or a serious electrical shock may result.

5. Operate the starter button to turn the engine over. A fat blue spark must be evident across the spark plug electrodes or between the tester terminals.
6. If the spark is good at the spark plug or tester, the ignition system is functioning properly. Check for one or more of the following possible malfunctions:
   a. Faulty fuel system component. Refer to *Electronic Diagnostic System* (this chapter).
   b. Engine damage (low compression).
   c. Engine flooded.
7. If the spark was weak or if there was no spark, note the following:
   a. Check for a problem on the input side of the ignition system as described in *Electronic Diagnostic System* (this chapter).
   b. Retest with a spark tester, or use a new spark plug. If there is still no spark, make sure the spark plug cap is installed correctly.
   c. If there is no spark, the ignition coil is faulty.
   d. Troubleshoot the ignition system as described in *Electronic Diagnostic System* (this chapter).
8. Install the spark plug as described in Chapter Three.

Engine is Difficult to Start

1. After attempting to start the engine, remove the spark plug as described in Chapter Three and check for the presence of fuel on the plug tip. Note the following:
   a. If there is fuel present on the plug tip, go to Step 3.
   b. If there is an excessive amount of fuel on the plug, check for a clogged or plugged air filter.
2. Perform the fuel pump testing procedures in Chapter Eight. Note the following:
   a. If the fuel pump operation is correct, go to Step 3.
   b. If there is fuel low fuel pressure, check for a clogged fuel pump filter.
   c. If fuel pump operation is faulty, replace the fuel pump and retest the fuel delivery system.
3. Perform the spark test as described in this chapter. Note the following:
   a. If the spark is weak or if there is no spark, go to Step 4.
   b. If the spark is good, go to Step 5.
4. If the spark is weak or if there is no spark, check the following:
   a. Fouled spark plug.
   b. Damaged spark plug.
   c. Loose or damaged spark plug wire.
   d. Loose or damaged spark plug cap.
   e. Faulty ECU.
   f. Faulty crankshaft position sensor.
   g. Faulty ignition coil.
   h. Faulty lean-angle sensor.
   i. Faulty engine stop switch.
   j. Faulty ignition switch.
   k. Dirty or loose-fitting terminals.
5. If the engine turns over but does not start, the engine compression is probably low. Check for the following possible malfunctions:
   a. Leaking cylinder head gasket.
   b. Bent or stuck valve(s).
   c. Incorrect valve timing.

d. Worn cylinder and/or pistons rings.

6. If the spark is good, try starting the engine by following normal starting procedures. If the engine starts but then stops, check for the following conditions:

a. Leaking or damaged intake duct.
b. Contaminated fuel.
c. Incorrect ignition timing.
d. Faulty throttle position sensor.
e. Faulty crankshaft position sensor.
f. Defective fuel injector.

Engine Will Not Crank

If the engine will not turn over, check for one or more of the following possible malfunctions:

1. Blown main fuse.
2. Discharged battery.
3. Defective starter or starter relay.
4. Seized piston.
5. Seized crankshaft bearings.
6. Broken connecting rod.
7. Locked-up transmission or clutch assembly.
8. Defective starter clutch.

ENGINE PERFORMANCE

If the engine runs, but performance is unsatisfactory, refer to the following procedure(s) that best describes the symptom(s). All models are equipped with a self-diagnostic engine management system. Refer to *Electronic Diagnostic System* in this chapter for identification of malfunctioning components that may cause a performance problem.

NOTE

The ignition timing is not adjustable. If incorrect ignition timing is suspected, inspect the ignition timing as described in Chapter Three. If the timing is incorrect, a defective ignition system component is indicated. Refer to ***Electronic Diagnostic System*** *in this chapter.*

Engine Will Not Idle

1. Clogged air filter element.
2. Fouled or improperly gapped spark plug(s).
3. Leaking head gasket.
4. Leaking or damaged intake duct.
5. Vacuum leak.
6. Incorrect ignition timing: faulty ECU or crankshaft position sensor.
7. Obstructed throttle body or defective fuel injector.
8. Low engine compression.
9. Faulty ignition coil.
10. Faulty coolant temperature sensor.

Poor Overall Performance

1. Support the ATV so the rear wheels are off the ground. Rotate the rear wheels by hand. If the wheels turn without dragging or binding, perform Step 2. If the wheels do not spin freely, check for the following conditions:

a. Dragging rear brake.
b. Damaged rear axle assembly.

2. Check the clutch adjustment and operation. If the clutch slips, refer to *Clutch* in this chapter.

3. If Step 1 and Step 2 did not locate the problem, test ride the ATV and accelerate with gradual throttle opening. If the engine hesitates, stumbles or acceleration does not match the throttle opening, check for one or more of the following problems:

a. Clogged air filter.
b. Clogged or damaged muffler.
c. Worn or fouled spark plugs.
d. Faulty fuel pump.
e. Obstructed throttle body or defective fuel injector.
f. Faulty coolant temperature sensor.
g. Faulty throttle position sensor.
h. Faulty intake air temperature sensor.
i. Faulty intake air pressure sensor.
j. Faulty ignition coil.
k. Incorrect ignition timing: faulty ECU or crankshaft position sensor.
l. Low engine compression.
m. Worn or damaged valve train assembly.
n. Engine overheating. See Engine Overheating in this section.

4. If the engine surges, check the following:

a. Fuel pump pressure.
b. Defective fuel injector.
c. Faulty coolant temperature sensor.

5. If the engine knocks during acceleration or when running at high speed, check for one or more of the following possible malfunctions:

a. Incorrect type of fuel.
b. Lean fuel mixture.
c. Incorrect ignition timing: faulty ECU or crankshaft position sensor.
d. Excessive carbon buildup in combustion chamber.
e. Worn pistons and/or cylinder bores.
f. Worn bearing(s).
g. Faulty intake air temperature sensor.
h. Faulty intake air pressure sensor.

Poor Idle or Low Speed Performance

1. Check for damaged intake duct and air box hose clamps.
2. Check the fuel system (Chapter Eight).

3. Perform the spark test as described in this chapter. Note the following:
   a. If the spark is good, go to Step 4.
   b. If the spark is weak, test the ignition system as described in this chapter.
4. Check the ignition timing as described in Chapter Three. Note the following:
   a. If the ignition timing is incorrect, check the ignition system (Chapter Nine).
   b. If the ignition timing is correct, recheck the fuel system.
5. Obstructed throttle body or defective fuel injector.
6. Faulty coolant temperature sensor.
7. Faulty throttle position sensor.
8. Faulty intake air temperature sensor.
9. Faulty intake air pressure sensor.
10. Faulty ignition coil.

Poor High Speed Performance

1. Check the fuel system (Chapter Eight).
2. Check ignition timing as described in Chapter Three. If ignition timing is correct, perform Step 4.
3. If the timing is incorrect, test the following components:
   a. ECU (Chapter Eight).
   b. Crankshaft position sensor (Chapter Nine).
   c. Ignition coil (Chapter Nine).
4. Incorrect valve timing and worn or damaged valve springs can cause poor high-speed performance. If the camshafts were timed just prior to the ATV experiencing this type of problem, the cam timing may be incorrect. If the cam timing was not set or changed, and all of the other inspection procedures in this section failed to locate the problem, inspect the camshafts and valve assembly.

Engine Overheating

Cooling system malfunction

1. Low coolant level.
2. Air in cooling system.
3. Clogged radiator, hose or engine coolant passages.
4. Thermostat stuck closed.
5. Worn or damaged radiator cap.
6. Damaged water pump.
7. Damaged fan motor switch.
8. Damaged fan motor.
9. Faulty coolant temperature sensor.

Other causes

1. Improper spark plug heat range.
2. Low oil level.
3. Oil not circulating properly.
4. Valves leaking.
5. Excessive carbon buildup in combustion chamber.
6. Dragging brake(s).
7. Clutch slip.
8. Incorrect ignition timing: faulty ECU or crankshaft position sensor.
9. Lean fuel mixture.

Engine Not Reaching Operating Temperature

1. Thermostat stuck open.
2. Damaged fan motor switch.
3. Faulty coolant temperature sensor.

Engine Backfires

1. Restricted fuel flow.
2. Faulty fuel pump.
3. Incorrect ignition timing: faulty ECU or crankshaft position sensor.
4. Faulty coolant temperature sensor.
5. Faulty throttle position sensor.
6. Faulty intake air temperature sensor.
7. Faulty intake air pressure sensor.

Engine Misfires During Acceleration

1. Restricted fuel flow.
2. Faulty fuel pump.
3. Faulty coolant temperature sensor.
4. Faulty intake air temperature sensor.
5. Faulty intake air pressure sensor.
6. Faulty ignition coil.

ELECTRONIC DIAGNOSTIC SYSTEM

The electronic control unit (ECU) includes a self-diagnostic function that monitors electrical components of the ignition and fuel injection systems. Whenever an error is detected, the ECU stores the malfunction and sets a fault code. It also turns on the engine trouble warning light (B, **Figure 2**) in the indicator light panel. The engine trouble warning light will either stay on continuously or will blink depending on the fault.

Note that some malfunctions may not trigger a fault code. If this occurs, refer to this chapter and to the wiring diagrams at the end of this manual to assist in troubleshooting the problem.

Under normal operating conditions, the engine trouble warning light is illuminated for 1.4 seconds after the ignition switch is turned on. The light should blink while the start button is being pressed. If the warning light does not come on or blink as described, check for a blown bulb or other problem in the circuit.

Read through the following sections before beginning diagnostic system troubleshooting. Refer to Chapter Eight or Chapter Nine prior to replacing any component(s). If the procedures are not followed carefully, an incorrect diagnosis may occur. Do not overlook the possibility that something as simple as a loose electrical connector or vacuum hose may be the source of a problem. If the source of a fault code cannot be determined, take the ATV to a dealership as soon as possible for troubleshooting and repair.

Trouble Codes and Diagnostic Codes

There are two different types of codes:

1. Trouble Codes. If a problem occurs within the system, the rider is notified by the engine trouble warning light. The engine trouble warning light remains on during operation or it blinks after the engine stops if a fault code exists in the ECU. The ATV may or may not be able to be started and ridden, depending on the type of the malfunction. Refer to **Table 1** for trouble codes.
2. Diagnostic Codes: After a trouble code is displayed, this can be cross-referenced to the diagnostic code. The FI diagnostic tool (Yamaha part No. YU-03182/90890-03182) is necessary to read the diagnostic code on 2006-2008 models. On 2009-2012 models, diagnostic codes may be read on the instrument panel display.

Refer to *Reading Diagnostic Codes* in this section. The FI diagnostic tool will display specification data for a particular component associated with the diagnostic code. Refer to **Table 2** for diagnostic codes.

Reading Trouble Codes

Two methods are available to read trouble codes. The engine trouble warning light will blink in a sequence that can be converted to the trouble code number. Trouble codes may also be read using the FI diagnostic tool. The FI diagnostic tool also provides a diagnostic code to assist in troubleshooting.

Using the engine trouble warning light

1. Run the engine, and then stop the engine using the engine stop switch.
2. Observe the engine trouble warning light (B, **Figure 2**). A blinking light indicates a trouble code exists in the ECU.
3. Read the trouble code by counting the long flashes and short flashes. Refer to **Figure 4**. A long flash represents tens digits. For instance, four long flashes represents 40. Short flashes represent single digits. For instance, six short flashes represent 6. Note in **Figure 4** that one long flash followed by three short flashes represents trouble code 13.
4. The lowest numbered trouble code is displayed.

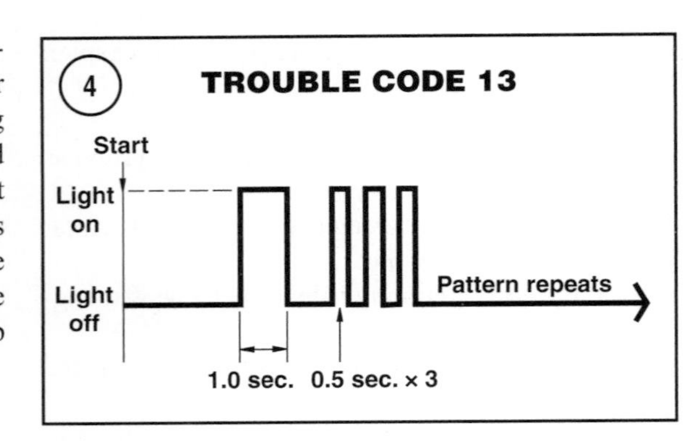

Using the FI Diagnostic Tool (except 2009-2012 models)

1. Remove the seat as described in Chapter Fifteen.
2. Make sure the ignition switch is off and the engine stop switch is set at run.
3. Remove the cap on the diagnostic connector (**Figure 5**).
4. Connect the FI diagnostic tool to the diagnostic connector.
5. Run the engine. The diagnostic tool will display engine rpm and coolant temperature. If a fault exists, the orange warning light on the tool will illuminate.
6. Using the engine stop switch, stop the engine.
7. Read the trouble code on the FI diagnostic tool. The lowest numbered trouble code is displayed.

Reading Diagnostic Codes

Trouble codes and diagnostic codes may be read using the FI diagnostic tool (Yamaha part No. YU-03182/90890-03182) or by reading the code(s) displayed on the instrument panel of 2009-2012 models. Use one of the following procedures to access diagnostic codes.

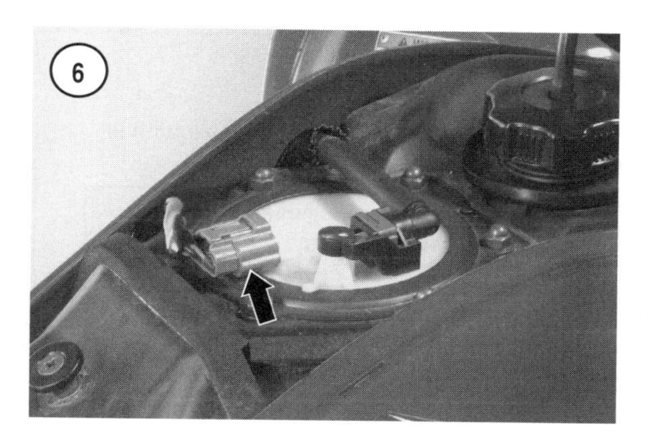

Using the FI Diagnostic Tool (except 2009-2012 models)

1. Remove the seat as described in Chapter Fifteen.
2. Make sure the ignition switch is off and the engine stop switch is set at run.
3. Remove the fuel tank cover as described in Chapter Fifteen.
4. Disconnect the fuel pump connector (**Figure 6**) from the fuel pump.
5. Remove the cap on the diagnostic connector (**Figure 5**).
6. Connect the diagnostic tool to the diagnostic connector.
7. Press and hold the MODE button on the diagnostic tool. Then, turn the ignition switch on.

NOTE
The diagnostic tool may display CO or DIAG modes. Depress the up button as needed so the DIAG mode appears on the tool screen. Do not use the CO adjustment mode.

8. When DIAG appears on the screen, press the mode button to set the tool in diagnostic mode.
9. Press the up or down buttons for 1 second or longer to scroll through the diagnostic codes (D01-D70).
10. Select the diagnostic code that applies to the item that was verified with the trouble code.
11. Refer to **Table 2** and verify the operation of the sensor/actuator by performing the instruction in the action column.
12. Turn the ignition switch off to cancel the diagnostic mode process.
13. Disconnect the diagnostic tool from the diagnostic connector.
14. Install the cap onto the diagnostic connector (**Figure 5**).
15. Connect the fuel pump connector (**Figure 6**) to the fuel pump.
16. Install the fuel tank cover as described in Chapter Fifteen.
17. Install the seat as described in Chapter Fifteen.

Using the Instrument Panel on 2009-2012 Models

1. Make sure the ignition switch is off and the engine stop switch is set at off.
2. Remove the fuel tank cover as described in Chapter Fifteen.
3. Disconnect the fuel pump connector (**Figure 6**) from the fuel pump.
4. Press and hold the SELECT and RESET buttons simultaneously on the instrument panel, and then turn the ignition switch to ON. Continue to hold down the buttons for at least 8 seconds.

NOTE
The panel characters will disappear, then DIAG will appear.

5. When DIAG appears, press the SELECT and RESET buttons for at least 2 seconds to set the tool in diagnostic mode.
6. Press the SELECT button for 1 second or longer to scroll up through the diagnostic codes (D01-D70). Press the RESET button to scroll down.
7. Select the diagnostic code that applies to the item that was verified with the trouble code.
8. Refer to **Table 2** and verify the operation of the sensor/actuator by performing the instruction in the action column.
9. Turn the engine stop switch to on to actuate the sensor or actuator.
10. Turn the ignition switch off to cancel the diagnostic mode process.
11. Connect the fuel pump connector (**Figure 6**) to the fuel pump.
12. Install the fuel tank cover as described in Chapter Fifteen.

Fail-safe Operation

If the warning light stays on continuously, the ATV may or may not operate, depending on the fault code.

When a problem with a sensor/actuator is detected by the ECU, the ECU processes the information and enters a pre-programmed specification for the sensor/actuator function. This fail-safe action, depending on the fault code, may allow ATV operation. It also may be necessary to stop operation of the ATV, depending on what area(s) of the system is affected.

If the warning light is blinking, the ATV will cease to operate and it cannot be started or ridden. At this time one of the following fault codes may exist:

1. No. 12: Crankshaft position sensor.
2. No. 30: Lean angle cut-off switch (latch up detected).
3. No. 33: Ignition coil (faulty ignition)

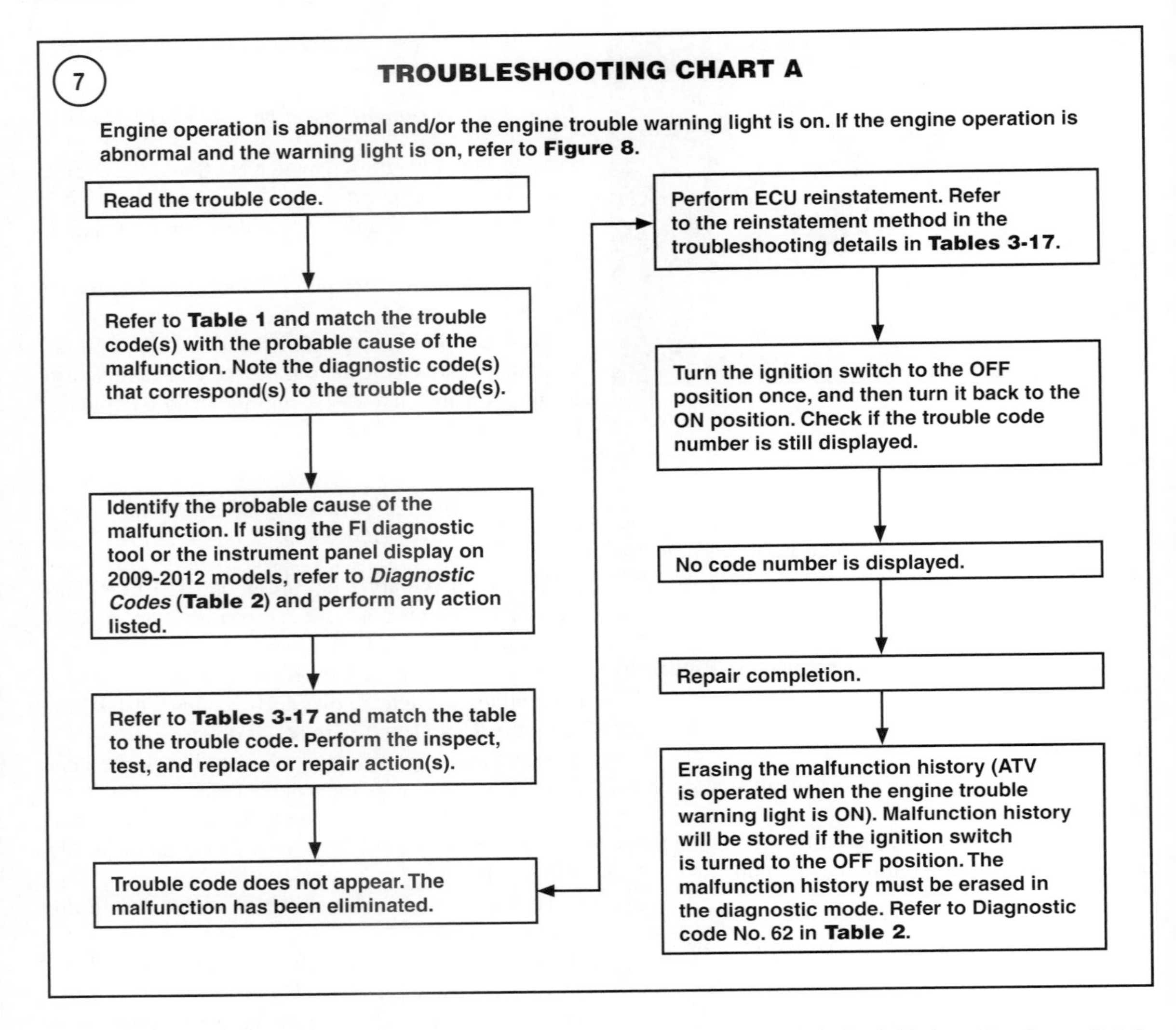

4. No. 41: Lean angle cut-off switch (open or short circuit).
5. No. 50: ECU internal malfunction (memory check error).

Troubleshooting

Refer to **Figure 7** and **Figure 8** for an outline of the diagnostic steps. Refer to **Figure 7** if a fault code is present. Refer to **Figure 8** if an abnormal engine condition is occurring and no fault code is present.

Use the fault code information (**Table 1**) and, if appropriate, diagnostic code information (**Table 2**), along with the corresponding display data to diagnose the fault(s). Refer to **Tables 3-17** by specific individual fault code for testing procedures.

ENGINE NOISE

Noise is often the first indicator of something wrong with the engine. In many cases, damage can be avoided or minimized if the rider immediately stops the ATV and diagnoses the source of the noise. Any time engine noises are ignored, even when the ATV seems to be running correctly, the rider risks causing more damage and possibly injury.

Pinging During Acceleration

1. Poor quality or contaminated fuel.
2. Lean fuel mixture.
3. Excessive carbon buildup in combustion chamber.
4. Misadjusted or faulty throttle position sensor.
5. Faulty ECU.
6. Faulty crankshaft position sensor.

Knocks, Ticks or Rattles

1. Loose exhaust system.
2. Loose/missing body fasteners.
3. Incorrect valve clearance.
4. Excessive connecting rod bearing clearance.

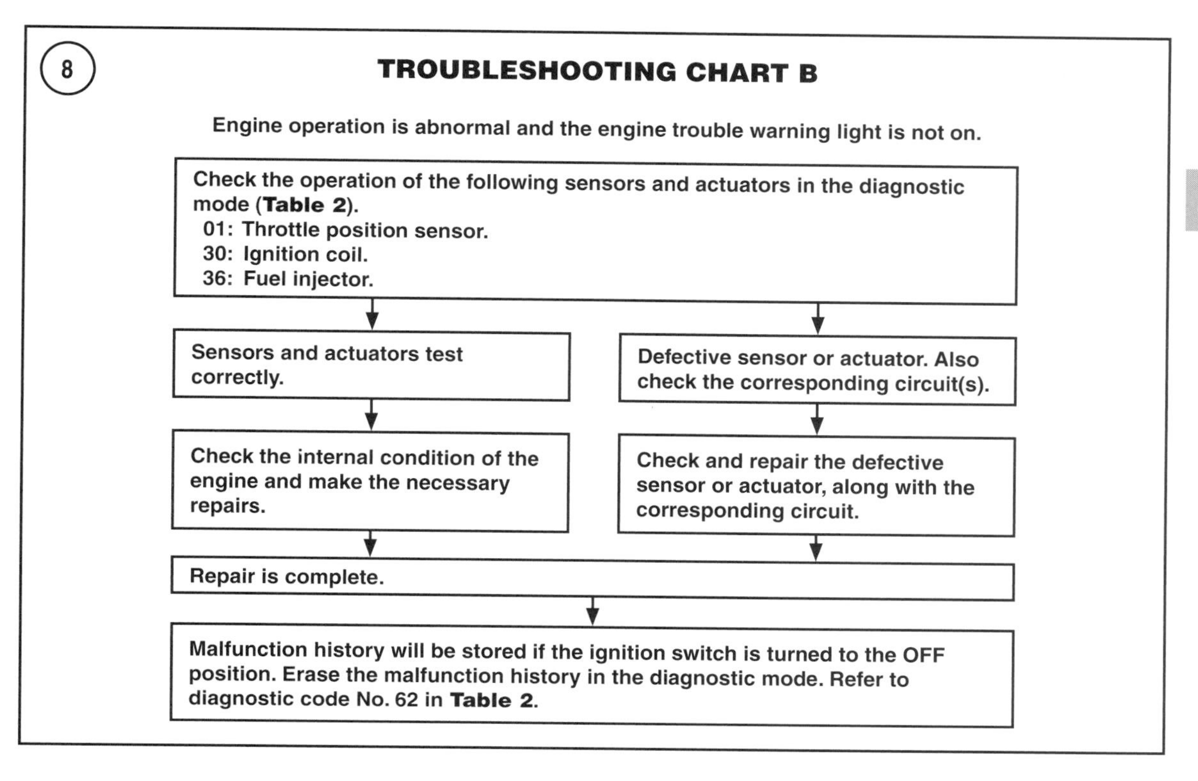

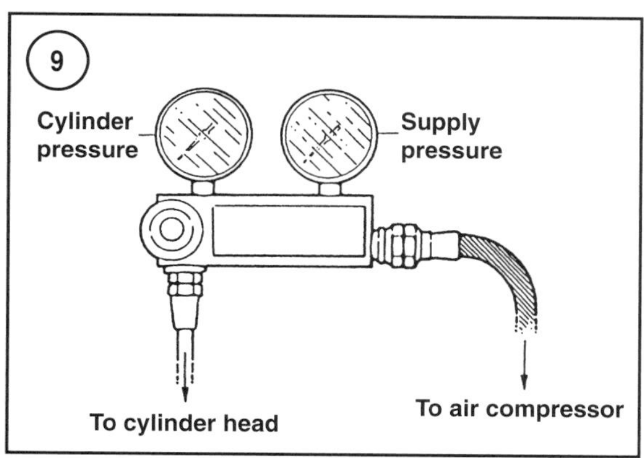

ENGINE LEAKDOWN TEST

The condition of the piston rings and valves can be accurately checked with a leakdown tester. With both valves in the closed position, this tester is screwed into the spark plug hole and air pressure is applied to the combustion chamber. The gauge on the tester is then observed to determine the rate of leak from the combustion chamber. An air compressor is required to use the leakdown tester (**Figure 9**).

1. Start the engine and allow it to reach operating temperature.
2. Shut off the engine and remove the air filter assembly.
3. Secure the throttle in the wide open position.
4. Remove the spark plug.
5. Set the piston to TDC on the compression stroke.
6. Install the leakdown tester following the manufacturer's instructions. The tester must not leak around the spark plug threads.
7. Make the test following the manufacturer's instructions for the tester. When pressure is applied to the cylinder, make sure the engine remains at TDC. If necessary, put the transmission in gear.
8. While the cylinder is under pressure, listen for air leaks at the following areas.
   a. Exhaust pipe. If a leak is detected, an exhaust valve is leaking.
   b. Throttle body: If a leak is detected, an intake valve is leaking.
   c. Crankcase breather tube. If a leak is detected, the piston rings are leaking.
9. Service a cylinder with a leakdown of 10% or more.

CLUTCH

The two main clutch problems are clutch slip (clutch does not fully engage) and clutch drag (clutch does not fully disengage). Both of these problems are usually caused by incorrect clutch adjustment, a worn clutch lever or a worn release lever at the engine. Perform the following inspections before removing the clutch:

1. Check the clutch cable routing from the handlebar to the engine. Make sure that the cable is free when

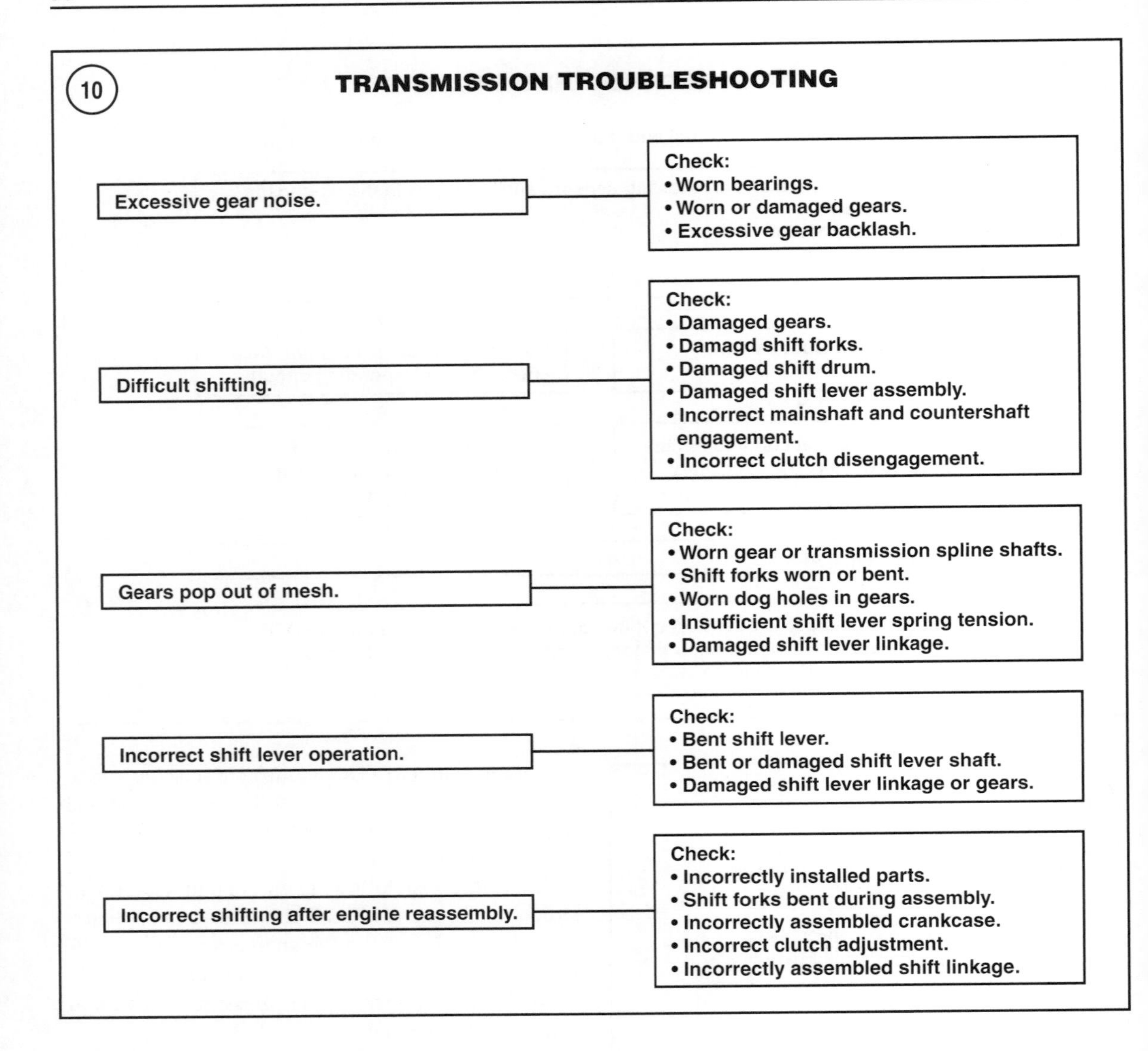

the handlebars are turned lock to lock and that the cable ends are installed correctly.

2. With the engine off, pull and release the clutch lever. If the lever is hard to pull, or the action is rough, check for the following:
   a. Damaged cable.
   b. Incorrect cable routing.
   c. Cable not lubricated.
   d. Damaged lever and perch assembly at the handlebar.
   e. Damaged release lever at the engine.
3. If the cable is installed correctly, does not drag and the clutch lever moves without excessive roughness or binding, check the clutch lever adjustment as described in Chapter Three. Note the following:
   a. If the clutch lever cannot be adjusted to the specifications in Chapter Three, the clutch cable is stretched or damaged.
   b. If the clutch cable and its adjustment are good, the friction plates may be worn.

Clutch Slipping

When the clutch slips, the engine accelerates faster than what the actual forward speed indicates. Because the clutch plates are spinning against each other, excessive heat is quickly built up in the assembly. This causes plate wear, warp and spring fatigue. One or more of the following can cause the clutch to slip:

1. Clutch wear or damage.
   a. Incorrect clutch adjustment.
   b. Weak or damaged clutch springs.
   c. Loose clutch springs.
   d. Worn friction plates.
   e. Warped steel plates.
   f. Clutch release mechanism wear or damage.
2. Clutch/transmission oil:
   a. Low oil level.
   b. Oil additives.
   c. Incorrect oil viscosity.

Clutch Dragging

When the clutch drags, the plates are not separating completely. This will cause the ATV to creep or lurch forward when the transmission is put into gear. Once underway, shifting is difficult. If this condition is not corrected, it can cause transmission gear and shift fork damage due to the abnormal grinding and actions of the parts. One or more of the following can cause the clutch to drag:

1. Clutch wear or damage.
   a. Clutch release mechanism wear or damage.
   b. Incorrect push lever and pushrod engagement.
   c. Damaged clutch pushrod.
   d. Warped steel plates.
   e. Swollen friction plates.
   f. Warped pressure plate.
   g. Incorrect clutch spring tension.
   h. Incorrectly assembled clutch.
   i. Loose clutch nut.
   j. Burnt primary driven gear bushing.
   k. Notched clutch hub splines.
   l. Notched clutch housing grooves.
2. Clutch transmission oil:
   a. Oil level too high.
   b. Incorrect oil viscosity.

Clutch Noise

Excessive clutch noise is usually caused by worn or damaged parts and is more noticeable at idle or low engine speeds. Clutch noise can be caused by the following conditions:

1. Wear on the clutch bushing or clutch housing bore. The noise is reduced or eliminated when a load is placed on the clutch housing.
2. Excessive axial play in the clutch housing.
3. Excessive friction disc-to-clutch housing clearance.
4. Excessive clutch housing-to-primary drive gear backlash.
5. Worn or damaged clutch housing and primary drive gear teeth.
6. Excessive wear in the clutch pushrod assembly.

TRANSMISSION

Transmission problems are often difficult to distinguish from problems with the clutch and external shift mechanism. Often, the symptoms may indicate a problem in one area, while the actual problem is in another area. For example, if the gears grind during shifting, the problem may be caused by a dragging clutch, not a damaged transmission. Of course, if the clutch is not repaired, the transmission will eventually become damaged too. Therefore, evaluate all of the variables that exist when the problem occurs and always start with the easiest inspections on the troubleshooting chart (**Figure 10**).

If the transmission exhibits abnormal noise or operation, drain the engine oil and check for contamination or metal particles. Examine a small quantity of oil under bright light. If a metallic cast or pieces of metal are seen, excessive wear and/or part failure is occurring. Some transmission noises are caused by the following:

1. Insufficient oil level.
2. Contaminated oil.
3. Incorrect oil viscosity.
4. Worn or damaged transmission gear(s).
5. Excessive gear side play.
6. Worn or damaged crankshaft-to-transmission bearings.

EXTERNAL SHIFT MECHANISM

The external shift mechanism includes all transmission shifting components that are not inside the crankcase. This includes the shift lever, shift shaft, torsion spring, reverse shift lever, shift guide, shift drum stopper, and the stopper lever. These parts are located at the rear of the engine, behind the right crankcase cover (**Figure 11**). Refer to Chapter Six for additional information and procedures. Troubleshoot as follows:

NOTE

When shifting a constant-mesh transmission, one of the transmission shafts must be turning. Have an assistant turn a rear wheel (with chain installed), so the gears can be shifted and the action of the linkage viewed.

1. Make sure the clutch is properly adjusted and in good condition. If the clutch is good, continue with the procedure.

2. Support the ATV with the rear wheels off the ground.
3. Remove the clutch as described in Chapter Six.
4. Turn the rear wheel and shift the transmission. Note the following:
   a. Make sure the torsion spring (A, **Figure 11**) is fitted around the pin and the shift shaft is engaged with the roller (B) on the shift lever assembly.
   b. The stopper lever roller (C, **Figure 11**) is spring-loaded and should move in and out of the shift drum detents. Each detent represents a different gear selection. The raised detent is the neutral position. If the parts are in place, but shifting is not correct, remove and inspect the external shift components as described in Chapter Six. Continue with the procedure, if necessary.
5. Check the shift drum as follows:
   a. Remove the external shift components as described in Chapter Six.
   b. Shift the transmission into neutral (if possible) and make a mark on the crankcase that aligns with the neutral detent on the shift drum stopper (**Figure 12**).
   c. While turning the rear wheel or mainshaft, turn the shift drum to change gears. Each time the shift drum moves and a new detent mark aligns with the crankcase mark, the transmission should be in another gear.
   d. The transmission should shift into each gear. If the shift drum cannot be turned, or if it locks into a particular gear position, the transmission is damaged. A locked shift drum indicates a damaged shift fork, seized bearing or gear, or a damaged shift drum.
6. If necessary, disassemble the crankcase and transmission as described in Chapter Five and Chapter Seven.
7. Assemble and install all removed parts as described in the appropriate chapters.

ELECTRICAL TESTING

Refer to Chapter Nine for specific electrical system test procedures. Refer to the procedures in *Engine Starting System* in this chapter for troubleshooting typical problems with the starting system. Perform the troubleshooting steps before disassembling and bench testing components. Refer to the wiring diagram at the back of the manual.

Before testing a component, check the electrical connections related to that component. Disconnect each connector and inspect the electrical terminals for corrosion or damage. If necessary, clean the terminals before reconnecting the connector. When reconnecting a connector make sure the individual male and female terminals properly mate. If the terminals are bent or damaged, they may be pushed out of the connector, causing an open circuit. Make sure the connectors attach securely and that locking connectors fully lock.

ENGINE STARTING SYSTEM

Starter Turns Slowly

1. Weak battery.
2. Loose or corroded battery terminals or cables.
3. Loose or corroded starter cable.
4. Worn or damaged starter.

Starter Turns, but Does Not Crank Engine

1. Worn or damaged starter clutch.
2. Damaged teeth on starter shaft or drive gears.

Starter Does Not Operate

If the starter does not operate, refer to **Figure 13** for troubleshooting the possible cause of the problem. If necessary, perform the starter relay test (Chapter Nine) before disassembling and bench testing components.

BRAKES

The brake system is critical to riding performance and safety. Inspect the brakes frequently and replace worn or damaged parts immediately.

When checking brake pad wear, the pads in each caliper should be squarely in contact with the disc. Uneven pad wear on one side of the disc can indicate a warped or damaged disc, caliper or pad pins.

The front and rear brake systems require DOT 4 brake fluid. Always use new fluid, from a sealed container. Refer to **Figure 14** to isolate brake problems.

(13)

STARTING SYSTEM TROUBLESHOOTING: STARTER WILL NOT TURN

Check	Action
Check battery charge.	• Charge battery and retest. • Replace battery if charge won't hold.
Inspect fuse.	• Replace blown fuse.
Inspect connections to battery, starter and starter relay.	• Clean and tighten connections. • Test cables for shorts.
Test starter motor by connecting a heavy gauge wire between the positive battery terminal and starter terminal.	• If the starter does not turn, replace the starter. • If the starter motor turns, check for a loose or damaged cable, or faulty relay.
Test the starter relay. The relay should make an audible click when the start switch is in the start position.	• If the relay does not click, remove and bench test it. If the relay now works, test the relay's voltage and ground circuits.
Perform starter relay ground circuit test.	• Loose or dirty connector. • Shorted wire harness. • Faulty neutral switch. • Faulty clutch diode. • Faulty clutch switch.
Perform starter relay voltage check.	• Loose or dirty connector. • Blown fuse. • Faulty ignition switch. • Faulty engine stop switch. • Faulty starter switch. • Shorted wire harness.

14

BRAKE TROUBLESHOOTING

Problem	Check
Brake fluid leaks.	Check: • Loose or damaged line fittings. • Worn caliper piston seals. • Scored caliper piston or bore. • Loose banjo bolts. • Damaged oil line washers. • Leaking master cylinder diaphragm. • Leaking master cylinder secondary seal. • Cracked master cylinder housing. • Too high brake fluid level. • Loose or damaged master cylinder.
Brake overheating.	Check: • Warped brake disc. • Incorrect brake fluid. • Caliper piston and/or brake pads binding. • Riding brakes during operation.
Brake chatter.	Check: • Warped brake disc. • Incorrect caliper alignment. • Loose caliper mounting bolts. • Loose front axle nut and/or clamps. • Worn wheel bearings. • Damaged hub. • Restricted brake hydraulic line. • Contaminated brake pads.
Brake locking.	Check: • Incorrect brake fluid. • Plugged passages in master cylinder. • Caliper piston and/or brake pads binding. • Warped brake disc.
Insufficient brakes.	Check: • Air in brake lines. • Worn brake pads. • Low brake fluid. • Incorrect brake fluid. • Worn brake disc. • Worn caliper piston seals. • Glazed brake pads. • Leaking primary cup seal in master cylinder. • Contaminated brake pads and/or disc.
Brake squeal.	Check: • Contaminated brake pads and/or disc. • Dust or dirt collected behind brake pads. • Loose parts.

STEERING AND HANDLING

Correct steering and handling problems as soon as they are detected, because loss of control may occur. Check the following areas:

1. Tires:
   a. Incorrect/uneven air pressure.
   b. Punctured/damaged tire.
2. Wheels:
   a. Loose lug nuts.
   b. Incorrect toe in.
   c. Damaged wheel bearings.
   d. Damaged wheel.
3. Handlebars:

a. Loose handlebars.
b. Tight steering shaft holder.
c. Damaged steering shaft bearing or bushing.

4. Brakes:
   a. Brake pads dragging.
   b. Misadjusted parking brake.
5. Rear axle and swing arm:
   a. Loose/damaged axle bearing holder.
   b. Loose shock absorber.
   c. Worn shock absorber bushings.
   d. Worn swing arm pivot.
   e. Bent axle.
6. Front axle:
   a. Loose wheel hub.
   b. Worn/damaged tie rods.
   c. Loose shock absorbers.
   d. Worn shock absorber bushings.
   e. Damaged wheel hub.
7. Frame:
   a. Bent/broken frame.
   b. Broken weld on frame member.
   c. Broken engine mounting bracket.

Table 1 TROUBLE CODES

Trouble code number	Symptoms	Probable cause of malfunction	Diagnostic code number
12	Normal signals are not received from the crankshaft position sensor Engine unable to start	Open or short in wiring harness Defective crankshaft position sensor Malfunction in the ECU Improperly installed sensor	–
13	Intake air pressure sensor, open or short circuit detected Engine able to start	Open or short circuit in wiring harness Defective intake air pressure sensor Malfunction in the ECU	03
14	Faulty intake air pressure sensor hose system, causing constant application of the atmospheric pressure sensor Engine able to start	Hose is detached, clogged or damaged Defective intake air pressure sensor Malfunction in the ECU	03
15	Throttle position sensor, open or short circuit detected Engine able to start	Open or short circuit in wiring sub-lead Open or short circuit in wiring harness Defective throttle position sensor Malfunction in the ECU Improperly installed throttle position sensor	01
16	Stuck throttle position sensor detected Engine able to start	Stuck throttle position sensor Malfunction in the ECU	01
21	Coolant temperature sensor, open or short circuit detected Engine able to start	Open or short circuit in wiring harness Faulty coolant temperature sensor Improperly installed sensor Malfunction in the ECU	06
22	Intake temperature sensor, open or short circuit detected Engine able to start	Open or short circuit in wiring harness Defective intake temperature sensor Improperly installed sensor Malfunction in the ECU	05
30	Lean angle sensor, lock-up detected Engine unable to start	ATV overturned Malfunction in the ECU	08

(continued)

Table 1 TROUBLE CODES (continued)

Trouble code number	Symptoms	Probable cause of malfunction	Diagnostic code number
33	Open circuit detected in primary lead of ignition coil Engine unable to start	Open or short circuit in wiring harness Malfunction in the ignition coil Malfunction in a component of the ignition cut-off circuit Malfunction in the ECU	30
41	Lean angle sensor, open or short cicuit detected Engine unable to start	Open or short circuit in wiring harness Defective lean angle sensor Malfunction in the ECU	08
42	No signals received from speed sensor; open or short circuit detected in neutral switch Engine able to start	Open or short circuit in wiring harness Defective speed sensor Malfunction in the vehicle speed sensor detected Defective neutral switch Malfunction in the engine side of the neutral switch Malfunction in the ECU	07, 21
43	ECU unable to monitor battery voltage (open circuit in monitor line to ECU) Engine able to start	Open circuit in wiring harness Malfunction in the ECU	09
44	An error is detected while reading or writing on EEPROM Engine able to start	Malfunction in the ECU; the program and data are not properly written on or read from the internal memory	60
46	Abnormal power to fuel injection system	Charging system malfunction (Refer to Chapter Nine)	–
50	Faulty ECU memory; when this malfunction is detected, trouble code number might not appear on diagnostic tool Engine unable to start	Malfunction in the ECU; the program and data are not properly written on or read from the internal memory	–

Table 2 DIAGNOSTIC CODES

Diagnostic code	Component	Description of action	Data displayed on diagnostic tool
01	Throttle angle	Displays the throttle angle: • Check with the throttle closed • Check with the throttle open	Fully closed position (15-20°) Fully open position (95-100°)
03	Pressure difference (atmospheric pressure: intake air pressure)	Displays the intake air pressure	Displayed value must change when throttle is operated while starting engine
05	Intake air temperature	Displays the intake air temperature: • Check the temperature in the air filter housing case as close to the sensor as possible	Compare to the value displayed on the diagnostic tool

(continued)

Table 2 DIAGNOSTIC CODES (continued)

Diagnostic code	Component	Description of action	Data displayed on diagnostic tool
06	Coolant temperature	Displays the coolant temperature: • Check the coolant temperature as close to the sensor on the thermostat housing as possible	Compare it to the value displayed on the diagnostic tool
07	Vehicle speed pulse	Displays the accumulation of the vehicle pulses that are generated when the rear wheel is rotated	(0 to 999; resets to 0 after 999) Good if the pulse count appears on the diagnostic tool
08	Lean angle sensor	Displays the lean angle sensor values	Upright: 0.4 to 1.4 volts Overturned; 3.7 to 4.4 volts
09	Fuel system voltage (battery voltage)	Displays the fuel system voltage (battery voltage) Engine stop switch in on position	0 to 16.7 volts Normally, approximately 12 volts
21	Neutral switch	Displays that the switch is on or off	Neutral: on In gear: off
30	Ignition coil	After one second has elapsed from the time the engine stop switch has been turned from the OFF to ON position, it actuates the ignition coil five times (at one second intervals) and illuminates the engine trouble warning light • Connect an ignition tester (Yamaha part No. 90890-06754/YM-34487 or an equivalent) • If the engine stop switch is on, turn it off once, and then turn it back on Check that the spark was generated five times with the engine stop switch in the ON position	Engine trouble warning light flashes five times
36	Fuel Injector	After one second has elapsed from the time the engine stop switch has been turned from the OFF to ON position, it actuates the fuel injector five times (at one second intervals) and illuminates the engine trouble warning light • If the engine stop switch is on, turn it off once and then turn it back on Check for the sound of the fuel injector operating five times with the engine switch in the ON position	Engine trouble warning light flashes five times
50	Fuel injection system relay	After one second has elapsed from the time engine stop switch has been turned from the OFF to ON position, it actuates the fuel injection system relay five times (at one second intervals) and illuminates the engine trouble warning light • If the engine stop switch is on, turn it off once, and then turn it back on Check for the sound of the fuel injection system relay operating five times with the engine switch in the ON position	Engine trouble warning light flashes five times (the warning light is off when the relay is on and the light is on when the relay is off)

(continued)

Table 2 DIAGNOSTIC CODES (continued)

Diagnostic code	Component	Description of action	Data displayed on diagnostic tool
51	Radiator cooling fan motor relay	After one second has elapsed from the time engine stop switch has been turned from the OFF to ON position, it actuates the radiator cooling fan relay five times and illuminates the engine trouble warning light • If the engine stop switch is on, turn it off once and then turn it back on Check for the sound of the radiator cooling fan motor relay operating five times with the engine switch in the ON position (at that time, the cooling fan motor rotates)	Engine trouble warning light flashes five times (the warning light is on for two seconds and then off for three seconds)
60	EEPROM fault	–	(01) Displays when a malfunction has been noted (00) Displays when there is no malfunction history
61	Malfunction history code display	Displays trouble code(s) of a malfunction that occured once and which has been corrected • If multiple malfunctions have been detected, different codes are displayed at two-second intervals, and the process is repeated	(12 to 50) (00) Displays when there is no malfunction history
62	Malfunction history code erasure	• Displays trouble code(s) of a malfunction that occured once and which has been corrected • Erases the history codes only when the engine stop switch is turned from the OFF to the ON position. If the engine stop switch is on, turn if off once and then turn it back on	(00 to 15) (00) Displays when there is no malfunction history
70	Control Number	Displays the program control number	(00 to 255)

Table 3 TROUBLE CODE 12: NORMAL SIGNALS ARE NOT RECEIVED FROM THE CRANKSHAFT POSITION SENSOR

Possible cause	Inspect, test and replace or repair
Sensor installation	Check the sensor for correct installation within the crankcase Check for looseness or pinching Tighten the mounting screw if necessary
Crankshaft position sensor faulty	Test the crankshaft position sensor as described in Chapter Nine Replace if necessary If the sensor is good, proceed to the next steps
Open or short circuit detected in the wiring harness	Repair or replace if there is an open or short in the sensor circuit Check continuity between the sensor coupler and the ECU coupler connectors as follows: 1. Blue/yellow to blue/yellow 2. Black/blue to black/blue

(continued)

Table 3 TROUBLE CODE 12: NORMAL SIGNALS ARE NOT RECEIVED FROM THE CRANKSHAFT POSITION SENSOR (continued)

Possible cause	Inspect, test and replace or repair
Electrical connector faulty	Inspect the electrical connector(s) for any loose or pulled-out pins Check the locking condition of the electrical connector(s) Repair or replace the electrical connector(s) within the circuit if necessary
Reinstatement method after sensor problem is corrected	Cranking the engine

Table 4 TROUBLE CODE 13: OPEN OR SHORT CIRCUIT DETECTED IN THE INTAKE AIR PRESSURE SENSOR (USE DIAGNOSTIC CODE NO. 03)

Possible cause	Inspect, test and replace or repair
Sensor installation	Check the sensor for correct installation
Defective intake air pressure sensor	Test the intake air pressure sensor as described in Chapter Eight Replace if necessary If the sensor is good, proceed to the next steps
Open or short circuit detected in the wiring harness and/or sub-lead	Repair or replace if there is an open or short in the sensor circuit Check continuity between the sensor coupler and the ECU coupler connectors as follows: 1. Black/blue to black/blue 2. Pink/blue to pink/blue 3. Blue to blue
Electrical connector faulty	Inspect the electrical connector(s) for any loose or pulled-out pins Check the locking condition of the electrical connector(s) Repair or replace the electrical connector(s) within the circuit if necessary
Reinstatement method after sensor problem is corrected	Turn the ignition switch to the ON position

Table 5 TROUBLE CODE 14: CLOGGED OR DETACHED HOSE IN THE INTAKE AIR PRESSURE SENSOR (USE DIAGNOSTIC CODE NO. 03)

Possible cause	Inspect, test and replace or repair
Sensor installation	Check the sensor for correct installation Check for looseness or pinching
Intake air pressure sensor faulty	Test the intake air pressure sensor as described in Chapter Eight Replace if necessary Refer to trouble code No. 13 If sensor is good, proceed to the next steps
Intake air pressure sensor hose detached	Repair or replace the sensor hose
Sensor malfunction at intermediate voltage	Check and repair the connection Replace sensor if necessary

(continued)

Table 5 TROUBLE CODE 14: CLOGGED OR DETACHED HOSE IN THE INTAKE AIR PRESSURE SENSOR (USE DIAGNOSTIC CODE NO. 03) (continued)

Possible cause	Inspect, test and replace or repair
Electrical connector faulty	Inspect the electrical connector(s) for any loose or pulled-out pins Check the locking condition of the electrical connector(s) Repair or replace the electrical connector(s) within the circuit if necessary
Reinstatement method after sensor problem is corrected	Start the engine and operate it at idle

Table 6 TROUBLE CODE 15: OPEN OR SHORT CIRCUIT DETECTED IN THE THROTTLE POSITION SENSOR (USE DIAGNOSTIC CODE NO. 01)

Possible cause	Inspect, test and replace or repair
Sensor installation	Check the sensor for correct installation on the on the throttle body housing as described in Chapter Eight Check for looseness or pinching Check that the sensor is installed in the correct position on the throttle body as described in Chapter Eight
Throttle position sensor faulty	Test the throttle position sensor as described in Chapter Eight Replace if necessary If sensor is good, proceed to the next steps
Open or short circuit detected in wiring harness	Repair or replace if there is an open or short in the sensor circuit Check continuity between the sensor coupler and the ECU coupler connectors as follows: 1. Black/blue to black/blue 2. Yellow to yellow 3. Blue to blue
Electrical connector faulty	Inspect the electrical connector(s) for any loose or pulled-out pins Check the locking condition of the electrical connector(s) Repair or replace the electrical connector(s) within the circuit if necessary
Reinstatement method after sensor problem is corrected	Turn the ignition switch to the ON position

Table 7 TROUBLE CODE 16: STUCK THROTTLE POSITION SENSOR (USE DIAGNOSTIC CODE NO. 01)

Possible cause	Inspect, test and replace or repair
Sensor installation	Check the sensor for correct installation on the end of the throttle body housing for looseness as described in Chapter Eight Check for looseness or pinching Tighten the screws if necessary Check that the sensor is installed in the correct position on the throttle body as described in Chapter Eight Readjust if necessary

(continued)

Table 7 TROUBLE CODE 16: STUCK THROTTLE POSITION SENSOR (USE DIAGNOSTIC CODE NO. 01) (continued)

Possible cause	Inspect, test and replace or repair
Throttle position sensor faulty	Test the throttle position sensor as described in Chapter Eight Replace if necessary
Reinstatement method after sensor problem is corrected	Start the engine and operate it at idle. Then, rapidly increase engine speed

Table 8 TROUBLE CODE 21: OPEN OR SHORT CIRCUIT DETECTED IN THE COOLANT TEMPERATURE SENSOR (USE DIAGNOSTIC CODE NO. 06)

Possible cause	Inspect, test and replace or repair
Sensor installation	Check the sensor installation as described in Chapter Eight Check for looseness or pinching
Coolant temperature sensor faulty	Test the coolant temperature sensor as described in Chapter Eight Replace if necessary If sensor is good, proceed to the next steps
Open or short circuit detected in wiring harness	Repair or replace if there is an open or short in the sensor circuit Check continuity between the sensor coupler and the ECU coupler connectors as follows: 1. Black/blue to black/blue 2. Black/yellow to black/yellow
Electrical connector faulty	Inspect the electrical connector(s) for any loose or pulled-out pins Check the locking condition of the electrical connector(s) Repair or replace the electrical connector(s) within the circuit if necessary
Reinstatement method after sensor problem is corrected	Turn the ignition switch to the ON position

Table 9 TROUBLE CODE 22: OPEN OR SHORT CIRCUIT DETECTED IN THE INTAKE TEMPERATURE SENSOR (USE DIAGNOSTIC CODE NO. 05)

Possible cause	Inspect, test and replace or repair
Sensor installation	Check the sensor for correct installation within the air box Check for looseness or pinching
Intake temperature sensor faulty	Test the intake temperature sensor as described in Chapter Eight Replace if necessary If sensor is good, proceed to the next steps
Open or short circuit detected in wiring harness and/or sub-lead	Repair or replace if there is an open or short in the sensor circuit Check continuity between the sensor coupler and the ECU coupler connectors as follows: 1. Black/white to black/white 2. Brown/white to brown/white

(continued)

Table 9 TROUBLE CODE 22: OPEN OR SHORT CIRCUIT DETECTED IN THE INTAKE TEMPERATURE SENSOR (USE DIAGNOSTIC CODE NO. 05) (continued)

Possible cause	Inspect, test and replace or repair
Electrical connector faulty	Inspect the electrical connector(s) for any loose or pulled-out pins Check the locking condition of the electrical connector(s) Repair or replace the electrical connector(s) within the circuit if necessary
Reinstatement method after sensor problem is corrected	Turn the ignition switch to the ON position

Table 10 TROUBLE CODE 30: THE ATV HAS OVERTURNED (USE DIAGNOSTIC CODE NO. 08)

Possible cause	Inspect, test and replace or repair
Sensor installation	Check the sensor for correct installation Check for looseness or pinching Tighten the screws if necessary
Lean angle sensor faulty	Test the lean angle sensor as described in Chapter Eight If faulty, replace the switch If switch is good, proceed to the next steps
Electrical connector faulty	Inspect the electrical connector(s) for any loose or pulled-out pins Check the locking condition of the electrical connector(s) Repair or replace the electrical connector(s) within the circuit if necessary
Reinstatement method after switch problem is corrected	Turn the ignition switch first to the OFF, then the ON position

Table 11 TROUBLE CODE 33: MALFUNCTION DETECTED IN THE PRIMARY LEAD OF THE IGNITION COIL (USE DIAGNOSTIC CODE NO. 30)

Possible cause	Inspect, test and replace or repair
Ignition coil installation	Check the primary lead for correct installation on the ignition coil Test the ignition coil primary and secondary circuits as described in Chapter Nine Replace if necessary If the ignition coil is good, proceed to the next steps
Open or short circuit detected in wiring harness	Repair or replace if there is an open or short in the ignition coil circuit Check continuity in the orange wire between the ignition coil coupler and the ECU coupler Check continuity in the red/black wire between the ignition coil coupler and the engine stop switch coupler
Electrical connector faulty	Inspect the electrical connector(s) for any loose or pulled-out pins Check the locking condition of the electrical connector(s) Repair or replace the electrical connector(s) within the circuit if necessary
Reinstatement method after ignition coil problem is corrected	Start the engine and operate at idle speed

Table 12 TROUBLE CODE 41: OPEN OR SHORT CIRCUIT DETECTED IN THE LEAN ANGLE SENSOR (USE DIAGNOSTIC CODE NO. 08)

Possible cause	Inspect, test and replace or repair
Sensor installation	Check the sensor for correct installation Check for looseness or pinching Tighten the screws if necessary
Lean angle sensor is defective	Test the lean angle sensor described in Chapter Eight Replace if necessary If sensor is good, proceed to the next steps
Open or short circuit detected in wiring harness	Repair or replace if there is an open or short in the sensor circuit Check continuity between the sensor coupler and the ECU coupler as follows: 1. Black/blue to black/blue 2. Yellow/green to yellow/green 3. Blue to blue
Electrical connector faulty	Inspect the electrical connector(s) for any loose or pulled-out pins Check the locking condition of the electrical connector(s) Repair or replace the electrical connector(s) within the circuit if necessary
Reinstatement method after sensor problem is corrected	Turn the ignition switch to the ON position

Table 13 TROUBLE CODE 42: NORMAL SIGNALS ARE NOT RECEIVED FROM THE SPPED SENSOR. OPEN OR SHORT CIRCUIT DETECTED IN THE NEUTRAL SWITCH (USE DIAGNOSTIC CODE NO. 07 [SPEED SENSOR], NO. 21 [NEUTRAL SWITCH])

Possible cause	Inspect, test and replace or repair
Speed sensor installation	Check the sensor for correct installation on the top surface of the crankcase Check for looseness or pinching Tighten mounting screw if necessary
Speed sensor faulty	Test the speed sensor as described in Chapter Eight Replace if necessary If the sensor is good, proceed to the next steps
Open or short circuit detected in speed sensor wiring harness	Repair or replace if there is an open or short in the sensor circuit Check continuity between the sensor coupler and the ECU coupler connectors as follows: 1. Blue to blue 2. White to white 3. Black/blue to black/blue
Gear related to the speed sensor faulty	Identify and replace the transmission gear as described in Chapter Seven
Electrical connector faulty	Inspect the electrical connector(s) for any loose or pulled-out pins Check the locking condition of the electrical connector(s) Repair or replace the electrical connector(s) within the circuit if necessary
Neutral switch installation	Check the switch for correct installation on the left side of the crankcase Check for looseness or pinching Tighten the switch if necessary

(continued)

Table 13 TROUBLE CODE 42: NORMAL SIGNALS ARE NOT RECEIVED FROM THE SPPED SENSOR. OPEN OR SHORT CIRCUIT DETECTED IN THE NEUTRAL SWITCH (USE DIAGNOSTIC CODE NO. 07 [SPEED SENSOR], NO. 21 [NEUTRAL SWITCH]) (continued)

Possible cause	Inspect, test and replace or repair
Neutral switch faulty	Test the neutral switch as described in Chapter Nine Replace if necessary If the switch is good, proceed to the next steps
Open or short circuit detected in neutral switch wiring	Repair or replace if there is an open or short in the switch circuit Check continuity between the neutral switch coupler and the relay unit coupler as follows: Sky blue to sky blue
Stopper pin on the shift drum faulty	Replace the shift drum stopper pin as described in Chapter Seven
Electrical connector faulty	Inspect the electrical connector(s) for any loose or pulled-out pins Check the locking condtion of the electrical connector(s) Repair or replace the electrical connector(s) within the circuit if necessary
Reinstatement method after sensor and/or switch problem is corrected	Start the engine and ride the ATV at a speed of 20-30 km/h (12-19 mph) to reset the speed sensor (also applies to the neutral switch)

Table 14 TROUBLE CODE 43: ABNORMAL POWER TO THE FUEL INJECTOR AND FUEL PUMP (USE DIAGNOSTIC CODE NO. 09)

Possible cause	Inspect, test and replace or repair
Fuel pump relay faulty	Test the pump relay as described in Chapter Eight Replace if necessary If the relay unit is good, proceed to the next steps
Open or short circuit detected in wiring	Repair or replace if there is an open or short in the circuit Check continuity between the ECU coupler and the fuel pump relay coupler as follows: 1. Blue/red to blue/red 2. Red/blue to red/blue Check continuity in the brown/green to red wire between the fuel pump relay coupler and the battery terminal Check continuity in the red/black to red/black wire between the fuel pump relay coupler and the engine stop switch coupler
Electrical connector faulty	Inspect the electrical connector(s) for any loose or pulled-out pins Check the locking condition of the electrical connector(s) Repair or replace the electrical connector(s) within the circuit if necessary
Reinstatement method after relay problem is corrected	Start the engine and run it at idle

Table 15 TROUBLE CODE 44: ERROR CODE IS DETECTED WHILE READING OR WRITING ON EEPROM (IMPROPER CYLINDER IDENTIFICATION [USE DIAGNOSTIC CODE NO. 60])

Possible cause	Inspect, test and replace or repair
ECU faulty	Execute diagnostic code No. 60 Check the faulty cylinder Replace if necessary
Reinstatement method after ECU problem is corrected	Turn the ignition switch to the ON position

Table 16 TROUBLE CODE 46: ABNORMAL POWER TO THE FUEL INJECTION SYSTEM (NO RELEVENT DIAGNOSTIC CODE)

Possible cause	Inspect, test and replace or repair
Battery faulty	Check the battery as described in Chapter Nine Replace if necessary
Regulator/rectifier	Test the regulator/rectifier as described in Chapter Nine Replace if necessary
Open or short circuit detected in wiring harness	Repair or replace if there is an open or short in the circuit Check continuity in the red to red wire between the battery terminal and the ignition switch coupler Check continuity in the brown to brown wire between the ignition switch coupler and the ignition fuse Check the continuity in the brown to brown wire between the ignition fuse and the ECU coupler
Electrical connector faulty	Inspect the electrical connector(s) for any loose or pulled-out pins Check the locking condition of the electrical connector(s) Repair or replace the electrical connector(s) within the circuit if necessary
Reinstatement method after problem is corrected	Turn the ignition switch to the ON position

Table 17 TROUBLE CODE 50: FAULTY ECU MEMORY (WHEN THIS MALFUNCTION IS DETECTED IN THE ECU, THE TROUBLE CODE NUMBER MIGHT NOT APPEAR ON THE DIAGNOSTIC TOOL OR PANEL DISPLAY)

Possible cause	Inspect, test and replace or repair
ECU faulty	Replace the ECU
Reinstatement method after ECU problem is corrected	Turn the ignition switch to the ON position

CHAPTER THREE

LUBRICATION, MAINTENANCE AND TUNE-UP

This chapter describes lubrication, maintenance and tune-up procedures. Procedures that require more than minor disassembly or adjustment are covered in the appropriate subsequent chapter. Specifications are in **Tables 1-7** located at the end of this chapter.

To maximize the service life of the ATV and gain the utmost in safety and performance, it is necessary to perform periodic inspections and maintenance. Minor problems found during routine service can be corrected before they develop into major ones. A neglected ATV will be unreliable and may be dangerous to ride.

Table 1 lists the recommended lubrication, maintenance and tune-up intervals. If the ATV is operated in extreme conditions, it may be appropriate to reduce the interval between some maintenance items.

PRE-RIDE INSPECTION

Perform the following checks before the first ride of the day. If a component requires service, refer to the appropriate section or chapter.

1. Inspect all fuel lines and fittings for leaks.
2. Check fuel tank level.
3. Check engine oil level.
4. Check the throttle operation for proper operation in all steering positions. Open the throttle all the way and release it. The throttle should close quickly with no binding or roughness.
5. Check that the brake lever and pedal operate properly with no binding.
6. Check the brake fluid level in the brake reservoirs. Add DOT 4 brake fluid if necessary.
7. Check clutch operation.
8. Inspect the front and rear suspension for loose components. Turn the handlebar from side to side and check steering play. Service the steering assembly if excessive play is noted. Make sure the handlebar cables do not bind.
9. Check tire pressure.
10. Check wheel condition.
11. Check drive chain condition and adjustment.
12. Check the exhaust system for looseness or damage.
13. Check fastener tightness, especially engine, steering and suspension mounting hardware.
14. Check headlight and taillight operation.
15. Check that all switches work properly.
16. Inspect the air box check hose for contamination.
17. Start the engine, and then stop it with the engine stop switch. If the engine stop switch does not operate properly, test the switch as described in *Switches* (Chapter Nine).

TUNE-UP

Perform the maintenance tasks in **Table 1** at the specified intervals.

The frequency of tune-ups depends on ATV usage. Creating a record that contains the type of operation and when tune-ups occur will help establish the frequency for future tune-ups.

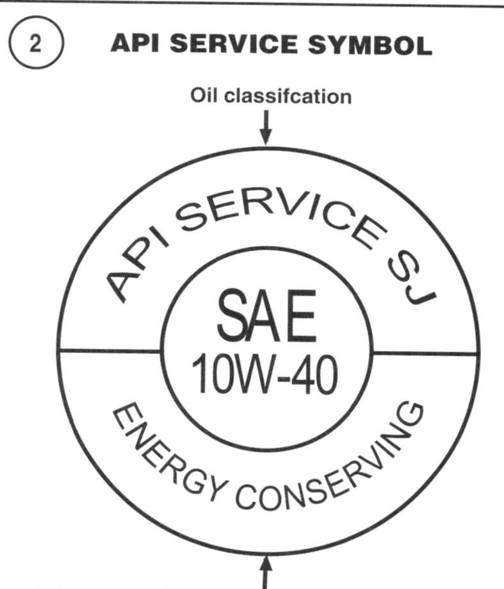

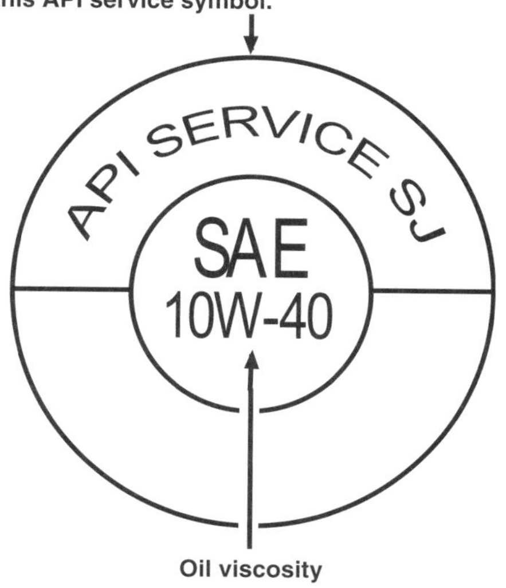

Determine which tasks are included in the tune-up by evaluating the operating conditions. For instance, air filter service is dictated by the amount of airborne debris.

As a guideline, the following items may be included in a tune-up:

1. Air filter.
2. Engine oil and filter.
3. Spark plug.
4. Fuel system.
5. Valve adjustment.
6. Engine compression.
7. Ignition timing.
8. Wheels and tires.
9. Suspension components.
10. Brake system.
11. Fasteners.

ENGINE OIL

Engine Oil Selection

Regular oil and filter changes contribute more to engine longevity than any other maintenance. **Table 1** lists the recommended oil and filter change intervals. If an ATV is operated in dusty conditions, the oil gets dirty quicker and should be changed more frequently than recommended.

Oil requirements for ATV engines are more demanding than those for automobile engines. Oils specifically designed for ATVs contain special additives to prevent premature viscosity breakdown, protect the engine from oil oxidation resulting from higher engine operating temperatures and provide lubrication qualities designed for engines operating at higher rpm. Consider the following when selecting engine oil:

1. Do not use oil additives or oil with graphite or molybdenum additives. These may adversely affect clutch operation.
2. Do not use vegetable, non-detergent or castor-based racing oils.
3. The Japanese Automobile Standards Organization (JASO) has established an oil classification for ATV engines. JASO ATV-specific oils are identified by the JASO T 903 Standard. The JASO label (**Figure 1**) appears on the oil container and identifies the two separate ATV oil classifications—MA and MB. The ATV manufacturer recommends the MA classification. JASO classified oil also uses the Society of Automotive Engineers (SAE) viscosity ratings.
4. When selecting American Petroleum Institute (API) classified oil, use only high-quality ATV oil with an SG or higher classification that does not display the Energy Conserving designation on the circular API service label (**Figure 2**) found on the oil container.

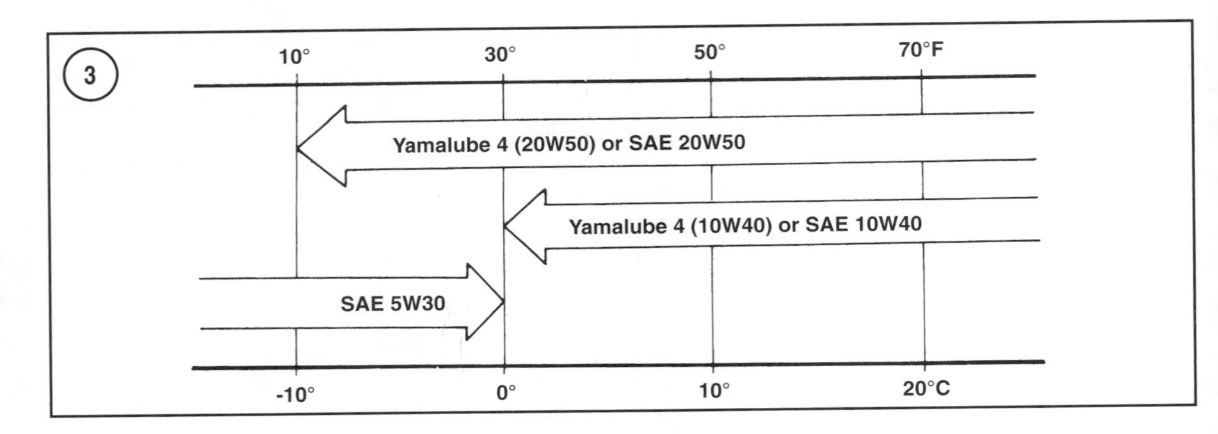

5. **Figure 3** indicates when different viscosity oils can be used, depending on the ambient temperature.

Engine Oil Level Check

Check the engine oil level with the dipstick cap mounted on the right side of the engine.

1. Park the ATV on level ground and set the parking brake.

NOTE
Due to the large quantity of oil contained in the engine and oil tank, and the dry sump design, the engine must be run for the period specified to be sure the oil in the oil tank reaches its normal operating level.

2. Start the engine. If the engine is at normal operating temperature, let it run 5 minutes. If the engine is cold, run the engine for 10 minutes.
3. Shut off the engine and let the oil drain into the crankcase for a few minutes.
4. Unscrew and remove the dipstick cap (**Figure 4**). Wipe the dipstick clean. Reinsert it onto the threads in the hole, but do not screw it in. Remove the dipstick and check the oil level.
5. The level is correct when it is between the two dipstick lines (**Figure 5**).
6. If necessary, add the recommended oil type (**Table 3**) through the dipstick opening in the tank to correct the level.
7. Replace the dipstick O-ring if damaged.
8. Install the dipstick and tighten it securely.

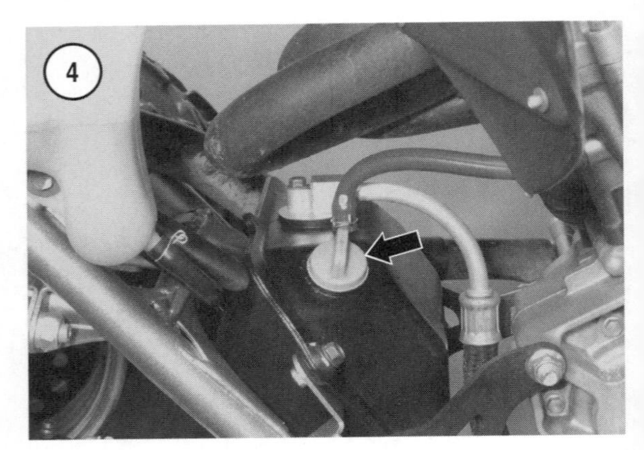

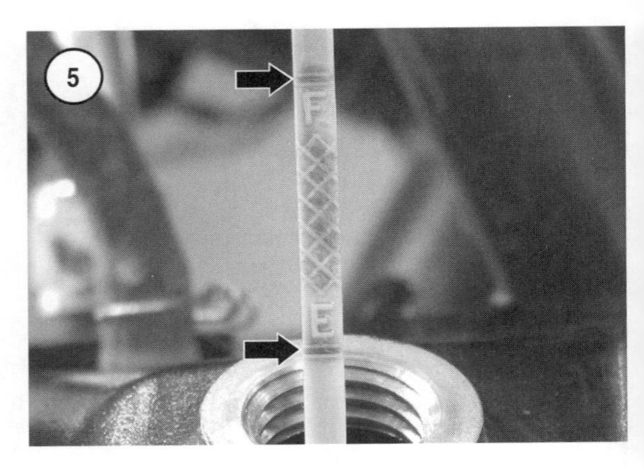

Engine Oil and Filter Change

NOTE
There are a number of ways to discard used oil safely. The easiest way is to pour it from the drain pan into a clean gallon plastic bleach, juice or milk container for disposal. Some service stations and oil retailers will accept used oil for recycling. Do not discard oil in household trash or pour it onto the ground. Never add other fluids to any engine oil to be recycled.

Change the oil and filter at the intervals recommended in **Table 1**. If the machine is used in extreme conditions (hot, cold, wet or dusty) change the oil more often. Use the oil type recommended in **Table 3**.

Always change the oil when the engine is warm. Contaminants will remain suspended in the oil and will drain more completely and quickly.

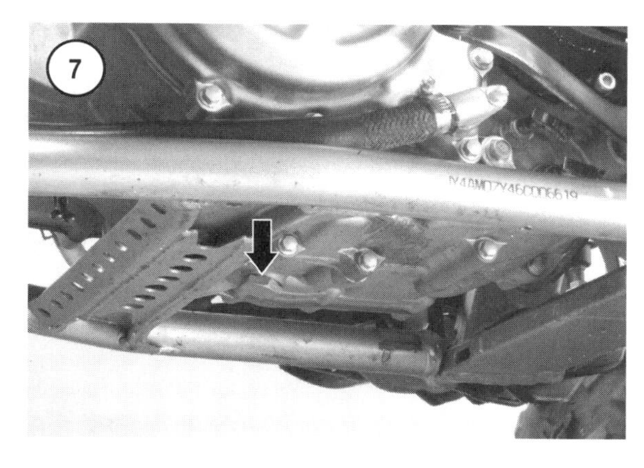

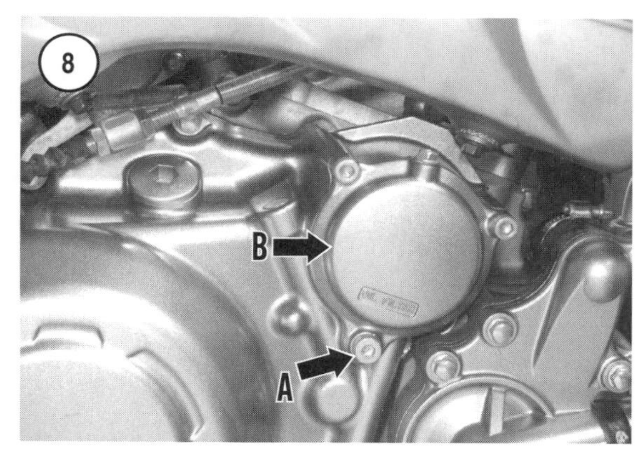

WARNING
Prolonged contact with used engine oil may cause skin cancer. Minimize contact with the engine oil.

1. Park the machine on level ground and set the parking brake.
2. Remove the engine skidplate (Chapter Fifteen).
3. Wipe the area around the dipstick, and then loosen the dipstick (**Figure 4**).
4. Place a drain pan below the oil tank drain bolt (**Figure 6**) and then remove the bolt. Allow the oil to drain from the oil tank.
5. Place a drain pan below the crankcase drain bolt (**Figure 7**). Remove the drain bolt and allow the oil to drain from the engine.
6. Remove the oil filter drain bolt (A, **Figure 8**) and allow the oil to drain.
7. Remove and replace the oil filter as follows:
   a. Remove the bolts that secure the oil filter cover (B, **Figure 8**) and remove the cover.
   b. Remove the oil filter (A, **Figure 9**).
   c. Wipe the filter housing and cover clean. Do not use compressed air to clean the housing. Debris can be blown into the passageways.
   d. Inspect the O-ring on the filter cover (B, **Figure 9**) and the O-ring in the oil passageway (C). Replace the O-ring(s) if hard, cracked or damaged.
   e. Install a new oil filter into the housing.
   f. Install the oil filter cover and bolts. Tighten the cover bolts to 10 N•m (89 in.-lb.).
   g. Install the oil filter drain bolt (A, **Figure 8**). Tighten the bolt to 10 N•m (89 in.-lb.).
8. Install new sealing washers on the engine and oil tank drain bolts.
9. Install the drain bolts. Tighten the crankcase drain bolt (**Figure 7**) to 23 N•m (17 ft.-lb.). Tighten the oil tank drain bolt (**Figure 6**) to 19 N•m (14 ft.-lb.).
10. Fill the oil tank and engine with the required quantity and type of motor oil. Refer to **Table 3** for oil capacity.
11. Insert the dipstick and screw into place.
12. Slightly loosen the oil gallery bolt (**Figure 10**) on the cylinder head so oil circulation can be verified after the engine is started.
13. Start the engine and allow it to idle. As the engine idles, check the following:
    a. Make sure that oil weeps from the oil gallery bolt within one minute. If oil is not present within this time, immediately shut off the engine and diagnose the problem. If oil is present, tighten the oil gallery bolt to 10 N•m (89 in.-lb.).
    b. Leaks at the drain bolts.

AIR FILTER

A clogged air filter decreases the efficiency and operating life of the engine. Never run the engine without a properly installed air filter. Dust that enters the engine can cause engine wear and clog throttle body passages.

Service the air filter at the interval in **Table 1**. Clean the air filter more often when racing, riding in sand or in wet and muddy conditions.

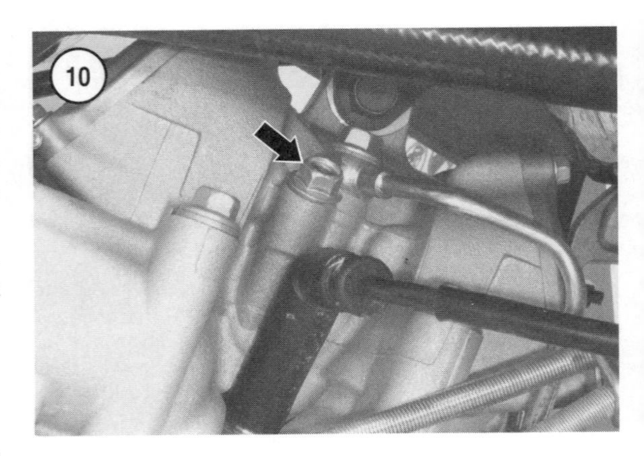

Air Box Check Hose

A check hose (**Figure 11**) is mounted in the bottom of the air box. If the check hose is filled with dirt and water, check the air box and air filter for contamination.

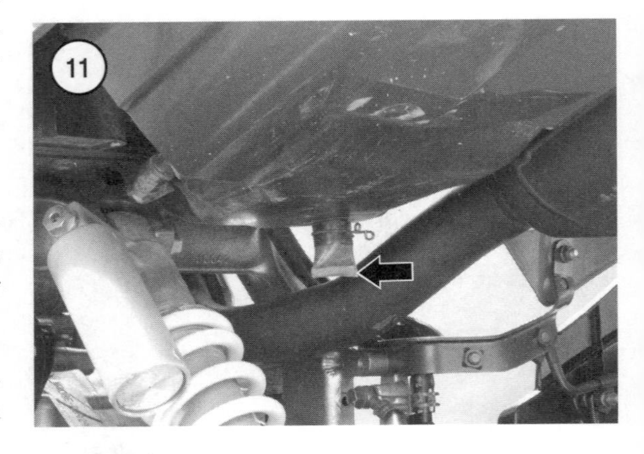

Filter Element

The following procedure covers the original equipment foam filter element. Follow the manufacturer's instructions if equipped with an aftermarket air filter element.

1. Remove the seat as described in Chapter Fifteen.
2. Disengage the spring clamps (**Figure 12**) that secure the cover to the air box. Remove the cover from the air box.
3. If necessary, wipe the inside of the air box to prevent any loose dust or dirt from falling into the intake part of the air box when removing the air filter.
4. Remove the bolt and washer (A, **Figure 13**) securing the air filter to the air box. Remove the air filter (B, **Figure 13**).
5. Inspect the intake tract from the air box to the throttle body for dirt or other residue.

CAUTION
To prevent air leaks and dirt from entering the engine, make sure all connections between the throttle body, air boot and air box are sealed properly.

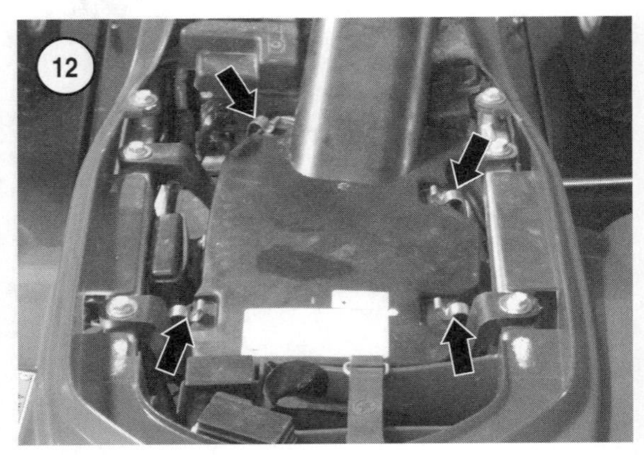

6. Cover the air box opening with a clean shop rag.
7. Carefully pull the foam element off the frame (**Figure 14**).
8. Before cleaning the air filter, check it for brittleness, separation or other damage. Replace the filter if damaged.

WARNING
Do not clean the air filter element with gasoline.

CAUTION
To prevent damage to the filter, do not wring or twist it during cleaning.

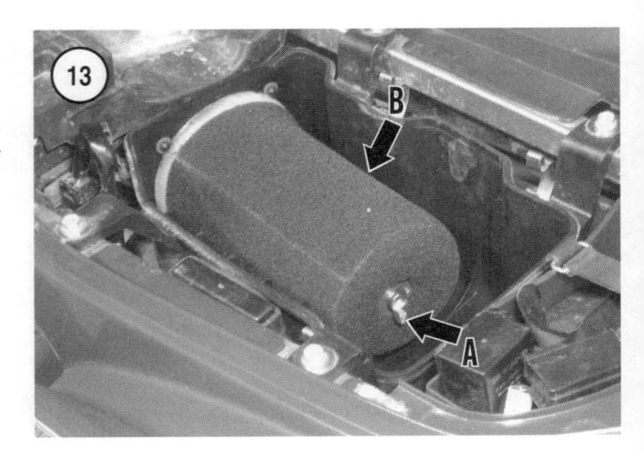

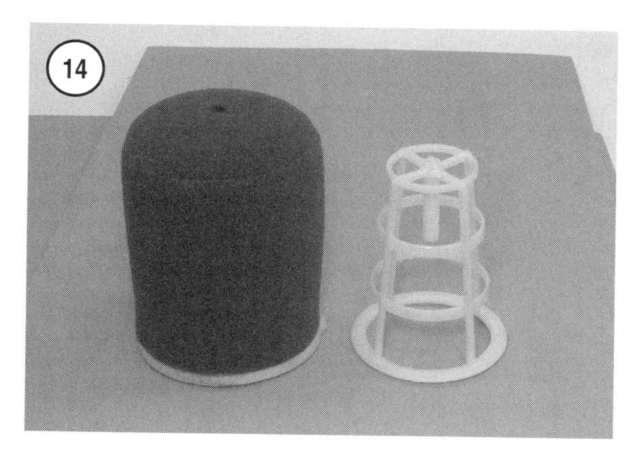

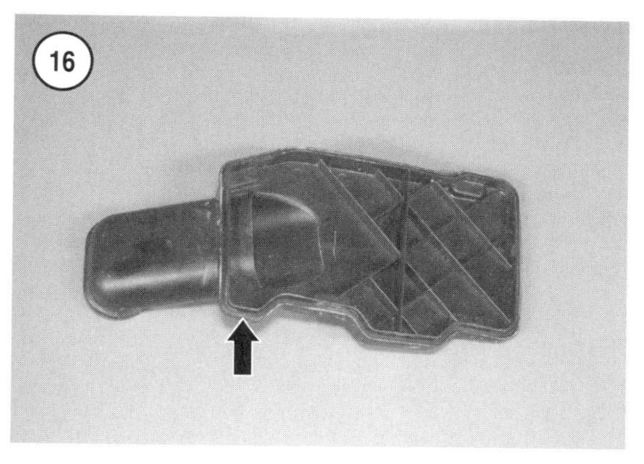

9. Soak the air filter in a container filled with kerosene or an air filter cleaner. Gently squeeze the filter to dislodge and remove the oil and dirt from the filter pores. Swish the filter around in the cleaner a few times. Then, remove the air filter and set it aside to air-dry.
10. Fill a clean pan with warm soapy water.
11. Submerge the filter into the pan and gently work the soap solution into the filter pores. Soak and squeeze (gently) the filter to clean it.
12. Rinse the filter under warm water while gently squeezing it.
13. Repeat the cleaning steps until there are no signs of dirt being rinsed from the filter.
14. After cleaning the element, inspect it again. Replace the air filter if it is torn or broken in any area. Do not run the engine with a damaged element as it may allow dirt to enter the engine.
15. Set the filter aside to air-dry.
16. Clean the retaining bolt and washer and dry thoroughly.

CAUTION
A damp filter will not trap fine dust. Make sure the filter is completely dry before oiling it.

NOTE
Proper application of the filter oil requires squeezing oil into the filter. Nitrile gloves are recommended.

17. Oil the filter as follows:
   a. Place the air filter into a gallon size storage bag.

NOTE
Oil designed for use in foam air filters is recommended. If unavailable, clean engine oil may be used.

   b. Pour air filter oil onto the filter to soak it completely.
   c. Gently squeeze and release the filter to soak filter oil into the filter pores. Repeat until the entire filter is saturated with oil.
   d. Remove the filter from the bag and check the pores for uneven oiling. This is indicated by light or dark areas on the filter. If necessary, soak the filter and squeeze it again.
   e. When the filter oiling is even, squeeze the filter a final time.
   f. Remove the air filter from the bag and inspect it for any excess oil or uneven oiling. Remove any excess oil from the filter with a paper towel.
18. Slide the air filter onto the frame, making sure the frame is centered properly inside the air filter.
19. Apply a coat of lithium grease to the foam sealing surface (**Figure 15**) on the open end of the filter. The grease will help seal the air filter against the air box.
20. Install the air filter into the air box.
21. Install the washer and retaining bolt (A, **Figure 13**). Tighten securely.
22. Make sure there are no gaps between the filter and the air box. If so, loosen the filter bolt and reposition the air filter.
23. Check the gasket (**Figure 16**) installed in the groove on the bottom side of the air box cover. Replace the gasket if missing or damaged.
24. Install the air box cover and secure it with the spring clamps (**Figure 12**).
25. Install the seat as described in Chapter Fifteen.

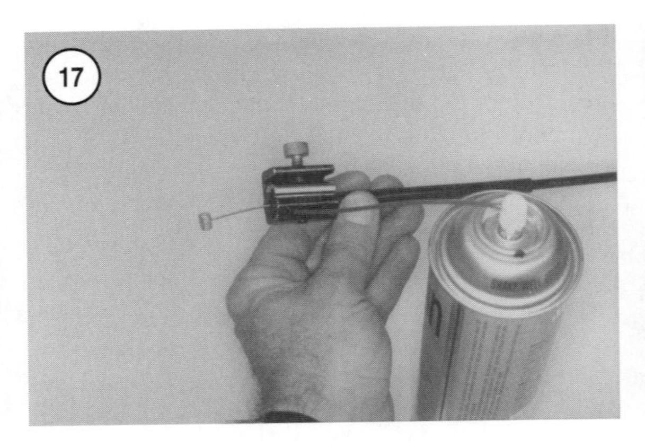

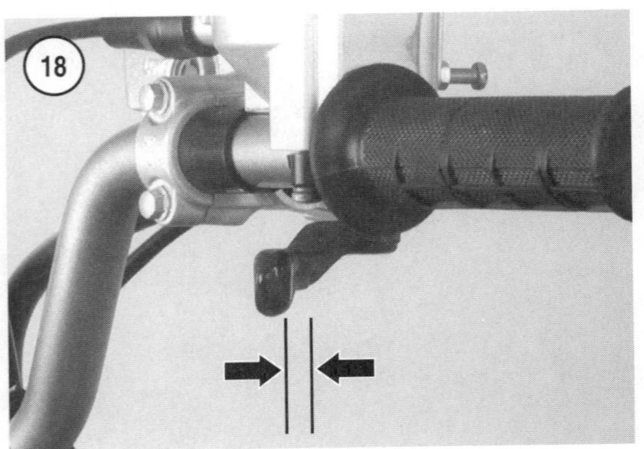

CONTROL CABLE INSPECTION AND LUBRICATION

Clean and lubricate the throttle and clutch whenever cable operation becomes sluggish or stiff. At the same time, check the cables for wear and damage or fraying that could cause the cables to bind or break. The most positive method of cable lubrication involves using a cable lubricator (**Figure 17**) and a can of cable lubricant.

CAUTION
Do not use chain lubricant to flush and lubricate the control cables.

1. Disconnect both clutch cable ends as described in Chapter Six.
2. Disconnect both throttle cable ends as described in Chapter Eight.
3. Disconnect both reverse cable ends as described in Chapter Six.

CAUTION
Do not lubricate the throttle cable while it is attached to the throttle body. Doing so will expel dirt and debris into the cable housing on the throttle body.

4. Attach a cable lubricator to one end of the cable, following the manufacturer's instructions (**Figure 17**).
5. Tie a plastic bag around the opposite cable end to catch the excess lubricant.
6. Fit the nozzle of the cable lubricant into the hole in the lubricator.
7. Hold a rag over the lubricator. Then, press and hold the button on the lubricant can. Continue until lubricant drips from the opposite end of the cable sheath.
8. Disconnect the cable lubricator, and then pull the inner cable back and forth to help distribute the lubricant.
9. Allow time for excess lubricant to drain from the cable before reconnecting it.
10. Apply a light coat of grease to the upper throttle cable ends before reconnecting them.

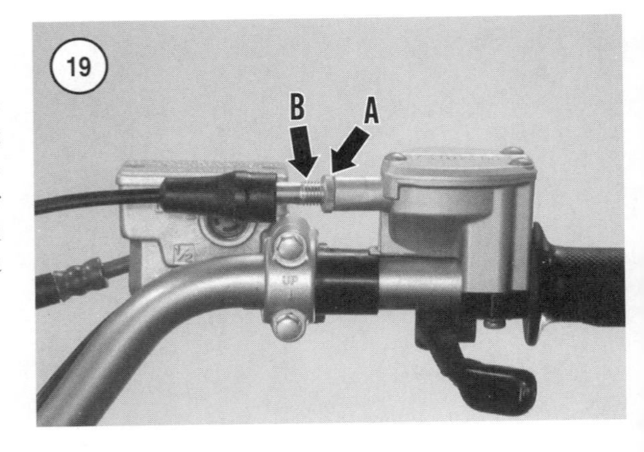

11. Lubricate the clutch and reverse cable ends with grease.
12. Reconnect the cables as described in the appropriate chapter.
13. Adjust the cables as described in this chapter.

THROTTLE CABLE AND SPEED LIMITER ADJUSTMENT

Throttle Cable

WARNING
A damaged or misadjusted throttle cable will prevent the engine from idling properly.

Cable wear and stretch affect throttle body operation. Normal amounts of cable wear and stretch can be controlled by the free play adjustments described in this section. If the cables cannot be adjusted within their limits, the cables are excessively worn or damaged and require replacement.

Free play (**Figure 18**) is the distance the throttle lever can be pushed until resistance from the throttle shaft can be felt. While measuring at the end of the throttle lever, set the throttle cable free play to 2-4 mm (0.08-0.16 in.). Excessive cable stretch will de-

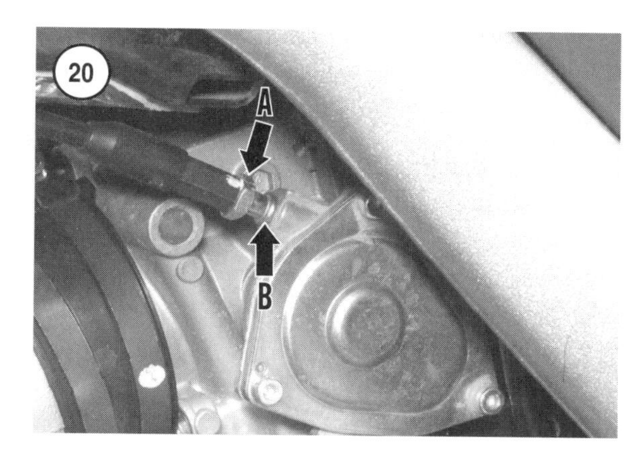

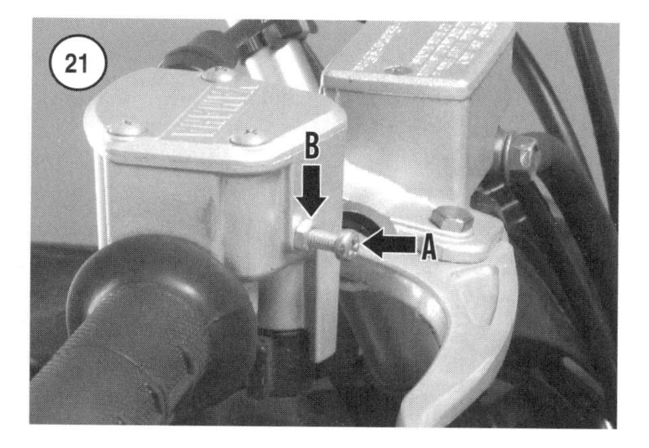

lay throttle response. Insufficient cable free play may cause an excessively high idle.

Minor adjustments can be made at the throttle grip adjuster. Major adjustments can be made at the throttle cable adjuster on the throttle body.

1. Before adjusting the throttle cable, operate the throttle lever and make sure it opens and closes properly with the handlebar turned in different positions. If not, check the throttle cable for damage or improper routing.
2. Operate the throttle lever and measure the amount of free play travel (**Figure 18**) until the cable play is taken up. If the free play measurement is incorrect, perform the following.
3. At the throttle housing, slide back the rubber boot on the cable adjuster. Loosen the throttle cable adjuster locknut (A, **Figure 19**) and turn the adjuster (B) to obtain proper free play. Tighten the locknut.
4. If the adjustment cannot be corrected at the throttle housing adjuster, turn in the throttle cable adjuster (B, **Figure 19**) all the way. Slide back the rubber boot and loosen the locknut (A, **Figure 20**) at the throttle body. Turn the adjuster (B, **Figure 20**) out as required, making sure the adjuster does not come all the way out. Complete adjustment by turning the adjuster at the throttle grip. Tighten the locknuts at both ends of the cable.
5. Slide the rubber boots back over the cable adjusters.

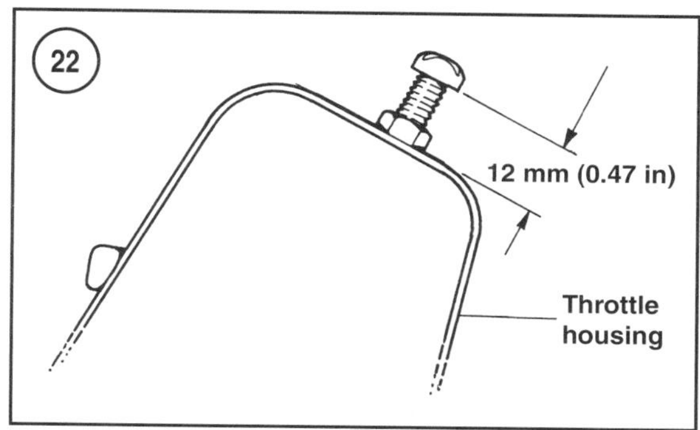

6. If the throttle cable cannot be adjusted properly, the cable has stretched excessively and must be replaced.
7. Make sure the throttle lever operates freely from a fully closed to fully open position.
8. Start the engine and allow it to idle in neutral. Turn the handlebar from side to side. If the idle increases, the throttle cable is routed incorrectly or there is not enough cable free play.

Speed Limiter

WARNING

Do not operate the vehicle with the speed limiter screw removed from the housing. Do not exceed the 12 mm (0.47 in.) adjustment limit. If adjusting the speed limiter for a beginning rider, start and ride the vehicle after adjustment to determine if a safe maximum speed has been achieved.

The throttle housing is equipped with a speed limiter (A, **Figure 21**) that can be set to prevent the rider from opening the throttle all the way. The speed limiter can be set for beginning riders or to control engine rpm when breaking in a new engine.

The speed limiter adjustment (**Figure 22**) is set by varying the length of the speed limiter screw, measured from the throttle housing to the bottom of the screw head. The standard speed limiter setting is less than 12 mm (0.47 in.).

1. Check throttle cable free play as described in this chapter. If necessary, adjust throttle cable free play.
2. Loosen the locknut (B, **Figure 21**).
3. Turn the speed limiter screw (A, **Figure 21**) in or out as required. Do not exceed the 12 mm (0.47 in.) adjustment limit. Tighten the locknut (B, **Figure 21**).

CLUTCH LEVER

Clutch Lever Adjustment

The clutch lever free play changes due to clutch cable and clutch plate wear. Maintain the clutch lever free play within the specification. Insufficient free play causes clutch slip and premature clutch plate wear. Excessive free play causes clutch drag and rough shift lever operation.

NOTE
Clutch cable adjustment is possible at the clutch lever or at the inline cable adjuster. Make minor adjustments at the clutch lever. Make major adjustments at the inline cable adjuster.

1. Determine the clutch lever free play (**Figure 23**) at the end of the clutch lever. If the free play is more or less than 5-10 mm (0.20-0.39 in.), adjust the cable as follows:
   a. At the clutch lever, slide back the rubber boot on the cable adjuster.
   b. Loosen the clutch lever adjuster locknut (A, **Figure 24**).
   c. Turn the clutch lever adjuster (B, **Figure 24**) as required to obtain the specified amount of free play.
2. If the proper amount of free play cannot be achieved by adjusting the clutch lever adjuster, the clutch cable inline adjuster must be moved. Perform the following:
   a. Turn the clutch lever adjuster (B, **Figure 24**) in all the way.
   b. Loosen the clutch cable inline adjuster locknut (A, **Figure 25**). Turn the adjuster nut (B, **Figure 25**) as required to obtain the correct free play. Tighten the locknut. If necessary, fine-tune the adjustment at the clutch lever adjuster.
3. If the correct free play cannot be obtained, either the cable has stretched to the point that it needs to be replaced or the clutch discs are worn. Refer to Chapter Six for clutch cable and clutch service.

Clutch Lever Pivot Bolt Lubrication

Periodically, remove the clutch lever pivot bolt and lubricate with lithium grease.

REVERSE CABLE

Adjustment (2006-2008 Models)

The reverse knob free play continually changes due to the reverse cable wearing and stretching over time. For proper reverse gear engagement, adjust the reverse cable to the specification listed in this procedure.

1. Make sure the reverse control knob is in the disengaged position.
2. Measure the distance from the pivot pin (A, **Figure 26**) on the reverse lever to the cable housing

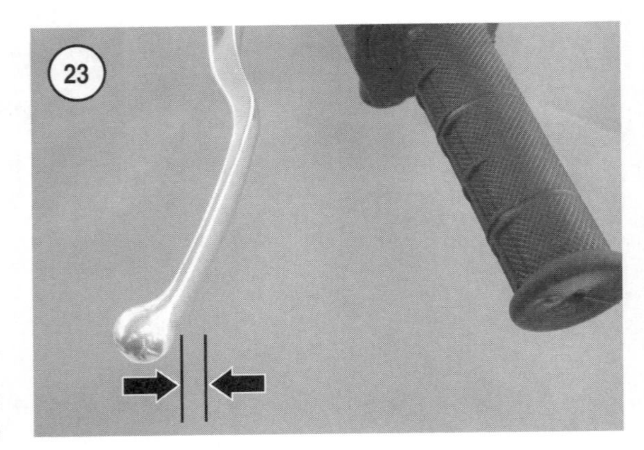

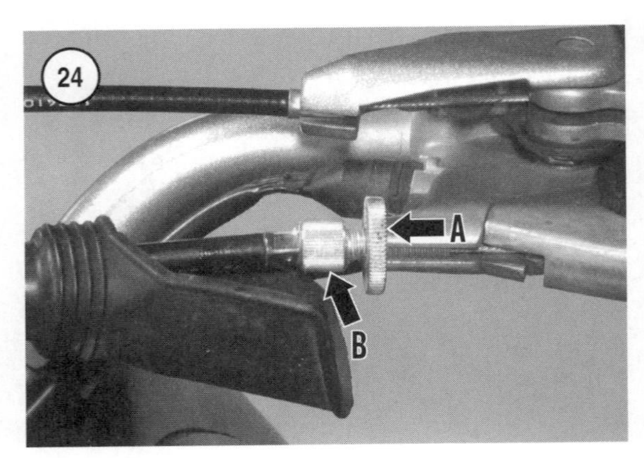

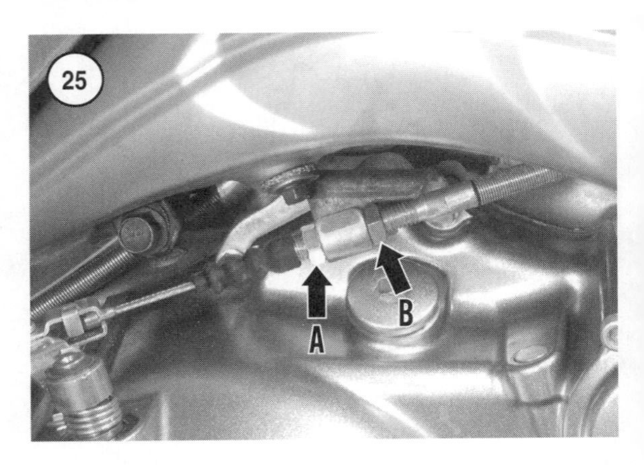

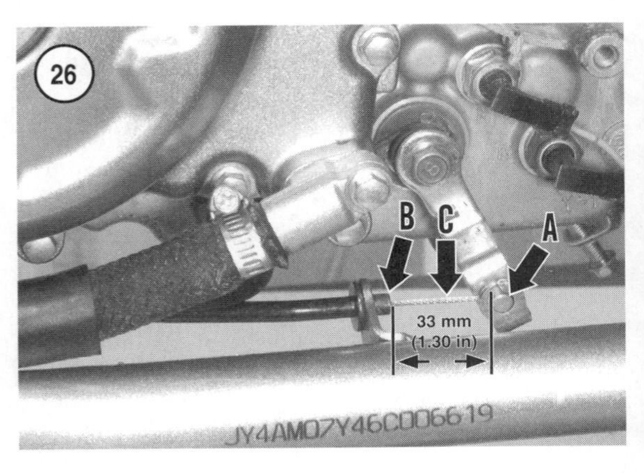

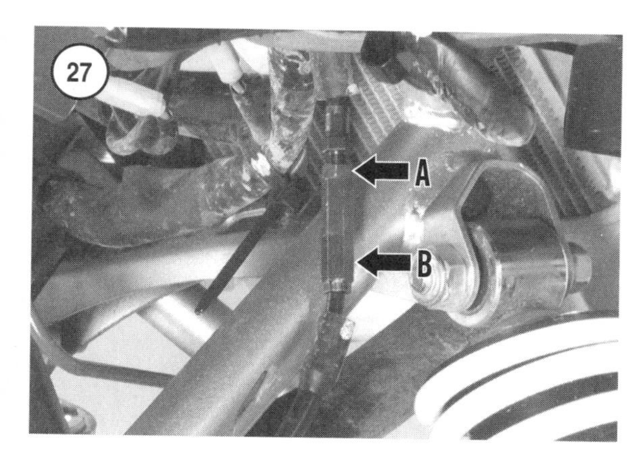

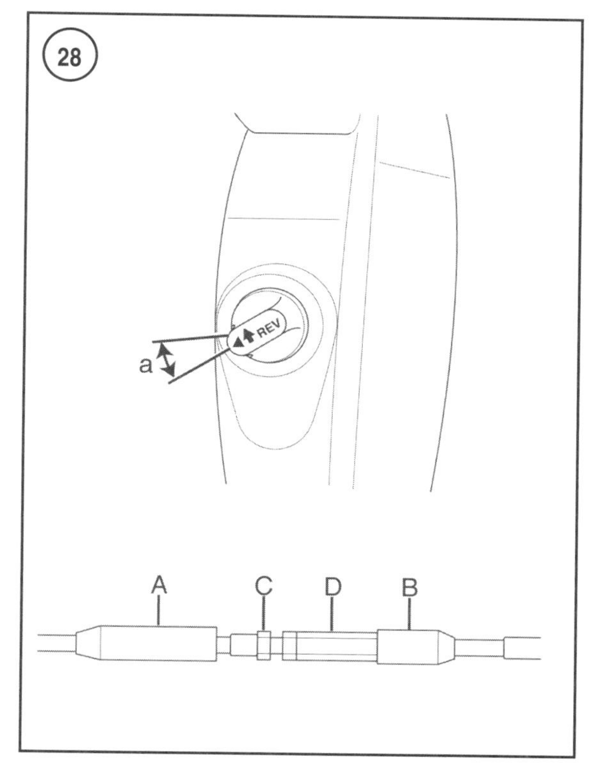

(B). The distance should be 33 mm (1.30 in.). There should be no slack in the control cable (C, **Figure 26**).

3. Adjust the reverse control cable as needed using the inline cable adjuster adjacent to the front, right shock absorber. Loosen the locknut (A, **Figure 27**) and turn the adjuster (B). Tighten the locknut.
4. Recheck the adjustment as needed until the proper specification is reached.

Adjustment (2009-on Models)

The reverse knob free play continually changes due to the reverse cable wearing and stretching over time. For proper reverse gear engagement, adjust the reverse cable to the specifications listed in this procedure.

1. Make sure the reverse control is in the disengaged position.
2. Rotate the knob and check for the specified rotational free play:
   a. 2009-2012 models, 0 mm (0 in.).
   b. 2012-on models: 2.0-2.4 mm (0.08-0.16 in.).
3. Adjust the reverse control cable free play as necessary as follows:
   a. Slide back the rubber boots (A and B, **Figure 28**).
   b. Loosen the locknut (C, **Figure 28**).
   c. Secure the reverse shift lever so it does not move.
   d. Turn the adjust nut (D, **Figure 28**) until the reverse control cable is taught or a length of 33 mm (1.30 in.) in length between the pivot pin (A, **Figure 26**) on the reverse lever to the cable housing (B). There should be no slack in the control cable. (C, **Figure 26**).
   e. Tighten the locknut (C, **Figure 28**).
   f. Slide back the rubber boots (A and B, **Figure 28**).
4. Recheck the adjustment as needed until the proper rotational free play specification is achieved.

BRAKES

This section describes routine service procedures for the front and rear disc brakes. Refer to **Table 1** for service intervals.

Brake Pad Wear

Remove the front wheels and inspect the brake pads for wear, scoring, grease or oil contamination, or other damage. A small mirror helps when checking rear brake pad wear. Inspect the thickness of the friction material on each pad. Each brake pad is equipped with a wear indicator. If any one pad on the front or rear is worn to its wear limit grooves, or measures 1.0 mm (0.04 in.) or less, replace both pads. Refer to Chapter Fourteen for brake pad service.

Front Brake Lever Adjustment

The brake lever position is adjustable to suit rider preference. There must be zero free play when the lever boss (A, **Figure 29**) contacts the master cylinder actuator bolt (B). Adjust the brake lever position as follows:

1. Push the brake lever forward.
2. Loosen the locknut (C, **Figure 29**).

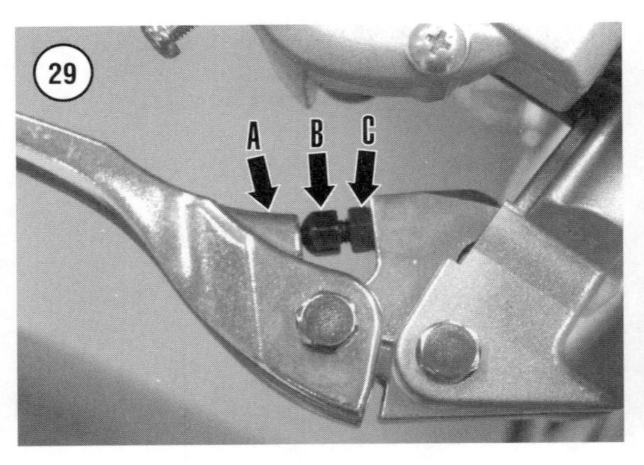

3. Pull the brake lever toward the handlebar grip until the lever boss (A, **Figure 29**) just contacts the actuator bolt (B).
4. Turn the actuator bolt (B, **Figure 29**) so the lever is in the desired position.
5. Tighten the locknut (C, **Figure 29**).
6. Check the adjustment. If free play still exists, bleed the front brake as described in Chapter Fourteen.

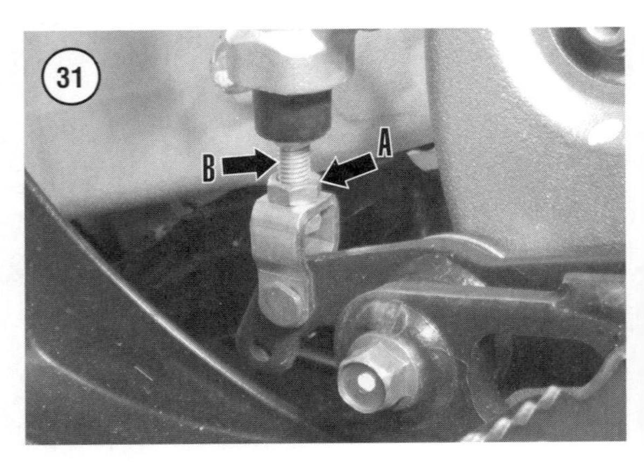

Rear Brake Pedal Height Adjustment

1. Apply the rear brake a few times and allow the pedal to come to rest. Make sure the return spring is installed and in good condition.
2. Measure the pedal height dimension as shown in **Figure 30**. The correct height dimension is 15.3 mm (0.60 in.) below the footrest.
3. If necessary, loosen the locknut (A, **Figure 31**) and turn the pushrod (B) to adjust the pedal height.
4. Tighten the locknut and recheck the height dimension.
5. Lift the rear wheels and verify that the brake is not dragging. If so, repeat the adjustment procedure.

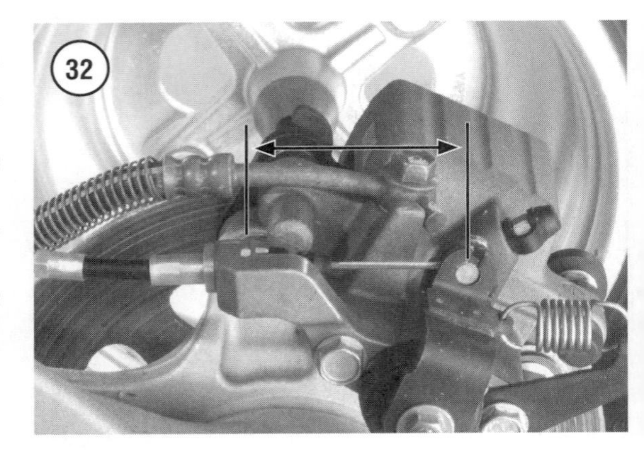

Parking Brake Cable Adjustment (2006-2012 Models)

The parking brake cable must be properly adjusted to ensure that it fully engages and disengages.

1. Measure the cable length (**Figure 32**) between the cable holder and the centerline of the brake lever. The specified length is 58-60 mm (2.28-2.36 in.).
2. To adjust the cable, push back the boot and loosen the locknut (A, **Figure 33**). Turn the cable adjuster (B, **Figure 33**) until the proper length is achieved. Tighten the locknut and reposition the boot.
3. Lift the rear wheels and verify that the brake is not dragging. If so, repeat the adjustment procedure.

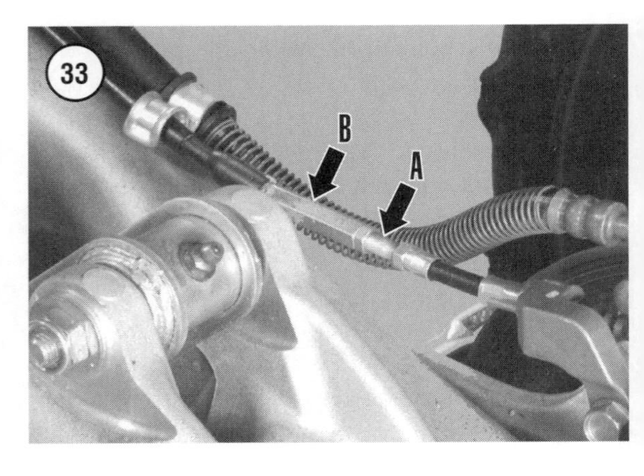

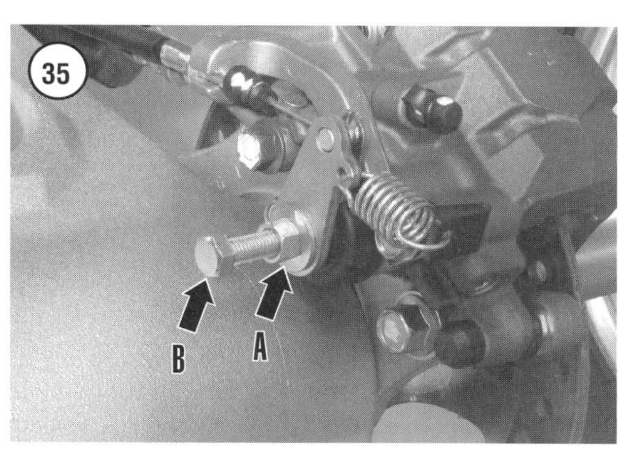

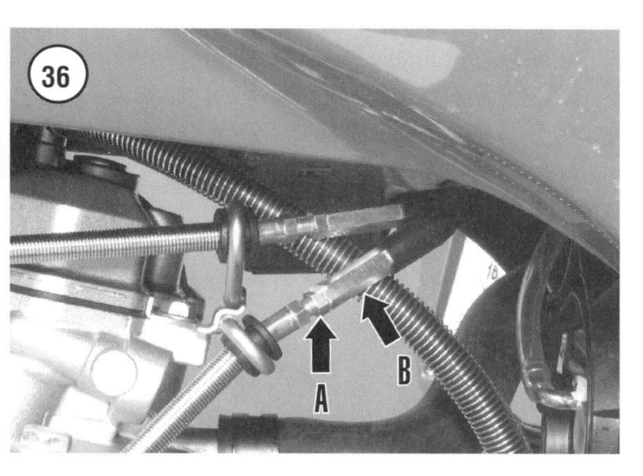

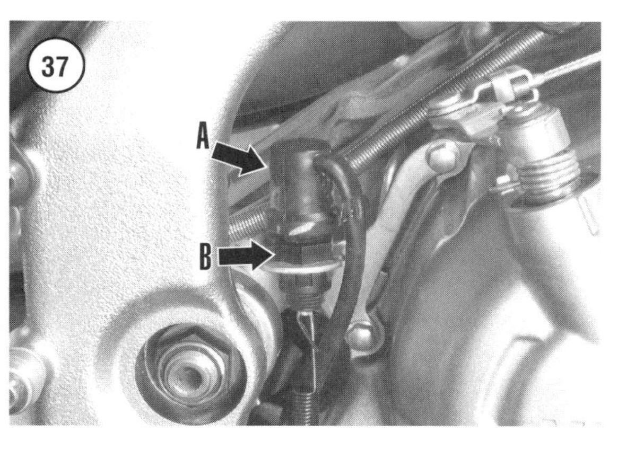

Parking Brake Adjustment (2013-on Models)

The parking brake cable must be properly adjusted to ensure it fully engages and disengages.

1. Measure the cable length between the cable holder (**Figure 34**) and the centerline of the brake lever. The specified length is 47-51 mm (1.8-2.0 in.).
2. At the parking brake, loosen the locknut (A, **Figure 35**) and the adjuster bolt (B).
3. On the inline cable adjuster, push back the boot and loosen the locknut (A, **Figure 36**). Turn the adjuster (B, **Figure 36**) until the proper length is achieved. Tighten the locknut and reposition the boot.
4. At the parking brake, turn the adjuster bolt (B, **Figure 35**) clockwise until resistance is felt. Turn it back 1/8 turn counterclockwise. Hold the adjuster bolt and tighten the locknut to 16 N•m (11 ft.-lb.). There should be no play at the handlebar lever.
5. Lift the rear wheels and verify that the brake is not dragging. If so, repeat this adjustment.

Rear Brake Light Switch Adjustment

1. Turn the ignition switch on.
2. Depress the brake pedal and watch the brake light. The brake light should come on just before feeling pressure at the brake pedal. If necessary, adjust the rear brake light switch by performing the following.
3. To adjust the brake light switch, hold the switch body (A, **Figure 37**) and turn the adjusting nut (B). To make the light come on earlier, turn the adjusting nut and move the switch body up. Move the switch body down to delay the light coming on.
4. Check that the brake light comes on when the pedal is depressed and goes off when the pedal is released. Readjust if necessary.
5. Turn the ignition switch off.

Brake Fluid Level Inspection

WARNING
If any reservoir is empty, or if the brake fluid level is so low that air is entering the brake system, bleed the brake system as described in Chapter Fourteen. Simply adding brake fluid to the reservoir does not restore the brake system to its full effectiveness.

WARNING
Use brake fluid marked DOT 4. Others may vaporize and cause brake failure. Do not mix different brands or types of

brake fluid, as they may not be compatible. Do not use a silicone-based (DOT 5) brake fluid, as it can cause brake component damage and brake system failure.

CAUTION
Be careful when handling brake fluid. Do not spill it on painted or plastic surfaces, as it will damage them. Wash the area immediately with soap and water and rinse thoroughly.

CAUTION
Do not remove the cover on either the front or rear brake reservoirs unless the reservoirs are level.

Maintain the brake fluid level in the front and rear master cylinder reservoirs above the minimum level line. If the fluid level is low in either reservoir, check for loose or damaged hoses or loose fittings. If there are no visible fluid leaks, check the brake pads for excessive wear. As the brake pads wear, the caliper piston moves farther out of the bore, thus causing the brake fluid level to drop in the reservoir. Also, check the master cylinder bore and the brake caliper piston areas for signs of brake fluid. If there is a noticeable fluid leak, that component requires overhaul to replace the damaged part. Check the brake pads for wear as described in this section. Refer to Chapter Fourteen for brake service.

1. Park the ATV on level ground.
2. Clean the area around the reservoir cover before removing the cover to avoid contaminating the reservoir.

CAUTION
When adding brake fluid to the reservoirs, inspect the reservoir diaphragm for tearing, cracks or other damage. A damaged diaphragm will allow moisture to enter the reservoir and contaminate the brake fluid.

3A. On the front reservoir, perform the following:
   a. Turn the handlebar so the master cylinder reservoir is level.
   b. Observe the brake fluid level through the inspection window (**Figure 38**) on the master cylinder reservoir.
   c. The brake fluid level must be above the lower level mark on the reservoir.
   d. Remove the two screws, and then remove the cover and diaphragm.

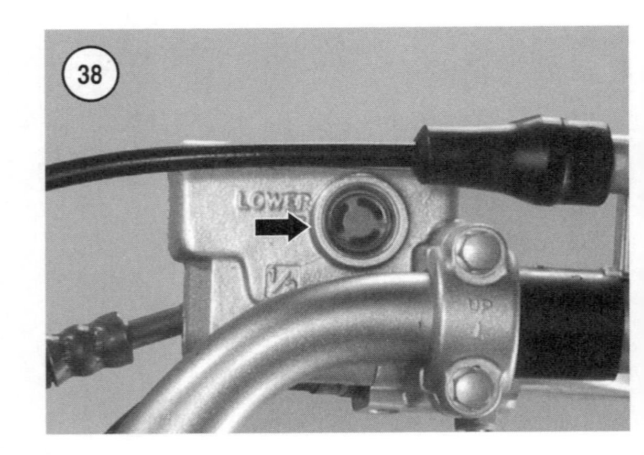

   e. Add fresh DOT 4 brake fluid up to the upper level mark inside the reservoir.
   f. Replace the cover and diaphragm if damaged.
   g. Install the diaphragm and cover. Then, install the screws and tighten them securely.

3B. On the rear reservoir, perform the following:
   a. Remove the seat as described in Chapter Fifteen.
   b. The brake fluid level must be above the lower level mark (A, **Figure 39**) on the reservoir.
   c. Remove the front fender rear mounting bolt and move the fender aside for access to the rear master cylinder reservoir cap.
   d. Unscrew the reservoir cap and remove the cap and diaphragm.
   e. Add fresh DOT 4 brake fluid up to the upper level mark (B, **Figure 39**) on the reservoir.
   f. Replace the top cap and diaphragm. Install the side cover.

Brake Hose Replacement

Replace the brake hoses if they become swollen or damaged. Refer to Chapter Fourteen for service procedures.

Brake Fluid Change

WARNING
Use brake fluid marked DOT 4 only. Others may vaporize and cause brake failure. Dispose of any unused fluid in a safe manner. Never reuse brake fluid. Contaminated brake fluid can cause brake failure.

Every time a fluid reservoir cap is removed, a small amount of dirt and moisture enters the brake system. The same thing happens if a leak occurs or if any part of the hydraulic system is loosened

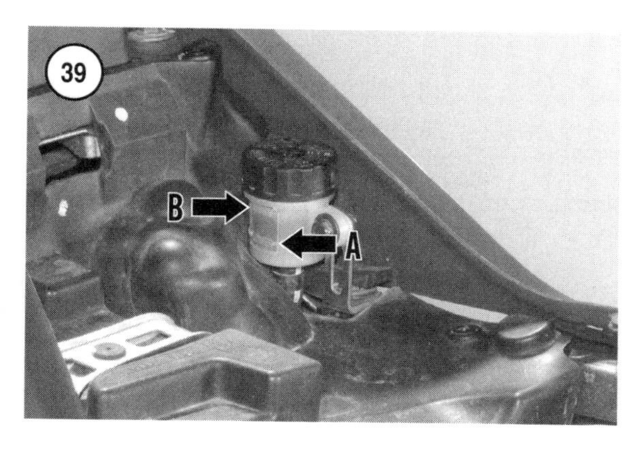

or disconnected. Dirt can clog the system and cause unnecessary wear. Water in the brake fluid can vaporize at high brake system temperatures, impairing hydraulic action and reducing stopping ability.

To maintain peak performance, change the brake fluid every year and when rebuilding a caliper or master cylinder. To change brake fluid, follow the brake bleeding procedure in Chapter Fourteen.

Brake Lever Pivot Bolt Lubrication

Periodically remove the brake lever pivot bolt and lubricate it with lithium grease.

DRIVE CHAIN

Drive Chain Lubrication

Lubricate the drive chain at the interval in **Table 1**. A properly maintained drive chain will provide maximum service life and reliability. The manufacturer recommends SAE 10W/30 engine oil or their O-ring chain and cable lubricant.

CAUTION
Not all commercial chain lubricants are recommended for use on O-ring drive chains. Make sure the product is formulated for O-ring chains.

NOTE
On an O-ring drive chain, the chain lubrication is used mainly to keep the O-rings pliable and to prevent the side plates and rollers from rusting. The actual chain lubrication is enclosed within the chain by the O-rings.

1. Ride the ATV a few miles to warm the drive chain. A warm chain increases lubricant penetration.
2. Park the ATV on level ground. Support the ATV securely with the rear wheels off the ground.
3. Oil the bottom chain run with SAE 10W/30 engine oil or a commercial chain lubricant recommended for use on O-ring equipped drive chains. Concentrate on getting the oil down between the side plates on both sides of the chain. Do not over lubricate.
4. Rotate the chain and continue lubricating until the entire chain has been lubricated.
5. Turn the rear wheels slowly and wipe off excess oil from the chain with a shop cloth. Also wipe off lubricant from the wheel and tire, and rear of the ATV.
6. Remove the ATV support.

Drive Chain Cleaning

Clean the drive chain after riding over dusty or sandy conditions. A properly maintained chain provides maximum service life and reliability.

CAUTION
All models are equipped with an O-ring drive chain. Clean the chain with kerosene only. Solvents and gasoline cause the rubber O-rings to swell. The drive chain then becomes so stiff it cannot move or flex. If this happens, the drive chain must be replaced. High pressure washers and steam cleaning can also damage the O-rings.

Because all models are equipped with an endless drive chain, it is not practical to break the chain in order to clean it. This section describes how to clean the drive chain while it is installed.

1. Ride the ATV a few miles to warm the drive chain. A warm chain increases lubricant penetration.
2. Park the ATV on level ground. Support the ATV securely with the rear wheels off the ground.
3. Place some stiff cardboard and a drain pan underneath the drive chain.

NOTE
Do not splash the kerosene when cleaning the drive chain in the following steps. Make sure to keep kerosene off the rear tires and other parts as much as possible.

4. Soak a thick rag in kerosene, and then wipe it against the section of chain that is exposed on the lower chain run. When this section of the chain is clean, turn the rear wheels to expose the next section and clean it. Repeat until all of the chain is clean. To remove stubborn dirt, scrub the rollers and side plates with a soft brush. To avoid catching fingers and rag between the chain and sprocket, do not rotate

the rear wheels when cleaning the chain. Clean one section of the chain at a time.

5. Turn the rear wheels slowly and wipe the drive chain dry with a thick shop cloth.
6. Remove all kerosene from the ATV.
7. Lubricate the drive chain as previously described in this section.

Drive Chain and Sprocket Inspection

Frequently check the chain and both sprockets for excessive wear and damage.

1. Clean the drive chain as described in this section.
2. Park the ATV on level ground. Support the ATV securely with the rear wheels off the ground.
3. Turn the rear wheels and inspect both sides of the chain for missing or damaged O-rings.
4. At the rear sprocket, pull one of the links away from the driven sprocket. If the link pulls away more than 1/2 the height of the sprocket tooth, the chain is excessively worn.
5. Inspect the inner plate chain faces (**Figure 40**). They should be polished on both sides. If they show considerable uneven wear on one side, the sprockets are not aligned properly. Severe wear requires replacement of not only the drive chain but also the drive and driven sprockets.
6. Inspect the drive and driven sprockets for the following defects:
   a. Undercutting or sharp teeth.
   b. Broken teeth.
7. Check the drive sprocket nut and the driven sprocket nuts for looseness. If loose, tighten to the torque specified in **Table 7**.
8. If excessive chain or sprocket wear is evident, replace the drive chain and both sprockets as a complete set. If only the drive chain is replaced, the worn sprockets will cause rapid chain wear.

Drive Chain Adjustment

The drive chain must have adequate play so it can adjust to the actions of the swing arm when the machine is in use. Too little play can cause the chain to become excessively tight and cause unnecessary wear to the driveline components. Too much play can cause excessive looseness and possibly cause the chain to jump off the sprocket(s).

1. There must be no weight on the ATV.
2. With the transmission in neutral, move the ATV so the chain rotates and determine when the chain is tightest along its top length (least amount of play).
3. Measure the free play (**Figure 41**) in the top length of chain. The free play specification is 25-35 mm (0.98-1.38 in.).

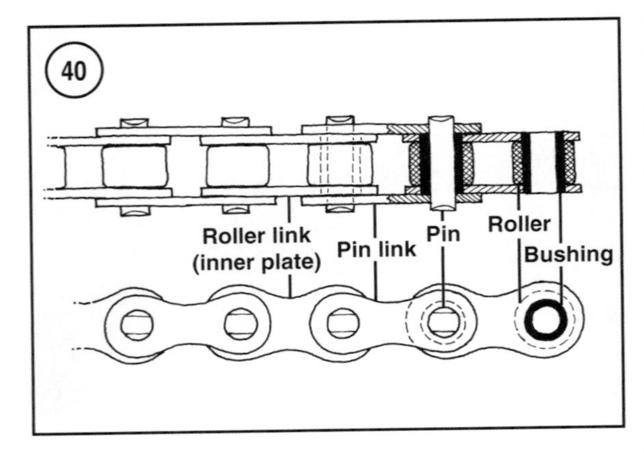

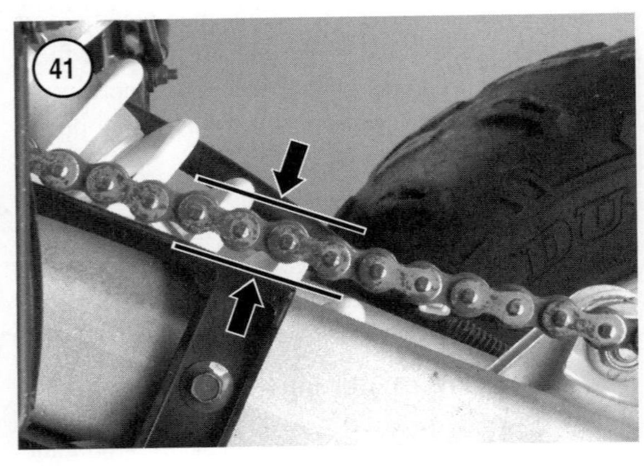

4. If necessary, adjust the chain play as follows:
   a. Loosen the pinch bolts on the axle hub in the reverse of the sequence shown in **Figure 42**.

NOTE
The rear axle hub is eccentric shaped. Rotating the hub causes the rear axle to move laterally.

   b. Insert a rod (**Figure 43**) into one of the holes in the axle hub.
   c. Make sure the transmission is in neutral.

NOTE
Move the ATV slowly in the following step. The axle hub will rotate when the rod presses against a driven sprocket spoke.

   d. Move the ATV forward to loosen the drive chain, or rearward to tighten the drive chain.
   e. Remove the rod and measure free play again.
   f. When free play is correct, tighten the axle hub pinch bolts to lock the setting.
   g. Using the sequence shown in **Figure 42**, tighten the axle hub pinch bolts to 21 N•m (15.5 ft.-lb.).

42

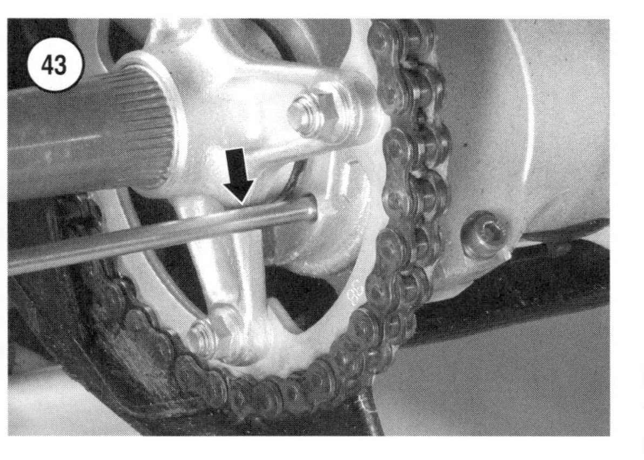
43

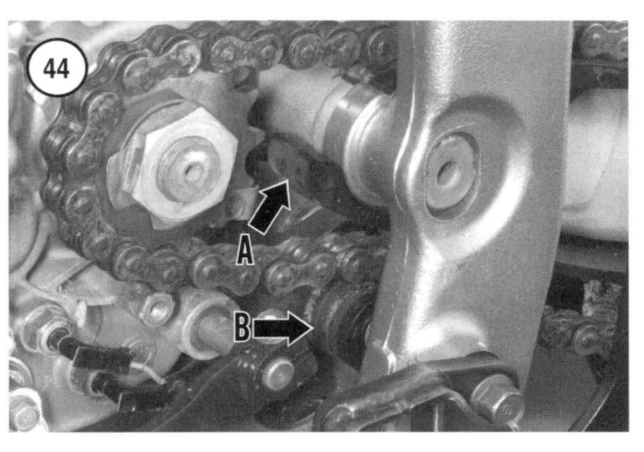

44

5. If free play cannot be adjusted within the limits of the adjuster, the chain is excessively worn. Replace the chain as described in Chapter Eleven.

Drive Chain Slider and Rollers Inspection

These parts support the chain and protect the frame and swing arm. Inspect the following for wear or damage:

1. Chain slider (A, **Figure 44**).
   a. Inspect the upper and lower surface of the slider for wear or damage. The chain will contact the swing arm, possibly causing severe damage, if the slider is worn or missing.
   b. Check the mounting bolt for tightness.
2. Chain roller (B, **Figure 44**).
   a. Clean and inspect the chain roller attached to the frame. Replace the roller if worn or seized.
   b. Check the mounting bolt for tightness. If loose, tighten the bolt to 32 N•m (24 ft.-lb.).

TIRES AND WHEELS

Tire Pressure

WARNING
Always inflate both tire sets (front and rear) tires to the correct air pressure. If the ATV is run with unequal air pressures, the ATV may run toward one side, causing poor handling.

CAUTION
Do not overinflate the tires as they can be permanently damaged.

Check and adjust tire pressure to maintain good traction and handling and to get the maximum service life from the tire. Refer to **Table 2** for specifications. Check tire pressure when the tires are cold.

Tire Inspection

WARNING
Do not ride the ATV with damaged or excessively worn tires. A tire in this condition can cause loss of control. Replace damaged or severely worn tires immediately.

The tires take a lot of punishment due to the variety of terrain they are subjected to. Inspect them daily for excessive wear, cuts, abrasions or punctures. If a nail or other object is found in a tire, mark its location with a light crayon before removing it. Service the tire as described in Chapter Eleven.

To gauge tire wear, inspect the height of the tread knobs. If the average tread knob height measures 3 mm (0.12 in.) or less (**Figure 45**), replace the tire as described in Chapter Eleven.

Wheel Inspection

Inspect the wheels for damage. Rim damage may be sufficient to cause an air leak or affect wheel alignment. Improper wheel alignment can cause vibration and result in an unsafe riding condition.

Make sure the wheel nuts (**Figure 46**) are tightened securely on each wheel. Tighten the wheel nuts in a crossing pattern to 45 N•m (33 ft.-lb.).

FRONT WHEEL BEARING INSPECTION

Inspect the front wheel bearings at the intervals in **Table 1**. To replace the seals and wheel bearings, refer to the service procedures in Chapter Twelve.

Check the front wheel bearings as follows:

1. Support the ATV so the front wheel is off the ground.
2. Remove the front wheel as described in Chapter Eleven.
3. Push the caliper in to push the piston into their bores. This will move the pads away from the disc.
4. Install the front wheel.
5. Spin the wheel while checking for excessive wheel bearing noise or other damage. Stop the wheel.

WARNING
A faulty ball joint can cause excessive wheel movement. Determine whether wheel movement is due to faulty bearings or ball joints.

6. Grab the wheel at two points and rock it. There should be no play at the wheel bearings. If any movement can be seen or felt, check the front wheel bearings for excessive wear or damage (Chapter Twelve).

WARNING
Do not ride the ATV until the brakes operate correctly.

7. Spin the wheel while applying the brake several times to reposition the pads against the disc.

STEERING SYSTEM

Steering System Inspection

Inspect the steering system at the interval in **Table 1**. If any of the steering fasteners are loose, refer to Chapter Twelve for the correct service procedures and torque specifications.

1. Park the ATV on level ground and set the parking brake.
2. Visually inspect all components of the steering system. Repair or replace damaged components as described in Chapter Twelve.
3. Check the shock absorbers as described in this chapter.
4. Remove the handlebar cover as described in Chapter Fifteen. Check that the handlebar holder bolts are tight. Reinstall the handlebar cover.

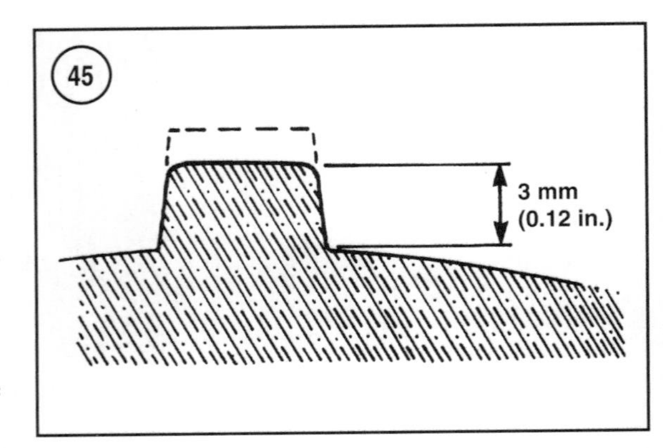

5. Make sure the front axle nuts are tight and that all cotter pins are in place.
6. Check that the cotter pins are in place on all other steering components. If any cotter pin is missing, check the nut for looseness. Tighten the nut to the specified torque and install a new cotter pin as described in Chapter Twelve.
7. Check the steering shaft play as follows:
   a. Support the ATV with the front wheels off the ground.
   b. To check steering shaft radial play, move the handlebar from side to side (without attempting to move the wheels). If radial play is excessive, the upper steering bushing is probably worn or the bushing holder mounting bolts (**Figure 47**) are loose. Replace the upper bushing or tighten the bushing holder bolts as necessary.
   c. To check steering shaft thrust play, lift up and then push down on the handlebar. If there is excessive thrust play, check the lower steering shaft nut (**Figure 48**) for looseness. If the nut is tightened properly, check the lower steering shaft bearing for excessive wear or damage.
   d. If necessary, service the steering shaft as described in Chapter Twelve.
   e. Lower the ATV so that all four tires are on the ground.

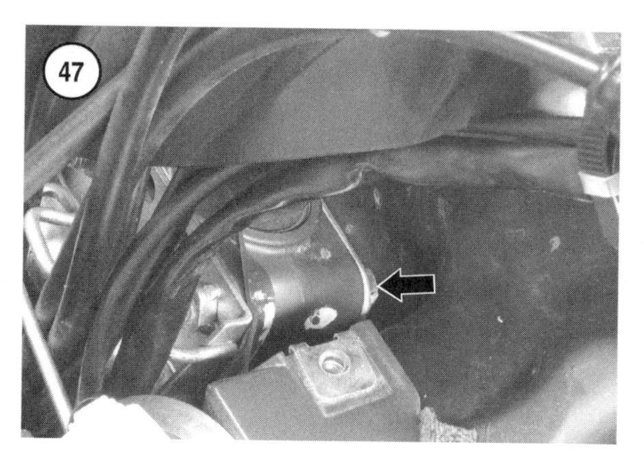

8. Check the steering knuckle and tie rod ends as follows:
   a. Turn the handlebar quickly from side to side. If there is appreciable looseness between the handlebar and tires, check the tie rod ends for excessive wear or damage.
   b. Service the steering knuckle and tie rods as described in Chapter Twelve.

Toe-in Adjustment

Check the toe-in adjustment periodically to prevent abnormal tire wear and to inspect for faulty steering components as described in Chapter Twelve.

FRONT SUSPENSION

All models are equipped with an independent front suspension that includes upper and lower control arms. A coil-over type shock absorber is attached to each lower control arm. Most models are equipped with an oil-dampened shock that allows spring preload adjustment. Later Special Edition (SE) and all 2009 models are equipped with a gas-charged shock absorber that also allows rebound and compression adjustments.

Shock Absorber Inspection

1. Check the front shock absorbers for oil leaks, a bent damper rod or other damage.
2. If necessary, replace the shock absorbers as described in Chapter Twelve.

Shock Spring Preload Adjustment (Except SE and All 2009-On Models)

WARNING
Adjust both shock absorbers to the same spring preload; otherwise, an unstable riding condition exists.

The front spring preload adjustment can be performed with the shock mounted on the ATV. Adjust spring preload by turning the notched adjustment ring (**Figure 49**) on the shock absorber. Rotate the adjustment ring using a suitable tool. The preload positions are numbered 1 (softest) through 5 (heaviest), which appear on the side of the shock absorber body.

Shock Spring Preload Adjustment (SE and All 2009-On Models)

CAUTION
The spring preload must be maintained within the specifications listed in ***Table 4****. If the minimum specification is exceeded, the spring may coil bind when the shock comes near full compression. This will overload and weaken the spring.*

NOTE
One complete turn of the adjuster moves the spring 1.5 mm (0.06 in.). Tightening the adjuster increases spring preload and loosening it decreases preload.

The spring preload adjustment can be performed with the shock mounted on the ATV. Adjust spring preload by changing the position of the adjuster (**Figure 50**) on the shock body.

1. Support the ATV with the front wheels off the ground.
2. Clean the threads on the shock body.
3. Measure the existing spring preload length. Measure the spring from end to end. Do not include the thickness of the adjuster or the spring seat. Record the measurement for reference.
4. Loosen the spring locknut (A, **Figure 50**) with a spanner wrench. If the adjuster (B, **Figure 50**) turns with the locknut, strike the locknut with a punch and hammer to break the adjuster loose from the locknut.
5. Turn the adjuster to change the spring preload dimension within the limits specified in **Table 4**. Measure and record the dimension for reference.
6. Lightly lubricate the threads on the shock body with engine oil. Then hold the adjuster and tighten the spring locknut to the torque listed in **Table 7**.

Shock Rebound Damping (SE and All 2009-On Models)

The rebound damping adjustment affects the rate of shock absorber extension after it has been compressed. This adjustment has no effect on shock compression. If rebound damping is set too low, the front wheel may bottom on subsequent bumps.

The rebound damping adjuster (**Figure 51**) is located at the bottom of the shock. Turning the clicker type adjuster changes the rebound damping in the shock. Refer to **Table 4** for standard and total adjustment positions. Set rebound damping as follows:

NOTE

Due to production changes, the number of detent positions may vary. Verify the total number of detent positions by turning the adjuster from full in to full out.

1. For the standard setting, turn the adjuster screw clockwise until it stops (this is the full hard position). Turn the adjuster screw counterclockwise the number of clicks (standard) in **Table 4**. When the standard setting is reached, the slit in the adjuster will align with the reference mark on the shock body.
2. Turn the adjuster as needed to obtain the desired rebound damping. To increase the rebound damping (harder), turn the adjuster clockwise. To decrease the rebound damping (softer), turn the adjuster counterclockwise.

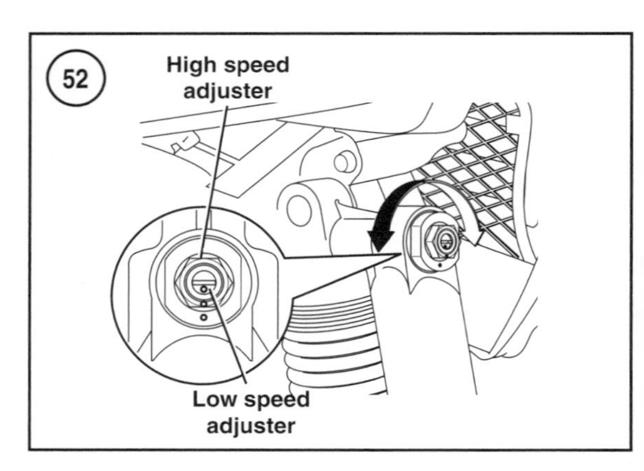

3. Make sure the adjuster is located in one of the detent positions and not in between any two settings.

Shock Compression Damping (SE and All 2009-On Models)

Compression damping controls the shock absorber rate when hitting a bump. This setting has no effect on the rebound rate of the shock. The shock is equipped with low- and high-speed adjusters. Both compression damping adjusters (**Figure 52**) are located above the shock reservoir. Turning either adjuster clockwise

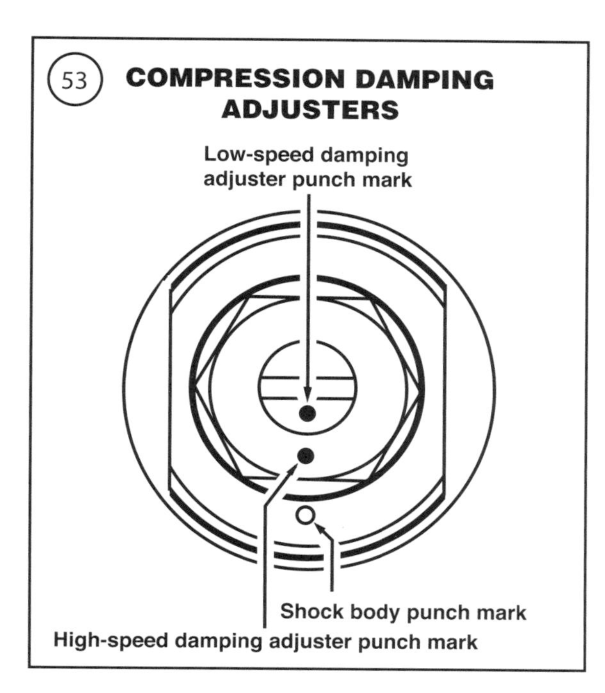

increases damping (stiffens). Turning either adjuster counterclockwise decreases damping (softens). Refer to **Table 4** for the standard compression settings. Set compression damping as follows:

1. To set the high-speed adjuster to its standard setting, turn the hex-head adjuster (**Figure 52**) clockwise until it stops (this is the full hard position). Then turn it counterclockwise the number of turns (standard) listed in **Table 4**. When the standard setting is reached, the high-speed damping adjuster punch mark will align with the shock body punch mark (**Figure 53**).
2. To set the low-speed adjuster to its standard setting, turn the center adjuster screw (**Figure 52**) clockwise until it stops (this is the full hard position). Then turn it counterclockwise the number of clicks (standard) in **Table 4**. When the standard setting is reached, the low-speed adjuster punch mark will align with the shock body punch mark (**Figure 53**).

3. Turn the adjuster(s) as needed to obtain the desired compression damping.

Shock Nitrogen Pressure (SE Models)

Refer all nitrogen pressure adjustment to a dealership or suspension specialist.

Control Arm And Ball Joint Inspection

1. Support the ATV so the front wheel is off the ground.

WARNING
Faulty wheel bearings can cause excessive wheel movement. Determine whether wheel movement is due to faulty bearings or ball joints.

2. Grab the wheel at two vertical points and rock it. There should be no wheel play. If any movement can be seen or felt, check the ball joints (**Figure 54**) for excessive wear or damage (Chapter Twelve).
3. Remove the front wheel.
4. Attempt to move the control arms laterally. Movement indicates worn or damaged control arm bushings. Refer to Chapter Twelve for inspection and service procedures.

Control Arm Lubrication

NOTE
Clean the grease fitting with a clean cloth before and after injecting grease.

Lubricate the control arm bushings at the intervals specified in **Table 1**. Inject lithium grease into the grease fittings (**Figure 55**) on the control arms.

REAR SUSPENSION

Shock Absorber Inspection

1. Check the rear shock absorber for oil leaks, a bent damper rod or other damage.
2. If necessary, replace the shock absorber as described in Chapter Thirteen.

Shock Spring Preload Adjustment

The rear spring preload adjustment can be performed with the shock mounted on the ATV. Adjust spring preload by changing the position of the adjuster (**Figure 56**) on the shock body.

CAUTION
*The spring preload must be maintained within the specifications listed in **Table 5** or **Table 6**. If the minimum specification is exceeded, the spring may coil bind when the shock comes near full compression. This will overload and weaken the spring.*

1. Support the ATV with the rear wheels off the ground.
2. Clean the threads on the shock body.
3. Measure the existing spring preload length. Measure the spring from end to end. Do not include the thickness of the adjuster or the spring seat. Record the measurement for reference.

NOTE
For tool accessibility, it may be necessary to remove the muffler as described in Chapter Four.

4. Loosen the spring locknut (A, **Figure 56**) with a spanner wrench. If the adjuster turns with the locknut, strike the locknut with a punch and hammer to break the adjuster loose from the locknut.

NOTE
One complete turn of the adjuster moves the spring 1.5 mm (0.06 in.). Tightening the adjuster increases spring preload and loosening it decreases preload.

5. Turn the adjuster (B, **Figure 56**) to change the spring preload dimension within the limits specified in **Table 5** or **Table 6**. Record the measurement for reference.
6. Lightly lubricate the threads on the shock body with engine oil. Hold the adjuster (B, **Figure 56**) and tighten the spring locknut (A) to 42 N•m (31 ft.-lb.).
7. If removed, install the muffler (Chapter Eight).

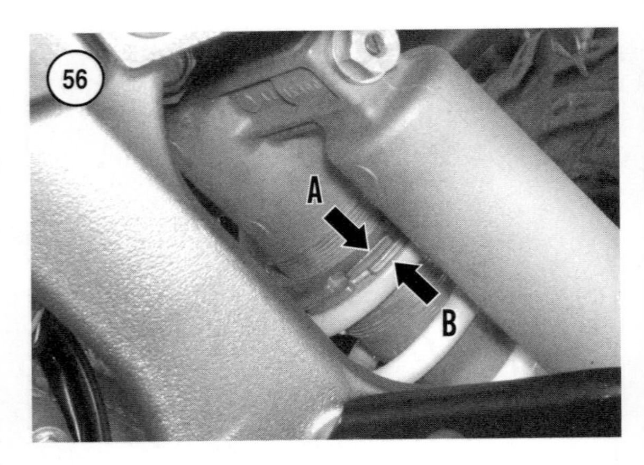

Shock Rebound Damping

The rebound damping adjustment affects the rate of shock absorber extension after it has been compressed. This adjustment has no effect on shock compression. If rebound damping is set too low, the rear wheels may bottom on subsequent bumps.

The shock absorber is equipped with a clicker type damping adjuster at the bottom of the shock (**Figure 57**). Each click of the adjuster screw represents one adjustment or position change. See **Table 5** or **Table 6** for standard and total adjustment positions. Set rebound damping as follows:

1. For the standard setting, turn the adjuster screw clockwise until it stops (full hard position). Turn the adjuster counterclockwise the number of clicks (standard) in **Table 5** or **Table 6**. When the standard setting is reached, the slit in the adjuster will align with the reference mark on the shock body.
2. Turn the adjuster as needed to obtain the desired rebound damping. To increase the rebound damping, turn the adjuster clockwise. To decrease the rebound damping, turn the adjuster counterclockwise.
3. Make sure the adjuster is located in one of the detent positions and not in between any two settings.

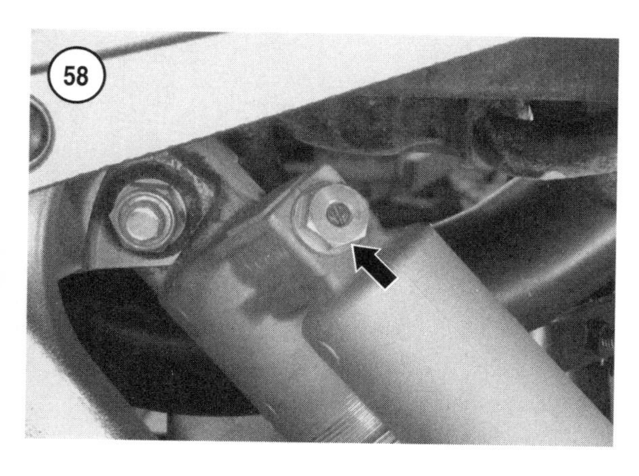

58

59

Shock Compression Damping

All models are equipped with a rear shock absorber that permits adjustment of compression damping. Later Special Edition (SE) and all 2009 models are equipped with a shock absorber that has two-stage (low/high) compression adjustment. A shock absorber equipped with a two-stage compression adjustment is identified by a hex adjuster at the top of the shock absorber.

Except SE and all 2009 models

Compression damping controls the shock absorber rate when hitting a bump. This setting has no effect on the rebound rate of the shock. The compression damping adjuster is located at the top of the shock (**Figure 58**). Turning the adjuster clockwise increases (stiffens) damping. Turning the adjuster counterclockwise decreases (softens) damping. Refer to **Table 5** for the standard compression setting. Set compression damping as follows:

1. Turn the adjuster to the maximum hard position (clockwise). Do not force the adjuster beyond its normal range of travel.
2. Turn the adjuster counterclockwise so the reference punch marks align. This is the standard position.
3. Turn the adjuster as needed to obtain the desired compression damping.

SE and all 2009 models

Compression damping controls the shock absorber rate when hitting a bump. This setting has no effect on the rebound rate of the shock. The shock is equipped with low- and high-speed adjusters. Both compression damping adjusters are located at the top of the shock (**Figure 59**). Turning either adjuster clockwise increases (stiffens) damping. Turning either adjuster counterclockwise decreases (softens) damping. Refer to **Table 6** for the standard compression settings. Set compression damping as follows:

1. To set the high-speed adjuster to its standard setting, turn the hex-head adjuster (**Figure 59**) clockwise until it stops (this is the full hard position). Then, turn it counterclockwise the number of turns (standard) listed in **Table 6**. When the standard setting is reached, the high-speed damping adjuster punch mark will align with the shock body punch mark (**Figure 53**).
2. To set the low-speed adjuster to its standard setting, turn the center adjuster screw (**Figure 59**) clockwise until it stops (full hard position). Then, turn it counterclockwise the number of clicks (standard) listed in **Table 6**. When the standard setting is reached, the low-speed adjuster punch mark will align with the shock body punch mark (**Figure 53**).
3. Turn the adjuster as needed to obtain the desired compression damping.

Swing Arm and Linkage Inspection and Lubrication

1. Support the ATV securely and remove the rear wheels as described in Chapter Eleven.
2. Check for loose rear suspension components.
3. Check for damaged seals.
4. Check the tightness of the rear suspension fasteners.
5. Lubricate the swing arm bearings with lithium grease at the intervals specified in **Table 1**. Do not remove the bearings. Refer to Chapter Thirteen.

BATTERY

The original equipment battery is a maintenance-free type. Maintenance-free batteries do not require periodic electrolyte inspection and water cannot be added. Refer to Chapter Nine for battery procedures.

COOLING SYSTEM

WARNING
Antifreeze is toxic. Do not dispose of coolant containing antifreeze into storm sewers, septic systems, or onto the ground. Place used antifreeze in the original container and dispose of it according to local regulations. Do not store coolant where it is accessible to children or animals.

CAUTION
*Do not reuse the old coolant, as it deteriorates with use. Do not operate the cooling system with only distilled water, even in climates where antifreeze protection is not required; doing so will promote internal engine corrosion. Refer to **Coolant Change**.*

Check the cooling system for leaks at the interval in **Table 1**.

Coolant Level

Check the coolant level at the interval in **Table 1**.

It is important to keep the coolant level at the FULL mark (A, **Figure 60**) on the coolant reserve tank.

1. Check the level with the engine at normal operating temperature and the ATV on a level surface.
2. If the level is low, remove the reservoir tank cap and add coolant to the reserve tank, not to the radiator.

Coolant Change

Drain and flush the cooling system at the interval in **Table 1**. Refill with a 50:50 mixture of ethylene glycol antifreeze (formulated for aluminum engines) and distilled water.

WARNING
Replace the coolant in the cooling system when the engine and coolant are cold. Severe injury can occur if the system is drained while it is hot.

CAUTION
Do not allow coolant to contact painted surfaces. If contact does occur, immediately wash the surface with water.

1. Park the ATV on level ground.
2. Remove the front fender panel as described in Chapter Fifteen.

3. Place a drain pan under the right side of the engine, below the water pump. Remove the drain bolt (**Figure 61**) from the bottom of the water pump.
4. As coolant begins to drain from the engine, stand to the side and slowly loosen the radiator cap (**Figure 62**) so the flow from the engine increases. Be ready to reposition the drain pan.
5. Place a drain pan under the left side of the engine, below the coolant reservoir.
6. Detach the lower hose (B, **Figure 60**) and allow coolant to drain from the reservoir and hose.

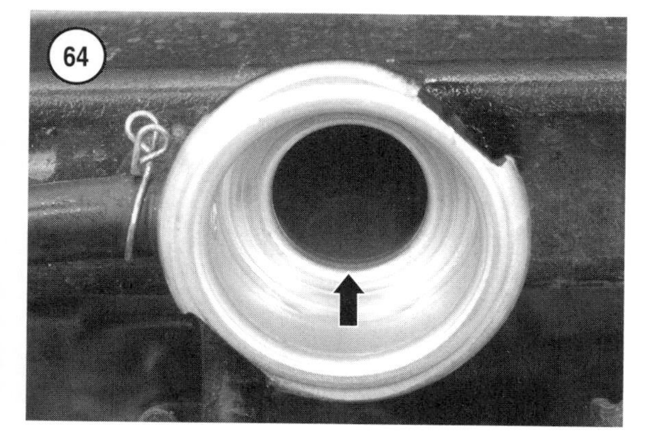

7. Check the reserve tank. If dirt or other buildup is in the tank, remove the mounting bolts and wash the tank.
8. Flush the cooling system and reserve tank with clean water. Check that all water drains from the system. Applying light air pressure to the radiator can aid in purging water from the passages.
9. Inspect the condition of:
   a. Radiator hoses. Check for leaks, cracks and loose clamps.
   b. Radiator core. Check for leaks, debris and tightness of mounting bolts.
   c. Radiator fan. Check for damaged wiring and tight connections.
10. Install a new seal washer on the coolant drain bolt. Then, install and tighten the bolt to 10 N•m (89 in.-lb.).
11. Connect the hose to the reserve tank.
12. Remove the air bleed bolt (**Figure 63**).

NOTE
When bubble-free coolant flows from the bleed bolt hole while filling the cooling system, reinstall the bleed bolt.

13. Fill the radiator to the bottom of the filler neck (**Figure 64**) with the amount of coolant mixture specified in **Table 3**.
14. Reinstall the bleed bolt and tighten to 10 N•m (89 in.-lb.).
15. Install the radiator cap.
16. Fill the reserve tank to the full mark.
17. Start the engine and allow the coolant to circulate for about one minute. Shut off the engine and do the following:

WARNING
Cover the cap with shop cloths, and then open the cap slowly. Do not remove the cap until all pressure is relieved.

   a. Remove the radiator cap and check the coolant level. If necessary, add coolant to bring the level to the bottom of the filler neck.
   b. Install the radiator cap.
18. Start the engine and allow it to reach operating temperature. Shut off the engine and check the following:
   a. Check for leaks at the drain plug, hoses and reserve tank.
   b. Check the level in the reserve tank. If necessary, remove the cap from the reserve tank and fill it to the full mark.
19. Rinse the frame and engine where coolant was splashed.
20. Install the front fender panel.

FUEL INJECTION

Idle Speed Adjustment

NOTE
Seat and fuel tank removal may be necessary to connect a tachometer in the following procedure.

1. Check the air filter for cleanliness. If necessary, clean the filter as described in this chapter.
2. Connect a tachometer to the engine following the manufacturer's instructions.
3. Make sure the throttle cable free play is correct. Check and adjust as described in this chapter.
4. Start and allow the engine to reach operating temperature.
5. Adjust the idle speed using the idle speed knob (**Figure 65**).
6. Adjust the idle speed to 1500-1700 rpm. Open and close the throttle a few times to make sure the idle speed returns to the proper setting.
7. Turn off the engine and disconnect the tachometer.
8. If removed, install the seat and fuel tank.

Fuel Hose

Periodically inspect the fuel system hoses. Replace cracked or deteriorated hoses. Make sure all hose clamps are in place and secure. Refer to Chapter Eight.

CRANKCASE BREATHER HOSES

Periodically inspect the breather hoses. Replace any cracked or deteriorated hoses. Make sure the hose clamps are in place and tight. Refer to Chapter Eight.

SPARK PLUG

Spark Plug Removal

1. Grasp the spark plug cap (**Figure 66**) as near the spark plug as possible and pull it off the plug. If it is stuck to the plug, twist it slightly to break it loose.

CAUTION
Whenever the spark plug is removed, dirt around it can fall into the plug hole. This can cause engine damage.

2. Blow away any dirt that has collected around the spark plug.

NOTE
If the plug is difficult to remove, apply penetrating oil around the base of the plug and let it soak about 10-20 minutes.

3. Remove the spark plug using a spark plug socket.
4. Inspect the plug carefully. Look for broken center porcelain, excessively eroded electrodes and excessive carbon or oil fouling.

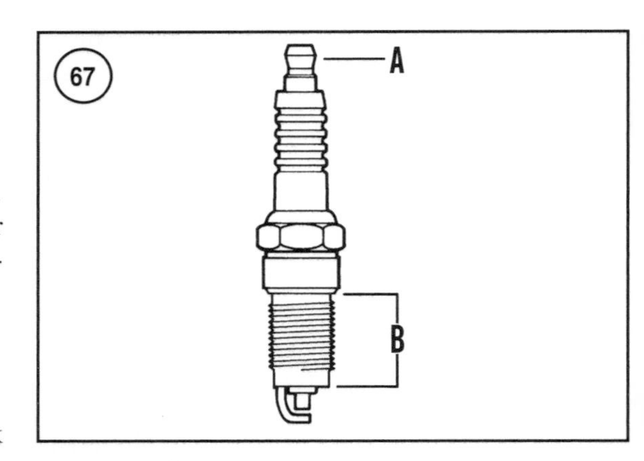

Spark Plug Gapping and Installation

Carefully adjust the electrode gap on a new spark plug to ensure a reliable spark. Use a spark plug gapping tool and a wire feeler gauge.

1. If so equipped, remove the terminal nut (A, **Figure 67**) from the end of the plug.
2. Insert a wire feeler gauge between the center and side electrode of the plug (**Figure 68**). The correct gap is listed in **Table 2**. If the gap is correct, a slight drag will be felt while pulling the wire through. If there is no drag, or the gauge will not pass through, bend the side electrode with a gapping tool (**Figure 69**) to set the proper gap.
3. Apply antiseize compound to the plug threads before installing the spark plug. Do not use engine oil on the plug threads.

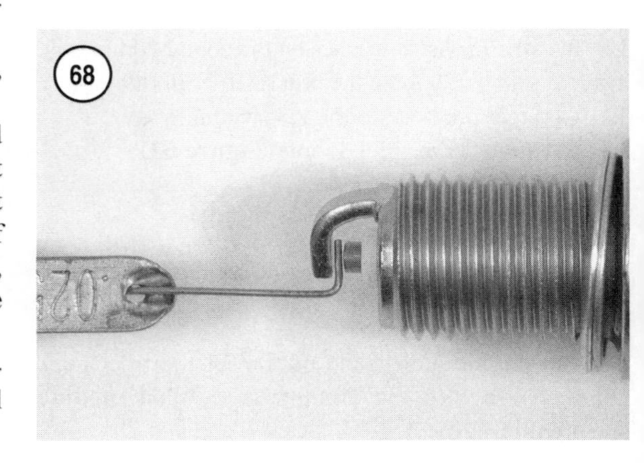

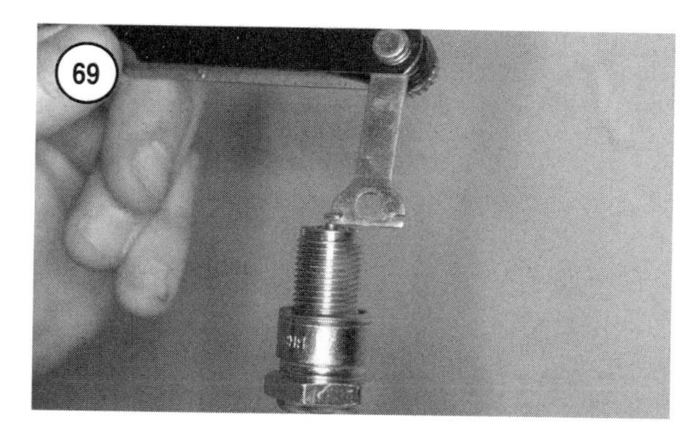

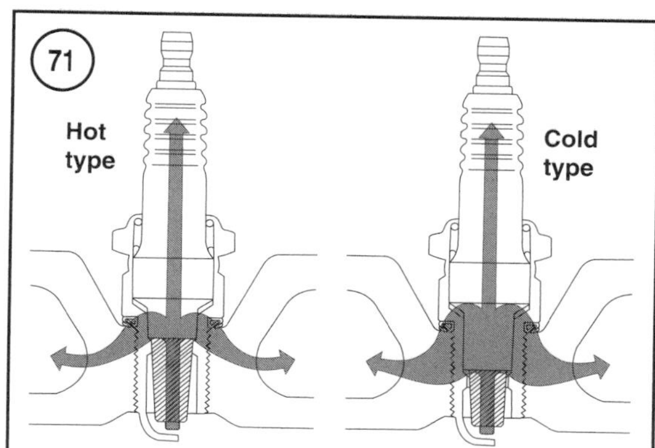

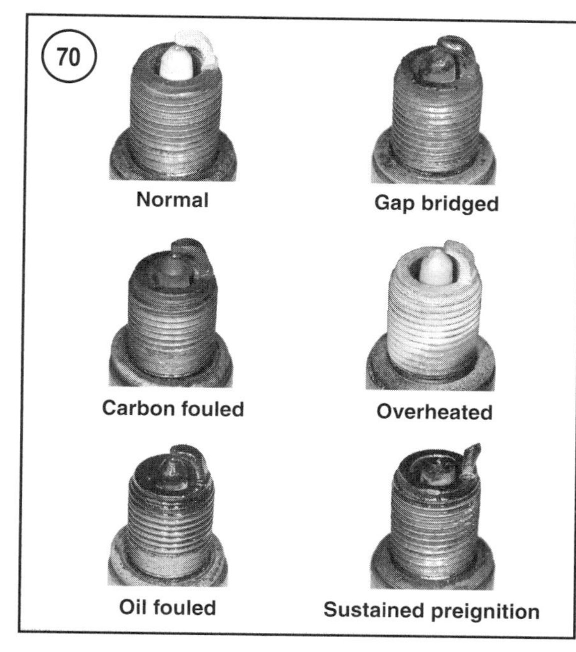

4. Screw the spark plug in by hand until it seats. Very little effort should be required. If force is necessary, the plug may be cross-threaded. Unscrew it and try again.

CAUTION
Do not overtighten. This may crush the gasket and cause a compression leak or damage the cylinder head threads.

5. Tighten the spark plug to 13 N•m (115 in.-lb.).

Inspection

Reading a spark plug that has been in use can provide information about spark plug operation, air/fuel mixture composition and engine operating conditions (such as oil consumption due to wear). Before checking the spark plug, operate the ATV under a medium load for approximately 10 km (6 miles). Avoid prolonged idling before shutting off the engine. Remove the spark plug as described in this section. Examine the plug and compare it to the plug appearance and operating conditions shown in **Figure 70**.

When reading a plug to evaluate the air/fuel mixture, install a new plug. Operate the ATV at the desired rpm range and load sufficiently to cause color on the plug insulator.

Heat range

Spark plugs are available in various heat ranges that are either hotter or colder than the original plugs (**Figure 71**). Select plugs of the heat range designed for the anticipated loads and operating conditions. Use of the incorrect heat range can cause the plug to foul or overheat and cause piston damage.

In general, use a hot plug for low speeds and low temperatures. Use a cold plug for high speeds, high engine loads and high temperatures. The plug should operate hot enough to burn off unwanted deposits, but not so hot that it burns itself or causes preignition. A spark plug of the correct heat range shows a light tan color on the insulator after the plug has been in service.

The reach (B, **Figure 67**), or length, of a plug is also important. A plug that is too short causes excessive carbon buildup, hard starting and plug fouling. A plug that is too long causes overheating or may contact the top of the piston. Both conditions cause engine damage.

Table 2 lists the standard heat range spark plug.

Normal condition

If the plug has a light tan- or gray-colored deposit and no abnormal gap wear or erosion, good engine, carburetion and ignition condition are indicated. The plug in use is of the proper heat range and may be serviced and returned to use.

Carbon fouled

Soft, dry, sooty deposits covering the entire firing end of the plug are evidence of incomplete combustion. Even though the firing end of the plug is dry, the plug's insulation decreases. An electrical path is formed that lowers the voltage from the ignition system. Engine misfiring is a sign of carbon fouling. Carbon fouling can be caused by one or more of the following:
1. Rich fuel mixture.
2. Spark plug heat range too cold.
3. Clogged air filter.
4. Retarded ignition timing.
5. Ignition component failure.
6. Low engine compression.
7. Prolonged idling.

Oil fouled

The tip of an oil-fouled plug has a black insulator tip, a damp oily film over the firing end and a carbon layer over the entire nose. The electrodes are not worn. An oil-fouled spark plug may be cleaned in an emergency, but it is better to replace it. It is important to correct the cause of fouling before the engine is returned to service. Common causes for of oil fouling are:
1. Low idle speed or prolonged idling.
2. Ignition component failure.
3. Spark plug heat range too cold.
4. Engine not broken in.

Gap bridging

Plugs with this condition exhibit gaps shorted out by combustion deposits between the electrodes. If this condition is encountered, check for an improper oil type or excessive carbon in the combustion chamber. Be sure to locate and correct the cause of this condition.

Overheating

Badly worn electrodes and premature gap wear, along with a gray or white blistered porcelain insulator surface are signs of overheating. The most common cause for this condition is using a spark plug of the wrong heat range (too hot). If a hotter spark plug has not been installed, but the plug is overheated, consider the following causes:
1. Lean fuel mixture.
2. Ignition timing too advanced.
3. Engine lubrication system malfunction.
4. Engine vacuum leak.
5. Improper spark plug installation (too tight).

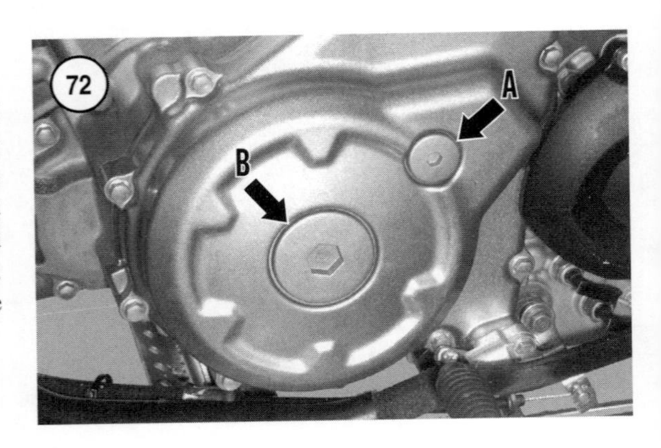

6. No spark plug gasket.

Worn out

Corrosive gases formed by combustion and high voltage sparks have eroded the electrodes. Spark plugs in this condition require more voltage to fire under hard acceleration. Replace with a new spark plug.

Preignition

If the electrodes are melted, preignition is almost certainly the cause. Check for throttle body mounting or intake manifold leaks and over-advanced ignition timing. It is also possible that a plug of the wrong heat range (too hot) is being used. Find the cause of the preignition before returning the engine to service.

IGNITION TIMING

All models are equipped with an electronic ignition system. Ignition timing is not adjustable. Check the ignition timing to make sure all components within the ignition system are working correctly. If the ignition timing is incorrect, troubleshoot the ignition system as described in Chapter Two. Incorrect ignition timing can cause a loss of engine performance and efficiency. It may also cause overheating.

Before starting this procedure, check all electrical connections related to the ignition system. Make sure all connections are tight and free from corrosion and that all ground connections are clean and tight.

1. Start the engine and let it warm approximately 2-3 minutes. Verify that the engine idles at 1500-1700 rpm. Shut off the engine.

NOTE
Seat removal (Chapter Fifteen) may be necessary to connect a timing light in the following procedure.

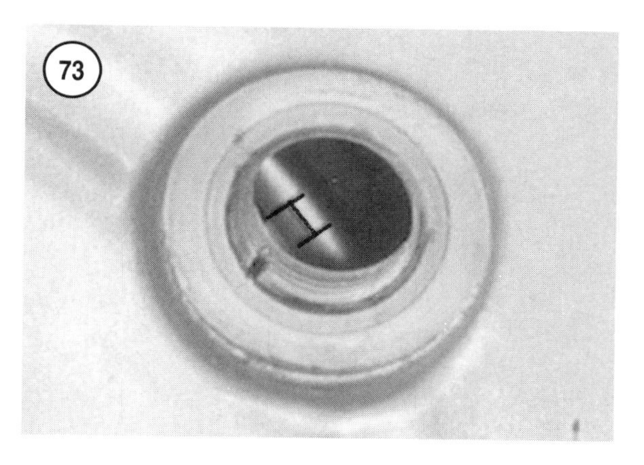
73

2. Attach a timing light following the manufacturer's instructions.
3. Remove the timing plug (A, **Figure 72**) from the left crankcase cover.
4. Run the engine at idle speed while directing the timing light into the crankcase timing hole.
5. Timing is correct if the H mark (A, **Figure 73**) aligns with the index notch (B) in the cover.
6. If the timing mark does not align with the index notch, the timing is incorrect. Refer to Chapter Nine and test the ignition system.
7. Turn off the engine and disconnect the test equipment.
8. Install the timing plug into the crankcase cover, and tighten it to 6 N•m (53 in.-lb.).
9. If removed , install the seat (Chapter Fifteen).

COMPRESSION TEST

A compression test is one of the quickest ways to check the internal condition of the engine, including the piston rings, pistons, and head gasket. Check the compression at each tune-up, record the readings and compare them with the readings at the next tune-up. The manufacturer does not specify a standard compression pressure. However, measuring and recording the compression pressure will help spot any developing problems.

1. Before starting the compression test, make sure the following items are correct:
   a. The cylinder head bolts are tightened to the specified torque. Refer to Chapter Four.
   b. The valves are properly adjusted as described in this chapter.
   c. The battery is fully charged to ensure proper engine cranking speed.
2. Warm the engine to normal operating temperature. Turn the engine off.
3. Remove the spark plug as described in this chapter.
4. Ground the spark plug wire as described in *Spark Test* (Chapter Two).

NOTE
A screw-in type compression gauge with a flexible adapter is required for this procedure. Before using this gauge, check the condition of the rubber gasket on the end of the adapter. This gasket must seal the spark plug hole and cylinder to ensure accurate compression readings. Replace the seal if it is cracked or starting to deteriorate.

5. Install the tip of a compression gauge into the cylinder head following the manufacturer's instructions (Refer to *Measuring Tools* in Chapter One).

CAUTION
Do not operate the starter more than absolutely necessary. When the spark plug lead is disconnected, the electronic ignition will produce the highest voltage possible and the coil may overheat and be damaged.

6. *Open the throttle completely* and turn the engine over until there is no further rise in pressure. Maximum pressure is usually reached within 4-7 seconds. Record the pressure reading.
7. Remove the compression gauge from the cylinder.
8. If the compression pressure is low based on previous readings, the low reading may be due to a valve or ring problem. To determine which, pour about a teaspoon of engine oil into the spark plug hole and repeat the procedure.
   a. If the compression increases significantly, the piston rings are probably worn.
   b. If the compression does not increase, the valves are leaking.
9. Install the spark plug.

VALVE CLEARANCE ADJUSTMENT

The engine is equipped with two intake valves and two exhaust valves. The valves must be adjusted correctly so they will completely open and close. Valves that are out of adjustment can cause poor performance and engine damage.

Perform the valve clearance measurements and adjustments with the engine cool, at room temperature. Refer to **Table 2** for valve clearance specifications. The exhaust valves are located at the front of the engine and the intake valves are located at the rear of the engine.

1. Remove the seat and front fender as described in Chapter Fifteen.
2. Remove the fuel tank as described in Chapter Eight.

3. Remove the spark plug as described in this chapter.
4. Remove the front and rear rocker covers (**Figure 74**).
5. Remove the camshaft sprocket cover (**Figure 75**).
6. Remove the timing plug (A, **Figure 72**) and the flywheel nut plug (B).
7. Set the engine at TDC as follows:
   a. Fit a socket onto the flywheel nut (**Figure 76**) and turn the crankshaft counterclockwise until the I mark (A, **Figure 77**) on the flywheel aligns with the index notch (B) in the timing hole.
   b. Verify the engine is at TDC by checking the location of the I mark (A, **Figure 78**) on the camshaft sprocket. The I mark must align with the reference boss (B, **Figure 78**) on the cylinder head. If the alignment is not as shown, rotate the crankshaft one full turn counterclockwise and realign the flywheel I mark.
8. Insert a flat feeler gauge (A, **Figure 79**) between the adjusting screw and the valve stem. When the clearance is correct, there will be a slight drag on the feeler gauge when it is inserted and withdrawn.
9. To correct the clearance, perform the following:
   a. Loosen the adjuster locknut (B, **Figure 79**).
   b. Screw the adjuster (C, **Figure 79**) in or out so there is a slight resistance felt on the feeler gauge.
   c. Hold the adjuster to prevent it from turning any farther and tighten the locknut to 14 N•m (10 ft.-lb.).
   d. Recheck the clearance to make sure the adjuster did not turn after the correct clearance was achieved; readjust if necessary.
10. Inspect the O-ring gaskets on each rocker cover and on the camshaft sprocket cover. Replace the O-ring(s) if damaged or hardened.
11. Install the rocker covers and the camshaft sprocket cover. Install the cable guide (**Figure 80**) on the lower left bolt for the exhaust rocker cover. Tighten the mounting bolts to 10 N•m (89 in.-lb.).
12. Inspect the O-ring gaskets on the timing plug and flywheel nut plug. Replace the O-ring(s) if damaged or hardened.
13. Install the spark plug as described in this chapter.
14. Install the fuel tank as described in Chapter Eight.
15. Install the seat and front fender as described in Chapter Fifteen.
16. Install the timing plug and tighten to 6 N•m (53 in.-lb.).

74

75

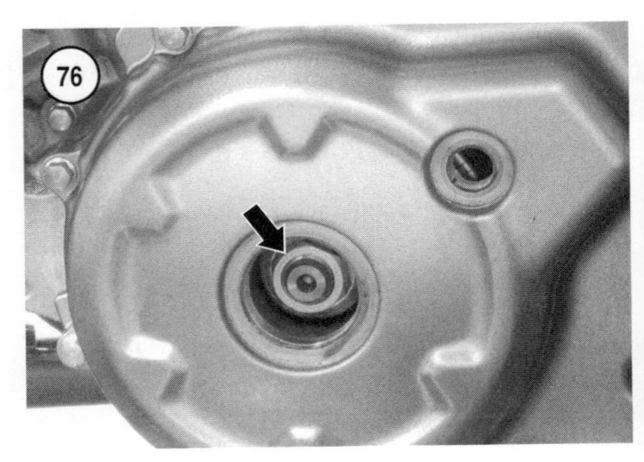
76

77

17. Install all the flywheel nut plug and tighten to 10 N•m (89 in.-lb.).

EXHAUST SYSTEM

Refer to Chapter Four for service and repair procedures.

Inspection

1. Inspect the exhaust system for cracks or dents that could alter performance. Refer all repairs to a qualified dealership or welding shop.
2. Check all fasteners and mounting points for loose or damaged parts.

Spark Arrestor Cleaning

Clean the spark arrestor at the intervals specified in **Table 1**.

WARNING
Do not spray solvents or other combustible liquids into the muffler to aid in removing buildup. If solvents are used to clean the spark arrester, use compressed air to completely dry the part before installing it in the muffler. An explosion and/or fire could occur if solvents are present in the muffler.

1. Park the ATV in an open area, away from combustible materials.
2. Remove the purge bolt (**Figure 81**) in the bottom of the muffler.
3. Start the engine.
4. Wearing gloves, use a rubber mallet to tap on the surface of the muffler as the engine speed is raised and lowered. Also, momentarily place a folded shop cloth over the end of the muffler to force exhaust pressure out of the plug opening.
5. When no more carbon particles are purged, stop the engine and replace the plug. Allow the muffler to cool. Tighten the purge bolt to 27 N•m (20 ft.-lb.).
6. Remove the bolt (**Figure 82**) securing the spark arrestor to the muffler.
7. Remove the spark arrestor and brush it clean.
8. Install the spark arrestor and tighten the bolt to 8 N•m (71 in.-lb.).

FASTENERS

Vibration can loosen many of the fasteners on the ATV. Check the tightness of all fasteners at the interval in **Table 1**. Pay particular attention to:

1. Engine mounting hardware.
2. Cylinder head bracket bolts.
3. Engine crankcase covers.
4. Handlebar.
5. Shift lever.
6. Brake pedal and lever.
7. Exhaust system.
8. Steering and suspension components.

Table 1 MAINTENANCE SCHEDULE*

Every 20-40 hours.
- Clean air filter.

Initial month.
- Check idle speed.
- Check valve clearance.
- Check cooling system for leaks.
- Check and adjust engine coolant level.
- Check spark plug.
- Change engine oil and replace oil filter.
- Check drive chain tension and adjustment.
- Clean and lubricate drive chain.
- Check brake system.
- Check clutch operation and adjust as necessary.
- Check wheels and tires.
- Check steering system.
- Check front wheel toe-in.
- Check front wheel bearings.
- Check fastener tightness.
- Check headlight and brake light operation.
- Check throttle operation and adjust as necessary.
- Lubricate throttle cable.

Initial 3 months.
- Check idle speed.
- Check cooling system for leaks.
- Check and adjust engine coolant level.
- Check spark plug.
- Check drive chain tension and adjustment.
- Clean and lubricate drive chain.
- Check brake system.
- Check steering system.
- Check front wheel toe-in.
- Check fastener tightness.
- Check headlight and brake light operation.
- Lubricate control cables and other moving parts.
- Check throttle operation and adjust as necessary.
- Lubricate throttle cable.

Initial 6 months and every 6 months thereafter.
- Check valve clearance.
- Check cooling system for leaks.
- Check and adjust engine coolant level.
- Check spark plug.
- Change engine oil and replace oil filter.

(continued)

Table 1 MAINTENANCE SCHEDULE* (continued)

Initial 6 months and every 6 months thereafter (continued)
Check drive chain tension and adjustment.
Clean and lubricate drive chain.
Check brake system.
Check clutch operation and adjust as necessary.
Check operation reverse lock and adjust if necessary.
Check wheels and tires.
Check steering system.
Check front wheel toe-in.
Check front wheel bearings.
Check fastener tightness.
Check idle speed.
Check crankcase breather system.
Check exhaust system.
Clean spark arrestor.
Check fuel hose.
Check front suspension.
Check rear suspension.
Lubricate front suspension.
Lubricate rear suspension.
Check headlight and brake light operation.
Lubricate control cables and other moving parts.
Check throttle operation and adjust as necessary.
Lubricate throttle cable.
Every 2 years.
Replace coolant.
Replace seals in brake master cylinders and calipers.
Every 4 years.
Replace brake hoses.
*Consider this maintenance schedule as a guide to general maintenance and lubrication intervals. Harder than normal use and operation in severe operating conditions will require more frequent attention to most maintenance items.

Table 2 MAINTENANCE AND TUNE-UP SPECIFICATIONS

Brake pad wear limit	1.0 mm (0.04 in.)
Brake pedal height (below footrest)	15.3 mm (0.60 in.)
Clutch lever free play	5-10 mm (0.98-1.38 in.)
Drive chain free play	25-35 mm (0.98-1.38 in.)
Idle Speed	1500-1700 rpm
Parking brake cable length	
2006-2012 models	58-60 mm (2.28-2.36 in.)
2013-on models	47-51 mm (1.85-2.01 in.)
Reverse cable length	33 mm (1.30 in.)
Radiator cap pressure relief	93.3-122.7 kPa (13.3-17.4 psi)
Spark plug	
Type	CR8E (NGK)
Plug gap	0.7-0.8 mm (0.028-0.031 in.)
Throttle lever free play	2-4 mm (0.08-0.16 in.)
Throttle speed limiter	Less than 12 mm(0.47 in.)
Tire inflation pressure	4.0 psi (27.5 kPa)
Tire tread knob height (min.)	3 mm (0.12 in.)
Valve clearance (cold)	
Intake	0.09-0.13 mm (0.0035-0.0051 in.)
Exhaust	0.16-0.20 mm (0.0063-0.0079 in.)

3

Table 3 RECOMMENDED LUBRICANTS, FLUIDS AND CAPACITIES

Brake fluid	DOT 4
Cooling system	
Coolant type	High quality ethylene-glycol*
Coolant capacity (2006-2012 models)	
Radiator and engine	1.61 L (1.70 US qt.)
Reservoir	0.25 L (0.26 US qt.)
Coolant capacity (2013-on models)	
Radiator and engine	1.68 L (1.78 US qt.)
Reservoir	0.25 L (0.26 US qt.)
Drive chain	Chain lubricant suitable for O-ring type chains or engine oil
Engine oil	
Grade	Yamalube 4, API SG (non-friction modified)
Viscosity	Refer to text
Capacity	
Oil change only	1.75 L (1.85 US qt.)
Oil and filter change	1.85 L (1.96 US qt.)
After disassembly (engine dry)	2.30 L (2.43 US qt.)
Fuel	
Type	Unleaded
Octane	Pump octane of 86 or higher
Fuel tank	
Capacity, including reserve	11.0 L (2.9 U.S. gal.)
Reserve only	
2006-2012 models	2.6 L (0.70 U.S. gal.)
2013-on models	2.9 L (0.77 U.S. gal.)

*Coolant must not contain silicate inhibitors as they can cause premature wear to the water pump seals. See text for further information.

Table 4 FRONT SUSPENSION SPECIFICATIONS (SE AND ALL 2009-ON MODELS)

Front shock absorber spring preload	
2006-2008 models	
Standard length	255 mm (10.04 in.)
Minimum length	246.5 mm (9.7 in.)
Maximum length	261.5 mm (10.3 in.)
2009-2014 models	
Standard length	255 mm (10.04 in.)
Minimum length	246.5 mm (9.7 in.)
Maximum length	261.5 mm (10.3 in.)
2015-on models	
Standard length	262 mm (10.31 in.)
Minimum length	268 mm (10.55 in.)
Maximum length	253 mm (9.69 in.)
Front shock rebound damping adjusting positions1	
2006-2014 models	
Minimum	20 clicks out
Standard	12 clicks out
Maximum	
2006-2008 models	1 click out
2009-2014 models	3 click out
2015-on models	
Minimum	30 clicks out
Standard	18 clicks out
Maximum	1 click out
Front shock compression damping adjusting positions*	
Fast compression damping	
2006-2014 models	
Minimum	3 turns out
Standard	1 1/4 turn out
Maximum	Fully turned in

(continued)

Table 4 FRONT SUSPENSION SPECIFICATIONS (SE AND ALL 2009-ON MODELS) (continued)

Front shock compression damping adjusting positions* (continued)	
Fast compression damping (continued)	
2015-on models	
Minimum	18 clicks out
Standard	9 clocks out
Maximum	1 click out
Slow compression damping	
2006-2012-on models	
Minimum	20 clicks out
Standard	9
Maximum	1 click out
2013-2014-on models	
Minimum	20 clicks out
Standard	16 clicks out
Maximum	1 click out
2015-on models	
Minimum	18 clicks out
Standard	10 clicks out
Maximum	1 click out

* From the fully turned-in position.

Table 5 REAR SUSPENSION SPECIFICATIONS (EXCEPT SE AND ALL 2009 MODELS)

Rear shock absorber spring preload	
Standard length	236 mm (9.29 in.)
Minimum length	228 mm (8.98 in.)
Maximum length	243 mm (9.57 in.)
Rear shock rebound damping adjusting positions*	
Minimum	20
Standard	12
Maximum	3
Rear shock compression damping adjusting positions*	
Minimum	12
Standard	7
Maximum	2

*Counter-clockwise from the fully turned-in position.

Table 6 REAR SUSPENSION SPECIFICATIONS (SE AND ALL 2009-ON MODELS)

Rear shock absorber spring preload	
2006-2012 models	
Standard length	233 mm (9.17 in.)
Minimum length	228 mm (8.97 in.)
Maximum length	243 mm (9.56 in.)
2013-2014 models	
Standard length	233 mm (9.17 in.)
Minimum length	243 mm (9.56 in.)
Maximum length	228 mm (8.97 in.)
2015-on models	
Standard length	228.5 mm (9.00 in.)
Minimum length	238.5 mm (9.39 in.)
Maximum length	223.5 mm (8.80 in.)
Rear shock rebound damping adjusting positions*	
2006-2008 models	
Minimum	20 clicks out
Standard	12 clicks out
Maximum	3 clicks out

(continued)

Table 6 REAR SUSPENSION SPECIFICATIONS (SE AND ALL 2009-ON MODELS) (continued)

Rear shock rebound damping adjusting positions* (continued)	
2009-2014 models	
Minimum	20 clicks out
Standard	13 clicks out
Maximum	3 clicks out
2015-on models	
Minimum	30 clicks out
Standard	18 clicks out
Maximum	1 clicks out
Rear shock compression damping adjusting positions*	
Fast compression damping	
2006-2014 models	
Minimum	4 turns out
Standard	2 turns out
Maximum	Fully turned in
2015-on models	
Minimum	2 turns out
Standard	1 1/4 turns out
Maximum	Fully turned in
Slow compression damping*	
2006-2014 models	
Minimum	16 clicks out
Standard	11 clicks out
Maximum	1 click out
2015-on models	
Minimum	18 clicks out
Standard	10 clicks out
Maximum	1 click out

*From the fully turned-in position.

Table 7 MAINTENANCE TORQUE SPECIFICATIONS

Item	N•m	in.-lb.	ft.-lb.
Air bleed bolt	10	89	–
Axle hub pinch bolts	21	186	–
Camshaft sprocket cover bolts	10	88	–
Coolant drain bolt	10	88	–
Crankcase oil drain bolt	23	–	17
Drive sprocket nut	85	–	63
Driven sprocket nuts	72	–	53
Exhaust purge bolt	27	–	20
Flywheel nut plug			
2006-2012 models	10	89	–
2013-on models	2	1.4	–
Front shock absorber spring locknut	42	–	31
Oil filter cover bolts	10	89	–
Oil filter drain bolt	10	89	–
Oil gallery bolt	10	89	–
Oil tank drain bolt	19	168	–
Rear shock absorber spring locknut	42	–	30
Rocker cover bolts	10	89	–
Spark arrestor bolt	8	71	–
Spark plug	13	115	–
Valve adjuster locknut	14	124	–
Wheel nuts	45	–	33

CHAPTER FOUR

ENGINE TOP END

This chapter provides information for removal, inspection and installation of the engine top end components. These include the exhaust system, cylinder head, valves, cylinder, piston, piston rings and camshaft.

Tables 1-5 are located at the end of this chapter.

EXHAUST SYSTEM

Removal/Installation

Refer to **Figure 1** or **Figure 2**.

WARNING
Do not remove the exhaust pipe(s) or muffler while they are hot.

1. Remove the heat shield (**Figure 3**).
2. Loosen the muffler clamp bolt (**Figure 4**).
3. While supporting the muffler, remove the muffler mounting bolts (A, **Figure 5**). Then remove the muffler (B, **Figure 5**).

4A. On 2006-2014 models, perform the following:
   a. Loosen the left exhaust pipe clamp bolt (A, **Figure 6**).
   b. Remove the left exhaust pipe retaining nuts (B, **Figure 6**).Then remove the left exhaust pipe (C, **Figure 6**).
   c. Remove the right exhaust pipe retaining nuts (D, **Figure 6**). Then remove the right exhaust pipe (E, **Figure 6**).

4B. On 2015-on models, remove the exhaust pipe retaining nuts. Then remove the exhaust pipe.

5. Reverse the removal steps to install the exhaust system while noting the following:
   a. Apply threadlock to the heat shield mounting bolts and tighten to 8 N•m (71 in.-lb.).
   b. Install a new gasket (**Figure 7**) to the exhaust port(s).
   c. Install all of the exhaust pipe nuts and finger-tighten them to hole the pipe(s) in place against the cylinder head. Then tighten the nuts to 20 N•m (14 ft.-lb.).
   d. Install a new gasket (**Figure 8**) into the muffler pipe, and on 2006-2014 models, the right exhaust pipe, so the chamfered end faces out. Push the gasket so it is recessed 1.0-1.5 mm (0.04-0.06 in.) in from the end of the pipe.
   e. Tighten the exhaust pipe clamp bolt (A, **Figure 6**) 16 N•m (12 ft.-lb.).
   f. Tighten the muffler mounting bolt to 38 N•m (28 ft.-lb.).
   g. Make sure the tab on the clamp (**Figure 4**) engages the slot in the muffler pipe.
   h. Tighten the muffler clamp bolt (**Figure 4**) 18 N•m (13 ft.-lb.).

AIR INDUCTION SYSTEM (2015-ON MODELS)

Air Injection

The air induction system burns the unburned exhaust gases by injecting fresh secondary air, from the air filter case, through the air cut-off valve, through the cylinder head reed valve and into the exhaust port, thus reducing the hydrocarbon emissions (**Figure 9**).

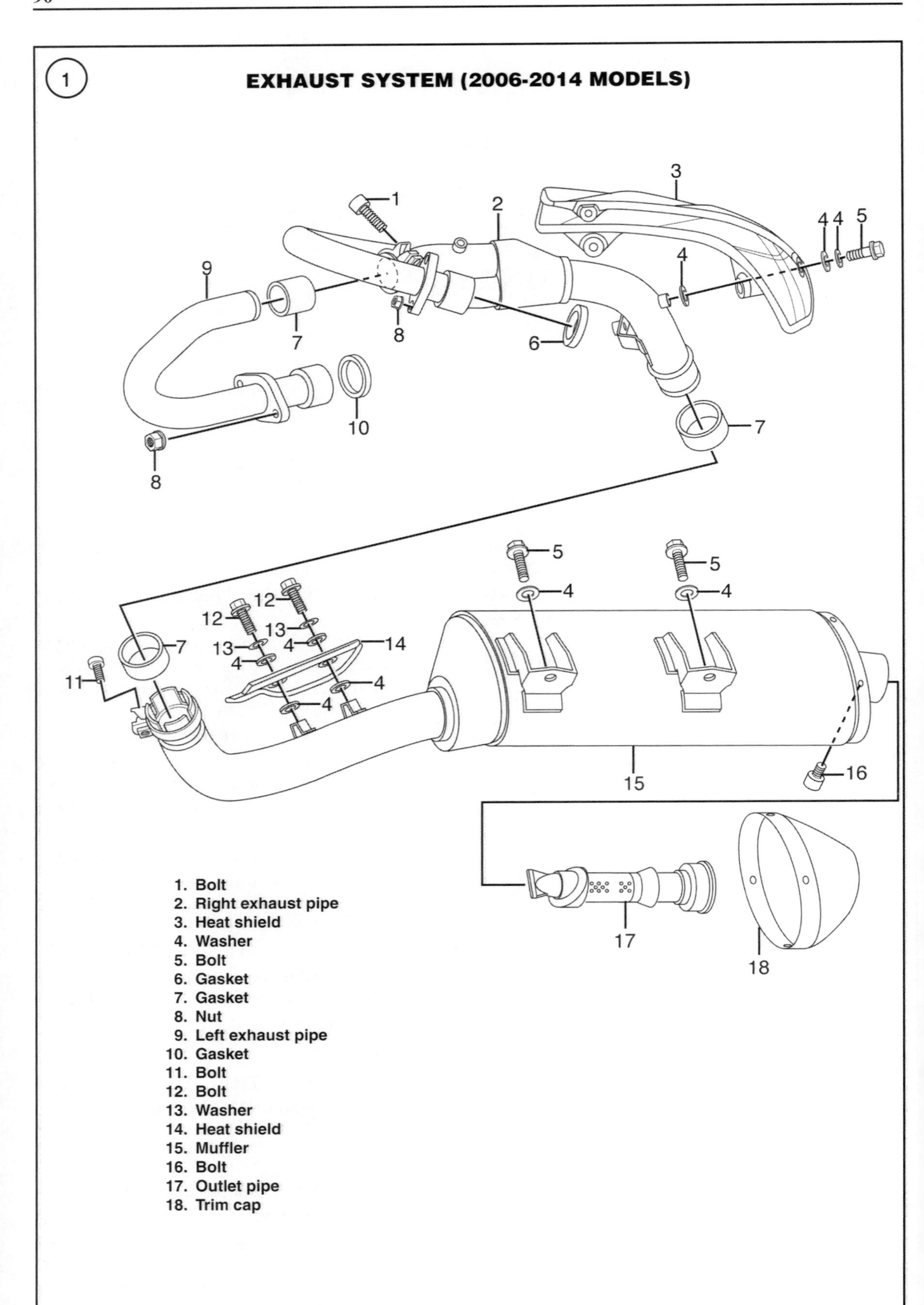
1
EXHAUST SYSTEM (2006-2014 MODELS)
1. Bolt
2. Right exhaust pipe
3. Heat shield
4. Washer
5. Bolt
6. Gasket
7. Gasket
8. Nut
9. Left exhaust pipe
10. Gasket
11. Bolt
12. Bolt
13. Washer
14. Heat shield
15. Muffler
16. Bolt
17. Outlet pipe
18. Trim cap

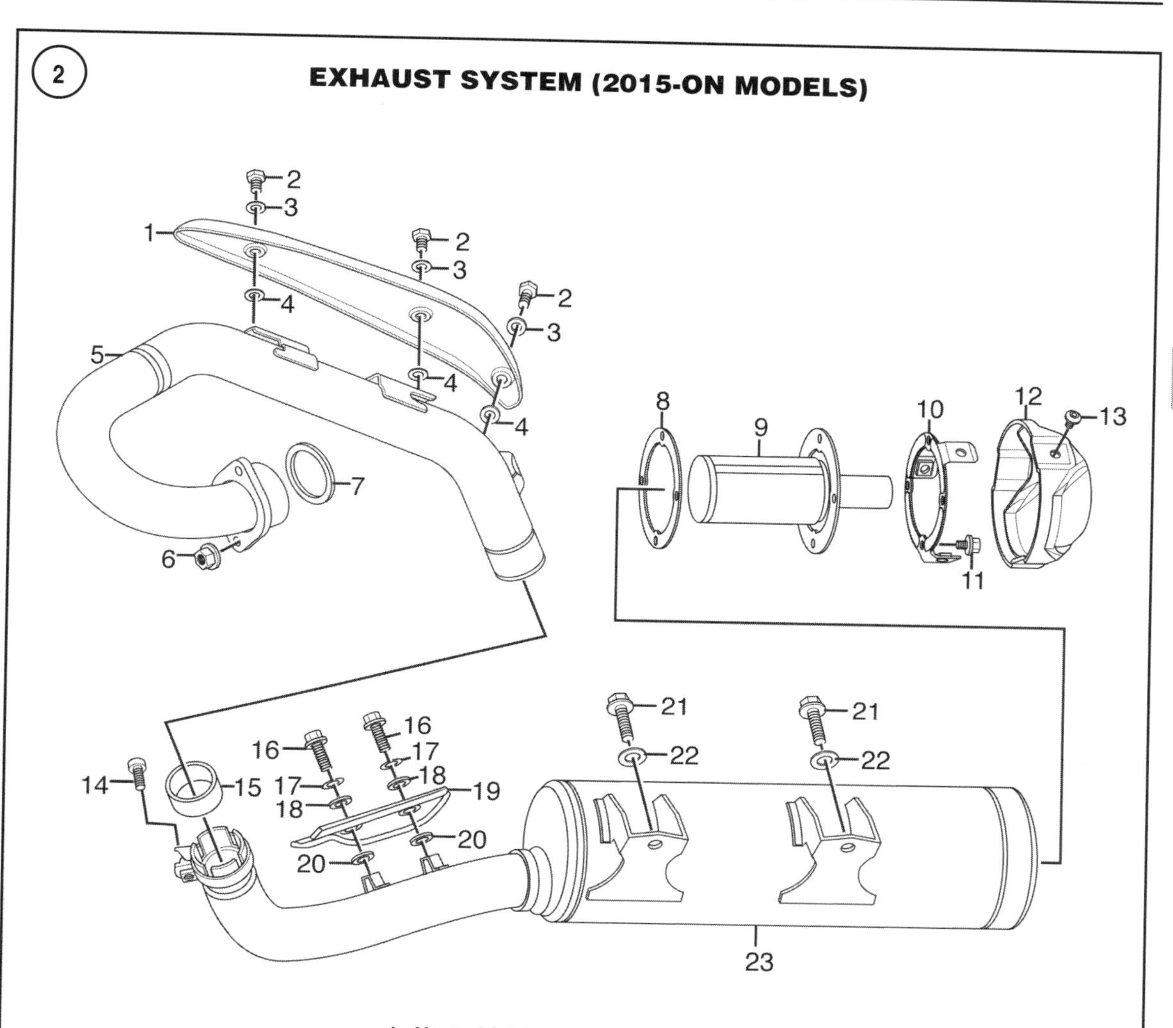

2 EXHAUST SYSTEM (2015-ON MODELS)

1. Heat shield
2. Bolt
3. Washer
4. Washer
5. Exhaust pipe
6. Nut
7. Gasket
8. Gasket
9. Spark arrester
10. Plate
11. Screw
12. Trim cap
13. Screw
14. Bolt
15. Gasket
16. Bolt
17. Washer
18. Washer
19. Heat shield
20. Washer
21. Flange bolt
22. Muffler

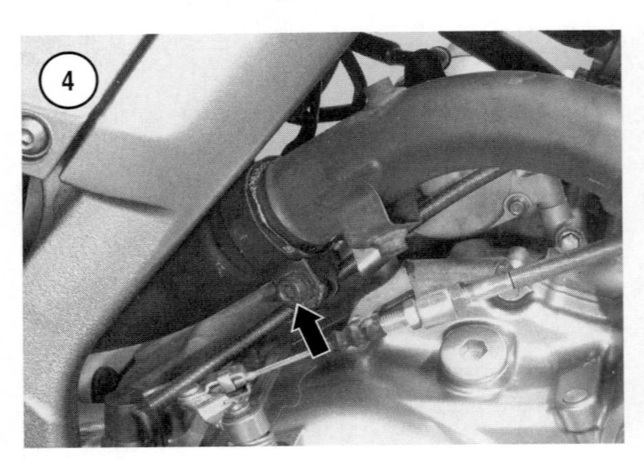

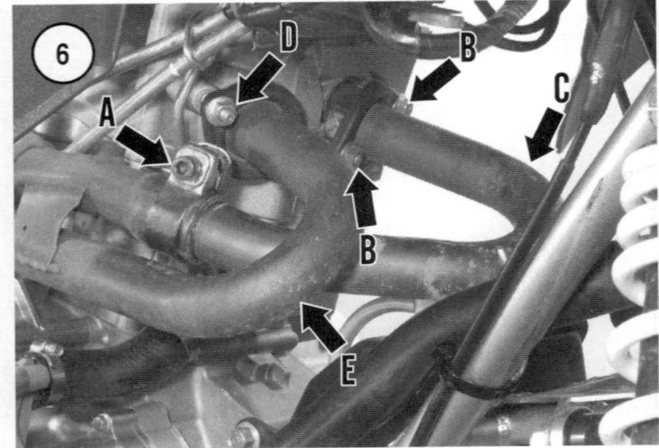

When there is a negative pressure at the exhaust port, the reed valve opens, allowing the secondary air to flow into the exhaust port.

Air Cut-off Valve

The air cut-off valve (**Figure 10**) is controlled by the ECU relating to exhaust combustion conditions. The air cut-off valve usually remains open to allow air to flow during idle and then closes off the air flow when the ATV is being driven.

If the coolant temperature is below the specified degree, the air cut-of valve will remain open and allow air to flow into the exhaust pipe until the coolant temperature reaches a higher degree.

Testing

Intake air temperature sensor

1. Remove the seat as described in Chapter Fifteen.
2. Remove the fuel tank as described in Chapter Eight.

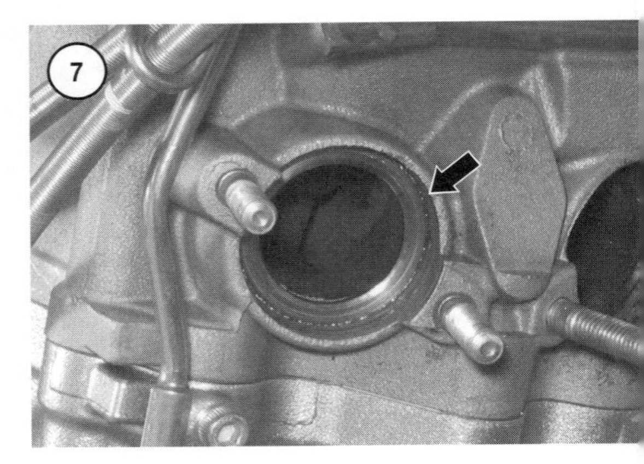

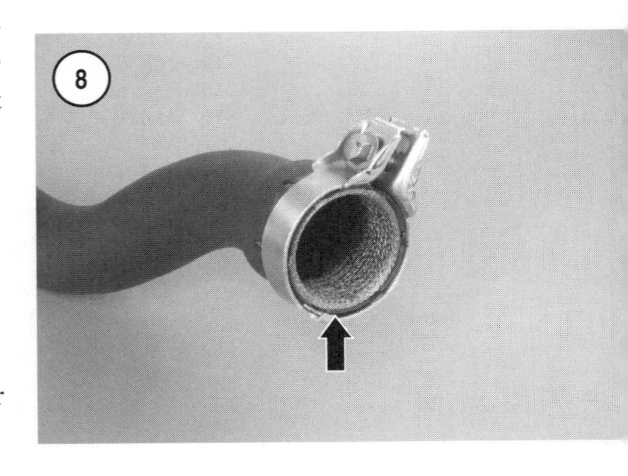

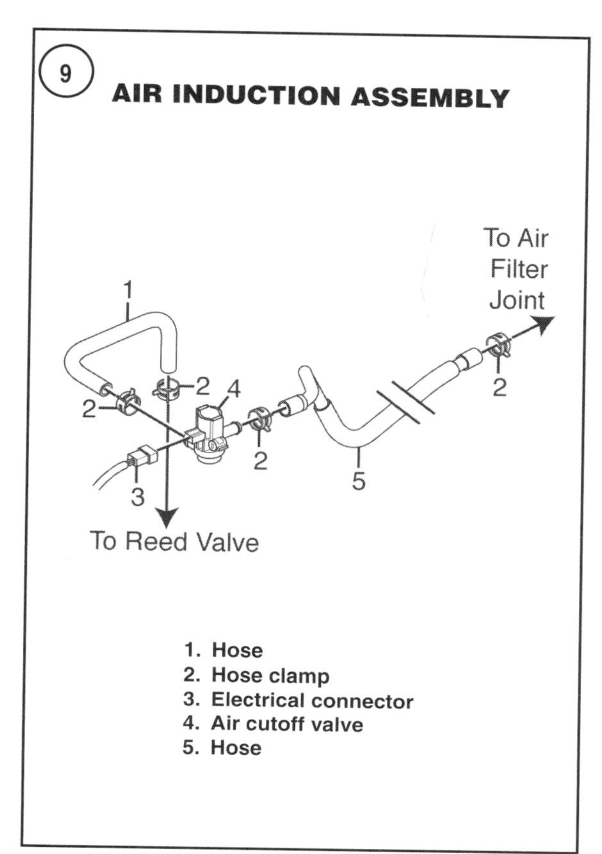

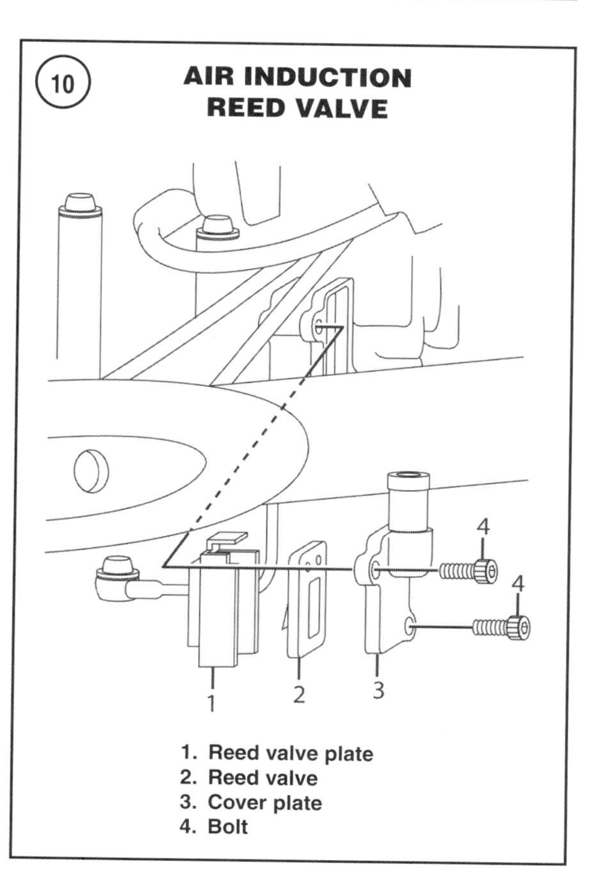

WARNING
Never subject the intake air temperature sensor to a strong shock nor drop it. It must be replaced if dropped.

3. Carefully disconnect the connector from intake air temperature sensor (**Figure 11**) and remove sensor from the air filter air box intake duct.
4. Connect an ohmmeter to the two terminals (brown/white and black/blue) and measure the sensor resistance. The specified resistance is 2.21-2.69 ohms. If the resistance results do not match the specification, replace the sensor.
5. Install the sensor into the air filter air box intake duct.
6. Connect the connector onto intake air temperature sensor (**Figure 11**). Press on until it locks in place.
7. Install the fuel tank as described in Chapter Eight.
8. Install the seat as described in Chapter Fifteen.

Air cut-off valve solenoid

1. Remove the seat as described in Chapter Fifteen.
2. Remove the fuel tank as described in Chapter Eight.
3. Disconnect the connector from the air cut-off valve solenoid located behind the radiator on the frame rail.
4. Connect an ohmmeter to the two terminals (red/blue and brown/red) (**Figure 12**) and measure the sensor resistance. The specified resistance is 20-24 ohms. If the resistance results do not match the specification, replace the sensor.
5. Connect the connector onto the air cut-off valve solenoid.
6. Install the fuel tank as described in Chapter Eight.
7. Install the seat as described in Chapter Fifteen.

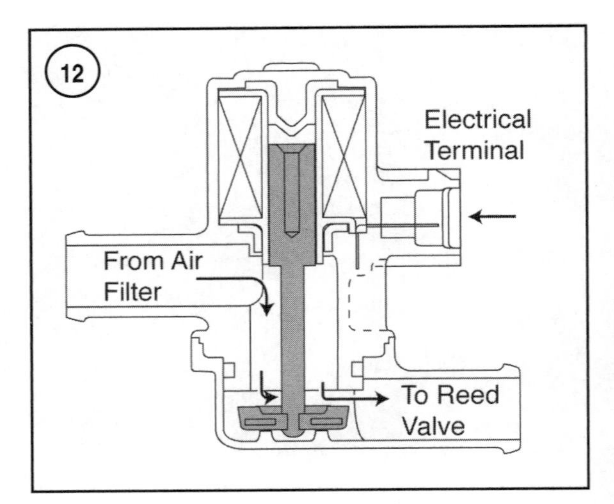

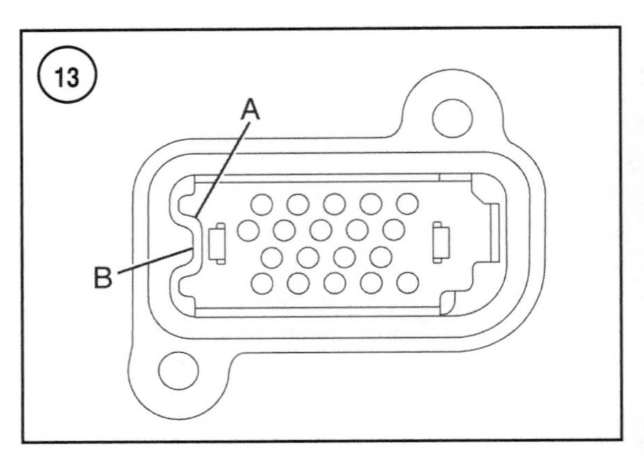

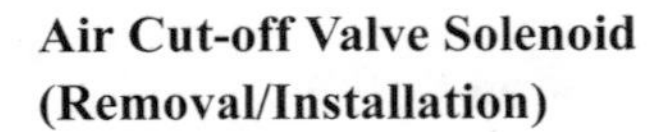

Air Cut-off Valve Solenoid (Removal/Installation)

Refer to **Figure 9**.

1. Remove the seat as described in Chapter Fifteen.
2. Remove the fuel tank as described in Chapter Eight.
3. Disconnect the connector from the air cut-off valve solenoid located behind the radiator on the frame rail.
4. Loosen the hose clamps and disconnect both hoses from the air cut-off valve solenoid.
5. Remove the fasteners and remove the air cut-off valve solenoid from the frame.
6. Install the air cut-off valve solenoid and tighten the fasteners securely.
7. Connect both hoses onto the air cut-off valve solenoid and tighten the hose clamps.
8. Connect the connector onto the air cut-off valve solenoid.
9. Install the fuel tank as described in Chapter Eight.
10. Install the seat as described in Chapter Fifteen.

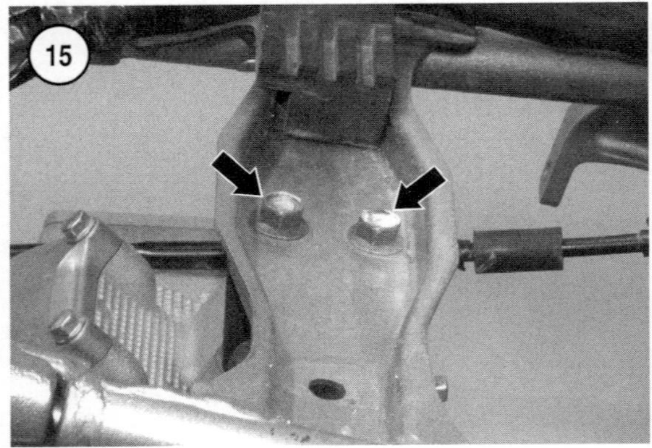

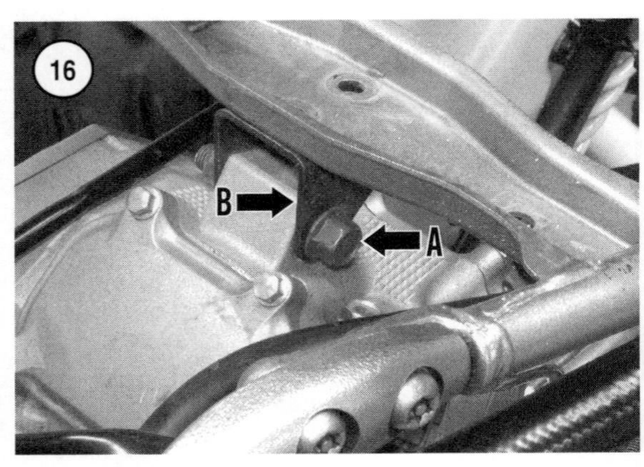

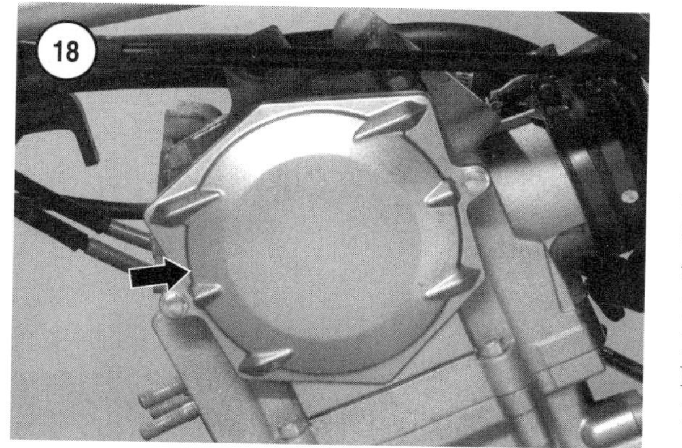

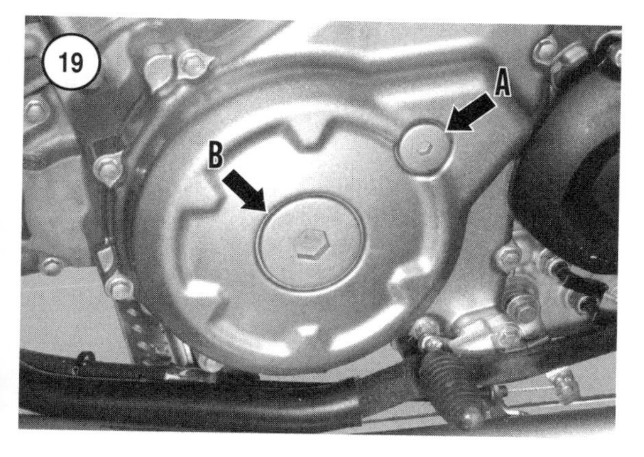

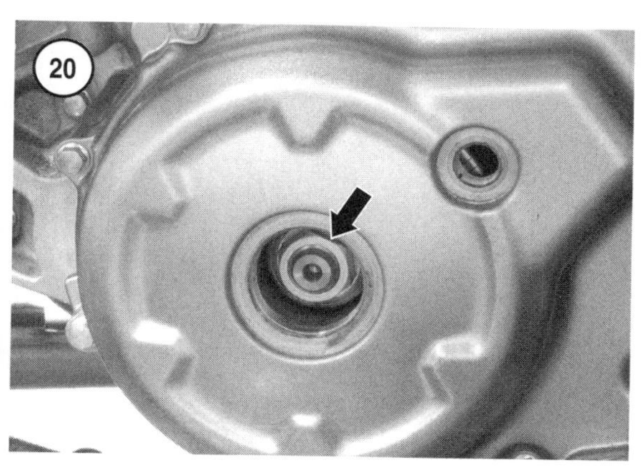

Reed Valve (Removal/Installation)

Refer to **Figure 10**.

1. Remove the seat as described in Chapter Fifteen.
2. Remove the fuel tank as described in Chapter Eight.
3. Remove the exhaust pipe heat shield.
4. Loosen the clamp and disconnect the hose from the reed valve cover plate.
5. Remove the two mounting bolts and remove the cover plate, reed valve and reed valve plate from the cylinder head.
6. Install the reed valve plate into the cylinder head.
7. Align the reed valve notch (A, **Figure 13**) with the projection (B) on the cylinder head reed valve seat, and install the reed valve.
8. Install the cover plate and two mounting bolts and tighten securely.
9. Connect the hose onto the cover plate and tighten the clamp securely.
10. Install the heat shield.
11. Install the fuel tank as described in Chapter Eight.
12. Install the seat as described in Chapter Fifteen.

CYLINDER HEAD

This section describes removal, inspection and installation of the cylinder head. After the cylinder head is removed, refer to the appropriate sections in this chapter for further disassembly, inspection and assembly procedures. The cylinder head can be removed with the engine mounted in the frame. If possible, perform a compression test (Chapter Three) and leakdown test (Chapter Two) prior to cylinder head removal.

Removal

1. Drain the coolant as described in Chapter Three.
2. Remove the exhaust system, and on 2015-on models disconnect the hose from the reed valve cover plate on the cylinder head as described in this chapter.
3. Remove the throttle body as described in Chapter Eight.
4. Loosen the clamp and detach the radiator hose (A, **Figure 14**) from the thermostat cover.
5. Disconnect the coolant temperature sensor connector (B, **Figure 14**).
6. Remove the upper mounting bracket bolts (**Figure 15**).
7. Remove the upper engine mounting bolt (A, **Figure 16**) and bracket (B).
8. Remove the spark plug. This will make it easier to turn the engine by hand.
9. Remove the exhaust (A, **Figure 17**) and intake (B) rocker covers.
10. Remove the camshaft sprocket cover (**Figure 18**).
11. Remove the timing plug (A, **Figure 19**) and the flywheel nut plug (B).
12. The engine must be set to top dead center (TDC) on its compression stroke before removing the sprocket bolts and cam sprocket. Perform the following:
    a. Fit a socket onto the flywheel nut (**Figure 20**) and turn the crankshaft counterclockwise until

the I mark on the flywheel is aligned with the index notch in the timing hole (**Figure 21**).

b. Verify that the camshaft sprocket index mark (A, **Figure 22**) aligns with the cylinder head boss (B). If these marks are not aligned, turn the crankshaft one revolution counterclockwise and align the flywheel I mark with the index notch.

c. When the camshaft sprocket and flywheel marks are properly aligned, all rocker arms will have a valve clearance, indicating that the intake and exhaust valves are closed. Move each rocker arm by hand. There should be some movement or free play.

13. Remove the oil pipe banjo bolts (A, **Figure 23**).
14. Remove the oil pipe retaining bolt (B, **Figure 23**), and then remove the oil pipe (C).
15. Loosen, but do not remove, the cam chain tensioner cap bolt (A, **Figure 24**).
16. Remove the cam chain tensioner mounting bolts (B, **Figure 24**) and remove the tensioner (C) from the cylinder block.
17. Secure the cam chain with safety wire. This will prevent the chain from falling into the cylinder chain tunnel.
18. Hold the flywheel nut (**Figure 20**) with a wrench and loosen the camshaft sprocket bolts (A, **Figure 25**).
19. Remove the camshaft sprocket bolts (A, **Figure 25**). Separate the camshaft sprocket (B) from the camshaft and remove it.

NOTE
The camshaft and both rocker arms can be removed with the cylinder head mounted in the frame as described in this chapter.

20. Remove the cylinder head bolts on the left side (A, **Figure 26**) of the engine.
21. Remove the lower cylinder head bolts at the front (**Figure 27**) and rear (**Figure 28**) of the engine.
22. Using a crossing pattern, loosen each of the upper cylinder head mounting bolts (D, **Figure 16** and

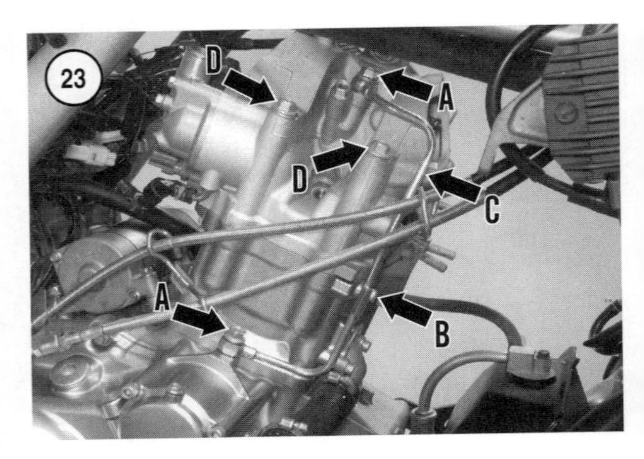

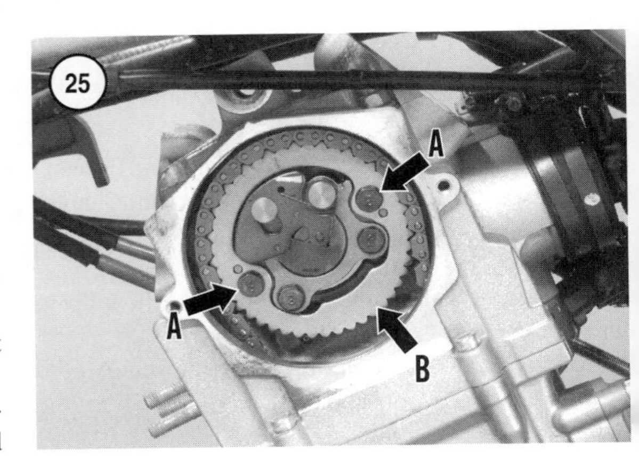

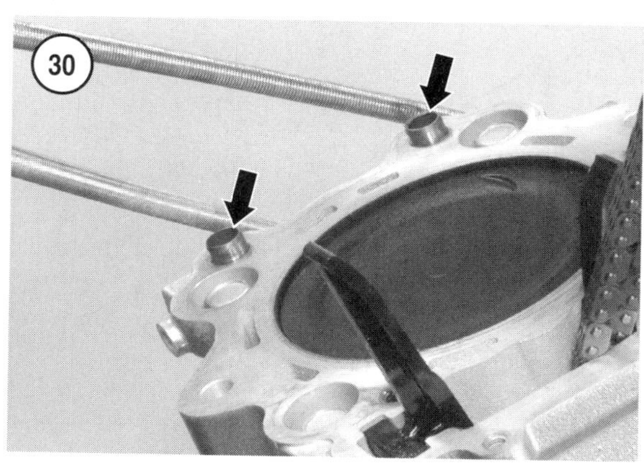

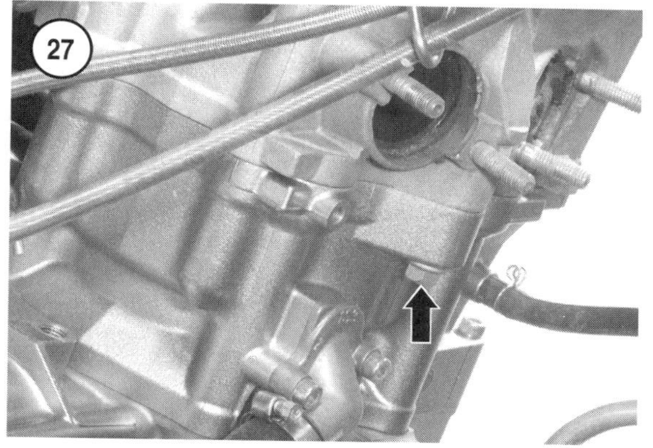

28

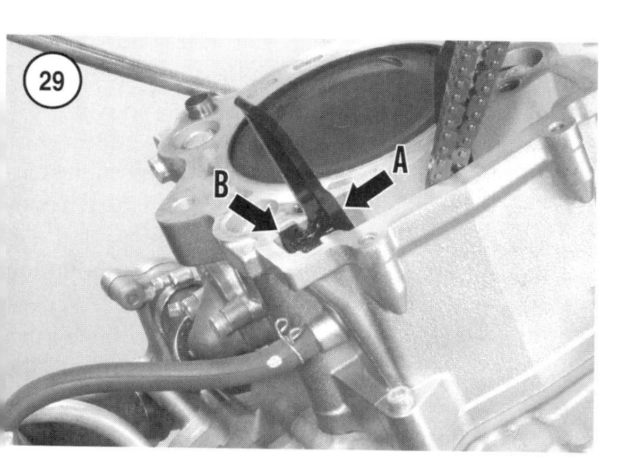

B, **Figure 26**) a half turn at a time until all of the bolts are loose.

23. Tap the cylinder head with a rubber mallet to break it free from the head gasket.
24. Remove the cylinder head.
25. Remove the cylinder head gasket.
26. If necessary, remove the front cam chain guide (A, **Figure 29**).
27. Remove the dowel pins (**Figure 30**) from the top of the cylinder block.
28. Cover the cylinder block with a clean shop rag or paper towels.
29. If necessary, remove the camshaft and rocker arms as described in this chapter.
30. If wear or damage is evident on the timing chain or guides, refer to *Camshaft Chain and Guides* in Chapter Five.
31. Inspect the cylinder head assembly as described in this section.

Installation

1. Remove all gasket material from the cylinder head and cylinder block mating surfaces.
2. If removed, install the following components as described in this chapter:
   a. Valves.
   b. Camshaft.
   c. Rocker arms and shafts.
3. Install both cylinder head dowel pins (**Figure 30**).
4. If removed, install the front cam chain guide (A, **Figure 29**) into the cylinder head chain guide slot (B).
5. Install a new cylinder head gasket.
6. Install the cylinder head and direct the cam chain and its safety wire through the cylinder head chain tunnel. Tie the safety wire to the frame.

NOTE

Two different length cylinder head mounting bolts are used. The longer mounting bolts are installed on the left side.

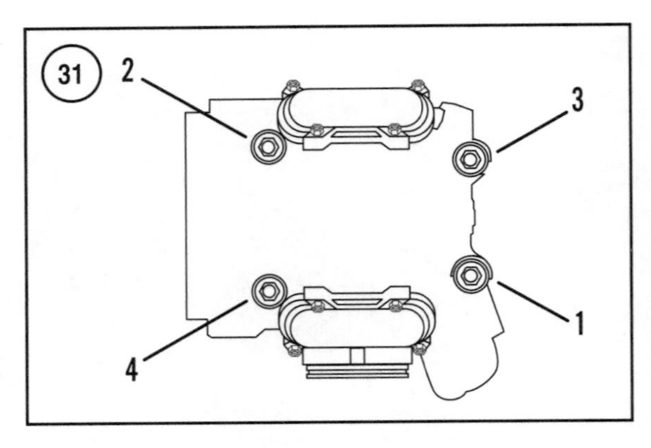

7. Lubricate the upper cylinder head bolt threads with molybdenum disulfide grease and install the bolts. Using the sequence shown in **Figure 31**, tighten the head bolts in 2-3 steps to 35 N•m (26 ft.-lb.).
8. Lubricate the threads with engine oil, and then install the front (**Figure 27**) and rear (**Figure 28**) lower cylinder head bolts. Tighten them to 38 N•m (28 ft.-lb.).
9. Install the left side cylinder head bolts (A, **Figure 26**) and tighten to 10 N•m (89 in.-lb.).
10. Make sure the camshaft is positioned so the decompressor cam (**Figure 32**) is at the top. If not, rotate the camshaft.

CAUTION
Because of chain slack, the cam chain can easily slip off of the crankshaft sprocket. Pull up on the chain and make sure it is properly engaged with the crankshaft sprocket.

11. If the crankshaft was rotated away from TDC, perform the following:

CAUTION
The cam chain must be kept tight against its sprocket when turning the crankshaft. Otherwise, the chain can roll off the sprocket and bind in the lower end, causing chain damage.

a. Lift the cam chain and make sure it is engaged with the crankshaft cam chain sprocket. Hold the chain in this position when turning the crankshaft.
b. With a wrench on the flywheel nut (**Figure 20**), turn the crankshaft counterclockwise and align the I mark on the flywheel with the index notch (**Figure 21**).

12. Remove the safety wire from the top of the cam chain and reconnect it lower on the chain so it may be removed after installing the cam sprocket.

13. Align the cam sprocket so that its timing mark faces out and is positioned up. Then, install the cam chain onto the cam sprocket.
14. Place the cam sprocket onto the camshaft and install the cam sprocket mounting bolts finger-tight.
15. Verify that the cam sprocket timing mark (A, **Figure 22**) aligns with the cylinder head boss (B). If not, remove the sprocket and reposition it on the cam chain.
16. When the timing marks are correct, tighten the cam sprocket mounting bolts to 20 N•m (15 ft.-lb.).
17. Install the cam chain tensioner as follows:

a. Remove the cam chain tensioner cap bolt, washer and spring (**Figure 33**).
b. Depress the cam chain tensioner one-way cam (A, **Figure 34**) and push the tensioner rod (B) into the tensioner body until it stops and locks in place.
c. Install a new gasket onto the cam chain tensioner so the raised bead is toward the tensioner end.
d. Install the tensioner and tighten the mounting bolts to 10 N•m (89 in.-lb.).
e. Install the spring, washer and cap bolt. Push the cap bolt into position and thread it into the tensioner body. Tighten the tensioner cap bolt (A, **Figure 24**) to 20 N•m (15 ft.-lb.).

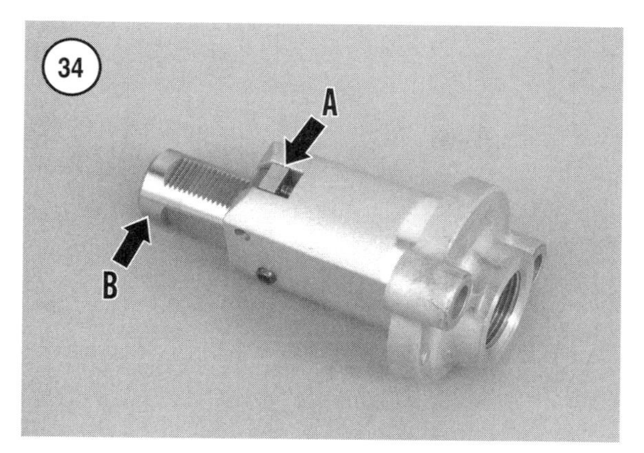

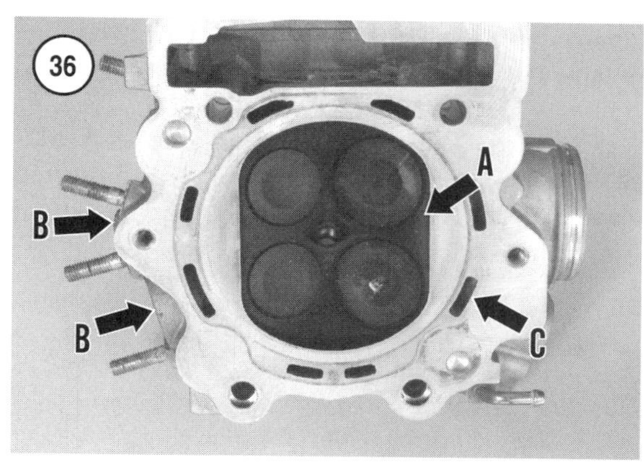

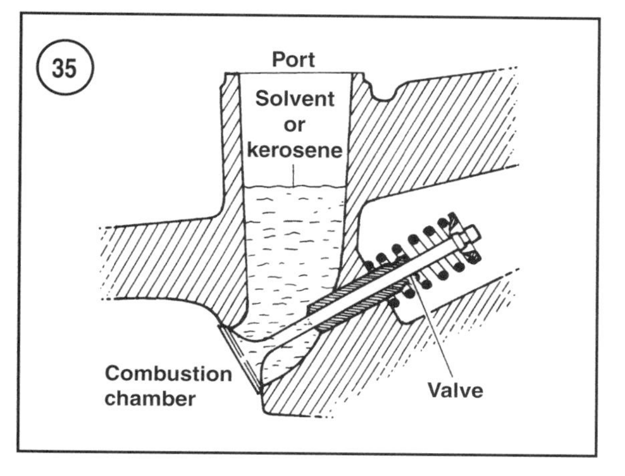

18. Check valve adjustment as described in Chapter Three.
19. Lubricate the O-ring. Install it and the camshaft sprocket cover (**Figure 18**). Tighten the cover mounting bolts to 10 N•m (89 in.-lb.).
20. Install the oil pipe (C, **Figure 23**) and the oil pipe retaining bolt (B). Tighten the retaining bolt to 10 N•m (89 in.-lb.).
21. Install the oil pipe banjo bolts (A, **Figure 23**) with new washers on both sides of the fitting. Tighten the banjo bolts to 20 N•m (15 ft.-lb.).
22. Install the upper engine bracket. Tighten the upper engine bracket bolts to 33 N•m (24 ft.-lb.).
23. Install the upper engine mounting bolt and tighten to 40 N•m (30 ft.-lb.).
24. Install the spark plug and tighten to 13 N•m (115 in.-lb.). Reconnect the spark plug cap.
25. Connect the coolant temperature sensor connector.
26. Attach the radiator hose to the thermostat cover and tighten the clamp.
27. Install the throttle body as described in Chapter Eight.
28. On 2015-on models connect the hose onto the reed valve cover plate on the cylinder head as described in this chapter.
29. Install the exhaust system as described in this chapter.
30. Refill the radiator and reservoir with coolant as described in Chapter Three.

Inspection

Before removing the valves from the cylinder head, perform a solvent test to check the valve face-to-valve seat seal.

1. Remove the cylinder head as described in this chapter.
2. Support the cylinder head with the exhaust ports facing up (**Figure 35**). Pour solvent or kerosene into the ports. Immediately check the combustion chambers for fluid leaking past the exhaust valves.
3. Repeat the test for the intake valves.
4. If there is fluid leaking around one or both sets of valves, the valve(s) is not seating correctly. The following conditions will cause poor valve seating:
   a. A bent valve stem.
   b. A worn or damaged valve seat.
   c. A worn or damaged valve face.
   d. A crack in the combustion chamber.
5. Remove all gasket material from the cylinder head mating surfaces. Do not scratch or gouge the surfaces.

CAUTION
If the valves are removed from the head, the valve seats are exposed and can be damaged from careless cleaning. A damaged valve seat will not seal properly.

6. Remove all carbon deposits from the combustion chamber (A, **Figure 36**) and exhaust ports (B). Use solvent and a fine wire brush or hardwood scraper. Do not use sharp-edged tools such as screwdrivers or putty knives.
7. Inspect the spark plug hole threads. If the threads are dirty or mildly damaged, use a spark plug thread

tap to clean and straighten the threads. Use kerosene or tap-cutting fluid to lubricate the threads as the tap is turned.

If the threads are galled, stripped or cross-threaded, install a steel thread insert (HeliCoil) following the manufacturer's instructions.

CAUTION

If the head was bead-blasted, wash the entire assembly in hot soapy water to remove all blasting media. Chase all threads and carefully clean the entire head. Blasting debris that remains in the head will contaminate the engine oil and damage other parts of the engine.

8. Clean the entire cylinder head assembly in fresh solvent.
9. Inspect the cylinder head for cracks in the combustion chamber, water jackets (C, **Figure 36**) and exhaust port. If cracks are found, have a dealership or machine shop determine if the cylinder head can be repaired. If not, replace the head.
10. Inspect the cylinder head for warp as follows:
   a. Place a machinist's straightedge across the cylinder head as shown in **Figure 37**.
   b. Attempt to insert a flat feeler gauge between the straightedge and the machined surface of the head. If clearance exists, record the measurement.
   c. Repeat this process several times, laying the straightedge both across and diagonally on the head in several locations on the head.
11. Compare the measurements to the warp service limit in **Table 2**. If cylinder warp is excessive, have a dealership or machine shop determine if the cylinder head can be repaired. If the clearance is close to the service limit, true the head as follows:
   a. Tape a sheet of 400-600 grit emery paper to a thick sheet of glass or to a surface plate.
   b. Place the head on the emery paper and move the head in a figure-eight pattern.
   c. Rotate the head at regular intervals so material is removed evenly.
   d. Check the progress often, measuring the clearance with the straightedge and feeler gauge in multiple locations on the cylinder head.

CAMSHAFT AND ROCKER ARMS

A single camshaft is mounted in the cylinder head. The chain-driven camshaft is supported by ball bearings. A decompressor assembly on the camshaft opens the exhaust valves during starting. The camshaft and both rocker arms can be removed with the

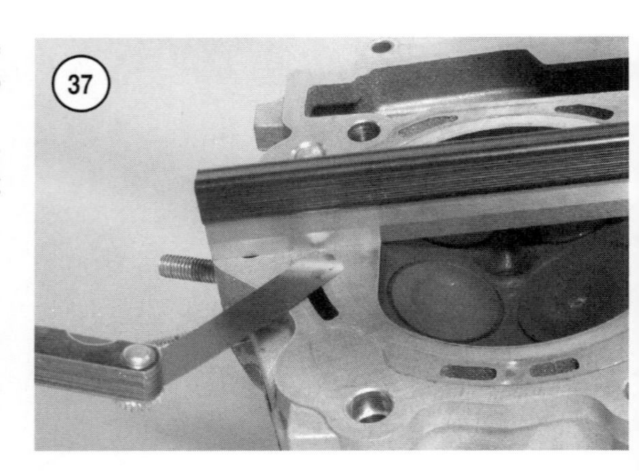

cylinder head installed on the engine, or after cylinder head removal.

Tools

A slide hammer set (Yamaha part No. YU-01083) or equivalent is required to remove the rocker arms shafts from the cylinder head. A suitable tool may also be fabricated using a threaded shaft with M6 × 1.00 mm threads.

NOTE

Although the following images depict the cylinder head removed from the engine, the camshaft can be removed with the cylinder head installed on the engine.

Removal

Refer to **Figure 38** or **Figure 39**.

1. If servicing the camshaft with the cylinder head installed, perform Steps 8-12 and Steps 15-19 in *Cylinder Head Removal* (this chapter).
2. Remove the retaining bolts (A, **Figure 40**), and then remove the decompressor weight assembly (B).
3. Remove the retaining bolts (A, **Figure 41**), and then remove the bearing retainer (B).

NOTE

Mark the rocker arm shafts so they may be installed in their original positions.

NOTE

If necessary, apply heat to the shaft boss on the cylinder head to ease removal of the rocker arm shaft.

4. Use one of the following methods to remove the rocker shaft(s). Make sure to protect the cylinder head surfaces.

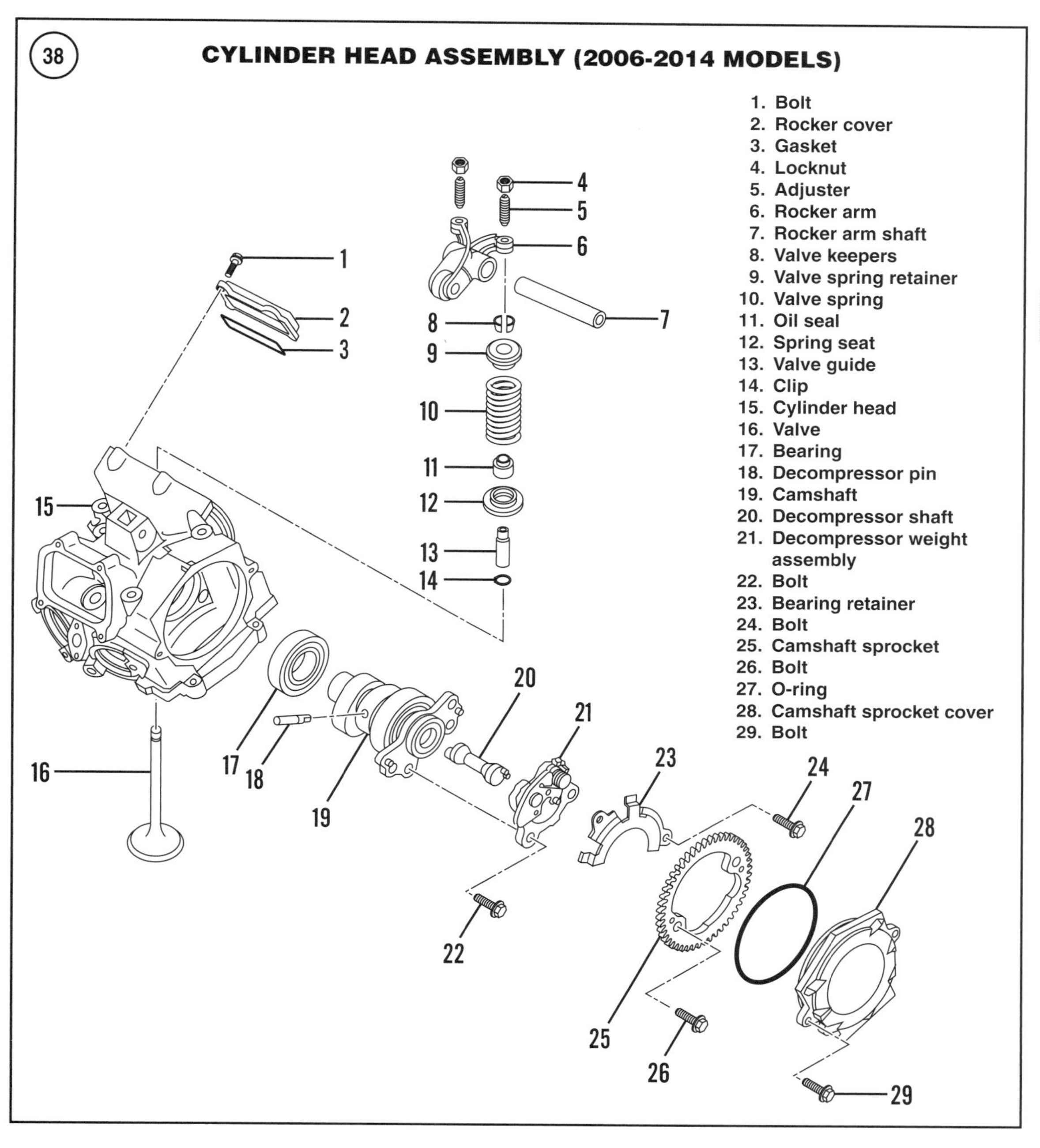

a. Thread the slide hammer into the rocker arm shaft. Operate the slide hammer and remove the rocker arm shaft.

b. Thread a suitable bolt or all-thread into the rocker arm shaft so it will bear against a draw-bar as shown in **Figure 42**. Turn the bolt or the nut on the threaded shaft to extract the rocker arm shaft.

5. Remove the rocker arm (**Figure 43**).

6. Repeat the removal procedure for the opposite rocker shaft and rocker arm.

NOTE

*When removing the camshaft, the decompressor shaft (A, **Figure 44**) or pin (B) in the camshaft lobe may fall out.*

7. Carefully pull the camshaft out of the cylinder head (**Figure 45**).

8. Remove the decompressor pin (A, **Figure 45**) and decompressor shaft (B) from the camshaft.

Camshaft Inspection

Refer to **Table 3** for specifications.

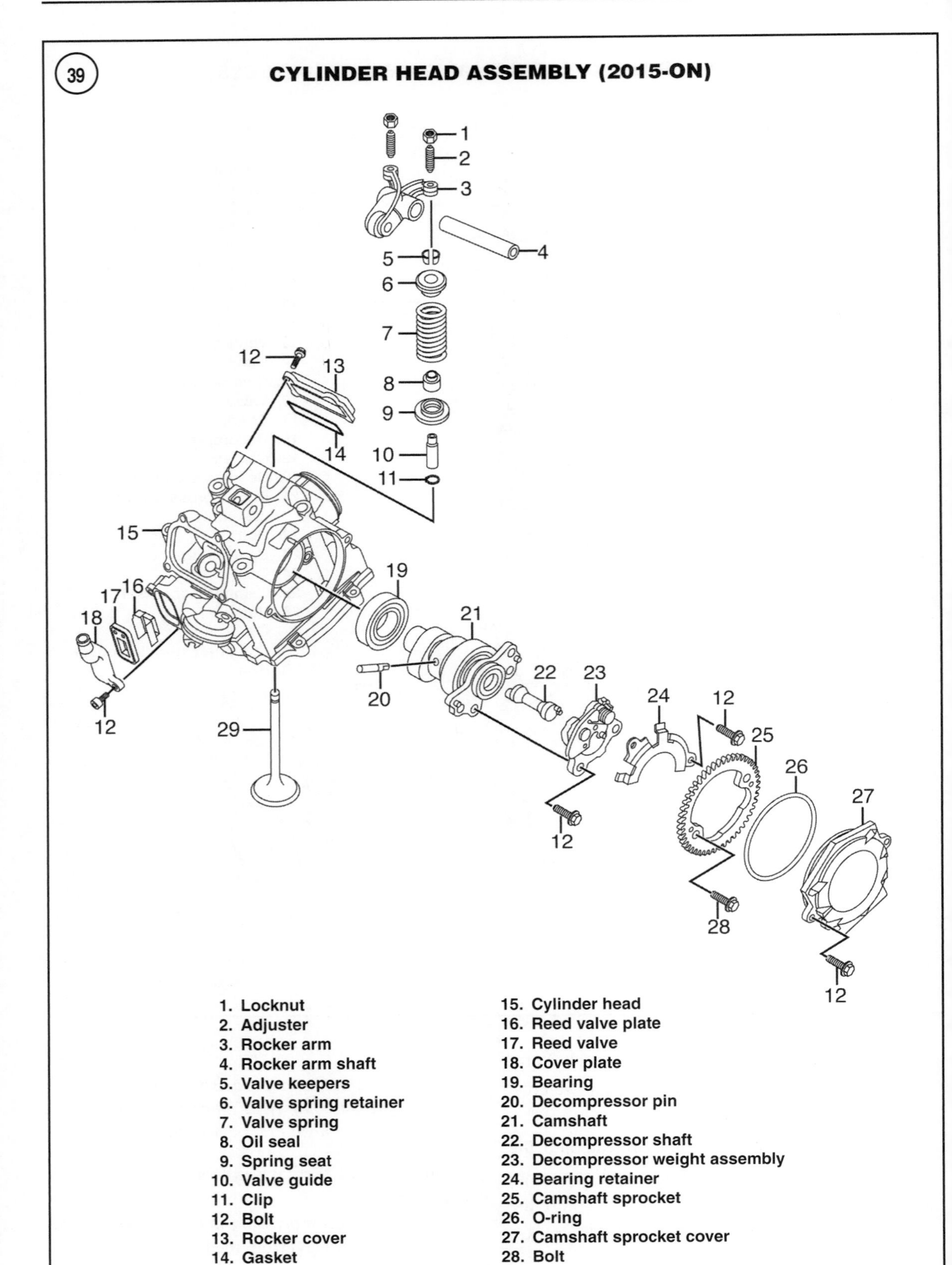
39
CYLINDER HEAD ASSEMBLY (2015-ON)
1
2
3
4
5
6
7
8
9
10
11
12
13
14
15
16
17
18
19
20
21
22
23
24
25
26
27
28
29
1. Locknut
2. Adjuster
3. Rocker arm
4. Rocker arm shaft
5. Valve keepers
6. Valve spring retainer
7. Valve spring
8. Oil seal
9. Spring seat
10. Valve guide
11. Clip
12. Bolt
13. Rocker cover
14. Gasket
15. Cylinder head
16. Reed valve plate
17. Reed valve
18. Cover plate
19. Bearing
20. Decompressor pin
21. Camshaft
22. Decompressor shaft
23. Decompressor weight assembly
24. Bearing retainer
25. Camshaft sprocket
26. O-ring
27. Camshaft sprocket cover
28. Bolt

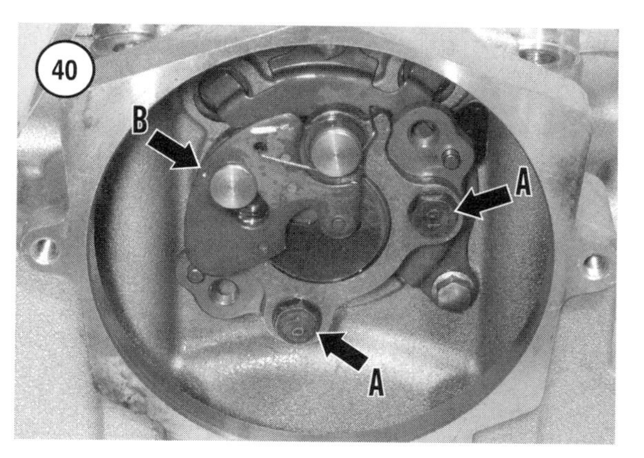

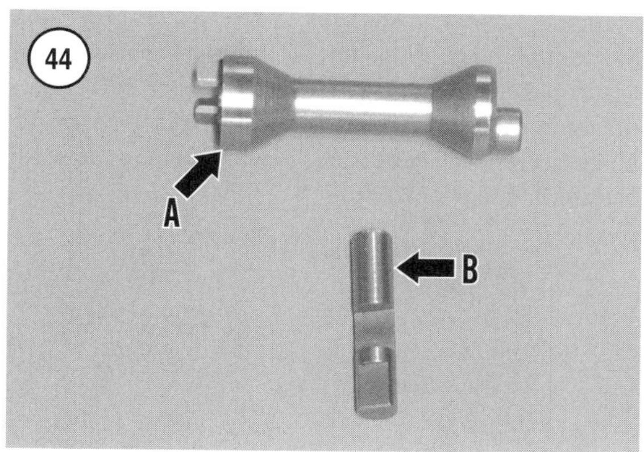

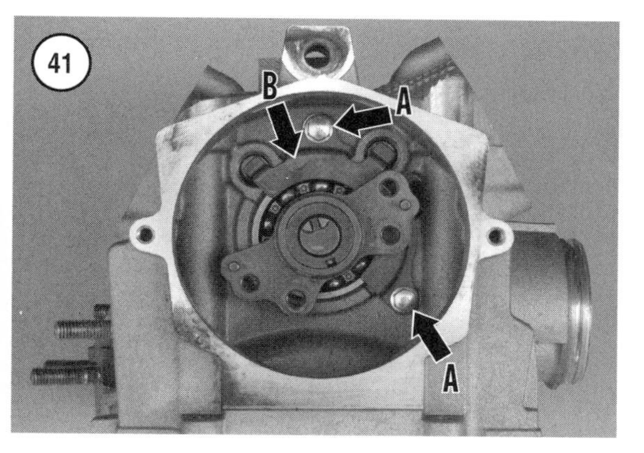

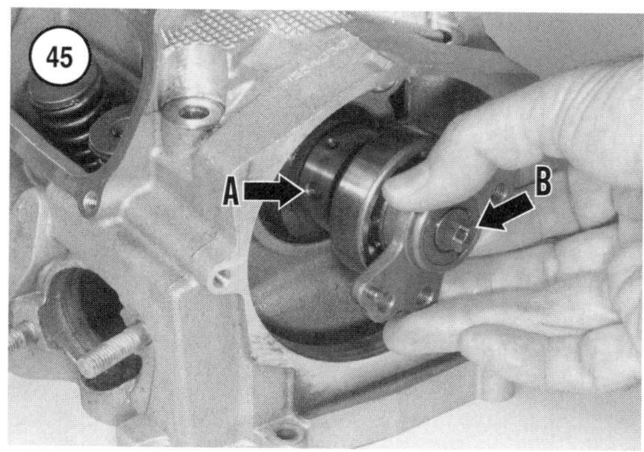

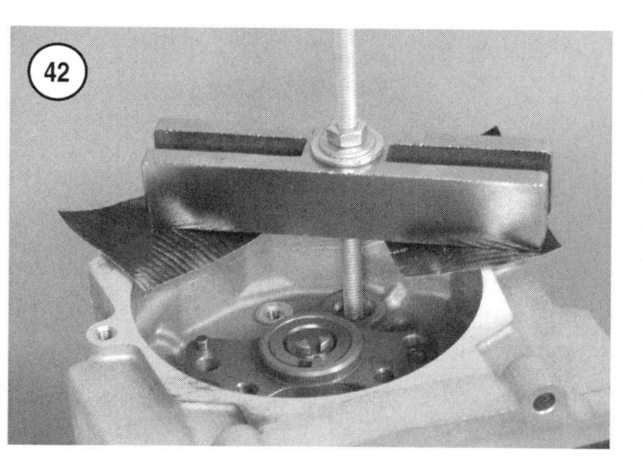

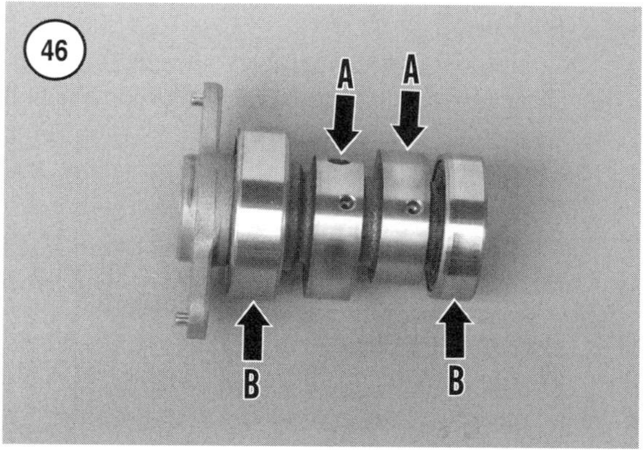

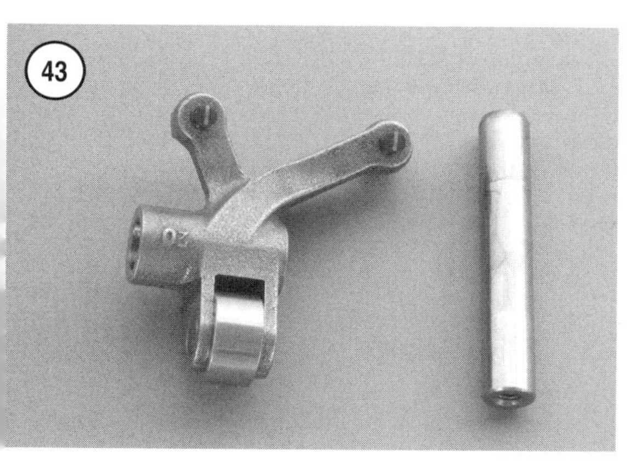

1. Check the cam lobes (A, **Figure 46**) for wear. The lobes should not be scored and the edges should be square.
2. Even though the cam lobe surface appears to be satisfactory, with no visible signs of wear, each lobe must be measured with a micrometer. Measure both the lobe height and the base circle diameter as shown in **Figure 47**. Replace the camshaft if worn beyond the service specifications.

CAUTION
The left camshaft bearing is not removable; do not disassemble the camshaft assembly.

3. Inspect the camshaft bearings (B, **Figure 46**). Make sure the bearings turn smoothly with no roughness, binding or excessive play. Inspect each for signs of overheating. Check the bearing shield for damage. If replacement is necessary, press the right camshaft bearing off the camshaft.

NOTE

If the sprockets are worn, also check the camshaft chain, chain guides and chain tensioner for damage, as described in Chapter Five.

4. Inspect the camshaft sprocket (**Figure 48**) for broken or chipped teeth. Also check the teeth for cracking or rounding. If the camshaft sprocket is damaged or severely worn, inspect the sprocket mounted on the crankshaft.

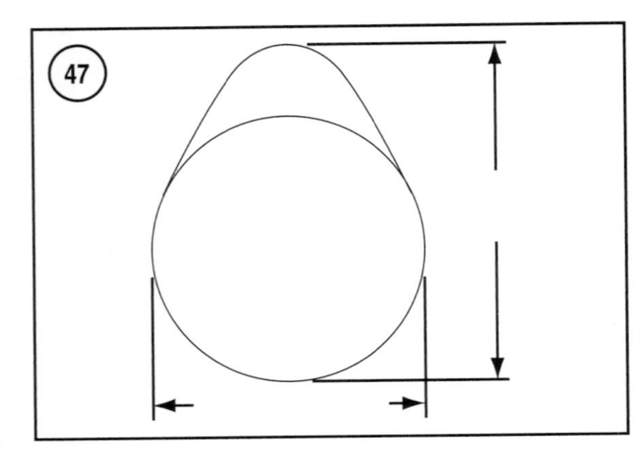

Rocker Arms and Shafts Inspection

1. Clean all parts in solvent. Dry with compressed air.
2. Inspect the rocker arm roller (A, **Figure 49**) for damage. Make sure the roller turns freely without excessive play.
3. Inspect the adjusters (B, **Figure 49**). Check for scratches, flat spots, uneven wear and scoring. Replace the valve adjuster if damaged.
4. Inspect the rocker arm shaft (C, **Figure 49**) for wear or scoring.
5. Calculate rocker arm shaft clearance as follows:
   a. Measure rocker arm inside bore diameter and record the measurement.
   b. Measure rocker arm shaft outer diameter and record the measurement.
   c. Subtract the measurement in sub-step b from the measurement in sub-step a to determine rocker arm shaft clearance. Replace the worn part(s) if the clearance exceeds the specification in **Table 2**.
6. Repeat for the other rocker arm assembly.

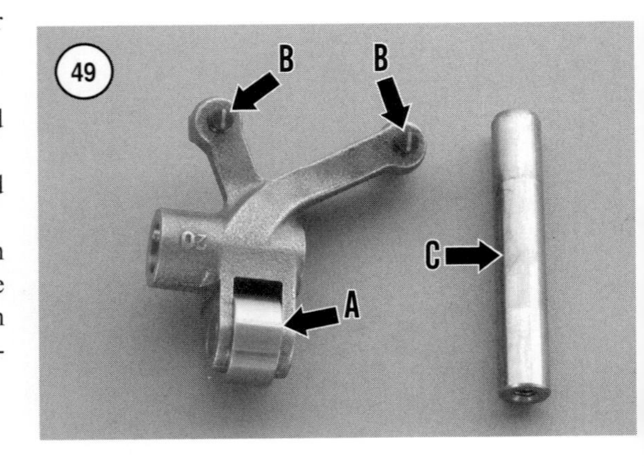

Decompressor Inspection

1. Inspect the decompressor weight assembly (A, **Figure 50**), shaft (B) and pin (C) for wear or damage.

NOTE

Lubricate the decompressor components with engine oil to ensure free movement.

2. Check decompressor operation as follows:
   a. Install the pin (A, **Figure 51**) into the camshaft so the rounded end is out. The notch (B, **Figure 51**) must be toward the sprocket end of the camshaft.

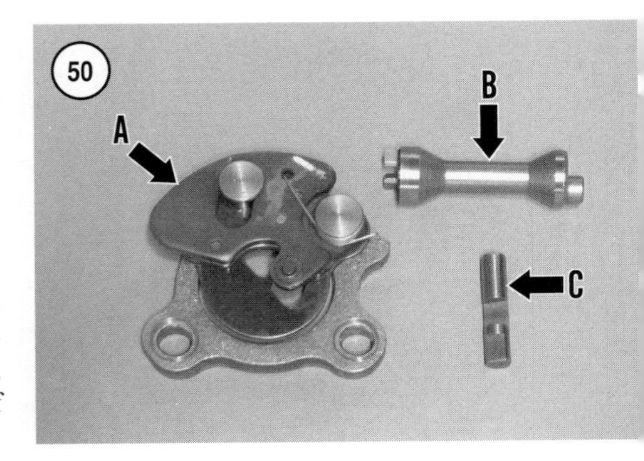

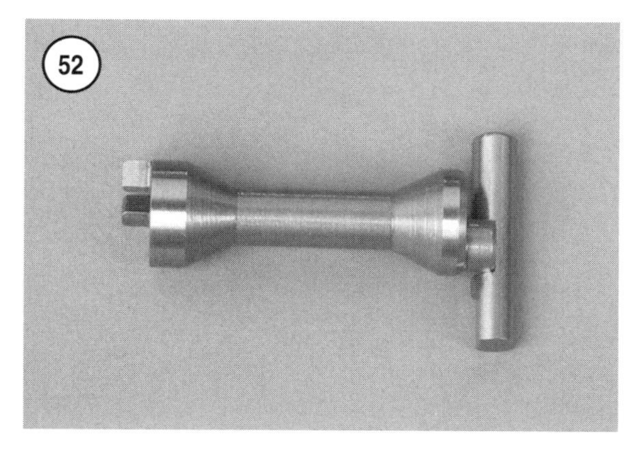

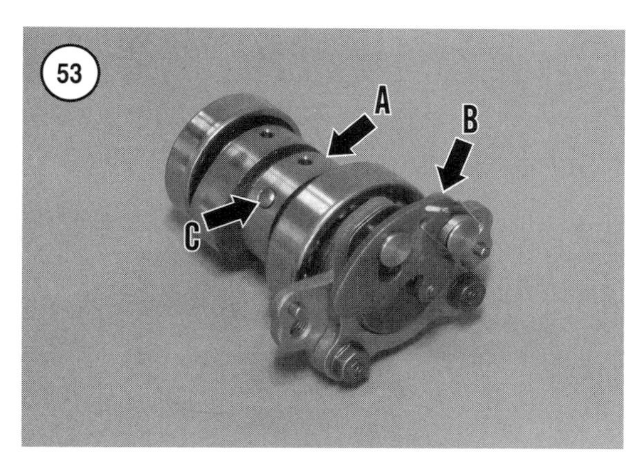

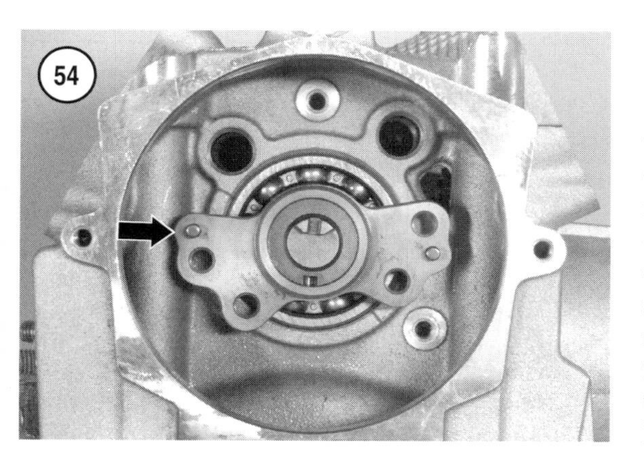

b. Insert the shaft into the camshaft so the pin end enters first. Make sure the shaft boss engages the notch in the pin as shown in **Figure 52**. Rotating the shaft should extend the pin.

c. Mount the decompressor weight assembly on the camshaft (A, **Figure 53**) so the weight plate properly engages the shaft tabs. Install the mounting bolts and tighten to 20 N•m (15 ft.-lb.).

d. Push the weight cam (B, **Figure 53**) and check decompressor operation. The decompressor pin (C, **Figure 53**) should extend above the cam without binding in the mechanism.

e. Remove the decompressor components.

Installation

1. If removed, install the right camshaft bearing so the sealed side is toward the camshaft. The open side of the bearing must be flush with the end of the camshaft.
2. Lubricate the decompressor pin (A, **Figure 51**) with molybdenum disulfide oil and insert it into the camshaft so the rounded end is out. The notch (B, **Figure 51**) must be toward the sprocket end of the camshaft.
3. Lubricate the decompressor shaft with molybdenum disulfide oil and insert it into the camshaft so the pin end enters first. Make sure the shaft boss engages the notch in the pin as shown in **Figure 52**. Rotating the shaft should extend the pin.
4. Lubricate the cam lobes with molybdenum disulfide oil. Lubricate the bearings with engine oil.
5. Install the camshaft so the flanges are positioned as shown in **Figure 54**.
6. Lubricate each rocker arm shaft and rocker arm bore with engine oil. Lubricate the rocker arm roller with engine oil. Lubricate the valve stem ends with molybdenum disulfide oil.

CAUTION
Install the rocker arms and shafts in their original positions.

7. Install the rocker arm shaft so the threaded end faces out. Partially drive the rocker arm shaft into the cylinder head and position the rocker arm in the cylinder head. The valve adjusters on the rocker arm must face out.
8. Continue to drive the rocker arm shaft through the cylinder head until it aligns and enters the rocker arm and then bottoms. Repeat the process to install the remaining rocker arm assembly.
9. Install the bearing retainer (B, **Figure 41**). Tighten the retaining bolts (A, **Figure 41**) to 10 N•m (89 in.-lb.).

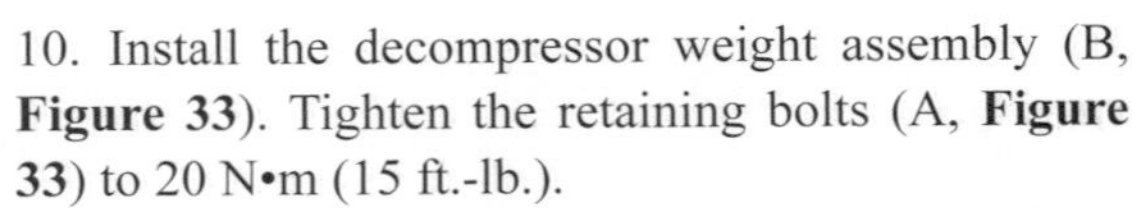

10. Install the decompressor weight assembly (B, **Figure 33**). Tighten the retaining bolts (A, **Figure 33**) to 20 N•m (15 ft.-lb.).
11. Install the cylinder head and camshaft sprocket as described in this chapter.

CAM CHAIN AND GUIDE

The cam chain is driven by a sprocket on the left end of the crankshaft. Refer to Chapter Five for cam chain service information.

VALVES

To remove and install the valves in this section, a valve spring compressor is required.

Valve Removal

Refer to **Figure 38** or **Figure 39**.

CAUTION
Do not remove the valve guides unless they require replacement.

1. Remove the cylinder head as described in this chapter.
2. Remove the rocker arms as described in this chapter.

CAUTION
All components of each valve assembly must be kept together. Mark all parts during removal so that they will be installed in their original locations. Place each valve set into a labeled plastic bag, divided carton or small box. Do not mix components from the different valve sets during assembly, or excessive wear may result.

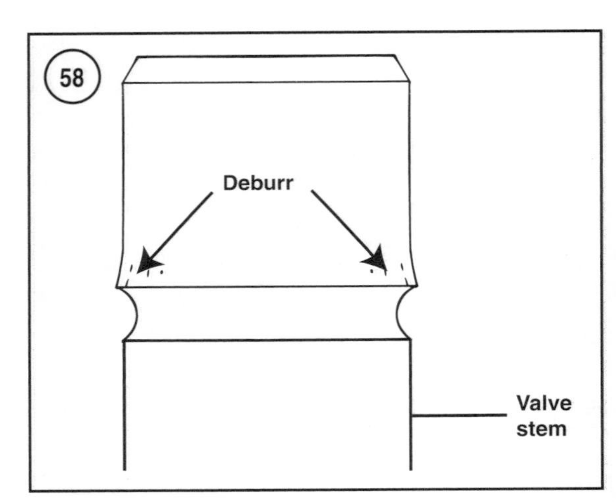

3. Install a valve spring compressor onto the valve assembly (**Figure 55**).
4. Tighten the valve spring compressor until the valve keepers separate. Lift the valve keepers (**Figure 56**) out through the valve spring compressor using needlenose pliers or tweezers.
5. Gradually loosen the valve spring compressor and remove it from the head.
6. Remove the spring retainer and valve spring (**Figure 57**).

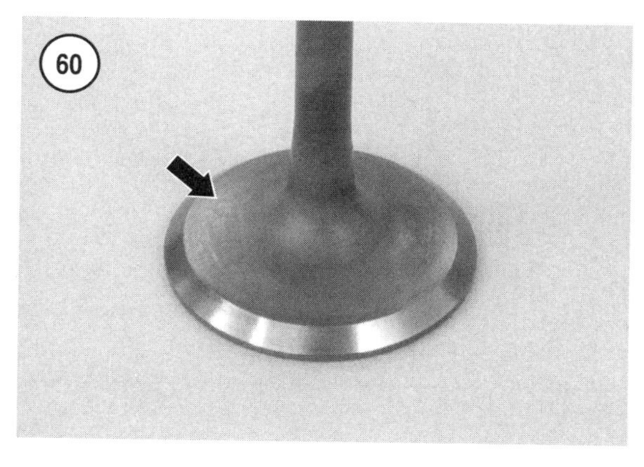

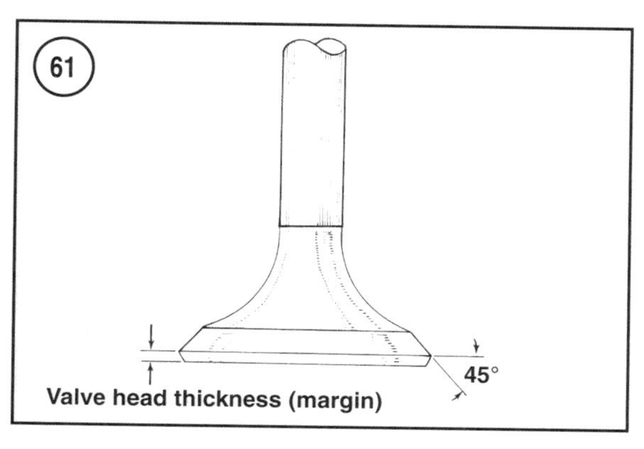

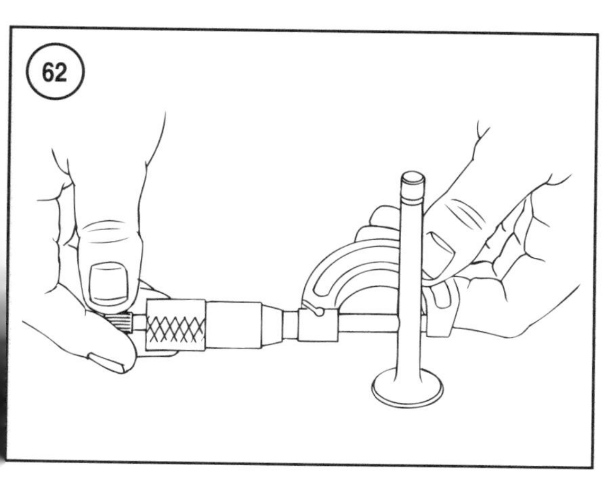

CAUTION
*Remove any burrs from the valve stem grooves (**Figure 58**) before removing the valves; otherwise the valve guides will be damaged as the valve stems are passed through them.*

NOTE
If a valve is difficult to remove, it may be bent, causing it to stick in the valve guide. This condition will require valve and valve guide replacement.

7. Pull the oil seal (A, **Figure 59**) off the valve guide and discard it.
8. Remove the spring seat (B, **Figure 59**).
9. Repeat for the remaining intake and exhaust valves as necessary.

Valve Component Inspection

Inspect one assembly at a time, repeating the procedure until each assembly is inspected.
1. Clean the valve assembly in solvent.

CAUTION
Condition of the valve seating surface is critical. It must not be damaged. Do not scrape the seating surface or place the valve where it could roll off the work surface.

2. Inspect the valve head as follows:
   a. Inspect the top (**Figure 60**) and perimeter of each valve. Check for burning or other damage on the top and seating surface. Replace the valve if damage is evident. If the valve face is uniform, with only minor wear, lap the valve face as described in this chapter.
   b. Measure the margin (thickness) (**Figure 61**). Record the measurement. Replace the valve if the measurement is not within the specification in **Table 2**.
3. Inspect the valve stem for wear and roughness. Also check the end of the valve stem for mushrooming. Measure the valve stem outside diameter (**Figure 62**) with a micrometer. Record the measurement. Replace the valve if the measurement is not within the specification in **Table 2**.
4. Place the valve in a V-block and measure valve stem runout with a dial indicator. Record the measurement. Replace the valve if the measurement is not within the specification in **Table 2**. If the valve is replaced, also replace the valve guide and oil seal.
5. Clean the valve guides so they are free of all carbon and varnish. Use solvent and a stiff, narrow, spiral brush such as one designed for cleaning firearms.

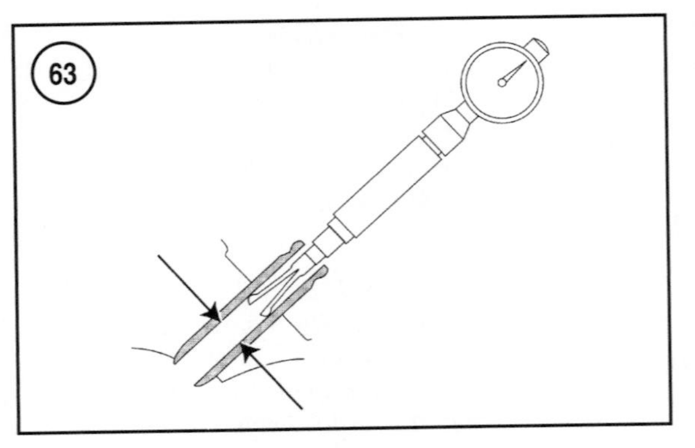

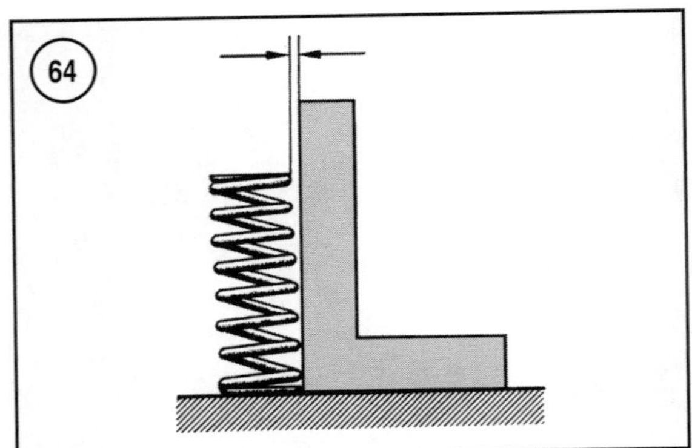

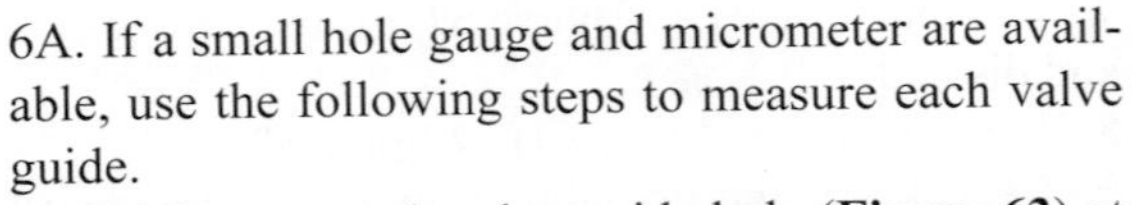

6A. If a small hole gauge and micrometer are available, use the following steps to measure each valve guide.

a. Measure each valve guide hole (**Figure 63**) at the top, center and bottom. Record the measurements.
b. Refer to **Table 2** to determine if the valve guide inside diameter is within the service limit. Replace any guide if it is not within the service limit.
c. Subtract the valve stem measurement from the largest valve guide measurement. Refer to **Table 2** to determine if the valve stem-to-valve guide clearance is within the service limit. If the parts are not within the service limit, replace the part(s).

6B. If a small hole gauge and micrometer are not available, perform the following:

a. Insert the appropriate valve into the guide.
b. With the valve head off the seat, rock the valve stem in the valve guide. Rock the valve in several directions, checking for any perceptible play. If movement is detected, the valve guide and/or valve is worn.
c. Have a dealership or machine shop accurately measure the valves and guides to determine which part(s) require replacement.

NOTE

Intake valve springs are identified by a blue paint mark. Exhaust valve springs are identified by a red paint mark.

7. Check each valve spring as follows:
   a. Visually check the spring for damage.
   b. Stand the spring vertically, and then place a square next to the spring to check for distortion or tilt (**Figure 64**). Refer to **Table 2** to determine if the spring is within the service limit.
   c. Measure each valve spring length (**Figure 65**) with a caliper. Refer to **Table 2** to determine if the spring is within the service limit.

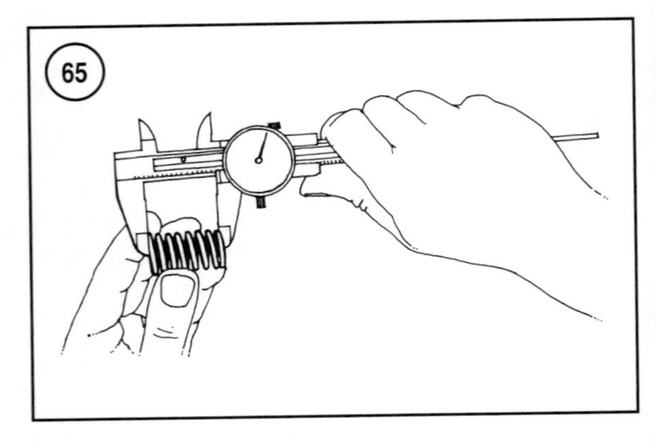

   d. Measure valve spring pressure (**Figure 66**) using a compression tool and compare to specifications in **Table 2**. Replace weak or damaged springs.
8. Inspect the valve spring seat and keepers for wear or damage.
9. Inspect the valve seats in the cylinder head to determine if they must be reconditioned.
   a. Clean and dry the valve seat and valve mating area with contact cleaner.
   b. Lightly coat the valve seat with Prussian Blue (gear-marking compound).
   c. Install the appropriate valve into the guide, and then lightly tap the valve against the seat so the compound transfers to the valve contact area.
   d. Remove the valve from the guide. At several locations, measure the width of the valve seat imprint on the valve (**Figure 67**) with a caliper. Refer to **Table 2** to determine if the valve seat width is within the service limit. Regrind the valve seat if any width measurement exceeds the service limit as described in this chapter. Always regrind a valve seat that is burned or worn.
10. Clean all compound residue from the valves and seats.

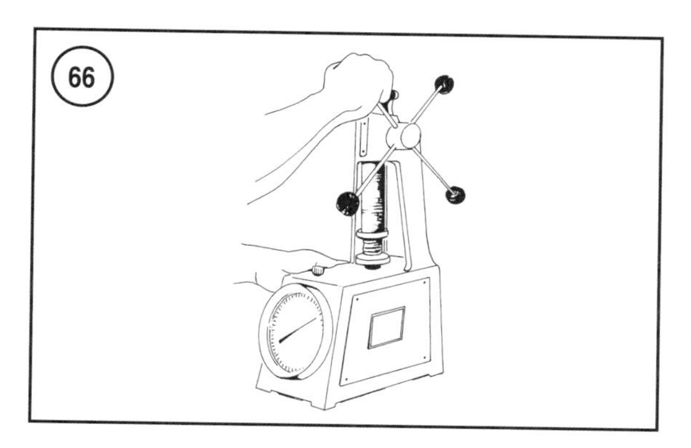

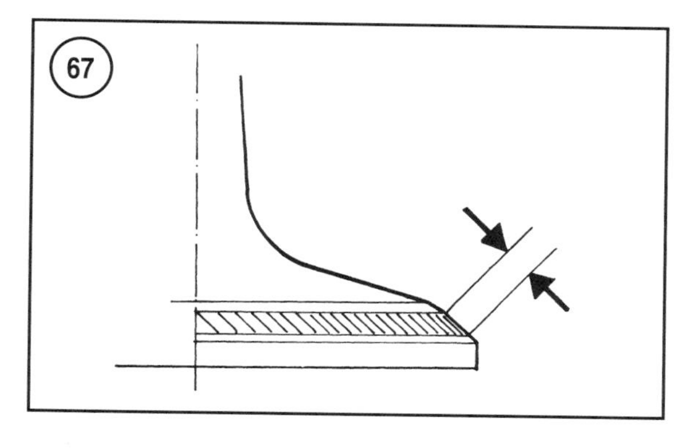

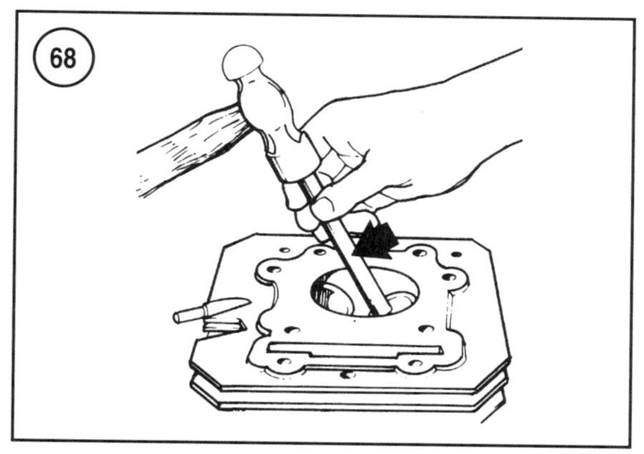

Valve Guide Replacement

CAUTION

Do not remove the valve guides unless they require replacement.

1. The valve guides must be removed and installed with the following tools or their equivalents:

   a. Valve guide remover (Yamaha part No. YM-04064-A/90890-04064).

   b. Valve guide installer (Yamaha part No. YM-04065-A/90890-04065).

   c. Valve guide reamer (Yamaha part No. YM-04066/90890-04066).

NOTE

Before driving the valve guides out of the cylinder head, place the new valve guides in the freezer. The freezing temperature will shrink the new guides slightly and ease installation.

2. When purchasing new valve guides, also purchase new valve guide clips. Install a clip on each valve guide prior to installing the guides in the following steps.

WARNING

Wear heavy gloves when handling the hot cylinder head.

CAUTION

Do not heat the cylinder head with a torch (propane or acetylene). Never bring a flame into contact with the cylinder head. The direct heat may warp the cylinder head.

3. The valve guides are installed with a slight interference fit. Heat the cylinder head to a temperature of approximately 212-300° F (100-150° C) in an oven or on a hot plate.
4. Remove the cylinder head from the oven or hot plate and place onto wood blocks with the combustion chamber facing up.
5. Drive the old valve guide out from the combustion chamber side of the cylinder head with the valve guide remover (**Figure 68**).
6. After the cylinder head cools, check the valve guide bores for carbon or other contamination. Clean the bores thoroughly.
7. Reheat the cylinder head to approximately 212-300° F (100-150° C).
8. Remove the cylinder head from the oven or hot plate and place it on wood blocks with the combustion chamber facing down.
9. Using the valve guide installer, drive the new valve guide into the cylinder head until the clip on the guide bottoms in the clip recess.
10. After the cylinder head has cooled to room temperature, ream the new valve guides as follows:

   a. Coat the valve guide and valve guide reamer with cutting-oil.

CAUTION

Always rotate the valve guide reamer in the same direction when installing and removing it from the guide. If the reamer is rotated in the opposite direction, the guide will be damaged and will require replacement.

b. Insert the reamer from the top side and rotate the reamer. Continue to rotate the reamer and work it down through the entire length of the new valve guide. Apply additional cutting oil during this procedure.
c. While rotating the reamer in the same direction, withdraw the reamer from the valve guide.
d. Measure the valve guide inside diameter with a small hole gauge. Then measure the small hole gauge with a micrometer to determine the valve guide inside diameter. The valve guide should be within the service specifications in **Table 2**. Continue reaming until this specification is reached.

11. Repeat for the other valve guide.
12. Thoroughly clean the cylinder head and valve guides with solvent to wash out all metal particles. Dry with compressed air.
13. Lightly oil the valve guides to prevent rust.
14. The valve seats must be refaced with a 45 ° cutter after replacing valve guides. Reface the valve seats as described in V*alve Seat Reconditioning* (this section).

Valve Seat Reconditioning

Before reconditioning the valve seats, inspect and measure them as described in this section. The valve and seat angle is 45° (**Figure 61**). No other angles are cut above or below the valve face.

CAUTION
Work slowly and make light cuts during reconditioning. Excessive valve seat cutting will lower the valves into the cylinder head, which will affect valve adjustment, and may require cylinder head replacement.

NOTE
Follow the manufacturer's instructions when using valve seat cutters.

1. Install the 45° cutter onto the valve tool and lightly cut the seat to remove roughness.
2. Measure the valve seat width in the cylinder head (**Figure 69**) with a caliper. Compare the measurement to the specification in **Table 2**.
3. When the valve seat width is within specification, clean the valve seat and valve mating areas.
4. Lightly coat the valve seat with Prussian Blue.
5. Install the appropriate valve into the guide, and then press the valve against the seat.
6. Remove the valve and evaluate where the seat has contacted the valve.
   a. The seat contact area should be in the center of the valve face area.

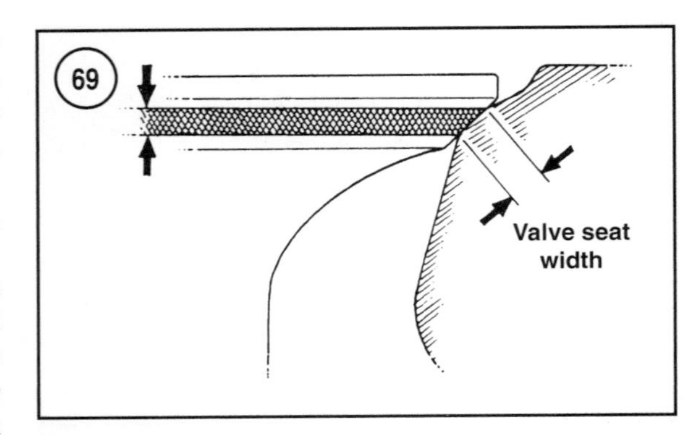

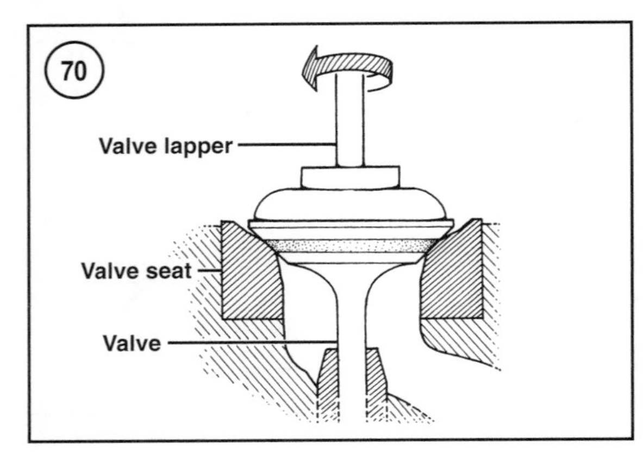

   b. If the seat is high on the valve face area, the valve head may not be within specification, or the seat diameter in the cylinder head is excessive.
   c. If the seat is low on the valve face area, the valve may need to be machined so it fits lower in the seat. Do not continue to cut the valve seat in the cylinder head in order to accommodate the valve. If the seat diameter is excessive, replace the cylinder head.
7. When the seat width is correct, lap the valve as described in this section.

Valve Lapping

Valve lapping restores the seal between the seat and valve without machining if the surfaces are not excessively worn. Lap valves and seats that have been inspected and are within specifications or when the seats have been reconditioned.

1. Lightly coat the valve face with fine-grade lapping compound.
2. Lubricate the valve stem, and then insert the valve into the head.
3. Wet the suction cup on the lapping tool and press it onto the head of the valve (**Figure 70**).
4. Spin the stick back and forth between the hands to lap the valve to the seat. Every 5 to 10 seconds,

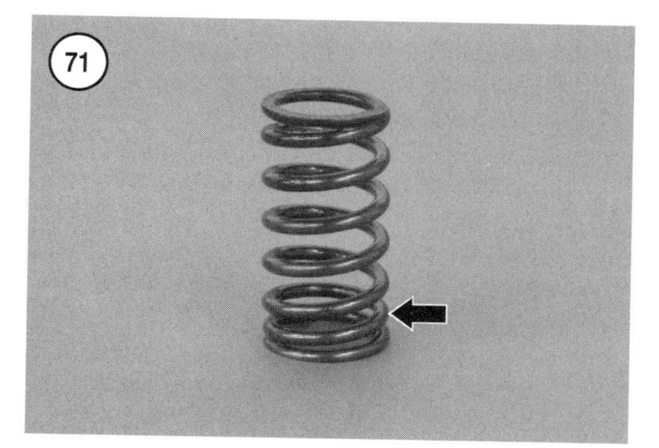

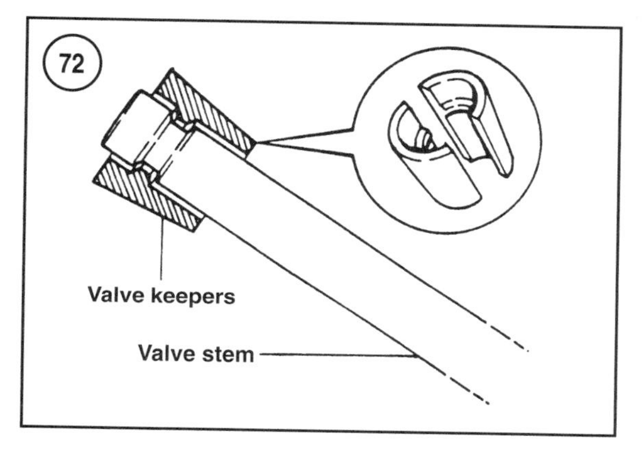

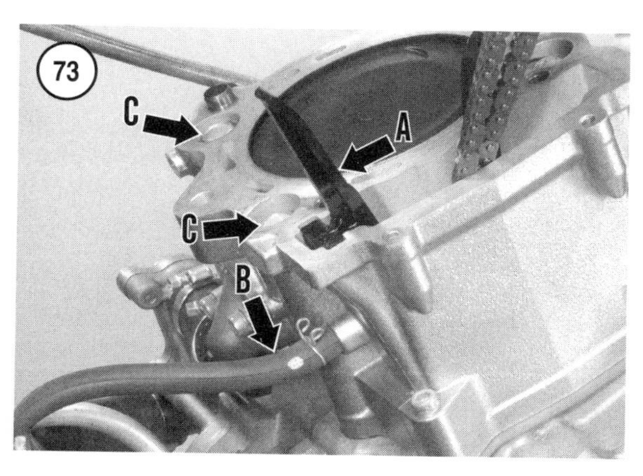

rotate the valve 180° and continue to lap the valve into the seat.

5. Frequently inspect the valve seat. Stop lapping the valve when the valve seat is smooth, even and highly polished. Identify each lapped valve so it will be installed in the correct seat during assembly.

6. Clean the valves and cylinder head in solvent and remove all lapping compound. Any abrasive allowed to remain in the head will cause premature wear and damage to other engine parts.

7. After valve installation, perform a solvent test as described in this chapter. If leaking is detected, remove that valve and repeat the lapping process.

Valve Installation

Perform the following procedure for each set of valve components. All components must be clean and dry. Refer to **Figure 38** or **Figure 39**.

1. Lubricate and install a new oil seal on the valve guide.
2. Coat the valve stem with molybdenum disulfide oil.
3. Insert the appropriate valve into the cylinder head. Rotate the valve as the stem passes through the seal. Hold the valve in place.
4. Install the spring seat into the head.
5. Install the valve springs so the tightly wound spring coils (**Figure 71**) of the spring contact the spring seat.
6. Install the spring retainer.
7. Install a valve spring compressor over the valve assembly. Place the tool squarely over the valve head and spring retainer.
8. Tighten the compressor until the spring retainer is compressed just far enough to install the valve keepers.
9. Insert the keepers into the groove in the valve stem (**Figure 72**).
10. Slowly relieve the pressure on the valve spring and remove the compressor from the head.
11. Tap the end of the valve stem with a soft mallet to ensure that the keepers are fully seated in the valve stem groove.
12. After all the valves are installed, test the valve face-to-seat seal with solvent as described in this chapter.
13. Install the cylinder head as described in this chapter.

CYLINDER

Removal

The cylinder and piston can be removed with the engine in the frame.

1. Remove the cylinder head as described in this chapter.
2. Remove the front cam chain guide (A, **Figure 73**).
3. Detach the oil tank breather hose (B, **Figure 73**).
4. Detach the coolant hose from the coolant joint (**Figure 74**).
5. Remove the lower cylinder mounting bolts (**Figure 75**).
6. Remove the upper cylinder mounting bolts (C, **Figure 73**).
7. Loosen the cylinder by tapping around the base.

CAUTION

Locating dowels that remain in the underside of the cylinder may fall out during cylinder removal.

8. Slowly remove the cylinder from the crankcase, routing the cam chain through the chain tunnel. Secure the cam chain after it passes through the cylinder.
9. Remove the base gasket.
10. If necessary, remove the dowels (A, **Figure 76**).

NOTE

*Fabricate a piston holding fixture as shown in **Figure** 77. Place the tool (B, **Figure** 76) under the piston and straddling the connecting rod. This will limit piston movement and prevent the piston from contacting the crankcase.*

11. Stuff a shop cloth into the crankcase to prevent entrance of small parts and debris.
12. Inspect the cylinder as described in this section.

Inspection

1. If necessary, remove the coolant joint (**Figure 78**) and its O-ring.
2. Remove all gasket residue from the cylinder and crankcase surfaces.
3. Wash the cylinder in solvent and dry with compressed air.
4. Inspect the cylinder bore for obvious scoring or gouges. Damage may indicate replacement is required.
5. Inspect the overall condition of the cylinder, as well as the coolant passages (**Figure 79**) for deposits.
6. Measure the cylinder for wear, taper and out of round. Measure the inside diameter of the cylinder with a bore gauge or inside micrometer as follows:

NOTE

The cylinder is hardened and cannot be bored. If it is not within specification, replace the cylinder.

a. Measure the cylinder at three points (**Figure 80**) along the bore axis. At each point, measure in line (X measurement) with the piston pin, and 90° to the pin (Y measurement). Record and identify the six measurements.
b. Cylinder wear- Use the largest measurement recorded (X or Y) and compare it to the piston diameter to determine the piston-to-cylinder clearance as described in this chapter. Compare the measurement to the specification in **Table 4**. If the clearance is not within the service limit, determine whether the piston, cylinder or both require replacement.
c. Cylinder out of round- Determine the largest Y measurement made. Determine the smallest X measurement made. Determine the difference between the two measurements. Compare

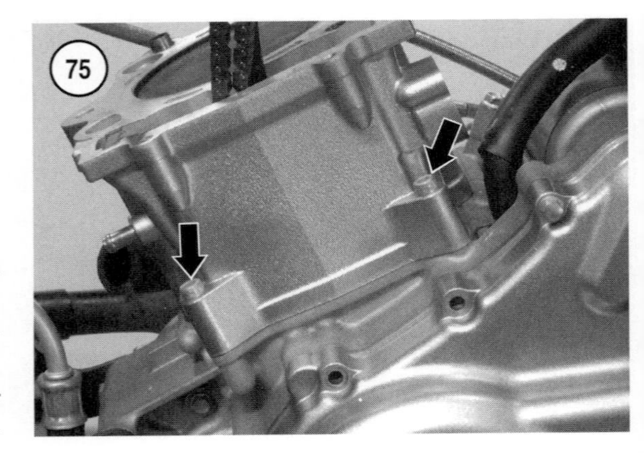

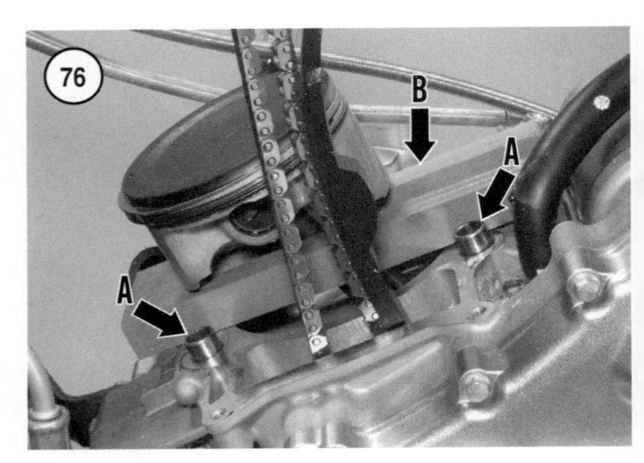

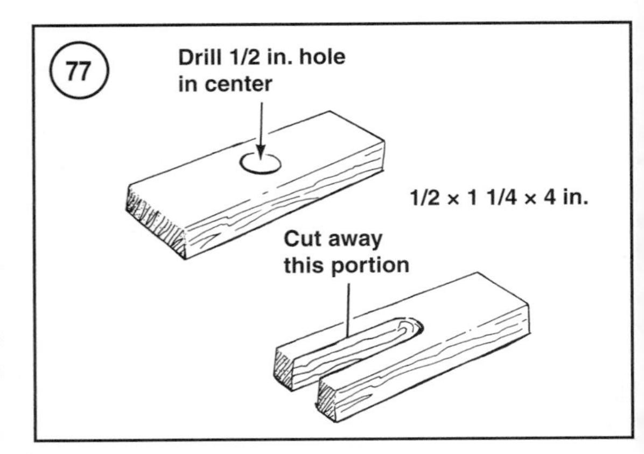

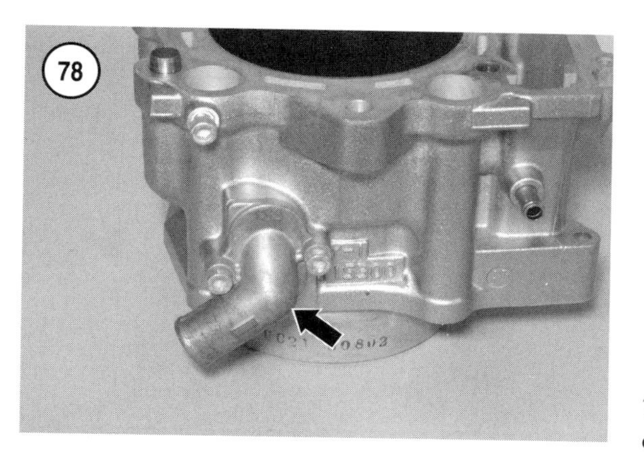

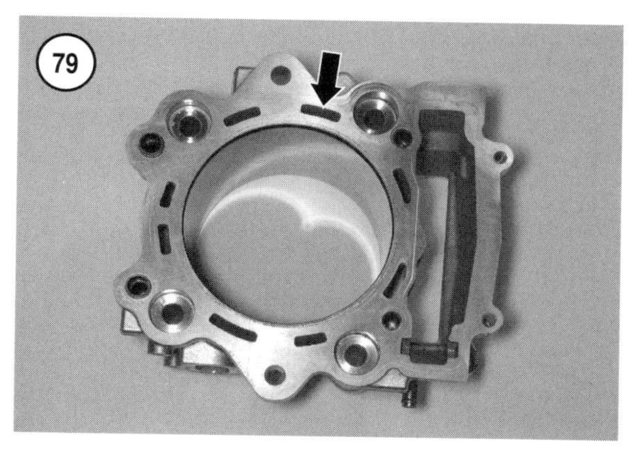

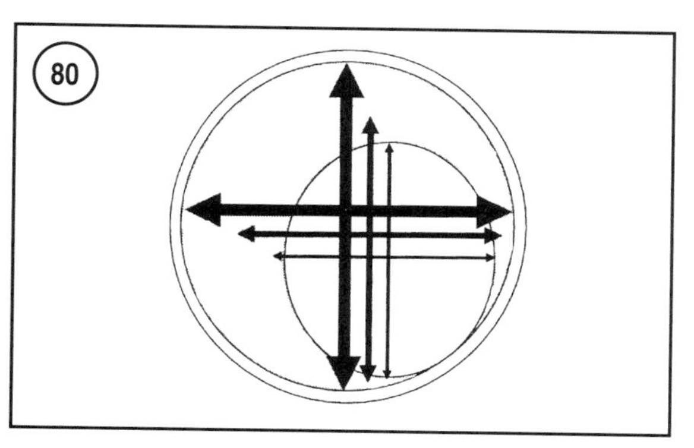

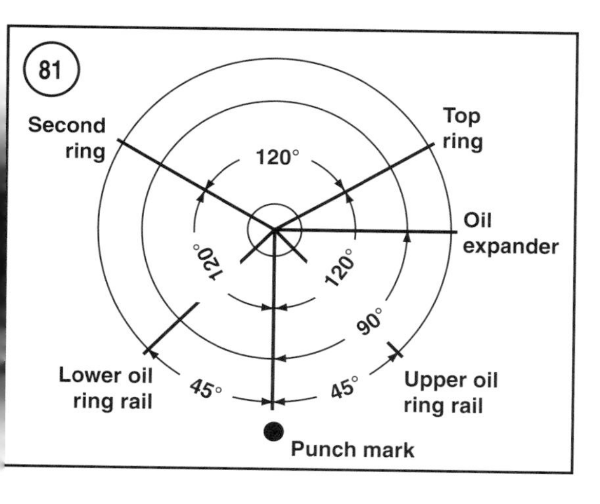

the result to the service limit in **Table 4**. If the cylinder bore is not within the service limit, replace the cylinder.

d. Cylinder taper- Determine the largest X or Y measurement made at the top of the cylinder. Determine the largest X or Y measurement made at the bottom of the cylinder. Determine the difference between the two measurements. Compare the result to the service limit in **Table 4**. If the cylinder bore is not within the service limit, replace the cylinder.

7. If the cylinder requires replacement, provide the dealership or machine shop with the piston and rings.

CAUTION

If the cylinder is within all service limits, lightly deglaze the cylinder. Excessive deglazing may damage the hardened bore. Do not remove the carbon ridge at the top of the cylinder bore. Removal of the buildup will promote oil consumption.

CAUTION

Wash the cylinder as described in this section. Solvents will not remove the fine grit left in the cylinder. This grit will cause premature wear of the rings and cylinder.

8. Wash the cylinder in hot soapy water to remove all residue left from deglazing. Check the cleanliness by passing a clean, white cloth over the bore. No residue should be evident. When the cylinder is thoroughly clean and dry, lightly coat the cylinder bore with oil to prevent corrosion. Wrap the cylinder in plastic until engine reassembly.

9. Perform any service to the piston assembly before installing the cylinder.

Installation

1. Make sure all gasket material is removed from all mating surfaces.
2. If removed, install the dowels (A, **Figure 76**) into the crankcase.
3. Install a new base gasket onto the crankcase.
4. Lubricate the following components with engine oil:
   a. Piston and rings.
   b. Piston pin and small end of connecting rod.
   c. Cylinder bore.
5. Support the piston so the cylinder can be lowered into place.
6. Stagger the piston ring gaps on the piston as shown in **Figure 81**.

7. Lower the cylinder onto the piston, routing the cam chain and rear cam chain guide through the chain tunnel. As the piston enters the cylinder, compress each ring so it can enter the cylinder. When the bottom ring is in the cylinder, remove the holding fixture and lower the cylinder onto the crankcase. Secure the cam chain so it cannot fall into the engine.
8. Lubricate the bolt threads and bolt flanges of the large cylinder mounting bolts with engine oil.
9. Install the upper cylinder mounting bolts (C, **Figure 73**). Using a crossing pattern, tighten the bolts to 15 N•m (11 ft.-lb.). Retighten in a crossing pattern to 50 N•m (37 ft.-lb.).
10. Install the lower cylinder mounting bolts (**Figure 75**) and tighten to 10 N•m (89 in.-lb.).
11. If removed, install the coolant joint and O-ring. Tighten the mounting bolts to 10 N•m (89 in.-lb.).
12. Install the cylinder head as described in this chapter.

PISTON AND PISTON RINGS

Piston Removal

1. Remove the cylinder as described in this chapter.
2. Before removing the piston, hold the rod and try to rock the piston from side to side (**Figure 82**). If rocking (not sliding) motion is detected, this indicates wear on the piston pin, pin bore, rod bushing or a combination of all three parts. Inspection of each component is necessary to determine which parts require replacement.
3. Stuff shop rags around the connecting rod and in the cam chain tunnel to prevent debris and small parts from falling into the crankcase.
4. Remove the circlips (**Figure 83**) from the piston pin bore. Discard the circlips.

CAUTION
Install new circlips during assembly.

5. Push the piston pin out of the piston by hand. If the pin is tight, make the tool shown in **Figure 84** to remove it. Do not drive out the piston pin, as this may damage the piston pin, connecting rod or piston.
6. Lift the piston off the connecting rod.
7. Inspect the piston and piston pin as described in this section.

Piston Inspection

1. Remove the piston rings as described in this section.

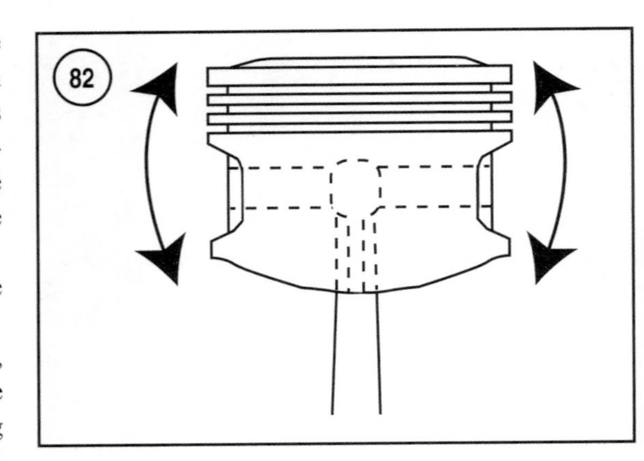

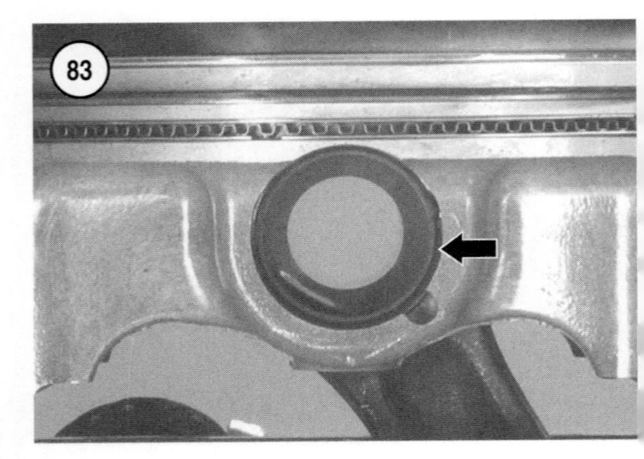

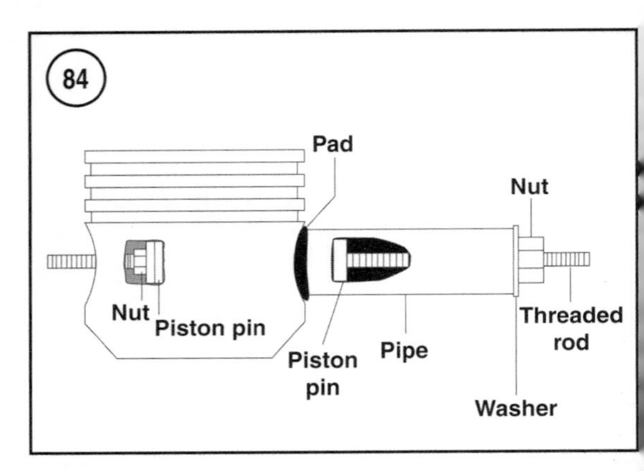

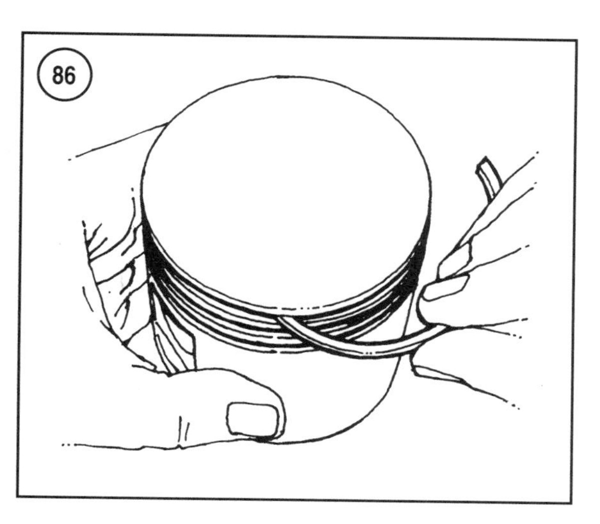
86

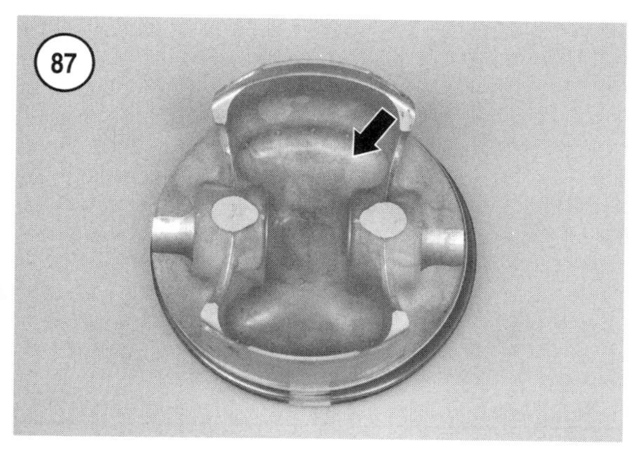
87

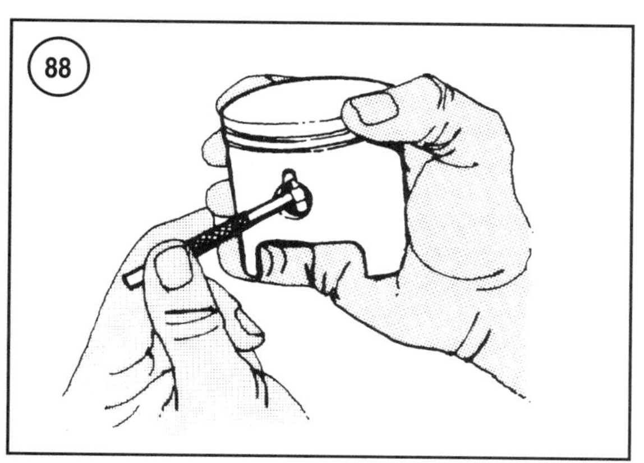
88

CAUTION
Do not use a wire brush to clean the piston.

2. Clean the carbon from the piston crown (**Figure 85**) using a soft scraper and solvent. Do not use tools that can gouge or scratch the surface. This type of damage can cause hot spots on the piston when the engine is running.
3. Clean the piston pin bore, ring grooves and piston skirt. Clean the ring grooves with a soft brush (such as a toothbrush), or use a broken piston ring (**Figure 86**) to remove carbon and oil residue. Polish any mild galling or discoloration off the piston skirt with fine emery cloth and oil.
4. Inspect the piston crown for signs of wear or damage. If the piston is pitted, overheating is likely occurring. This can be caused by a lean fuel mixture and/or preignition. If damage is evident, perform troubleshooting procedures as described in Chapter Two.
5. Inspect the ring grooves for dents, nicks, cracks or other damage. The grooves should be square and uniform around the circumference of the piston. Particularly inspect the top compression ring groove. It is lubricated the least and is nearest the combustion process with its related high temperatures. If the oil ring appears worn, or if it was difficult to remove, the piston has likely overheated and distorted. Replace the piston if any type of damage is detected.
6. Inspect the piston skirt. If the skirt shows signs of severe galling or partial seizure (bits of metal imbedded in the skirt), replace the piston.
7. Inspect the interior (**Figure 87**) of the piston. Check the crown, skirt, piston pin bores and bosses for cracks or other damage. Check the circlip grooves for cleanliness and damage. Replace the piston if necessary.
8. Measure the piston pin bores (**Figure 88**) with a small hole gauge and micrometer. Measure each bore horizontally and vertically. Record the measurements. Compare the largest measurement to the specifications in **Table 4**. Record this measurement to determining the piston pin-to-piston bore clearance.
9. Inspect the piston ring-to-ring groove clearance as described in this section.

Piston-to-Cylinder Clearance Check

Calculate the clearance between the piston and cylinder to determine if the parts can be reused. If parts are not within specification, replace the cylinder, the piston or both. Clean and dry the piston and cylinder before measuring.

1. Measure the outside diameter of the piston. Measure 10 mm (0.39 in.) up from the bottom edge of the piston skirt and 90° to the direction of the piston pin (**Figure 89**). Record the measurement.
2. Determine the clearance by subtracting the piston measurement from the largest cylinder measurement. Determine the cylinder measurements as described in this chapter. If the clearance exceeds the specification in **Table 4**, replace the piston, the cylinder or both to achieve the proper clearance.

4

Piston Pin and Connecting Rod Inspection

1. Clean the piston pin in solvent, and then dry.
2. Inspect the pin for wear or discoloration from overheating.
3. Inspect the piston pin bore in the connecting rod (**Figure 90**). Check for scoring, uneven wear, and discoloration from overheating.
4. Lubricate the piston pin and slide it into the connecting rod. Slowly rotate the pin and check for radial play (**Figure 91**). If play is detectable, one or both of the parts are worn. Specifications for the connecting rod are not available. Therefore, measure the piston pin where it contacts the rod. If it is within specification, replace the rod. If the pin is not within specification, replace the pin and recheck for play in the connecting rod. If play still exists, replace the rod.
5. Determine the piston-to-piston pin clearance as follows:
   a. Measure the piston pin at both ends (**Figure 92**), using a micrometer. Record the measurements. Replace the pin if any measurements exceed the service limit in **Table 4**.
   b. Subtract the smallest piston pin measurement from the largest piston pin bore measurement taken as described in *Piston Inspection* (this section). Replace the piston and pin if they exceed the service limit in **Table 4**.

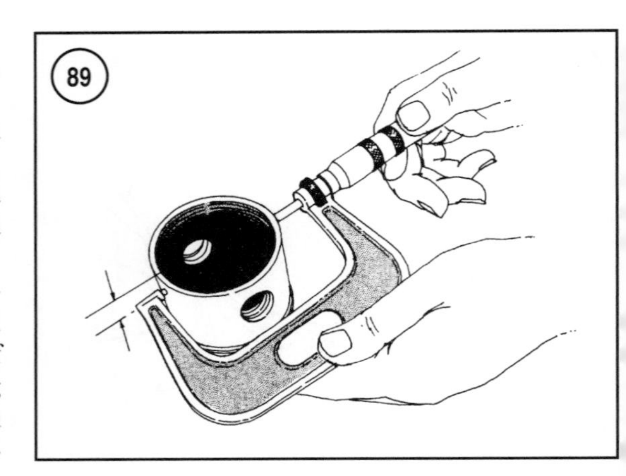
89

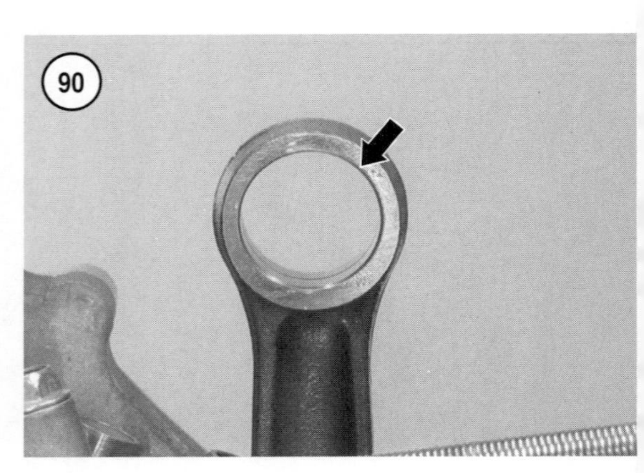
90

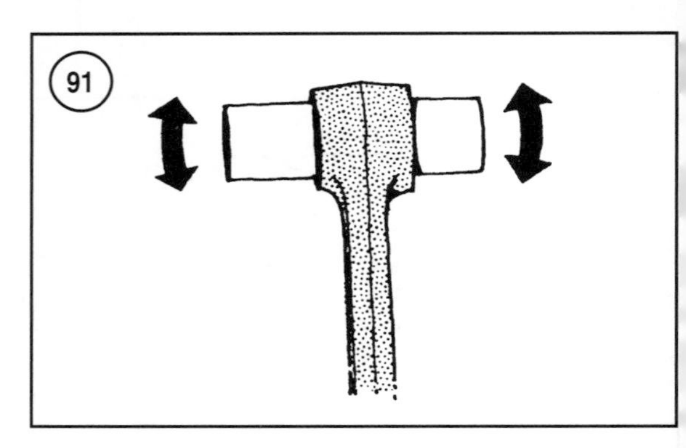
91

Piston Ring Removal and Inspection

WARNING
The piston ring edges are sharp. Be careful when handling them.

NOTE
*There are two ways to remove the rings: with a ring expander tool (**Figure 93**) or by hand (**Figure 94**). The ring expander tool is useful because it removes the rings without damaging them or scratching the piston. If this tool is not available, remove the rings by carefully spreading the end gaps with two thumbs and sliding them off the top of the piston.*

NOTE
The top and second rings have identification marks near their end gaps. These marks are not always visible on used rings. If the rings are going to be reused, mark them for location and direction during disassembly. On original equipment pistons and rings, the top ring is wider than the second ring.

1. Remove the piston rings from the piston, starting with the top ring and working down.
2. Remove the oil ring assembly by first removing the top rail, followed by the bottom rail. Remove (by hand) the expander ring last.
3. Clean and inspect the piston as described in this chapter.
4. Check the piston ring-to-ring groove clearance as follows:
   a. Clean the rings and grooves so accurate measurements can be made with a flat feeler gauge.
   b. Install the top ring into the groove so the ring is fully seated in the groove.

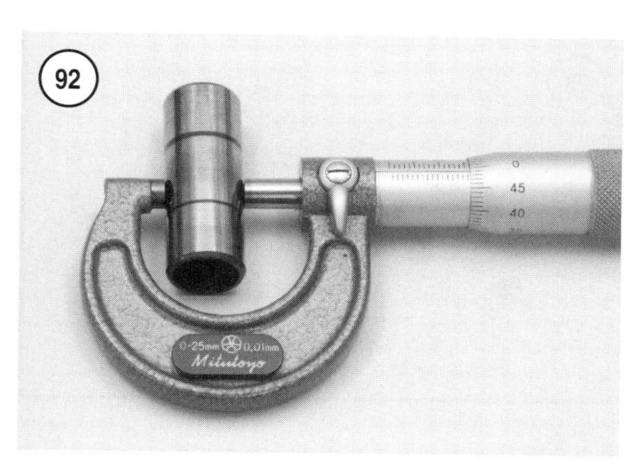

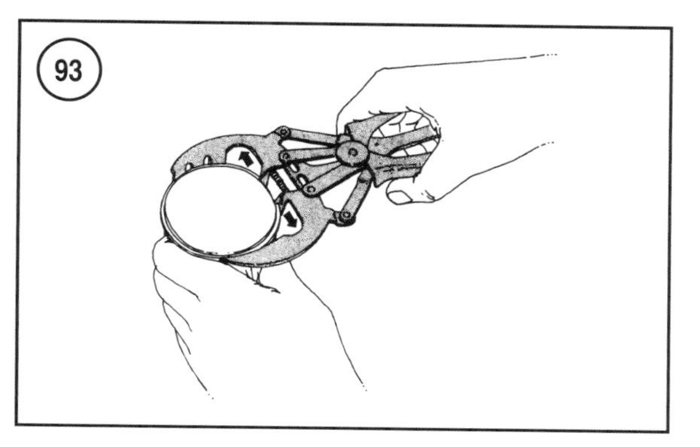

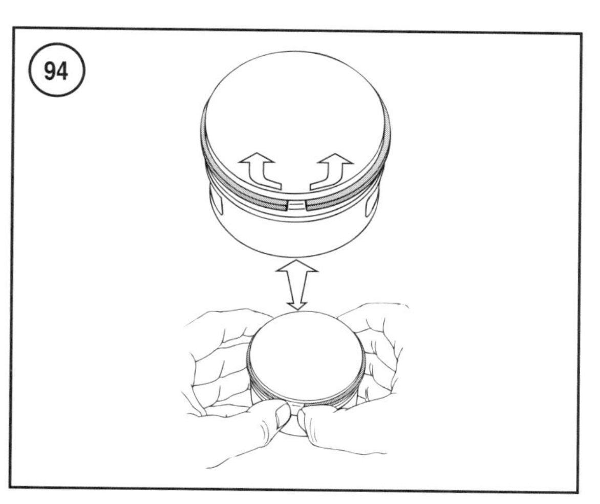

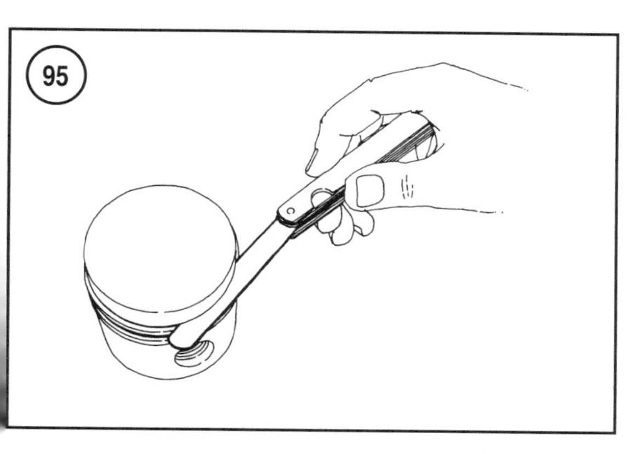

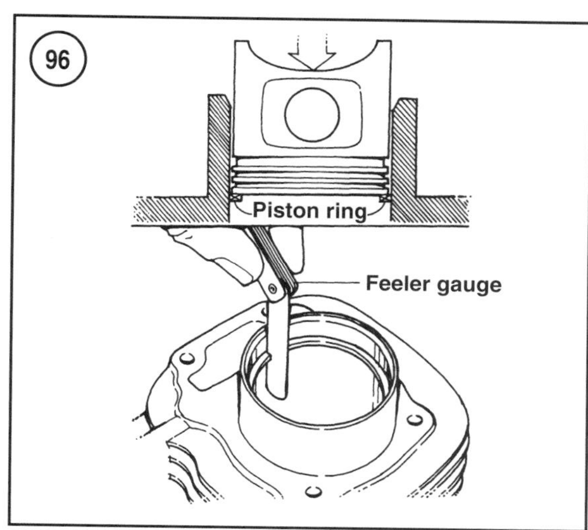

c. Insert a flat feeler gauge between the ring and groove (**Figure 95**). Record the measurement. Repeat this step at other points around the piston. Replace the rings if any measurement exceeds the service limit in **Table 4**. If excessive clearance remains after new rings are installed, replace the piston.

d. Repeat the process for the second compression ring. The oil control ring side clearance is not measured.

5. Inspect the end gap of each ring as follows:
   a. Insert a ring into the bottom of the cylinder. Use the piston to push the ring squarely into the cylinder (**Figure 96**) approximately 10 mm (0.039 in.).
   b. Measure the end gap with a feeler gauge (**Figure 96**). Replace the rings as a set if any gap measurement exceeds the service limit in **Table 4**. If new rings are installed, gap the new rings after the cylinder has been serviced. If the new ring gap is too small, carefully widen the gap using a fine-cut file as shown in **Figure 97**. Work slowly and measure often.

NOTE

Measure only the ring rails of the oil control ring. It is not necessary to measure the expander spacer.

6. Roll each ring around its piston groove (**Figure 98**) and check for binding or snags. Repair minor damage with a fine-cut file.

Piston Ring Installation

If installing new piston rings, hone or deglaze the cylinder. This is necessary to roughen and crosshatch the cylinder surface. The newly honed surface is im-

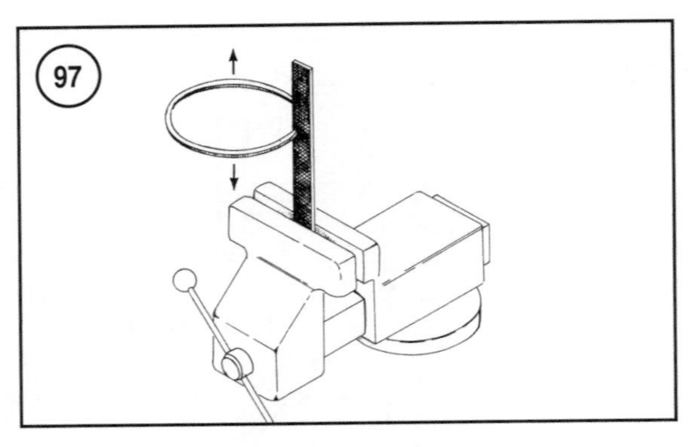

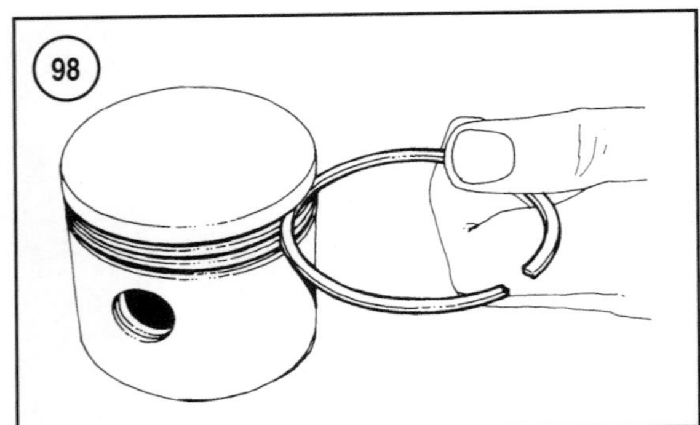

portant in controlling wear and lubrication of the new rings, helping them seat and seal properly. A dealership or machine shop can hone the cylinder for a minimal cost. Refer to *Cylinder Inspection* in this chapter to determine if the cylinder should be honed.

1. Check that the piston and rings are clean and dry.
2. Install the oil control, middle and top rings into their respective grooves as follows:

WARNING
Piston ring edges are sharp. Be careful when handling.

CAUTION
When installing the top and middle rings, check that the top mark, or manufacturer's numbers are facing up. The oil control ring is not marked.

CAUTION
*Install rings using a ring expander (**Figure 93**) or by hand (**Figure 94**). Spread the rings just enough to clear the piston.*

a. Install (by hand) the oil ring expander into the bottom groove.
b. Install the oil ring rails into the bottom groove; one above and one below the expander.
c. Install the middle ring. Make sure the top mark, or manufacturer's number, is facing up.
d. Install the top ring. Make sure the top mark, or manufacturer's number, is facing up.

3. Make sure all rings rotate freely in their grooves.
4. Adjust the ring gaps as described in *Cylinder Installation* (this chapter).

Piston Installation

1. Install the piston rings onto the piston as described in this section.
2. Make sure all parts are clean and ready to install.

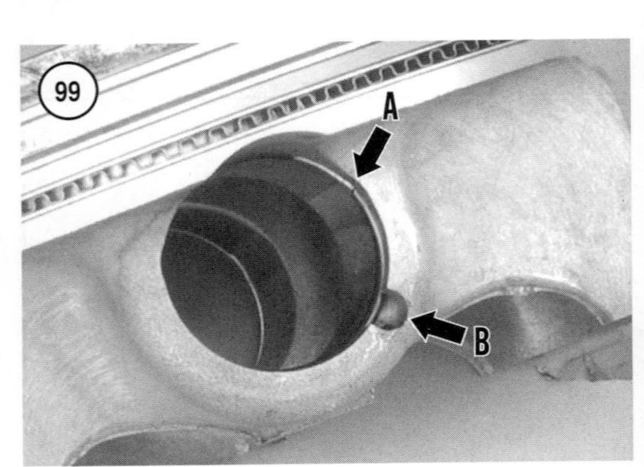

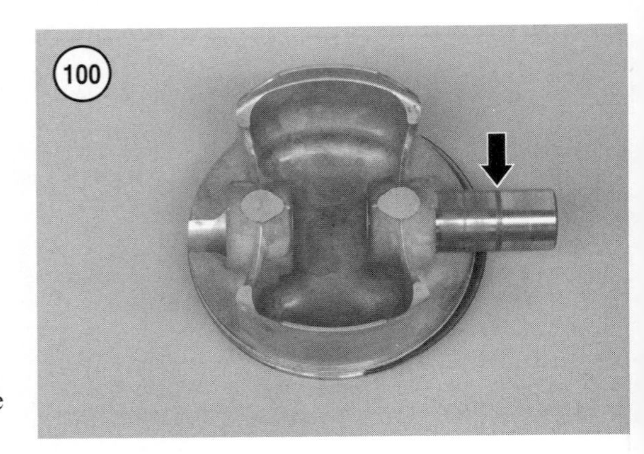

CAUTION
Never install used circlips. Severe engine damage could occur. Circlips fatigue and distort during removal, even though they appear reusable.

3. Install a new circlip into the piston bore groove so the gap (A, **Figure 99**) does not align with the notch (B) on the piston.
4. Lubricate the piston pin, piston pin bores and connecting rod bore with engine oil.
5. Start the piston pin into the open piston pin bore (**Figure 100**).
6. Install the piston onto the connecting rod so the punch mark (A, **Figure 101**) stamped on the piston

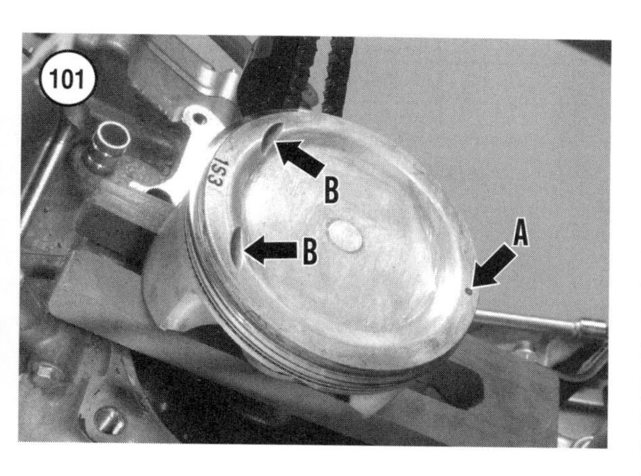

crown is forward. Make sure the two intake valve indentions (B, **Figure 101**) on the piston crown face the intake (rear) side of the engine.

CAUTION
The piston must be installed correctly to accommodate piston pin offset and prevent the valves from striking the piston. Failure to install the piston correctly can damage the engine.

7. Align the piston with the rod, then slide the pin through the rod and into the opposite piston pin bore.
8. Install the remaining piston pin circlip into the piston bore groove so the gap (A, **Figure 99**) does not align with the notch (B) on the piston.
9. Position the ring end gaps as shown in **Figure 81**.
10. Install the cylinder as described in this chapter.
11. Refer to Chapter Five for break-in procedures.

Table 1 GENERAL ENGINE SPECIFICATIONS

Item	Specification
Cylinder arrangement	Single-cylinder
Engine type	Four-stroke, SOHC, four-valve head
Bore × stroke	102 × 84 mm (4.02 × 3.31 in.)
Displacement	686 cc (41.86 cu. in.)
Compression ratio	9.2:1
Ignition type	Electronic
Ignition timing	9 degrees BTDC @ 1600 rpm
Ignition advancer type	Throttle position sensor and electronic
Cooling system	Liquid cooled
Lubrication system	
Type	Dry sump, forced pressure
Oil pump	Trochoid

Table 2 CYLINDER HEAD SPECIFICATIONS

Item	Standard mm (in.)	Service limit mm (in.)
Cylinder head warp	–	0.03 (0.0012)
Rocker arm inside diameter	12.000-12.018 (0.4724-0.4731)	–
Rocker shaft outside diameter	11.981-11.991 (0.4717-0.4721)	–
Rocker arm-to-shaft clearance	0.009-0.037 (0.0004-0.0015)	–
Valve clearance (cold)		
Intake	0.09-0.13 mm (0.0035-0.0051 in.)	–
Exhaust	0.16-0.20 mm (0.0063-0.0079 in.)	–
Valve guide inside diameter		
Intake and exhaust	6.000-6.012 (0.2362-0.2367)	6.050 (0.2382)
Valve stem outside diameter		
Intake	5.975-5.990 (0.2352-0.2358)	5.945 (0.2341)
Exhaust	5.960-5.975 (0.2346-0.2352)	5.930 (0.2335)
Valve stem runout	–	0.01 (0.0004)
Valve stem-to-guide clearance		
Intake	0.010-0.037 (0.0004-0.0015)	0.08 (0.0031)
Exhaust	0.025-0.052 (0.0010-0.0020)	0.10 (0.0039)
Valve face width		
Intake and exhaust	2.26 (0.089)	–

(continued)

Table 2 CYLINDER HEAD SPECIFICATIONS

Item	Standard mm (in.)	Service limit mm (in.)
Valve seat width		
Intake and exhaust	1.0-1.2 (0.039-0.047)	1.6 (0.063)
Valve margin (thickness)		
Intake and exhaust	0.8-1.2 (0.0315-0.0472)	–
Valve spring free length		
Intake and exhaust	38.79 (1.53)	36.85 (1.45)
Valve spring pressure		
Intake and exhaust	169-199 N @ 35.00 mm (37.99-44.73 lb. @ 1.38 in.)	–
Valve spring tilt limit	1.7 mm (0.07 in.)	

Table 3 CAMSHAFT SPECIFICATIONS

Item	Standard mm (in.)	Service limit mm (in.)
Camshaft		
Cam lobe height		
Intake	43.300-43.400 (1.7047-1.7087)	43.200 (1.7008)
Exhaust	43.129-43.229 (1.6980-1.7019)	43.029 (1.6941)
Cam base circle diameter		
Intake	37.026-37.126 (1.4577-1.4617)	36.926 (1.4538)
Exhaust	37.057-37.157 (1.4589-1.4629)	36.957 (1.4550)
Camshaft runout	–	0.03 (0.0012)

Table 4 CYLINDER AND PISTON SPECIFICATIONS

Item	Standard mm (in.)	Service limit mm (in.)
Cylinder		
Bore	102.00-102.010 (4.0157-4.0161)	–
Out of round	–	0.05 (0.002)
Taper	–	0.05 (0.002)
Piston		
Outside diameter*	101.955-101.970 (4.0140-4.0146)	–
Piston-to-cylinder clearance	0.030-0.055 (0.0012-0.0022)	0.13 (0.005)
Piston-pin bore inside diameter	23.004-23.015 (0.9057-0.9061)	23.045 (0.9073)
Piston pin outside diameter	22.991-23.000 (0.9052-0.9055)	22.971 (0.9044)
Piston pin clearance	0.004-0.024 (0.0002-0.0009)	0.074 (0.0029)
Piston rings		
Ring-to-groove clearance		
Top	0.030-0.070 (0.0012-0.0028)	0.12 (0.005)
Second	0.030-0.070 (0.0012-0.0028)	0.12 (0.005)
Ring end gap (installed)		
Top	0.20-0.35 (0.008-0.014)	0.60 (0.024)
Second	0.75-0.90 (0.03-0.04)	1.25 (0.049)
Oil ring (side rails)	0.20-0.70 (0.008-0.028)	–
Ring thickness		
Top and second	1.20 (0.047)	–

*Measured at a point 10 mm (0.39 in.) from the bottom of the piston shirt. See text for information.

Table 5 ENGINE TOP END TORQUE SPECIFICATIONS

Item	N•m	in.-lb.	ft.-lb.
Cam chain tensioer cap bolt	20	–	15
Cam chain tensioner mounting bolts	10	89	–
Cam sprocket mounting bolts	20	–	15
Camshaft bearing retainer bolts	10	89	–
Coolant joint bolts	10	89	–
Cylinder bolts*			
Upper bolts	50	–	37
Lower bolts	10	89	–
Cylinder head bolts*			
Upper bolts (Figure 24)	35	–	26
Lower bolts (Figures 20 and 21)	38	–	28
Left side bolts (Figure 19)	10	89	–
Cylinder head side cover bolts	10	89	–
Decompressor weight assembly bolts	20	–	15
Exhaust pipe clamp bolt	16	–	12
Exhaust pipe nuts	20	–	15
Heat shield bolts	8	71	–
Muffler clamp bolt	18	–	13
Muffler mounting bolts	38	–	28
Oil pipe banjo bolts	20	–	15
Oil pipe retaining bolt	10	89	–
Spark plug	13	115	–
Upper engine bracket bolts	33	–	24
Upper engine mounting bolt	40	–	29.5

*Refer to tightening procedure in text.

4

CHAPTER FIVE

ENGINE LOWER END

This chapter describes service procedures for the following lower end components:

1. Crankcase covers.
2. Torque limiter.
3. Starter idle gear.
4. Flywheel.
5. Starter clutch.
6. Camshaft chain and guides.
7. Primary drive gear.
8. Balancers.
9. Oil pump.
10. Crankshaft.
11. Crankcase.

Throughout the text there is reference to the left and right sides of the engine. This refers to the engine as it sits in the vehicle's frame, not as it sits on the workbench.

Refer to **Table 1** and **Table 2** at the end of this chapter.

SERVICING ENGINE IN FRAME

Many engine components can be serviced with the engine mounted in the frame. The following components can be serviced with the engine mounted in the frame:

1. Cylinder head cover.
2. Camshafts.
3. Cylinder head.
4. Cylinder and piston.
5. Water pump.
6. Clutch.
7. Oil pump.
8. Fuel injection.
9. Alternator.
10. Starter.
11. Exhaust system.

ENGINE

Removal/Installation

1. Park the vehicle on a level surface and set the parking brake.
2. Drain the engine oil as described in Chapter Three.
3. Drain the engine coolant as described in Chapter Three.
4. Disconnect the electrical cable from the negative battery terminal (Chapter Nine).
5. Remove the exhaust system, and on 2015-on models disconnect the hose from the reed valve cover plate on the cylinder head as described in this chapter.
6. Remove the fuel tank as described in Chapter Eight.
7. Remove the throttle body as described in Chapter Eight.
8. Remove the drive sprocket as described in Chapter Eleven.
9. Remove the right footrest as described in Chapter Fourteen.

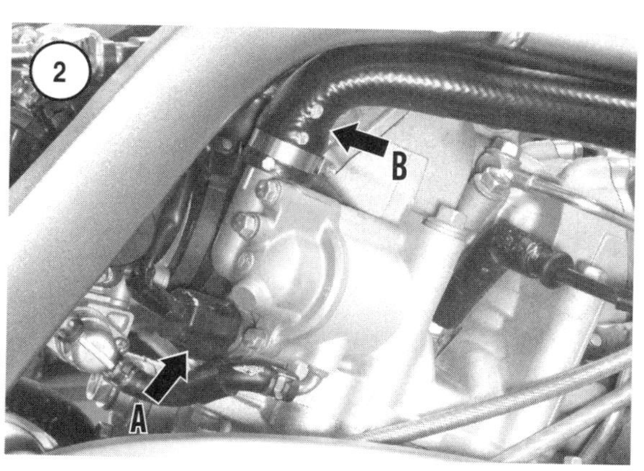

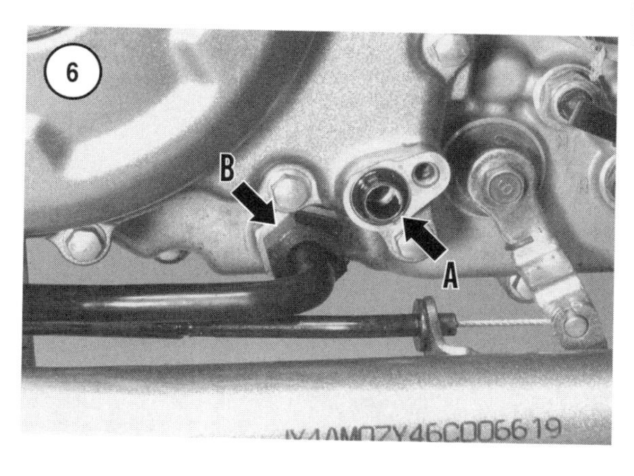

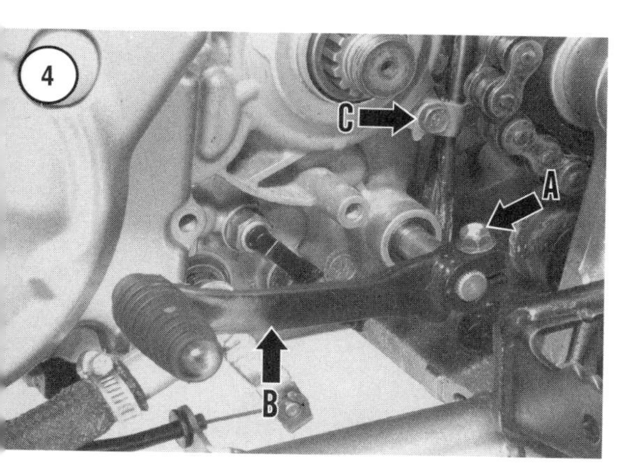

10. Disconnect the spark plug cap from the spark plug.

11. Push back the boot, then disconnect the wire connector (**Figure 1**) from the starter motor terminal.

12. Disconnect the coolant temperature sensor connector (A, **Figure 2**).

13. Remove the crankcase bolt (A, **Figure 3**) that secures the ground wire terminal.

14. Remove the speed sensor retaining bolt (B, **Figure 3**) to release the wire clamp. Reinstall the bolt to secure the sensor.

15. Disconnect the connectors for the speed sensor, stator and crankshaft position sensor above the rear of the engine.

16. Remove the clamp bolt (A, **Figure 4**), and then remove the shift lever (B).

17. Remove the seal retainer bolt (C, **Figure 4**) that secures the wire clamp.

18. Detach the oil return hose fitting after removing the retaining bolt (**Figure 5**). Do not lose the dowel and O-ring (A, **Figure 6**) which may remain in the engine.

19. Unscrew the oil intake line fitting (B, **Figure 6**).

20. Pull off the connectors from the terminals on the neutral switch (A, **Figure 7**) and the reverse switch (B).

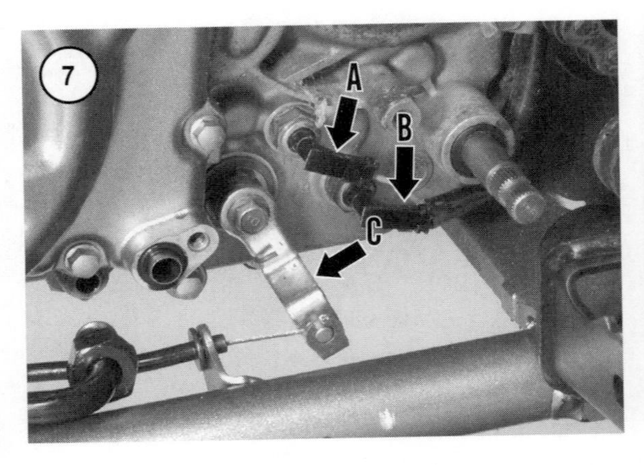

21. Refer to Chapter Three and adjust the reverse cable to obtain maximum slack. Detach the reverse cable end from the reverse lever (C, **Figure 7**).
22. Remove the clutch and parking brake cable retaining brackets (**Figure 8**).
23. Refer to Chapter Three and adjust the clutch cable to obtain maximum slack. Detach the clutch cable end from the clutch release lever (A, **Figure 9**). Loosen the adjustment nuts and separate the cable from the bracket (B, **Figure 9**).
24. Remove the rear brake light switch holder bracket (**Figure 10**) from the right crankcase cover.
25. Refer to Chapter Fourteen and detach the parking brake cable from the brake lever and swing arm. It is not necessary to detach the front end of the cable. This prevents cable interference during engine removal.
26. Loosen the clamp and detach the radiator hose (B, **Figure 2**) from the thermostat cover.
27. Loosen the clamp and detach the radiator hose (**Figure 11**) from the water pump.
28. Verify that all engine wiring or hoses have been disconnected from the frame.
29. If the engine is going to be disassembled, consider removing the following parts for ease of service and weight reduction during engine removal.
   a. Alternator (Chapter Nine).

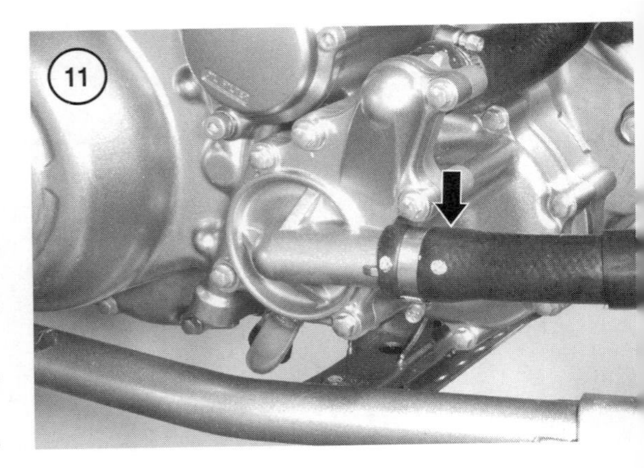

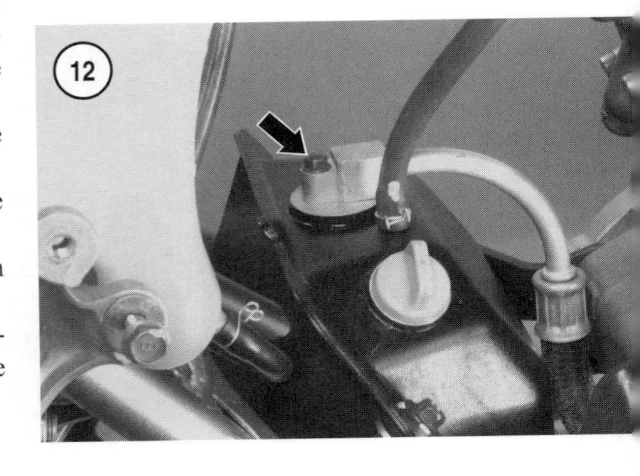

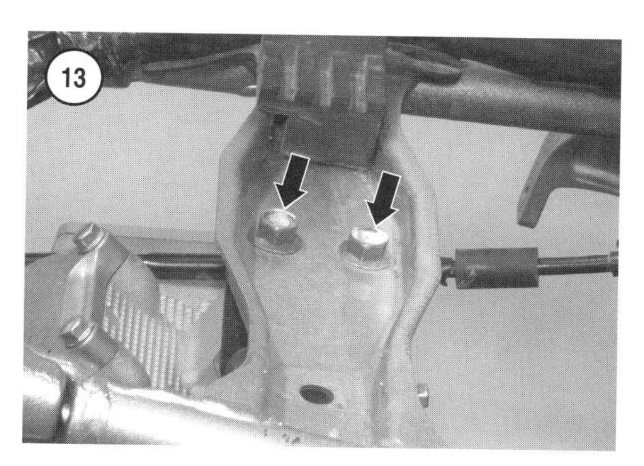

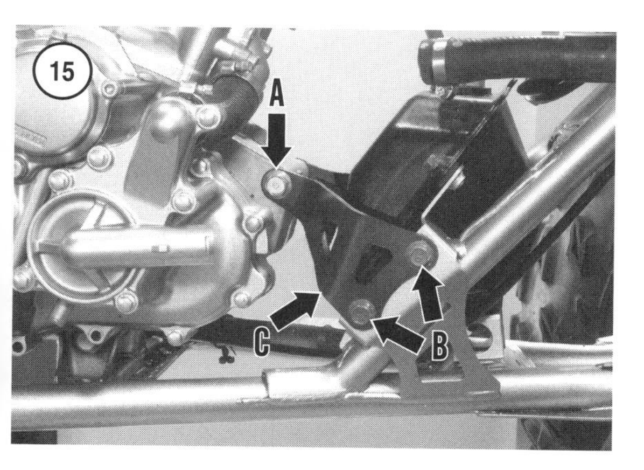

b. Starter (Chapter Nine).
c. Cylinder head (Chapter Four).
d. Cylinder and piston (Chapter Four).
e. Clutch (Chapter Six).
f. External shift mechanism (Chapter Six).
g. Oil pump (this chapter).

30. Remove the engine skidplate as described in Chapter Fifteen.

31. Remove the bolt (**Figure 12**) securing the oil return line fitting on the top of the oil tank and move the oil line out of the way. Cover the dowel and O-ring in the top of the tank to prevent contamination.

32. Place tape or other material on the frame to protect it and the engine.

33. If the cylinder head remains in place, remove the upper mounting bracket bolts (**Figure 13**).

34. Remove the upper engine mounting bolt (A, **Figure 14**) and bracket (B).

35. Place a jack underneath the engine and support the engine with just enough pressure to remove weight from the lower engine mounting bolts when removing them. Place a block of wood between the jack and engine to protect the engine crankcase.

36. Remove the nut, and then remove the front mounting bolt (A, **Figure 15**).

37. On each side, remove the mounting bracket bolts (B, **Figure 15**). Then, remove the brackets (C, **Figure 15**).

38. Remove the nut (**Figure 16**), and then remove the lower mounting bolt.

NOTE

The rear mounting bolt also serves as the swing arm pivot bolt. Pull out the bolt just enough to allow engine removal. Allow the bolt to remain in the left side of the swing arm so it will stay in place.

39. Remove the nut and washer (**Figure 17**). Then, withdraw the rear mounting bolt just enough to release the engine.

40. Remove the engine through the right side of the frame.

41. Reverse the removal steps to install the engine while noting the following:

a. Lubricate the rear engine mounting bolt before installation. The bolt also serves as the swing arm pivot bolt.

b. Install and finger-tighten all engine mounting bolts. Then, tighten the bolts to the specified torque once they have all been installed.

c. Tighten the upper engine bracket bolts to 33 N•m (24 ft.-lb.).

d. Tighten the upper engine mounting bolt to 40 N•m (30 ft.-lb.).

e. Tighten the rear engine mounting bolt to 100 N•m (74 ft.-lb.).

f. Tighten the lower engine mounting bolt to 66 N•m (49 ft.-lb.).

g. Tighten the front engine mounting bolt to 66 N•m (49 ft.-lb.).

h. Tighten the front engine mounting bracket bolts to 41 N•m (30 ft.-lb.).

i. Tighten the oil intake line fitting (B, **Figure 6**) to 35 N•m (26 ft.-lb.).

j. Make sure the dowel and O-ring are installed in the engine (**Figure 6**) and oil tank holes.

k. Tighten the oil return hose fitting bolt (**Figure 5**) to 10 N•m (89 in.-lb.).

l. Tighten the oil tank return line fitting bolt (**Figure 12**) to 10 N•m (89 in.-lb.).

m. Install the right footrest and rear brake pedal as described in Chapter Fourteen.

n. Tighten the clutch and parking brake cable bracket bolt to 7 N•m (62 in.-lb.).

o. Fill the engine with oil as described in Chapter Three.

p. Fill the cooling system as described in Chapter Three.

q. Adjust the throttle cable, clutch cable, reverse cable and drive chain as described in Chapter Three.

r. Start the engine and check for leaks and proper operation.

s. If the engine was overhauled, observe the *Engine Break-in* procedure in this chapter.

LEFT CRANKCASE COVER

The left crankcase cover must be removed for access to the flywheel, stator, torque limiter and starter idle gear.

Removal and Installation

1. Disconnect the electrical cable from the negative battery terminal (Chapter Nine).

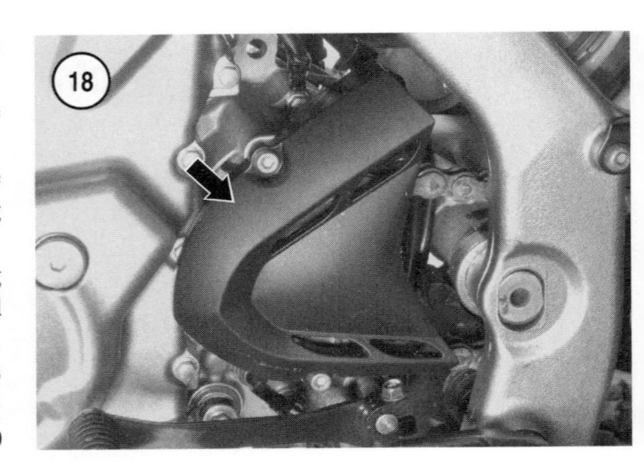

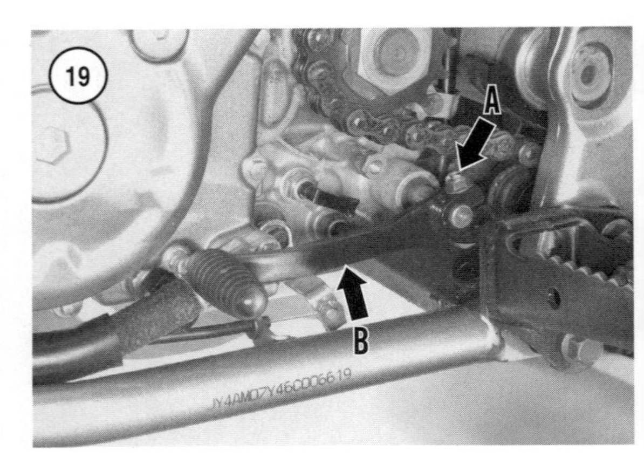

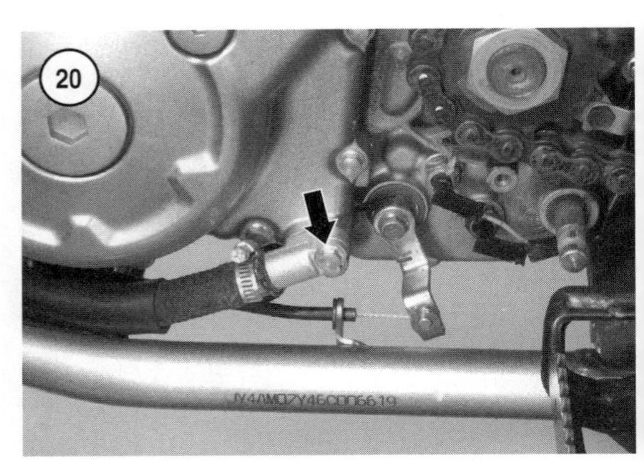

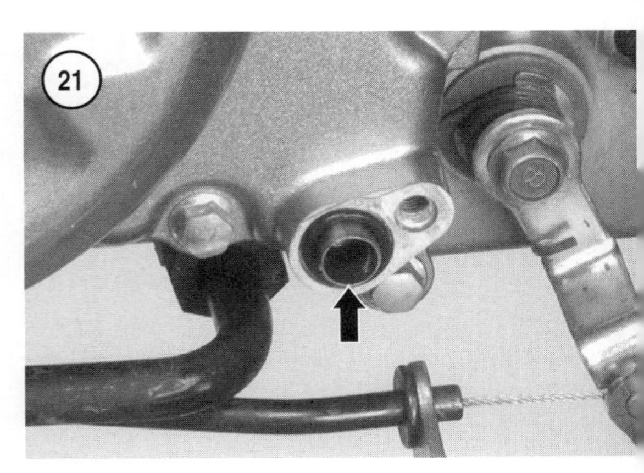

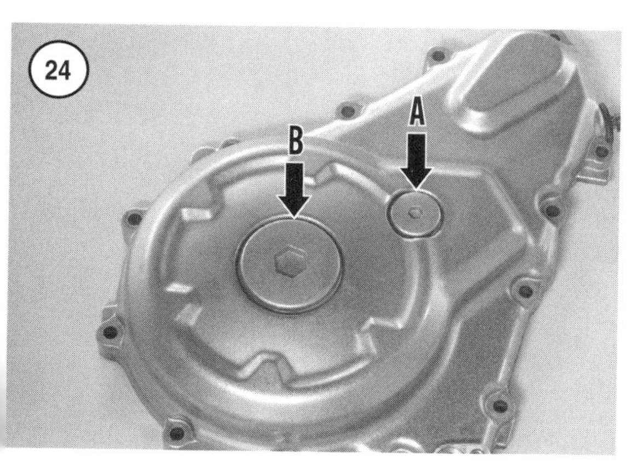

2. Drain the engine oil as described in Chapter Three.
3. Remove the front fender as described in Chapter Fifteen.
4. Disconnect the round 3-wire stator connector and the white 2-wire crankshaft position sensor connector located above the rear of the engine.
5. Detach the plastic bands securing the stator and crankshaft position sensor wires. Note the wire routing for reinstallation.
6. Remove the drive sprocket cover (**Figure 18**).
7. Remove the clamp bolt (A, **Figure 19**), and then remove the shift lever (B).
8. Remove the bolt (**Figure 20**) securing the oil return hose fitting. Do not lose the dowel and O-ring (**Figure 21**) which may remain in the fitting or in the cover.
9. Loosen the fourteen bolts securing the left crankcase cover (**Figure 22**) 1/4 turn at a time in a crossing pattern until fully loosened. Remove the bolts and cover. If necessary, lightly tap the cover to free it from the engine.
10. Remove and discard the gasket.
11. Account for the two dowels (**Figure 23**) that may remain in the crankcase or cover.
12. Remove the timing plug (A, **Figure 24**) and the flywheel nut plug (B) from the cover and inspect the O-ring on each plug. Lubricate the O-rings.
13. If necessary, inspect the stator and crankshaft position sensor as described in Chapter Nine.
14. Reverse the removal steps to install the left crankcase cover while noting the following:
   a. Make sure both dowels (**Figure 23**) are in place.
   b. Install a new cover gasket.
   c. Using a crossing pattern, tighten the left crankcase cover bolts evenly to 10 N•m (89 in.-lb.).
   d. Tighten the oil return hose fitting bolt (**Figure 20**) to 10 N•m (89 in.-lb.).
   e. Tighten the timing plug (A, **Figure 24**) to 6 N•m (53 in.-lb.) and the flywheel nut plug (B) to 10 N•m (89 in.-lb.).
   f. Tighten the drive sprocket cover bolts to 10 N•m (89 in.-lb.).

TORQUE LIMITER

The ATV is equipped with a torque limiter that prevents damage to the starter and engine components should kickback occur.

Removal/Inspection/Installation

1. Remove the left crankcase cover as described in this chapter.
2. Remove the torque limiter (**Figure 25**) by pulling it straight out from the crankcase.

CAUTION
The torque limiter is available only as a unit assembly. Do not disassemble the torque limiter.

NOTE
If the gear teeth on the torque limiter are damaged, also inspect the gear teeth on the starter idle gear.

3. Inspect the torque limiter for damaged gear teeth (A, **Figure 26**) or other damage. Inspect the shaft (B, **Figure 26**) on the torque limiter for scoring or other damage.
4. Inspect the bearing bore (**Figure 27**) in the crankcase.
5. Inspect the bearing bore (**Figure 28**) in the cover. Replace the cover if damaged. Also inspect the shaft on the torque limiter where it enters the cover.
6. Install the torque limiter, making sure the gear teeth engage properly with the starter and starter idle gear.
7. Install the left crankcase cover as described in this chapter.

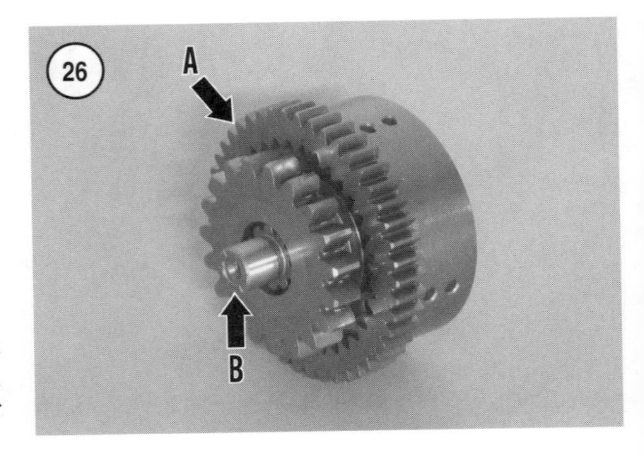

STARTER IDLE GEAR

Removal/Inspection/Installation

1. Remove the torque limiter as described in this chapter.
2. Remove the idle gear (A, **Figure 29**) and the shaft (B).
3. Inspect the idle gear for abnormal wear or tooth damage. Replace if necessary.
4. Inspect the shaft for abnormal wear or damage. Replace if necessary.
5. Make sure the shaft fits snugly in the bores in the crankcase and crankcase cover.
6. Installation is the reverse of the removal steps. Lubricate all parts with engine oil before installation.

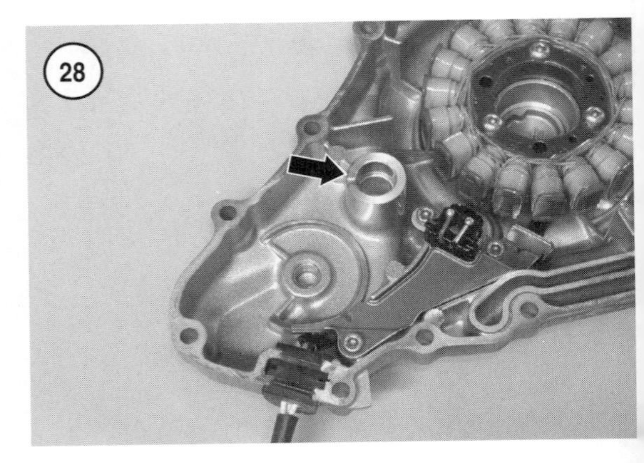

FLYWHEEL (ALTERNATOR ROTOR) AND STARTER CLUTCH

The alternator rotor, mounted on the flywheel, contains the magnets that energize the alternator stator coils. The alternator rotor and flywheel are available only as a unit assembly. The flywheel can be removed with the engine in the frame.

Tools

Special tools are required to remove the flywheel from the crankshaft. Before starting the procedure, obtain the following:

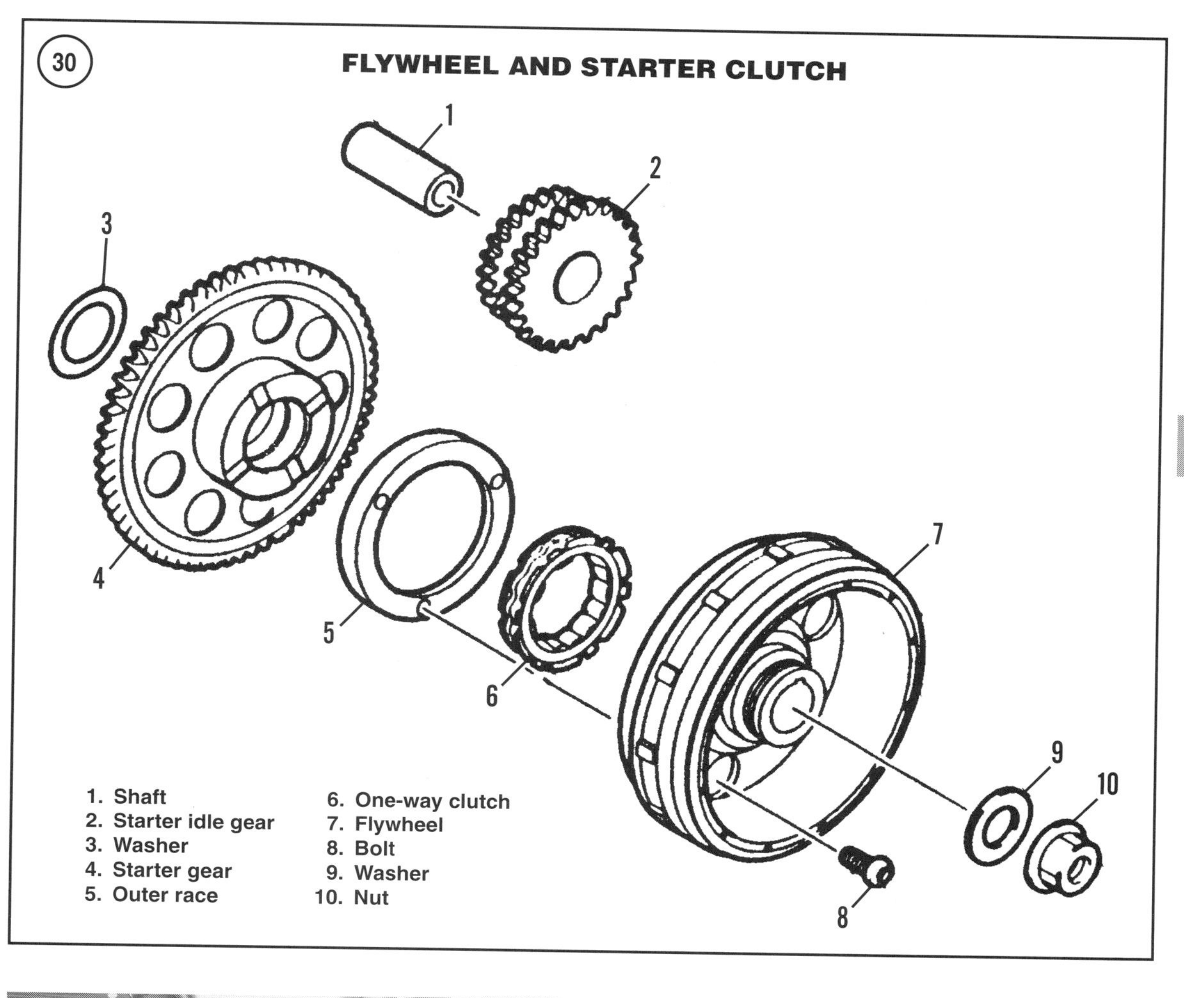

1. Flywheel puller (Yamaha part No. YM-01404; Motion Pro part No. 08-0349 or an equivalent).
2. Flywheel holder (Yamaha part No. 90890-01701 or an equivalent).

Removal

Refer to **Figure 30**.

1. Remove the left crankcase cover as described in this chapter.

CAUTION

Do not damage or disfigure any projections on the flywheel rim when holding the flywheel. Doing so will affect crankshaft position sensor operation.

2. Prevent flywheel rotation using a flywheel holding tool (A, **Figure 31**).
3. Loosen the flywheel retaining nut (B, **Figure 31**). Then, remove the nut and washer.

CAUTION

Do not try to remove the flywheel without a puller. Any attempt to do so will damage the crankshaft and flywheel.

CAUTION

If the flywheel cannot be removed, do not force the puller. Excessive force will strip the flywheel threads, causing damage. Take the engine to a dealership to have the flywheel removed.

4. Thread the flywheel puller (**Figure 32**) onto the flywheel. Make sure the puller fully engages the flywheel threads. Tighten the puller bolt against the crankshaft end.
5. Hold the puller flats with a wrench and gradually tighten the flywheel puller bolt until the flywheel pops off the crankshaft taper.
6. Remove the puller from the flywheel.
7. Remove the flywheel and starter clutch assembly.
8. Remove the Woodruff key (A, **Figure 33**).
9. Remove the starter gear (B, **Figure 33**).
10. Remove the washer (**Figure 34**).
11. Inspect and lubricate the parts as described in this section.
12. Reverse the removal steps to install the flywheel and starter clutch while noting the following:
    a. Lubricate the starter gear and crankshaft with engine oil.
    b. Rotate the starter gear clockwise while installing the flywheel to engage the starter clutch.
    c. Tighten the flywheel nut to 60 N•m (44 ft.-lb.).

Inspection

1. Check starter clutch operation as follows:
    a. With the starter gear facing up, turn the gear counterclockwise. The gear should turn freely and smoothly in that direction (**Figure 35**).
    b. Attempt to turn the gear clockwise. The gear should not turn.
    c. If the gear turns in both directions or is always locked, disassemble and inspect the clutch assembly.
2. Remove the starter gear from the flywheel. Extract the gear from the clutch while turning the gear counterclockwise.
3. Clean and inspect the clutch assembly (**Figure 30**).
    a. Inspect the starter gear teeth (A, **Figure 36**) for wear or damage.

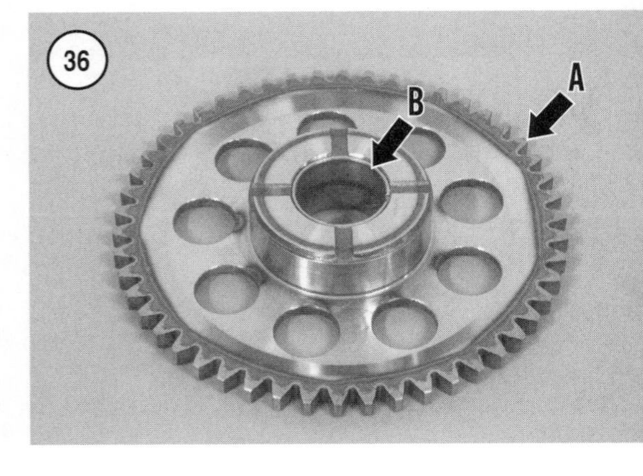

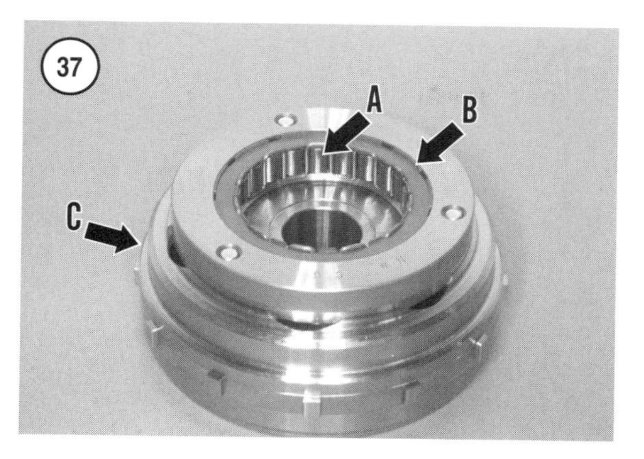

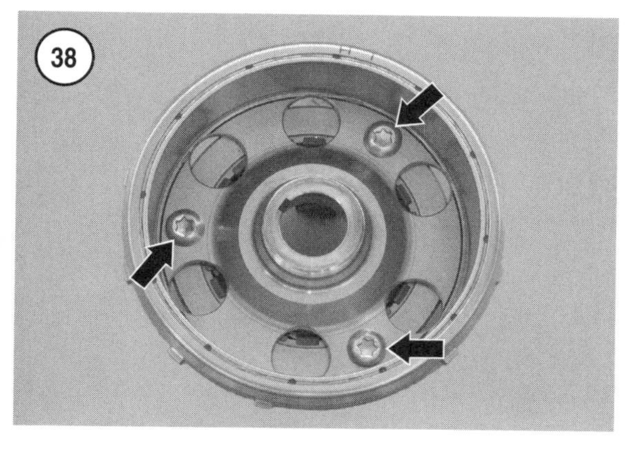

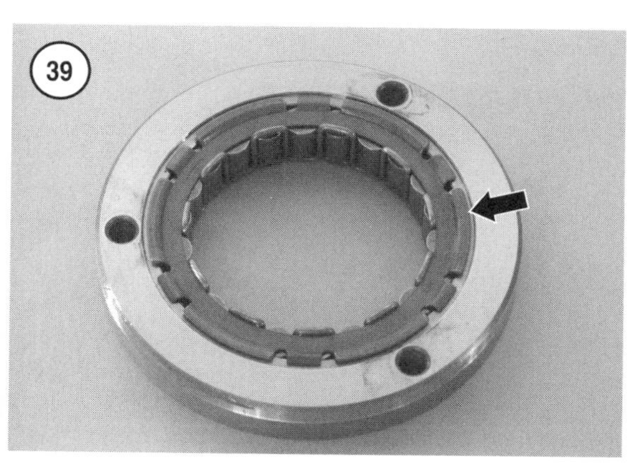

b. Inspect the starter gear bushing (B, **Figure 36**) and crankshaft for damage. Install the gear onto the crankshaft. The gear should rotate smoothly with no play.

c. Inspect the clutch rollers (A, **Figure 37**). The rollers should be undamaged and operate smoothly.

4. To replace the one-way clutch, perform the following:
   a. Secure the flywheel with a strap or band wrench.
   b. Using an impact driver, remove the one-way clutch mounting bolts (**Figure 38**).
   c. Separate the clutch assembly (B, **Figure 37**) from the flywheel (C).
   d. Install the one-way clutch into the outer race so the flange on the one-way clutch fits into the recess in the outer race as shown in **Figure 39**.
   e. Apply a medium-strength threadlock to the threads of each mounting bolt.
   f. Install the one-way clutch mounting bolts finger-tight. Then, tighten the bolts to 30 N•m (22 ft.-lb.).
5. Lubricate the clutch rollers with engine oil.
6. Install the starter gear into the flywheel. Turn the starter gear counterclockwise and twist it squarely into the flywheel. When the starter gear is fully seated, check that it turns only in the counterclockwise direction.
7. Clean and inspect the flywheel components.

WARNING

Replace the flywheel if damaged. The flywheel can fly apart at high crankshaft speeds, causing severe personal injury and damage to the ATV.

   a. Inspect the flywheel for cracks and damage.
   b. Inspect the taper in the bore of the flywheel and on the crankshaft for damage.

NOTE

A bent or sheared Woodruff key will cause flywheel misalignment, resulting in incorrect ignition timing.

   c. Inspect the Woodruff key (A, **Figure 33**), crankshaft keyway, flywheel nut and washer for damage.

CAMSHAFT CHAIN AND GUIDES

The camshaft chain and guides (**Figure 40**) are located behind the flywheel and starter clutch on the left side of the crankcase. The front camshaft chain guide can be removed after cylinder head removal.

5

Removal/Inspection/Installation

1. Remove the cylinder head as described in Chapter Four.
2. Remove the flywheel and starter clutch as described in this chapter.
3. If not previously removed, remove the front chain guide (A, **Figure 40**).
4. Remove the rear cam chain guide retaining bolts (B, **Figure 40**).
5. Remove the rear chain guide (C, **Figure 40**).
6. Lower the chain (D, **Figure 40**) through the crankcase and remove it from the crankshaft sprocket.
7. Inspect the camshaft chain (A, **Figure 41**) for wear and damage. Check for excessive play between the links, indicating worn rollers and pins. If chain replacement is necessary, also inspect the crankshaft drive sprocket and the camshaft driven sprocket.
8. Inspect the guides (B, **Figure 41**) for excessive wear (grooves), cuts or other damage. Replace if excessively worn or damaged.
9. Reverse the removal steps to install the camshaft chain and guides. Tighten the rear cam chain guide retaining bolts to 10 N•m (89 in.-lb.).

RIGHT CRANKCASE COVER

The right crankcase cover must be removed for access to the clutch, external shift mechanism, oil pump, balancer gears and primary drive gears.

Removal and Installation

1. Drain the engine oil as described in Chapter Three.
2. Remove the exhaust pipe as described in Chapter Four.
3. Remove the oil tube upper banjo bolt (**Figure 42**).
4. Remove the oil tube retainer bolt (A, **Figure 43**) and oil tube lower banjo bolt (B). Remove the oil tube (C, **Figure 43**).
5. Refer to Chapter Three and adjust the clutch cable to obtain maximum slack. Detach the clutch cable end from the clutch release lever (A, **Figure 44**) and the cable bracket (B).
6. Remove the engine oil filter as described in Chapter Three.
7. Remove the water pump as described in Chapter Ten.
8. Remove the right footrest and rear brake pedal as described in Chapter Fourteen.
9. Remove the bolts securing the crankcase cover (A, **Figure 45**) to the engine. If necessary, lightly tap the cover to loosen it from the engine.
10. Account for the two dowels (**Figure 46**) that may remain in the crankcase or cover.

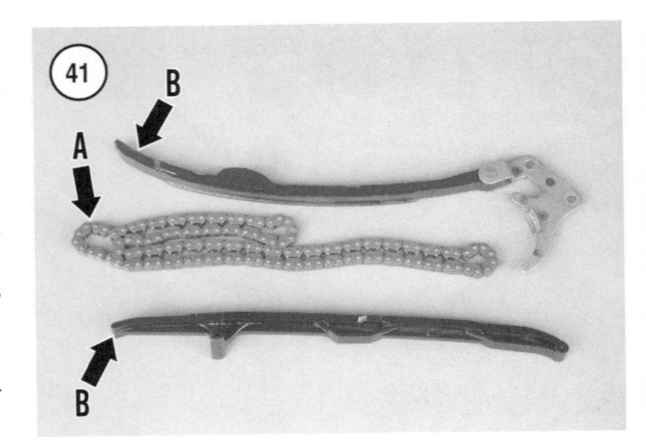

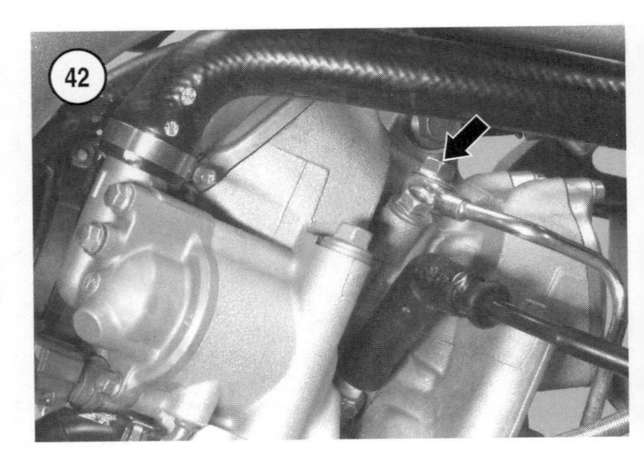

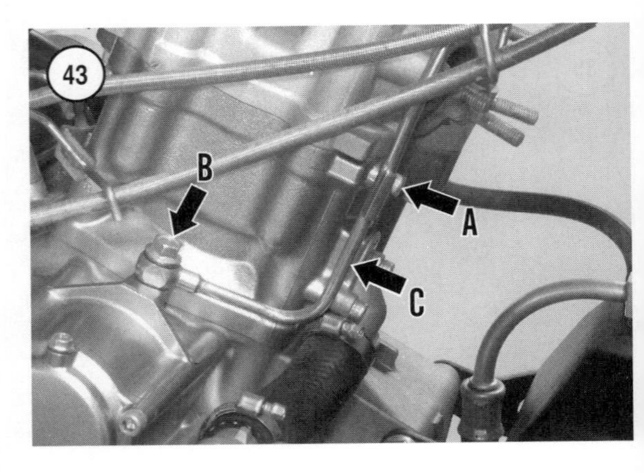

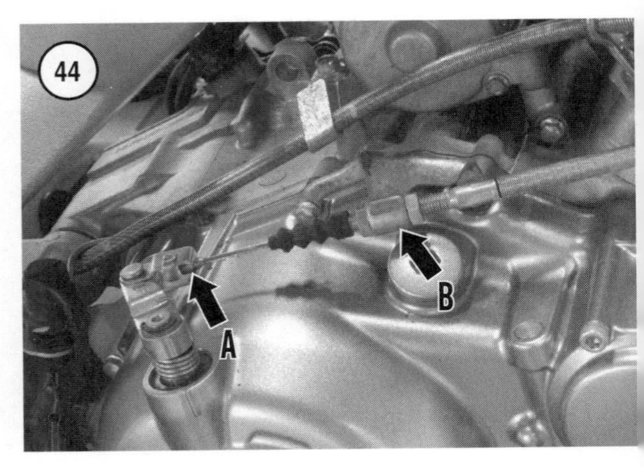

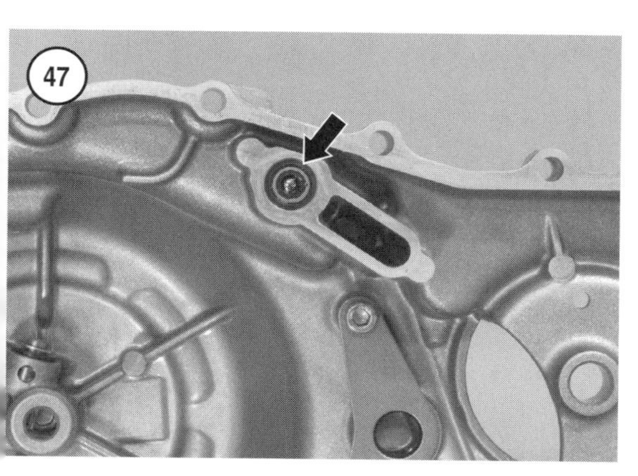

11. Remove and discard the cover gasket.
12. Inspect the oil check valve (**Figure 47**). The check ball should move freely, and then seat firmly under spring pressure. If necessary, replace the check valve assembly.
13. Inspect the crankshaft end seal (A, **Figure 48**). If damaged, remove the seal retainer (B) and replace the seal. Apply threadlock to the seal retainer bolt threads and tighten to 10 N•m (89 in.-lb.). Lubricate the seal.
14. Reverse the removal steps to install the right crankcase cover. Note the following:

   a. Make sure both dowels (**Figure 46**) are in place.
   b. Install a new cover gasket.
   c. Note the position of the clutch cable bracket (B, **Figure 45**), rear brake light switch bracket (C), wire clamp (D) and water pump vent hose holder (E).
   d. Using a crossing pattern, tighten the right crankcase cover bolts in several steps to 10 N•m (89 in.-lb.).
   e. Install new sealing washers on the oil tube banjo bolts. Tighten the oil tube banjo bolts to 20 N•m (15 ft.-lb.).
   f. Tighten the oil tube retainer bolt to 10 N•m (89 in.-lb.).
   g. Install the water pump as described in Chapter Ten.
   h. Install the oil filter as described in Chapter Three.
   i. Install the right footrest and rear brake pedal as described in Chapter Fourteen.
   j. Fill the engine with oil as described in Chapter Three.
   k. Fill the cooling system as described in Chapter Three.
   l. Check for leaks after running the engine.

OIL PUMP

Removal/Installation

Refer to **Figure 49**.

1. Remove the clutch assembly as described in Chapter Six.
2. Remove the retaining bolts (A, **Figure 50**), and then remove the outer oil baffle plate (B).
3. Remove the snap ring (A, **Figure 51**) and driven gear (B) from the shaft.
4. Remove the two mounting bolts (A, **Figure 52**), then remove the inner oil baffle plate (B).
5. Remove the remaining mounting bolt (C, **Figure 52**) and remove the oil pump (D).
6. Remove the gasket and two O-rings (**Figure 53**).
7. Disassemble, inspect and assemble the oil pump as described in this section.
8. Reverse the preceding steps to install the oil pump. Note the following:

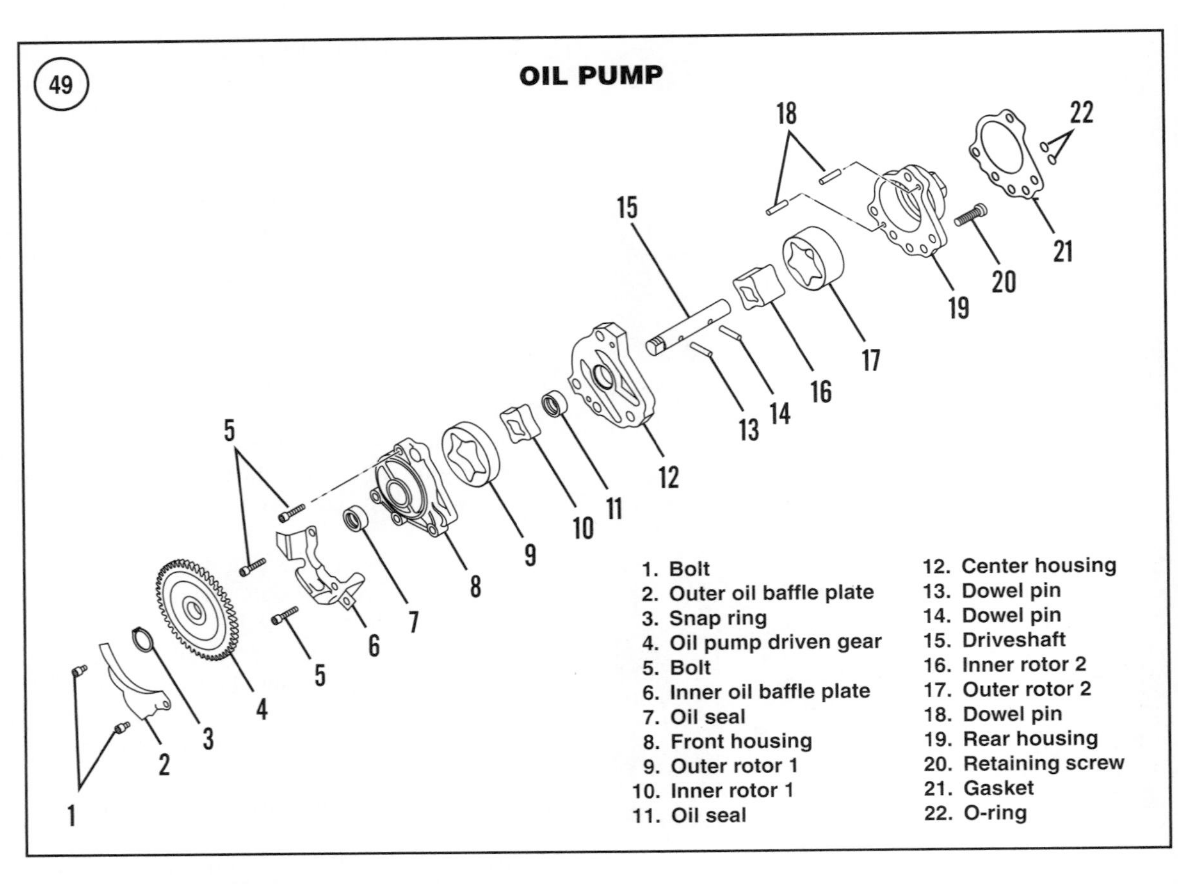
49
OIL PUMP
1
2
3
4
5
6
7
8
9
10
11
12
13
14
15
16
17
18
19
20
21
22
1. Bolt
2. Outer oil baffle plate
3. Snap ring
4. Oil pump driven gear
5. Bolt
6. Inner oil baffle plate
7. Oil seal
8. Front housing
9. Outer rotor 1
10. Inner rotor 1
11. Oil seal
12. Center housing
13. Dowel pin
14. Dowel pin
15. Driveshaft
16. Inner rotor 2
17. Outer rotor 2
18. Dowel pin
19. Rear housing
20. Retaining screw
21. Gasket
22. O-ring

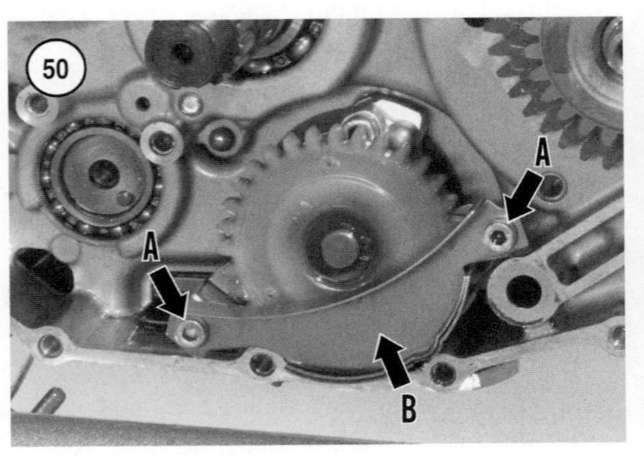
50
A
A
B

52
D
C
A
A
B

51
B
A

53

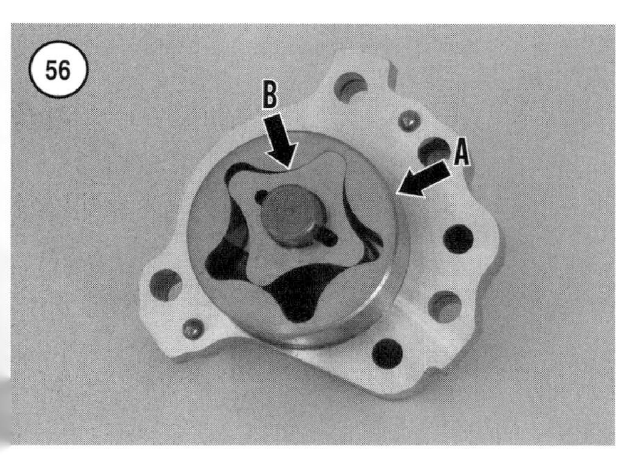

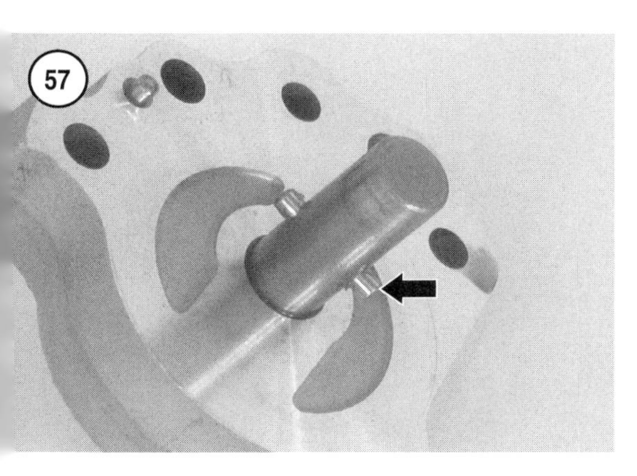

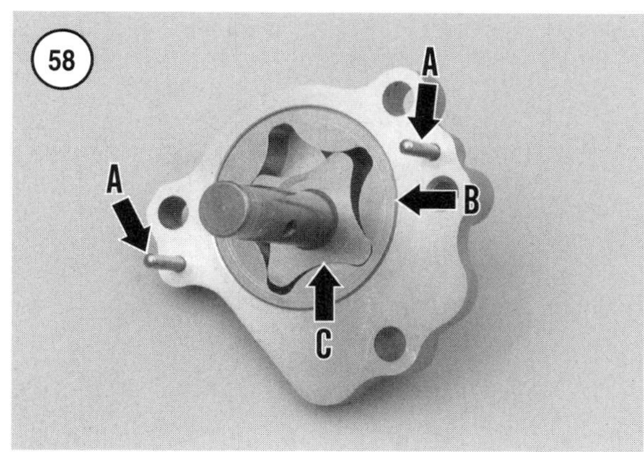

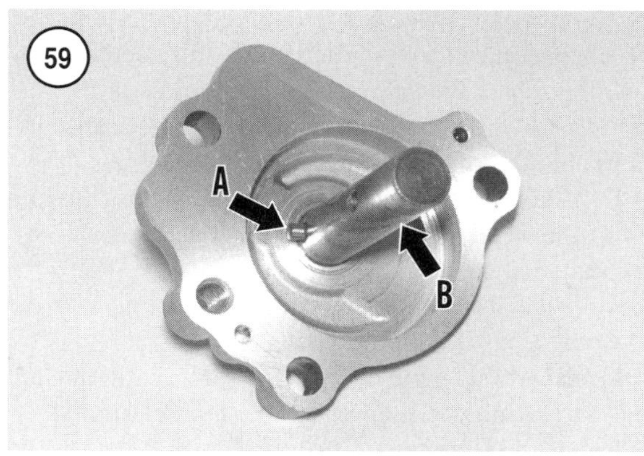

a. Fill the pump with engine oil prior to mounting.
b. Install a new oil pump gasket and O-rings.
c. Tighten the oil pump mounting bolts to 10 N•m (89 in.-lb.).
d. Install the driven gear with the dished side facing out.
e. Install a new snap ring for the driven gear with the sharp edge facing out.
f. Apply threadlock to the threads of the mounting bolts for the outer baffle plate before installing. Tighten the bolts to 4 N•m (35 in.-lb.).

Disassembly/Assembly

Refer to **Figure 49**.

1. Remove the retaining screw (**Figure 54**) from the back of the oil pump housing.
2. Lift off the rear housing (**Figure 55**).
3. Remove the outer rotor 2 (A, **Figure 56**) and inner rotor 2 (B).
4. Remove the pin (**Figure 57**) from the shaft.
5. Separate the center housing from the front housing and remove the dowels (A, **Figure 58**).
6. Remove the outer rotor 1 (B, **Figure 58**) and inner rotor 1 (C) from the front housing.
7. Remove the pin (A, **Figure 59**) from the driveshaft (B).

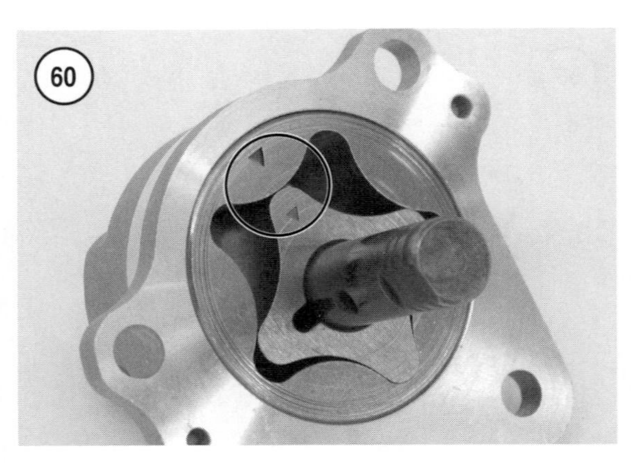

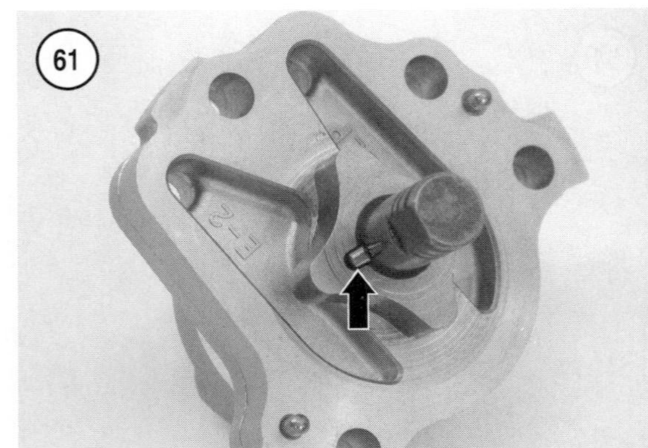

8. Remove the driveshaft from the housing.
9. Inspect the parts as described in this section.
10. Lubricate the parts with engine oil.
11. Install the number 2 rotor set into the rear housing, with the rotor marks (**Figure 60**) aligned.
12. Install the driveshaft and pin, engaging the pin with the inner rotor. The grooves on the driveshaft should face out.
13. Install the dowels and center housing, with the bushing seal facing out.
14. Install the number 1 inner rotor with the pin groove facing out, then install the pin (**Figure 61**).
15. Install the number 1 outer rotor. There is no alignment required for this rotor set.
16. Install the front housing with the bushing seal facing out.
17. With the assembly held tight, check that the three grooves on the driveshaft (**Figure 62**) are visible. If not, check assembly.
18. Apply threadlock to the threads of the oil pump retaining screw (**Figure 54**). Install and tighten the screw to 7 N•m (62 in.-lb.).
19. Check that the pump shaft turns smoothly.
20. Install the oil pump as described in this section.

Inspection

1. Clean the parts in solvent.
2. Inspect all parts for wear or damage.
3. Inspect the pump driveshaft, driven gear and pins (**Figure 63**) for wear or scoring.
   a. The pins should firmly fit in the shaft.
   b. The pump driveshaft should fit in the pump housing with minimal perceptible play.
   c. If the driven gear is worn or damaged, also inspect the drive gear on the clutch housing.
4. Inspect the rotor sets.
   a. Inspect each rotor set (**Figure 64**) for wear or scoring. When assembled, the inner rotor and pin of each set should fit firmly on the shaft.

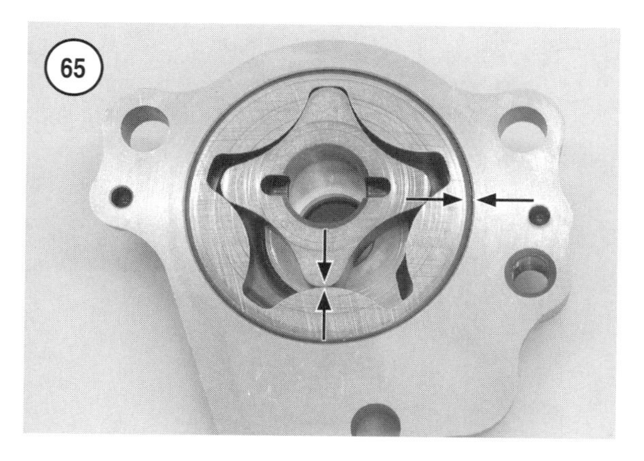

   b. Check the tip clearance at the inner rotor and the body clearance at the outer rotor-to-housing gap (**Figure 65**). Refer to **Table 1** for specifications.

5. Assemble the oil pump as described in this section.

CRANKSHAFT AND BALANCER DRIVE GEARS

Removal

NOTE

The following procedure describes complete removal of the crankshaft gears and the balancer gears. Individual gears may be removed using the appropriate steps without removing all gears.

1. Remove the clutch as described in Chapter Six.
2. Remove the oil baffle plate (**Figure 66**).
3. Loosen the nuts securing the crankshaft gears and balancer gears as follows:
   a. Bend the lockwashers (**Figure 67**) away from the nuts.

CAUTION

Inserting a screwdriver or other tool into the gear teeth to prevent gear rotation may cause gear tooth breakage.

   b. Place a discarded gear or gear holding tool (**Figure 68**) at the mesh point of the primary drive gear and balancer gear. This jam gear will prevent the gears from turning so the retaining nuts on the primary drive gear and balancer gears can be loosened.
   c. Loosen the nut on the crankshaft (A, **Figure 69**), front balancer shaft (B) and rear balancer shaft (C).
   d. Remove the gear holder.
4. Remove the nut and lockwasher. Then, remove the front balancer driven gear (B, **Figure 69**) and/or rear balancer driven gear (C).

5. Remove the nut and washer securing the crankshaft gears. Then, remove the following gears:
   a. Water pump drive gear (**Figure 70**).
   b. Primary drive gear (**Figure 71**).
   c. Balancer drive gear (A, **Figure 72**).

Inspection

1. Wash and dry all parts so they can be carefully inspected.
2. Inspect the gear teeth and keyway for wear and damage.
3. Inspect the drive key (B, **Figure 72**) in each shaft. Replace if damaged.
4. Replace any damaged parts.

Installation

1. Install the following gears onto the crankshaft:
   a. Balancer drive gear (A, **Figure 72**) with timing marks (C and D) visible.
   b. Primary drive gear (**Figure 71**) with the flat side out.
   c. Water pump drive gear (**Figure 70**) with the flat side out.
2. Lubricate the crankshaft nut with molybdenum disulfide oil, then install a new lockwasher and the nut onto the crankshaft. Do not tighten the nut.
3. Using the crankshaft nut, rotate the crankshaft so the timing marks (C and D, **Figure 72**) on the balancer drive gear are located as shown.
4. Install the balancer driven gears so the timing marks (**Figure 73**) on the balancer drive gear and balancer driven gear are aligned.
5. Lubricate the balancer driven gear nuts with engine oil. Then, install a new lockwasher and the nut onto each balancer shaft. Do not tighten the nut.
6. Using the same procedure performed during gear removal, place a gear holder tool or discarded gear against the gear teeth to prevent rotation.

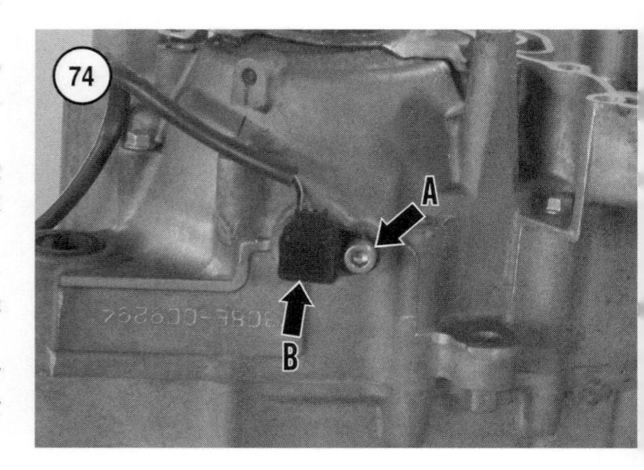

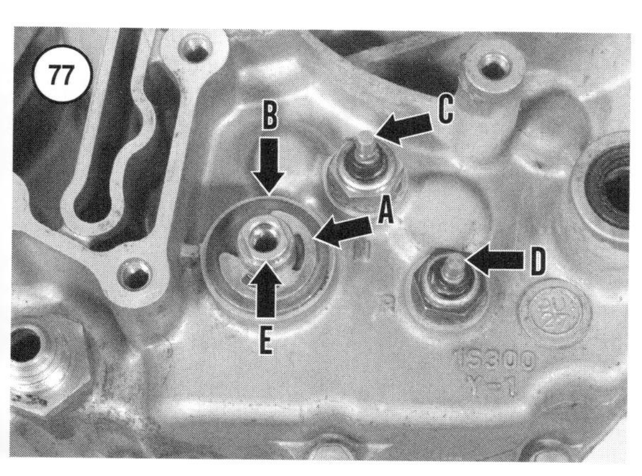

7. Tighten the front balancer driven gear nut to 60 N•m (44 ft.-lb.).
8. Tighten the crankshaft nut to 110 N•m (81 ft.-lb.).
9. Tighten the rear balancer driven gear nut to 60 N•m (44 ft.-lb.).
10. Bend the lockwashers against the flats on the nuts (**Figure 67**).

CRANKCASE

The following procedures describe the disassembly and reassembly of the crankcase. The crankcase halves must be split for access to the crankshaft and transmission assemblies.

Disassembly

As components are removed, keep each part or assembly separated from the other components. Keep seals and O-rings with their respective parts.

1. Prior to disassembly of the crankcase, remove the following parts if not removed during engine removal:
   a. Starter (Chapter Nine).
   b. Piston (Chapter Four).
   c. Torque limiter.
   d. Starter idle gear.
   e. Flywheel.
   f. Cam chain and guides.
   g. Clutch (Chapter Six).
   h. Oil pump.
   i. External shift mechanism (Chapter Six).
   j. Crankshaft drive gears.
   k. Balancer driven gears.
2. Remove the speed sensor retaining bolt (A, **Figure 74**).
3. Remove the speed sensor (B, **Figure 74**) and its O-ring.
4. Place the engine on wooden blocks with the left side facing up (**Figure 75**).
5. Remove the bolt (A, **Figure 76**), and then remove the reverse shift lever (B) and spring from the reverse lockout shaft.
6. Remove the snap ring (A, **Figure 77**) and washer (B) from the reverse lockout shaft.
7. Remove the neutral switch (C, **Figure 77**) and reverse switch (D).
8. Remove the oil fitting (**Figure 78**) and its O-ring.
9. Remove the crankcase seal retainer (**Figure 79**).
10. Remove the spacer (**Figure 80**) from the countershaft.
11. Remove the O-ring (**Figure 81**) from the groove in the countershaft.

12. Working in a crossing pattern, loosen each crankcase bolt (**Figure 82**) 1/4 turn. Continue to loosen the bolts until they can be removed by hand. Remove the bolts, along with the clutch cable holder and hose guide.
13. Grasp both halves of the crankcase and turn it over so the right case faces up.
14. Remove the crankcase bolts (**Figure 83**) from the right side.

CAUTION

Do not hammer or pry on areas of the crankcase halves that are not reinforced. Do not pry on gasket surfaces.

15. Loosen the crankcase halves by tapping around the perimeter with a soft mallet.
16. Using a soft mallet, alternately tap on reinforced bosses on the right crankcase half while carefully prying in small increments at the pry points. Work slowly and separate the crankcase halves equally. If binding occurs, reseat the crankcase halves and start again.
17. Slowly raise and remove the right crankcase half.
18. Account for the crankcase dowel (**Figure 84**) at each end and at the bottom of the crankcase. These may remain in either crankcase half. The dowel at the bottom of the crankcase half is also fitted with an O-ring (**Figure 85**).

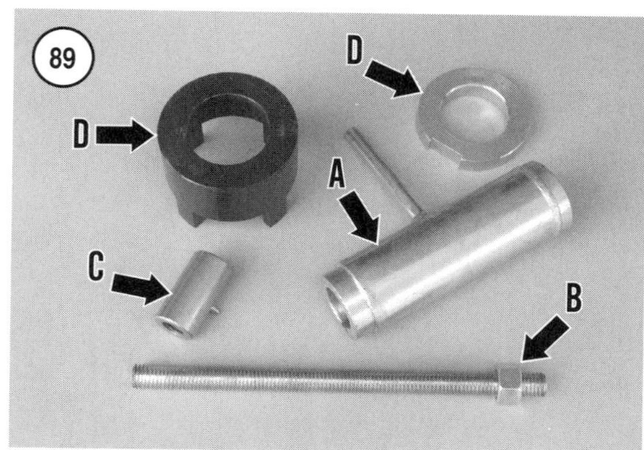

19. If necessary, remove the transmission from the left crankcase half as described in Chapter Seven.
20. Remove the front balancer (A, **Figure 86**) and rear balancer (B) from the crankcase.

CAUTION
Do not attempt to drive the crankshaft out of the crankcase. Doing so will damage the crankshaft and bearing.

NOTE
A crankshaft removal tool (Yamaha part No. 90890-01135, or an equivalent), is required to remove the crankshaft.

21. To remove the crankshaft, attach the crankshaft separating tool and bolts to the left crankcase half and crankshaft (**Figure 87**).
22. Tighten the center bolt to push the crankshaft out of the crankcase half.
23. Inspect the crankcase and crankshaft assembly as described in this chapter.
24. Remove the bolts (A, **Figure 88**) securing the oil strainer (B) in the right crankcase half. Remove the oil strainer from the crankcase.

Assembly

Tools

The following crankshaft installation tools, or their equivalent, are required to pull the crankshaft into the bearing. Refer to **Figure 89**. A crankshaft installation tool is also available from K&L Supply Co. at ATV dealerships.

1. Pot (A, **Figure 89**), Yamaha part No. 90890-01274.
2. Bolt (B, **Figure 89**), Yamaha part No. 90890-01275.
3. Adapter (C, **Figure 89**), Yamaha part No. 90890-04130.
4. Spacers (D, **Figure 89**), Yamaha part No. 90890-04081.

Procedure

NOTE
Prior to assembly, lubricate all O-rings and the lip of each seal. Wrap splined shafts with tape to prevent damage to the seals. Lubricate all bearings and the transmission and crankshaft assemblies with engine oil.

1. Insert the crankshaft into the bearing in the left crankcase half. Hold the connecting rod at TDC using a rubber band so the rod cannot contact the crankcase during crankshaft insertion.

CAUTION
Do not use a hammer to drive the crankshaft into the bearing.

2. Thread the adapter (**Figure 90**) onto the crankshaft. Then, thread the bolt into the adapter.
3. Place the spacers and pot over the bolt (**Figure 91**). The lower spacer must seat parallel to the case.
4. Thread the nut onto the bolt and against the pot.
5. While holding the connecting rod at TDC, tighten the installation tool nut until the crankshaft bearing seats against the crankcase.
6. Remove the installation tool from the crankshaft. Install the flywheel nut on the end of the crankshaft to protect the threads during crankcase assembly.
7. Install the front balancer (A, **Figure 86**) and the rear balancer (B) into the crankcase.
8. Install the transmission as described in Chapter Seven. When installed, make sure all shift fork pins engage with the shift drum. Spin the shafts and turn the shift drum in both directions by hand to check operation. Make sure all gears engage properly. It is normal for the shift fork shafts to move as they are fixed to the forks.
9. Install the oil strainer (B, **Figure 88**) onto the right crankcase half. Apply threadlock to the retaining bolts. Tighten the bolts (A, **Figure 88**) to 10 N•m (89 in.-lb.).

10. Insert the dowels into the case. Install the O-ring (**Figure 85**) onto the dowel at the bottom of the crankcase half.
11. Make sure all mating surfaces are clean and dry.
12. Apply a nonhardening, liquid gasket sealant such as Yamabond 1215 or Yamabond 4 to all mating surfaces on the right crankcase half, including the inner mating surfaces (**Figure 92**).
13. Make sure the connecting rod is at TDC.
14. Seat the right crankcase half squarely onto the left. If necessary, use a soft mallet to seat the crankcase. Do not raise the crankcase once it is seated.
15. Install and finger-tighten the proper length crankcase bolts (**Figure 93**) into the left crankcase half at the following locations.
   a. 30 mm (A, **Figure 93**).
   b. 70 mm (B, **Figure 93**).
   c. 90 mm (C, **Figure 93**).
16. Using a crossing pattern, tighten the bolts in three steps to 10 N•m (89 in.-lb.).
17. Insert the crankcase bolts (**Figure 83**) into the right crankcase half. Using a crossing pattern, tighten the bolts in three steps to 10 N•m (89 in.-lb.).
18. Install the washer (B, **Figure 77**) and snap ring (A) onto the reverse lockout shaft.
19. Check the transmission for proper shifting as follows:

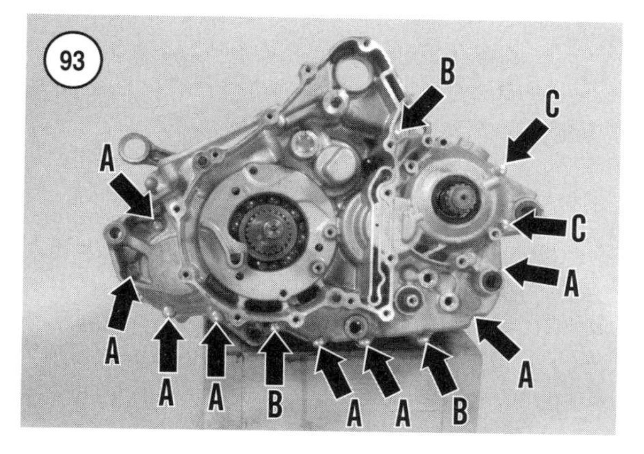

a. Install the shift drum stopper (**Figure 94**).
b. Turn the shift drum stopper to the neutral position. The mainshaft and countershaft should turn independently of one another.
c. Turn the mainshaft while turning the shift drum stopper fully clockwise. This is the first gear position. The mainshaft and countershaft should be meshed together.
d. Turn the shift drum stopper counterclockwise while checking the remaining gears for proper engagement. The mainshaft and countershaft should mesh whenever the transmission is in gear.
e. To check reverse gear, turn the shift drum stopper clockwise to first gear. Place the shift lever onto the reverse lockout shaft (E, **Figure 77**). While moving the shift lever forward, turn the shift drum stopper clockwise. The transmission should now be in reverse. Turn the shift drum stopper counterclockwise while moving the reverse shift lever to the rear. The transmission should shift to first gear. Attempt to turn the shift drum stopper clockwise while the reverse shift lever is fully rearward. The transmission must not shift into reverse.
f. Remove the shift drum stopper when the function test is completed. If the transmission did not engage properly, disassemble the crankcase and inspect the transmission for proper assembly or damaged parts.

20. Install the O-ring (**Figure 81**) into the countershaft groove.
21. Place the spacer (**Figure 80**) onto the countershaft with the notches inward.
22. Install the crankcase seal retainer (**Figure 79**). Tighten the bolts to 10 N•m (89 in.-lb.).
23. Install the neutral switch (C, **Figure 77**) and reverse switch (D). Install a new washer on each switch. Tighten each switch to 17 N•m (13 ft.-lb.).
24. Install the oil fitting (**Figure 78**) and a new O-ring. Tighten the fitting to 50 N•m (37 ft.-lb.).
25. Install the reverse shift lever (B, **Figure 76**) and spring onto the reverse shift shaft. Tighten the bolt to 13 N•m (115 in.-lb.).
26. Install the speed sensor (B, **Figure 74**) and a new O-ring. Lubricate the O-ring with engine oil.
27. Temporarily install the speed sensor holder bolt. The bolt will be removed later to install the wire holder after engine installation.
28. Continue with engine assembly and installation as described in this chapter and Chapter Four.

Inspection

1. Remove the oil seals as described in this chapter and Chapter One.
2. Remove all sealer and residue from the gasket surfaces.
3. Clean the crankcase halves with solvent.
4. Using clean solvent, flush each bearing.

WARNING
When drying a bearing with compressed air, do not allow the bearing to rotate. The air can spin the bearing at excessive speed, possibly causing the bearing to destruct.

5. Dry the cases with compressed air.
6. Blow through each oil passage with compressed air.
7. Lightly oil the engine bearings before inspecting their condition.
8. Inspect the bearings for roughness, pitting, galling and play. Replace any bearing that is not in good condition. Always replace the opposite bearing in the crankcase at the same time.
9. Inspect the cases for fractures around all mounting and bearing bosses, stiffening ribs and threaded holes. If repair is required, have the cases inspected by a dealership or machine shop that is experienced in repairing precision aluminum castings.
10. Check all threaded holes for damage or buildup. Clean threads with the correct size metric tap. Lubricate the tap with kerosene or tap fluid.

CRANKCASE SEAL AND BEARING REPLACEMENT

Refer to Chapter One for general bearing and seal removal and installation techniques.

Refer to this section for specific removal and installation techniques that are unique to this engine.

Countershaft Seal Replacement

When replacing the countershaft seal, located in the left crankcase half, care must be taken when prying the seal from the crankcase. Oil passages are located in the recess behind the oil seal. To prevent damage when prying the seal, do not insert the seal removal tool any deeper than necessary.

Engine in frame

1. Remove the drive sprocket as described in Chapter Eleven.
2. Remove the crankcase seal retainer (**Figure 95**).
3. Remove the spacer (**Figure 96**).
4. Remove the O-ring (**Figure 97**) from the countershaft.

NOTE
Depending on the type of seal removal tool used, removing the shift lever will provide additional working room.

5. Using a suitable seal removal tool (**Figure 98**), extract the seal from the crankcase.
6. Install a new seal so the closed side is out. Use a suitable seal installation tool.
7. Install the O-ring (**Figure 97**) into the countershaft groove.
8. Place the spacer (**Figure 96**) onto the countershaft with the notches inward.
9. Install the crankcase seal retainer (**Figure 95**). Tighten the bolts to 10 N•m (89 in.-lb.).
10. If removed, install the shift lever and tighten the clamp bolt to 16 N•m (12 ft.-lb.).

Engine disassembled

1. Using a suitable seal removal tool, extract the seal from the crankcase.
2. Install a new seal so the closed side is out. Use a suitable seal installation tool.

Crankcase Bearings

NOTE
The left crankshaft main bearing remains on the crankshaft.

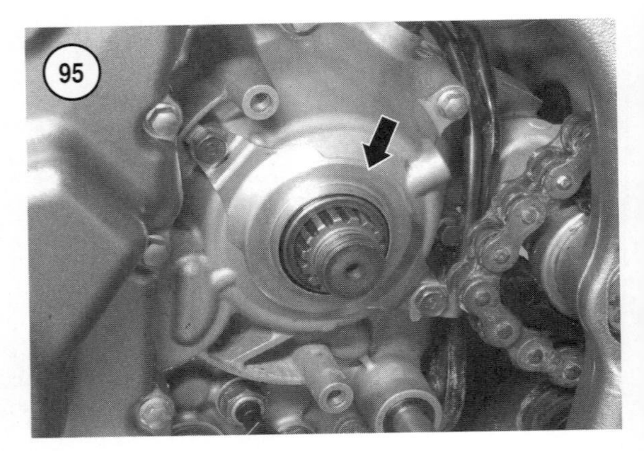
95

96

97

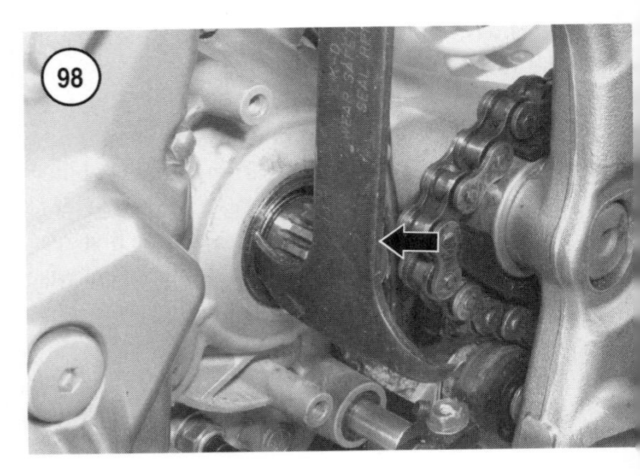
98

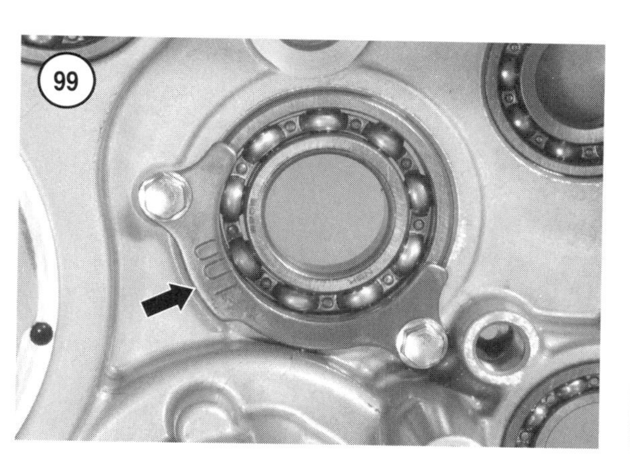

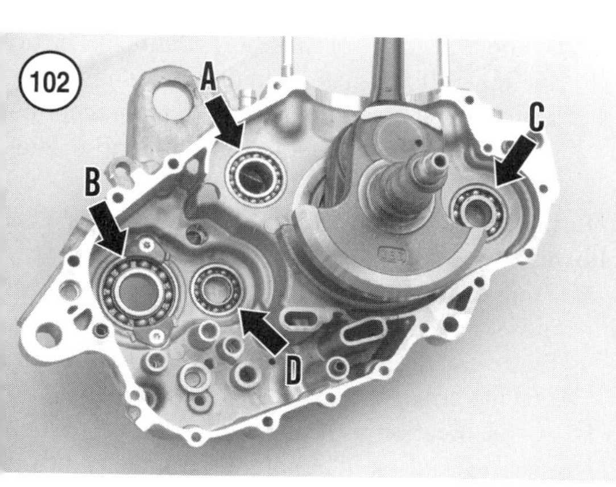

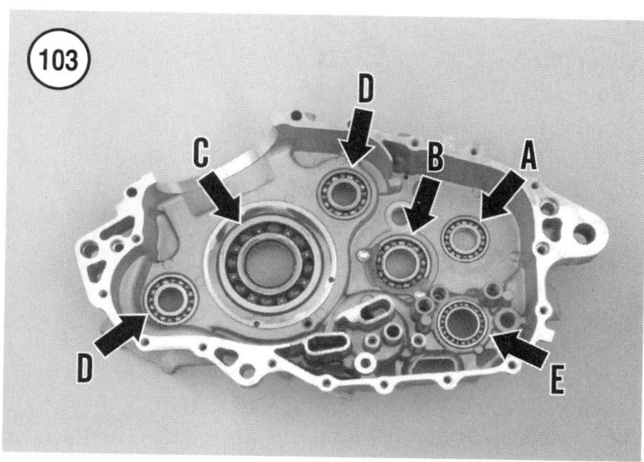

1. When replacing crankcase bearings, remove bearing retainers before attempting bearing removal. Note the following during installation:

   a. Install the mainshaft bearing retainer so the side marked OUT (**Figure 99**) is visible. Apply threadlock to the bolt threads and tighten to 10 N•m (89 in.-lb.).

NOTE

*If the countershaft bearing retainer is equipped with a depression adjacent to the bolt head, use a punch and depress the edge of the bolt head into the depression in the bearing retainer (**Figure 100**, typical).*

   b. The countershaft bearing retainers are secured by Torx head bolts (**Figure 101**). Apply threadlock to the bolt threads and tighten to 10 N•m (89 in.-lb.).
   c. Identify and record the size code of each bearing before it is removed from the case. This will eliminate confusion when installing the bearings into the correct bores.
   d. Record the location and orientation of each bearing in its bore. Note if the size code faces toward the inside or outside of the crankcase.

2. Inspect the oil seal behind the rear balancer shaft bearing (A, **Figure 102**) in the left crankcase half. Remove the bearing to replace the oil seal. Note seal orientation during removal.

3. The left crankcase half houses the following bearings:

   a. Rear balancer shaft bearing (A, **Figure 102**).
   b. Countershaft bearing (B, **Figure 102**).
   c. Front balancer shaft bearing (C, **Figure 102**).
   d. Mainshaft bearing (D, **Figure 102**).

4. The right crankcase half houses the following bearings:

   a. Countershaft bearing (A, **Figure 103**).
   b. Mainshaft bearing (B, **Figure 103**).
   c. Crankshaft bearing (C, **Figure 103**).

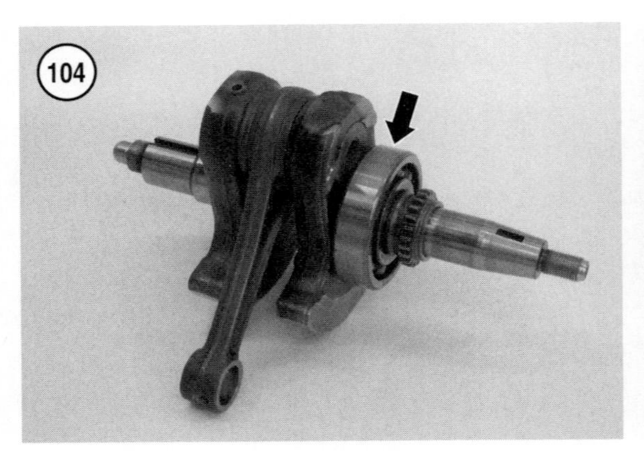

d. Balancer shaft bearing (D, **Figure 103**).
e. Shift drum bearing (E, **Figure 103**).

CRANKSHAFT

Inspection

Handle the crankshaft assembly carefully during inspection. Do not place the crankshaft where it could accidentally roll off the workbench. The crankshaft is an assembly-type, with its two halves joined by the crankpin. The crankpin is pressed into the flywheels and aligned, both vertically and horizontally, with calibrated equipment.

If the crankshaft assembly shows signs of wear, or is out of alignment, have a dealership inspect, overhaul or replace the crankshaft. Inspect the crankshaft assembly as follows:

1. Clean the crankshaft with solvent.
2. Dry the crankshaft with compressed air.
3. Blow through all oil passages with compressed air.

NOTE
The two halves of the crankshaft are available separately, if one side must be replaced. The left crankshaft end assembly includes the main bearing and cam chain sprocket.

4. Inspect the left main bearing (**Figure 104**) for roughness, pitting, galling and play. The bearing is not available separately.
5. Inspect the crankshaft bearing surfaces for scoring, heat discoloration or other damage.
6. Inspect the sprocket (A, **Figure 105**), shaft (B), shaft taper (C) and threads (D) for signs of wear or damage.
7. Inspect the piston pin end of the connecting rod (**Figure 106**) as follows:
   a. Inspect the rod end for scoring, galling or heat damage.

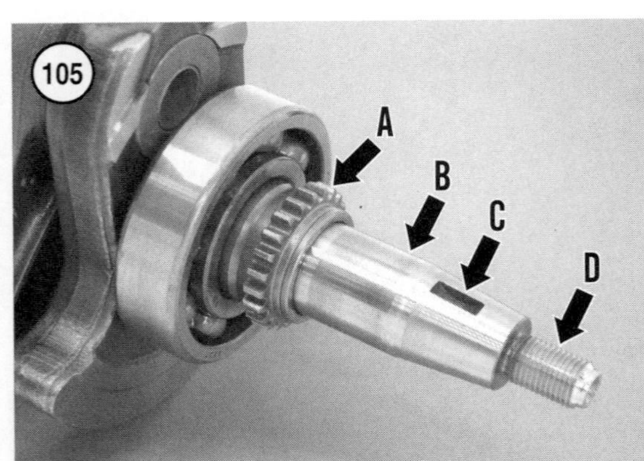

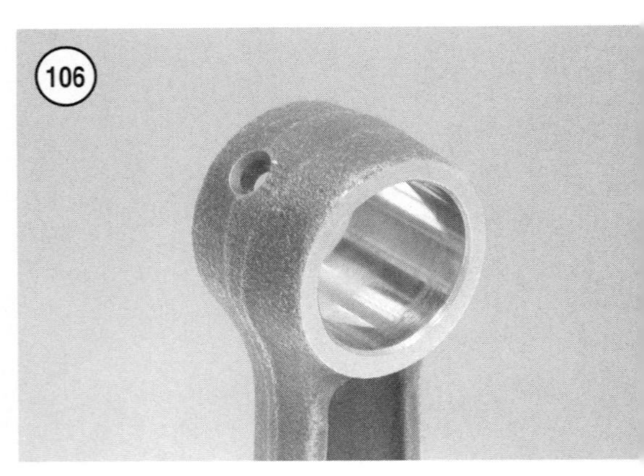

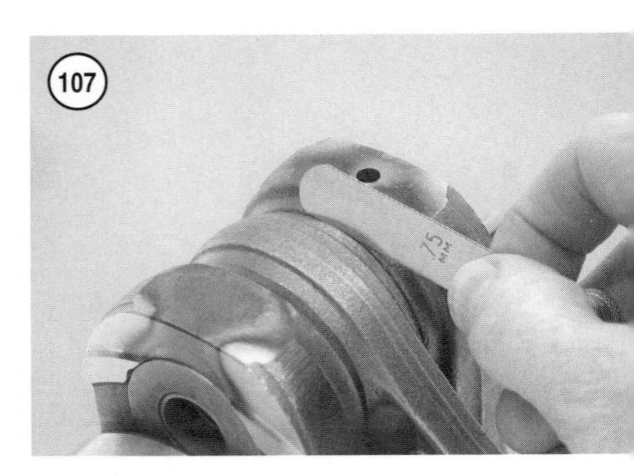

   b. A specification for the bore diameter is no available. If the piston pin does not show sign of wear, and fits in the bore with no perceptibl radial play, the rod end is considered in goo condition.
8. Inspect the crankpin end of the connecting rod a follows:
   a. Slide the connecting rod to one side and chec the connecting rod side clearance with a fla feeler gauge (**Figure 107**). Refer to **Table 1** fo service limits.
   b. A specification for connecting rod to crankpi clearance is not available. Check the rod man

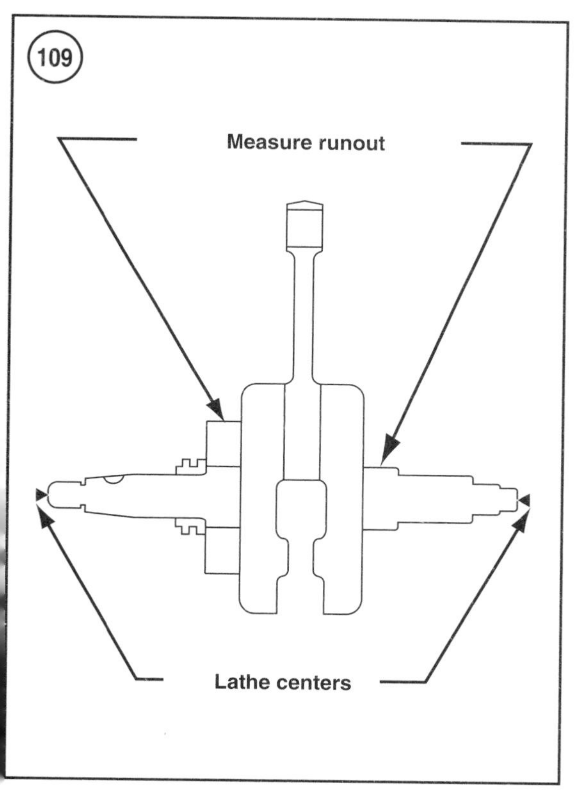

ually by grasping the rod and feeling for radial play in all directions. Play will not be evident for a rod in good condition. If in doubt about the condition, check with a dealership.

9. Measure the width of the crankshaft at the flywheels (**Figure 108**). Measure at the machined edge and at 90° intervals. Record the measurements. Have the crankshaft retrued if the measurements are not identical. Refer to **Table 1** for service limits.

10. Place the crankshaft between lathe centers (**Figure 109**) or equivalent and measure crankshaft runout with a dial indicator. Measure at both bearing surfaces. If the runout exceeds the service limit listed in **Table 1**, have the crankshaft trued by a dealership.

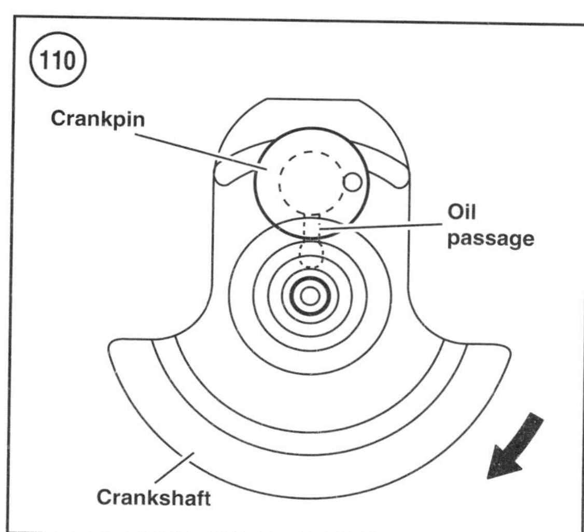

Crankshaft Overhaul

Crankshaft overhaul requires a hydraulic press with 20-ton (minimum) capacity, holding jigs, a crankshaft alignment jig, dial indicators and a micrometer or caliper. For this reason, refer crankshaft overhaul to a dealership or ATV repair shop specializing in crankshaft rebuilding. If having the crankshaft rebuilt, instruct the dealership or shop to align the crankshaft to the crankpin oil passages as shown in **Figure 110**.

ENGINE BREAK-IN

If the rings are replaced, a new piston is installed, the cylinder block is rebored or honed or if major lower end work is performed, the engine should be broken in just as though it were new. The performance and service life of the engine depends greatly on a careful and sensible break-in.

During break-in, oil consumption will be higher than normal. It is therefore important to check and correct the oil level frequently (Chapter Three). At no time during the break-in or later should the oil level be allowed to drop below the minimum level. If the oil level is low the oil will overheat, resulting in insufficient lubrication and increased wear.

For the first 0-10 hours, do not operate the engine above half throttle. The manufacturer recommends stopping the engine and allowing it to cool for approximately 5 to 10 minutes after each hour of operation. Avoid hard acceleration and prolonged steady running at one speed, no matter how moderate.

Between 10-20 hours, do not operate the engine above 3/4 throttle.

After 20 hours, operate the vehicle normally.

After one month, perform the maintenance procedures described in **Table 1** of Chapter Three.

Table 1 ENGINE SERVICE SPECIFICATIONS

	New mm (in.)	Service limit mm (in.)
Connecting rod		
Side clearance	0.35-0.65 (0.014-0.026)	1.00 (0.04)
Crankshaft dimensions		
Width (flywheel-to-flywheel)	74.95-75.00 (2.951-2.953)	–
Runout	–	0.03 (0.0012)
Oil pump		
Body clearance	0.09-0.15 (0.0035-0.0059)	0.22 (0.0087)
Tip clearance	Less than 0.12 (0.0047)	0.20 (0.0079)

Table 2 ENGINE TORQUE SPECIFICATIONS

Item	N•m	in.-lb.	ft.-lb.
Balancer driven gear nut	60	–	44
Clutch and parking brake cable bracket bolt	7	62	–
Countershaft bearing retainer bolts	10	89	–
Crankcase bolts	10	89	–
Crankshaft nut	110	–	81
Drive sprocket cover bolts	10	89	–
Flywheel nut	60	–	44
Flywheel nut plug	10	89	–
Front engine mounting bolt	66	–	49
Front engine mounting bracket bolts	41	–	30
Left crankcase cover bolts	10	89	–
Lower engine mounting bolt	66	–	49
Mainshaft bearing retainer bolts	10	89	–
Neutral switch	17	–	13
Oil fitting	50	–	37
Oil intake line fitting	35	–	26
Oil tube banjo bolt	20	–	15
Oil tube retainer bolt	10	89	–
Oil pump housing retaining screw	7	62	–
Oil pump mounting bolts	10	89	–
Oil return hose fitting bolt	10	89	–
Oil strainer bolts	10	89	–
Oil tank return line fitting bolt	10	89	–
Outer baffle plate bolts	4	35	–
Rear cam chain guide retaining bolts	10	89	–
Rear engine mounting bolt	100	–	74
Reverse shift lever bolt	13	115	–
Reverse switch	17	–	13
Right crankcase cover bolts	10	89	–
Seal retainer bolts	10	89	–
Shift lever clamp bolt	16	–	12
Speed sensor bolt	10	89	–
Starter one way clutch mounting bolts	30	–	22
Timing plug	6	53	–
Upper engine bracket bolts	33	–	24
Upper engine mounting bolt	40	–	29.5

CHAPTER SIX

CLUTCH AND EXTERNAL SHIFT MECHANISM

This chapter provides service procedures for the clutch, clutch release mechanism and external shift mechanism. Specifications are listed in **Table 1** and **Table 2**, located at the end of this chapter.

The clutch is a wet (operates in the engine oil) multi-plate design. The clutch assembly is located on the right side of the engine. The clutch hub is mounted on the splines on the transmission mainshaft. The outer clutch housing is driven by the primary drive gear on the crankshaft.

Pulling in the clutch lever on the handlebar actuates the clutch release mechanism on the right crankcase cover. The clutch release shaft bears against a pull rod that moves the pressure plate outward to disengage the clutch.

CLUTCH

The clutch assembly is located behind the right crankcase cover. The clutch may be serviced with the engine mounted in the frame after removing the crankcase cover.

Removal

Refer to **Figure 1**.

1. Remove the right crankcase cover as described in Chapter Five.
2. Slowly remove the clutch spring bolts (A, **Figure 2**). Loosen the bolts evenly in several steps. Remove the bolts and springs from the clutch.
3. Remove the pressure plate (B, **Figure 2**).
4. Remove the pull rod (**Figure 3**) from the bearing.

NOTE

Unless replacement is required, keep the clutch plates in the order removed.

5. Remove the steel plates and friction plates (**Figure 4**) from the clutch hub.
6. On 2006-2012 models, remove the circlip (**Figure 5**). The circlip is a wire ring that fits in a groove around the clutch hub. The wire ends extend through a hole in the hub (**Figure 6**). Lift up the ring using a screwdriver while compressing the wire ends with needlenose pliers (**Figure 5**) to release the wire from the hub.
7. Remove the steel plate (**Figure 7**).
8. Remove the friction plate (**Figure 8**).
9. Remove the damper spring and spring seat (**Figure 9**) from the clutch hub.

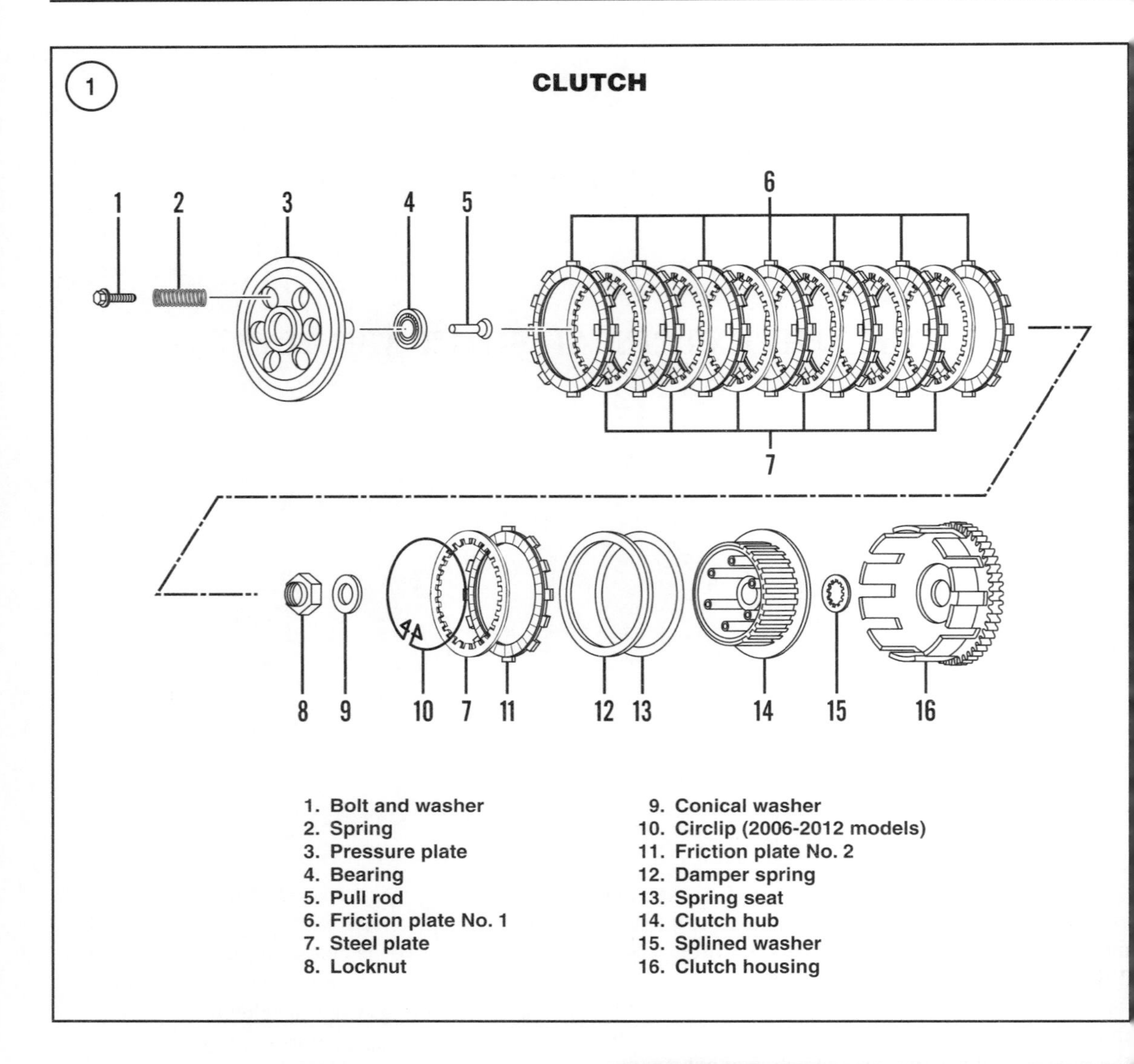

CAUTION
Be sure to unstake the clutch locknut where it contacts the mainshaft. This will prevent the nut from damaging the mainshaft threads during clutch removal.

NOTE
If necessary, use a die grinder or other metal removal tool to unstake the nut from the groove in the mainshaft. Cover the parts so that metal particles do not enter the clutch or engine.

10. Using a suitable punch, lift the staked portion of the nut away from the mainshaft.

CAUTION
To prevent damage, be sure to position the clutch holder tool squarely onto the clutch hub splines.

11. Attach a clutch holding tool (A, **Figure 10**) to the clutch hub.
12. While grasping the holding tool, loosen the clutch locknut (B, **Figure 10**).
13. Remove the clutch locknut and conical washer.
14. Remove the holding tool from the clutch hub.

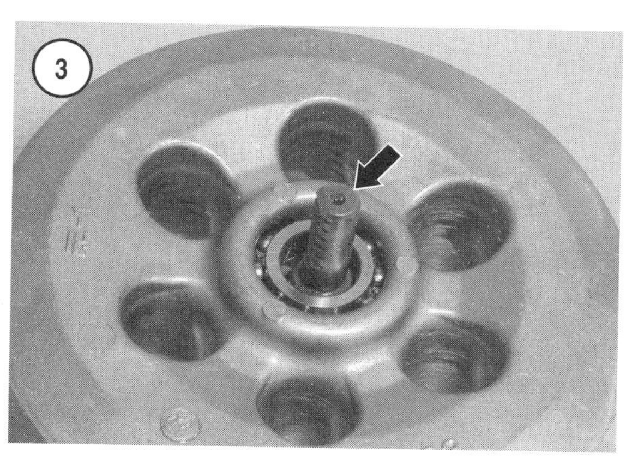
3

4

5

6

7

8

9

10
B
A

15. Remove the clutch hub (**Figure 11**) from the transmission mainshaft.
16. Remove the thrust washer (**Figure 12**) from the shaft.
17. Remove the clutch housing (**Figure 13**).
18. Inspect the clutch assembly as described in this section.

Inspection

Refer to **Table 1** for clutch specifications.

1. Clean and dry all parts.
2. Inspect the friction plates (**Figure 14**) as follows:

NOTE
If any friction plate is damaged or out of specification, replace all of the friction plates as a set.

NOTE
If the tangs are damaged, inspect the clutch housing slots carefully as described in this section.

   a. The friction material (A, **Figure 14**) used on the friction plates is bonded onto an aluminum plate. Inspect the friction material for excessive or uneven wear, cracks and other damage. Inspect the plate tangs (B, **Figure 14**) for damage. The sides of the tangs must be smooth where they contact the clutch housing slots; otherwise, the plates cannot engage and disengage correctly.
   b. Measure the thickness of each friction plate using a caliper (**Figure 15**). Measure at several places around the plate and refer to **Table 1** for service limits.
3. Inspect the steel clutch plates (**Figure 16**) as follows:
   a. Inspect the clutch plates for cracks, damage or color change. Overheated clutch plates will have a bluish discoloration.

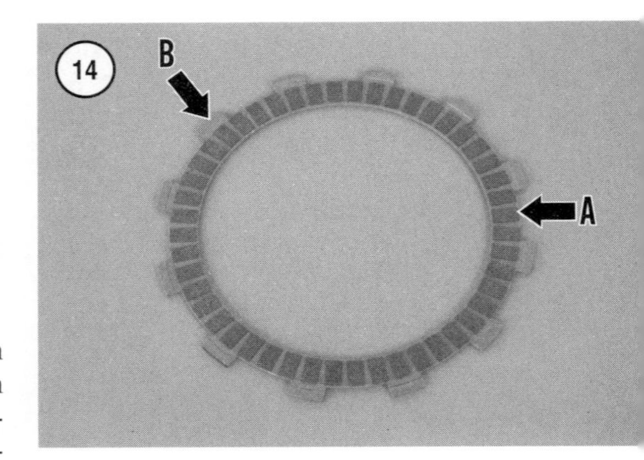

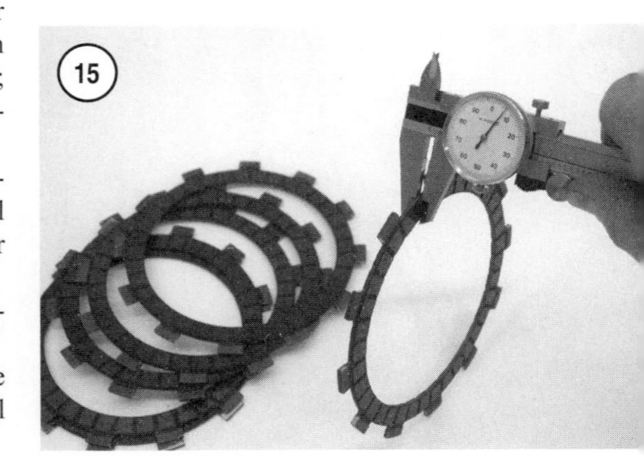

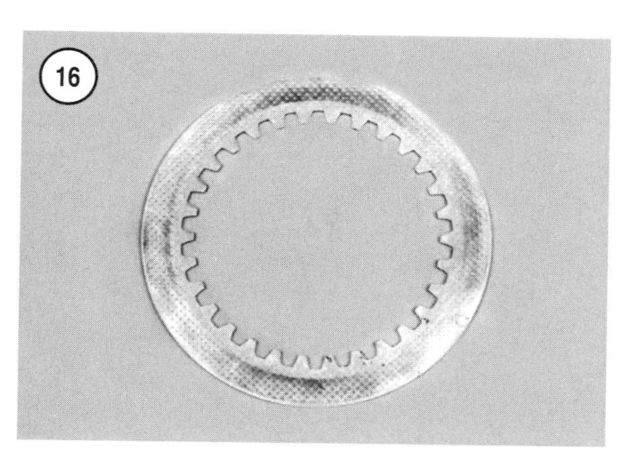

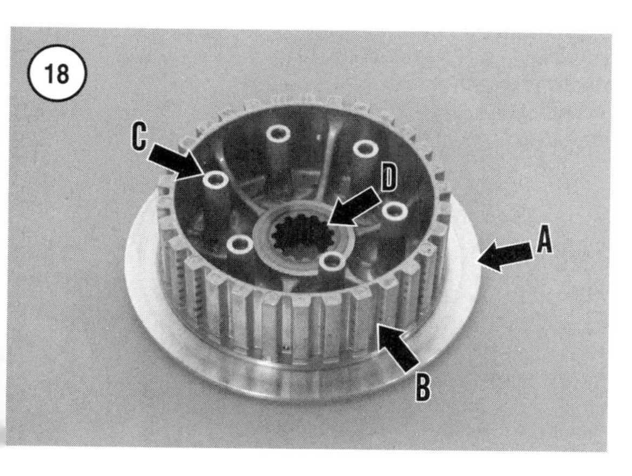

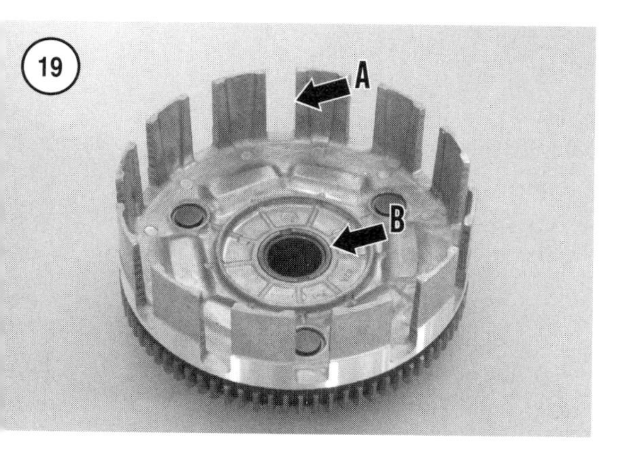

b. Check the clutch plates for an oil glaze buildup. Remove buildup by lightly sanding both sides of each plate with 400 grit sandpaper placed on a surface plate or piece of glass.

c. Place each clutch plate on a surface plate or piece of glass and check for warp with a feeler gauge (**Figure 17**). If the clutch plates are warped, compare the measurement to the service limit in **Table 1**. If any are warped beyond the specification, replace the entire set.

d. Measure the thickness of each steel clutch plate with a caliper. Measure at several places around the plate and refer to **Table 1** for service limits.

NOTE

If the clutch plate teeth are damaged, inspect the clutch hub splines carefully as described in this section.

e. The clutch plate inner teeth mesh with the clutch hub splines. Check the clutch plate teeth for any roughness or damage. The teeth contact surfaces must be smooth; otherwise, the plates cannot engage and disengage correctly.

4. Inspect the clutch hub for the following conditions:
   a. Galled or otherwise damaged plate contact surface (A, **Figure 18**).
   b. The clutch plate teeth slide in the clutch hub splines (B, **Figure 18**). Inspect the splines for rough spots, grooves or other damage. Repair minor damage with a file or oil stone. If the damage is excessive, replace the clutch hub.
   c. Damaged bolt towers and threads (C, **Figure 18**).
   d. Inspect the inner splines (D, **Figure 18**) for damage.
5. Inspect the clutch housing for the following conditions:
   a. The friction plate tangs slide in the clutch housing slots. Inspect the slots (A, **Figure 19**) for cracks or galling. Repair minor damage with a file. If the damage is excessive, replace the clutch housing.
   b. Inspect the bushing (B, **Figure 19**). The bushing is not available separately.

NOTE

If the clutch housing gear is excessively worn or damaged, check the primary drive gear assembly for the same wear conditions.

   c. Inspect the clutch housing gear (A, **Figure 20**) for excessive wear, pitting, chipped gear teeth or other damage.

6

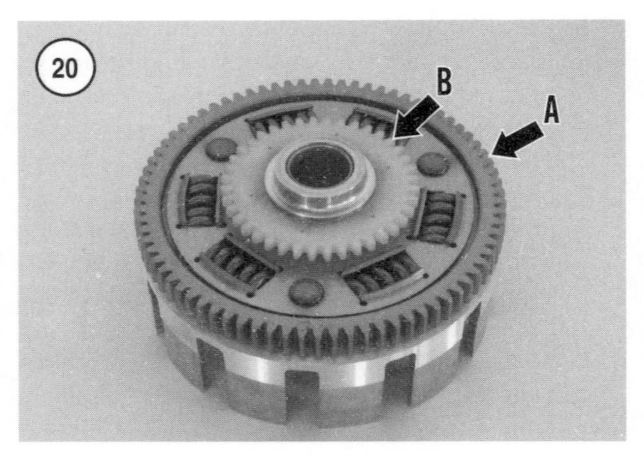

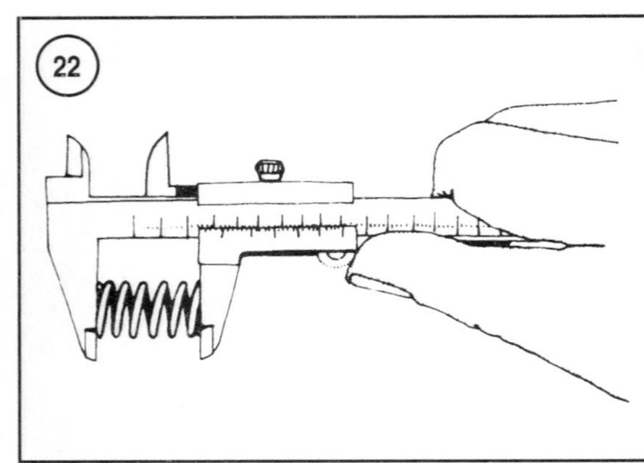

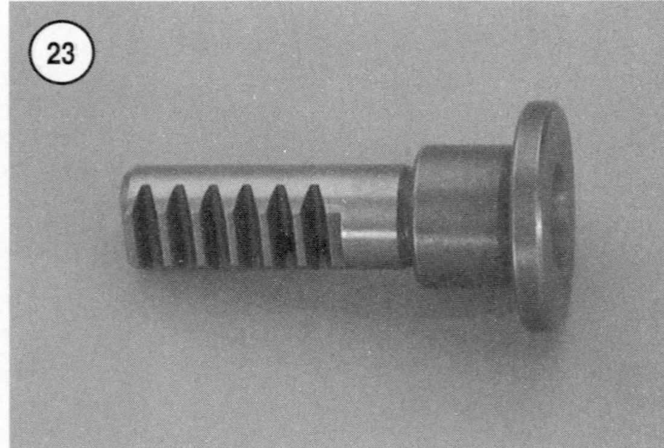

d. Inspect the oil pump drive gear (B, **Figure 20**).

6. Inspect the pressure plate (**Figure 21**) for the following conditions:

a. Galled or otherwise damaged plate contact surface (A, **Figure 21**).
b. Cracks or other damage.
c. Inspect the spring pockets (B, **Figure 21**) for damage.
d. Inspect the bearing (C, **Figure 21**). Replace if necessary.

7. Inspect the clutch springs for damage and free length (**Figure 22**). Replace the springs if the free length is less than the limit specified in **Table 1**.

8. Check the pull rod (**Figure 23**) for straightness and damage. Check the puller notch for excessive wear.

Installation

Refer to **Figure 1**. Where noted in the following procedure, lubricate components with engine oil.

NOTE
Make sure the primary gear and oil pump gear mesh properly when installing the clutch housing.

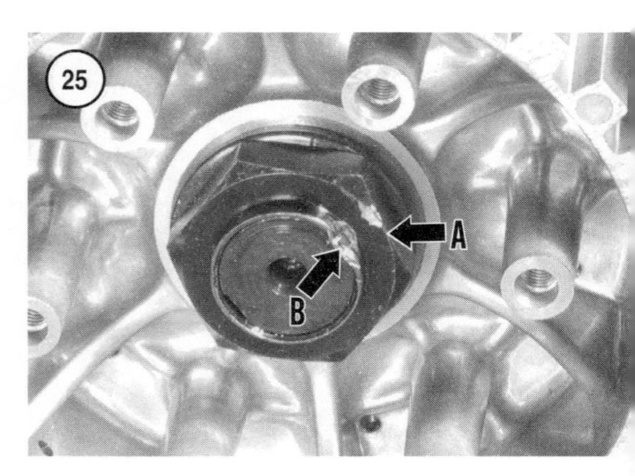

26

27

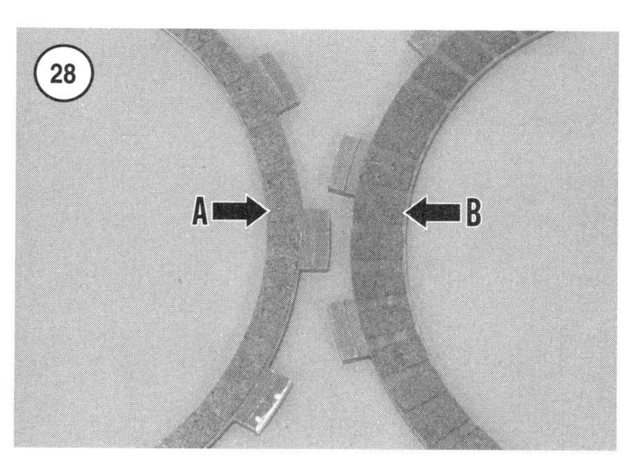

28

29

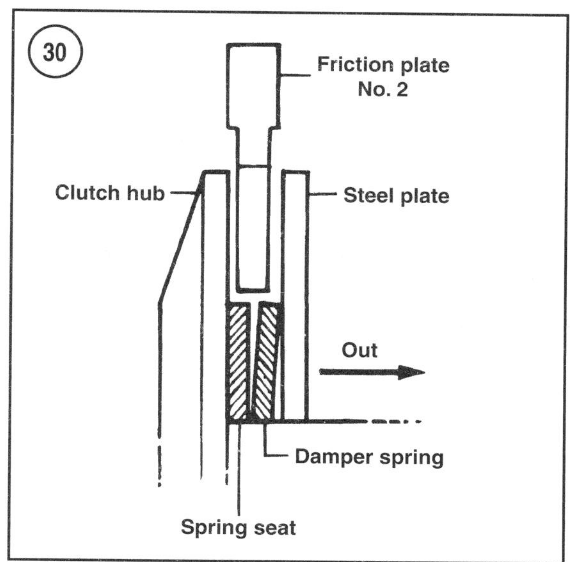

30

1. Lubricate the transmission mainshaft and clutch housing bore. Then, slide the housing (**Figure 13**) onto the shaft.
2. Place the thrust washer (**Figure 12**) onto the shaft.
3. Install the clutch hub (**Figure 11**) onto the shaft.
4. Install the conical washer (**Figure 24**) with the OUT mark facing toward the outside.
5. Install the clutch locknut finger-tight.
6. Hold the clutch hub using the tool when disassembling the clutch. Tighten the clutch locknut to 95 N•m (70 ft.-lb.).
7. Stake the clutch locknut (A, **Figure 25**) into the notch (B) in the mainshaft.
8. Remove the holding tool from the clutch hub.
9. Install the damper spring seat (**Figure 26**) onto the clutch hub.
10. Install the damper spring (**Figure 27**) onto the clutch hub so the side marked OUTSIDE (concave side) faces out.
11. Identify the single No. 2 friction plate in the clutch pack. The No. 2 friction plate (A, **Figure 28**) has a larger inside diameter than the remaining No. 1 friction plates (B).
12. Lubricate the friction plates and steel plates with engine oil.
13. Install friction plate No. 2 (**Figure 29**) around the damper spring seat and damper spring. Push it on until it is seated correctly.

NOTE
*Refer to **Figure 30** to verify correct assembly of the spring seat, spring and friction plate No. 2.*

14. Install a steel plate and push it on until it is completely seated against friction plate No. 2.

6

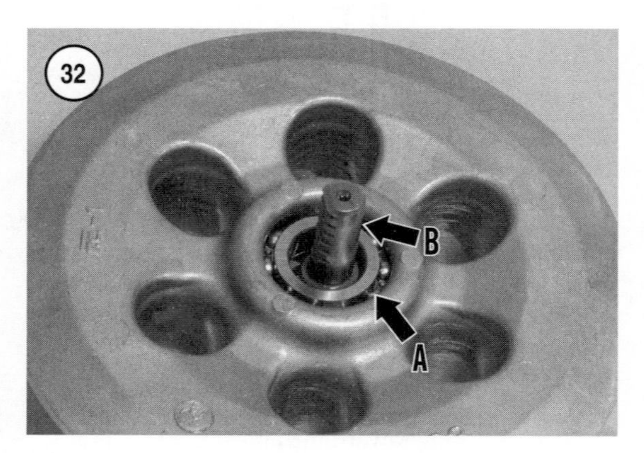

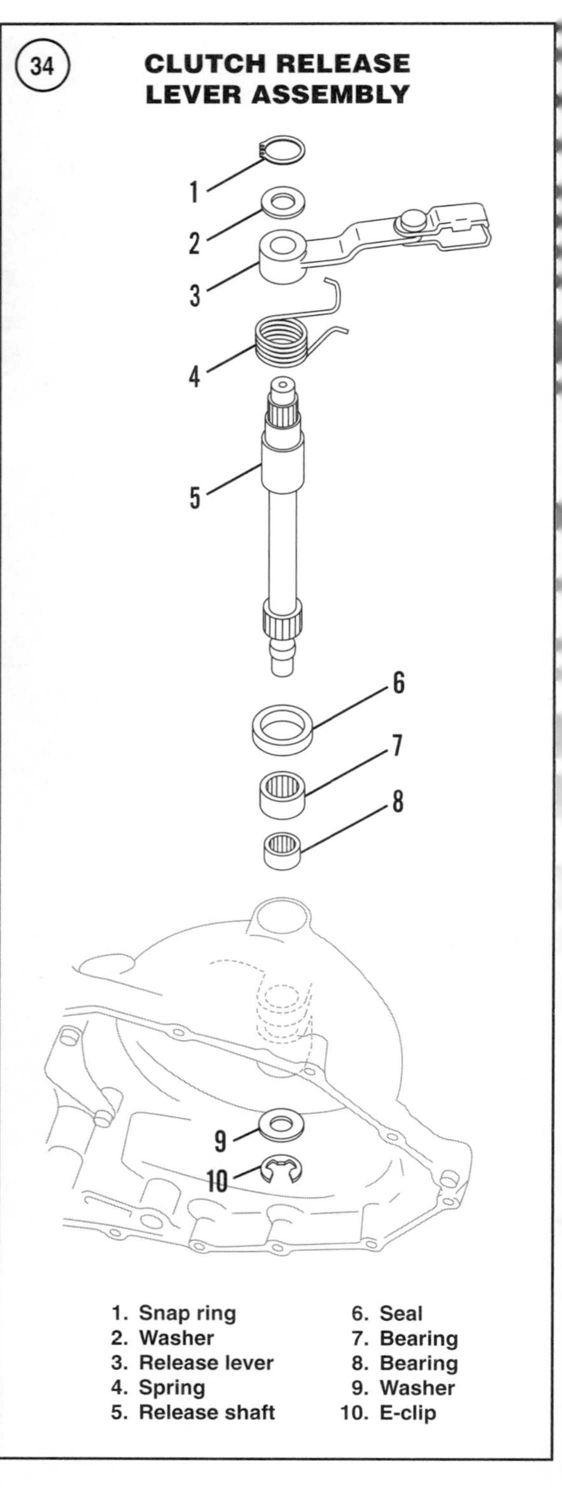

15. On 2006-2012 models, install a new circlip into the groove around the clutch hub (A, **Figure 31**). Insert the clip ends (B, **Figure 31**) through the hole in the hub. Be sure the clip ends (**Figure 6**) are fully inserted through the hole.

16. Beginning with a friction plate, alternately install friction plates and steel plates into the clutch housing and clutch hub.

17. If removed, install the bearing (C, **Figure 21**) into the pressure plate (A).

18. Lubricate the bearing (A, **Figure 32**) with engine oil, and then insert the pull rod (B).

19. Install the pressure plate (A, **Figure 33**).

20. Install the clutch springs (B, **Figure 33**) and the bolts with washers (C).

21. Using a crossing pattern, evenly tighten the clutch spring bolts in several steps to 8 N•m (71 in.-lb.).

22. Install the right crankcase cover as described in Chapter Five.

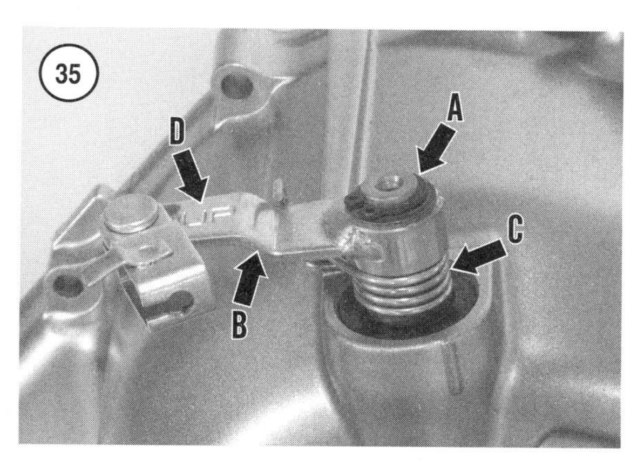

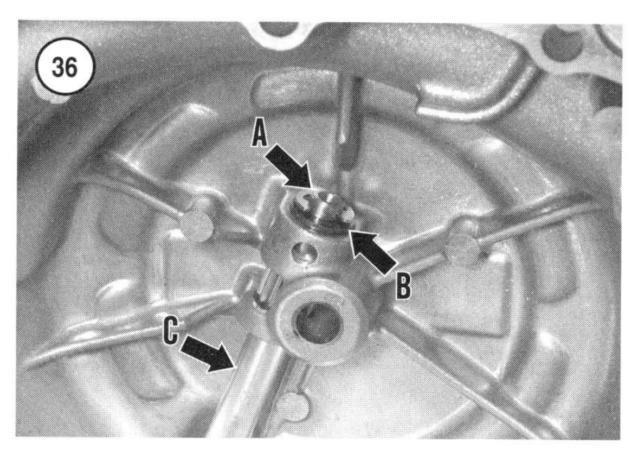

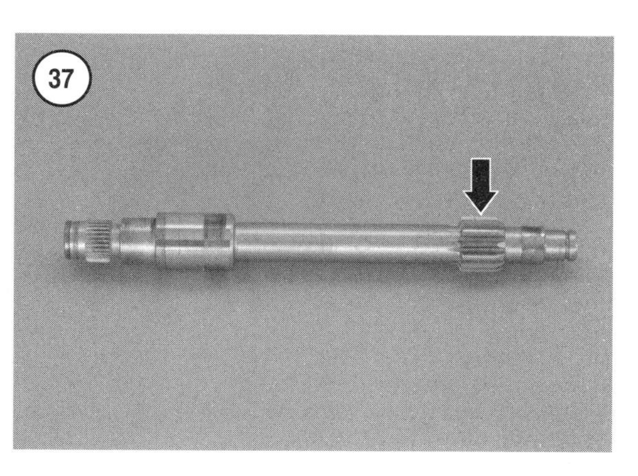

38

CLUTCH RELEASE LEVER ASSEMBLY

Removal/Inspection/Installation

The clutch release mechanism is located in the right crankcase cover. Refer to **Figure 34**.

1. Remove the right crankcase cover as described in Chapter Five.
2. Remove the snap ring (A, **Figure 35**) and washer from the outer end of the shaft.
3. Remove the release lever (B, **Figure 35**) and spring (C).
4. Remove the E-clip (A, **Figure 36**) and washer (B) from the inner end of the shaft.
5. Withdraw the shaft (C, **Figure 36**) from the cover.
6. Inspect all parts for wear or damage. Inspect the splines in the shaft and release lever (**Figure 37**) for damage.
7. Install the shaft into the clutch cover.
8. At the inner end of the shaft, install the washer (B, **Figure 36**) and E-clip (A). Make sure the E-clip is completely seated in the shaft groove.
9. Install the release lever and spring onto the outer end of the shaft. Install the lever on the shaft so the UP mark (D, **Figure 35**) on the top of the lever is up.
10. Install the washer and snap ring (A, **Figure 35**). Make sure the snap ring is completely seated in the shaft groove.

Oil Seal and Bearing Replacement

1. Carefully pry the seal (A, **Figure 38**) out of the cover using a screwdriver or seal puller.
2. Remove the upper bearing (B, **Figure 38**) or lower bearing (**Figure 39**) using a bearing puller.
3. Clean and dry the cover.
4. Install the new bearing(s) using a bearing driver or a suitable size socket.

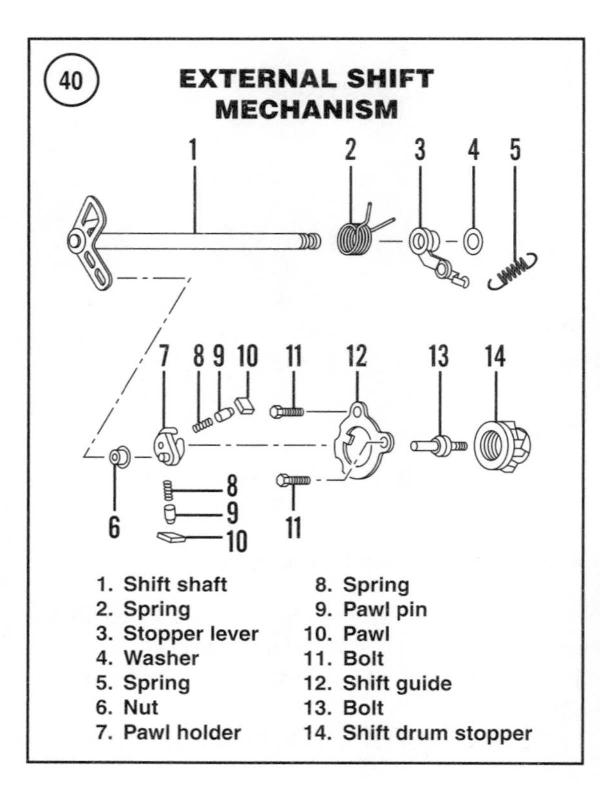

40

EXTERNAL SHIFT MECHANISM

1. Shift shaft
2. Spring
3. Stopper lever
4. Washer
5. Spring
6. Nut
7. Pawl holder
8. Spring
9. Pawl pin
10. Pawl
11. Bolt
12. Shift guide
13. Bolt
14. Shift drum stopper

5. Pack the seal lips with a waterproof grease. Then, press the seal into the cover with the closed side facing out.

EXTERNAL SHIFT MECHANISM

The external shift mechanism includes all parts related to transmission shifting that are not within the crankcase halves. This includes the shift lever, shift shaft and linkages that connect to the shift drum, located inside the crankcase. Other than the shift lever and reverse shift lever, all other components of the external shift mechanism are located behind the right crankcase cover.

The reverse shift lever is covered in *Reverse Shift Lever* (this chapter).

Removal

Refer to **Figure 40**.

1. Remove the shift lever clamp bolt (A, **Figure 41**).
2. Mark the location of the shift lever (B, **Figure 41**) on the shift shaft, and then remove the lever.
3. Remove the clutch as described in this chapter.
4. Detach the stopper lever spring (A, **Figure 42**).
5. Slowly pull the shift shaft (B, **Figure 42**) and spring (C) from the engine. Remove the shaft assembly (**Figure 43**).
6. Remove the shaft washer if it remains on the engine.
7. Remove the roller (**Figure 44**) from the pawl holder.

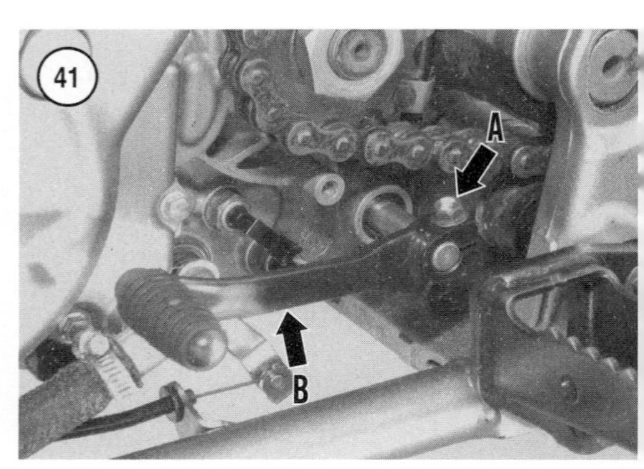

41

42

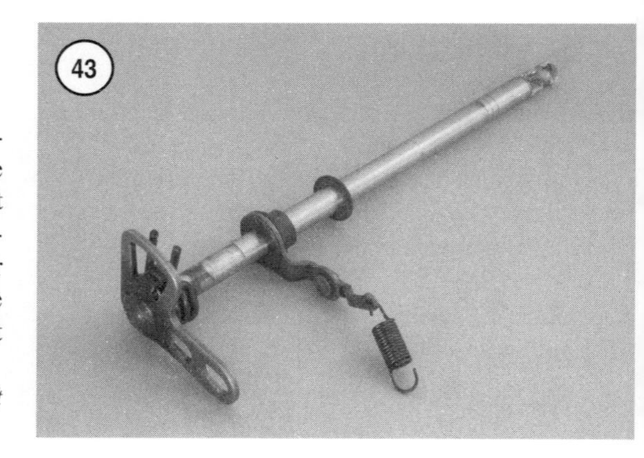

43

44

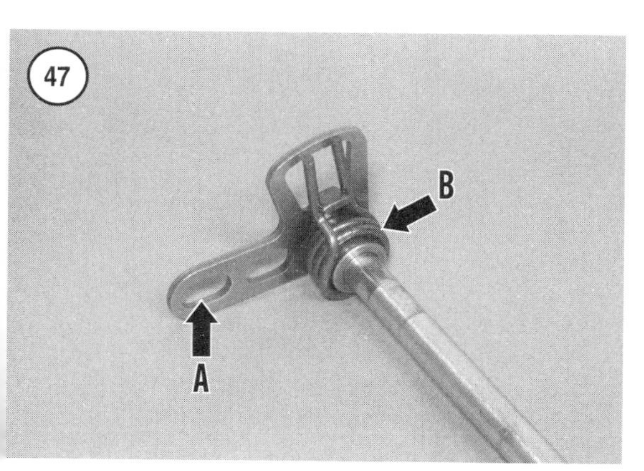

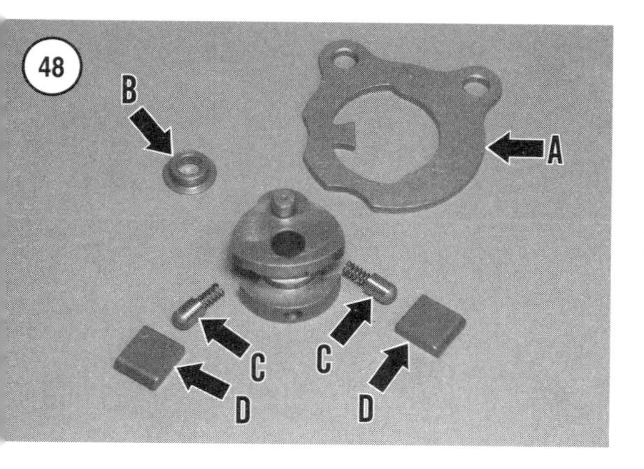

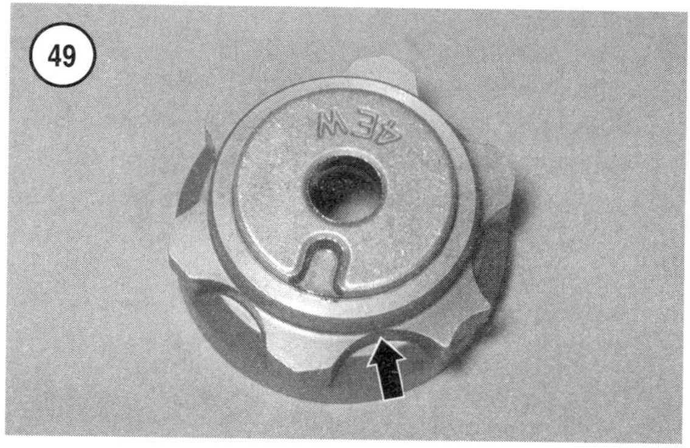

NOTE
Be careful when handling the pawl holder assembly. It contains loose pairs of springs, pawl pins and pawls.

8. Remove the bolts (A, **Figure 45**) securing the shift guide (B). Then, remove the shift guide (B, **Figure 45**) and the pawl holder assembly (C).
9. Remove the shift drum stopper bolt (A, **Figure 46**).
10. Remove the shift drum stopper (B, **Figure 46**).
11. Inspect the parts as described in this section.

Inspection

1. Inspect the shift shaft and spring assembly. Note the following:
   a. Inspect the splines on the shaft for damage.
   b. Inspect the shaft for straightness.
   c. Inspect the engagement hole (A, **Figure 47**) for wear. The hole should be symmetrical and not worn excessively.
   d. Inspect the spring (B, **Figure 47**) for wear and fatigue cracks.
   e. Replace any parts that are worn or damaged.
2. Inspect the pawl holder assembly, roller and shift guide. Note the following:
   a. Inspect the shift guide (A, **Figure 48**) for wear.
   b. Inspect the roller (B, **Figure 48**) for wear. The roller should be symmetrical, with no perceptible wear in any one area.
   c. Inspect the springs and pawl pins (C, **Figure 48**) for wear.
   d. Inspect the pawls (D, **Figure 48**) for wear at their square end. The ends must be square in order to stay engaged in the shift drum stopper.
   e. Replace any parts that are worn or damaged.
3. Inspect the shift drum stopper as follows:
   a. Inspect the detents (**Figure 49**) in the back of the stopper. The detents must not be worn, or faulty shifting will occur.
   b. Inspect the depressions in the front side of the stopper for wear or damage. If the depressions are rounded at their shoulders, the pawls in the

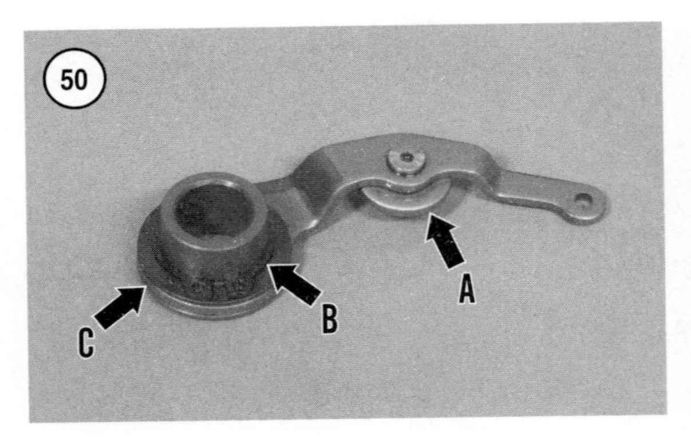

shift lever assembly can slip. Replace the stopper if it is worn or damaged.

4. Inspect the stopper lever assembly. Note the following:
   a. Inspect the roller (A, **Figure 50**) on the lever. It must be symmetrical and turn freely, but be firmly attached to the lever.
   b. Inspect the fit of the shouldered sleeve in the lever hole. The sleeve must fit in the hole firmly, but not bind or drag when the lever is pivoted. If necessary, replace the worn parts after removing the snap ring (B, **Figure 50**) and washer (C).
   c. Inspect the spring for wear or fatigue.
   d. Replace any parts that are worn or damaged.
5. Inspect the pin (A, **Figure 51**) on the end of the shift drum for wear or damage. The pin must be in good condition in order to properly engage with the notch in the back of the shift drum stopper.

Installation

Refer to **Figure 40**.

1. Install the shift drum stopper so the notch (B, **Figure 51**) on the back of the drum stopper engages the pin (A) on the shift drum.
2. Install the shift drum stopper bolt (A, **Figure 46**) and tighten to 30 N•m (22 ft.-lb.).
3. Insert the springs, pawl pins and pawls into the pawl holder, making sure that the rounded ends of the pawls are seated in the pawl holder (**Figure 52**). The pawls must compress and retract smoothly in the pawl holder. Lubricate the pawl assembly with engine oil.
4. Fit the pawl holder assembly into the shift guide (**Figure 53**).
5. Lubricate the shift drum stopper bolt with engine oil. Slide the pawl holder and shift guide assembly onto the shaft of the shift drum stopper bolt (**Figure 45**). Apply threadlock to the threads of the shift guide bolts (A, **Figure 45**), and tighten the bolts to 10 N•m (89 in.-lb.).
6. Place the roller (**Figure 44**) onto the pawl holder, installing the wide portion of the roller first. Lubricate the roller with engine oil.

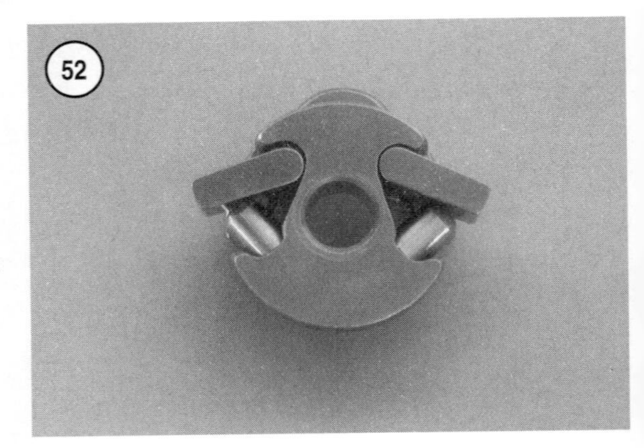

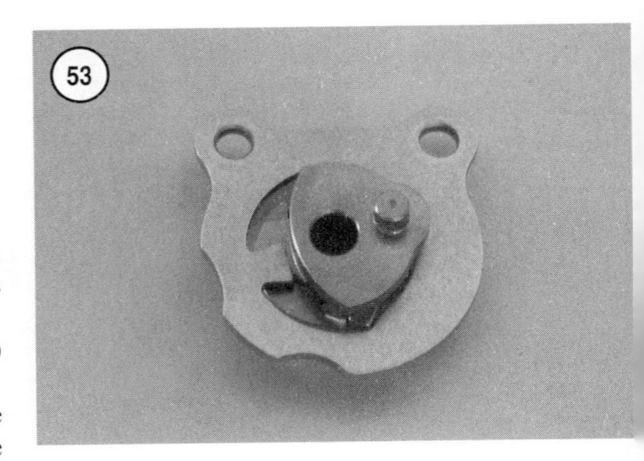

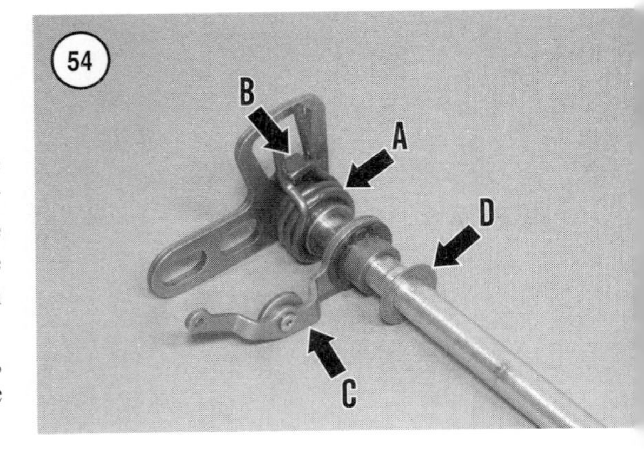

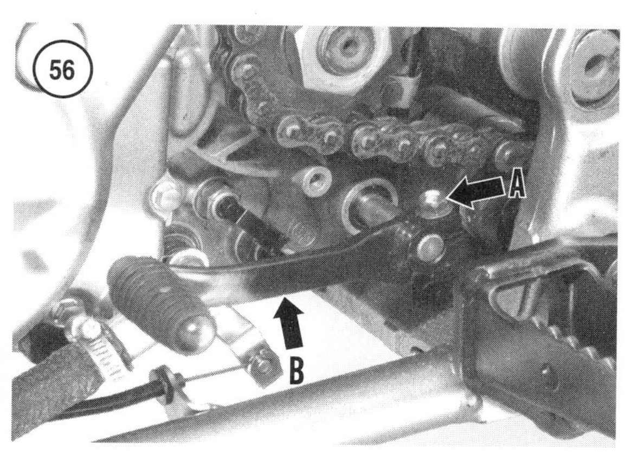

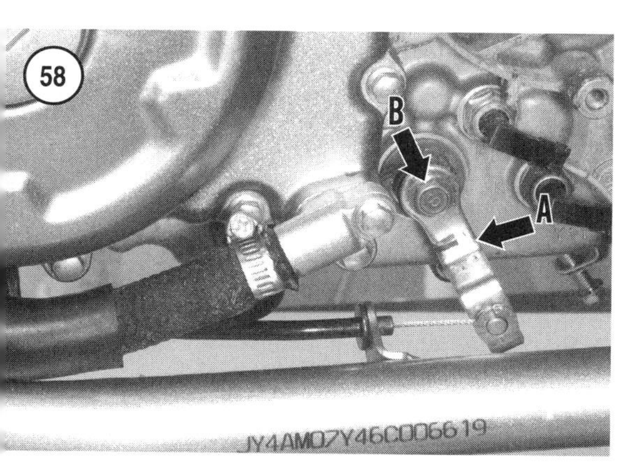

7. If removed, slide the spring (A, **Figure 54**) onto the shift shaft. The spring ends must press against the lever (B, **Figure 54**) on opposite sides.
8. Install the stopper lever (C, **Figure 54**) onto the shift shaft so the snap ring is toward the splined end of the shaft. Install the washer (D, **Figure 54**).
9. Lubricate the shift shaft.
10. Insert the shift shaft into the engine cases. As the lever and spring approach the engine, position the spring ends (A, **Figure 55**) on each side of the pin (B). Engage the roller (C, **Figure 55**) with the lever slot (D). Position the stopper lever roller (E, **Figure 55**) against the lower side of the shift drum stopper, and attach the stopper lever spring (F).
11. Lubricate the shift mechanism components.
12. Install the clutch as described in this chapter.
13. Install the shift lever in its original location on the shift shaft.
14. Install and tighten the shift lever clamp bolt to 16 N•m (12 ft.-lb.).

REVERSE SHIFT LEVER

The reverse shift lever is cable-actuated by the reverse shift knob mounted on the right, front fender. The reverse shift lever is located on the left side of the crankcase. Mounted on the reverse lockout shaft, moving the shift lever forward allows internal engagement of the reverse gear in the transmission.

Removal/Installation

1. Remove the shift lever clamp bolt (A, **Figure 56**). Mark the original location of the shift lever (B, **Figure 56**), and then remove it.
2. Push back the boots (A, **Figure 57**) on the reverse cable adjuster (B).
3. Loosen the locknut (C, **Figure 57**). Turn the adjuster (B, **Figure 57**) to obtain maximum cable slack at the reverse shift lever (A, **Figure 58**).
4. Remove the reverse shift lever retaining bolt (B, **Figure 58**).
5. Remove the reverse shift lever and spring.
6. Reverse the removal steps for installation while noting the following:
   a. Make sure the spring forces the shift lever rearward.
   b. Tighten the reverse shift lever retaining bolt to 13 N•m (115 in.-lb.).
   c. Adjust the reverse cable as described in Chapter Three.
   d. Install the shift lever in its original location.
   e. Install and tighten the shift lever clamp bolt to 16 N•m (12 ft.-lb.).

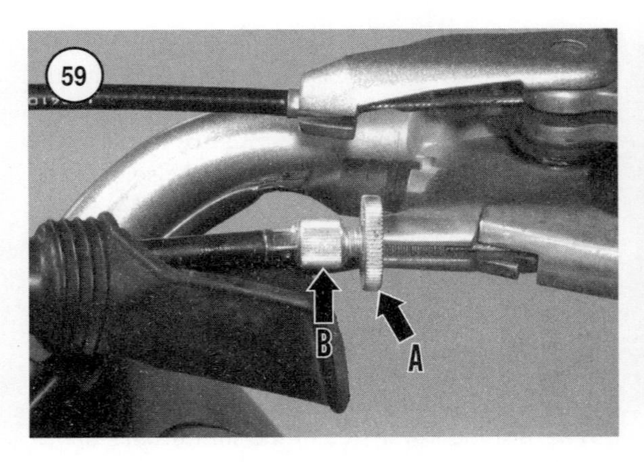

CLUTCH CABLE

Replacement

1. Loosen the clutch cable locknut (A, **Figure 59**) and loosen the adjuster (B) to allow maximum slack in the clutch cable.
2. Disconnect the cable end from the clutch hand lever.
3. Loosen the locknuts (**Figure 60**) at the lower clutch cable adjuster.
4. Bend out the lock tab on the clutch cable end retainer.
5. Remove the end of the clutch cable from the clutch lever, and release the cable from the cable bracket on the right crankcase cover.

NOTE
Prior to removing the cable, make a drawing of the cable routing through the frame. It is very easy to forget how it was run, once it has been removed. Replace the cable exactly as it was, avoiding any sharp turns.

6. Pull the clutch cable out from behind the steering head area and out of the retaining loop and clips on the frame.
7. Remove the cable and replace it with a new cable.
8. Install the cable by reversing the removal steps. Adjust the clutch as described in Chapter Three.

REVERSE CABLE

Replacement

1. Remove the shift lever clamp bolt (A, **Figure 56**). Mark the original location of the shift lever (B, **Figure 56**), and then remove it.
2. Push back the boots (A, **Figure 57**) on the reverse cable adjuster (B).
3. Loosen the locknut (C, **Figure 57**). Turn the adjuster (B, **Figure 57**) to obtain maximum cable slack at the reverse shift lever (A, **Figure 58**).

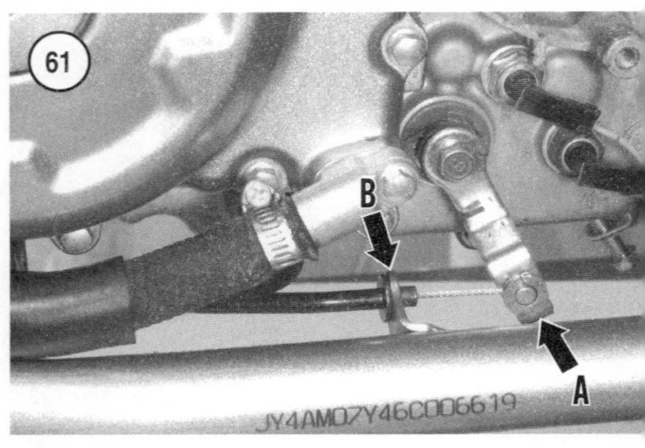

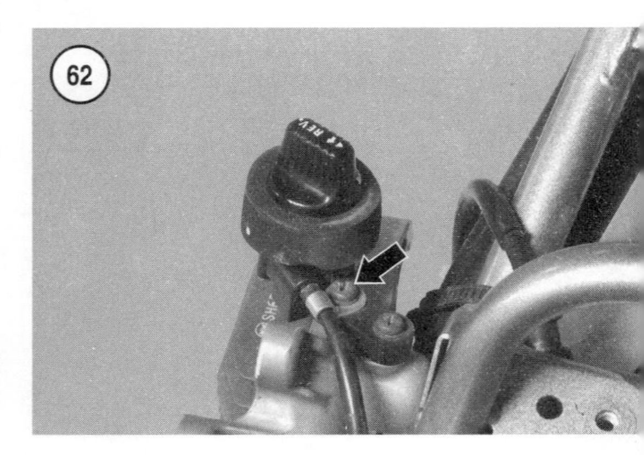

4. Disengage the cable end from the reverse shift lever (A, **Figure 61**).
5. Disengage the cable housing from the cable bracket (B, **Figure 61**).
6. Remove the front fender as described in Chapter Fifteen.
7. Remove the screw (**Figure 62**) securing the cable end. Then, pull the cable end out of the reverse knob housing.
8. Remove the cable while noting the location of any retaining clamps.
9. Install the new cable. Adjust the reverse cable as described in Chapter Three.
10. Install the shift lever in its original location. Install and tighten the clamp bolt to 16 N•m (12 ft.-lb.).

Table 1 CLUTCH SPECIFICATIONS

Item	Standard mm (in.)	Service limit mm (in.)
Clutch spring free length	50.0 (1.97)	48.0 (1.89)
Friction plate 1		
Quantity	7	–
Thickness	2.92-3.08 (0.115-0.121)	2.82 (0.111)
Friction plate 2		
Quantity	1	–
Thickness	2.90-3.10 (0.114-0.122)	2.80 (0.110)
Steel plate		
Quantity	7	–
Thickness	1.50-1.60 (0.059-0.063)	–
Warp	–	0.20 (0.008)

Table 2 CLUTCH TORQUE SPECIFICATIONS

Item	N•m	in.-lb.	ft.-lb.
Clutch locknut	95	–	70
Clutch spring bolts	8	71	–
Reverse shift lever retaining bolt	13	115	–
Shift drum stopper bolt	30	–	22
Shift guide bolts*	10	89	–
Shift lever clamp bolt	16	–	12

*Apply a medium-strength threadlock to the fastener threads.

CHAPTER SEVEN

TRANSMISSION AND INTERNAL SHIFT MECHANISM

This chapter covers service for the transmission and internal shift mechanism. The external shift mechanism is covered in Chapter Six. Transmission and internal shift mechanism service requires crankcase disassembly as described in Chapter Five.

Transmission specifications are listed in **Table 1** and **Table 2**, located at the end of this chapter.

TRANSMISSION SERVICE

1. Lubricate all parts with molybdenum disulfide oil.
2. Parts with two different sides, such as gears, snap rings and shift forks, can be installed backward. To maintain the correct alignment and position of the parts during disassembly, mark each part and store it in order using a divided container.
3. The snap rings are a tight fit on the transmission shafts and will bend and twist during removal. Install new snap rings during transmission assembly.
4. To avoid bending and twisting the new snap rings during installation, use the following installation technique:
   a. Open the new snap ring with a pair of snap ring pliers while holding the back of the snap ring with a pair of pliers (**Figure 1**).
   b. Slide the snap ring down the shaft and seat it into the correct transmission groove. Check the snap ring to make sure it seats in the groove completely.
5. When installing snap rings, align the snap ring opening with the shaft groove as shown in **Figure 2**.
6. Snap rings and flat washers have one sharp edg and one rounded edge (**Figure 3**). Install the sna rings with the sharp edge facing away from the gea producing the thrust.

TRANSMISSION AND INTERNAL SHIFT MECHANISM

Removal

1. Split the crankcase as described in *Crankcas Disassembly* (Chapter Five).
2. Remove the seal retainer (**Figure 4**).
3. Remove the spacer (**Figure 5**) from the drive en of the countershaft. Then, remove the O-ring (**Figur 6**).
4. Remove the snap ring (A, **Figure 7**), washer (B and reverse gear (C) from the countershaft.
5. Remove the bushing (**Figure 8**) if it did not re main in the reverse gear.
6. Remove the reverse countershaft assembl (**Figure 9**).

NOTE

To provide additional clearance when removing the shift drum, lift up the mainshaft and countershaft as needed. After shift drum removal, return the shafts to their original positions.

7. Remove the shift drum (**Figure 10**).
8. Remove the right shift fork, shaft and dog clutc (**Figure 11**) as an assembly.

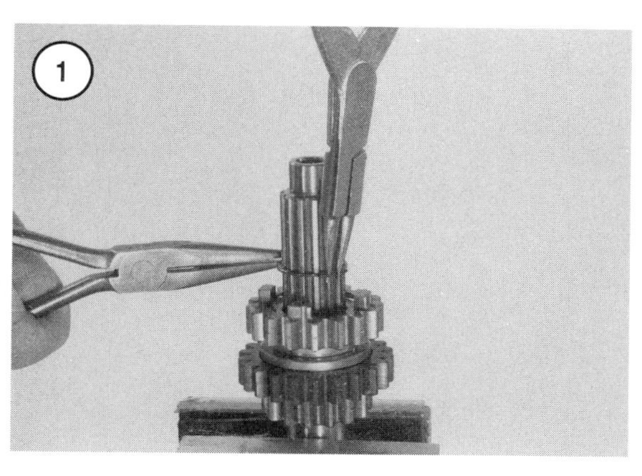
1

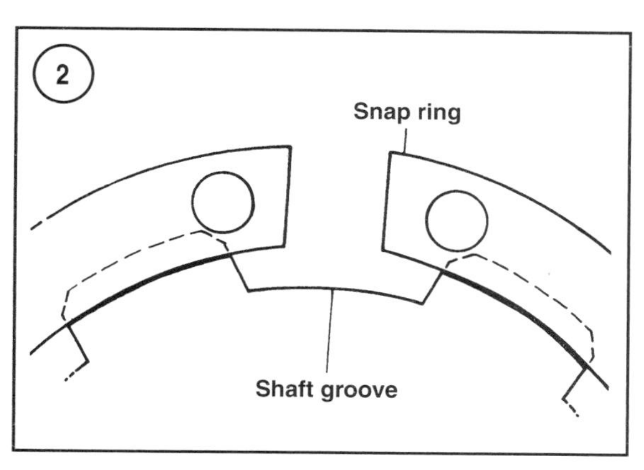
2
Snap ring
Shaft groove

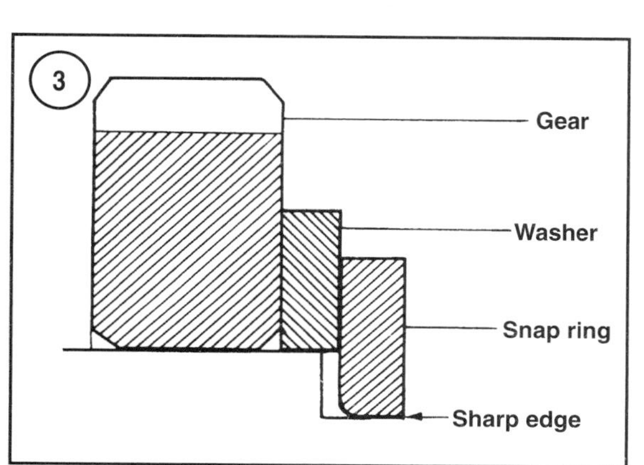
3
Gear
Washer
Snap ring
Sharp edge

4

5

6

7
C
B
A

8

9. Remove the center shift fork and shaft assembly (**Figure 12**).

10. Remove the left shift fork and shaft assembly (**Figure 13**).

11. Pull out both the countershaft assembly (A, **Figure 14**) and the mainshaft assembly (B) and remove them simultaneously as a unit (**Figure 15**).

12. Remove the reverse lockout shaft (**Figure 16**) and washer.

13. Prior to shaft disassembly, perform the *Preliminary Inspection* procedure as described in this section. Perform this even though the shafts may not be intended for service.

14. If necessary, service the transmission shafts as described in this chapter.

15. Wrap the transmission components in clean shop cloths and store in a box to avoid damage.

Installation

1. If necessary, replace the countershaft oil seal as follows:
   a. Remove the seal retainer if not previously removed.
   b. Remove the countershaft oil seal (**Figure 17**) using a suitable seal removal tool.
   c. Pack the lips of the oil seal with a waterproof bearing grease.
   d. Position the new oil seal with the manufacturer's marks facing out.
   e. Push in the seal until it bottoms.
2. Prior to installing any components, apply clean engine oil to all bearing surfaces.
3. Install the reverse lockout shaft (**Figure 16**) and washer.

NOTE
If necessary, identify the mainshaft and countershaft assemblies as described in the respective sections in this chapter.

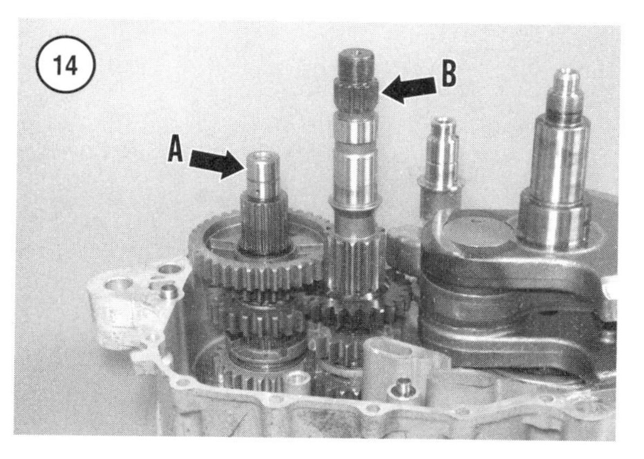

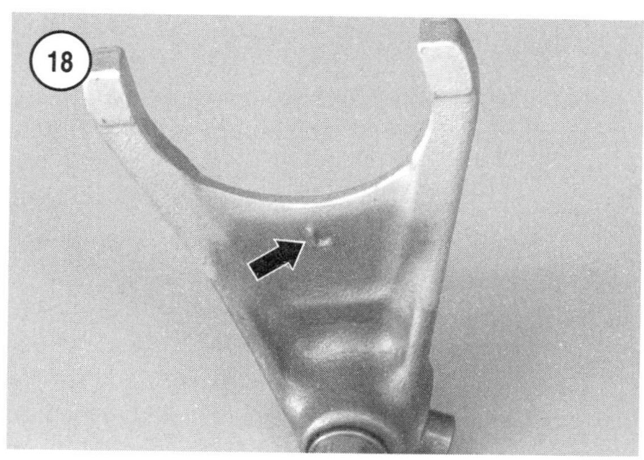

4. Assemble the mainshaft and countershaft assemblies together as a unit (**Figure 15**).
5. Install the countershaft (A, **Figure 14**) and mainshaft (B) assemblies into the crankcase together.

NOTE
*The shift forks are marked with a R (right), L (left) and C (center) (**Figure 18**). These marks relate to the engine as it sits in the frame, i.e. the R fork is on the right side of the engine. These marks must face the clutch (right side) of the engine.*

NOTE
It is necessary to move the mainshaft, countershaft and gears up and down to install the shift forks and shift drum. After fork and drum installation, make sure the shafts are fully seated in their bearings and that all components move correctly.

6. Install the left shift fork and shaft (**Figure 13**). Insert the shift fork ends into the groove on the countershaft fourth gear.
7. Install the center shift fork and shaft (**Figure 12**). Insert the shift fork ends into the groove on the mainshaft third gear.
8. Install the right shift fork and shaft (**Figure 11**). Insert the shift fork ends into the groove on the dog clutch.
9. Install the shift drum (**Figure 10**) while inserting the actuating pin on each shift fork into the appropriate groove on the shift drum.
10. Install the reverse countershaft assembly (**Figure 9**). Insert the step on the shaft end into the notch in the crankcase.
11. Install the bushing (**Figure 8**) onto the countershaft.
12. Install the reverse gear (C, **Figure 7**) onto the countershaft so the slotted side is toward the dog clutch.

13. Install the washer (B, **Figure 7**) and a new snap ring (A).
14. Install the O-ring (**Figure 6**) onto the countershaft.
15. Install the spacer so the notched end (A, **Figure 19**) is in.
16. Assemble the crankcase as described in Chapter Five.

Preliminary Inspection

1. Clean and inspect the shaft assemblies prior to disassembling them. Place the assembled shaft into a large can or plastic bucket and thoroughly clean the assembly with a petroleum-based solvent, such as kerosene, and a stiff brush. Dry the assembly with compressed air or let it sit on rags to drip dry. Do this for both shaft assemblies.
2. Visually inspect the components for excessive wear.

NOTE
Replace defective gears and their mating gears on the other shaft as well, even though it may not show as much wear or damage.

3. Check the gear teeth for chips, burrs or pitting. An oilstone may remove minor damage.
4. Carefully check the engagement dogs and slots. If any are chipped, worn, rounded or missing, replace the damaged gear.
5. Rotate the transmission bearings (**Figure 20** and **Figure 21**) by hand. Check for roughness, noise and radial play. Replace any bearing that is suspect as described in *Crankcase Bearings* (Chapter Five).
6. Inspect the inner and outer surfaces (B, **Figure 19**) of the spacer. If a groove exists where the spacer contacts the oil seal or O-ring, replace the spacer.

MAINSHAFT

Disassembly

Remove the parts from the mainshaft in the following order. Refer to **Figure 22**.

1. Clean and dry the assembled mainshaft (**Figure 23**).
2. Remove the snap ring (A, **Figure 24**).
3. Remove second gear (B, **Figure 24**).
4. Remove the tabbed spline lockwasher (A, **Figure 25**). Rotate the notched spline washer (B, **Figure 25**) to clear the spline groove and remove it.
5. Remove fourth gear (**Figure 26**).
6. Remove the spline bushing (**Figure 27**).
7. Remove the spline washer (**Figure 28**).
8. Remove the snap ring (A, **Figure 29**).
9. Remove third gear (B, **Figure 29**).
10. Remove the snap ring (A, **Figure 30**).
11. Remove the spline washer (B, **Figure 30**).
12. Remove fifth gear (**Figure 31**).

Inspection

Refer to *Transmission Inspection*.

Assembly

Refer to **Figure 22**.

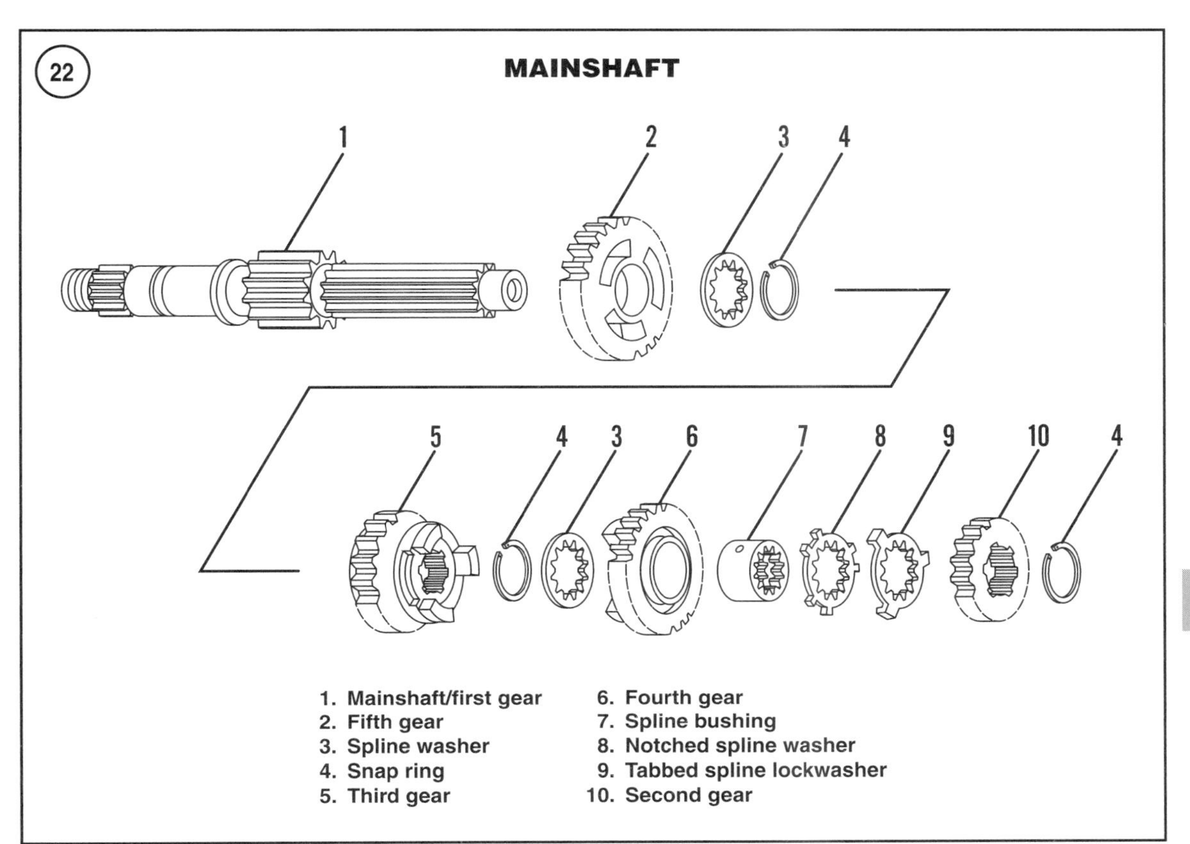
22
MAINSHAFT
1
2
3
4
5
4
3
6
7
8
9
10
4
1. Mainshaft/first gear
2. Fifth gear
3. Spline washer
4. Snap ring
5. Third gear
6. Fourth gear
7. Spline bushing
8. Notched spline washer
9. Tabbed spline lockwasher
10. Second gear

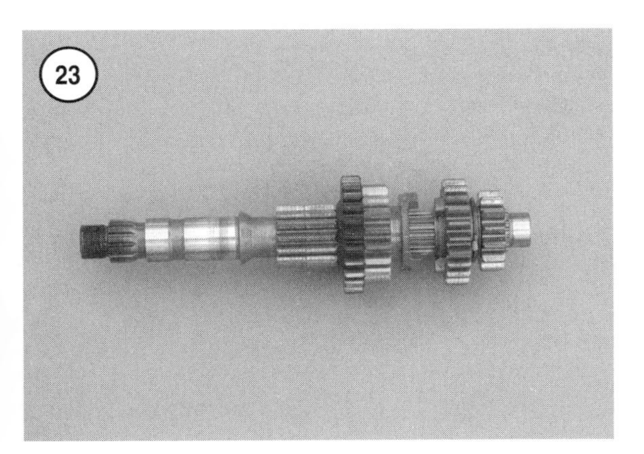
23

25
B
A

24
A
B

26

7

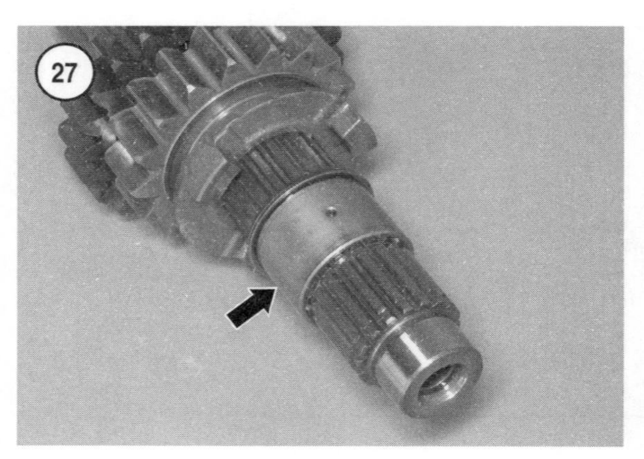

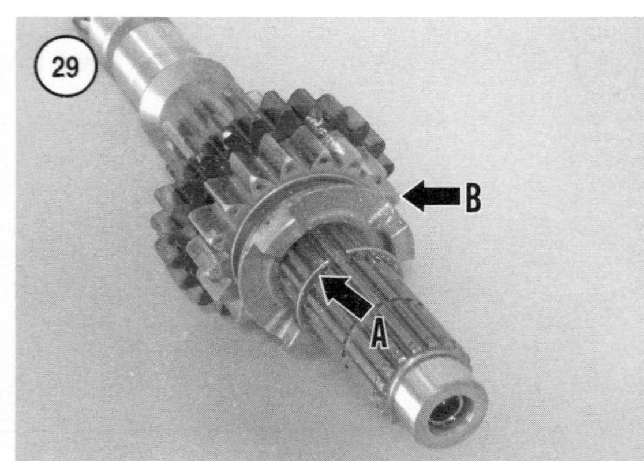

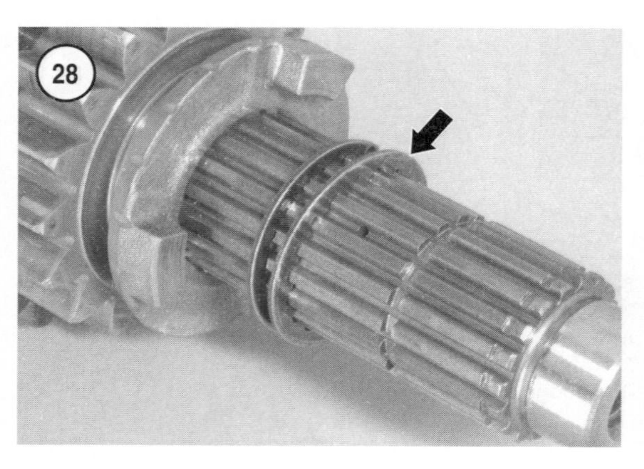

1. Install fifth gear (**Figure 31**) onto the mainshaft so the slots on the gear are toward the shaft end.
2. Install the spline washer (B, **Figure 30**).
3. Install a new snap ring (A, **Figure 30**).
4. Install third gear (B, **Figure 29**) so the end with the shift groove is toward the shaft end.
5. Install a new snap ring (A, **Figure 29**).
6. Install the spline washer (**Figure 28**).
7. Install the spline bushing so the oil hole in the bushing adjoins the oil hole in the mainshaft (**Figure 32**).
8. Install fourth gear (**Figure 26**) so the gear dogs are toward the third gear.
9. Slide on the notched spline washer (B, **Figure 25**). This washer is symmetrical (both sides are flat). Slightly rotate the spline washer so it is locked in the mainshaft groove and held in place by the splines.
10. Position the tabbed spline lockwasher (A, **Figure 25**) with the locking arms facing toward the notched spline washer (B).
11. Slide on the tabbed spline lockwasher and insert the locking arms into the notched spline washer as shown in **Figure 25**.
12. Install second gear (B, **Figure 24**).
13. Install the snap ring (A, **Figure 24**).
14. Wrap and store the assembly (**Figure 23**) until it is ready for installation into the crankcase. Install

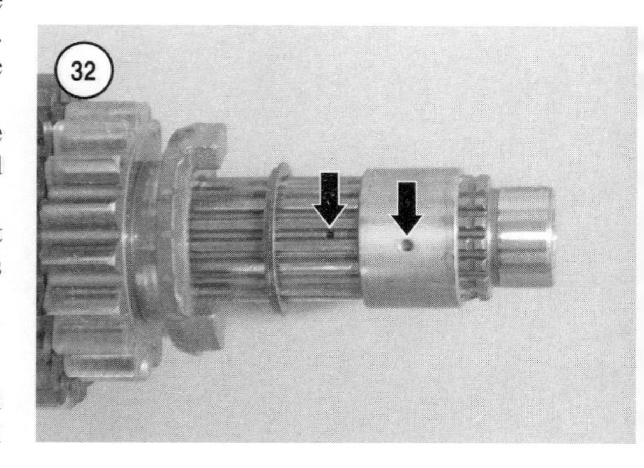

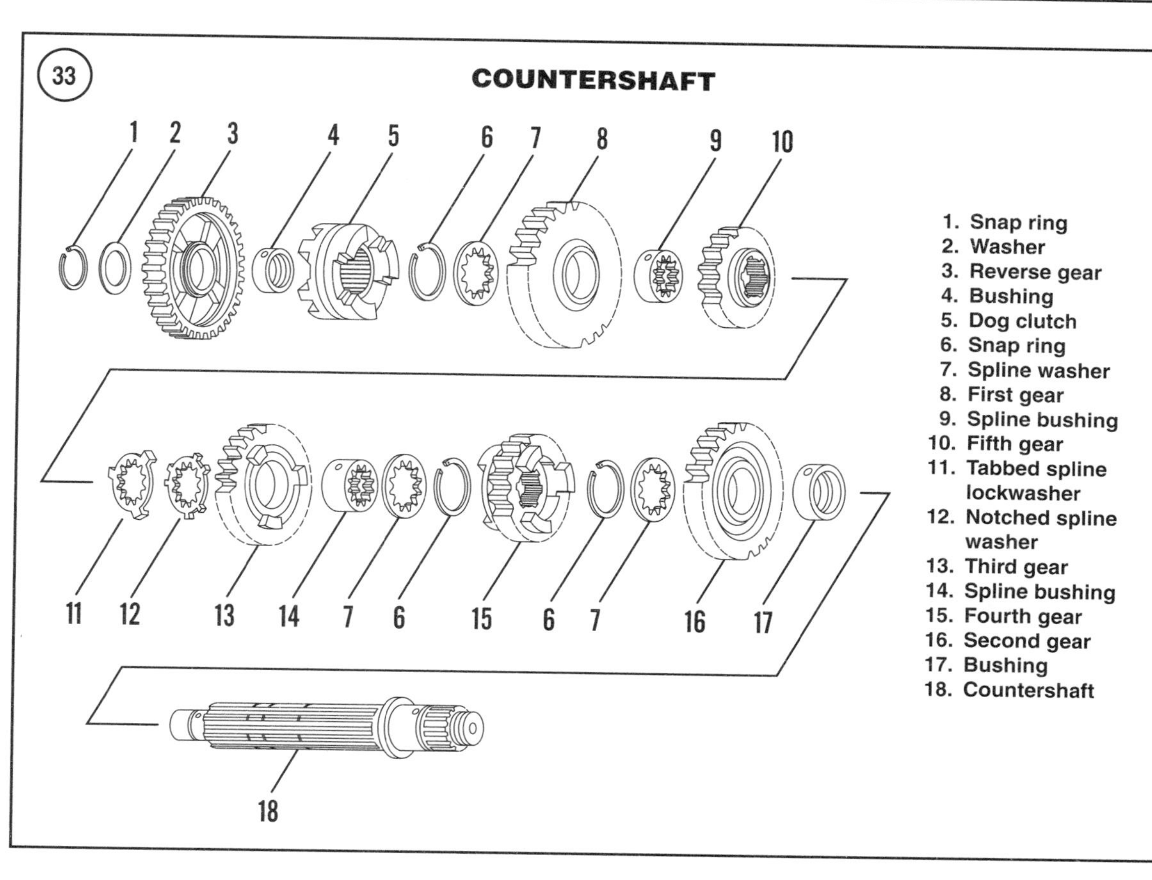

the complete transmission assembly as described in this chapter.

COUNTERSHAFT

Disassembly

Remove the parts from the countershaft in the following order. Refer to **Figure 33**.

1. Clean and dry the assembled countershaft (**Figure 34**).
2. Remove dog clutch (**Figure 35**).
3. Remove the snap ring (A, **Figure 36**) and spline washer (B).

7

4. Remove first gear (**Figure 37**).
5. Remove the spline bushing (**Figure 38**).
6. Remove fifth gear (**Figure 39**).
7. Remove the tabbed spline lockwasher (A, **Figure 40**). Rotate the notched spline washer (B, **Figure 40**) to clear the spline groove and remove it.
8. Remove third gear (**Figure 41**).
9. Remove the spline bushing (**Figure 42**).
10. Remove the spline washer (A, **Figure 43**) and snap ring (B).
11. Remove fourth gear (**Figure 44**).
12. Remove the snap ring (A, **Figure 45**) and spline washer (B).
13. Remove second gear (**Figure 46**).
14. Remove the bushing (**Figure 47**).

Inspection

Refer to *Transmission Inspection*.

Assembly

Refer to **Figure 33**.

1. Install the bushing (**Figure 47**).
2. Install second gear (**Figure 46**) so the slotted side is facing away from the threaded end of the shaft.

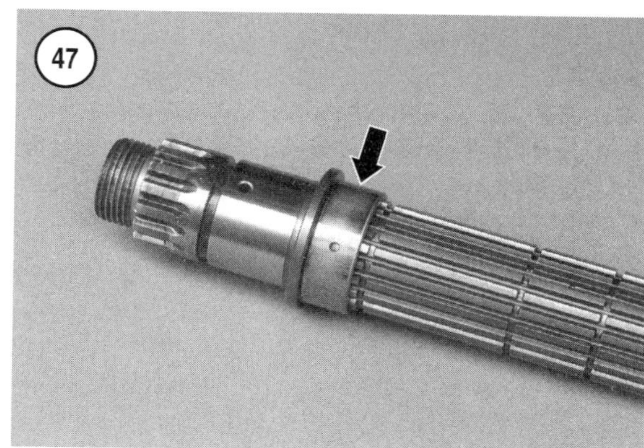

3. Install the spline washer (B, **Figure 45**) and a new snap ring (A).
4. Install fourth gear (**Figure 44**) so the end with the shift groove is facing away from the threaded end of the shaft.
5. Install a new snap ring (B, **Figure 43**) and the spline washer (A).

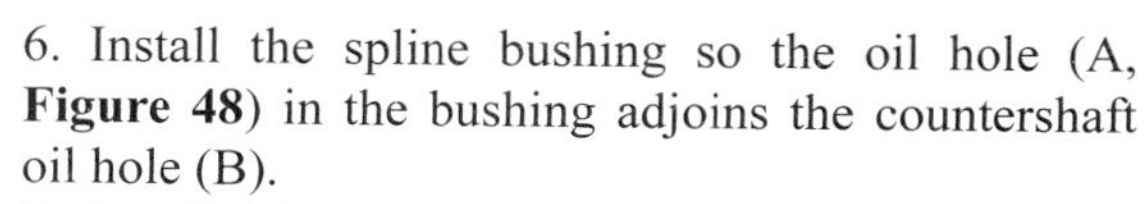
NOTE
The oil holes may not align. Position the bushing so its oil hole is over the spline next to the countershaft oil hole.

6. Install the spline bushing so the oil hole (A, **Figure 48**) in the bushing adjoins the countershaft oil hole (B).
7. Install third gear (**Figure 41**) so the slotted side is toward fourth gear.
8. Slide on the notched spline washer (B, **Figure 40**). This washer is symmetrical (both sides are flat). Slightly rotate the spline washer so it is locked in the countershaft groove and held in place by the splines.
9. Position the tabbed spline lockwasher (A, **Figure 40**) with the locking arms facing toward the notched spline washer (B).
10. Slide on the tabbed spline lockwasher and insert the locking arms into the notches in the spline washer as shown in **Figure 49**.

11. Install fifth gear (**Figure 39**).

NOTE
The oil holes may not align. Position the bushing so its oil hole is over the spline next to the countershaft oil hole.

12. Install the spline bushing (**Figure 38**) so the oil hole in the bushing adjoins the countershaft oil hole.
13. Install first gear (**Figure 37**) so the slotted side is facing away from the threaded end of the shaft.
14. Install the spline washer (B, **Figure 36**) and a new snap ring (A).
15. Install the dog clutch (**Figure 35**) so the side with four dogs is facing away the threaded end of the shaft.

REVERSE COUNTERSHAFT

Disassembly

Remove the parts from the reverse countershaft in the following order. Refer to **Figure 50**.

1. Clean and dry the assembled shaft (**Figure 51**).
2. Remove the snap ring (A, **Figure 52**) and washer (B).
3. Remove the reverse countershaft gear (**Figure 53**). The bushing may remain in the gear.
4. If the bushing remained on the shaft, remove the bushing (**Figure 54**).
5. If necessary, remove the remaining washer and snap ring.
6. Reverse the removal steps for installation.

TRANSMISSION INSPECTION

Shaft Inspection

1. Inspect each shaft for the following:
   a. Clean oil holes (A, **Figure 55**).
   b. Worn or-damaged splines (B, **Figure 55**).
   c. Rounded or damaged snap ring grooves (C, **Figure 55**).
   d. Damaged threads (A, **Figure 56**). Mildly damaged threads can be trued with a thread die.
   e. Wear, galling or other damage on the bearing/bushing surfaces (B, **Figure 56**). A blue discoloration on any surface indicates excessive heat.
   f. Broken or damaged gear teeth (C, **Figure 56**) on the mainshaft.
   g. Shaft runout. With the mainshaft or countershaft mounted between lathe centers or a centering jig, use a dial indicator to measure runout. Measure on a smooth surface near the center of the shaft. Refer to **Table 1** for the specification.

2. Assemble the shafts as described in this chapter.

Gear, Bushing and Washer Inspection

1. Inspect the gears for the following:
   a. Broken or damaged teeth (A, **Figure 57**).
   b. Worn, damaged or rounded dog slots (B, **Figure 57**).
   c. Scored, galled or fractured bore (C, **Figure 57**). The oil pockets should not be worn away. A blue discoloration indicates excessive heat.
   d. Worn or damaged shift fork groove (A, **Figure 58**).
   e. Worn or damaged splines (B, **Figure 58**).
   f. Worn, damaged or rounded gear dogs (C, **Figure 58**). Any wear on the dogs and mating recesses should be uniform. If the dogs are not worn evenly, the remaining dogs will be over stressed and possibly fail. Check the engagement of the dogs by placing the gears at their appropriate positions on the countershaft, then twisting the gears together. Check for positive engagement in both directions. If damage is evident, also check the condition of the shift forks as described in this chapter.

NOTE
The side of the gear dogs that carries the engine load will wear and eventually become rounded. The unloaded side of the dogs will remain unworn. Rounded dogs will cause the transmission to jump out of gear.

   g. Smooth gear operation on the shafts. Bored gears should fit firmly on the shaft, yet spin smoothly and freely. Splined gears should fit snugly at their position on the shaft, yet slide smoothly and freely from side to side. If a gear is worn or damaged, also replace the gear it mates to on the other shaft.

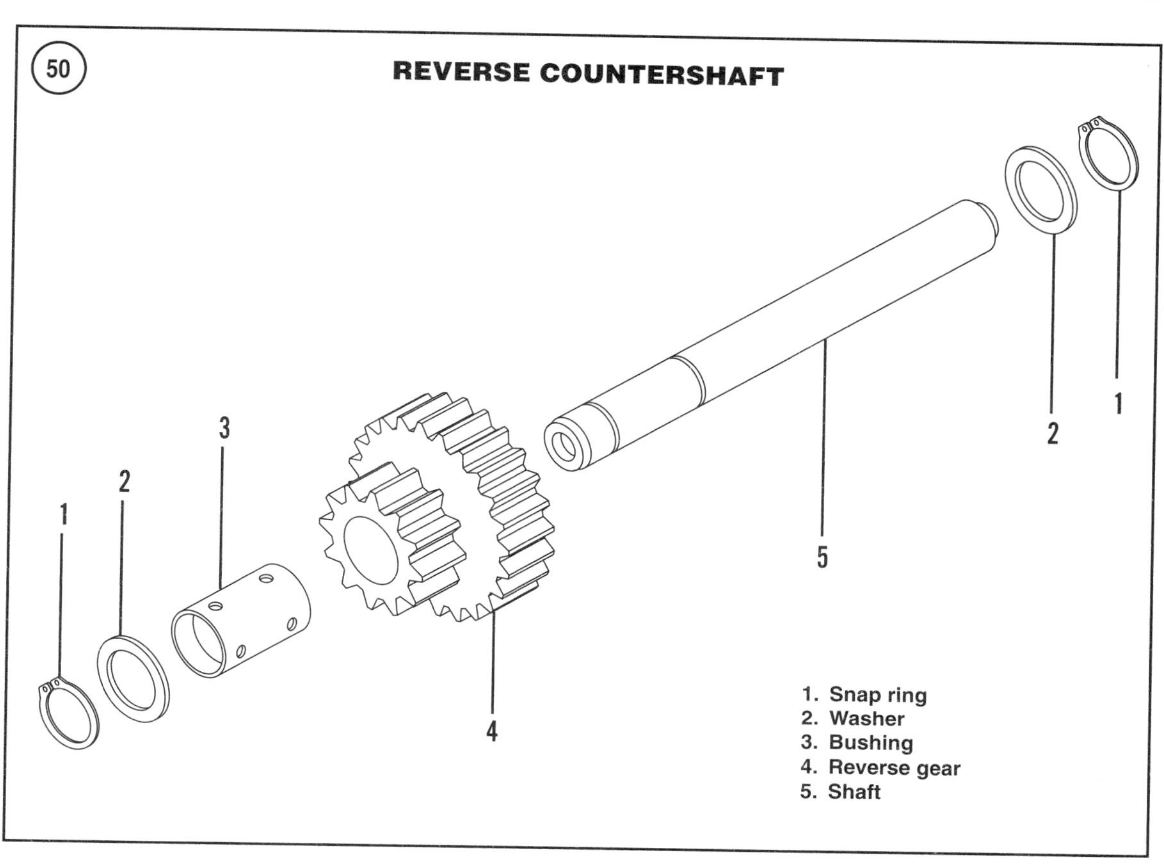
50
REVERSE COUNTERSHAFT
1
2
3
4
5
2
1
1. Snap ring
2. Washer
3. Bushing
4. Reverse gear
5. Shaft

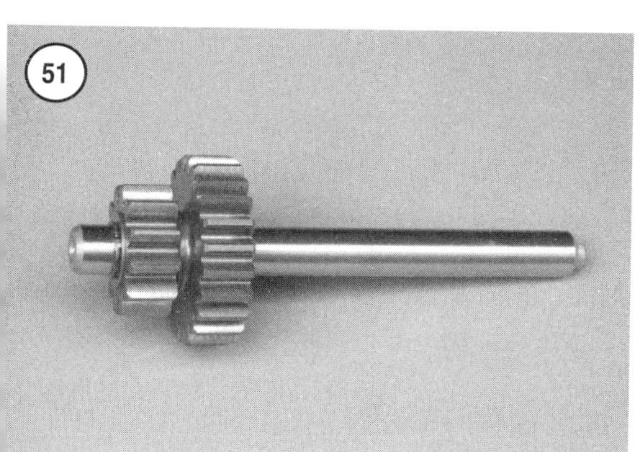
51

52
A
B

53

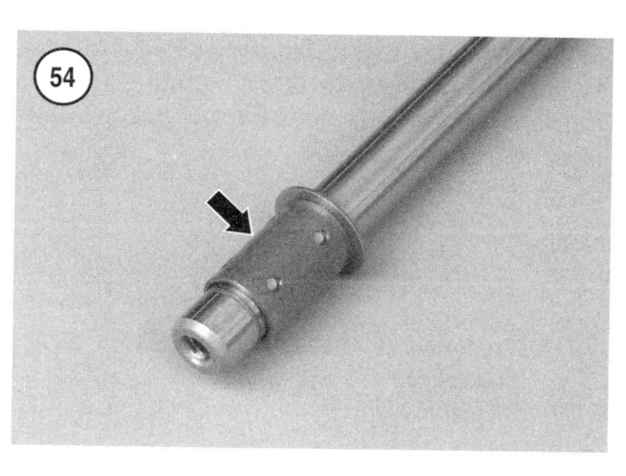
54

7

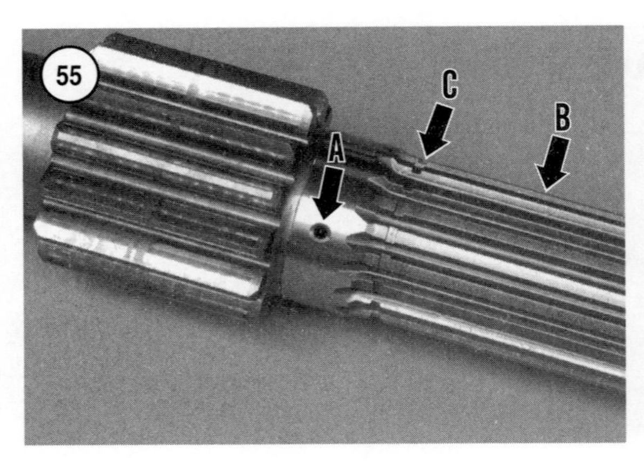

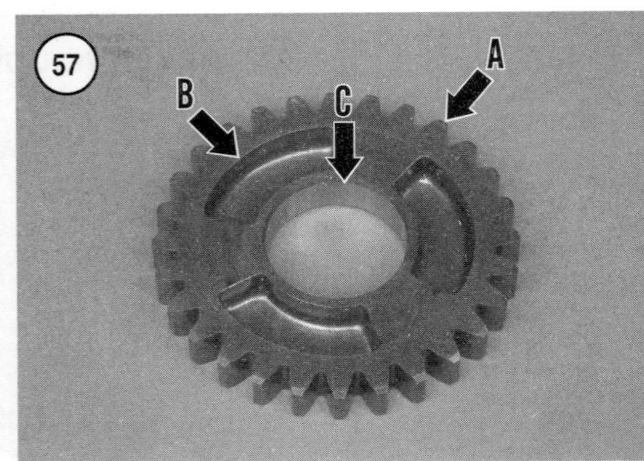

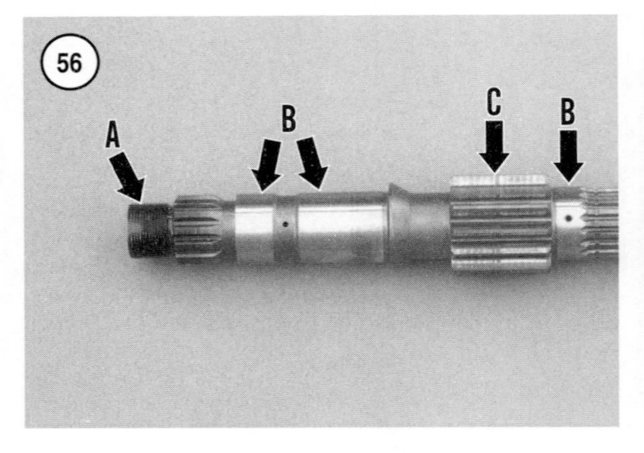

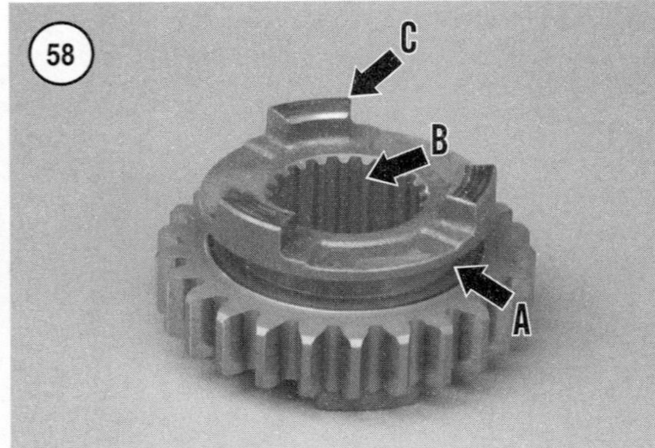

2. Inspect the bushing and gear bore (**Figure 59**). There should be no signs of wear or damage.
3. Install the parts onto their shafts as described in this chapter.

SHIFT DRUM AND FORKS

When the transmission is shifted, the shift drum and fork assembly engages and disengages pairs of gears on the transmission shafts. Cam grooves in the shift drum move the shift forks, which slide the gears along the mainshaft and countershaft.

It is important that the shift drum grooves, shift forks and mating gear grooves be in good condition. Too much wear between the parts will cause unreliable and poor engagement of the gears. This can lead to premature wear of the gear dogs and other parts.

Inspection

NOTE

The shift fork is retained on the shaft by circlips. The shift fork, shaft and clips are available only as a unit assembly.

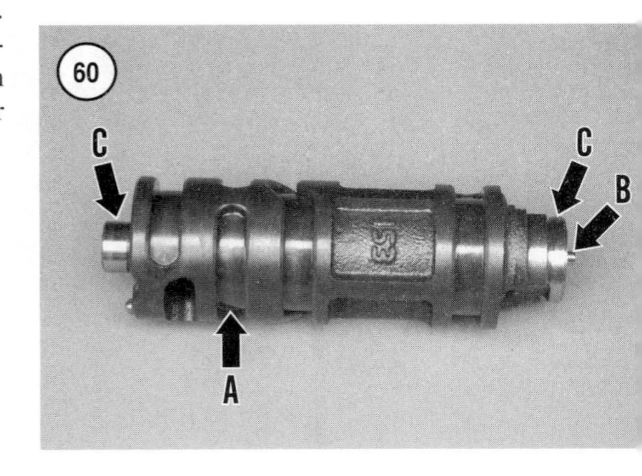

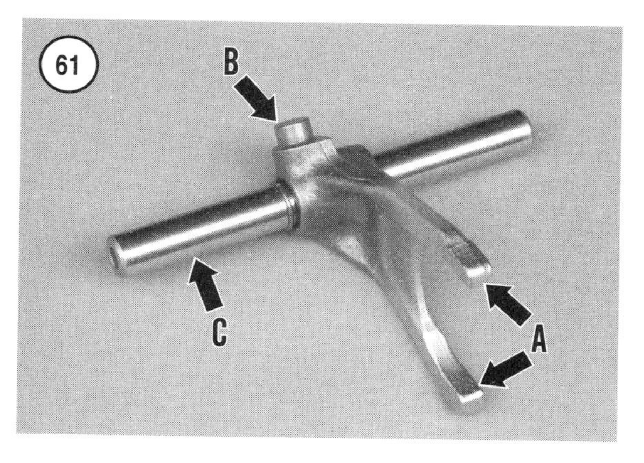

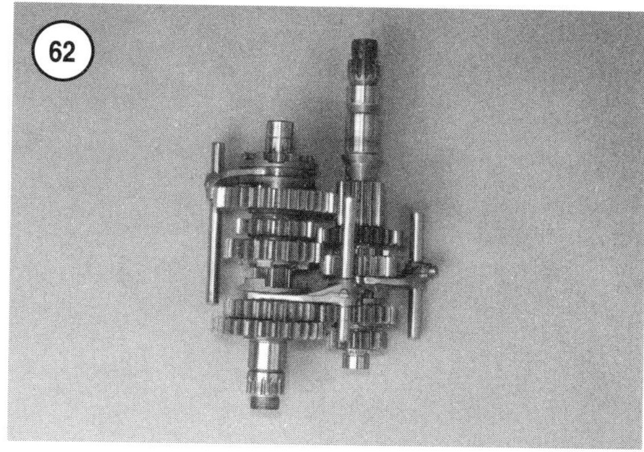

1. Clean all parts in solvent and dry with compressed air.
2. Inspect the shift drum. Check for:
   a. Worn or damaged grooves (A, **Figure 60**). The grooves should be a uniform width.
   b. Worn shift drum stopper pin (B, **Figure 60**).
   c. Worn or damaged bearing surfaces (C, **Figure 60**).
3. Inspect each shift fork for:
   a. Worn or damaged fingers (A, **Figure 61**).
   b. Worn or damaged guide pin (B, **Figure 61**). The pin should be symmetrical and not flat on the sides.
   c. Bends, cracks or scoring.
   d. Worn or damaged pivot shafts (C, **Figure 61**).
4. Inspect the fit of each fork guide pin with the appropriate groove in the shift drum. The pin should fit with slight lateral play.
5. Inspect the fit of each fork in the matching gear groove. Refer to **Figure 62** for correct fork and groove combinations. The forks should fit with slight lateral play.
6. Inspect the fit of each fork shaft in the corresponding bore in the right and left crankcase halves. The fork shaft should slide smoothly in the bore.

Table 1 TRANSMISSION SPECIFICATIONS

Transmission	Constant mesh, 5-speed forward, 1-speed reverse
Shift pattern	1-N-2-3-4-5
Primary reduction ratio	2.265 (77/34)
Final reduction ratio	2.714 (38/14)
Transmission gear ratios	
First gear	2.923 (38/13)
Second gear	2.000 (28/14)
Third gear	1.471 (25/17)
Fourth gear	1.136 (25/22)
Fifth gear	0.917 (22/24)
Reverse gear	4.462 (24/13 × 29/12)

Table 2 TRANSMISSION SHAFT SPECIFICATIONS

Item	Standard mm (in.)	Service limit mm (in.)
Countershaft runout	–	0.08 (0.003)
Mainshaft runout	–	0.08 (0.003)

CHAPTER EIGHT

FUEL INJECTION SYSTEM

This chapter covers the service procedures for the fuel injection system. Air filter service is covered in Chapter Three. Specifications are listed in **Tables 1-3** at the end of this chapter.

The fuel system consists of the fuel tank, fuel pump, fuel pump relay, fuel injector, throttle body, ECU and associated electrical components.

When working on the fuel system, observe the shop and safety practices outlined in Chapter One.

FUEL INJECTION (FI)

This section describes the components and operation of the electronic fuel injection system. The FI system consists of a fuel delivery system and electronic control system. Refer to **Figure 1**.

Components in the fuel delivery system include the fuel tank, fuel pump, fuel pump relay, throttle body and fuel injectors. The fuel pump resides in the fuel tank and directs fuel to the fuel injector at a regulated pressure of 324 kPa (47 psi). The fuel injector mounts on the throttle body, which is attached to the rear of the cylinder head.

The electronic control system consists of the electronic control unit (ECU) and sensors (**Figure 1**). The electronic control system determines the output of the fuel injector, as well as controlling ignition timing.

Idle speed is controlled by the fast idle plunger unit attached to the bottom of the throttle body. An adjustable idle speed screw regulates air entering the engine when the throttle body plate is closed at idle.

Engine coolant passing through the fast idle plunger unit heats the throttle body.

Refer to Chapter Two for fuel injection system troubleshooting procedures.

Electronic Control Unit (ECU) and Sensors

The electronic control unit (ECU) is mounted on the side of the air box. The ECU contains a program map that determines the optimum fuel injection and ignition timing based on input from the sensors.

The sensors (**Figure 1**), their locations and functions are as follows:

1. The throttle position sensor, located on the throttle body and attached directly to the throttle shaft, indicates throttle angle. The ECU determines the air volume entering the engine based on the throttle angle.
2. The coolant temperature sensor is located in the cylinder head. The ECU adjusts the injector opening time based on input from this sensor.
3. The intake air temperature sensor is located on the top of the intake tube from the air box. The ECU determines the air density and adjusts the injector opening time based on input from this sensor.
4. The intake air pressure sensor is attached to the fuel injection pipe on the throttle body. The sensor monitors atmospheric pressure and sends this information to the ECU.

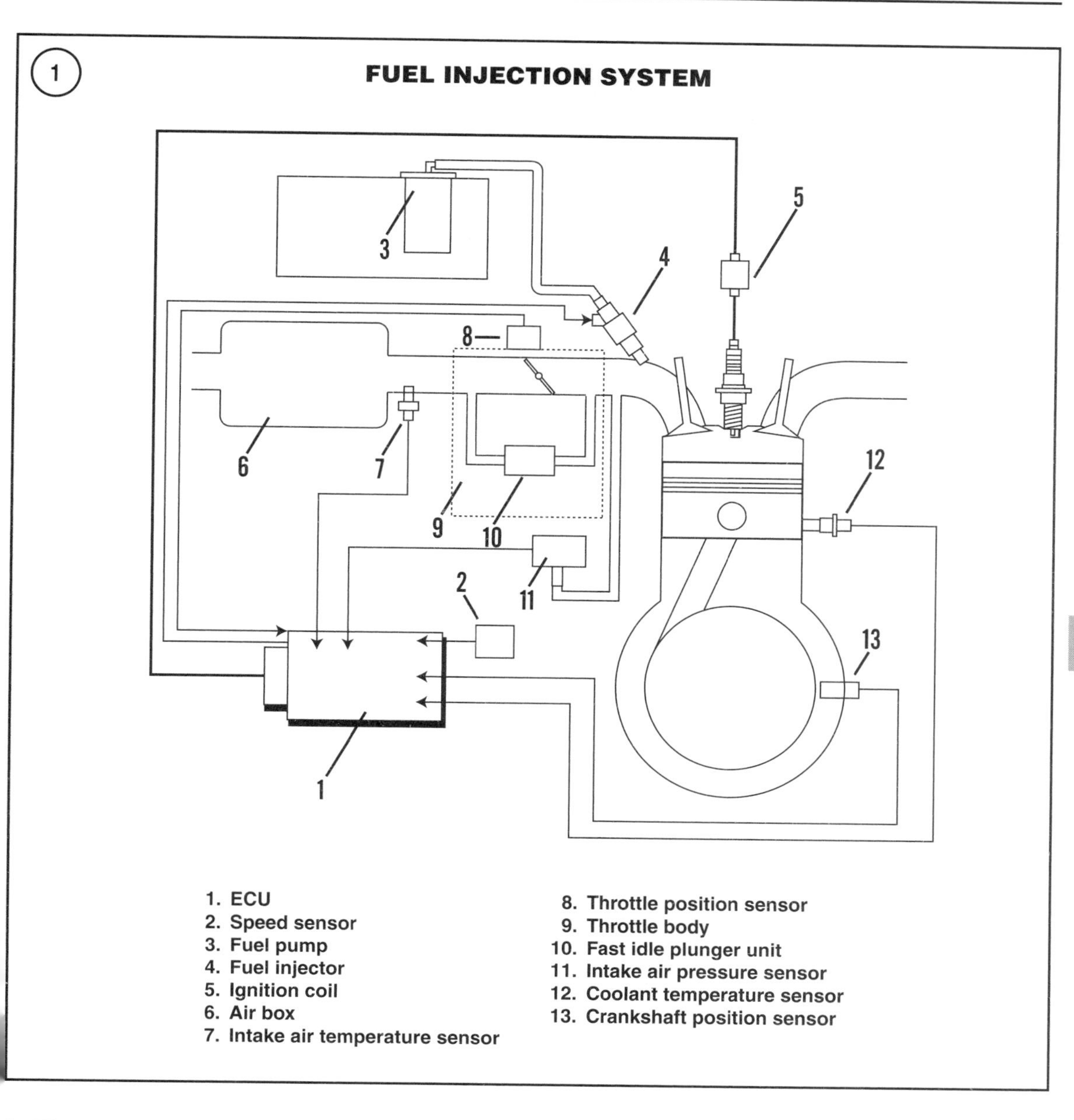

5. The crankshaft position sensor is located inside the left crankcase cover. The sensor provides engine speed and crankshaft position to the ECU.
6. The speed sensor mounted on the upper, rear of the crankcase informs the ECU of vehicle speed.
7. The lean-angle sensor, located under the seat and forward of the battery, interrupts the ignition and shuts off the engine if the ATV lean angle exceeds 55-75° from vertical.

Fuel Delivery System

Fuel pump and filters

The fuel pump is located inside the fuel tank. The pump hangs from a plate attached to the top of the fuel tank. A filter at the inlet of the fuel pump prevents contaminants in the gasoline from entering the fuel pump. A pressure regulator maintains the fuel system pressure. A fuel sensor triggers the low-fuel level warning light.

Fuel pressure regulator

A fuel pressure regulator within the fuel pump unit maintains fuel pressure at 324 kPa (47 psi).

Fuel injector

The multiple-orifice fuel injector consists of a solenoid plunger, needle valve and housing. The injector operates at a constant pressure.

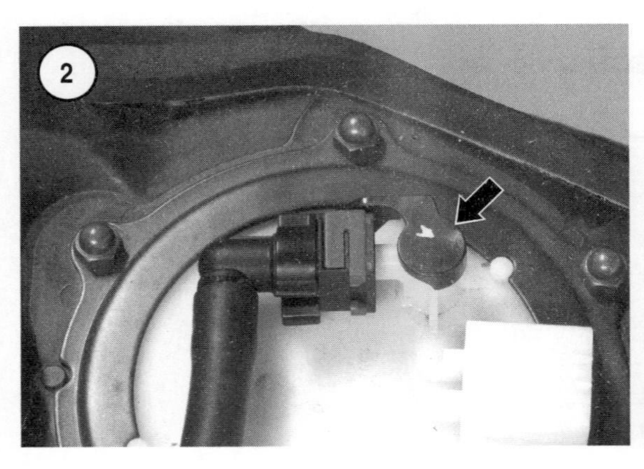

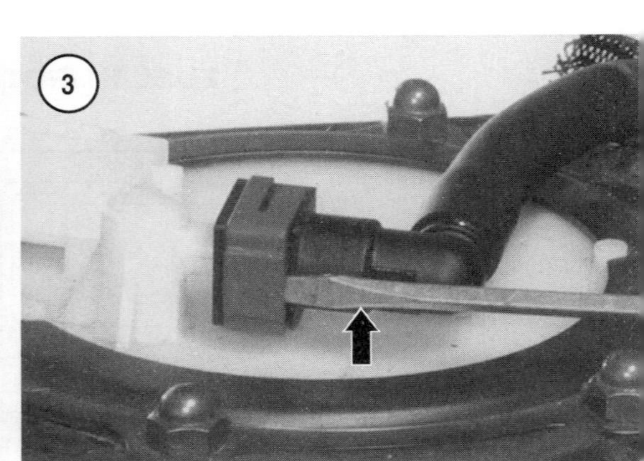

Throttle Body

The throttle body is attached to the intake tube at the rear of the cylinder head. The throttle body contains the throttle lever-controlled primary throttle valve. Mounted on the throttle body is the throttle position sensor.

Fuel Injection System Fuse

The fuel injection system is protected by a 10 amp fuse. Refer to Chapter Nine for fuse replacement.

FUEL DELIVERY SYSTEM TESTS

The following tests evaluate the performance of the fuel delivery system components (fuel pump, pressure regulator and filters).

WARNING
Before disconnecting the fuel fittings and hoses, turn the ignition switch to OFF and allow the system to internally release fuel pressure.

WARNING
Some fuel may spill from the fuel hoses when performing this procedure. Because gasoline is extremely flammable and explosive, perform this procedure away from all open flames (including appliance pilot lights) and sparks. Do not smoke or allow someone who is smoking in the work area. Always work in a well-ventilated area. Wipe up any spills immediately.

Fuel Pump Operation Test

1. Turn the ignition switch on and listen for operation of the fuel pump.

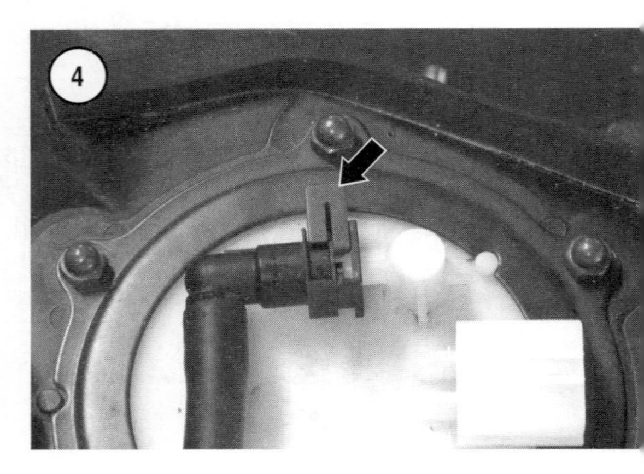

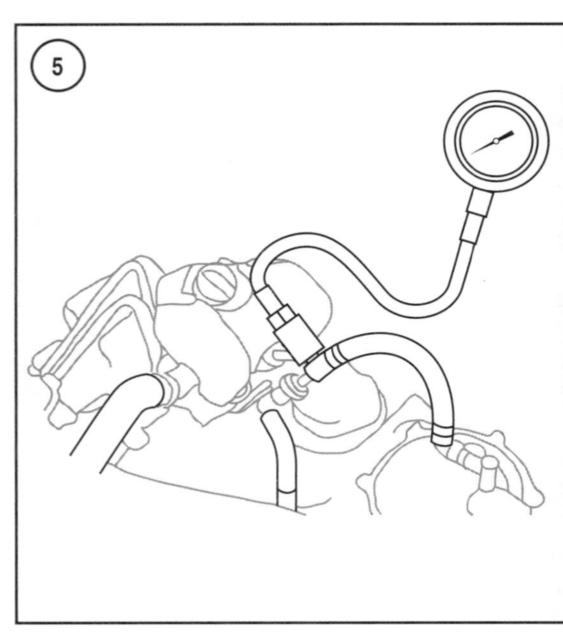

2. If no sound is heard, check the fuel injection system fuse (Chapter Nine).
3. Test the fuel pump relay and the lean-angle sensor as described in this chapter. If both of these components are within specification, replace the fuel pump.

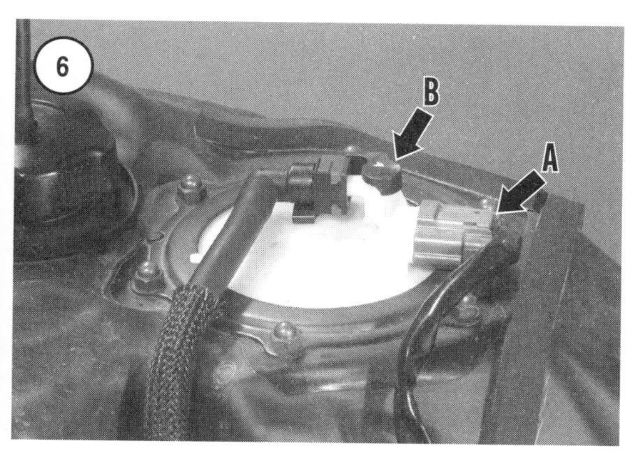

Fuel Pressure Test

The following procedure requires a fuel hose adapter (Yamaha part No. YM-03176/90890-03176 or an equivalent) and fuel pressure gauge (Yamaha part No. YU-03153/90890-03153 or an equivalent).

1. Remove the fuel tank cover as described in Chapter Fifteen.
2. Disconnect the fuel hose connector as follows:
   a. Lift up the fuel connector retainer (**Figure 2**).
   b. Insert a screwdriver (**Figure 3**) into the connector clamp and pry out the clamp (**Figure 4**).
   c. Separate the fuel hose connector from the fuel pump tube.
3. Connect the fuel hose adapter to the fuel pump tube and the fuel hose.
4. Connect the fuel pressure gauge to the fuel hose adapter (**Figure 5**).
5. Start the engine and run it at idle. Read the fuel pressure and compare with the specification in **Table 1**.
6. If fuel pressure is less than specified, check for a leak in the fuel system or a clogged fuel filter. If no problem is found, replace the fuel pump.
7. If fuel pressure exceeds specification, the fuel pump pressure regulator is faulty. Replace the fuel pump.
8. Remove the test gauge and hose adapter.

CAUTION

*Make sure the fuel connector clamp (**Figure 4**) fully engages the fitting and the hose is securely connected.*

9. Reconnect the fuel hose to the fuel pump tube.

FUEL TANK

Removal/Installation

1. Remove the front fender as described in Chapter Fifteen.
2. Disconnect the battery cable from the negative battery terminal as described in Chapter Nine.

WARNING

Make sure the engine is cold any time fuel may spill onto the engine.

3. Disconnect the electrical connector (A, **Figure 6**) from the fuel pump assembly.
4. Lift up the fuel connector retainer (B, **Figure 6**).
5. Insert a screwdriver (**Figure 3**) into the connector clamp and pry out the clamp (**Figure 4**).
6. Separate the fuel hose connector from the fuel pump tube.
7. Remove the front mounting bolt, washer and spacer (**Figure 7**) on each side.
8. Remove the rear mounting bolt and washer on each side (**Figure 8**). Note the flanged spacer on the underside of the tank mounting flange.
9. Remove the fuel tank.
10. Reverse the removal procedure to install the fuel tank while noting the following:
    a. Check that the rubber cushions and collars at the front and rear of the fuel tank are in good condition.
    b. Tighten the fuel tank mounting bolts to 7 N•m (62 in.-lb.).
    c. Check that the fuel cap gasket is in good condition.

CAUTION
*Make sure the fuel connector clamp (**Figure 4**) fully engages the fitting and the hose is securely connected.*

d. Check for leaks before and after starting the engine.

FUEL TANK PLATE

Removal/Installation

1. Remove the fuel tank as described in this chapter.
2. Detach the drain hose from the left side of the plate.
3. Note the location of wires and hoses enclosed in the holder (**Figure 9**) at the front of the fuel tank plate. Mark or tag the wires and hoses for reinstallation.
4. While disengaging from the throttle cable, remove the fuel tank plate (A, **Figure 10**).
5. Reverse the removal steps to install the fuel tank plate. Make sure the fuel tank cushions (B, **Figure 10**) are in place on the frame rails.

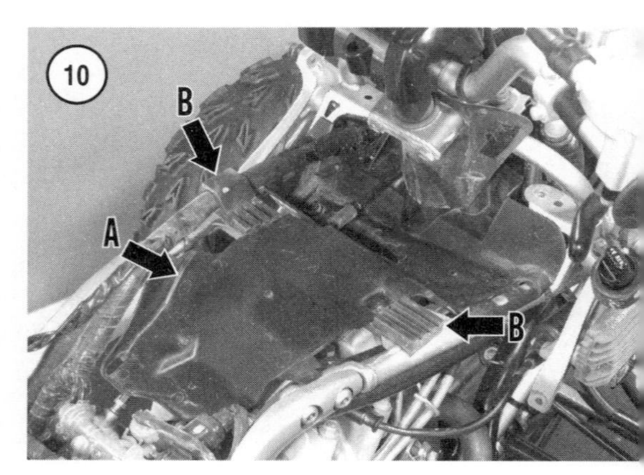

FUEL PUMP

NOTE
Other than the bottom cover components and pump mounting gasket, there are no parts available for the fuel pump assembly. It must be serviced as a unit.

The electric fuel pump is located inside the fuel tank. When the ignition switch is turned on, the fuel pump will operate for 3 seconds, and then stop. During engine starting or running, the ECU turns on the fuel pump.

A fuel level sender in the fuel pump assembly indicates to the ECU when a low fuel level occurs in the fuel tank. The ECU then illuminates the low fuel level warning light. An external resistor drops voltage for the fuel level sender circuit.

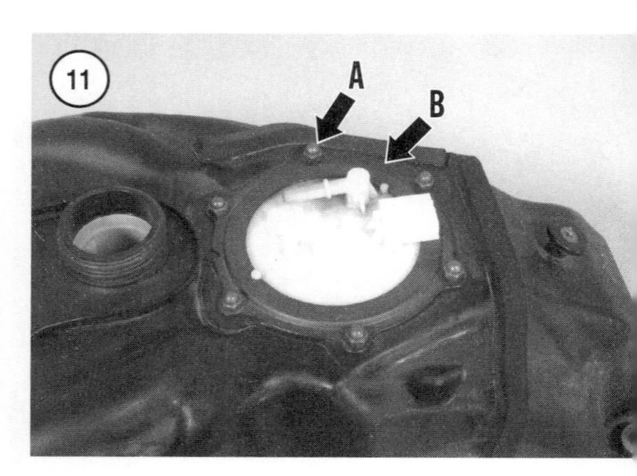

Removal/Installation

1. Remove the fuel tank as described in this chapter. Drain the fuel into a suitable container.
2. Set the fuel tank on towels or a blanket on the workbench.
3. Using a crossing pattern, evenly loosen the fuel pump mounting plate nuts (A, **Figure 11**). Then, remove the nuts.
4. Remove the mounting flange (B, **Figure 11**).

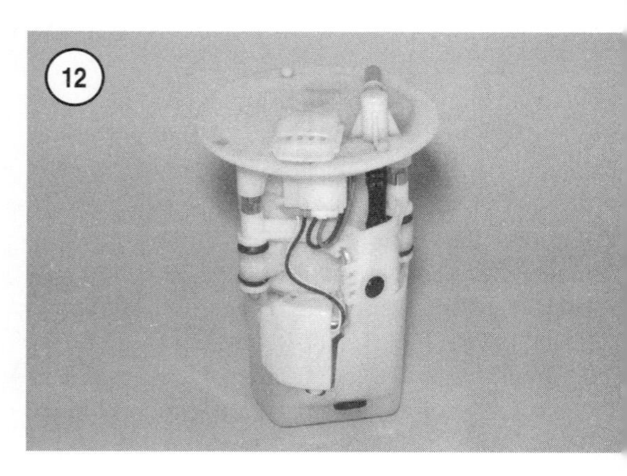

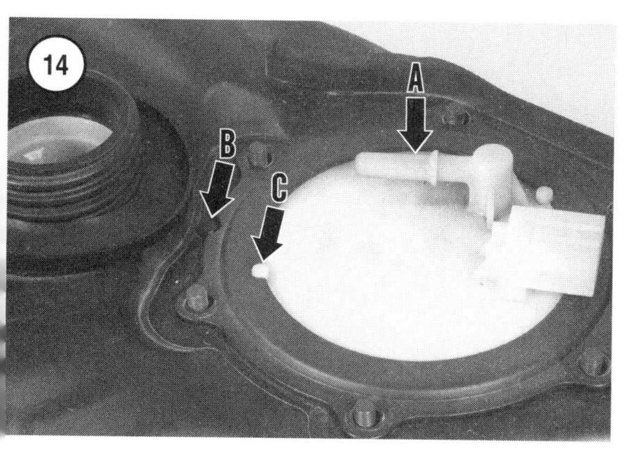

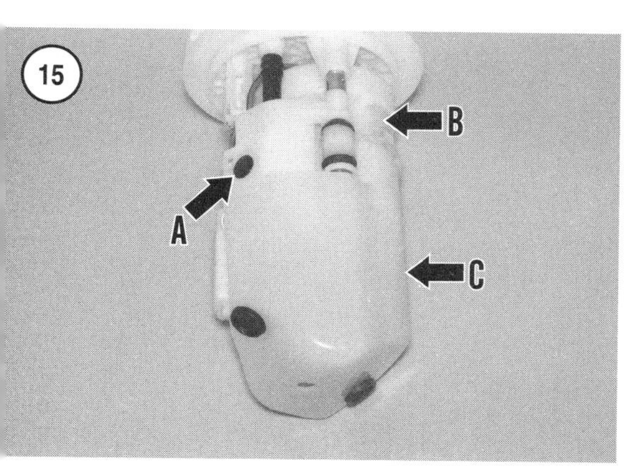

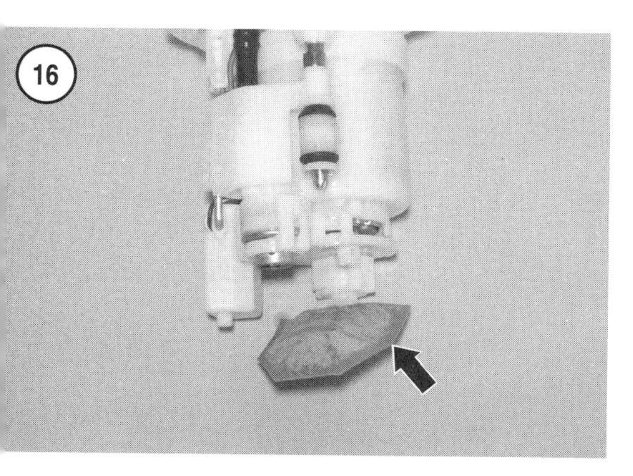

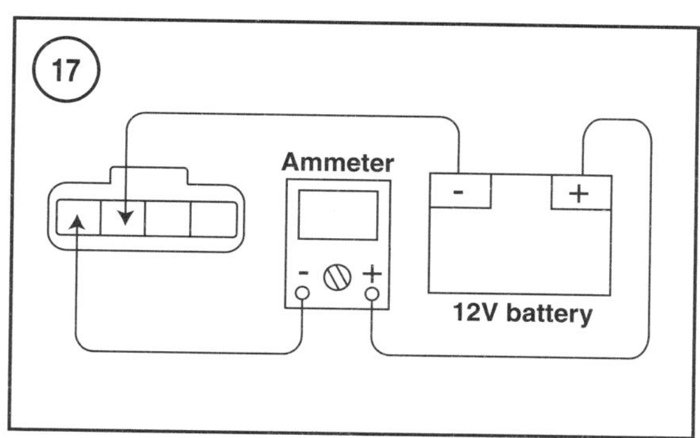

5. Pull the fuel pump assembly (**Figure 12**) from the tank. Remove and discard the fuel pump gasket (**Figure 13**).

6. Install the fuel pump by reversing the removal steps while noting the following:

   a. Install a new gasket (**Figure 13**).
   b. Install the fuel pump so the fuel tube (A, **Figure 14**) points toward the fuel tank filler opening.
   c. Install the mounting flange so the outer notch indexes with the fuel tank pin (B, **Figure 14**).
   d. Move the fuel pump as needed so the index pins (C, **Figure 14**) fit into the notches on the mounting flange.
   e. Install the nuts. Using a crossing pattern, evenly tighten the fuel pump mounting nuts to 7 N•m (62 in.-lb.) .

Inspection

1. Extract the cover retaining button (A, **Figure 15**).
2. Note the routing of the plastic strap (B, **Figure 15**), and remove the strap.
3. Remove the cover (C, **Figure 15**).
4. Inspect the inlet filter (**Figure 16**). Clean as needed.
5. Install the cover and secure it with the retaining button and plastic strap.

Fuel Level Sender Testing

1. Remove the fuel pump as described in this section.
2. Drain all gasoline from the fuel tank.
3. Position the fuel tank so the fuel pump mounting surface is horizontal.
4. Pour a low flash point fuel (such as kerosene) into the fuel tank so the fuel level measured to the fuel pump mounting surface is approximately 109.85 mm (4.32 in.) on 2006-2008 models or 79.5 mm (3.13 in.) on 2009 models.
5. Install the fuel pump into the fuel tank.
6. Connect a 12-volt battery and ammeter to the fuel pump terminals as shown in **Figure 17**.

8

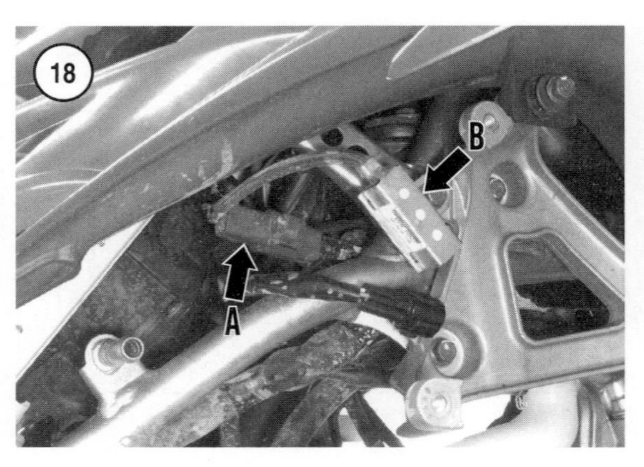

7. Compare the ammeter reading and measured fuel level with the specifications in **Table 2**.
8. If the fuel level sender is not operating properly, replace the fuel pump.

Fuel Level Sender Resistor Testing (2006-2008 models)

1. Remove the left headlight as described in Chapter Nine.
2. Disconnect the resistor connector (A, **Figure 18**).
3. Measure resistance between the black wire terminals in the resistor connector.
4. If measured resistance is not as specified in **Table 2**, replace the resistor (B, **Figure 18**).

FUEL PUMP RELAY

The fuel pump relay controls power to the fuel pump and fuel injector. The ECU controls relay operation. The fuel pump relay is contained in the relay unit, which also contains the starting circuit cut-off relay.

Removal/Installation

1. Remove the seat as described in Chapter Fifteen.
2. Pull the relay (**Figure 19**) off the mounting bracket.
3. Disconnect the connector, and remove the relay.
4. Installation is the reverse of removal.

Test

1. Remove the relay as described in this section.
2. Check the continuity between the brown/green wire terminal (A, **Figure 20**) and red/blue wire terminal (B). The relay should not have continuity.
3. Use jumpers to connect the positive terminal of a 12-volt battery to the red/black wire terminal

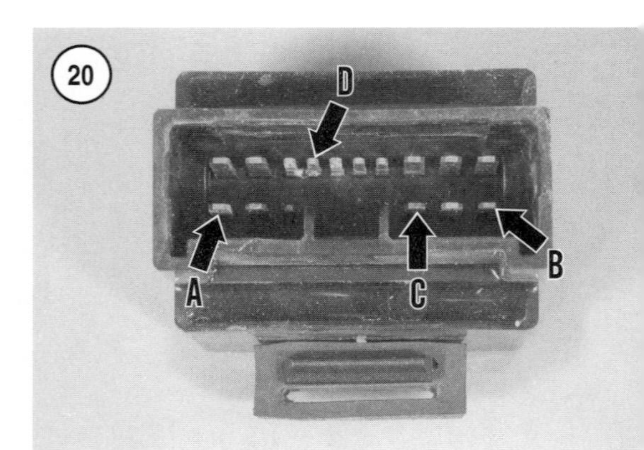

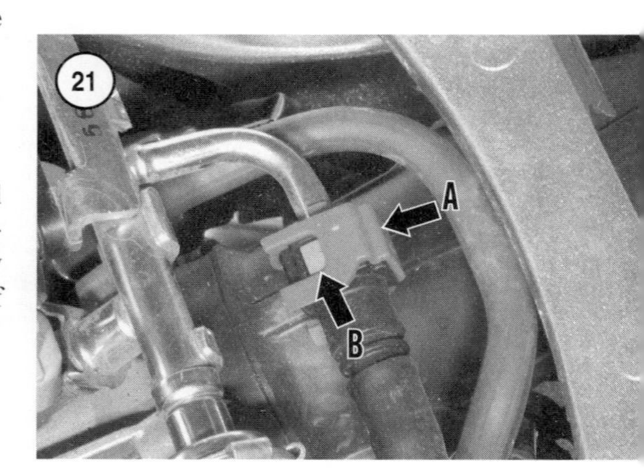

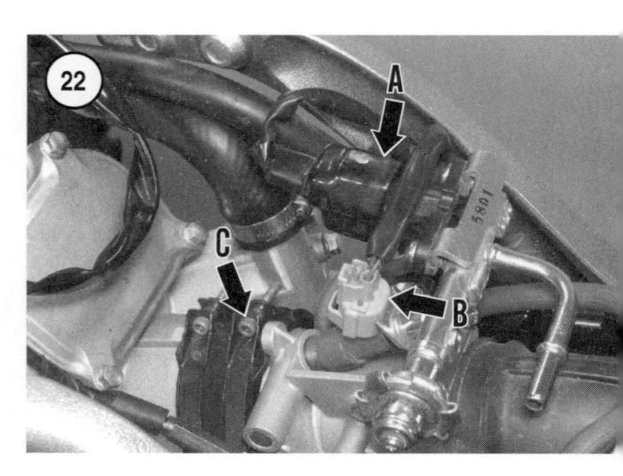

(C, **Figure 20**) on the relay; connect the negative battery terminal to the blue/red wire terminal (D).

4. Check the continuity between the brown/green wire terminal (A, **Figure 20**) and red/blue wire terminal (B). The relay should have continuity while voltage is applied.

5. Replace the relay if it fails either portion of this test.

THROTTLE BODY

Removal/Installation

1. Drain the engine coolant as described in Chapter Three.
2. Remove the fuel tank and fuel tank plate as described in this chapter.
3. Slide back the hose fitting cover (A, **Figure 21**). Push in the gray buttons on each side of the fitting (B) and detach the hose fitting from the fuel delivery pipe.
4. Disconnect the intake air pressure sensor connector (A, **Figure 22**).
5. Disconnect the fuel injector connector (B, **Figure 22**).
6. Disconnect the throttle position sensor connector (A, **Figure 23**).
7. Disconnect the intake duct hose (B, **Figure 23**) from the throttle body.
8. Detach the coolant hoses (**Figure 24**) from the fast idle plunger housing.
9. Disconnect the intake duct hose (**Figure 25**) from the fast idle plunger housing.
10. Refer to Chapter Three and adjust the throttle cable so there is maximum slack.
11. Remove the throttle cable housing cover (**Figure 26**) on the throttle body.
12. Rotate the throttle pulley on the throttle body as needed and disengage the cable end (**Figure 27**) from the throttle cable. Extract the throttle cable from the throttle housing.

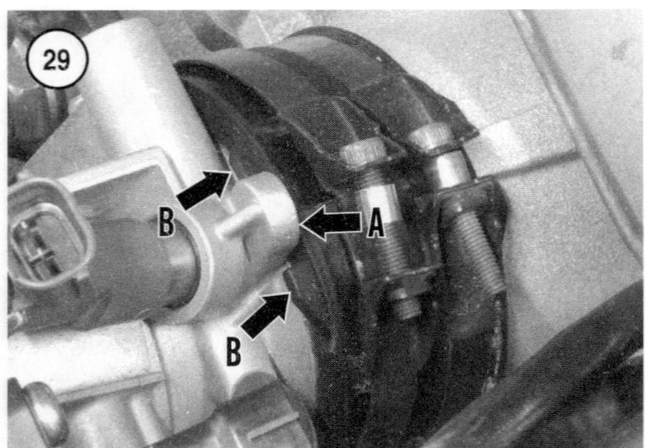

13. Loosen the intake tube clamp screw (C, **Figure 22**).
14. Loosen the intake duct clamp screw (**Figure 28**).
15. Remove the throttle body by working it out of the intake tube and intake duct.
16. Reverse the removal steps to install the throttle body while noting the following:
    a. Position the throttle body so the upper boss (A, **Figure 29**) fits between the ears on the intake tube (B).
    b. Make sure the hose clamps properly fit around the locating ribs on the intake tube and intake duct.
    c. Install the throttle cable as described in *Throttle Cable Replacement* (this chapter).
    d. Verify proper operation of the throttle.

Disassembly/Inspection/Reassembly

1. Remove the intake duct hose (**Figure 30**).
2. Remove the fuel delivery pipe retaining screws (A, **Figure 31**).
3. Disconnect the intake air pressure sensor hose (B, **Figure 31**).
4. Separate the fuel delivery pipe (C, **Figure 31**) and fuel injector from the throttle body.
5. If necessary, remove the throttle position sensor (**Figure 32**). Make marks on the throttle position sensor and throttle body so the sensor can be reinstalled in its original position.
6. If still in place, remove the throttle cable housing O-ring gasket (A, **Figure 33**).
7. While counting the turns, turn in the fast idle screw (B, **Figure 33**) just until it bottoms. Note the number of turns for future reference.
8. Turn out and remove the fast idle screw (A, **Figure 34**), large spring (B), spool (C) and small spring (D).

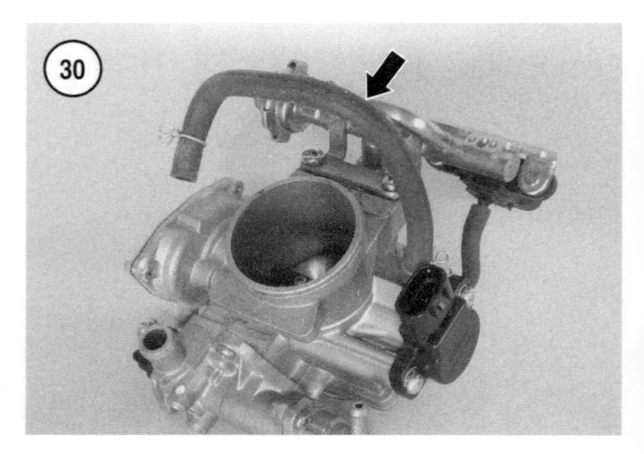

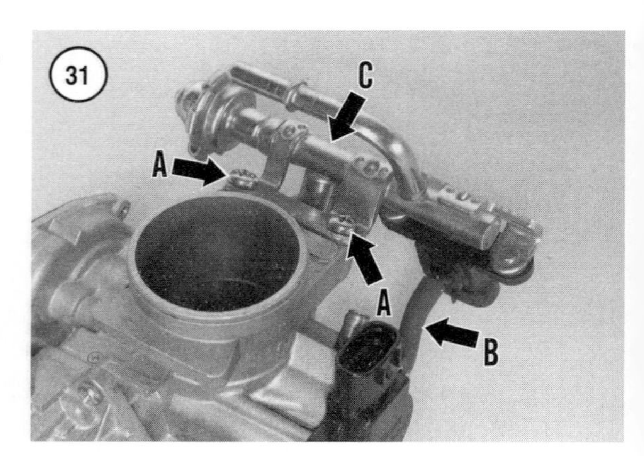

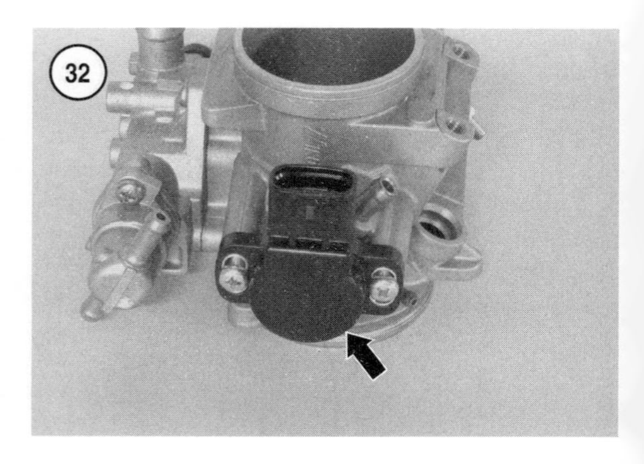

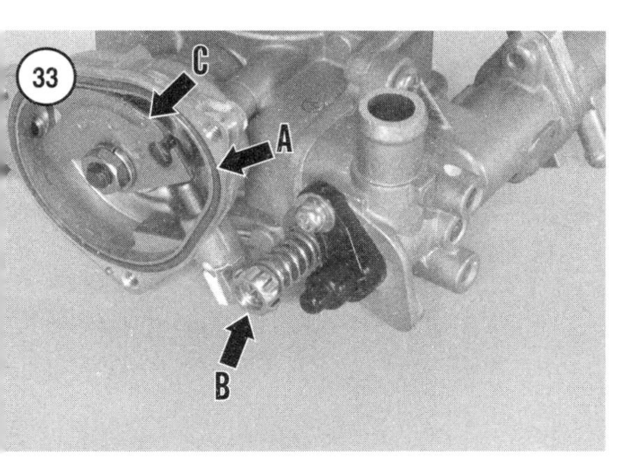

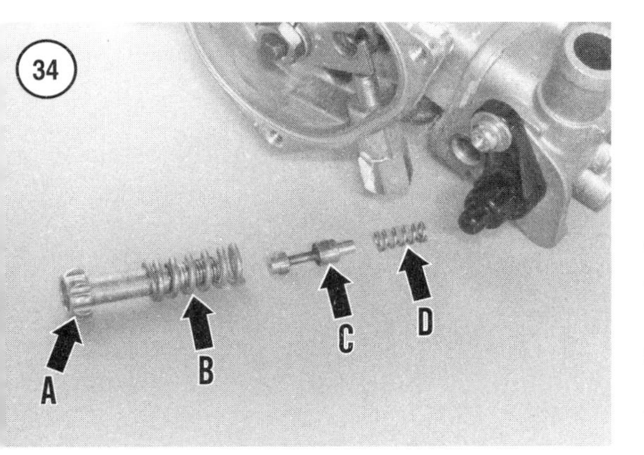

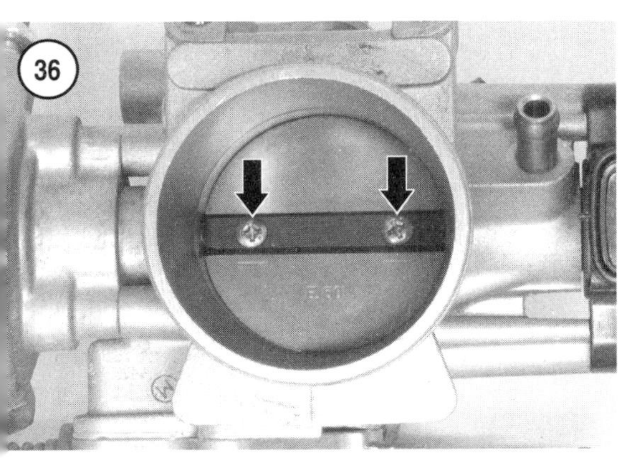

NOTE

Internal gaskets are not available for the fast idle plunger unit. Remove the unit from the throttle body only if a coolant leak is evident or erratic fast idle occurs.

9. If necessary, remove the fast idle plunger unit on the base of the throttle body (**Figure 35**).
10. Do not attempt to remove the throttle valve and screws (**Figure 36**).
11. Clean the throttle body bores and passages using fuel injection cleaner (available at auto parts stores).
12. Inspect the throttle body for cracks or other damage that could admit unfiltered air.
13. Operate the throttle valve using the throttle pulley (C, **Figure 33**). They must move smoothly.
14. Install the fast idle screw. Set the screw at the number of turns out noted during disassembly. Adjust the fast idle speed after throttle body installation as described in Chapter Three.
15. Install the fuel injector and fuel delivery pipe as described in *Fuel Injector* (this chapter).

FUEL INJECTOR

A multi-hole type fuel injector is mounted on the throttle body. The ECU controls the opening time of the injector. The fuel injector is not serviceable, but must be replaced as a unit.

Removal/Installation

1. Remove the fuel tank and fuel tank plate as described in this chapter.
2. Disconnect the intake air pressure sensor connector (A, **Figure 37**).
3. Disconnect the fuel injector connector (B, **Figure 37**).
4. Detach the intake air pressure sensor hose (C, **Figure 37**).

5. Slide back the hose fitting cover (A, **Figure 38**). Push in the gray buttons (B, **Figure 38**) on each side of the fitting and detach the hose fitting from the fuel pipe.
6. Remove the screws (A, **Figure 39**) securing the fuel delivery pipe (B).
7. Remove the fuel injector and fuel delivery pipe.

NOTE
The manufacturer does not offer the upper O-ring fuel injector seal (A, ***Figure 40****) separate from the injector. If leaking is evident, remove the injector and take the injector and O-ring to a dealership or service shop to find a suitable replacement. Run the engine and check for leaks after assembly.*

8. Remove the lower seal (A, **Figure 41**).
9. If necessary, pull the injector (B, **Figure 41**) out of the fuel delivery pipe (C).
10. Install a new lower seal onto the fuel injector.
11. Reverse the removal procedure to install the fuel injector and fuel delivery pipe. Make sure the mounting bore for the fuel injector in the throttle body is clean. Tighten the fuel delivery pipe mounting screws securely.

Inspection

1. Visually inspect the fuel injector for damage. Inspect the injector nozzle (B, **Figure 40**) for carbon buildup or damage.
2. Check the fuel injector terminals and the wiring connector for corrosion or damage.
3. Be sure the mounting bore for the fuel injector in the throttle body is clean.

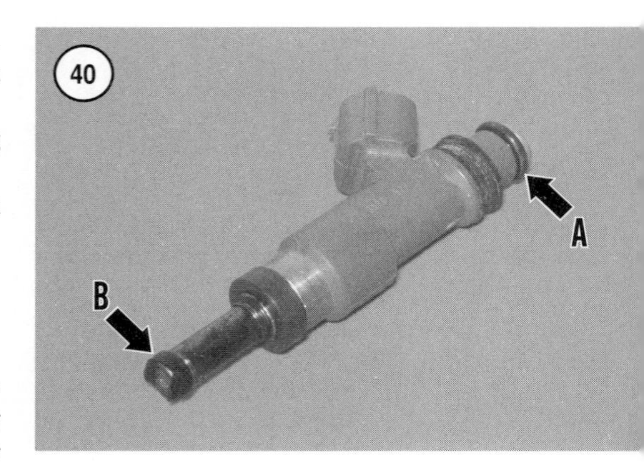

Fuel Injector Cleaning

A fuel injector must emit a satisfactory spray pattern for optimum engine performance. A dirty or clogged fuel injector nozzle will affect the injector spray pattern. Contact a dealership or service shop for referral to a company that tests and cleans fuel injectors. The nominal cost of this service is usually much less than the price of a new injector.

ECU

Testing

NOTE
The ECU is expensive. Be sure the ECU is faulty before purchasing a new unit. Most dealerships do not accept returned electrical components.

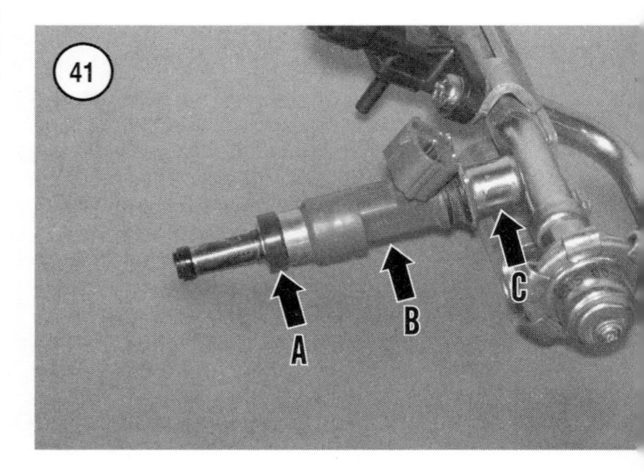

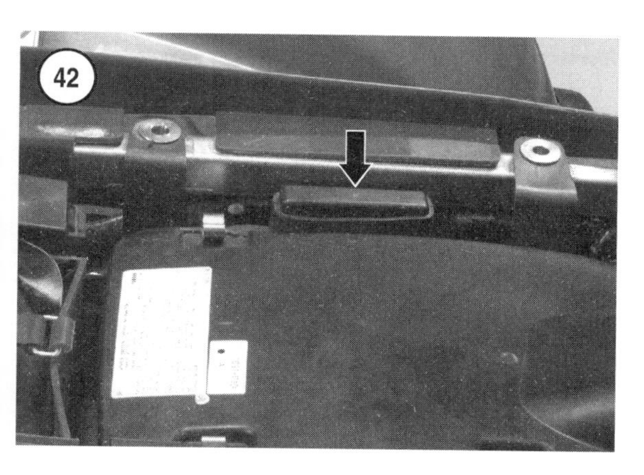

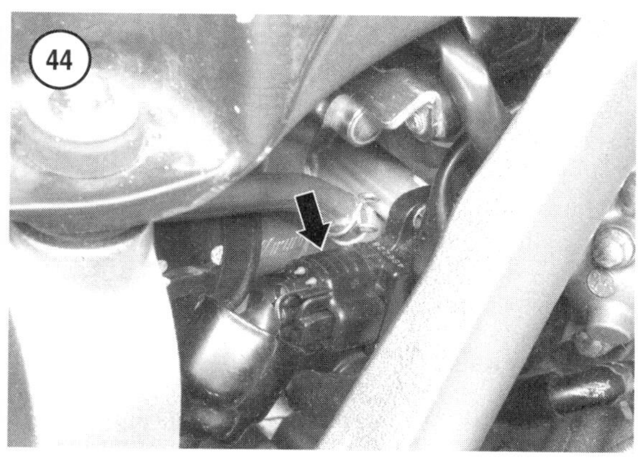

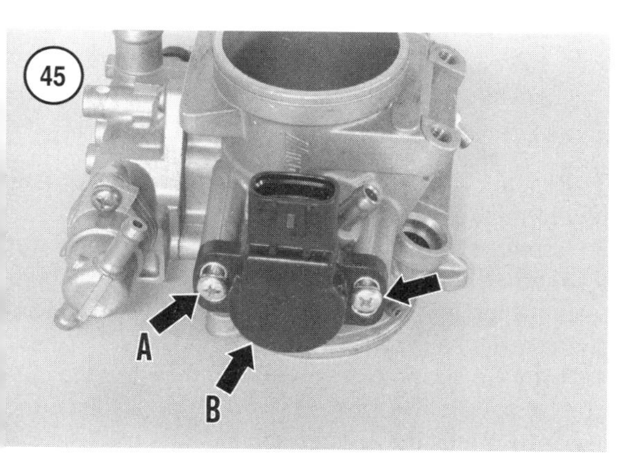

Test specifications for the ECU are not available. Determining whether the ECU is faulty requires eliminating other possible causes through troubleshooting. Refer to Chapter Two for troubleshooting procedures.

Removal/Installation

1. Disconnect the battery cable from the negative battery terminal as described in Chapter Nine.

NOTE
If necessary, remove the air box mounting bolts and move the air box slightly for access to the ECU.

2. Lift the ECU (**Figure 42**) and rubber holder off the bracket on the air box.
3. Disconnect the connector (**Figure 43**) from the ECU.
4. Reverse the removal steps to install the ECU. If removed, tighten the air box mounting bolts securely.

THROTTLE POSITION SENSOR

Adjustment

1. Make sure the engine idle speed is correct. Refer to Chapter Three.
2. Remove the front fender as described in Chapter Fifteen.
3. Pull back the connector boot. Using back probe pins, insert the voltmeter test leads into the connector (**Figure 44**) so the positive lead contacts the yellow wire and the negative lead contacts the black/blue wire.
4. Start and run the engine at idle.
5. Observe the voltmeter reading. The specified voltage is 0.63-0.73 volt. If the voltage is not within specification, perform Step 6.

NOTE
*The throttle body is shown removed in **Figure 45** for clarity. It is not necessary to remove the throttle body.*

6. Loosen the mounting screws (A, **Figure 45**) and slowly rotate the throttle position sensor (B) until the voltage reading is within specification.
7. Tighten the mounting screws securely.
8. Turn the ignition switch off.
9. Remove the tester leads and replace the rubber cover.
10. Install the front fender as described in Chapter Fifteen.

Removal/Installation

1. Remove the front fender as described in Chapter Fifteen.

2. Make marks on the throttle position sensor and throttle body so the sensor can be reinstalled in its original position.
3. Pull back the boot and disconnect the throttle position sensor connector (**Figure 44**).

NOTE
*The throttle body is shown removed in **Figure 45** for clarity. It is not necessary to remove the throttle body.*

4. Remove the sensor mounting screws (A, **Figure 45**).
5. Pull out and remove the throttle position sensor (B, **Figure 45**).
6. Reverse the removal steps to install the throttle position sensor while noting the following:
   a. Make sure the tab on the sensor fits into the slot in the throttle body shaft.
   b. If reinstalling the original sensor, align the marks made prior to removal.
   c. If installing a new or unmarked sensor, adjust the sensor as described in this section.

Test

1. Remove the throttle position sensor as described in this section.
2. Connect the positive test lead of an ohmmeter to the blue (**Figure 46**) terminal on the sensor and connect the negative lead to the black/blue terminal on the sensor.
3. The ohmmeter should indicate the maximum resistance listed in **Table 2**.
4. Connect the positive test lead of an analog ohmmeter to the yellow terminal on the sensor and connect the negative lead to the black/blue terminal on the sensor.

NOTE
The meter readings may differ slightly than those specified. The important factor is that the needle movement changes gradually and smoothly during the full range of movement.

5. Slowly open the throttle from the closed to the wide-open position and note the needle movement. The resistance should change gradually from 0 ohms to the maximum resistance listed in **Table 2**.
6. If the movement is erratic or not within specification, the sensor is defective and must be replaced.

INTAKE AIR PRESSURE SENSOR

Removal/Installation

1. Remove the fuel tank and fuel tank plate as described in this chapter.

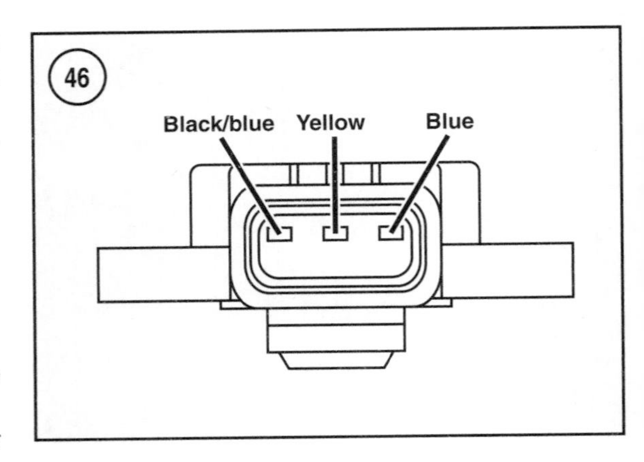

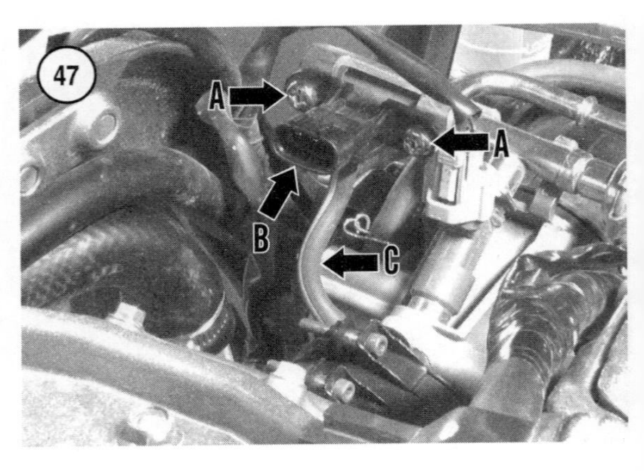

2. Disconnect the intake air pressure sensor connector (A, **Figure 37**).
3. Remove the sensor retaining screws (A, **Figure 47**).
4. Remove the sensor (B, **Figure 47**) after detaching the hose (C).
5. Installation is the reverse of removal. Tighten the retaining screws securely.

Output Voltage Test

1. Remove the fuel tank and fuel tank plate as described in this chapter.

NOTE
The connector must remain attached to the atmospheric pressure sensor during this test.

2. Reconnect the battery cable to the negative battery terminal.
3. Using back probe pins, insert the voltmeter test leads into the connector so the positive test lead contacts the pink/blue wire and the negative test lead contacts the black/blue wire.
4. Turn the ignition switch on and measure the output voltage. It should be 3.0-4.0 volts. Replace the sensor if it fails the voltage test.

INTAKE AIR TEMPERATURE SENSOR

CAUTION
The intake air temperature sensor is sensitive to shock. Handle it carefully.

Removal/Installation

1. Remove the seat as described in Chapter Fifteen.
2. Remove the battery retaining strap, then lift up the rubber cover over the intake duct for access to the sensor connector.
3. Disconnect the intake air temperature sensor connector (A, **Figure 48**).
4. Remove the sensor (B, **Figure 48**) from the intake duct.
5. Reverse the removal steps to install the sensor.

Resistance Test

NOTE
The following test specification applies for a sensor at 20° C (68° F).

1. Remove the intake air temperature sensor as described in this section.
2. Connect the positive test probe of an ohmmeter to the brown/white wire terminal in the sensor.
3. Connect the negative test probe to the black/white wire terminal in the sensor. The ohmmeter should read 2210-2690 ohms.
4. Replace the sensor if it fails the resistance test.

COOLANT TEMPERATURE SENSOR

Refer to Chapter Nine for replacement and testing procedures.

CRANKSHAFT POSITION SENSOR

Refer to Chapter Nine for replacement and testing procedures.

SPEED SENSOR

Voltage Test

1. Locate the white, 3-pin speed sensor connector (**Figure 49**).
2. Using back probe pins, insert the voltmeter test leads into the harness end of the speed sensor connector so the positive lead contacts the white terminal and the negative lead contacts the black/blue terminal.
3. Securely support the ATV with the rear wheels off the ground.
4. Turn the ignition switch on and slowly rotate the rear wheels.
5. The speed sensor is operating properly if the voltage cycles between 0.6 and 4.8 volts per each revolution of the wheel. Replace the speed sensor if the voltage is outside this range.

Removal/Installation

1. Disconnect the white, 3-pin speed sensor connector (**Figure 49**).
2. Remove the mounting screw (A, **Figure 50**) and wire guide.
3. Pull the speed sensor (B, **Figure 50**) from the top of the crankcase. Discard the speed sensor O-ring.
4. Installation is the reverse of removal. Install a new O-ring onto the speed sensor. Tighten the mounting screw securely.

LEAN-ANGLE SENSOR

Whenever the lean-angle sensor is activated, the ECU cuts off power to the fuel pump, ignition system and fuel injector circuits.

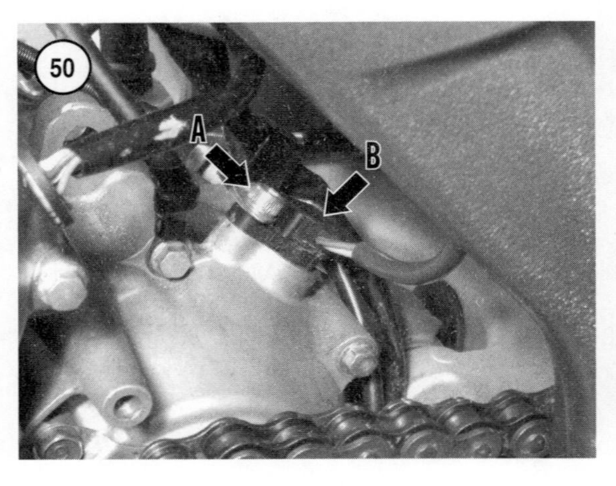

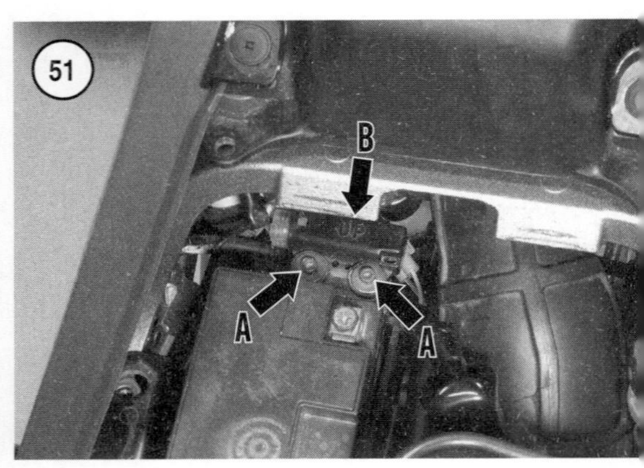

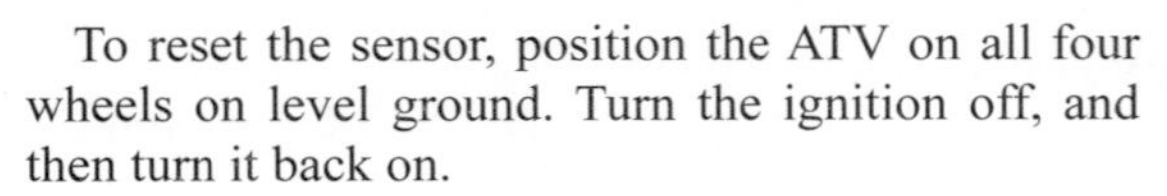

To reset the sensor, position the ATV on all four wheels on level ground. Turn the ignition off, and then turn it back on.

Removal/Installation

1. Disconnect the cable from the negative battery terminal as described in Chapter Nine.
2. Remove the screws (A, **Figure 51**) securing the lean-angle sensor (B), and lift up the sensor.
3. Disconnect the connector from the lean-angle sensor, and remove the sensor.
4. Installation is the reverse of removal. Install the sensor so the UP mark is facing up.

Output Voltage Test

1. Remove the lean-angle sensor as described in this section.
2. Plug the connector into the lean-angle sensor.
3. Turn the ignition switch on.
4. Using back probe pins, insert the voltmeter test leads into the connector so the positive lead contacts the blue terminal (A, **Figure 52**) and the negative lead contacts the yellow/green terminal (B).
5. Hold the lean angle sensor upright. Rotate the switch 65° clockwise and 65° counterclockwise. Measure the voltage in each direction.
6. Replace the lean angle sensor if either measurement is outside the output voltage range specified in **Table 2**.

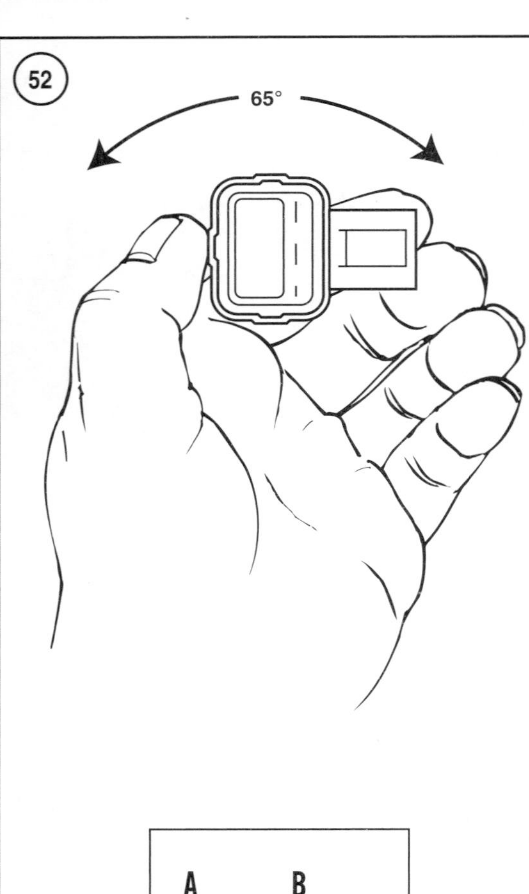

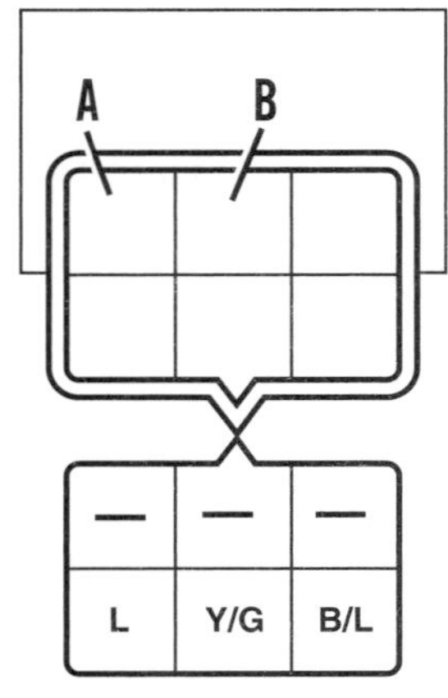

AIR BOX

Removal/Installation

Refer to **Figure 53**.
1. Remove the fuel tank as described in this chapter.
2. Remove the ECU as described in this chapter.

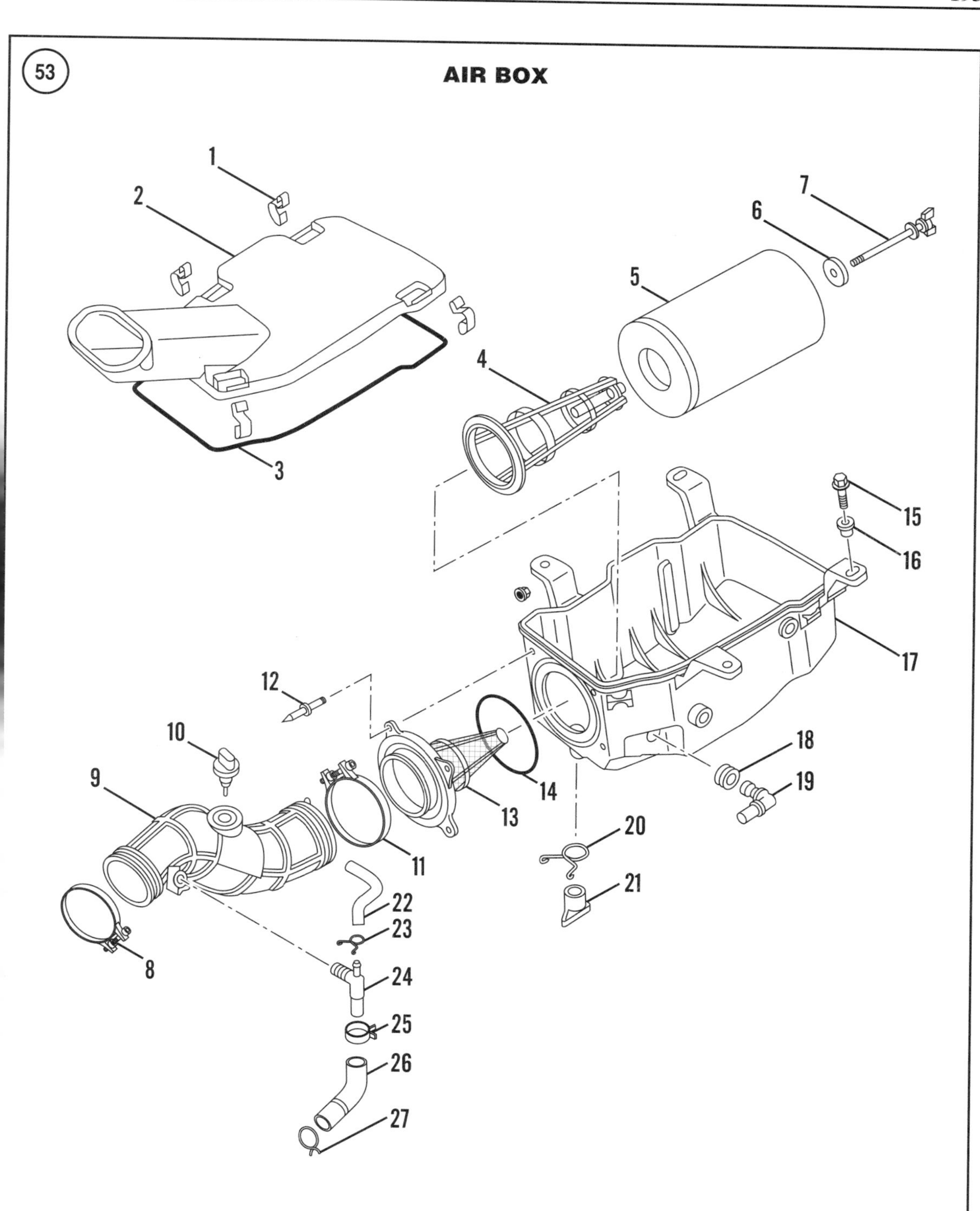

AIR BOX

1. Clip
2. Cover
3. Gasket
4. Guide
5. Air filter
6. Washer
7. Bolt
8. Clamp
9. Intake duct
10. Intake air temperature sensor
11. Clamp
12. Rivet
13. Guide holder
14. O-ring
15. Bolt
16. Flange collar
17. Air box
18. Grommet
19. Breather hose fitting
20. Clamp
21. Seal
22. Hose to throttle body
23. Clamp
24. Fitting
25. Clamp
26. Hose to fast idle plunger
27. Clamp

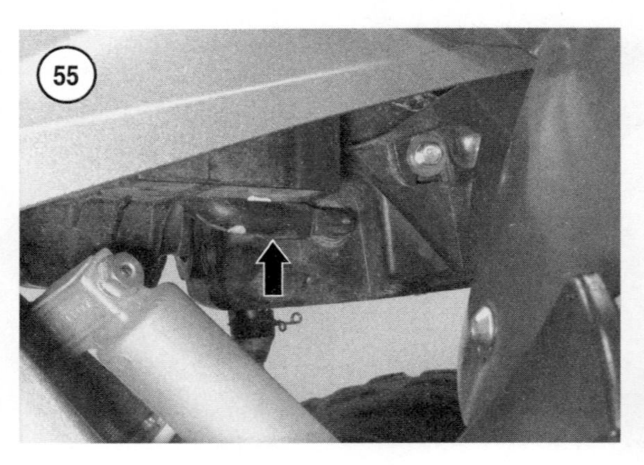

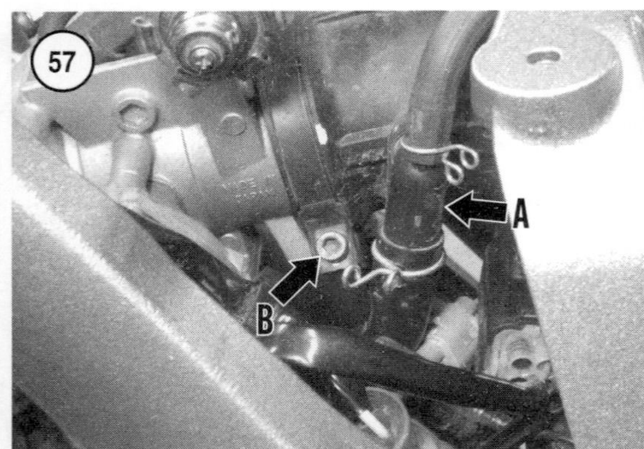

3. Disconnect the intake air temperature sensor connector (**Figure 54**).
4. Disconnect the breather hose (**Figure 55**) from the air box.
5. Disconnect the lower hose (**Figure 56**) from the intake duct fitting to the fast idle plunger unit on the throttle body.
6. Disconnect the throttle body hose (A, **Figure 57**) from the intake duct fitting.
7. Loosen the intake duct clamp screw (B, **Figure 57**).
8. If not removed during ECU removal, remove the air box mounting bolts (**Figure 58**).
9. Remove the air box (A, **Figure 59**) and intake duct (B) as an assembly.
10. If necessary, loosen the clamp (C, **Figure 59**) and separate the air box and intake duct.
11. Reverse the removal steps to install the air box and intake duct. Tighten the air box mounting bolts securely.

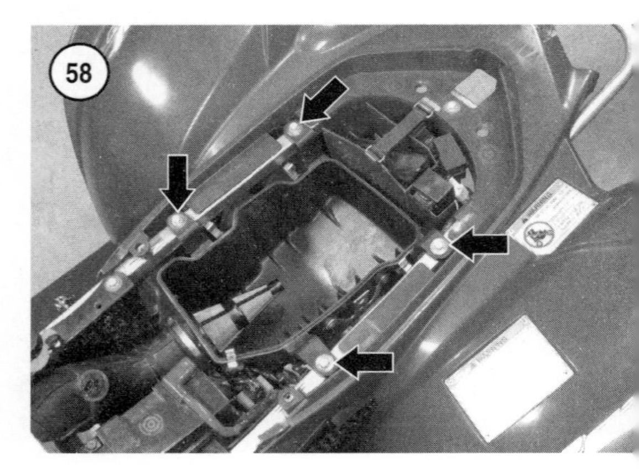

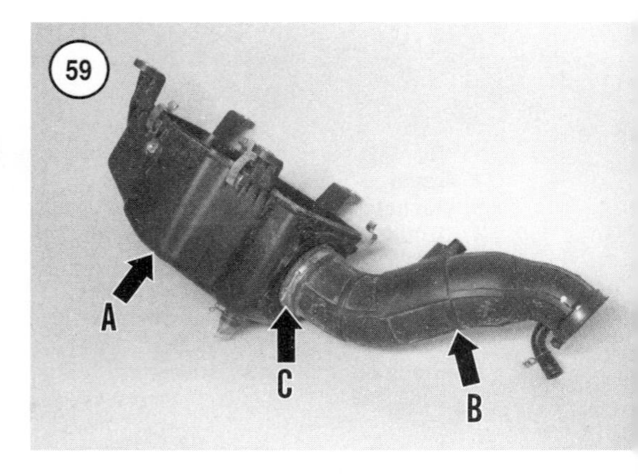

THROTTLE CABLE REPLACEMENT

1. Remove the fuel tank as described in this chapter.
2. Refer to Chapter Three and adjust the throttle cable so there is maximum slack.

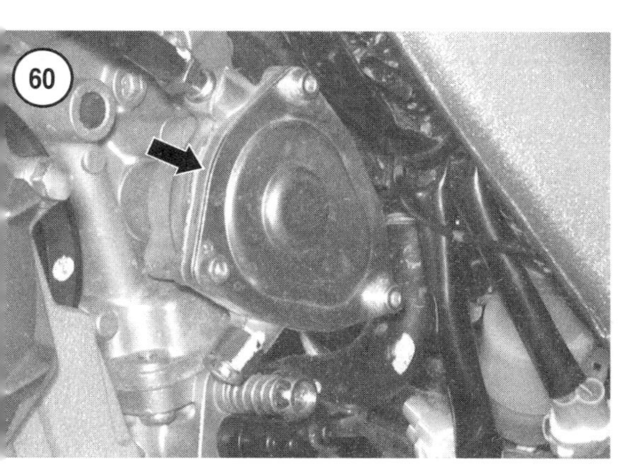

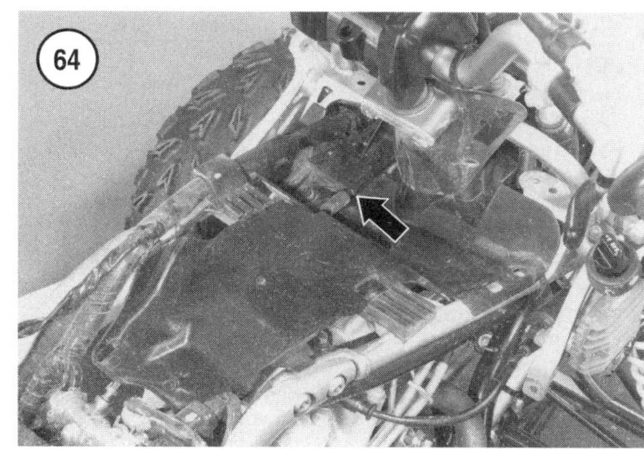

3. Remove the throttle cable housing cover (**Figure 60**) on the throttle body.

4. Rotate the throttle pulley (A, **Figure 61**) on the throttle body as needed and disengage the cable end from the throttle cable. Extract the throttle cable and cable housing fitting (B, **Figure 61**) from the throttle housing.

5. Remove the cover (**Figure 62**) on the handlebar throttle housing. Detach the cable end from the throttle lever (**Figure 63**) and remove the cable from the throttle housing.

6. Note the cable routing through the fuel tank plate (**Figure 64**), and remove the cable.

7. Reverse the removal steps to install the new cable. Note the following:

   a. Clean the housings and levers before assembly.
   b. Lubricate the cable and cable ends.
   c. After routing the rear end of the cable into the throttle body pulley, install the cable housing fitting (**Figure 65**) onto the cable so the flanged side is out.
   d. Adjust the throttle lever free play as described in Chapter Three.
   e. Verify proper throttle operation.

Table 1 FUEL SYSTEM SPECIFICATIONS

ECU type	Denso TBDF18
Fuel injector type	Denso 297500-0390/1
Throttle body type	Mikuni 44 EHS
Fuel pump	
Type	Denso 1S3
Output pressure	324 kPa (46.1 psi)
Fuel tank capacity	
Total (including reserve)	11.0 L (2.9 U.S. gal.)
Reserve only	
2006-2012 models	2.6 L (0.70 U.S. gal.)
2013-on models	2.9 L (0.77 U.S. gal.)
Fuel	Unleaded, 86 pump octane*

*Gasohol containing a maximum of 10 percent ethanol may be used.

Table 2 FUEL SYSTEM ELECTRICAL SPECIFICATIONS

Fuel sender current	
2006-2008 models	
Fuel level less than 109.85 mm (4.32 in.)	Less than 60 mA
Fuel level more than 109.85 mm (4.32 in.)	More than 135 mA
2009-on models	
Fuel level less than 79.5 mm (3.13 in.)	Less than 60 mA
Fuel level more than 79.5 mm (3.13 in.)	More than 135 mA
Fuel sender resistor resistance	68 ohms at 20° C (68° F)
Intake air pressure sensor output voltage	
2006-2012 models	3.0-4.0 volts
2013-on models	NA
Intake air temperature sensor output voltage	
2006-2012 models	3.0-4.0 volts
2013-on models	3.57-3.71 volts
Intake air temperature sensor resistance	2210-2690 ohms at 20° C (68° F)
Lean-angle sensor output voltage	
Less than 55-75	Approx. 1.0 volt
More than 55-75	Approx. 4.0 volts
Speed sensor output voltage	Cycle between 0.6 volts and 4.8 volts
Throttle position sensor	
Maximum resistance	
2006-2008 models	4000-6000 ohms at 20° C (68° F)
2009-on models	3080-5720 ohms at 20° C (68° F)
Operating resistance	0 ohm to 4000-6000 ohms at 20° C (68° F)
Output voltage	0.63-0.73 volt at idle

NA Information not available from manufacturer.

Table 3 FUEL SYSTEM TORQUE SPECIFICATIONS

Item	N•m	in.-lb.	ft.-lb.
Fuel pump mounting nuts	7	62	–
Fuel tank mounting bolts	7	62	–

CHAPTER NINE

ELECTRICAL SYSTEM

This chapter contains service and test procedures for the following systems/components:

1. Charging system.
2. Ignition system.
3. Starting system.
4. Lighting system.
5. Electrical components.
6. Switches.
7. Fuses.

Refer to **Tables 1-8** at the end of this chapter for specifications.

ELECTRICAL COMPONENT REPLACEMENT

Most dealerships and parts suppliers will not accept the return of any electrical part. If the exact cause of an electrical system malfunction cannot be determined, have a dealership retest that specific system to verify the test results. This may help avert the possibility of purchasing an expensive, unreturnable part that does not fix the problem.

Consider any test results carefully before replacing a component that tests only slightly out of specification, especially for resistance. A number of variables can affect test results dramatically. These include the testing meter's internal circuitry, ambient temperature and conditions under which the machine has been operated. All instructions and specifications have been checked for accuracy; however, successful test results depend to a great extent upon individual accuracy.

CONTINUITY TESTING

Circuits, switches, light bulbs and fuses can be checked for continuity (a completed circuit) using an ohmmeter connected to the appropriate color-coded wires in the circuit. Tests can be made at the connector or at the part. Use the following procedure as a guide to performing general continuity tests.

CAUTION

When performing continuity checks, do not turn on the ignition switch. Damage to parts and test equipment could occur. Also, verify that power from the battery is not routed directly into the test circuit, regardless of ignition switch position.

1. Refer to the wiring diagrams at the end of the manual and find the part to be checked.
2. Identify the wire colors leading to the part and determine which pairs of wires should be checked. For any check, the circuit should begin at the connector, pass through the part, then return to the connector.
3. Determine when continuity should exist.
   a. Typically, whenever a switch or button is turned on, it closes the circuit, and the meter should indicate continuity.
   b. When the switch or button is turned off, it opens the circuit, and the meter should not indicate continuity.
4. Trace the wires from the part to the nearest connector. Separate the connector.

5. Connect an ohmmeter to the connector half that leads to the part being checked. If the test is being made at the terminals on the part, remove all other wires connected to the terminals so they do not influence the meter reading.
6. Operate the switch/button and check for continuity.

ELECTRICAL CONNECTORS

All models are equipped with numerous electrical components, connectors and wires. Corrosion-causing moisture can enter these electrical connectors and cause poor electrical connections, leading to component failure. Troubleshooting an electrical circuit with one or more corroded electrical connectors can be time-consuming and frustrating.

When reconnecting electrical connectors, pack them in a dielectric grease compound. Dielectric grease is specially formulated for sealing and waterproofing electrical connections without interfering with current flow. Use only this compound or an equivalent designed for this specific purpose. Do not use a substitute that may interfere with the current flow within the electrical connector. Do not use silicone sealant.

After cleaning both the male and female connectors, make sure they are thoroughly dry. Apply dielectric grease to the interior of one of the connectors prior to connecting the connector halves. For best results, the compound should fill the entire inner area of the connector. On multi-pin connectors, also pack the backside of both the male and female side with the compound to prevent moisture from entering the connector. After the connector is fully packed, wipe all excess compound from the exterior.

NEGATIVE BATTERY TERMINAL

Some service procedures require disconnection of the battery cable from the negative battery terminal.

1. Turn the ignition switch to the OFF position.
2. Remove the seat as described in Chapter Fifteen.
3. Remove the air box cover.
4. Remove the rubber cover fasteners (A, **Figure 1**).
5. Remove the bracket retaining bolts (**Figure 2**).
6. Remove the rubber cover (B, **Figure 1**) and bracket (C).
7. Remove the bolt (A, **Figure 3**) and disconnect the cable from the negative battery terminal.
8. Move the cable out of the way and secure it so it cannot accidentally touch the battery terminal.
9. When the procedure has been completed, reconnect the cable to the negative battery terminal and tighten the bolt securely.

1

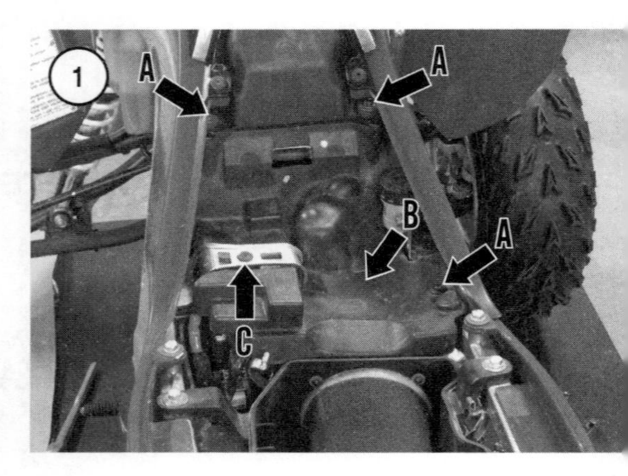

2

10. Install the rubber cover and battery bracke Tighten the bracket retaining bolts to 7 N•m (62 in lb.).
11. Install the air box cover.
12. Install the seat (Chapter Fifteen).

BATTERY

A sealed, maintenance-free battery is installed o all models. When replacing the battery, use a seale type; do not install a non-sealed battery. Refer t **Table 1** for battery specifications.

To prevent accidental shorts that could blow a fus when working on the electrical system, always dis connect the negative battery cable from the battery.

WARNING
Even though the battery is a sealed type, protect eyes, skin and clothing; electrolyte is corrosive and can cause severe burns and permanent injury. The battery case may be cracked and leaking electrolyte. If electrolyte gets into the eyes, flush both eyes thoroughly with clean, running water and get immediate medical attention. Always wear safety goggles when servicing the battery.

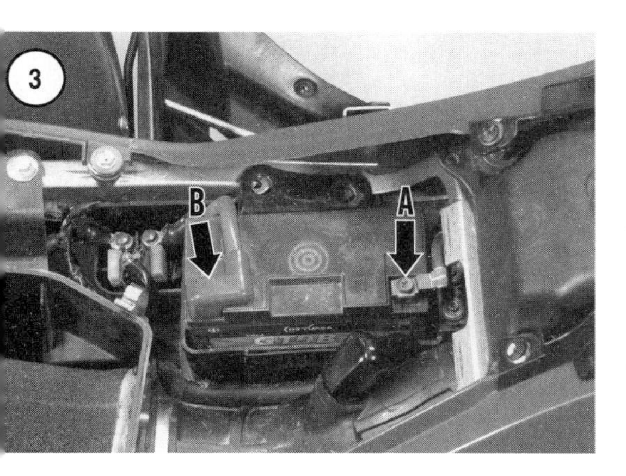

WARNING
While batteries are being charged, highly explosive hydrogen gas forms in each cell. Some of this gas escapes through filler cap openings and may form an explosive atmosphere in and around the battery. This condition can persist for several hours. Sparks, an open flame or a lighted cigarette can ignite the gas, causing an internal battery explosion and possible serious personal injury.

NOTE
Recycle the old battery. When replacing the old battery, be sure to turn in the old battery at that time. The lead plates and the plastic case can be recycled. Most vehicle dealerships accept old batteries in trade when purchasing a new one. Never place an old battery in household trash; it is illegal, in most states, to place any acid or lead (heavy metal) contents in landfills.

afety Precautions

Heed the following precautions to prevent an exlosion.

. Do not smoke or permit an open flame near any attery being charged or one which has been recently harged.
. Do not disconnect live circuits at the battery. A park usually occurs when a live circuit is broken.
. Take care when connecting or disconnecting a attery charger. Turn the power switch OFF before naking or breaking connections. Poor connections re a common cause of electrical arcs, which can ause explosions.
. Keep children and pets away from the charging quipment and the battery.

Removal/Installation

The battery is installed in the box located underneath the seat.

1. Read *Safety Precautions* in this section.
2. Disconnect the battery cable (A, **Figure 3**) from the negative battery terminal as described in this chapter.
3. Disconnect the positive battery cable (B, **Figure 3**) from the positive battery terminal.
4. Lift the battery out of the battery compartment.
5. After the battery has been serviced or replaced, install it by reversing the removal steps. Note the following:
   a. Install the battery into the battery box with the negative terminal toward the front of the ATV.

CAUTION
Be sure the battery cables are connected to their proper terminals. Connecting the battery backward reverses the polarity and damages the rectifier and ignition system.

   b. Always connect the positive battery cable first (B, **Figure 3**), and then the negative cable (A).
   c. Coat the battery leads with dielectric grease or petroleum jelly.
   d. Tighten the battery bracket retaining bolts to 7 N•m (62 in.-lb.).

9

Cleaning/Inspection

The battery electrolyte level cannot be serviced. Never attempt to remove the sealing bar cap from the top of the battery. The battery does not require periodic electrolyte inspection or refilling.

1. Read *Safety Precautions* in this section.
2. Remove the battery from the vehicle as described in this section. Do not clean the battery while it is mounted in the vehicle.
3. Clean the battery exterior with a solution of warm water and baking soda. Rinse thoroughly with clean water.
4. Inspect the physical condition of the battery. Look for bulges or cracks in the case, leaking electrolyte or corrosion buildup.
5. Check the battery terminal bolts and nuts for corrosion and damage. Clean parts with a solution of baking soda and water, and rinse thoroughly. Replace any damaged parts.
6. Check the battery cable clamps for corrosion and damage. If corrosion is minor, clean the battery cable clamps with a stiff brush. Replace excessively worn or damaged cables.

Testing

The maintenance-free battery can be tested while mounted in the vehicle. A digital voltmeter is required for this procedure. See **Table 1** for battery voltage readings for the maintenance free battery.

1. Read *Safety Precautions* in this section.

NOTE

To prevent false test readings, do not test the battery if the battery terminals are corroded. Remove and clean the battery and terminals as described in this section, and then reinstall it.

2. Connect a digital voltmeter between the battery negative and positive leads. Note the following:
   a. If the battery voltage is 13.0-13.2 volts (at 20° C [68° F]), the battery is fully charged.
   b. If the battery voltage is below 12.8 volts (at 20° C [68° F]), the battery is undercharged and requires charging.
3. If the battery is undercharged, recharge it as described in this section. Then, test the charging system as described in this chapter.

Charging

Refer to *Battery Initialization* (this section) if the battery is *new*.

To recharge a maintenance-free battery, a digital voltmeter and a charger (**Figure 4**) with an adjustable or automatically variable amperage output are required. If this equipment is not available, have the battery charged by a shop with the proper equipment. Excessive voltage and amperage from an unregulated charger can damage the battery and shorten service life.

The battery should only self-discharge approximately one percent of its given capacity each day. If a battery not in use, without any loads connected, loses its charge within a week after charging, the battery is defective.

If the vehicle is not used for long periods of time, an automatic battery charger with variable voltage and amperage outputs is recommended for optimum battery service life.

WARNING

During the charging process, highly explosive hydrogen gas is released from the battery. Charge the battery only in a well-ventilated area away from any open flames (including pilot lights on home gas appliances). Do not allow any smoking in the area. Never check the charge of the battery by connecting screwdriver blades or other metal objects between the terminals; the resulting spark can ignite the hydrogen gas.

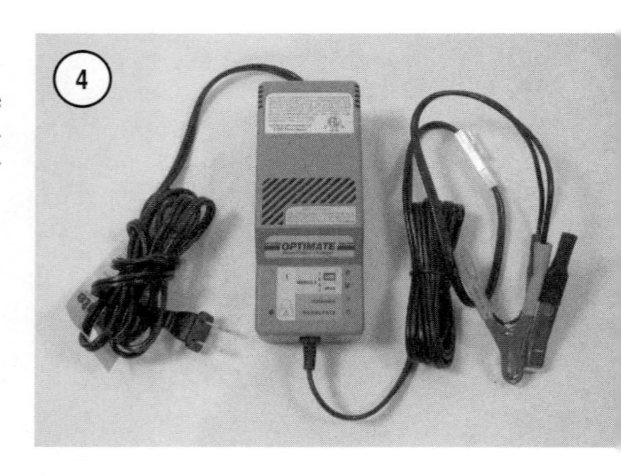

CAUTION

Always remove the battery from the vehicle before connecting the battery charger. Never recharge a battery in the frame; corrosive gasses emitted during the charging process will damage surfaces.

1. Remove the battery as described in this section.
2. Connect the positive charger lead to the positiv battery terminal and the negative charger lead to th negative battery terminal.
3. Set the charger at 12 volts and switch it on. Normally, a battery should be charged at a slov charge rate of 1/10 its given capacity. **Table 1** list the battery capacity and charge rate for all mod els.
4. After the battery has been charged, turn the char ger OFF, disconnect the leads and check the batter voltage with a digital voltmeter. It should be withi the limits specified in **Table 1**. If it is, and remain stable for one hour, the battery is charged.

Battery Initialization

A *new* battery must be fully charged before instal lation. Failure to do so reduces the life of the bat tery. Using a *new* battery without an initial charg causes permanent battery damage. That is, the bat tery will never be able to hold more than an 80% charge. Charging a *new* battery after it has been use will not bring its charge to 100%. When purchas ing a *new* battery from a dealership or parts store verify its charge status. If necessary, have them per form the initial or booster charge before acceptin the battery.

CHARGING SYSTEM

The charging system consists of the battery, alternator and a voltage regulator/rectifier. A 20-amp main fuse protects the circuit. Refer to the wiring diagrams at the end of this manual.

The stator coil assembly contains coils that generate alternating current which is then changed to direct current by the regulator/rectifier. The voltage regulator maintains constant voltage to the battery and additional electrical loads (such as lights or ignition) despite variations in engine speed and load.

Charging Voltage Test

This procedure tests charging system operation. It does not measure maximum charging system output. **Table 2** lists charging system test specifications.

To obtain accurate test results, the battery must be fully charged (13.0 volts or higher).

1. Start and run the engine until it reaches normal operating temperature, and then turn the engine OFF.

NOTE
Do not disconnect either battery cable when making this test.

2. Connect a digital voltmeter to the battery terminals.
3. Start the engine and allow it to idle.
4. Gradually increase engine speed to 5000 rpm and read the voltage indicated on the voltmeter. Compare this with the regulated voltage reading in **Table 2**.

NOTE
If the battery is often discharged, but charging voltage tests normal, the battery may be damaged.

5. If the regulated voltage is too low, check for an open or short circuit in the charging system wiring harness, an open or short in the alternator or a damaged regulator/rectifier.
6. If the regulated voltage is too high, check for a poor regulator/rectifier ground, a damaged regulator/rectifier or a damaged battery.

Regulator/Rectifier Removal/Installation

1. Disconnect the cable from the negative battery terminal as described in this chapter.
2. Disconnect the regulator/rectifier electrical connector (A, **Figure 5**).
3. Remove the bolts (B, **Figure 5**) securing the regulator/rectifier (C) to the frame bracket and remove the regulator/rectifier.
4. Install by reversing the removal steps. Make sure the electrical connector is secure and corrosion-free.

ALTERNATOR

The alternator consists of the flywheel rotor and stator coil assembly. The rotor is a part of the flywheel. The stator coil assembly is located inside the left crankcase cover. The stator coils generate voltage for the electrical system.

Refer to Chapter Five for removal and installation of the flywheel and left crankcase cover.

Rotor Testing

The rotor is permanently magnetized and cannot be tested except by replacing it with a known good one. The rotor can lose magnetism from old age or a sharp hit, such as dropping it onto a concrete floor. Replace the flywheel if the rotor is defective or damaged.

Stator Coil

Resistance test

The stator coil can be tested while mounted on the engine.

1. Disconnect the cable from the negative battery terminal as described in this chapter.
2. Remove the front fender as described in Chapter Fifteen.
3. Disconnect the regulator/rectifier electrical connector (A, **Figure 5**).
4. Measure resistance between each white wire terminal in the alternator end of the connector. **Table 2** lists the specified stator coil resistance.
5. Replace the stator if the resistance is not as specified.
6. Check continuity from each white stator wire to ground.

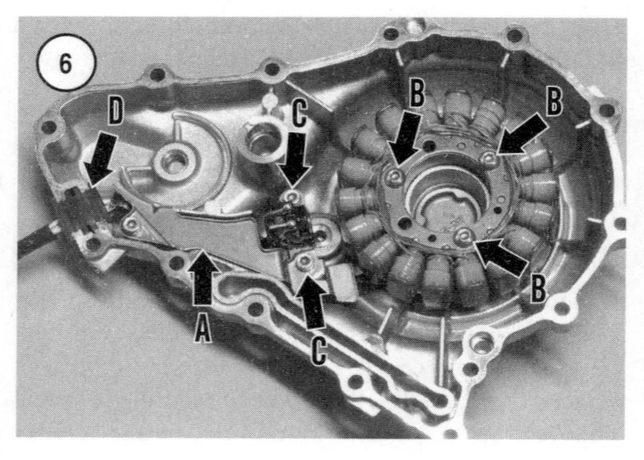

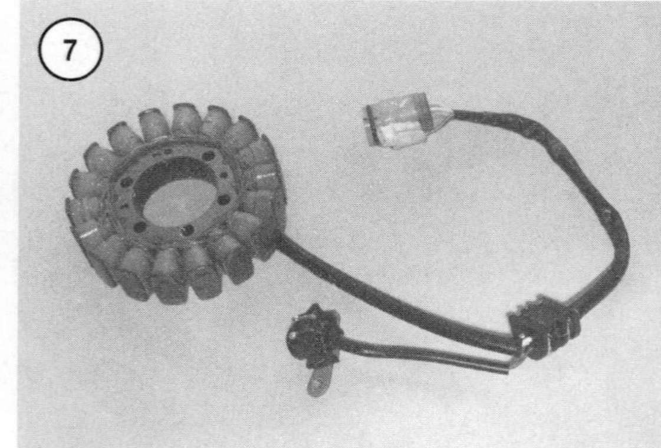

NOTE
Before replacing the stator assembly, check the electrical wires to and within the electrical connector, including the three-wire stator connector, for any breaks in the wire or poor connections.

7. Replace the stator coil if any white terminal has continuity to ground. Continuity indicates a short within the stator coil winding.
8. If the stator coil fails either of these tests, replace it as described in this section.
9. Make sure the electrical connector is secure and corrosion-free.
10. Connect the negative battery cable (this chapter).
11. Install the front fender (Chapter Fifteen).

Removal/installation

NOTE
The stator coil and crankshaft position sensor are wired together and must be serviced as a unit.

1. Remove the left crankcase cover as described in Chapter Five.
2. Remove the bolts securing the wire retainer (A, **Figure 6**) and remove the retainer.
3. Remove the stator coil mounting bolts (B, **Figure 6**).
4. Remove the crankshaft position sensor mounting bolts (C, **Figure 6**).
5. Pull the wire harness grommet (D, **Figure 6**) out of the crankcase cover notch.
6. Remove the stator coil and crankshaft position sensor assembly (**Figure 7**).
7. Do not clean the stator coils with solvent. Wipe off with a clean rag.
8. Install the stator coil by reversing the removal steps, while noting the following:

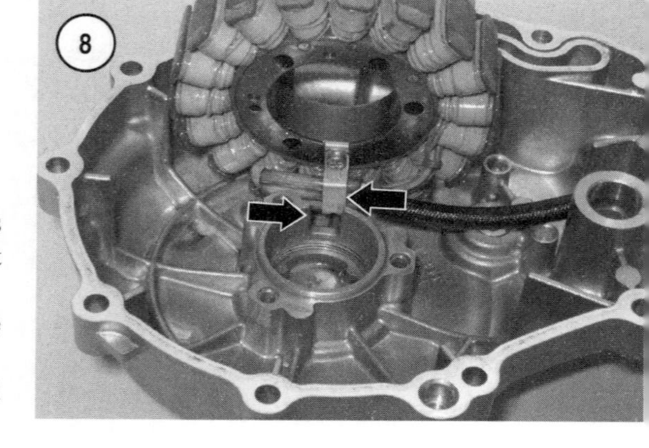

a. Apply sealant to the grooves in the wiring harness grommet before inserting it into the crankcase cover notch.
b. Insert the tab on the backside of the stator into the notch in the cover (**Figure 8**).
c. Apply threadlock to the mounting bolts for the stator coil, crankshaft position sensor and wire retainer.
d. Tighten the stator coil mounting bolts to 7 N•m (62 in.-lb.).
e. Tighten the crankshaft position sensor mounting bolts to 7 N•m (62 in.-lb.).
f. Tighten the stator wire retainer bolts to 7 N•m (62 in.-lb.).

IGNITION SYSTEM

The ATV is equipped with an electronic ignition system. Refer to the wiring diagrams at the end of this manual.

Ignition System Precautions

Certain measures must be taken to protect ignition system components.

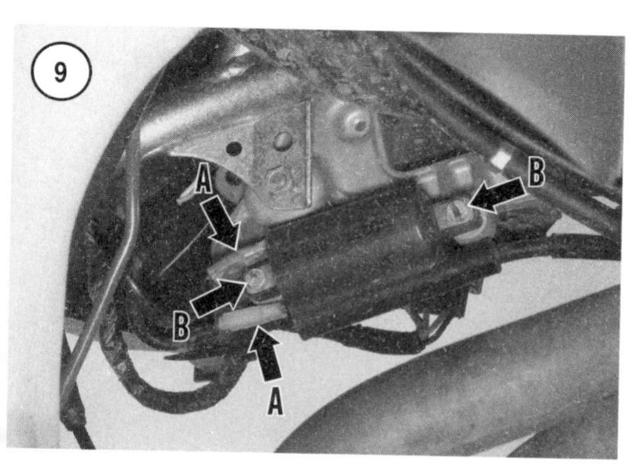

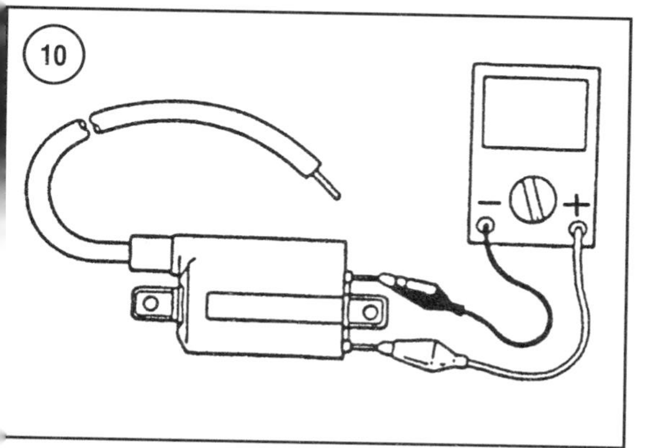

I. Never disconnect any of the electrical connec-
ions while the engine is running.
2. Keep all connections between the various units
lean and tight. Apply dielectric grease to all electri-
al connectors before reconnecting them. This will
elp seal out moisture.
. When operating the starter with the spark plug re-
noved, make sure the spark plug or a spark tester is
nstalled in the plug cap, and that the plug or tester
s grounded. If not, excessive resistance may damage
he ECU. See *Spark Test* in Chapter Two.
. Make sure the ECU is mounted correctly.

'roubleshooting

Refer to Chapter Two.

gnition Coil Assembly .emoval/Installation

Disconnect the spark plug lead from the spark
lug.
Disconnect the primary electrical wire connectors
\, **Figure 9**) from the ignition coil.
Remove the ignition coil mounting bolts (B,
igure 9).

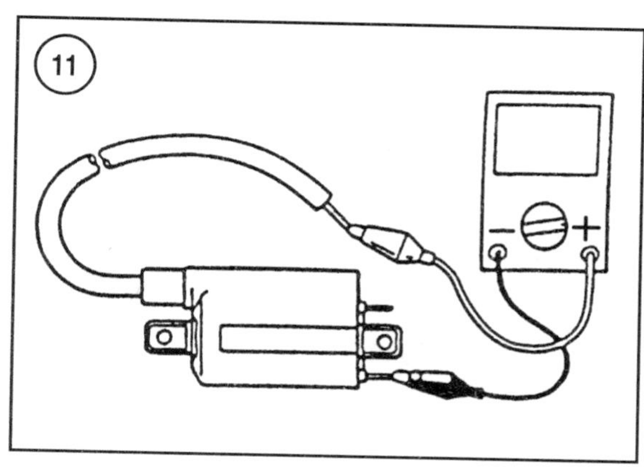

4. Remove the ignition coil with the spark plug lead.
5. Reverse the removal steps to install the ignition coil. Make sure the electrical connectors are corrosion-free and secure.

Ignition Coil Resistance Test

1. Disconnect the primary coil resistance terminal connectors (A, **Figure 9**).
2. Using an ohmmeter, measure the primary coil resistance between the positive and the negative terminals (**Figure 10**) on the side of the ignition coil. Record the measured resistance.
3. Disconnect the spark plug lead and remove the spark plug cap.
4. Measure the secondary coil resistance between the spark plug lead and the red/black wire terminal (**Figure 11**) on the ignition coil. Record the measured resistance.
5. If either measurement does not meet specification in **Table 3**, replace the coil. If the coil exhibits visible damage, replace it.

ECU Module

The ECU controls the ignition timing and fuel injection. Refer to Chapter Eight.

STARTER

The starting system consists of the starter, starter gears, starting circuit cutoff relay, starter relay, neutral switch, clutch switch and starter button. Refer to the wiring diagram at the end of this manual.

Table 4 lists starter specifications.

CAUTION
Do not operate the starter for more than five seconds at a time. Wait approximately ten seconds between starting attempts.

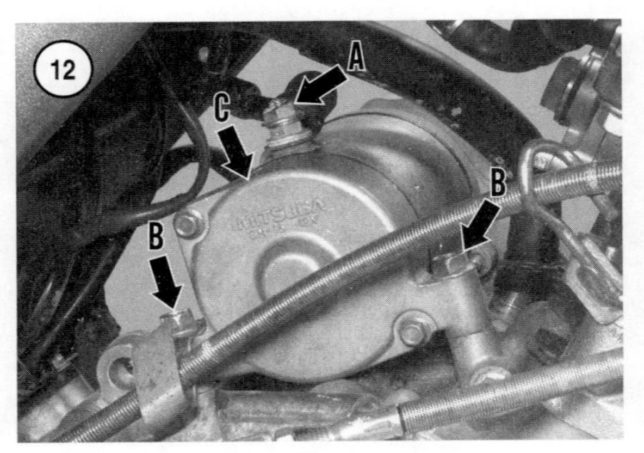

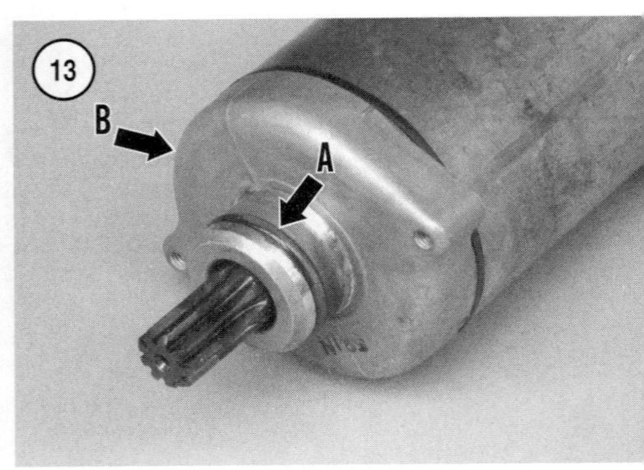

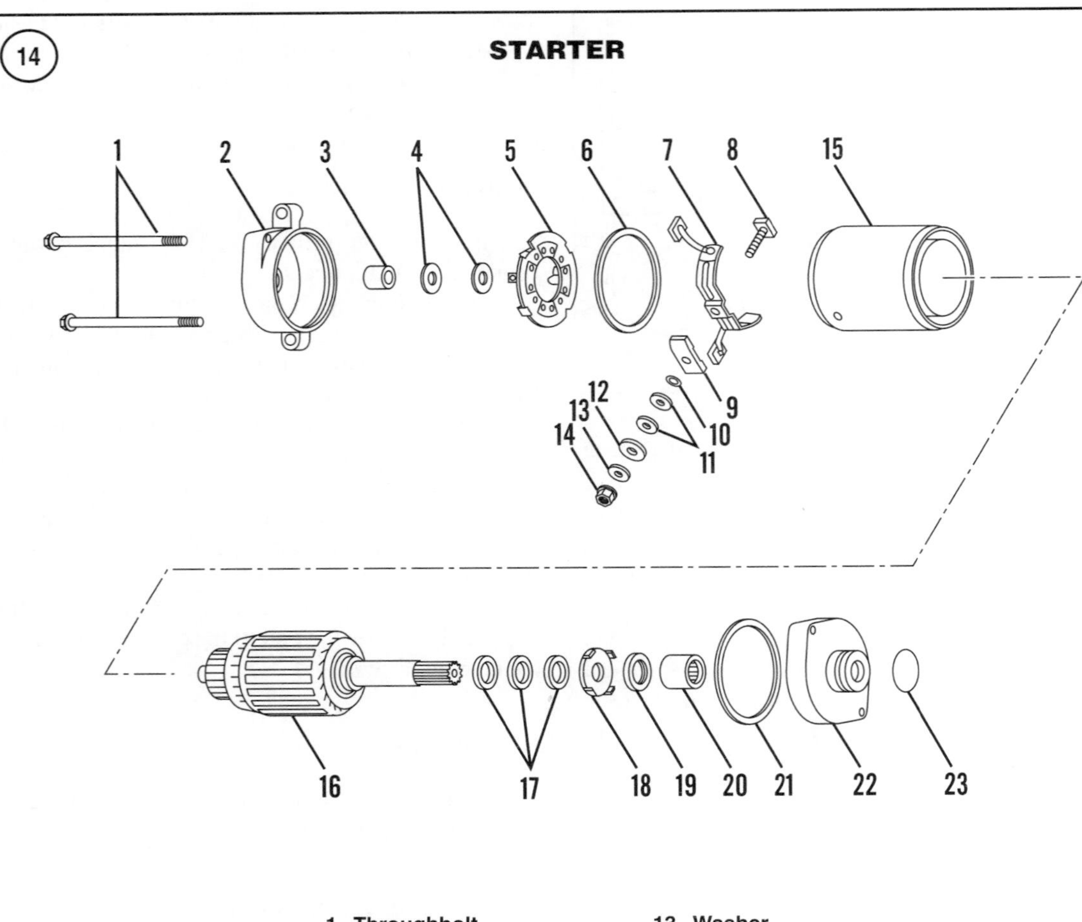

1. Throughbolt
2. Rear cover
3. Bushing
4. Shims
5. Brush plate
6. Seal ring
7. Brush holder
8. Terminal bolt
9. Insulator
10. O-ring
11. Insulated washers (small)
12. Insulated washer (large)
13. Washer
14. Nut
15. Case
16. Armature
17. Shims
18. Lockwasher
19. Seal
20. Bearing
21. Seal ring
22. Front cover
23. O-ring

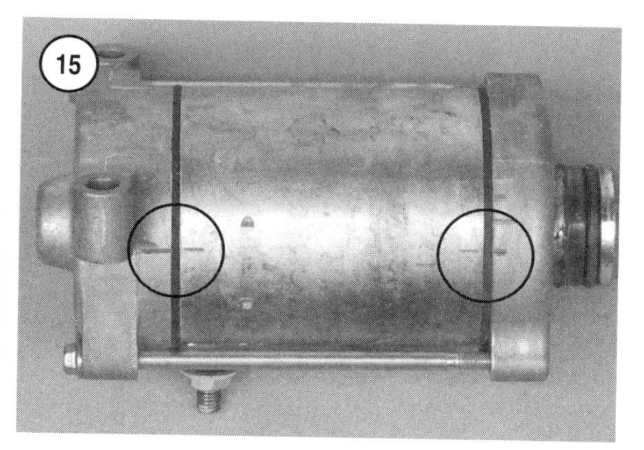
15

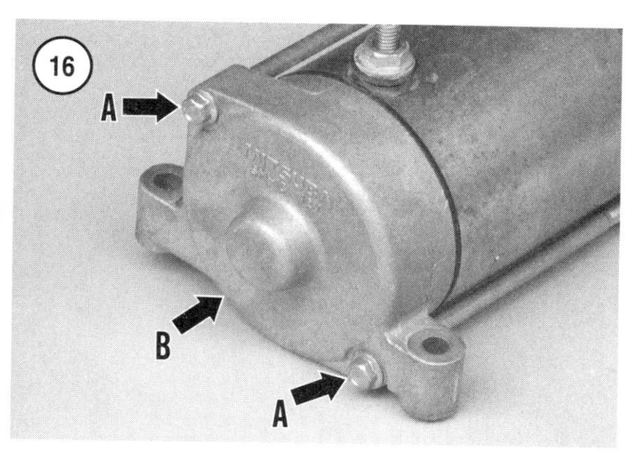

16

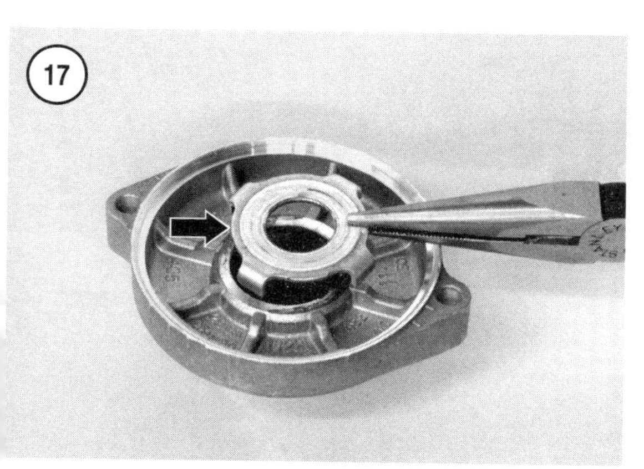
17

18

Troubleshooting

Refer to Chapter Two.

Removal/Installation

1. Disconnect the cable from the negative battery terminal as described in this chapter.
2. Remove the exhaust system as described in Chapter Four.
3. Push back the rubber cap, and then remove the nut and starter cable terminal (A, **Figure 12**) from the starter.
4. Remove the starter retaining bolts (B, **Figure 12**).
5. Remove the starter (C, **Figure 12**).
6. If necessary, service the starter as described in this section.
7. Install the starter by reversing the removal steps while noting the following:
   a. Lubricate the starter O-ring (A, **Figure 13**) with grease.
   b. Clean any rust or corrosion from the starter cable terminal.
   c. Tighten the starter mounting bolts to 10 N•m (89 in.-lb.). Note that the rear bolt also secures the parking brake clamp.

9

Disassembly

Refer to **Figure 14**.

NOTE
*Before disassembling the starter, locate the alignment marks on the starter case and both end covers (**Figure 15**) for assembly. If necessary, scribe new marks.*

1. Loosen the starter throughbolts (A, **Figure 16**) and remove them.

NOTE
Record the number, type and thickness of the shims and the washer used on both ends of the armature shaft. These shims and the washer must be installed in their original order and positions.

2. Slide the front cover (B, **Figure 13**) off the armature shaft, and remove the washers.
3. Remove the lockwasher (**Figure 17**) from the front cover.
4. Slide the rear cover (B, **Figure 16**) off the armature shaft and remove the shims (**Figure 18**).
5. Slide the starter case off the armature.
6. Remove the brush holder assembly (A, **Figure 19**).

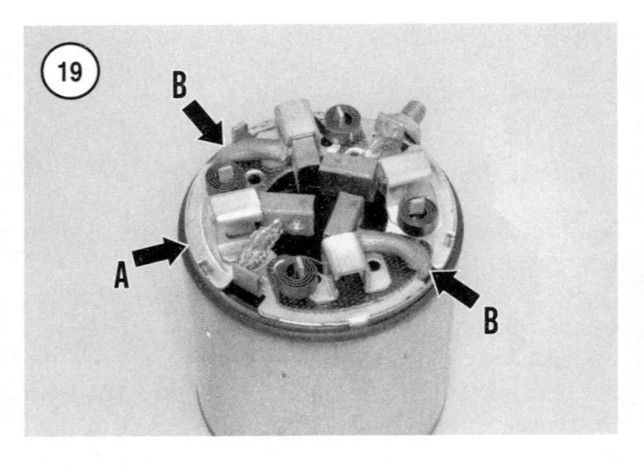

NOTE
Before removing the terminal bolt nut and washers, record their description and order. They must be reinstalled in the same order to insulate the positive brush set from the case.

7. Remove the nut and washers (**Figure 20**) securing the positive terminal bolt to the starter case.
8. Remove the terminal bolt, positive brush set (**Figure 21**), insulator and O-ring.

CAUTION
Immersing the armature coil or starter case in solvent will damage the insulation. Wipe the windings with a cloth lightly moistened in solvent and dry with compressed air.

9. Clean all grease, dirt and carbon from the components.
10. Inspect the starter as described in this section.

Assembly

1. Install the positive brush set (**Figure 21**) as follows:

NOTE
Reinstall all parts in the same order as noted during disassembly. This is essential in order to insulate the set of brushes from the starter case.

a. Install the insulator on top of the positive brush holder. Then, insert the brush holder into the starter case with the tab on the insulator facing toward the brush plate.
b. Install the terminal bolt through the brush holder, insulator and grommet.
c. Insert the terminal bolt through the starter case.
d. Install the two small insulated washers onto the terminal bolt.
e. Install the large insulated washer.

20

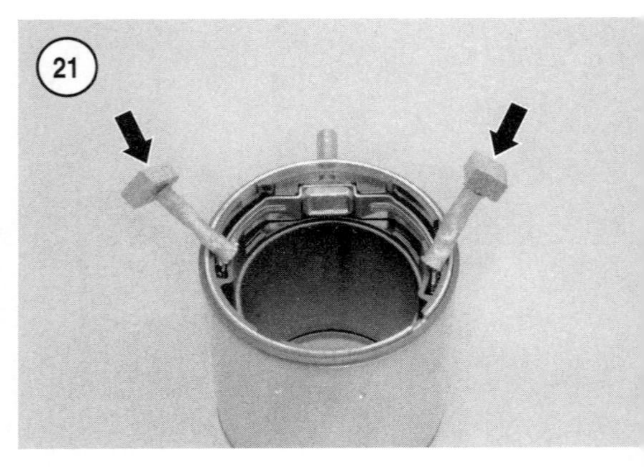

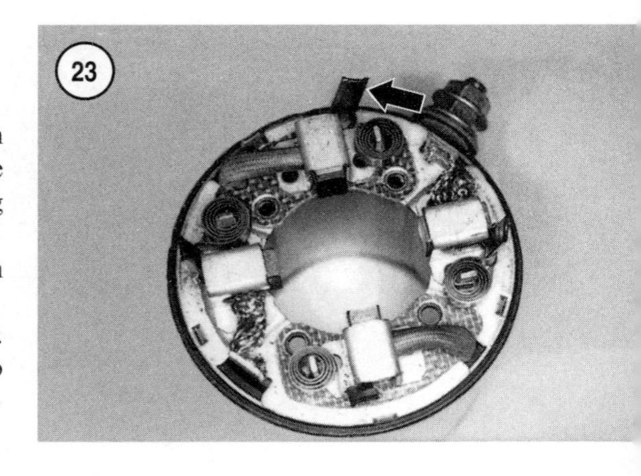

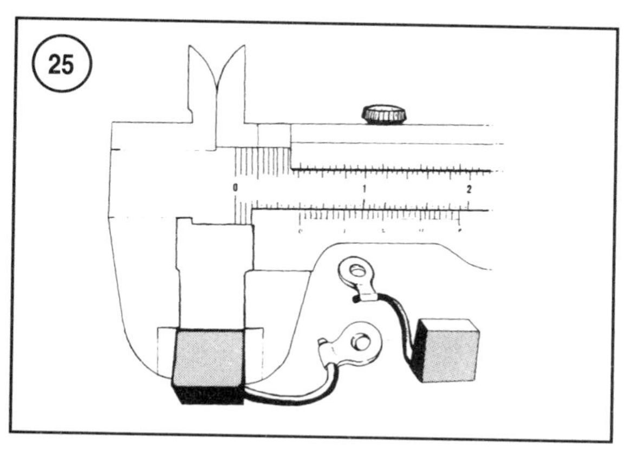

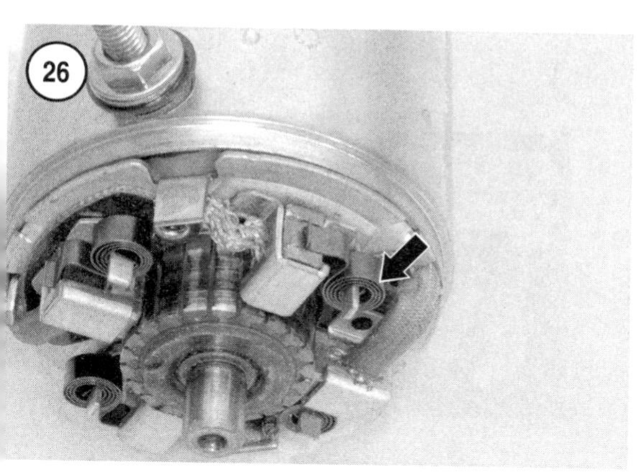

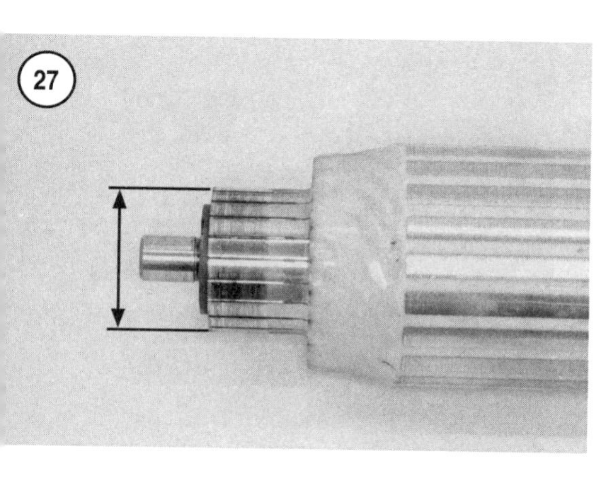

f. Install the steel washer.

g. Install the nut finger tight.

2. Install the negative brush plate onto the starter case, inserting the two positive brush wires through the plate notches (B, **Figure 19**). Align the brush plate locating tab (**Figure 22**) with the notch in the starter case.
3. Install the brushes into their receptacles. Install a small shim (**Figure 23**) between each spring and brush to reduce spring pressure on the brushes.
4. Position the commutator end of the armature toward the brush plate and slowly insert the armature into the front of the starter case. Do not damage the brushes during this step.
5. Remove the shims (**Figure 24**).
6. Make sure that each brush seats squarely against the commutator.
7. Install the shims (**Figure 18**) onto the commutator end of the shaft.
8. Install the seal ring into the rear case cover groove.
9. Check that the brush plate locating tab (**Figure 22**) is still aligned with the notch in the starter case.
10. Install the shims and insulated washer onto the front of the armature shaft, if so equipped.
11. Install the lockwasher (**Figure 17**) into the front cover. Make sure it is correctly seated.
12. Install the seal ring into the front cover groove.
13. Install the front cover (B, **Figure 13**).
14. Align the index marks (**Figure 15**) on all three components.

NOTE

If the throughbolt does not pass outside the starter case and through the end covers, the components are installed incorrectly.

15. Install the throughbolts (A, **Figure 16**) and tighten securely.

Inspection

Check with a dealership regarding starter replacement components. In most cases only the brush sets, O-ring and seal rings are available.

1. Measure the length of each brush (**Figure 25**) with a caliper and compare with the specification listed in **Table 4**. If any brush is too short, replace both brush sets together.
2. Inspect the brush springs (**Figure 26**) for fatigue, cracks or other damage. Replace the negative brush plate if the springs are severely worn or damaged. The positive brush plate is part of the brush replacement parts set.
3. Inspect the commutator (**Figure 27**) for abnormal wear or discoloration. Neither of these conditions can be repaired and both require replacement of the armature.

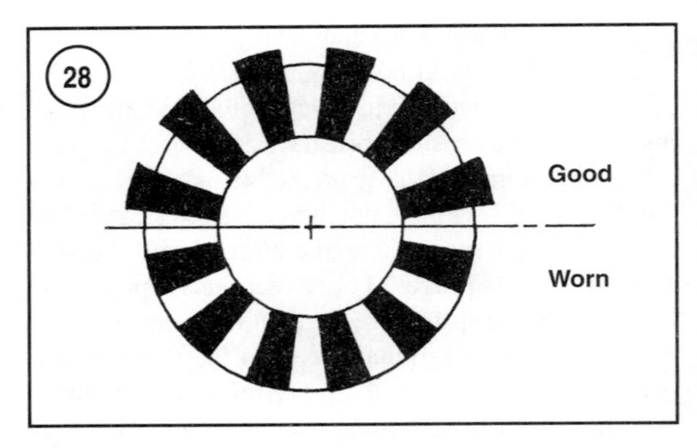

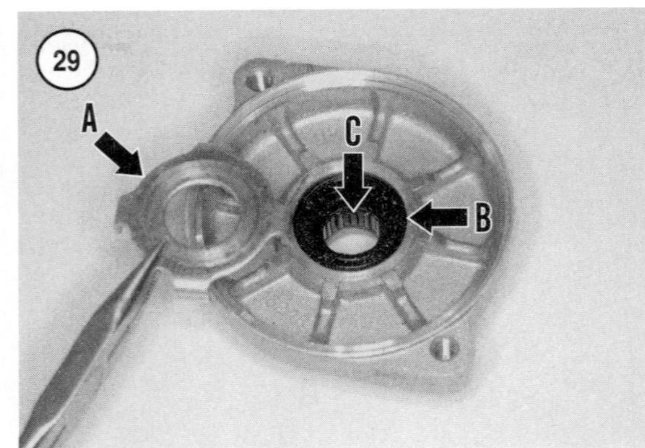

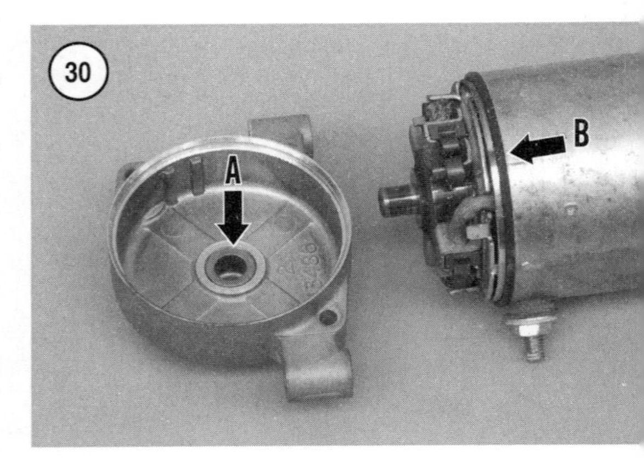

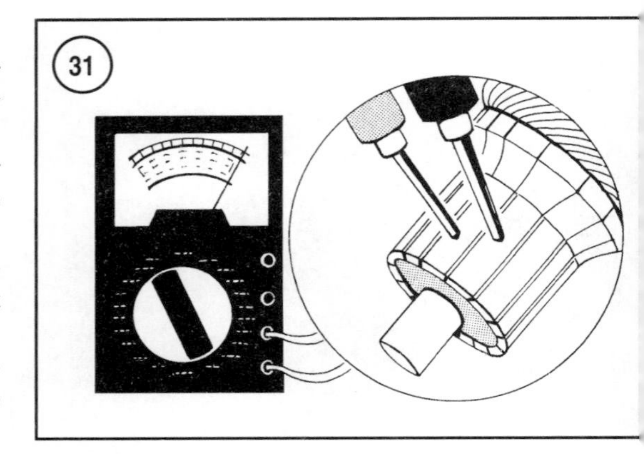

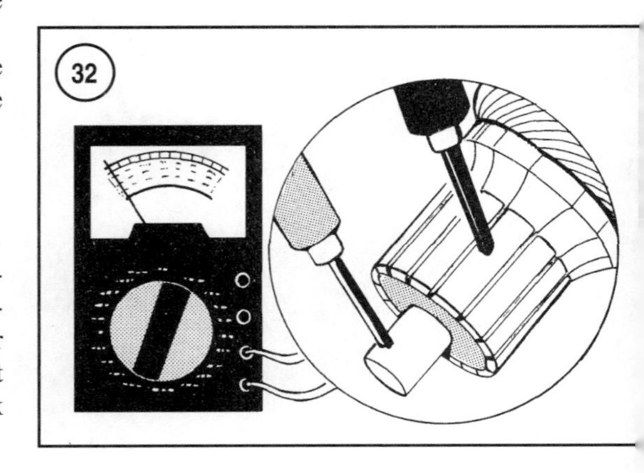

4. The mica in a good commutator is below the surface of the copper bars. On a worn commutator the mica and copper bars may be worn to the same level. If necessary, undercut the mica between each pair of bars. Refer to **Figure 28**.
5. Measure the outside diameter (**Figure 27**) of the commutator and compare to the specification in **Table 4**.
6. Check the armature shaft splines for wear or damage. If worn or damaged, also inspect the starter reduction gear for damage.
7. Remove the lockwasher (A, **Figure 29**) from the front cover. Inspect the oil seal (B, **Figure 29**) and needle bearing (C) for wear or damage.
8. Inspect the bushing (A, **Figure 30**) in the rear cover for severe wear or damage.
9. Use an ohmmeter to make the following tests:
   a. Check for continuity between the commutator bars (**Figure 31**); there should be continuity between pairs of bars.
   b. Check for continuity between the commutator bars and the shaft (**Figure 32**); there should be no continuity.
   c. If the commutator fails either of these tests, replace the starter assembly. The armature is not available separately.
10. Check for continuity between the positive terminal bolt and starter case (**Figure 33**); there should be no continuity.
11. Replace the seal rings (B, **Figure 30**) if they are worn or damaged.
12. Check the magnets bonded into the inner surface of the starter case. If damaged or loose, replace the starter assembly.

STARTING CIRCUIT CUTOFF SYSTEM

The starting circuit cutoff system uses a cutoff relay that does not allow current to the starter relay unless the transmission is in neutral or the clutch lever is pulled in. Included in the relay unit is a diode that prevents current flow from the neutral switch back through the clutch switch.

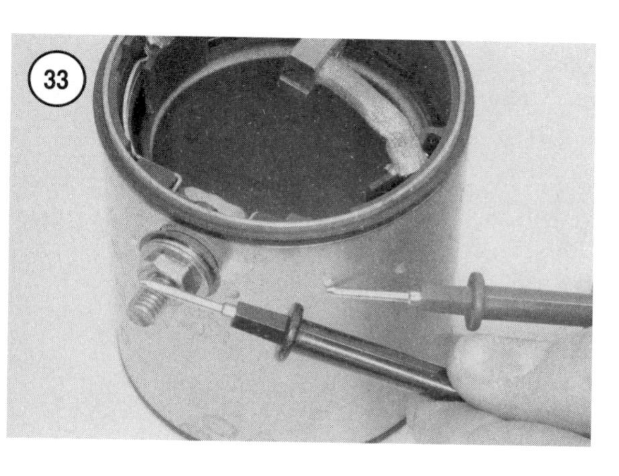
33

34

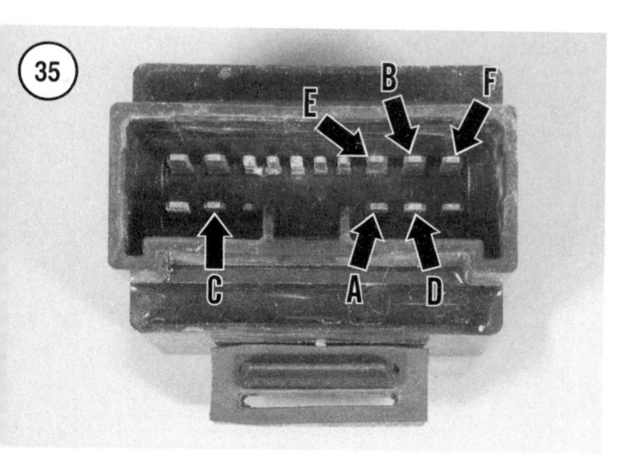

35

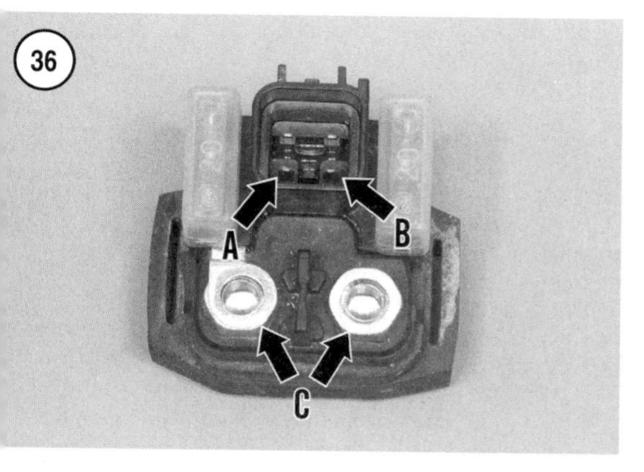

36

Removal/Installation

1. Disconnect the battery cable from the negative battery terminal as described in this chapter.
2. Remove the seat as described in Chapter Fifteen.
3. Remove the starting circuit cutoff relay (**Figure 34**) from the mounting bracket.
4. Disconnect the connector from the starting circuit cutoff relay.
5. Install by reversing the removal steps.

Relay Testing

1. Remove the relay as described in this section.
2. Disconnect the electrical connector from the relay unit.
3. Connect a fully charged 12-volt battery to the relay. Connect the positive battery terminal to the red/black wire terminal (A, **Figure 35**) and the negative battery terminal to the black/yellow wire terminal (B).
4. Connect the ohmmeter positive test lead to the blue/white wire terminal (C, **Figure 35**) on the relay and connect the negative test lead to the blue/black wire terminal (D) on the relay. The ohmmeter should show continuity.
5. Replace the relay if it fails this test.
6. Test the diode as follows:
   a. Using an ohmmeter, connect the positive test lead to the sky blue wire terminal (E, **Figure 35**) on the relay.
   b. Connect the negative test lead to the red/black wire terminal (A, **Figure 35**) on the relay. The ohmmeter should indicate continuity.
   c. Reverse the test leads and check continuity in the opposite direction. The ohmmeter should indicate no continuity.
   d. Repeat substeps a, b and c at the sky blue wire terminal (E, **Figure 35**) and the light green wire terminal (F).
   e. Replace the cutoff relay if it fails the diode test.

STARTER RELAY

Testing

1. Remove the starter relay as described in this section.
2. Check the continuity of the starter relay by performing the following:
   a. Connect the positive terminal of a fully charged 12-volt battery to the starter relay brown wire terminal (A, **Figure 36**).
   b. Connect the negative battery terminal to the blue/white relay terminal (B, **Figure 36**).
   c. Check for continuity between the starter relay terminals (C, **Figure 36**).
3. Replace the starter relay if it fails this test.

Removal/Installation

1. Disconnect the battery cable from the negative battery terminal as described in this chapter.
2. Disconnect the starter relay electrical connector (A, **Figure 37**).
3. Slide the rubber boots off the two large cable leads.
4. Disconnect the two large cable leads (B, **Figure 37**) from the starter relay.
5. Remove the starter relay from the mounting bracket.
6. Transfer the 20-amp main fuse and spare fuse to the new starter relay.
7. Install by reversing the removal steps.

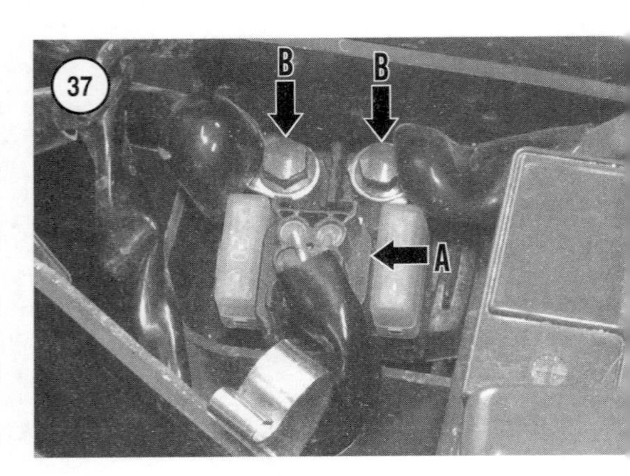

LIGHTS

The lights and related components used on the ATV include the headlights, headlight relay, taillight/ brake light and indicator lights.

Always use the correct wattage bulb as listed in **Table 5**. Using the wrong size bulb produces a dim light or causes the bulb to burn out prematurely.

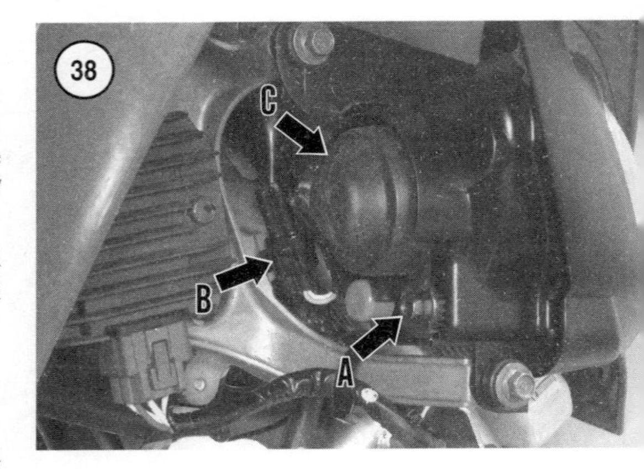

Headlight Adjustment

The headlight beam may be adjusted vertically by turning the adjustment bolt (A, **Figure 38**) on each headlight. Turn the bolt clockwise to lower the beam.

Headlight Bulb Replacement

WARNING
If the headlight just burned out or if it was just turned off, it will be hot! Do not touch the bulb until it cools.

1. Disconnect the headlight connector (B, **Figure 38**).
2. Pull back the rubber cover (C, **Figure 38**).
3. Push in the bulb holder, then turn it counterclockwise and remove the bulb holder.
4. Remove the bulb from the headlight housing.
5. Reverse the removal steps to install the bulb and headlight. Insert the bulb so the tab (**Figure 39**) fits into the slot in the headlight housing. If necessary, perform the *Headlight Adjustment* as described in this section.

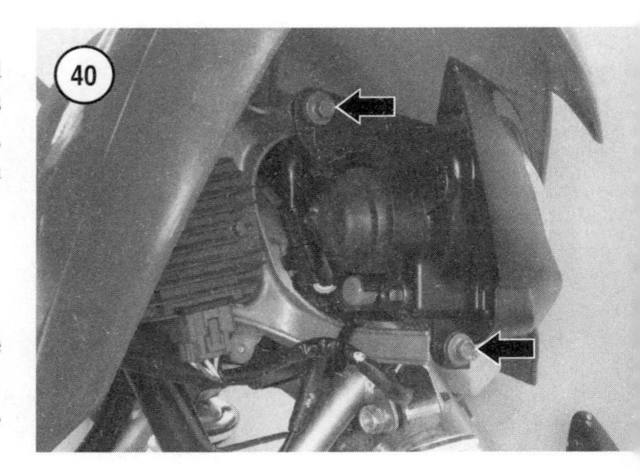

Headlight Housing Replacement

1. Disconnect the headlight connector (B, **Figure 38**).
2. Remove the headlight mounting bolts (**Figure 40**), washers and spacers. Then, remove the headlight.

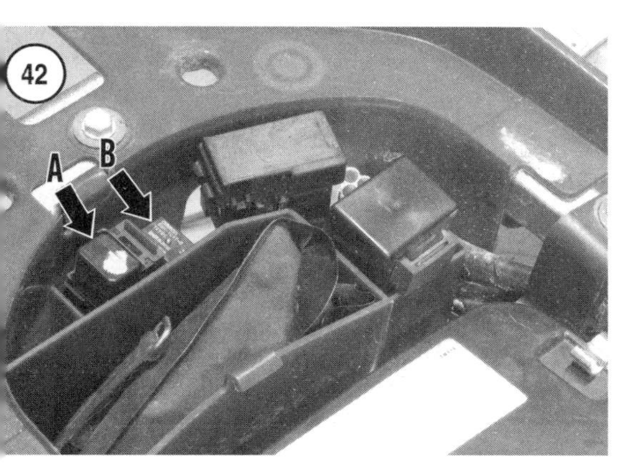

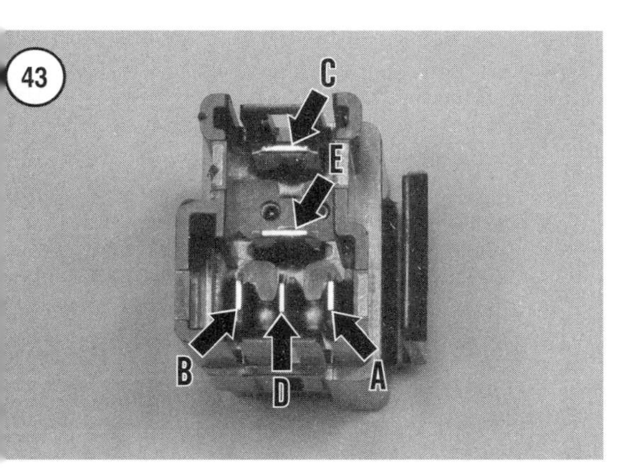

3. Reverse the removal steps to install the headlight housing. Push the inner housing grommet onto the mounting stud (**Figure 41**) on the frame.

Headlight Relay

Removal/installation

1. Disconnect the battery cable from the negative battery terminal as described in this chapter.
2. Disengage the headlight relay (A, **Figure 42**) from the rubber mount.

NOTE
Pry up the tabs on the relay nearest the connector.

3. Disconnect the electrical connector from the headlight relay.
4. Reverse the removal steps to install the relay.

Continuity test

1. Remove the headlight relay as described in this section.
2. Connect test leads to the headlight relay as follows:
   a. Jumper from 12-volt battery positive (A, **Figure 43**).
   b. Jumper from 12-volt battery negative (B, **Figure 43**).
   c. Ohmmeter positive test lead (C, **Figure 43**).
   d. Ohmmeter negative test lead (D, **Figure 43**).
3. There should be no continuity with battery voltage applied to the relay.
4. Disconnect the ohmmeter from the relay.
5. Connect test leads to the headlight relay as follows:
   a. Ohmmeter positive test lead (C, **Figure 43**).
   b. Ohmmeter negative test lead (E, **Figure 43**).
6. There should be continuity with battery voltage applied to the relay.
7. Replace the relay if it fails any portion of this test.

Taillight/Brake Light

The ATV is equipped with a LED-lighted taillight/brake light assembly. The entire assembly must be replaced if it is faulty.

Testing

1. Refer to Chapter Fifteen and remove the rear lower cover for access to the taillight/brake light connector (**Figure 44**).
2. Disconnect the taillight/brake light connector.

3A. To check the brake light circuit, connect the positive terminal of a 12-volt battery to the yellow wire terminal in the light end of the connector.
3B. To check the taillight circuit, connect the positive terminal of a 12-volt battery to the blue wire terminal in the light end of the connector.
4. Connect the negative battery terminal to the black wire terminal of the connector.
5. If the light does not illuminate, replace the taillight/brake light assembly.

Replacement

1. Remove the rear lower cover as described in Chapter Fifteen.
2. Remove the taillight housing mounting screws (**Figure 45**) and washers.
3. Remove the taillight/brake light assembly.
4. Reverse the removal steps to install the taillight/brake light assembly.

Indicator Lights

Indicator lights for coolant temperature, neutral, reverse, fuel level and engine trouble are mounted on a panel forward of the handlebar. Individual lights are not available.

Testing (2006-2008 models)

1. Remove the front fender panel as described in Chapter Fifteen.
2. Disconnect the indicator light connector (**Figure 46**).
3. To check the indicator lights, connect the positive terminal of a 12-volt battery to the brown wire terminal in the light end of the connector.
4. Refer to the wiring diagram at the back of this manual and connect the negative terminal of the battery to the wire terminal that corresponds to the indicator light.
5. Replace the indicator light unit if any light fails to illuminate.

Testing (2009 models)

Individual lights cannot be tested or replaced. If a malfunction occurs, eliminate possible causes such as a faulty sensor, wiring or connectors. Check operation with a known good unit before installing a new panel.

Replacement

1. Remove the front fender panel as described in Chapter Fifteen.

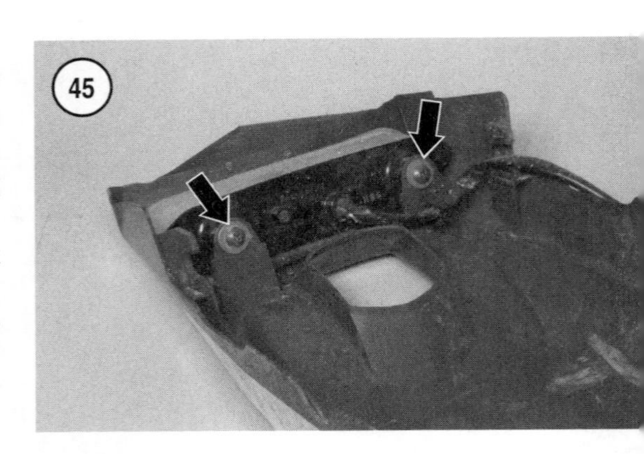

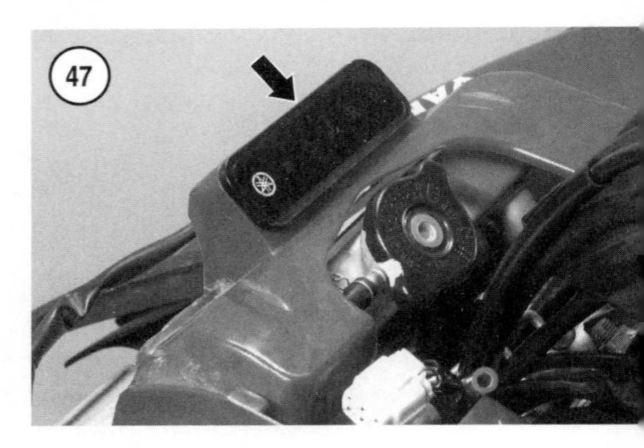

2. Disconnect the indicator light connector (**Figure 46**).
3. Remove the front grille as described in Chapter Fifteen.
4. Disengage the wiring harness from the retaining tabs on the front fender.
5. Lift the indicator light panel (**Figure 47**) out of the front fender.
6. Reverse the removal steps for installation.

COOLING SYSTEM

Radiator Fan Motor Testing

1. Disconnect the white electrical connector (**Figure 48**) under the front fender.

48

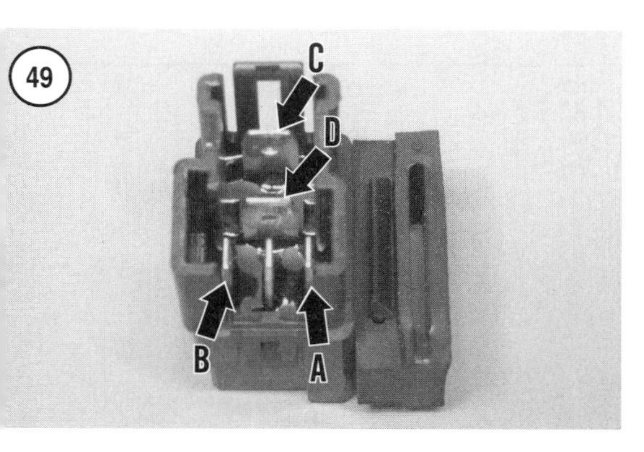

49

50

. Connect a fully charged 12-volt battery to the onnector as follows:

a. Positive battery lead to the blue terminal.
b. Negative battery lead to the black terminal.

. The fan motor should operate. If it is faulty, re-lace it as described in Chapter Ten.
. Reconnect the electrical connector.

:adiator Fan Motor Relay

emoval/installation

. Remove the headlight relay as described in this hapter.
. Disengage the fan motor relay (B, **Figure 42**) :om the rubber mount.

NOTE
Pry up the tabs on the relay nearest the connector.

3. Disconnect the electrical connector from the fan motor relay.
4. Reverse the removal steps to install the relay.

Continuity test

CAUTION
Reversing the battery connections to the relay as specified in this procedure will damage the relay. Operating the ATV with a damaged relay installed will damage the ECU.

1. Remove the fan motor relay as described in this section.
2. Connect test leads to the fan motor relay as follows:
   a. Jumper from 12-volt battery positive (A, **Figure 49**).
   b. Jumper from 12-volt battery negative (B, **Figure 49**).
   c. Ohmmeter positive test lead (C, **Figure 49**).
   d. Ohmmeter negative test lead (D, **Figure 49**).
3. There should be continuity with battery voltage applied to the relay.
4. Replace the relay if it fails any portion of this test.

Radiator Fan Motor Circuit Breaker Testing

A circuit breaker protects the fan circuit. The circuit breaker is contained in a small vinyl pack attached to the fan motor relay wires in the rear fender.

1. Remove the rear lower cover as described in Chapter Fifteen.
2. Unwrap the circuit breaker (**Figure 50**) and disconnect the leads.
3. Using an ohmmeter, measure the resistance between the circuit breaker leads.
4. If the resistance is greater than 0, replace the circuit breaker.

Coolant Temperature Sensor

Removal/installation

1. Drain the cooling system as described in Chapter Three.
2. Disconnect the electrical connector (**Figure 51**) from the sensor.
3. Unscrew and remove the sensor from the cylinder head.
4. Install a new washer onto the sensor.

9

5. Install the coolant temperature sensor and tighten it to 18 N•m (13 ft.-lb.).
6. Connect the electrical connector to the sensor.
7. Refill the cooling system as described in Chapter Three.

Testing

NOTE
Make sure the sensor terminals do not get wet.

1. Place the sensor (A, **Figure 52**) in a pan filled with a 50:50 coolant (water/antifreeze) mixture. Support the sensor so the threads are covered with the coolant and the sensor does not contact the pan.
2. Place a shop thermometer (B, **Figure 52**) in the pan. Use a thermometer that is rated higher than the test temperature.
3. Connect an ohmmeter to the terminals on top of the sensor.
4. Heat the coolant to a temperature above the highest test temperature listed in **Table 6**.
5. Allow the coolant to cool while checking resistance between the terminals on the sensor at the temperatures specified in **Table 6**.
6. If the resistance test results do not match the specifications listed in **Table 6**, replace the sensor.

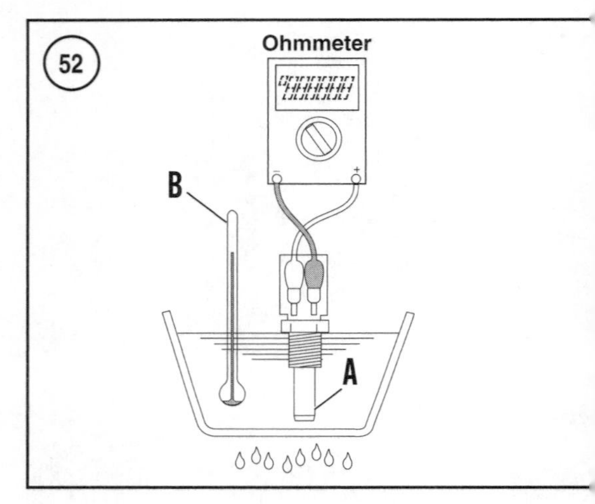

CRANKSHAFT POSITION SENSOR

The crankshaft position sensor is located inside the left crankcase cover.

Resistance test

The crankshaft position sensor can be tested while mounted on the engine.
1. Disconnect the battery cable from the negative battery terminal as described in this chapter.

NOTE
Note the wire colors in the wiring diagram to identify the crankshaft position sensor connector.

2. Disconnect the crankshaft position sensor electrical connector located above the rear of the engine.
3. Connect the negative probe of an ohmmeter to the green/white wire terminal and the positive probe to the blue/yellow wire terminal in the crankshaft position sensor end of the connector. Measure the resistance and refer to **Table 6**.
4. Replace the crankshaft position sensor if the resistance is not as specified.

Removal/installation

The stator coil and crankshaft position sensor ar wired together and must be serviced as a unit. Refe to *Stator Coil* in this chapter for removal and instal lation procedures.

SWITCHES

Left Handlebar Switch Housing

The left handlebar switch housing contains th headlight switch (A, **Figure 53**), engine stop switc (B) and starter switch (C). The switches can b checked for continuity using an ohmmeter connecte to the appropriate color-coded wires in the connecto plug. Refer to *Continuity Testing* in this chapter fo the test procedure and to the wiring diagrams at th end of the manual for the proper wire colors.

NOTE
The switches mounted in the left handlebar switch housing are not available separately. If one switch is damaged, the housing will have to be replaced as a unit.

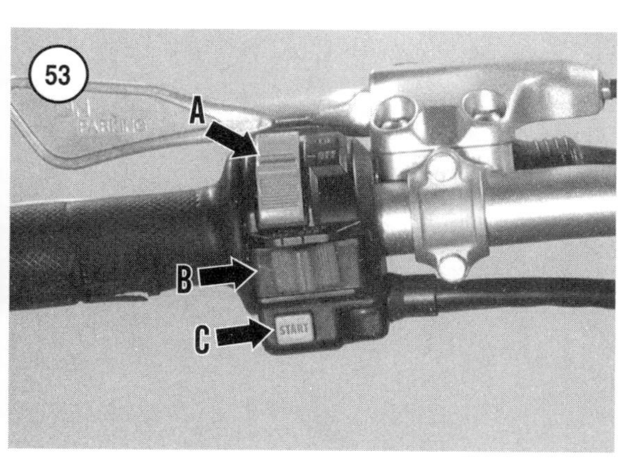

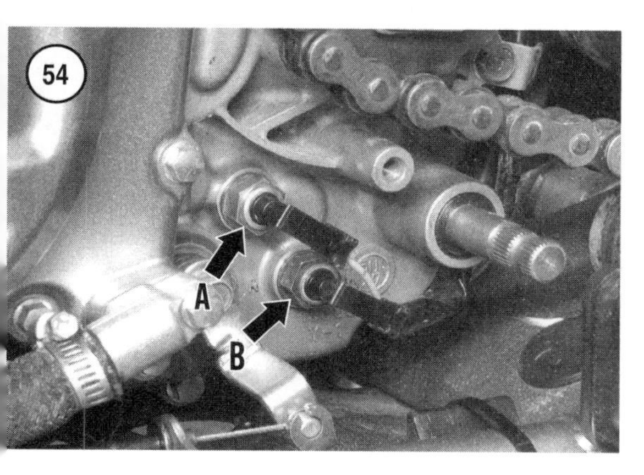

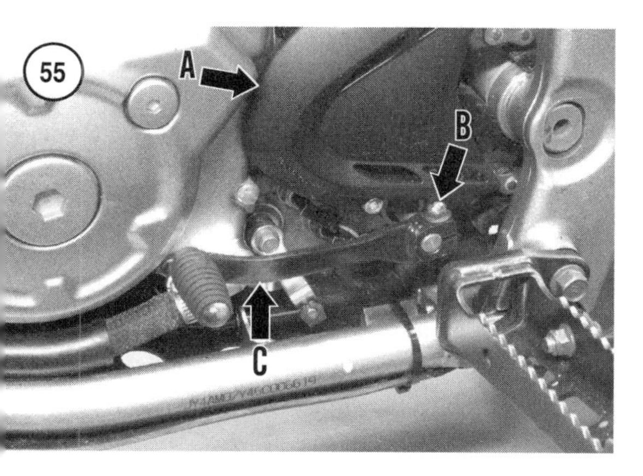

Replacement

1. Remove the front fender as described in Chapter Fifteen.
2. Remove or cut any clamps securing the switch wiring harness to the handlebar.
3. Pull back the large rubber boot and disconnect the switch assembly electrical connectors.
4. Remove the screws securing the switch to the handlebar and remove the switch assembly.
5. Install by reversing the removal steps.

Neutral Switch

The neutral switch (A, **Figure 54**) is mounted on the left crankcase.

Testing

1. Shift the transmission into neutral.
2. Disconnect the connector from the switch.
3. Connect one lead of an ohmmeter to the neutral switch terminal and the other ohmmeter lead to a good engine ground.
4. Read the ohmmeter scale with the transmission in neutral, and then in gear. Note the following:
   a. The ohmmeter must read continuity with the transmission in neutral.
   b. The ohmmeter must read infinity with the transmission in gear.
   c. If either reading is incorrect, check the wiring harness for damage or for any dirty or loose-fitting terminals. If the wiring harness is good, replace the neutral switch.
5. Reconnect the switch connector.
6. Start the engine and check the operation of the neutral switch indicator light with the transmission in neutral and in gear.

Replacement

1. Shift the transmission into neutral.
2. Remove the drive sprocket cover (A, **Figure 55**).
3. Remove the shift lever clamp bolt (B, **Figure 55**). Then, remove the shift lever (C, **Figure 55**).
4. Disconnect the electrical connector from the neutral switch (A, **Figure 54**).
5. Unscrew the neutral switch and washer from the crankcase.
6. Make sure the sealing washer (**Figure 56**) is installed on the neutral switch. Install the neutral switch into the lower crankcase and tighten it to 17 N•m (12.5 ft.-lb.).

9

7. Connect the electrical connector to the neutral switch. Push it on and make sure it is seated correctly.
8. Install the shift lever. and tighten the clamp bolt to 16 N•m (12 ft.-lb.).
9. Install the drive sprocket cover and tighten the mounting bolts to 10 N•m (89 in.-lb.).

Reverse Switch

The reverse switch (B, **Figure 54**) is mounted on the left crankcase.

Testing

1. Shift the transmission into neutral.
2. Disconnect the connector from the reverse switch.
3. Connect one lead of an ohmmeter to the reverse switch terminal and the other ohmmeter lead to a good engine ground.
4. Read the ohmmeter scale with the transmission in reverse, and then in the forward gears. Note the following:
   a. The ohmmeter must read infinity with the transmission in reverse.
   b. The ohmmeter must read continuity with the transmission in the forward gears.
   c. If either reading is incorrect, check the wiring harness for damage or for any dirty or loose-fitting terminals. If the wiring harness is good, replace the neutral switch.
5. Reconnect the switch connector.
6. Start the engine and check the operation of the reverse switch indicator light with the transmission in reverse.

Replacement

1. Shift the transmission into neutral.
2. Remove the drive sprocket cover (A, **Figure 55**).
3. Remove the shift lever clamp bolt (B, **Figure 55**). Then, remove the shift lever (C, **Figure 55**).
4. Disconnect the electrical connector from the reverse switch (B, **Figure 54**).
5. Unscrew the reverse switch and washer from the crankcase.
6. Make sure the sealing washer (**Figure 56**) is installed on the reverse switch. Install the reverse switch into the lower crankcase and tighten it to 17 N•m (12.5 ft.-lb.).
7. Connect the electrical connector to the reverse switch. Push it on and make sure it is seated correctly.

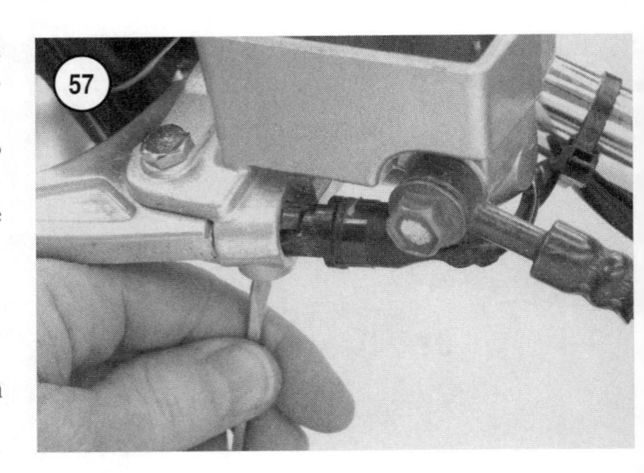

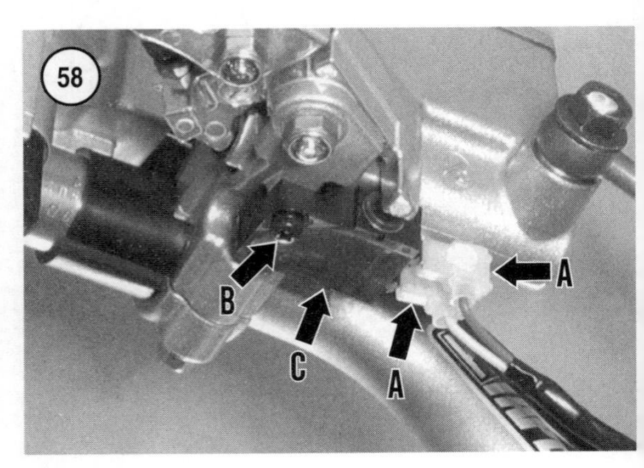

8. Install the shift lever and tighten the clamp bolt to 16 N•m (12 ft.-lb.).
9. Install the drive sprocket cover and tighten the mounting bolts to 10 N•m (89 in.-lb.).

Front Brake Light Switch

The front brake switch is mounted on the front master cylinder assembly.

Testing

The switch can be checked for continuity using an ohmmeter connected to the appropriate color-coded wires in the connector plug. Refer to *Continuity Testing* in this chapter for the test procedure and to the wiring diagrams at the end of the manual for the proper wire colors.

Removal/installation (2006 models)

1. Insert a small tool to depress the barb that retains the switch housing in the master cylinder (**Figure 57**).
2. Pull the switch out from the master cylinder.

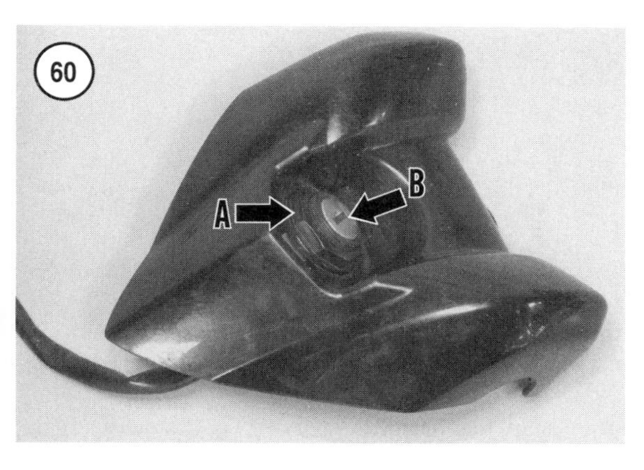

3. Disconnect the switch connector and remove the switch.
4. Reverse the removal steps to install the switch.
5. Check brake light operation.

Removal/installation (2007-on models)

1. Disconnect the two electrical connectors (A, **Figure 58**) from the front brake light switch.
2. Remove the mounting screw (B, **Figure 58**) and brake switch (C).
3. Reverse the removal steps to install the switch.
4. Check brake light operation.

Rear Brake Light Switch

Testing

1. Disconnect the brake light switch wires at the black electrical connector above the rear of the engine.
2. Connect the leads of an ohmmeter or continuity tester between the connector terminals. The tester should indicate continuity when the rear brake pedal is depressed and infinity when the pedal is released.
3. If necessary, replace the rear brake light switch if it fails to operate as described.

Removal/installation

1. Disconnect the brake light switch wires at the black electrical connector above the rear of the engine.
2. Detach the spring (A, **Figure 59**) from the brake light switch.
3. Unscrew the brake light switch from the mounting nut (B, **Figure 59**).

NOTE
The switch wires are secured by wire holders on the right crankcase cover and left crankcase. Remove the holder bolts to release the switch wires.

4. Note the routing of the switch wires and remove the switch.
5. Reverse the removal steps to install the brake light switch. Tighten the left and right crankcase cover bolts securing the wire holders to 10 N•m (89 in.-lb.).
6. Refer to Chapter Three and adjust the rear brake light switch.

Ignition Switch Replacement

1. Disconnect the gray ignition switch connector below the steering shaft bracket.
2. Remove the handlebar cover as described in Chapter Fifteen.
3. Unscrew the switch retaining nut (A, **Figure 60**), and remove the ignition switch (B).
4. Reverse the removal steps to install the ignition switch.
5. Turn the ignition switch on and check operation.

FUSES

Whenever a fuse blows, determine the cause before replacing the fuse. Usually, the trouble is a short circuit in the wiring. Worn-through insulation or a short to ground from a disconnected wire may cause this.

CAUTION
If replacing a fuse, make sure the ignition switch is turned to the OFF position. This lessens the chance of a short circuit.

CAUTION
Never substitute any metal object for a fuse. Never use a higher amperage fuse than specified. An overload could cause a fire and lead to the complete loss of the ATV.

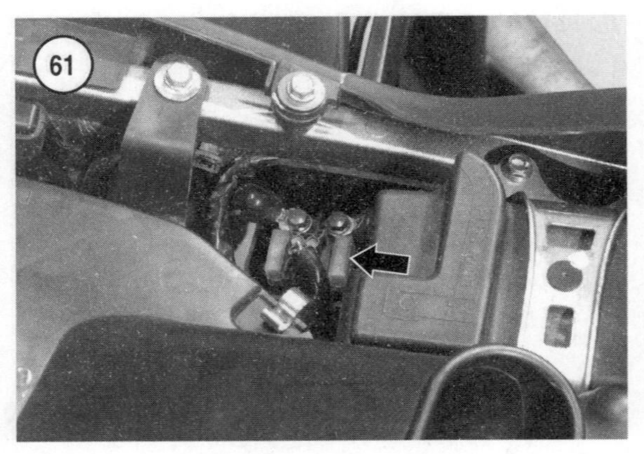

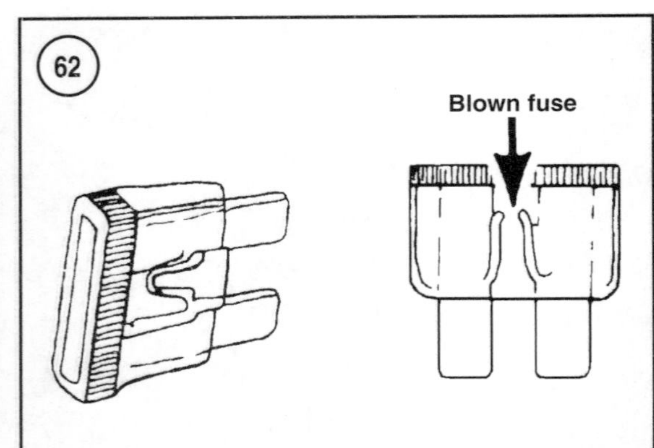

Main Fuse

The 20-amp main fuse is mounted on the starter relay switch located underneath the seat (**Figure 61**). To check or replace the main fuse, perform the following:

1. Turn the ignition switch to the OFF position.
2. Remove the seat as described in Chapter Fifteen.
3. Remove the main fuse (**Figure 61**). The adjacent fuse is a spare main fuse.
4. Remove the main fuse and inspect it. Replace the fuse if it has blown (**Figure 62**).
5. Install the new main fuse.
6. Install the seat as described in Chapter Fifteen.

Fuses

Fuses for the headlights, tail/brake light, ignition and fuel injection system are located in the fuse box (**Figure 63**) mounted underneath the seat. To identify an individual fuse and its amperage, refer to the decal mounted on the underside of the fuse box cover and review the wiring diagram located at the end of this book.

If a fuse in the fuse box blows, perform the following:

1. Turn the ignition switch to the OFF position.
2. Remove the seat as described in Chapter Fifteen.
3. Open the fuse box cover.

NOTE
There are spare fuses contained in the fuse box.

4. Remove and inspect the fuse. Replace the fuse if it has blown (**Figure 62**).

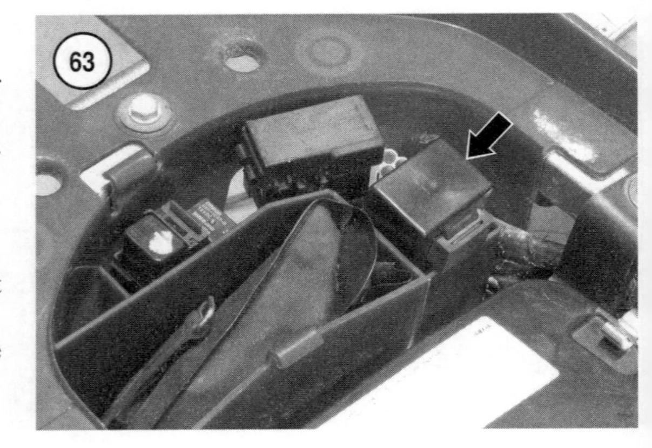

5. Close the fuse box cover.
6. Install the seat as described in Chapter Fifteen.

FUSE BOX

The fuse box is part of the main harness assembly and not available separately.

Removal/Installation

1. Remove the seat as described in Chapter Fifteen.
2. Disengage the latch on the side of the fuse box (**Figure 63**).
3. Lift the fuse box up to separate it from the rear fender.
4. Reverse the removal steps to install the fuse box.

WIRING DIAGRAMS

Color wiring diagrams for all models are located at the end of this manual.

Table 1 BATTERY SPECIFICATIONS

Type	GT9B-4, maintenance free (sealed)*
Capacity	12 volt 8.0 amp hour
Voltage (@ 68° F/20° C)	
Fully charged	13.0-13.2 volts
Charging required	Below 12.8 volts
State of charge	Voltage reading
100%	13.0-13.2
75%	12.8
50%	12.5
25%	12.2
0%	12.0 volts or less

*A maintenance free battery is installed on all models described in this manual. Because this type of battery requires a high-voltage charging system, do not install a standard type battery.

Table 2 ALTERNATOR AND CHARGING SYSTEM SPECIFICATIONS

Alternator	
Type	AC magneto
Model number	LMX58 (Denso)
Normal output	14 volts/17.2 amps @ 5000 rpm
Stator coil resistance	0.248-0.372 ohm*
Voltage regulator/rectifier	
Model number	SH650D-11 (Shindengen)
Regulator no-load regulated voltage	14.1-14.9 volts
Rectifier capacity	
2006-2012 models	18.0 amps
2013-on models	25.0 amps

*Test must be made at an ambient temperature of 20° C (68° F). Do not test when the engine or component is hot.

Table 3 IGNITION SYSTEM SPECIFICATIONS

Type	Electronic ignition
Ignition timing	9.0° BTDC @ 1600 rpm
Advancer type	Electronic
Ignition coil	
Model number	JO267 (Denso)
Primary resistance	3.4-4.6 ohms*
Secondary resistance	10,400-15,600 ohms*
Spark plug cap resistance	10,000 ohms

*Test must be made at an ambient temperature of 20° C (68° F). Do not test when the engine or component is hot.

Table 4 STARTER SYSTEM SPECIFICATIONS

Item	New mm (in.)	Service limit mm (in.)
Starter model number	SM-13 (Mitsuba)	
Brush length	12.5 (0.49)	5.0 (0.20)
Commutator outer diameter	28 (1.10)	27 (1.06)
Mica undercut	0.7 (0.03)	–

Table 5 BULB SPECIFICATIONS

Item	Size (all 12 volt), quantity
Headlight (high/low beam)	30W/30W (2)
Tail/brake light	LED
Indicator lights	LED

9

Table 6 TEST SPECIFICATIONS

Item	Test readings
Coolant temperature sensor	
At 20° C (68° F)	2320-2590 ohms
At 80° C (176° F)	310-326 ohms
At 110° C (230° F)	140-144 ohms
Crankshaft position sensor resistance	192-288 ohms*

*Test must be made at an ambient temperature of 20° C (68° F). Do not test when the engine or component is hot.

Table 7 FUSE SPECIFICATIONS

Fuel injection fuse	10 amp
Headlight fuse	
2006-2012 models	15 amp
2013-on models	10 amp
Ignition fuse	10 amp
Main fuse	
2006-2012 models	20 amp
2013-on models	30 amp
Signaling system fuse	10 amp

Table 8 ELECTRICAL SYSTEM TORQUE SPECIFICATIONS

Item	N•m	in.-lb.	ft.-lb.
Battery bracket bolts	7	62	–
Coolant temperature sensor	18	–	13
Crankshaft position sensor	7	62	–
Drive sprocket cover bolts	10	89	–
Neutral switch	17	–	12.5
Reverse switch	17	–	12.5
Shift lever clamp bolt	16	–	12
Starter mounting bolts	10	89	–
Stator coil mounting bolts	7	62	–
Stator wire retainer bolts	7	62	–

CHAPTER TEN

COOLING SYSTEM

This chapter describes the repair and replacement of cooling system components. **Table 1** and **Table 2** at the end of this chapter list cooling system specifications. For electrical test procedures, refer to Chapter Nine. For routine cooling system maintenance, refer to Chapter Three.

COOLING SYSTEM PRECAUTIONS/ INSPECTION

The pressurized cooling system consists of the radiator, water pump, radiator cap, thermostat, electric cooling fan and coolant reservoir.

WARNING
*Do not remove the radiator cap (**Figure 1**), remove the coolant drain plug or disconnect any coolant hoses when the engine and radiator are hot. The coolant is very hot and under pressure. Scalding fluid and steam may be emitted which could cause personal injury.*

WARNING
Antifreeze is toxic. Do not discharge coolant containing antifreeze into storm sewers, septic systems, or onto the ground. Place used antifreeze in the original container and dispose of it according to local regulations. Do not store coolant where it is accessible to children or animals.

CAUTION
*Drain and flush the cooling system at the interval listed in Chapter Three. Refill with a mixture of ethylene glycol antifreeze (formulated for aluminum engines) and distilled water. Do not reuse the old coolant, as it deteriorates with use. Do not operate the cooling system with only distilled water, even in climates where antifreeze protection is not required; doing so will promote internal engine corrosion. Refer to **Coolant Change** in Chapter Three.*

It is important to keep the coolant level to the FULL mark (**Figure 2**) on the coolant reserve tank.

1. Check the level with the engine at normal operating temperature and the ATV parked on a level surface.
2. If the level is low, remove the reservoir tank cap and add coolant to the reserve tank, not to the radiator.
3. Check the coolant hoses and clamps for looseness or damage.
4. Start the engine and allow it to idle. If steam is observed at the muffler, the head gasket might be damaged. If enough coolant leaks into the cylinder,

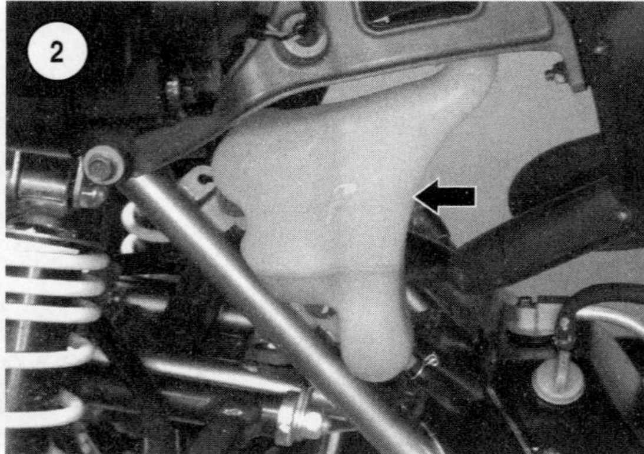

the cylinder could hydrolock, thus preventing the engine from being cranked. Coolant may also be present in the engine oil. If the oil on the dipstick is foamy or milky-looking, there is coolant in the oil. If so, correct the problem before returning the ATV to service.

CAUTION
If the engine oil is contaminated with coolant, change the oil and filter after performing the repair.

5. Check the radiator for clogged or damaged fins. Refer radiator repair to a dealership or a radiator repair shop.
6. Check all coolant hoses for cracks or damage. Replace all questionable parts. Make sure the hose clamps are tight, but not so tight that they cut the hoses. Refer to *Hoses and Hose Clamps* in this chapter.
7. When troubleshooting the cooling system for loss of coolant, pressure test the system as described in this chapter.

COOLING SYSTEM PRESSURE TEST

A cooling system tester is required to perform the following tests.

1. Park the ATV on level ground.
2. Remove the radiator cap (**Figure 1**).
3. Pressure test the radiator cap (**Figure 3**) using a cooling system tester. Refer to the manufacturer's instructions when making the tests. The specified radiator cap pressure is 93.3-122.7 kPa (13.5-17.8 psi). Replace the radiator cap if it does not hold pressure or if the relief pressure is too high or too low.
4. Pressure test the radiator and cooling system (**Figure 4**). Apply a pressure of 122.7 kPa (17.8 psi). If the cooling system will not hold the specified pressure, determine the source of the leak(s) and repair as needed.

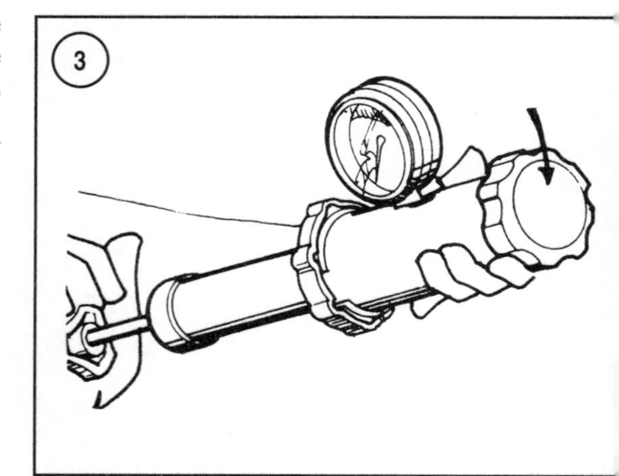

5. Reinstall the radiator cap (**Figure 1**).

HOSES AND HOSE CLAMPS

Hoses deteriorate with age. Replace them periodically or whenever they show signs of cracking or leaking. To be safe, replace the hoses every two years. The spray of hot coolant from a cracked hose can injure the rider. Loss of coolant can also cause the engine to overheat and cause damage.

Whenever any component of the cooling system is removed, inspect the hoses and clamps to determine if replacement is necessary.

Inspection

1. With the engine cool, check the cooling hoses for brittleness, hardness or cracks. Replace hoses in this condition.
2. With the engine hot, examine the hoses for swelling along the entire hose length. Replace hoses that show signs of swelling.
3. Check the area around each hose clamp. Signs of rust around clamps indicate a possible hose leak from a damaged or over-tightened clamp.

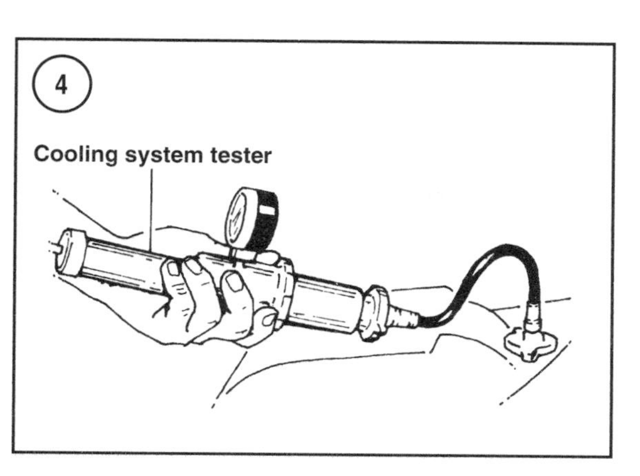

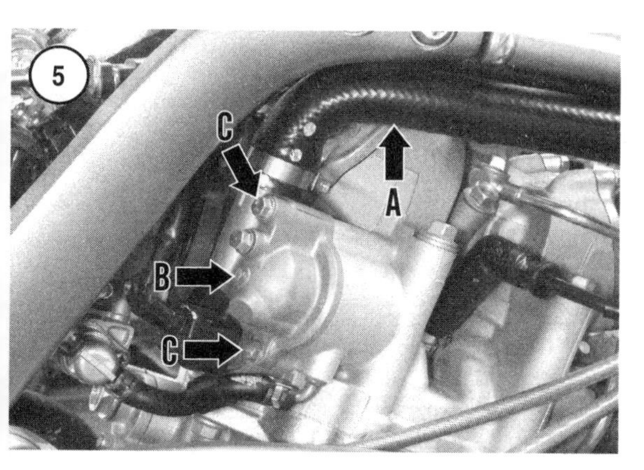

Replacement

Perform hose replacement when the engine is cool.

1. Drain the cooling system as described in *Coolant Change* (Chapter Three).
2. Loosen the hose clamps from the hose to be replaced. Slide the clamps along the hose and out of the way.

CAUTION
Do not apply excessive force to a hose when attempting to remove it. Many of the hose connectors are fragile and can be easily damaged.

3. Twist the hose end to break the seal and remove it from the connecting joint. If the hose has been on for some time, it may have become fused to the joint. If so, insert a small screwdriver or pick tool between the hose and joint. While working the tool around the joint, carefully pry the hose loose with a thin screwdriver.
4. Examine the connecting joint for cracks or other damage. Repair or replace parts as required. Remove rust and corrosion with a wire brush.
5. Inspect the hose clamps and replace if necessary. The hose clamps are as important as the hoses. If they do not hold the hose in place tightly, coolant will leak.

NOTE
If it is difficult to install a hose on a joint, apply some antifreeze into the end of the hose where it seats onto its connecting joint. This usually aids installation.

6. Slide the hose clamp over the outside of the hose and then install the hose over its connecting joint. Make sure the hose clears all obstructions and is routed properly.
7. With the hose positioned correctly on the joint, position the clamp back away from the end of the hose slightly. Tighten the clamp securely, but not so much that the hose is damaged.

NOTE
If installing coolant hoses onto the engine while it is removed from the frame, check the position of the hose clamp(s) to make sure it can be loosened when installed in the frame.

8. Refill the cooling system as described in *Coolant Change* (Chapter Three). Start the engine and check for leaks. Retighten hose clamps as necessary.

THERMOSTAT

Removal/Installation

1. Drain the cooling system as described in *Coolant Change* (Chapter Three).
2. Remove the front fender as described in Chapter Fifteen.
3. Remove the radiator cap (**Figure 1**).
4. Loosen the radiator hose clamp. Then, disconnect the radiator inlet hose (A, **Figure 5**) from the thermostat cover (B).
5. Remove the thermostat cover retaining bolts (C, **Figure 5**).
6. Remove the thermostat (A, **Figure 6**).

7. Inspect the O-ring (**Figure 7**) on the thermostat cover. If damaged, remove the O-ring and install a new one.
8. If necessary, test the thermostat as described in this section.
9. Install the thermostat by reversing the removal steps while noting the following:
   a. The thermostat will only fit one way in the housing, with the air bleed hole (B, **Figure 6**) facing upward.
   b. Tighten the thermostat cover bolts to 10 N•m (89 in.-lb.).
   c. Refill the cooling system with the recommended type and quantity of coolant as described in *Coolant Change* (Chapter Three).

Inspection

Test the thermostat to ensure proper operation as follows:

NOTE
Do not allow the thermometer or thermostat to touch the sides or bottom of the pan, or a false reading will result.

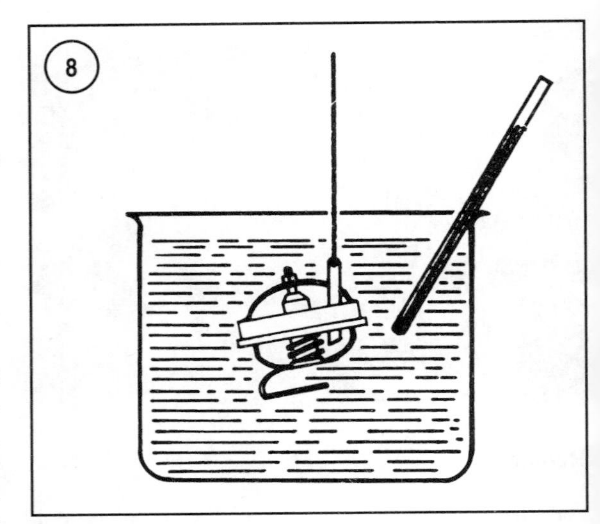

1. Suspend the thermostat in a pan of water (**Figure 8**) and place a thermometer in the pan of water. Use a thermometer that is rated higher than the test temperature.
2. Gradually heat the water and continue to gently stir the water until it reaches the temperature specified in **Table 1**. At this temperature, the thermostat should start to open.

NOTE
After the specified temperature is reached, it may take three to five minutes for the valve to open completely.

3. Make sure the thermostat is fully open at the temperature specified in **Table 1**.
4. Replace the thermostat if it remains open at normal room temperature or stays closed after the specified temperature has been reached during the test procedure. Make sure the replacement thermostat has the same temperature rating.

RADIATOR

Removal/Installation

1. Remove the front fender as described in Chapter Fifteen.
2. Drain the coolant as described in Chapter Three.
3. Disconnect the white fan motor connector.
4. Detach the upper (inlet) radiator hose (A, **Figure 9**) from the radiator.

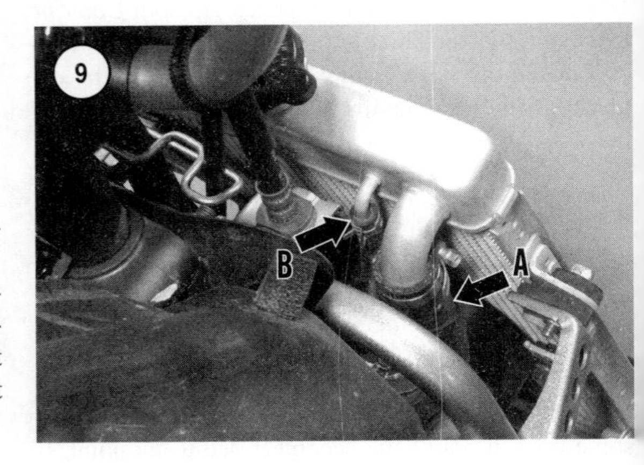

5. Detach the fast idle plunger hose (B, **Figure 9**) from the radiator.
6. Detach the coolant reservoir hose (A, **Figure 10**) from the radiator.
7. Detach the lower (outlet) radiator hose (**Figure 11**).

NOTE
Note the routing of the fan motor vent hose during removal.

. Remove the radiator retaining bolts (B, **Figure** **0**), and then remove the radiator.
. If necessary, remove the fan motor as described n this chapter.
0. Reverse the removal steps to install the radiator vhile noting the following:

a. Make sure the mounting grommets (A, **Figure 12**) are in good condition. Replace otherwise.
b. Tighten the radiator retaining bolts to 7 N•m (62 in.-lb.).
c. Refill the coolant system as described in Chapter Three.
d. Check for leaks.

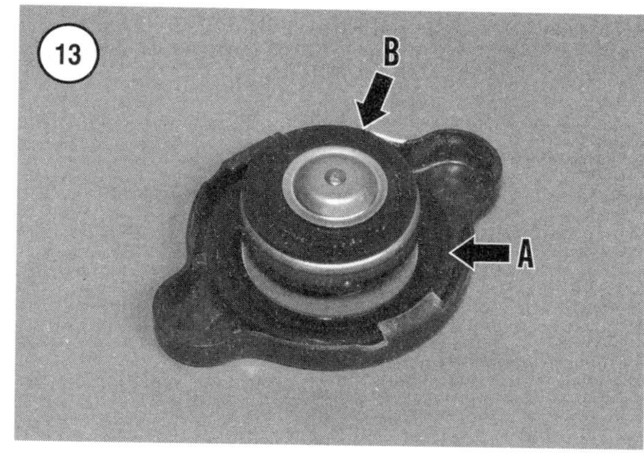

Inspection

1. Flush off the exterior of the radiator with a water hose on low pressure. Spray both the front and the back to remove all dirt and debris. Carefully use a whiskbroom or stiff paintbrush to remove any stubborn debris.

CAUTION
Do not press too hard on the cooling fins and tubes or they may be damaged and cause a leak.

2. Carefully straighten any bent cooling fins with a broad-tipped screwdriver.
3. Check for cracks or coolant leaks (usually a moss-green colored residue). If leaks, blockage or damage are evident, take the radiator to a radiator repair shop.
4. Check the mounting brackets for cracks or damage.
5. To prevent oxidation to the radiator, touch up any area where the black paint is worn off. Use good-quality spray paint. Do not apply heavy coats, as this decreases the cooling efficiency of the radiator.
6. Inspect the radiator cap top seal (A, **Figure 13**) and bottom seal (B) for deterioration or damage. Check the spring for damage. Pressure test the radiator cap as described in this chapter. Replace the radiator cap if necessary.

COOLANT RESERVOIR

Removal/Installation

1. Remove the front fender as described in Chapter Fifteen.
2. Drain the coolant as described in Chapter Three.
3. Detach the reservoir vent hose from the top of the reservoir.
4. Detach the bottom reservoir hose (A, **Figure 14**).

5. While holding the reservoir, remove the reservoir retaining bolts (B, **Figure 14**). Then, remove the reservoir.
6. Remove the reservoir cap, and pour any remaining coolant into a container.
7. Reverse the removal steps to install the reservoir.
   a. Tighten the coolant reservoir retaining bolts to 7 N•m (62 in.-lb.).
   b. Fill with coolant as described in Chapter Three.

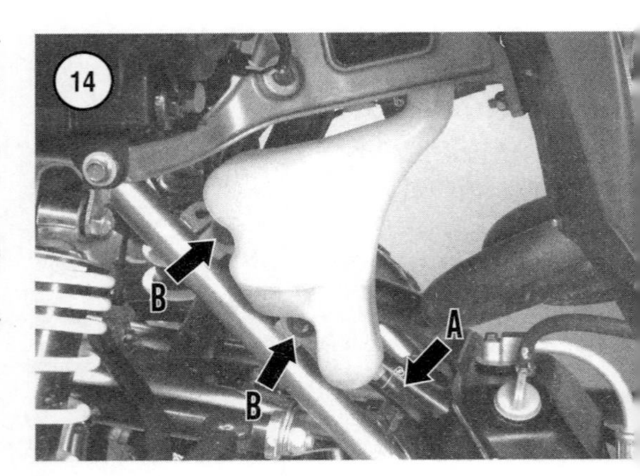

RADIATOR FAN

The radiator fan is mounted on the backside of the radiator.

Testing

To test the fan motor and relay, refer to Chapter Nine.

Removal/Installation

1. Remove the radiator as described in this chapter.
2. Remove the three fan motor retaining bolts (B, **Figure 12**) and then remove the radiator fan.
3. Reverse the removal steps to install the radiator fan. Tighten the fan motor retaining bolts securely.

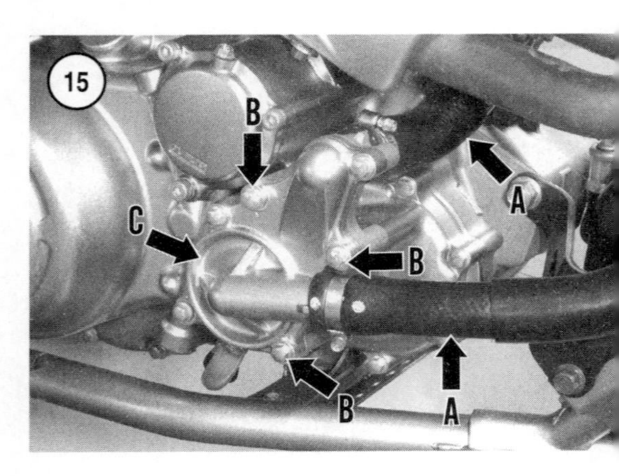

COOLANT TEMPERATURE SENSOR

All models are equipped with a coolant temperature sensor. The sensor is connected to the ECU, which controls radiator fan operation. Refer to Chapter Nine for service information.

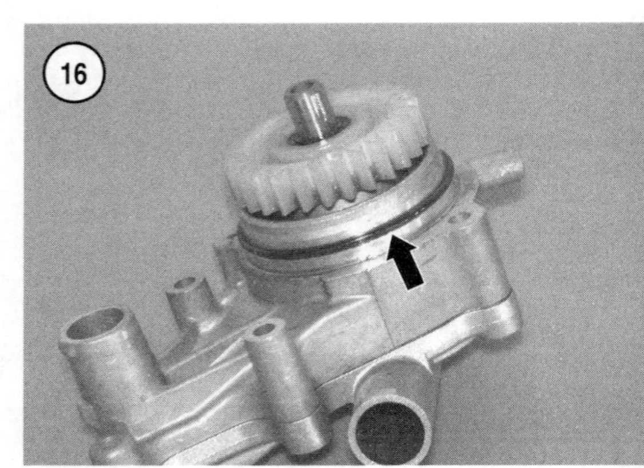

WATER PUMP

Removal/Installation

1. Drain the cooling system (Chapter Three).
2. Remove the hoses (A, **Figure 15**) from the water pump.

NOTE
The water pump bolts have varying lengths. Note bolt lengths during removal for proper installation.

3. Remove the bolts (B, **Figure 15**) securing the water pump to the engine.
4. Remove the water pump (C, **Figure 15**) by pulling it straight out from the engine.

NOTE
If necessary, lightly tap the pump to loosen it from the crankcase.

5. Reverse the removal steps to install the water pump while noting the following:
   a. Install a new O-ring (**Figure 16**) onto the water pump. Lubricate the O-ring.
   b. Install a new seal washer onto the bottom housing bolt (**Figure 15**).
   c. Tighten the water pump retaining bolts to 1 N•m (89 in.-lb.).
   d. Fill the cooling system (Chapter Three).

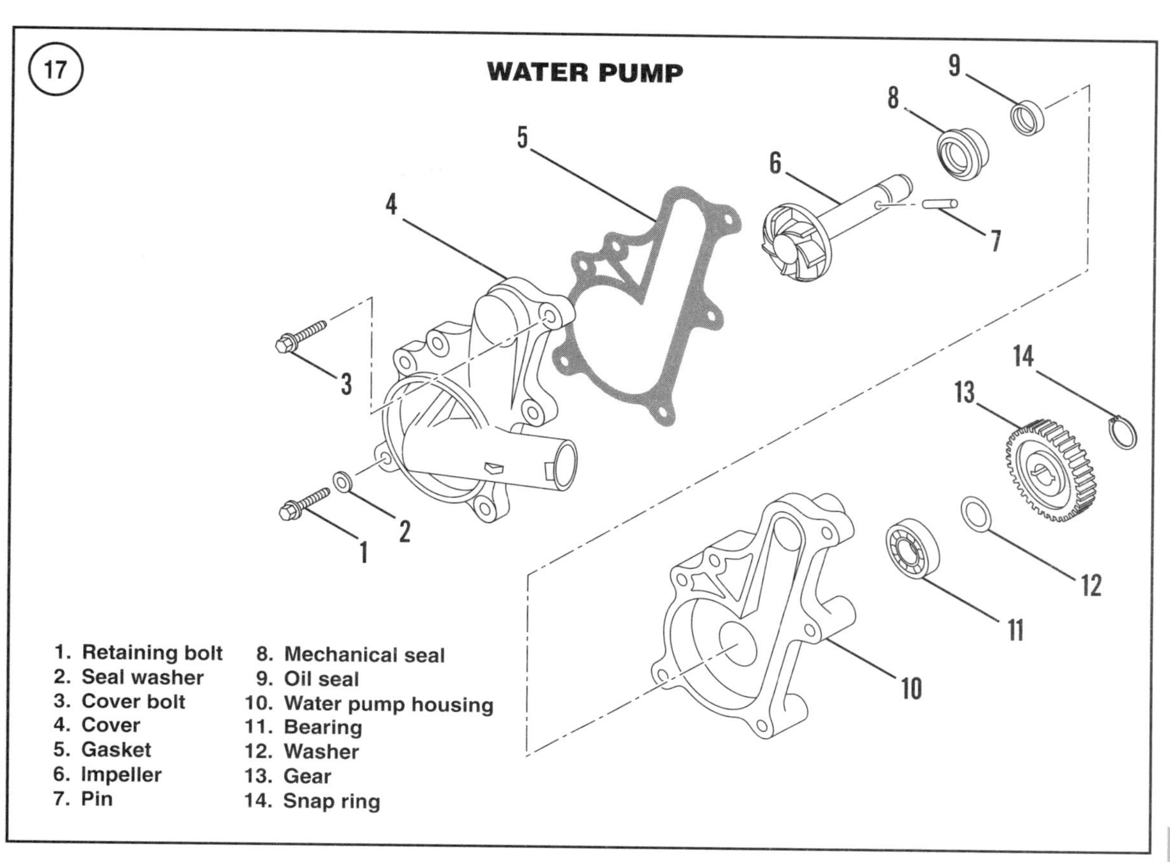

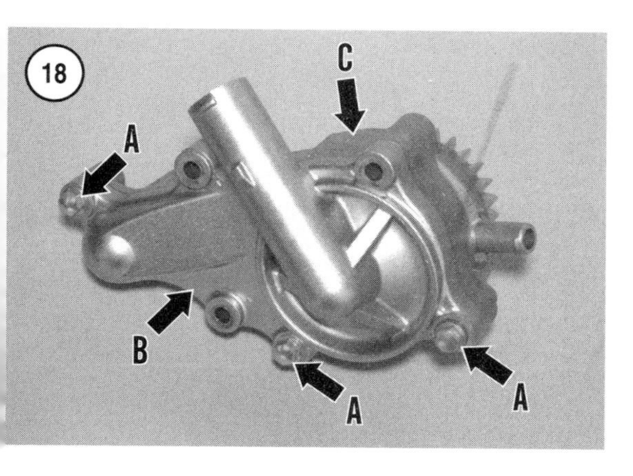

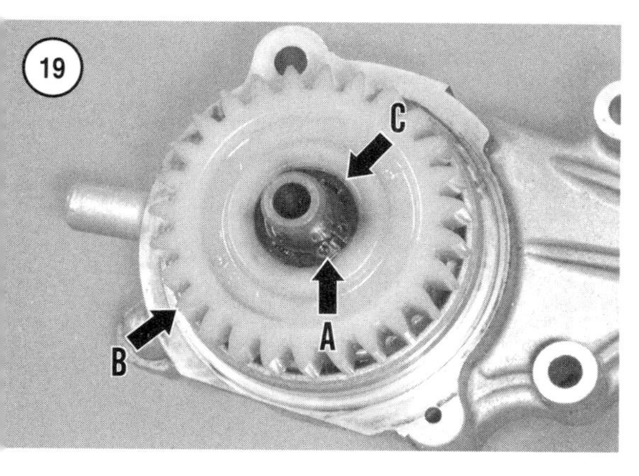

Disassembly/Inspection/Reassembly

Refer to **Figure 17**.

1. Remove the O-ring (**Figure 16**).
2. Remove the cover bolts (A, **Figure 18**). Then, separate the cover (B, **Figure 18**) from the housing (C). Discard the gasket.
3. Remove the snap ring (A, **Figure 19**).
4. Remove the gear (B, **Figure 19**).
5. Remove the pin (A, **Figure 20**) and washer (B).
6. Pull the impeller (**Figure 21**) and shaft out of the housing.
7. Inspect the parts as follows:

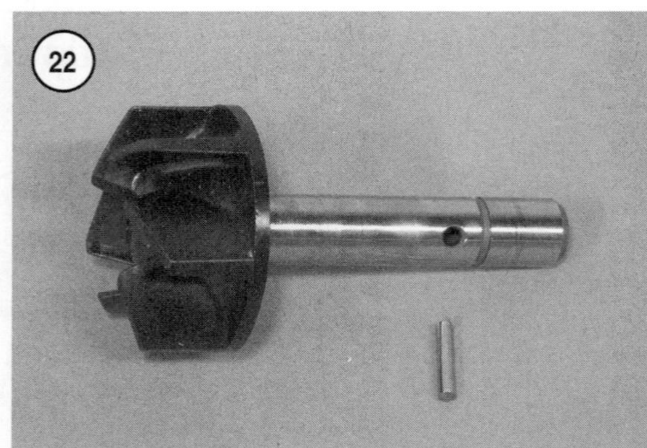

a. Inspect the impeller, shaft and pin for obvious damage (**Figure 22**).

b. Inspect the gear and the fit of the gear on the pin and shaft. It is normal for the gear to be loose on the pin. However, if the pin and gear seat are worn or damaged, replace the parts.

c. Inspect the contact surfaces of the impeller shaft and mechanical seal in the housing (**Figure 23**). In order to seal properly, both faces must be smooth and free of damage. When installed, the impeller seal should fit firmly against the seal in the housing. Because the seal in the housing is spring loaded, it maintains pressure on the seals and compensates for wear. If necessary, replace the mechanical seal and oil seal as described in this section.

d. Inspect the bearing in the housing (**Figure 24**). The bearing should turn smoothly with no play. If necessary, replace the bearing as described in this section.

e. Check the shaft for tilt in the impeller (**Figure 25**). Maximum allowable tilt is 0.15 mm (0.006 in.). If tilt is excessive, the two halves of the mechanical seal will not make full contact and leaking is possible. If necessary, remove and reseat the shaft in the impeller and seal.

f. Inspect the cover for damage and cleanliness.

8. Reverse the removal steps to assemble the water pump while noting the following:

a. Install the gear with the cupped side at the hub (C, **Figure 19**) facing out.

b. Install a new snap ring (A, **Figure 19**) with the sharp edge facing out.

c. Lubricate the bearing with engine oil.

d. Lubricate the face of the mechanical seal with coolant.

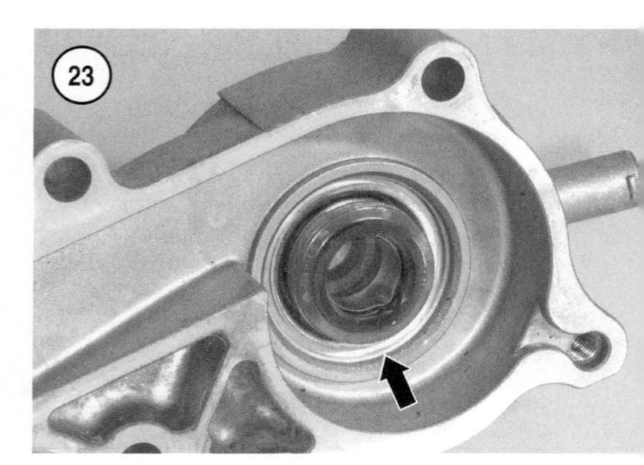

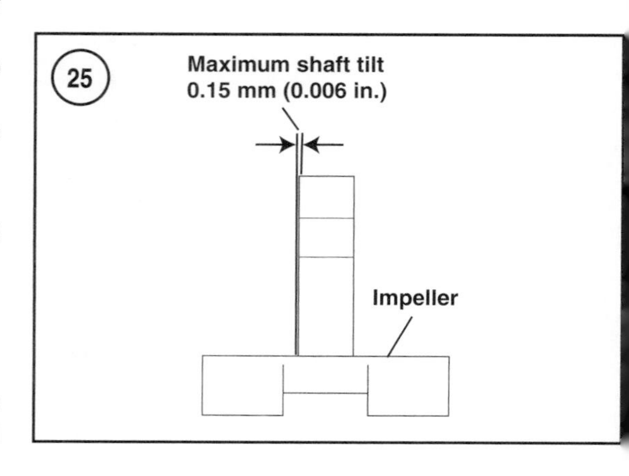

Bearing and Seal Replacement

The water pump contains a mechanical seal (**Figure 23**) and an oil seal (**Figure 26**). The mechanical seal

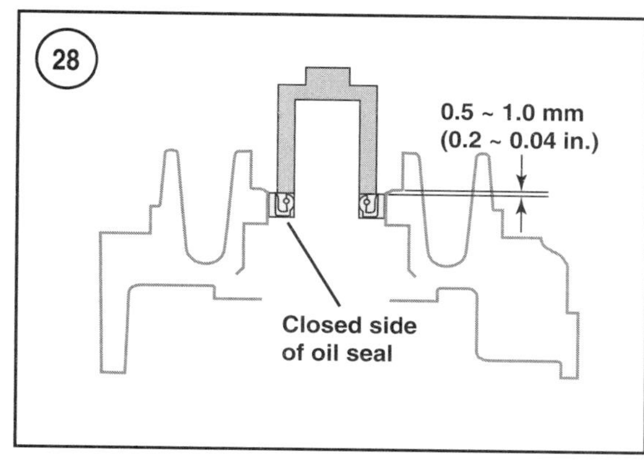

prevents coolant in the pump chamber from passing into the crankcase, while the oil seal prevents oil in the crankcase from passing into the pump chamber. A vent hose located between the seals allows leaking coolant or oil to drain to the outside of the engine. Whenever a leak is detected in the vent hose, the seals should be replaced.

1. Replace the mechanical seal in the housing as follows:
   a. Place a punch (**Figure 27**) against the back of the mechanical seal. Work around the seal and drive it from the bore. Avoid any contact with the surface of the bore. Do not attempt to pry the seal from the front side of the housing.
   b. Install a new seal using the proper tool (Yamaha part No. YM-33221-A/90890-04132 or an equivalent). Make sure the seal flange seats against the housing (**Figure 23**).
2. Replace the oil seal and bearing as follows:
   a. Remove the mechanical seal as previously described.
   b. Support the water pump housing with the bearing side down. Provide clearance for the bearing and seal to fall from the bore. Place a driver on the outside edge of the oil seal and drive it and the bearing from the bore.
   c. Clean and inspect the housing.
   d. Lubricate the outer circumference of the oil seal with coolant.
   e. Working from the bearing side of the housing, place the seal into the bore, with the closed side of the seal toward the inside of the housing (**Figure 26**). Note the required depth (**Figure 28**) that the seal must be driven into place. Press the seal into the bore using a driver or socket that fits on the outer edge of the seal. Check the seal depth.
   f. Apply engine oil to the outer surface of the bearing. Then, place the bearing into the housing bore with the manufacturer's marks facing out. Drive in the bearing until it is fully seated. Use a driver that fits on the outer race of the bearing.
   g. Install a new mechanical seal as described in this section.

Table 1 COOLING SYSTEM SPECIFICATIONS

Coolant type	Ethylene glycol containing corrosion inhibitors for aluminum engines
Coolant mixture	50/50 (antifreeze/soft or distilled water)
Coolant capacity	
Radiator and engine	1.61 L (1.70 US qt.)
Reservoir	0.25 L (0.26 US qt.)

(continued)

10

Table 1 COOLING SYSTEM SPECIFICATIONS (continued)

Radiator cap pressure relief	
2006-2014 models	93.3-122.7 kPa (13.3-17.4 psi)
2015-on models	107.9-137.3 kPa (15.6-14.9 psi)

Table 2 COOLING SYSTEM TORQUE SPECIFICATIONS

Item	N•m	in.-lb.	ft.-lb.
Coolant reservoir retaining bolts	7	62	–
Radiator retaining bolts	7	62	–
Thermostat cover bolts	10	89	–
Water pump cover bolts	11	97	–
Water pump retaining bolts	10	89	–

CHAPTER ELEVEN

WHEELS, TIRES AND DRIVE CHAIN

This chapter describes service procedures for the wheels, tires, drive chain and sprockets. Routine maintenance procedures for these components are found in Chapter Three. Refer to **Tables 1-4** at the end of this chapter for specifications.

WHEEL

Removal/Installation

1. Park the ATV on level ground and set the parking brake.
2. Loosen the wheel lug nuts (**Figure 1**).
3. Raise and support the ATV so the wheel is off the ground.
4. Remove the wheel nuts and washers from the studs. Then, remove the wheel from the hub. If more than one wheel will be removed, mark each wheel so it can be installed in its original location.
5. If a front wheel is damaged or dirty, remove the outer brake disc guard (**Figure 2**).
6. Clean the wheel nuts, washers and studs. If studs are broken or damaged, replace them.
7. If removed, install the outer brake disc guard onto the front wheel hub. Install the burred side against the hub.
8. Install the wheel onto the studs with the valve stem facing out.

WARNING

If more than one wheel has been removed, check that the tire direction arrow (on the tire sidewall, if applicable) is pointing forward when the wheel is mounted.

9. Install the washers and finger-tighten the wheel lug nuts.
10. Lower the ATV to the ground. Using a crossing pattern, evenly tighten the wheel lug nuts in several steps to 45 N•m (33 ft.-lb.).
11. Raise the ATV and spin the wheel, checking that the wheel runs true.
12. Lower the ATV to the ground.

Inspection

1. Inspect the wheel for damage which may affect true wheel rotation, tire seating or wheel strength. Replace a damaged wheel.

CAUTION

Do not remove the wheel bearings for inspection purposes as they can be damaged during the removal process. Remove the wheel bearings only if replacement is required.

2. Mount the wheel on its hub and tighten the wheel nuts to 45 N•m (33 ft.-lb.).
3. Support the ATV securely so the wheel can rotate freely.
4. Mount a dial indicator against the rim as shown in **Figure 3** to measure radial and lateral rim runout. Turn the tire slowly by hand and read movement indicated on dial indicator. See **Table 1** for rim runout limits. Note the following:
   a. If rim runout limit is excessive, first check the condition of the wheel assembly. If the wheel is bent or otherwise damaged, it may require replacement.
   b. If wheel condition is okay but runout is excessive, remove the wheel and inspect either the front (Chapter Twelve) or rear (Chapter Thirteen) hub.
5. Remove the dial indicator and lower the vehicle to ground.

TIRES

The ATV is equipped with tubeless, low pressure tires designed specifically for off-road use. Rapid tire wear will occur if the ATV is riden on paved surfaces.

Tools

The following tools are required to change a tire:
1. Bead breaker tool.
2. Tire irons.
3. Rim protectors.

Removal

CAUTION
If the tire is difficult to remove or install using the proper tools, do not take a chance on damaging the tire or rim sealing surface. Take the tire and wheel to a dealership and have them service the tire.

NOTE
*The severe operating conditions in which an ATV may operate can create a seal that makes tire bead and wheel separation extremely difficult. A heavy-duty tire breakdown tool (**Figure 4**) is available through ATV dealerships.*

1. Remove the valve stem cap and core and deflate the tire. Do not reinstall the core at this time.

1

2

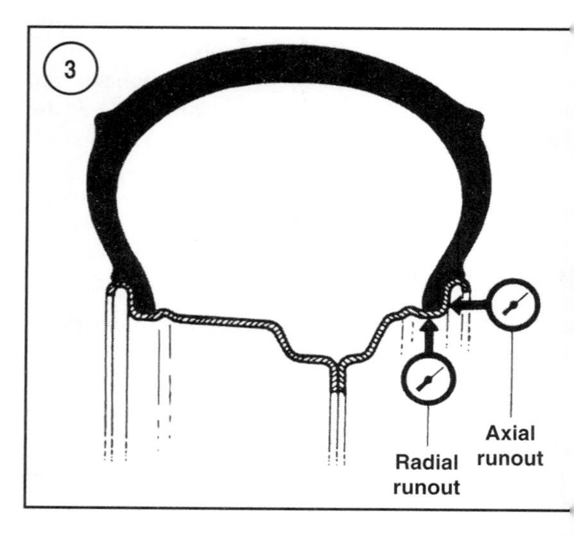

3

2. Lubricate the tire bead and rim flanges with a rubber lubricant. Press the tire sidewall/bead down to allow the lubricant to run into and around the bead area. Also apply lubricant to the area where the bead breaker arm will contact the tire sidewall.
3. Position the wheel into the bead breaker tool (**Figure 5**).
4. Slowly work the bead breaker tool, making sure the tool arm seats against the inside of the rim, and break the tire bead away from the rim.

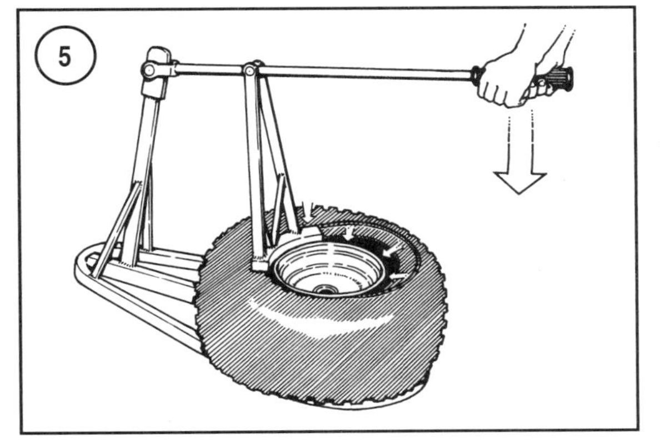

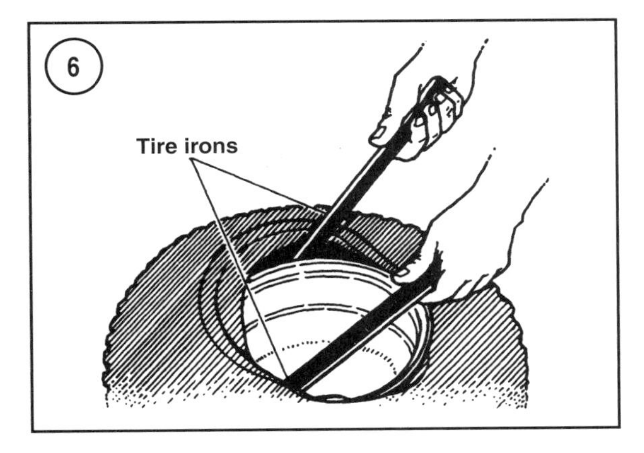

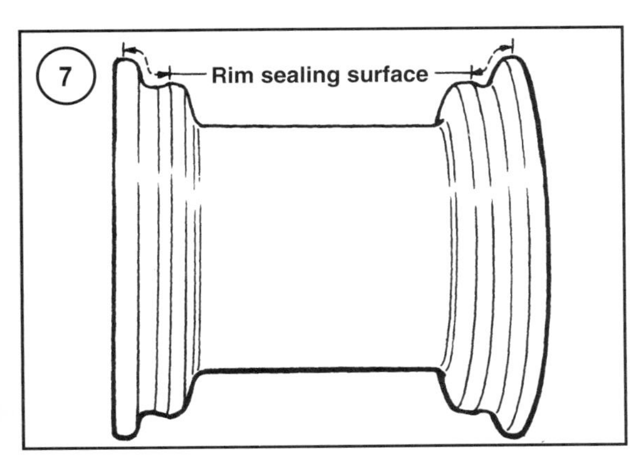

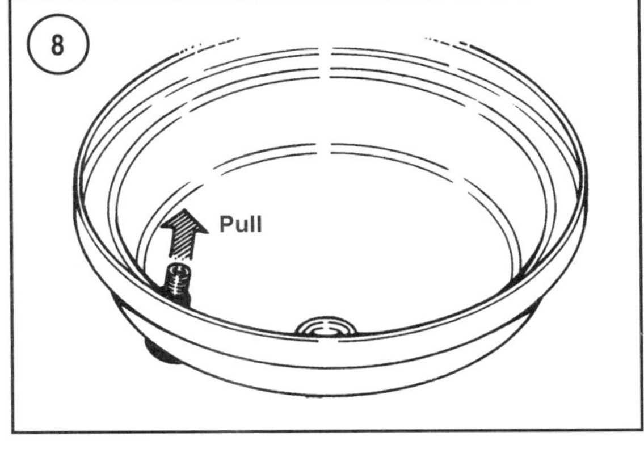

5. Apply hand pressure against the tire on either side of the tool to break the rest of the bead free from the rim.
6. If the rest of the tire bead cannot be broken loose, raise the tool, rotate the tire/wheel assembly and repeat the process until the entire bead is broken loose from the rim.
7. Turn the wheel over and repeat the procedure to break the opposite side loose.

CAUTION
When using tire irons in the following steps, work carefully so that the tire or rim sealing surfaces are not damaged. Damage to these areas may cause an air leak and require replacement of the tire or rim.

8. Lubricate the tire beads and rim flanges again with rubber lubricant. Pry the bead over the rim with two tire irons (**Figure 6**). Take small bites with the tire irons. Place rim protectors between the tire irons and the rim.
9. When the upper tire bead is free, lift the second bead up into the center rim well and remove it in the same manner.
10. Clean and dry the rim.

Inspection

1. Inspect the rim sealing surface (**Figure 7**) on both sides of the wheel. If the rim is bent, it may leak air.

NOTE
Special tools are available for installing this type of valve stem.

2. To replace the air valve, perform the following:
   a. Support the wheel and pull the valve stem out of the rim. Discard the valve stem.
   b. Lubricate the new valve stem with a rubber lubricant.
   c. Pull a new valve stem into the rim, from the inside out, until it snaps into place (**Figure 8**).

3. Inspect the tire for cuts, tears, abrasions or any other defects.
4. Clean the tire and rim of any lubricant used during removal.

Installation

WARNING
When mounting the tire, use only clean water as a tire lubricant. Other lubricants may leave a slippery residue on the tire that would allow the tire to slip on the rim, causing a loss of air pressure.

NOTE
The tire tread pattern on the original equipment tires is directional. Position the tire onto the rim so the rotation arrow on the tire sidewall faces in the correct direction of wheel rotation.

NOTE
If the tire is difficult to install, place the tire outside in the sun (or in the trunk of a car). The higher temperatures will soften the tire and help with installation.

1. Install the tire onto the wheel starting with the side opposite the valve stem. Push the first bead over the rim flange. Force the bead into the center of the rim to help installation (**Figure 9**).
2. Install the rest of the first bead with tire irons (**Figure 10**).
3. Repeat the procedure to install the second bead onto the rim.
4. Install the valve stem core, if necessary.

WARNING
Never exceed the maximum inflation pressure specified on the tire sidewall.

5. Apply water to the tire bead and inflate the tire to seat the tire onto the rim. Check that the rim lines on both sides of the tire are parallel with the rim flanges as shown in **Figure 11**. If the rim flanges are not parallel, deflate the tire and break the bead. Then lubricate the tire with water again and reinflate the tire.
6. When the tire is properly seated, remove the air valve to deflate the tire and wait one hour before putting the tire into service. After one hour, inflate the tire to the operating pressure listed in **Table 2**.
7. Check for air leaks and install the valve cap.

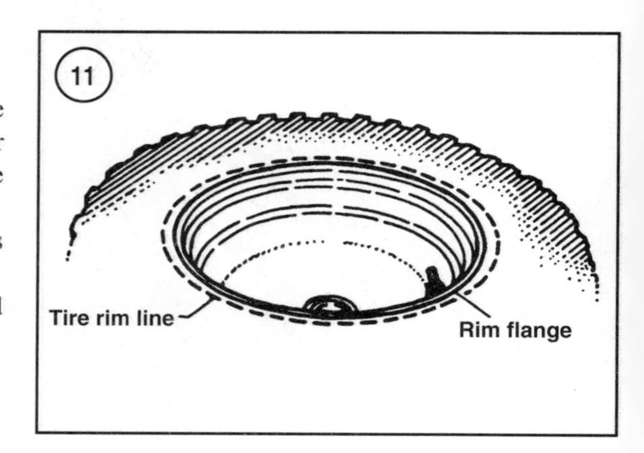

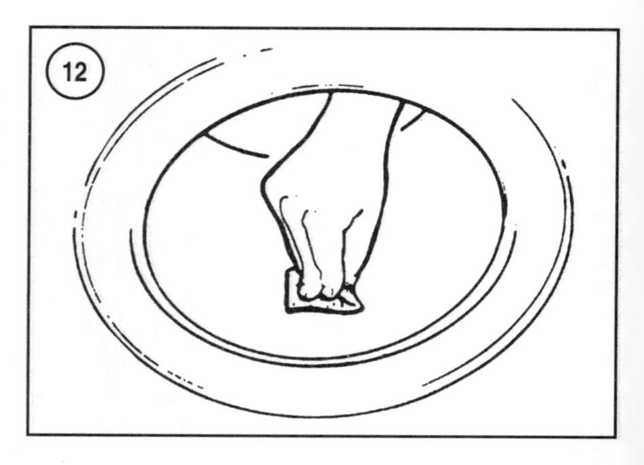

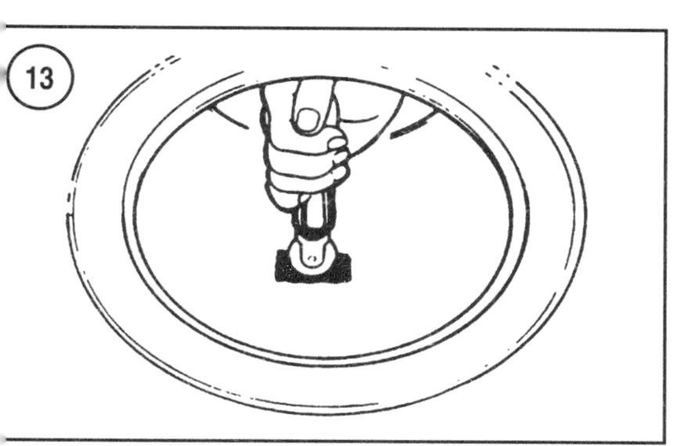

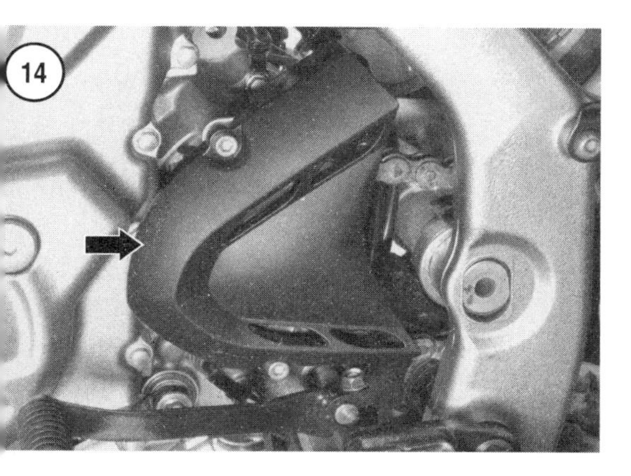

old Patch Repair

Use the manufacturer's instructions for the tire re-ir kit. If there are no instructions, use the following ocedure.

Remove the tire from the wheel as described in is section.

Prior to removing the object that punctured the e, mark the puncture location with chalk or crayon. emove the object.

Working on the inside of the tire, roughen an area ound the hole that is larger than the patch (**Figure 2**). Use the tool from the tire repair kit or a pocket ife. Do not scrape too vigorously or additional mage may occur.

4. Clean the area with a non-flammable solvent. Do not use an oil-based solvent as it will leave a residue, rendering the patch useless.
5. Apply a small amount of special cement to the puncture and spread it evenly.
6. Allow the cement to dry until it is tacky (usually 30 seconds or so is sufficient).
7. Remove the backing from the patch.

CAUTION
Do not touch the newly exposed rubber or the patch will not stick firmly.

8. Center the patch over the hole. Hold the patch firmly in place for about 30 seconds to allow the cement to dry. If available, use a roller (**Figure 13**) to press the patch into place.
9. Dust the area with talcum powder.

SPROCKETS

Check the condition of both sprockets and the drive chain, as described in Chapter Three. If either the chain or sprockets are worn, replace all drive components. Using new sprockets with a worn chain, or a new chain on worn sprockets will shorten the life of the new part.

Drive Sprocket and Cover Removal and Installation

1. Shift the transmission into gear and set the parking brake.
2. Remove the sprocket cover (**Figure 14**).

NOTE
The chain can now be removed from the drive sprocket without removing the sprocket. If the drive sprocket must be removed, leave the chain on the sprocket until the sprocket nut is loosened.

3. Bend the lockwasher tabs away from the sprocket nut (**Figure 15**). Then remove the nut, washer and sprocket from the shaft. Mark the outside face of the sprocket. If reused, install the sprocket in its original direction.
4. Clean and inspect the sprocket and chain (Chapter Three).

NOTE
If oil is leaking past the countershaft spacer, remove the spacer to determine the cause.

5. To inspect the seal and spacer, remove the seal retainer (**Figure 16**).

6. Twist and remove the output shaft spacer (**Figure 17**) and shaft O-ring (A, **Figure 18**).
   a. Clean and inspect the output shaft spacer (**Figure 19**). Inspect the inner and outer surfaces that contact the O-ring and crankcase seal. The surfaces should be smooth and free of corrosion or damage.
   b. If a leak is evident at the crankcase seal (B, **Figure 18**), replace the seal as described in *Countershaft Seal Replacement* (Chapter Five). Tighten the seal retainer bolts to 10 N•m (89 in.-lb.).
7. Reverse the removal steps to install the drive sprocket. Note the following:
   a. Install a new, lubricated O-ring (A, **Figure 18**) onto the countershaft. The O-ring must seat in the shaft groove.
   b. Install the countershaft spacer so the notched end faces in.
   c. If reusing the sprocket, check that the sprocket is installed in its original direction.
   d. Install a new lockwasher.
   e. Tighten the drive sprocket nut to 85 N•m (63 ft.-lb.).
   f. Use a chisel or punch to bend the tabs on the lockwasher against the sides of the drive sprocket nut.
   g. Tighten the sprocket cover bolts to 10 N•m (89 in.-lb.).
   h. Adjust the chain (Chapter Three).

Driven Sprocket Removal and Installation

If the drive sprocket will be replaced, loosen the drive sprocket shaft nut before raising the swing arm to remove the driven sprocket. The resistance of the machine sitting on the ground will aid in loosening the nut.

1. Shift the transmission into gear and set the parking brake.
2. Loosen the driven sprocket mounting bolts (**Figure 20**).
3. Remove the left rear wheel as described in this chapter.
4. Remove the sprocket from the hub.
5. Clean and inspect the sprocket, bolts and chain (Chapter Three).
6. Reverse the removal steps to install the driven sprocket. Note the following:

NOTE
Install the left rear wheel if necessary to move the axle forward.

   a. If necessary, move the axle forward as described in *Drive Chain Adjustment* (Chapter Three) to mount the chain.
   b. Tighten the driven sprocket bolts to 72 N•m (53 ft.-lb.).

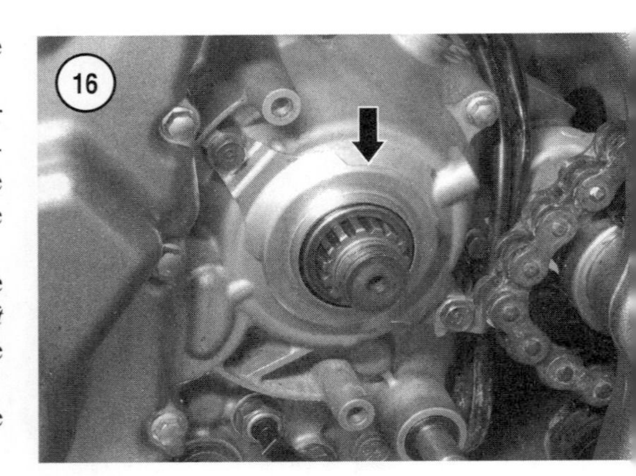
16

17

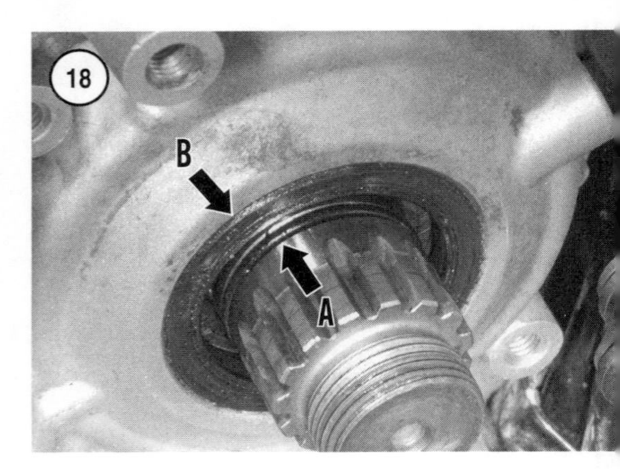

18

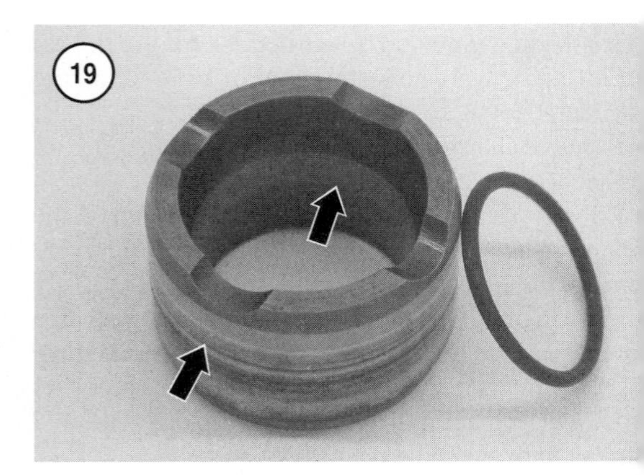
19

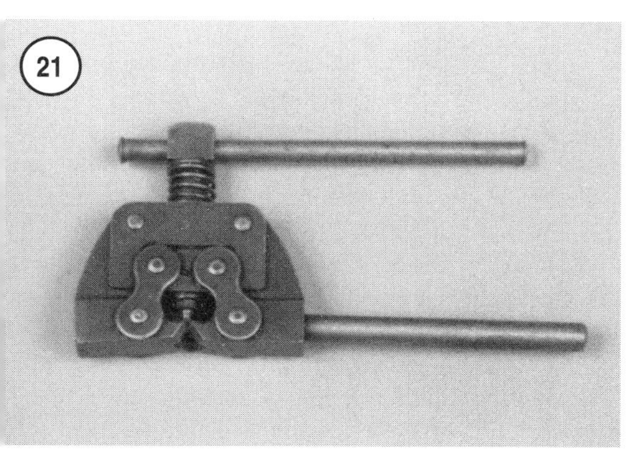

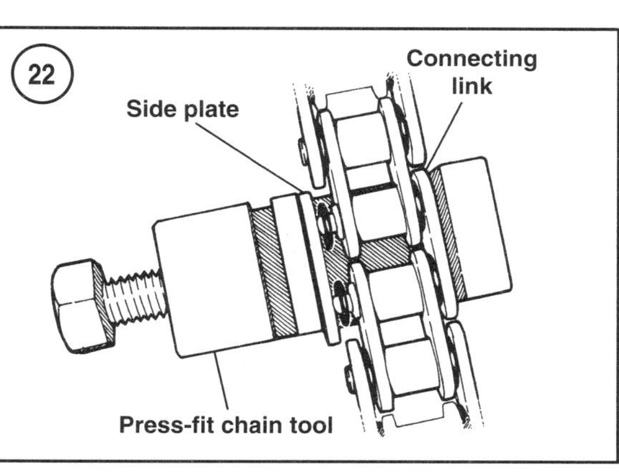

c. Adjust the chain (Chapter Three).

DRIVE CHAIN

Refer to Chapter Three for drive chain cleaning, lubrication, adjustment and measurement. Refer to **Table 3** in this chapter for drive chain specifications.

When checking the condition of the chain, also check the condition of the sprockets (Chapter Three). If either the chain or sprockets are worn, replace all drive components. Using new sprockets with a worn chain, or a new chain on worn sprockets will shorten the life of the new part.

The vehicle is originally equipped with an endless O-ring type chain. This type of chain is recommended because it is internally lubricated and requires minimal maintenance. The chain is permanently assembled, which increases reliability. However, to remove the chain, the swing arm must be partially disassembled so the chain can pass by the swing arm pivot.

Using a drive chain with a clip-type master link is not recommended. However, a chain that can be assembled using a permanent, press-fit master link is acceptable. If a chain breaker tool (**Figure 21**) and link riveting tool (**Figure 22**) are available, this can be a more convenient way to replace the chain, rather than disassembling the swing arm.

Read both procedures while noting the equipment and skill required.

Chain With No Master Link Removal and Installation

1. Increase drive chain slack as described in *Drive Chain Adjustment* (Chapter Three).
2. Remove the rear wheels as described in this chapter.
3. Remove the drive sprocket cover as described in this chapter.
4. Support the ATV so that the swing arm may be removed.
5. Remove the rear shock absorber as described in Chapter Thirteen.
6. Lift the chain off the sprockets.

WARNING
If necessary, get assistance in handling the swing arm.

NOTE
With the swing arm disconnected from the shock absorber and linkage, it is recommended to check the condition of the swing arm bearings as described in Chapter Thirteen.

7. Remove the swing arm pivot nut (**Figure 23**).

8. Remove the swing arm bolt (**Figure 24**) and pull back the swing arm.
9. Lower the swing arm and remove the chain.
10. Reverse the removal steps to install the chain. Note the following:
   a. Clean and inspect the bores in the swing arm, engine case and frame.
   b. Apply waterproof grease to the parts and bores.
   c. Tighten the swing arm pivot nut to 100 N•m (74 ft.-lb.).
   d. Adjust the chain (Chapter Three).

Chain With Press-Fit Master Link Removal and Installation

1. Increase drive chain slack as described in *Drive Chain Adjustment* (Chapter Three).
2. Support the machine so the rear wheels are off the ground.
3. Choose a convenient location along the drive chain for attaching a chain breaker tool (**Figure 21**).
4. Attach the tool to the drive chain and drive a link pin from the chain. Remove the chain.
5. Install the new chain and route it over the sprockets.
   a. Shift the transmission into neutral.
   b. If necessary, attach a wire to the end of the chain to route it behind the sprocket guard and over the drive sprocket.
   c. After the chain is routed over the sprockets, remove the chain slack and position the ends together. Shift the transmission into gear to prevent the drive sprocket from rotating.
6. Secure the chain ends with the master link. Check that the O-rings are on the master link pins. Insert the link from the back side of the chain.
7. Place the chain link sideplate on the master link. The identification marks must face out.
8. Stake the link pins using a chain riveting tool (**Figure 22**).
9. Adjust the chain (Chapter Three).

Table 1 TIRE AND WHEEL SPECIFICATIONS

Tires (2006-2012 models)	
Type	
Front	Dunlop KT341
Rear	Dunlop KT345
Size	
Front	AT21 x 7-10
Rear	AT20 x 10-9
Tires (2013-2014 models)	
Type	
Front	MAXXIS/M971Y
Rear	MAXXIS/M976Y
Size	
Front	AT21 x 7-10
Rear	AT20 x 10-9
Tires (2015-on models)	
Type	
Front	MAXXIS/MS13
Rear	MAXXIS/M976Y

(continued)

Table 1 TIRE AND WHEEL SPECIFICATIONS (continued)

Tires (2015-on models) (continued)	
Size	
Front	AT22 x 7-10
Rear	AT20 x 10-9
Wheels	
Front rim size	10 x 5.5 AT
Rear rim size	
2006-2008 models	9 x 8.5 AT
2009-on models	9 x 8.0 AT
Rim runout limit–radial or lateral	2.0 mm (0.08 in.)

Table 2 TIRE INFLATION PRESSURE

	kPa (psi)
Maximum	
Front	4.0 (27.5)
Rear	4.0 (27.5)
Minimum	
Front	3.6 (24.5)
Rear	3.6 (24.5)

Table 3 DRIVE CHAIN SPECIFICATIONS

Drive chain	
Manufacturer	Daido
Type	
2006-2014 models	520MXV
2015-on models	520VP2-T
Number of link	98
Drive chain slack	25-35 mm (0.98-1.38 in.)
Drive chain 15 link length limit	239.3 mm (9.42 in.)
Sprocket sizes	
Drive (front)	14 teeth
Driven (rear)	38 teeth

Table 4 WHEEL AND DRIVE CHAIN TORQUE SPECIFICATIONS

Item	N•m	in.-lb.	ft.-lb.
Chain roller mounting bolt	32	–	24
Drive sprocket cover bolts	10	89	–
Drive sprocket nut	85	–	63
Drive sprocket seal retainer bolts	10	89	–
Driven sprocket nuts	72	–	53
Swing arm pivot nut	100	–	74
Wheel lug nuts	45	–	33

CHAPTER TWELVE

FRONT SUSPENSION AND STEERING

This chapter provides service procedures for the front suspension and steering components. Refer to the **Table 1** and **Table 2** at the end of this chapter for specifications.

HANDLEBAR

Adjustment

1. Withdraw the fuel tank vent hose (A, **Figure 1**) from the handlebar cover.
2. Push up and remove the handlebar cover (B, **Figure 1**).
3. Loosen the rear (A, **Figure 2**), and then the front (B) handlebar holder bolts.
4. Tilt the handlebar to the desired position.
5. Tighten the front (B, **Figure 2**), and then the rear (A) handlebar holder bolts to 23 N•m (17 ft.-lb.).

Removal and Installation

1. Withdraw the fuel tank vent hose (A, **Figure 1**) from the handlebar cover.
2. Push up and remove the handlebar cover (B, **Figure 1**).
3. Remove cable and hose bands.
4. Remove the front master cylinder as described in Chapter Fourteen.
5. Remove the throttle housing clamp screws (A, **Figure 3**), clamp (B) and throttle housing (C). Plac the throttle housing out of the way.
6. Remove the clutch lever clamp screws (A, **Figur 4**) and clamp (B). Then, remove the clutch lever as sembly (C, **Figure 4**) and place it out of the way.
7. Remove the switch housing as described in *Le Handlebar Switch Housing Replacement* (Chapte Nine).
8. Remove the handlebar holder bolts (A and B **Figure 2**). Then, remove the handlebar.
9. If removal of the grips is necessary, use solvent o a spray lubricant to flood under the grip to soften th adhesive. Compressed air can also be used to lift an free the grips.
10. If replacing the handlebar, remove the space and install it on the new handlebar.
11. Inspect the handlebar as described in this sec tion.
12. Reverse the removal steps to install the handle bar while noting the following:
   a. The punch marks (**Figure 5**) on the handleba holders must face forward. Tighten the fron holder bolts, followed by the rear holder bolts Tighten all holder bolts to 23 N•m (17 ft.-lb. There should be a gap between the top and bot tom holders at the rear of the holders.
   b. Make sure the notch on the spacer engages th throttle housing (**Figure 6**).

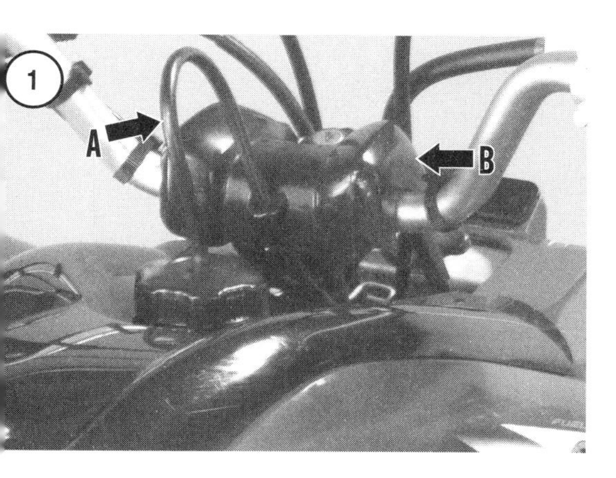

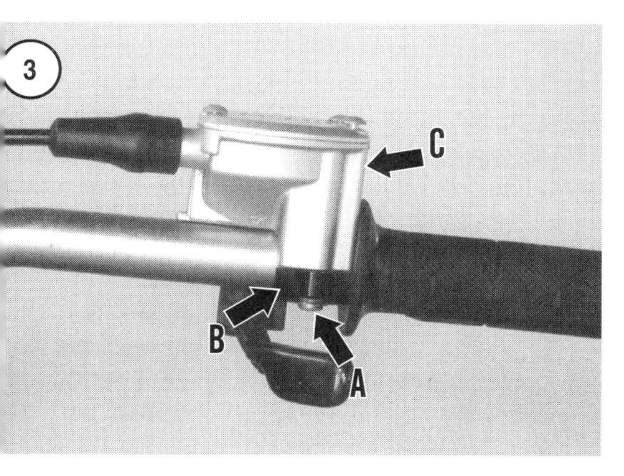

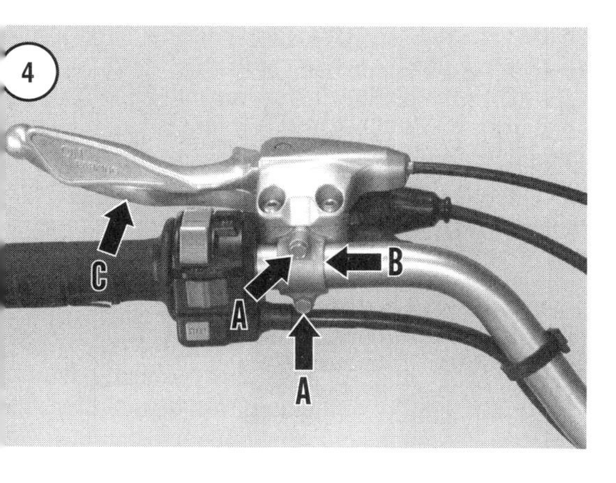

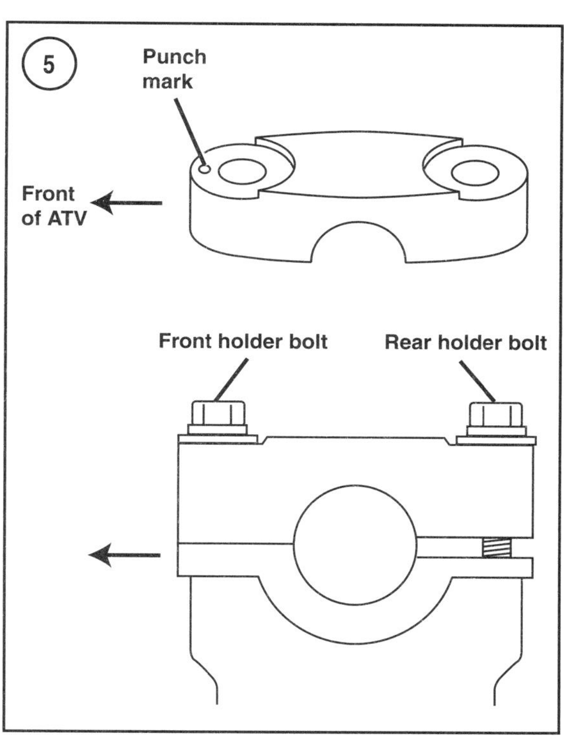

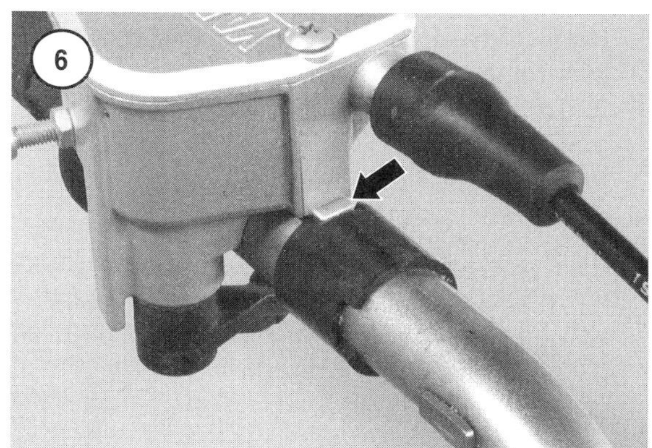

c. If new grips will be installed, clean the handlebar grip surface with solvent, such as electrical contact cleaner. Apply a hand grip cement following the manufacturer's instructions.

d. Check the riding position and adjust the handlebar, if necessary. Turn the handlebar side to side and check for cable binding.

Inspection

WARNING
Never attempt to straighten, weld or heat a damaged handlebar. The metal can weaken and possibly break when subjected to the shocks and stresses that occur when riding the ATV.

1. Inspect the handlebar for cracks, bends or other damage. If the handlebar is made of aluminum, check closely where the handlebar is clamped to the holders, and at the clutch lever. If cracks, scores or other damage is found, replace the handlebar. Damage in these areas can cause handlebar failure.
2. Inspect the threads on the mounting bolts and in the holders. Clean all residue from the threads. Replace damaged bolts.
3. Clean the handlebar holders and handlebar with solvent or electrical contact cleaner.

SHOCK ABSORBERS

Depending on model and year, the models are equipped with either an oil-dampened shock absorber or with a gas/oil dampened shock absorber that is identified by the external reservoir.

Removal/Installation

1. Support the vehicle with the front wheels off the ground.
2. Remove the lower shock absorber nut, washer and bolt (**Figure 7**).
3. Remove the upper shock absorber nut and bolt (**Figure 8**), then remove the shock absorber.
4. Inspect the shock absorber as described in this section.
5. Install the shock absorber by reversing the removal steps, while noting the following:

CAUTION
A self-locking nut is used on each shock absorber retaining bolt. Replace any nut that does not resist turning during installation.

a. Install a washer inside the nut on the lower shock retaining bolt.
b. Tighten the shock absorber retaining bolts to 48 N•m (35 ft.-lb.).

Inspection

1A. On oil-dampened shock absorbers, perform the following:
a. Inspect for oil leaks, particularly around the damper rod cover (A, **Figure 9**).
b. Inspect the spring (B, **Figure 9**) for damage. The spring is not available separately.

1B. On gas/oil-dampened shock absorbers, perform the following:
a. Inspect for oil leaks, particularly around the damper rod.
b. Inspect the damper rod (A, **Figure 10**) for bending, rust or other damage.

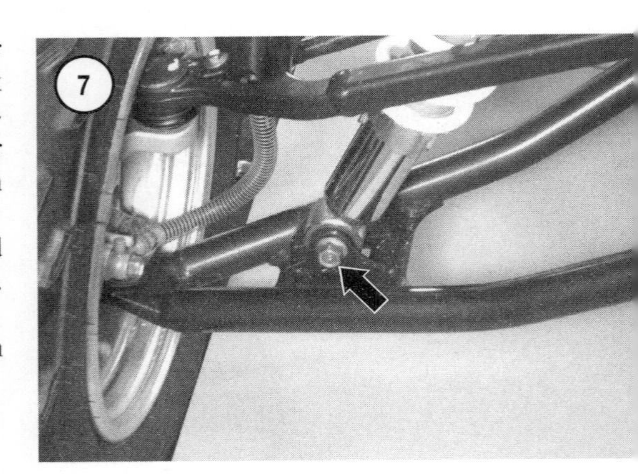

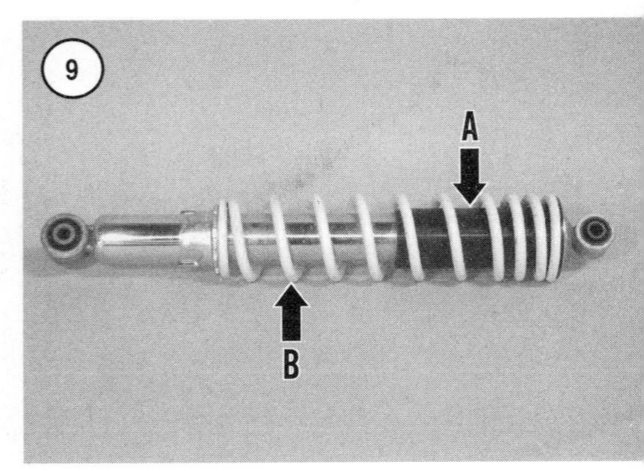

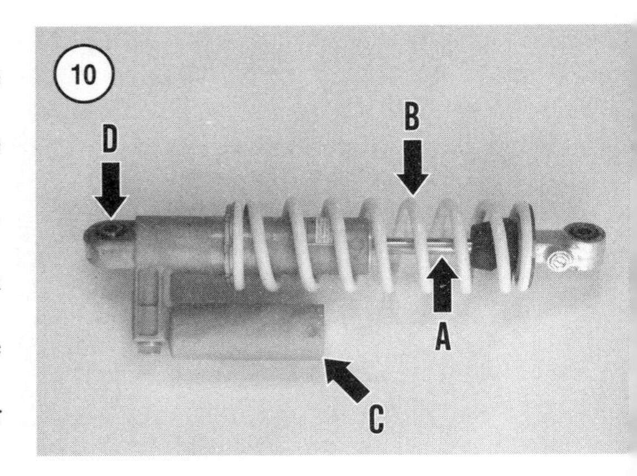

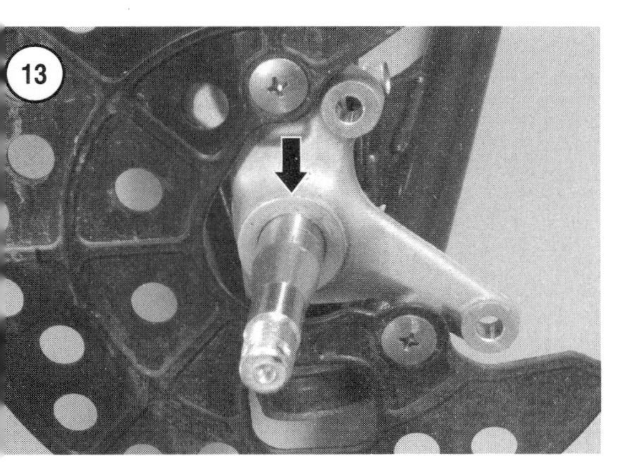

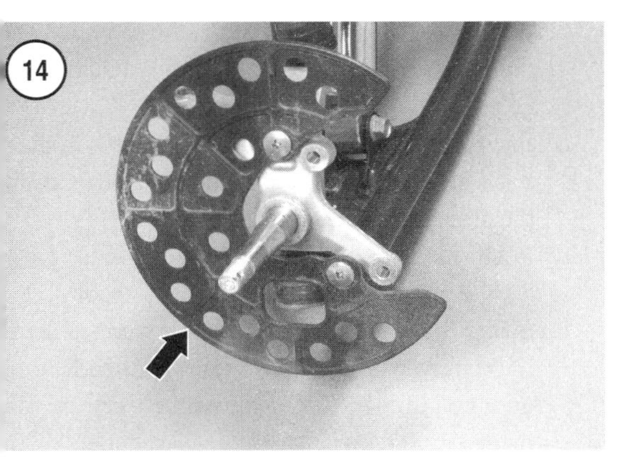

c. Inspect the spring (B, **Figure 10**) for damage. The spring is not available separately.
d. Inspect the reservoir (C, **Figure 10**) for damage.
e. Inspect the bearing, collar and seals in the upper end of the shock absorber (D, **Figure 10**) for wear or damage.

2. On all models, inspect the upper and lower mounting holes for damage and excessive wear.
3. If the shock is leaking, or it is time or replace the shock, refer service to a dealership or suspension specialist.

FRONT WHEEL HUB

Removal and Installation

1. Remove the front wheel and outer brake disc guard as described in Chapter Eleven.
2. Remove the front brake caliper as described in Chapter Fourteen.
3. Remove the hub cap.
4. Remove the cotter pin, axle nut (**Figure 11**) and washer.

NOTE
If the hub is corroded to the axle, place a drift against the back of the hub and tap it free. Do not strike the outer edge of the brake disc.

5. Remove the wheel hub assembly (**Figure 12**).
6. Remove the inner washer (**Figure 12**) from the axle.
7. Inspect and repair the front hub assembly as described in this section.
8. If additional suspension or steering components will be serviced, remove the inner brake disc guard (**Figure 14**).
9. If necessary, remove the brake disc from the hub as described in Chapter Fourteen.
10. Reverse the removal steps to install the front hub. Note the following:
  a. Inspect the steering knuckle before installing the hub. Check for cracks and damage on bearing surfaces (A, **Figure 15**) and threads (B).
  b. Tighten the axle nut to 70 N•m (52 ft.-lb.).
  c. Install a new cotter pin.

WARNING
Make sure the brakes operate correctly before riding the ATV.

  d. Install the caliper as described in Chapter Fourteen.
  e. Install the front wheel and outer brake disc guard as described in Chapter Eleven.

Inspection

1. Remove the spacers (**Figure 16**) from both sides of the hub.
2. Inspect the seals (A, **Figure 17**) for damage.
3. Turn each bearing inner race (B, **Figure 17**) by hand. The bearing should roll smoothly and quietly. If binding or roughness is detected, replace both bearings.
4. Check each bearing for axial and radial play (**Figure 18**). If obvious play is detected, replace the bearing. Replace both bearings if either bearing is worn or damaged.
5. Check the tightness of the bearings in the hub. Replace the bearings and/or hub if they are loose.
6. Install the spacers if the bearings and seals are in good condition.

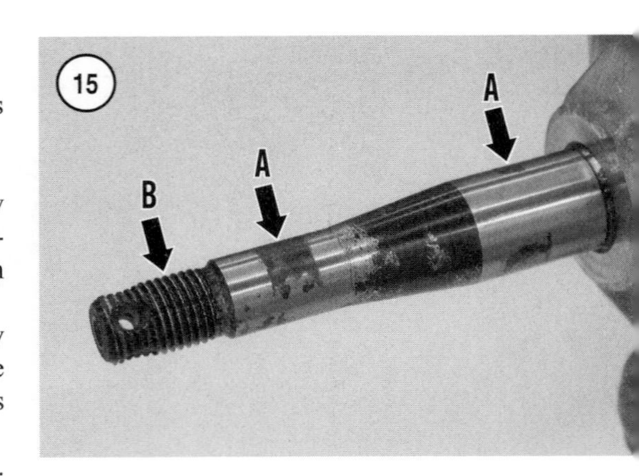

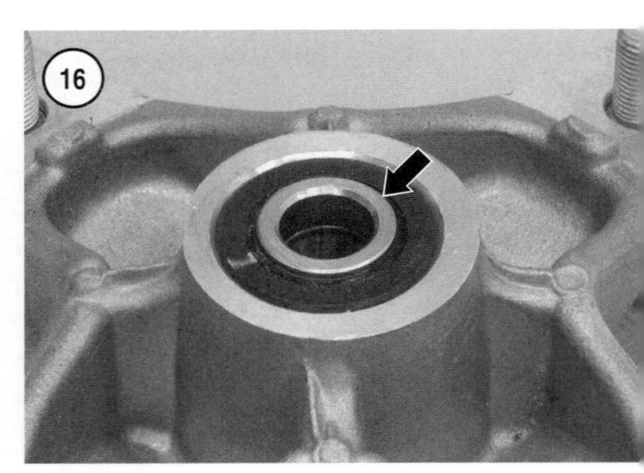

Bearing and Seal Replacement

Two methods for removing bearings from the front hub are provided in the following procedure. The first method uses a wheel bearing removal set and the second method uses common shop tools.

CAUTION
In the following procedure, do not allow the hub to rest on the brake disc. Support the hub to prevent pressure against the disc.

1. Pry the seals (A, **Figure 17**) from both sides of the hub. Protect the hub to prevent damage.
2. Examine the bearings. Note the following:
   a. The bearings are open on the outer face and shielded on the inner face. The new bearings must be installed with the open side facing out.
   b. If bearing damage is severe, determine which bearing is damaged the least. This bearing will be removed first.

3A. Remove the bearings using the wheel bearing removal set as follows:

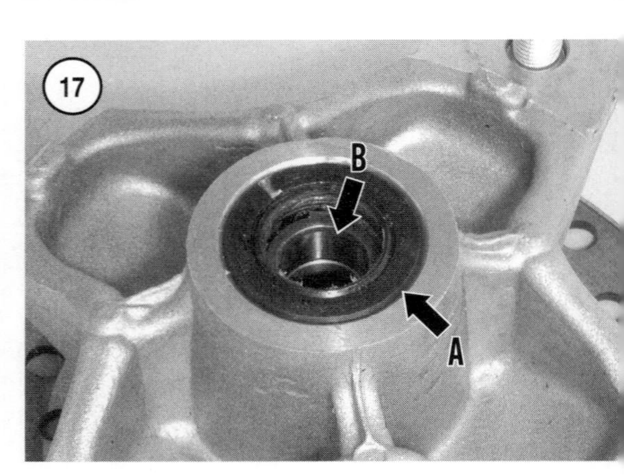

NOTE
*The tools used in this procedure are part of the Kowa Seiki Wheel Bearing Remover set (**Figure 19**). The set is available through ATV dealerships. The set is designed so a proper-size remover head can be wedged against the inner bearing race (**Figure 20**). The bearing can then be driven from the hub.*

   a. Select the appropriate-size remover head. The small, split end of the remover head must fit inside the bearing race.
   b. Insert the split end of the remover head into the bearing. Seat the remover head against the bearing.
   c. Insert the tapered end of the driver through the back side of the hub. Fit the tapered end into the slot of the remover head.
   d. Position the hub so the remover head is against a solid surface, such as a concrete floor.
   e. Strike the end of the driver so it wedges firmly in the remover head. The remover head should now be jammed tight against the inner bearing race.

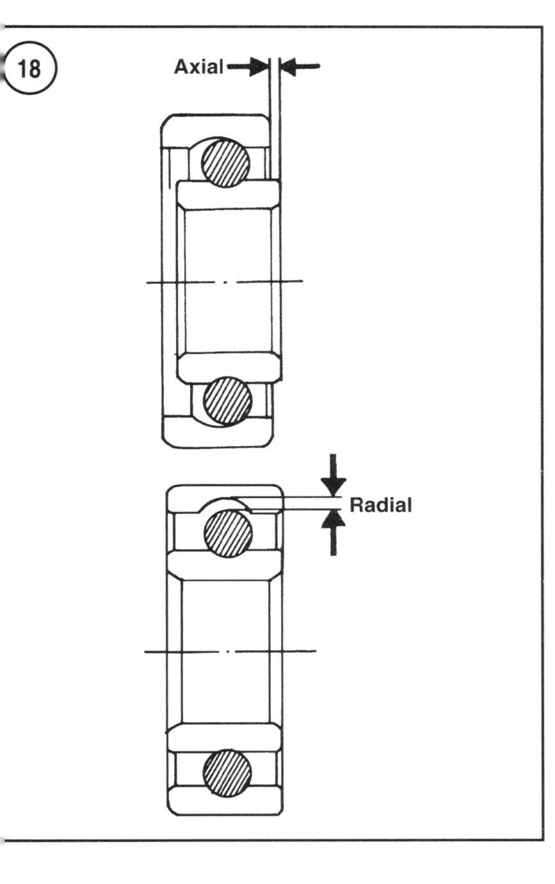

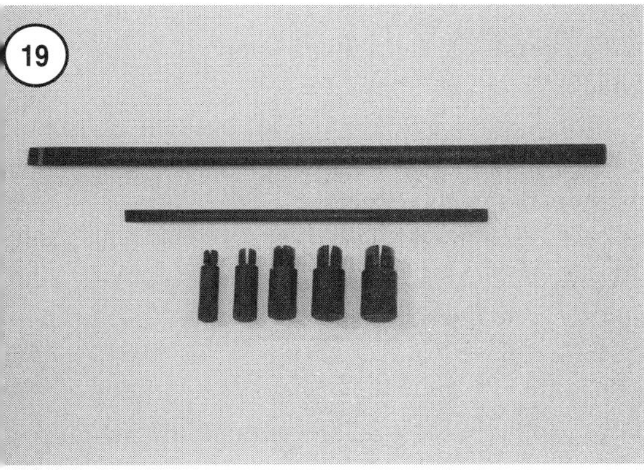

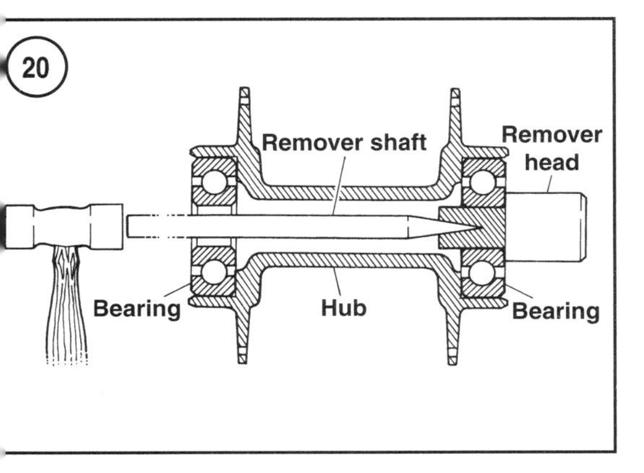

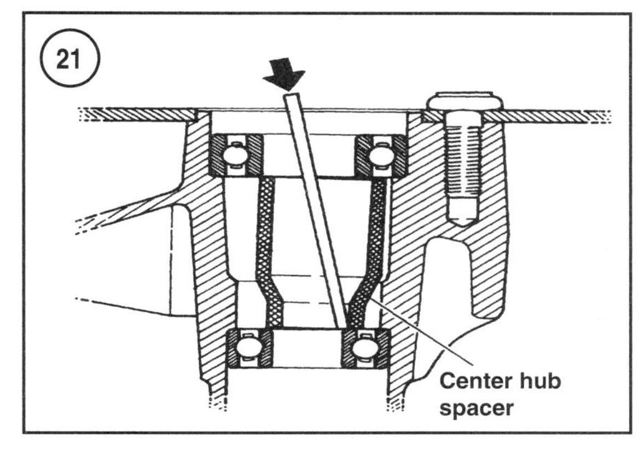

f. Reposition and support the assembly so the remover head is free to move and the driver can be struck again. Support the hub so there is no pressure applied to the outside of the brake disc.
g. Strike the driver, forcing the bearing and hub spacer from the hub.
h. Remove the driver from the remover head.
i. Repeat the procedure to remove the remaining bearing.

3B. Remove the bearings using a hammer, drift and heat gun, or propane torch. The purpose for using heat is to slightly expand the hub bores so the bearings can removed with minimal resistance. Remove the bearings as follows:

WARNING
When using a heat gun or propane torch to heat the hub, care must be taken to prevent burning finished or combustible surfaces. Work in a well-ventilated area and away from combustible materials. Wear protective clothing, including eye protection and insulated gloves.

a. Clean all lubricants from the wheel.
b. Insert a long drift into the hub. Move the hub spacer as needed for access to the bearing to be removed.
c. Heat the hub around the bearing to be removed. Keep the heat source moving at an steady rate and avoid heating the bearing. A large washer placed over the bearing will help insulate the bearing from the heat.
d. Turn the wheel over and use the drift to tap around the inner bearing race (**Figure 21**). To prevent cocking the bearing in the bore, tap in several different locations. Drive the bearing out of the hub.
e. Remove the hub spacer (**Figure 22**).
f. Heat the hub around the remaining bearing, and then drive out the remaining bearing.

4. Clean and inspect all parts.
5. Inspect the hub bore (**Figure 23**) for:
   a. Cracks, corrosion or other damage.
   b. Fit of the new bearings. If a bearing easily enters the hub bore, replace the hub. The bearings must be driven in for an interference fit.
6. Inspect the hub spacer for:
   a. Cracks, corrosion or other damage.
   b. Fit. Check the fit of the spacer against the back side of the bearings. It should fit flat against the bearings. Repair minor nicks and flaring with a file. Do not grind or shorten the spacer. The spacer must remain its full length, in order to prevent binding of the bearings when the axle is tightened.
7. Before installing the new bearings, apply waterproof grease to bearings that are not lubricated by the manufacturer. Work the grease into the cavities between the balls and races.
8. Refer to Chapter One and install the bearings as described. Note the following:
   a. Install each bearing so the open side is out.
   b. After installing one of the bearings, install the spacer (**Figure 22**) so the tapered end is toward the wheel side of the hub.
9. Install the seals as described in Chapter One. Note the following:
   a. Pack grease into the lips of the new seals.
   b. Lubricate the seal bores.
   c. Install the seal so the manufacturer's marks face out.
10. Install the spacers (**Figure 16**) on both sides of the hub.

TIE RODS

Removal and Installation

Refer to **Figure 24**.

1. Before removing the tie rods, make the following check for obvious play and wear.
   a. Park the ATV on level ground with the wheels pointing straight ahead.
   b. Lightly turn the handlebar toward the left, then right while observing the tie rod ends. It is not necessary to actually turn the wheels. If the tie rod ends move vertically (removing play) as pressure is applied, they are worn or damaged.
   c. Repeat the check with the wheels fully locked to the left, then the right. If vertical play is observed in this position, this also indicates worn tie rod ends.
2. To improve access, remove the front wheel as described in Chapter Eleven.

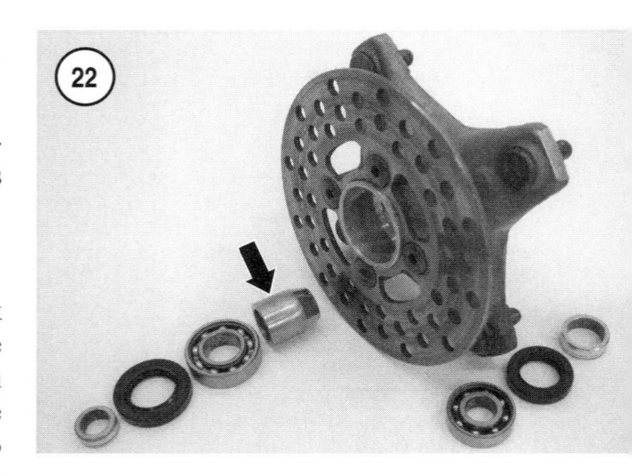
22

23

3. Remove the cotter pin, castle nut (**Figure 25**) an washer from the tie rod end attached to the steerin knuckle.
4. Install a hex nut (**Figure 26**) onto the tie rod stu threads so it is flush with the end of the stud. The n protects the stud threads.
5. Using as little force as required, tap the tie rod ba joint stud free of the steering knuckle. Unscrew the n and separate the tie rod from the steering knuckle.
6. If the tie rod end is seized in the bore, note th following:
   a. Apply heat to the area around the joint using heat gun or propane torch.
   b. Use a ball joint remover (**Figure 27**) to sepa rate the parts. If the tie rod end will be reuse there is a risk of tearing the rubber boot whe using this tool.
7. Repeat the procedure to remove the tie rod en (**Figure 28**) from the pitman arm. If the tie rod en is seized in the bore, and must be driven out, it ma be necessary to remove the upper control arm to gai the necessary clearance.
8. Reverse the removal steps to install the tie rod Note the following:
   a. Install the tie rods so the tie rod sleeve wrenc flats (**Figure 29**) are nearer the steering knuckl

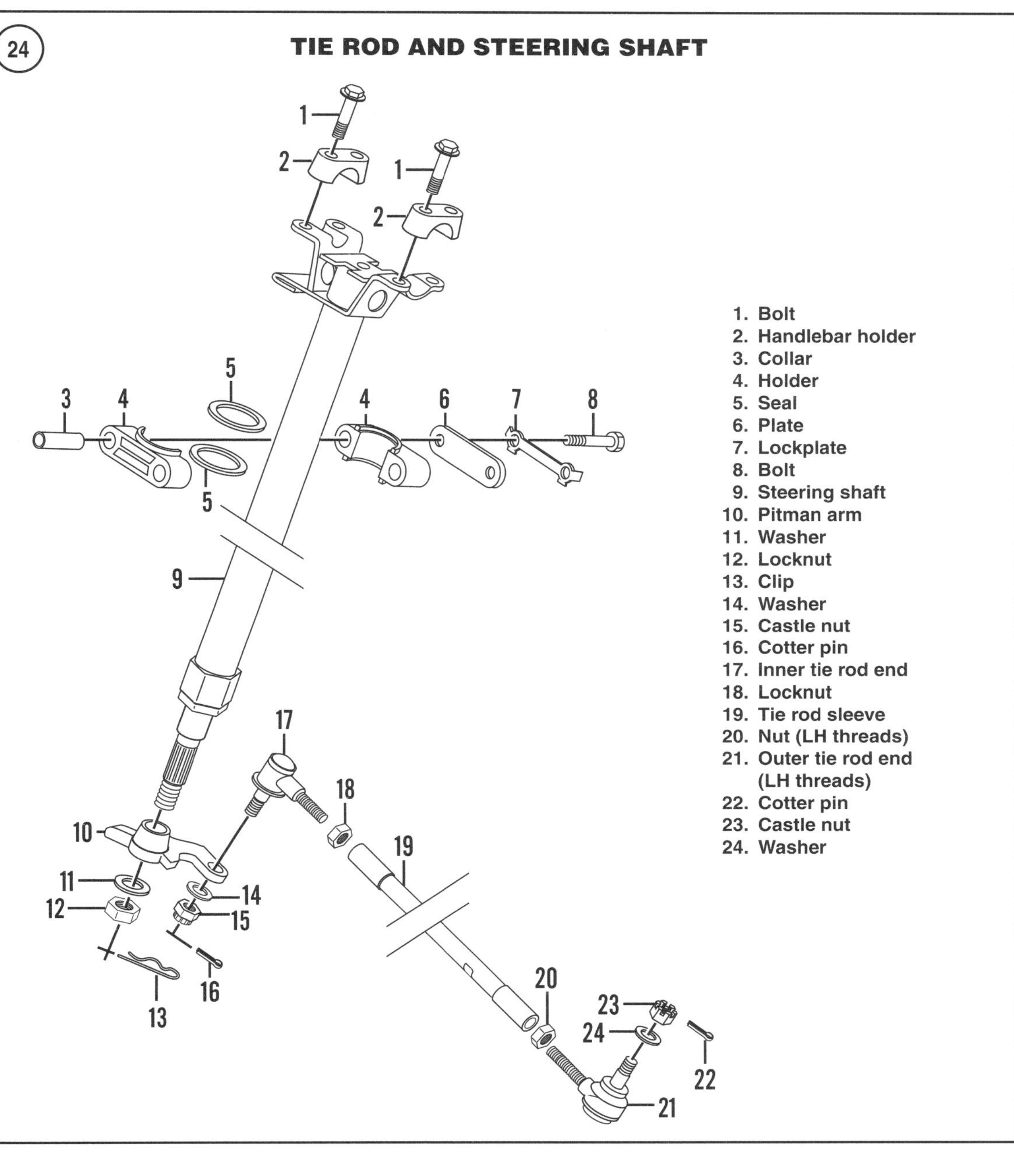
24
TIE ROD AND STEERING SHAFT
1
2
1
2
5
3
4
4
6
7
8
5
9
17
18
10
19
11
14
12
15
16
13
20
23
24
22
21
1. Bolt
2. Handlebar holder
3. Collar
4. Holder
5. Seal
6. Plate
7. Lockplate
8. Bolt
9. Steering shaft
10. Pitman arm
11. Washer
12. Locknut
13. Clip
14. Washer
15. Castle nut
16. Cotter pin
17. Inner tie rod end
18. Locknut
19. Tie rod sleeve
20. Nut (LH threads)
21. Outer tie rod end (LH threads)
22. Cotter pin
23. Castle nut
24. Washer

12

25

26

b. Tighten both tie rod ball joint nuts to 25 N•m (18.5 ft.-lb.).
c. Install new cotter pins.

9. Check toe-in adjustment as described in this section.

Inspection

NOTE
The tie rod ends are packed with grease and sealed. Do not immerse the tie rod ends in solvent or any other liquid that could penetrate the boots. Wipe the tie rod ends with a shop cloth prior to inspection.

1. Inspect the tie rod sleeve for straightness. Replace the tie rod sleeve if it is bent.
2. Inspect the ball joint boot for tears and the entry of moisture or dirt into the joint.
3. Grasp the ball joint (**Figure 30**) and swivel it in all directions, as well as vertically. Check for roughness, dryness and play. Replace the tie rod end if any wear is detected.

Tie Rod Ends Disassembly and Assembly

NOTE
The outer tie rod end and locknut have left-hand threads. The inner tie rod end and locknut have right-hand threads. Note which direction each set of parts must be turned when loosening and tightening the parts.

1. Measure and note the distance from the center of the tie rod stud to the locknut (**Figure 31**). This will provide a starting point for installation of the tie rod end.
2. Hold the tie rod sleeve with a wrench placed on the flats (A, **Figure 32**) of the sleeve.
3. Loosen the locknut (B, **Figure 32**) and remove the tie rod end (C).
4. Clean the tie rod end threads.
5. Thread the correct tie rod end into the tie rod sleeve.
6. Repeat the procedure for the remaining tie rod end.
7. Adjust the tie rod ends as follows:
   a. Turn the tie rod end into the sleeve until it is the same distance from the locknut as noted in Step 1. The distance should be same at both ends.
   b. Finger-tighten the locknuts to hold the positions. Tighten the tie rod end locknuts to 18 N•m (13 ft.-lb.) after the tie rods have been installed and the toe-in adjustment has been made.

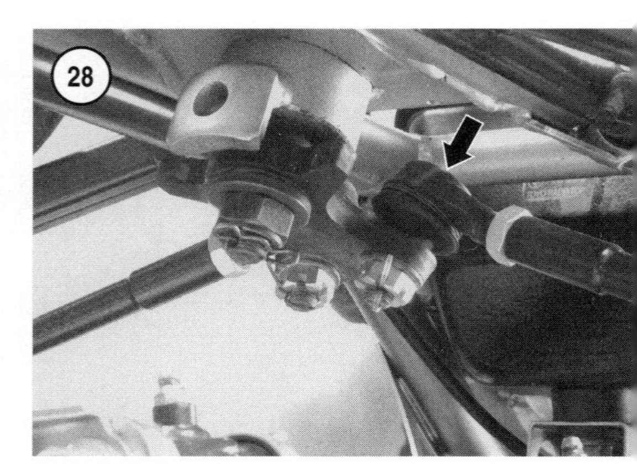

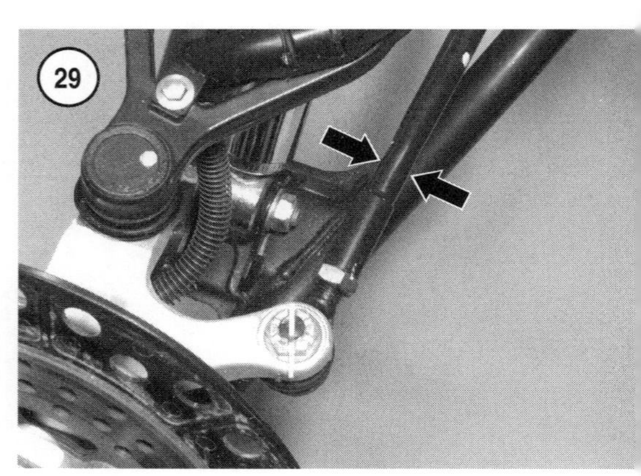

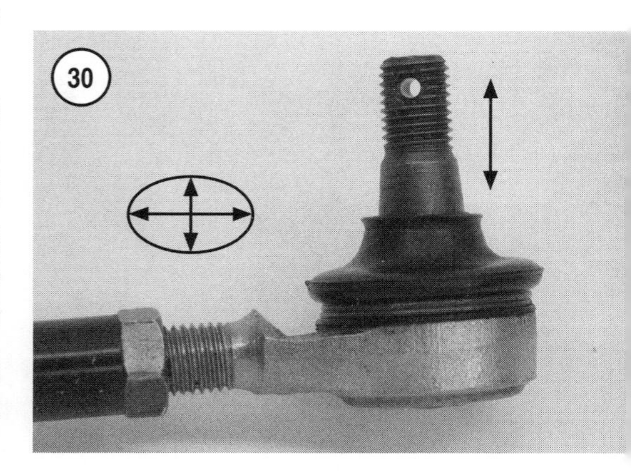

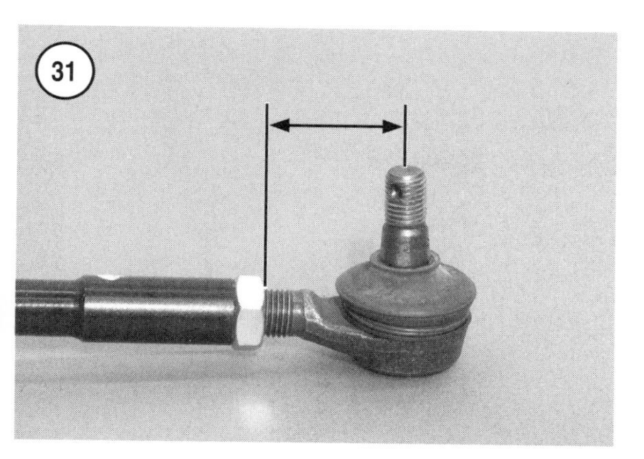

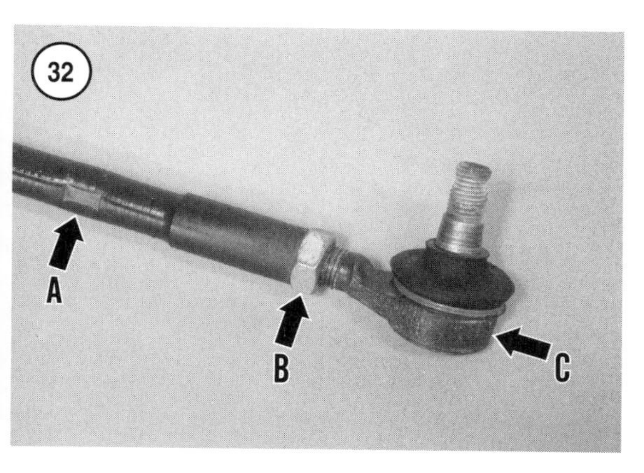

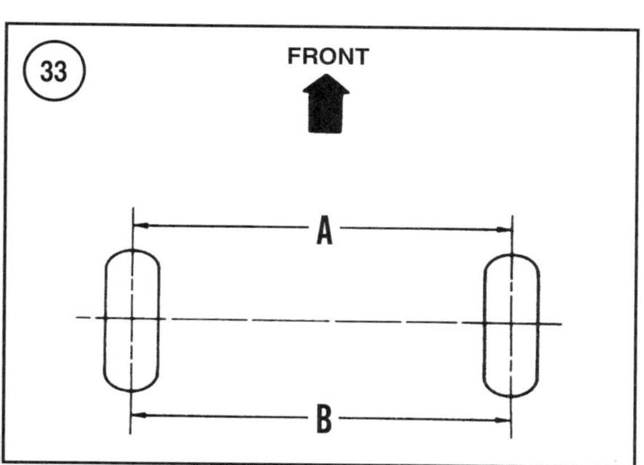

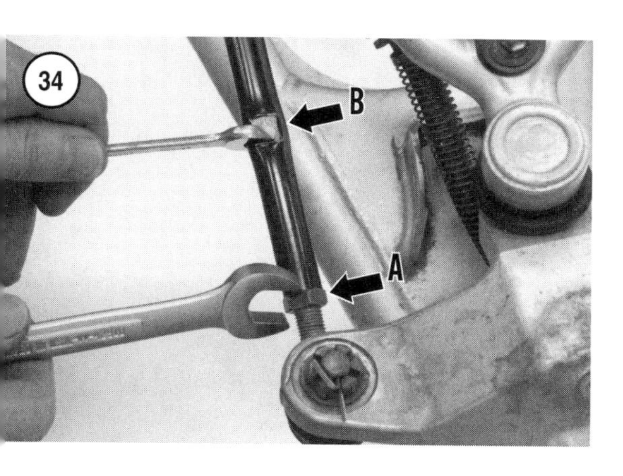

c. Check toe-in adjustment as described in this section.

Toe-in Adjustment

In order to maintain stable steering and minimize tire wear, the front wheels must be set for toe-in. When correctly set, the front of the tires will point in slightly, while the rear of the tires will point out. To check toe-in, measure the distance between the tires at the front and rear (**Figure 33**). If toe-in is incorrect, tie rod length is adjusted to bring the measurement to within specifications.

Proper toe-in adjustment cannot be achieved if the tie rods, wheel bearings or ball joints are worn. Replace worn parts before adjusting toe-in.

1. Inflate all tires to the recommended pressure listed in **Table 1**.
2. Park the ATV on level ground and set the parking brake.
3. Raise and support the ATV. The front wheels must be off the ground.
4. Point the handlebar straight ahead.
5. On the front of both tires, make a chalk mark at the center of the tread. The mark should be level with the centerline of the axle.
6. Measure distance A between the tires as shown in **Figure 33**. Record the measurement.
7. Rotate both wheels evenly until the marks are at the back of both tires, and level with the centerline of the axle.
8. Measure distance B between the tires as shown in **Figure 33**. Record the measurement.
9. Subtract measurement A from measurement B.
   a. If the difference is 2-12 mm (0.08-0.47 in.), toe-in is correct.
   b. If toe-in is not correct, adjust the alignment.
10. To change toe-in setting, adjust both tie rods equally as follows:

NOTE
The outer tie rod end and locknut is a left-hand thread. The inner tie rod end and locknut is a right-hand thread. Note which direction each set of parts must be turned when loosening and tightening the parts.

   a. Loosen both tie rod end locknuts (A, **Figure 34**) on each tie rod.

NOTE
If the tie rods are not adjusted identically, handlebar alignment will not be centered with the wheels.

   b. Equally turn each tie rod end with a wrench fitted to the flats (B, **Figure 34**) on the tie rod sleeve until the toe-in measurement is within the specification listed in **Table 1**.

c. Recheck the measurements.
d. Tighten the locknuts to 18 N•m (13 ft.-lb.) when toe-in is correct.
e. Turn the handlebar from side to side and check that all ball joints pivot properly.
f. Test ride the ATV slowly to ensure that all adjustments are correct.

STEERING KNUCKLE

Removal and Installation

1. Remove the front hub as described in this chapter.
2. Remove the inner brake disc guard (**Figure 35**).
3. Remove the outer tie rod end (**Figure 25**) as described in this chapter.
4. Remove the cotter pins and nuts (**Figure 36**) from the ball joint studs.
5. Remove the ball joints from the steering knuckle. Use one of the following methods:
   a. A ball joint remover (**Figure 27**), or similar tool, can be used to separate the parts (**Figure 37**). If the ball joint will be reused, there is a risk of tearing the rubber boot when using this tool.
   b. If a ball joint remover is not available, support the steering knuckle and thread a hex nut onto the stud. Use a heat gun to heat the area around the joint. Then, drive the ball joint from the steering knuckle. If the ball joint will be reused, avoid damaging the threads on the stud.
6. Inspect the steering knuckle as described in this section.
7. Reverse the removal steps to install the steering knuckle while noting the following:
   a. Tighten both ball joint nuts to 25 N•m (18.5 ft.-lb.).
   b. Install new cotter pins.

Inspection

1. Clean and dry the steering knuckle (**Figure 38**).
2. Inspect the following areas for cracks and other damage. If damage is detected, replace the steering knuckle.
   a. Cotter pin hole (A, **Figure 38**).
   b. Axle threads (B, **Figure 38**).
   c. Bearing surfaces (C, **Figure 38**).
   d. Bores (D, **Figure 38**).

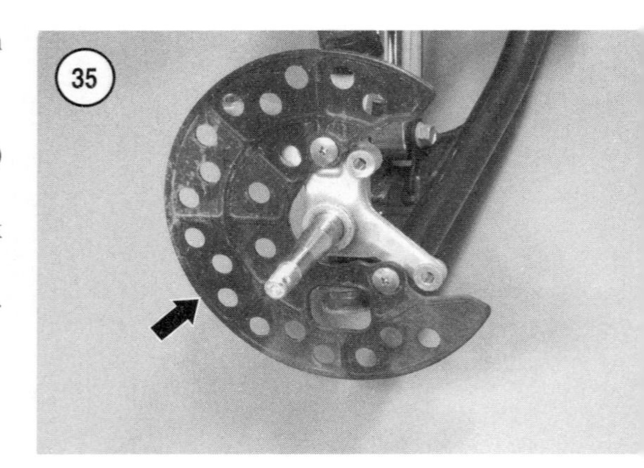

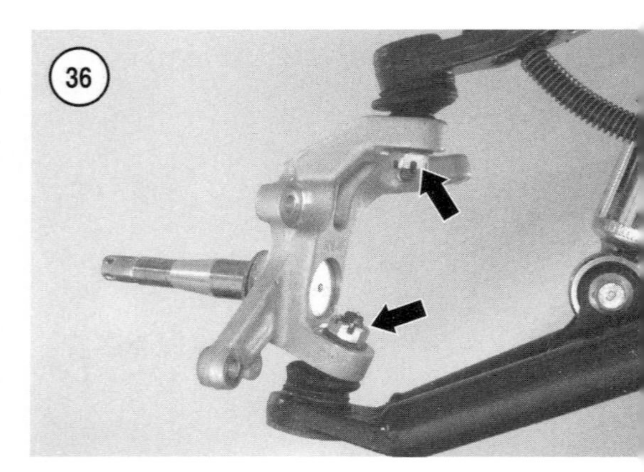

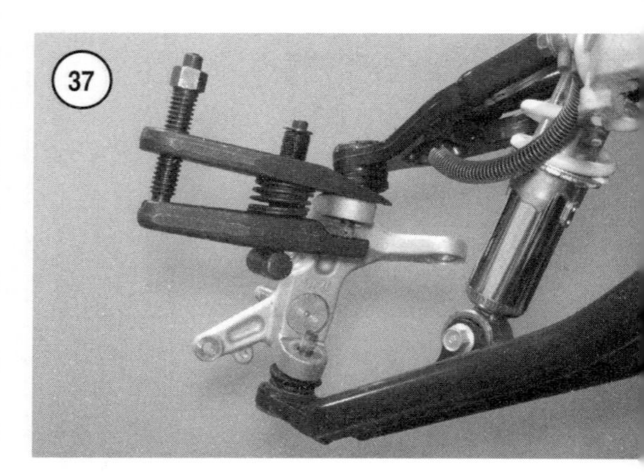

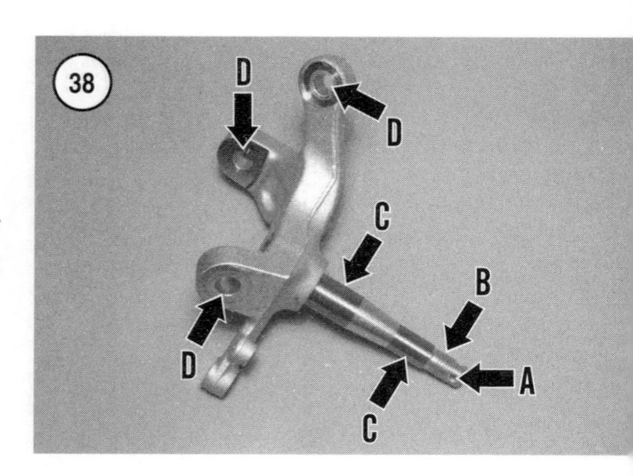

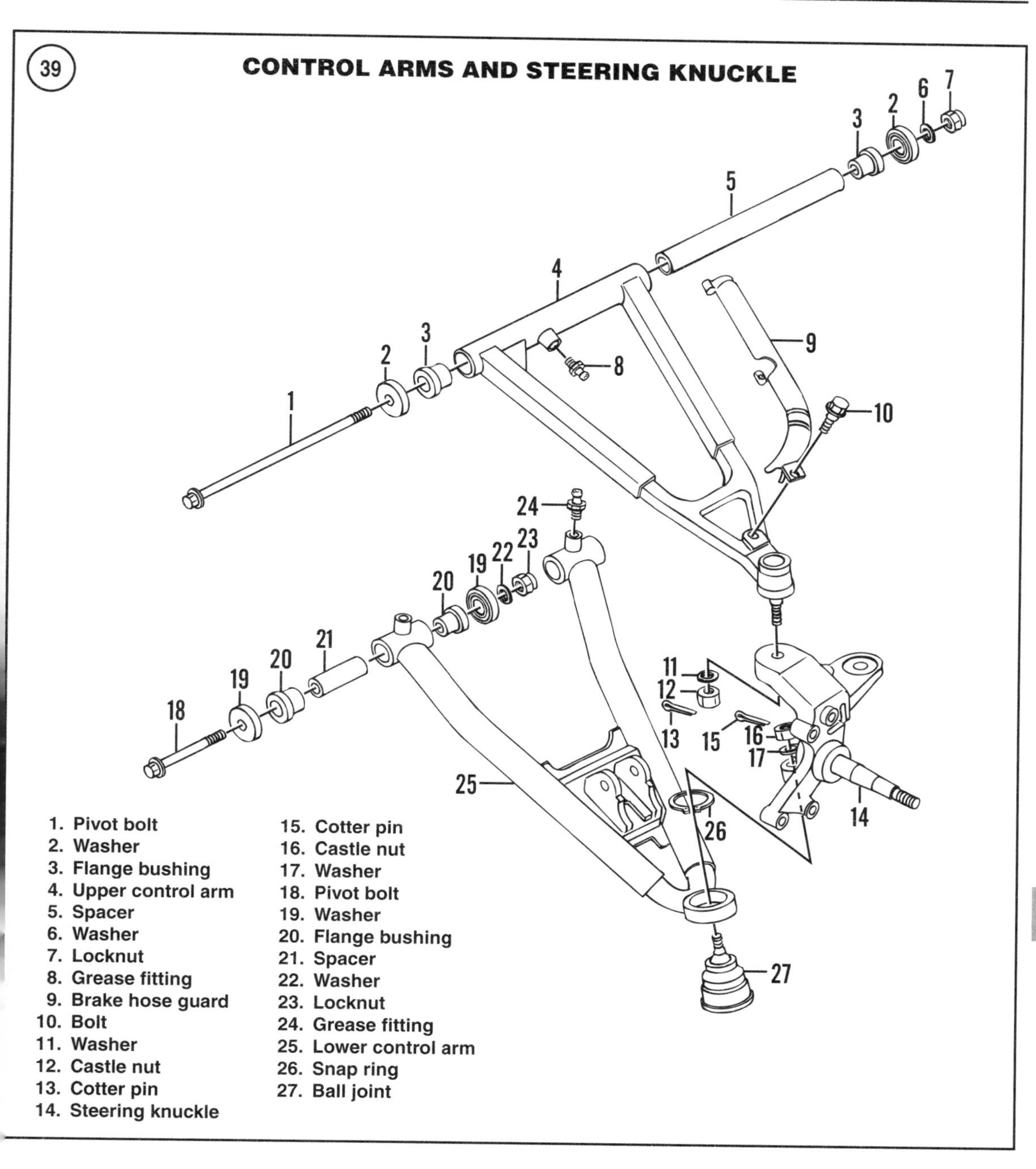

CONTROL ARMS

Removal and Installation

Refer to **Figure 39**.

The following procedure describes the complete removal of the control arms for reconditioning or replacement.

1. Remove the front bumper to allow control arm bolt removal.
2. Remove the front brake caliper as described in Chapter Fourteen.
3. Remove the lower mounting bolt (**Figure 40**) from the shock absorber. If increased work space is desired, remove the entire shock absorber as described in this chapter.
4. Remove the steering knuckle as described in this chapter.
5. Remove the brake hose guard (**Figure 41**) on the upper control arm.
6. Before removing the control arms, grasp each arm and leverage it side to side. If play is noticeable, check the bushings for wear.
7. Remove the pivot bolt (A, **Figure 42**) from the upper control arm, and then remove the control arm

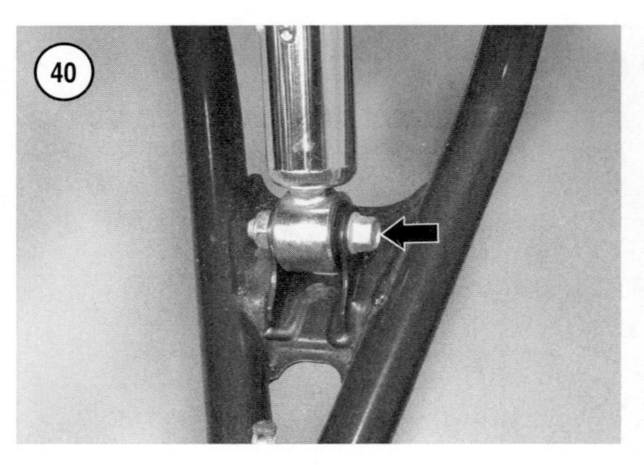

assembly (B). If both upper control arms are removed, identify the arms so they can be installed in their original positions.

8. Remove the pivot bolts (A, **Figure 43**) from the lower control arm, and then remove the control arm assembly (B). If both lower control arms are removed, identify the arms so they can be installed in their original positions.

9. Inspect the control arms as described in this section.

10. Reverse the removal steps to install the control arms. Note the following:

   a. If control arms on both sides have been removed, verify that they are being installed on the correct side of the ATV.
   b. Install the control arm pivot bolts so the heads face toward the front.
   c. Tighten the lower control arm pivot bolts to 55 N•m (40 ft.-lb.).
   d. Tighten the upper control arm pivot bolt to 38 N•m (28 ft.-lb.).
   e. Tighten the ball joint nuts to 25 N•m (18.5 ft.-lb.).
   f. Tighten the shock absorber retaining bolts to 48 N•m (35 ft.-lb.).

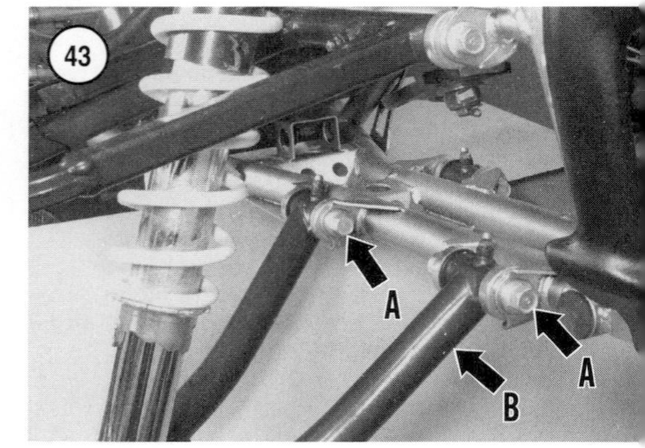

Inspection

NOTE

Unless the flange bushings are obviously damaged, do not remove them from the control arms. Removal may damage the synthetic bushing material.

1. Remove the caps (A, **Figure 44**) and pivot spacer (B) from the control arm. Keep all parts with their respective control arm.

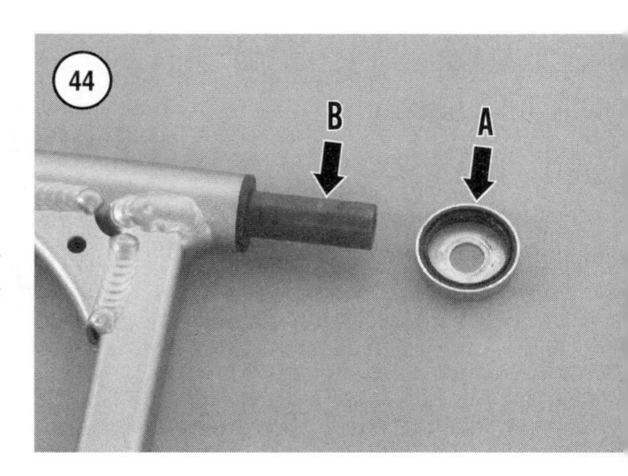

NOTE

The ball joints are packed with grease and sealed. Do not immerse the ball

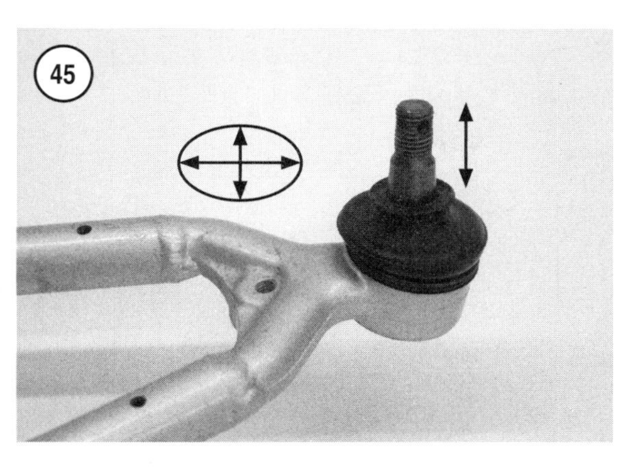

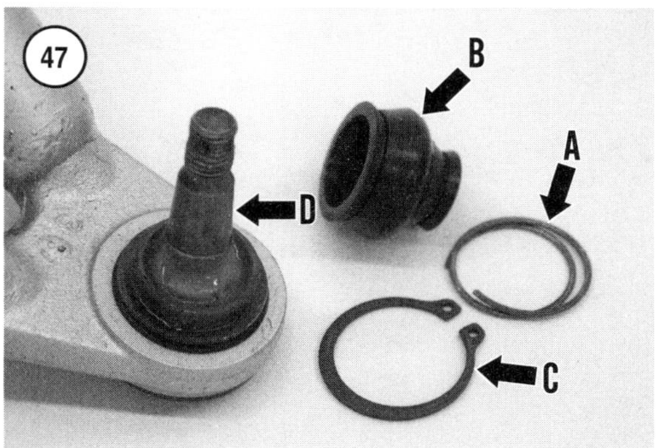

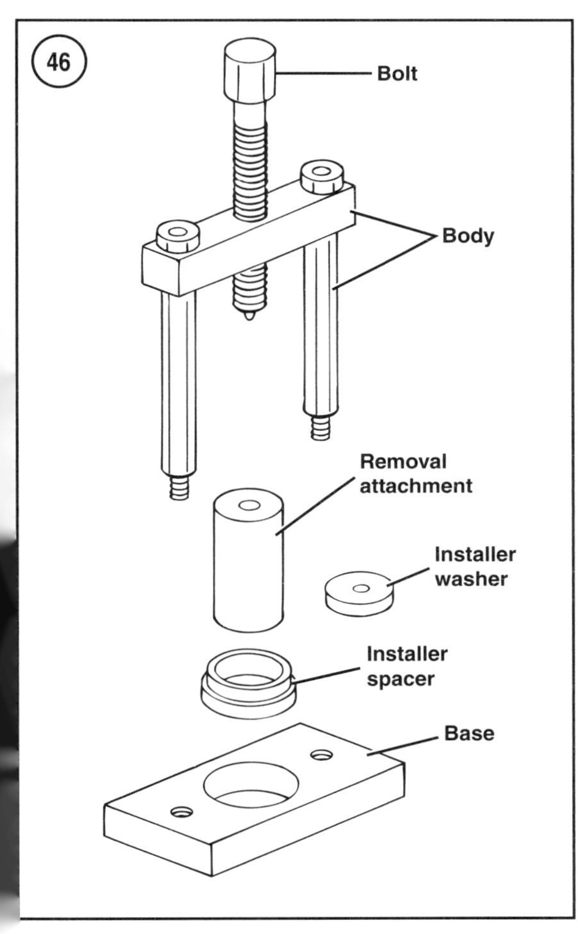

joints in solvent or any other liquid that could penetrate the boots. Wipe the ball joints clean with a shop cloth prior to inspection.

2. Clean the control arm parts.
3. Inspect all welded joints on the control arm. Check for fractures, bending or other damage. If damage is detected, replace the control arm.
4. Inspect the ball joint boots for tears and the entry of moisture or dirt into the joint.

NOTE
The upper ball joint is not replaceable. If lower ball joint replacement is required, refer to the procedure in this section.

5. Grasp each ball joint (**Figure 45**) and swivel it in all directions, as well as vertically. Check for roughness, dryness and play.
6. Inspect the control arm pivot assemblies as follows:
   a. Insert each pivot spacer (B, **Figure 44**) into its bushing and check for play. If necessary, remove a damaged bushing by carefully prying at the edge of the bushing. When the bushing is unseated, twist it from the bore. Install a new bushing by lightly tapping it into place with a soft mallet.
   b. Check the fit of the bolt in the spacer. If play is evident, replace the worn parts.
   c. Check the fit of each cap (A, **Figure 44**) on the control arm. The cap should fit snugly to prevent the entry of moisture and dirt into the bushing.

Lower Control Arm Ball Joint Replacement

Removal of the ball joint requires a ball joint removal/installation tool set (Yamaha part No. YM-01474/90890-01474 and part No. YM-01480/90890-01480 [**Figure 46**]), or an equivalent.

1. Remove the clip (A, **Figure 47**), boot (B) and snap ring (C) from the ball joint (D).
2. Drive out the ball joint by installing the tool as shown in **Figure 48**.
3. Center the bolt on the ball joint stud.
4. Center the base so the ball joint can pass through the hole in the base.
5. Turn the bolt and apply pressure to the ball joint, driving it from the control arm.
6. Force in the new ball joint by installing the tool as shown in **Figure 49**.

12

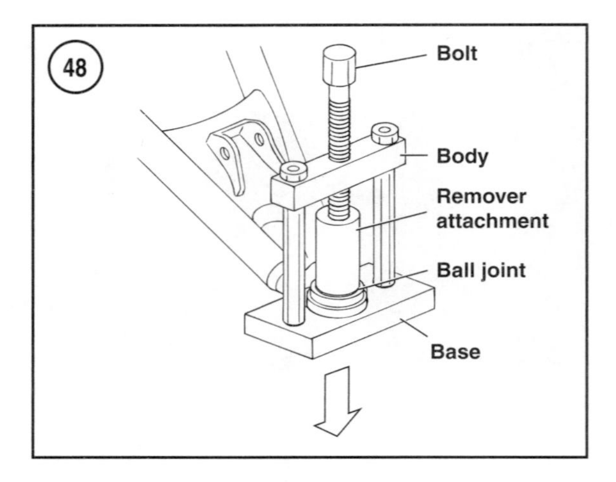

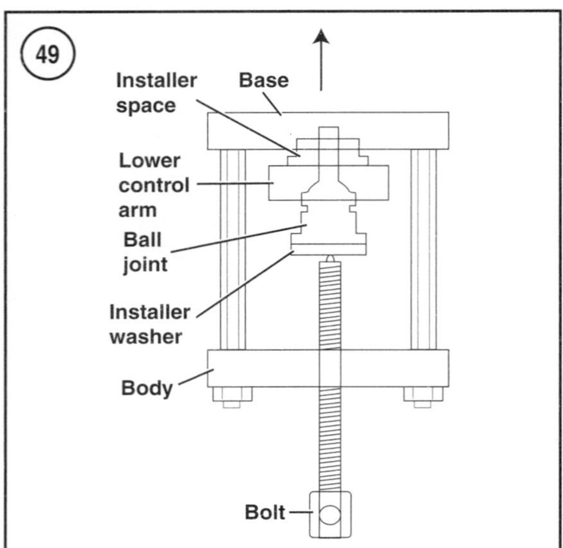

7. Check that all parts are aligned and the ball joint can pass into the control arm.
8. Turn the bolt and apply pressure to the ball joint, driving it into the control arm.
9. Lubricate the ball joint and boot interior with waterproof grease. Then, install the snap ring, boot and clip.

STEERING SHAFT

Removal and Installation

Refer to **Figure 24**.

1. Remove the front fender (Chapter Fifteen) and fuel tank (Chapter Eight).
2. Remove the handlebar as described in this chapter. Reposition and secure the handlebar out of the way. Avoid kinking the cables and brake hose. Keep the brake fluid reservoir upright.
3. Remove the pin, nut (**Figure 50**) and washer from the end of the steering shaft. If the pitman arm must also be removed, remove the tie rod ends as described in this chapter.
4. Bend the lockplate tabs away from the bolt heads. Then, remove the two bolts from the steering shaft holders (**Figure 51**).
5. Lift and remove the steering shaft from the lower bearing (**Figure 52**).
6. Inspect the steering shaft assembly as described in this section.
7. Reverse the removal steps to install the steering shaft while noting the following:
   a. Apply waterproof grease to the shaft splines, seals, bearing and steering shaft holder.
   b. When installing the steering shaft splines into the pitman arm splines, engage the master spline on the pitman arm (**Figure 53**) with the master spline on the shaft end (**Figure 54**).
   c. Tighten the steering shaft nut to 180 N•m (133 ft.-lb.).

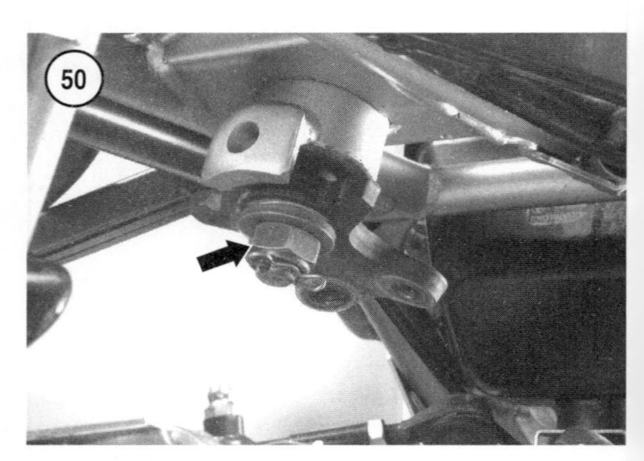

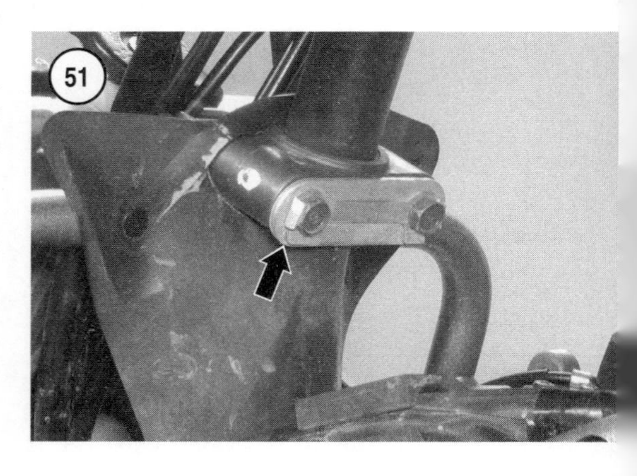

   d. Install a new lockplate onto the steering shaft holder.
   e. Tighten the steering shaft holder bolts to 23 N•m (17 ft.-lb.). Bend the lockplate tabs against the bolt heads.
   f. Check toe-in as described in this chapter.

52

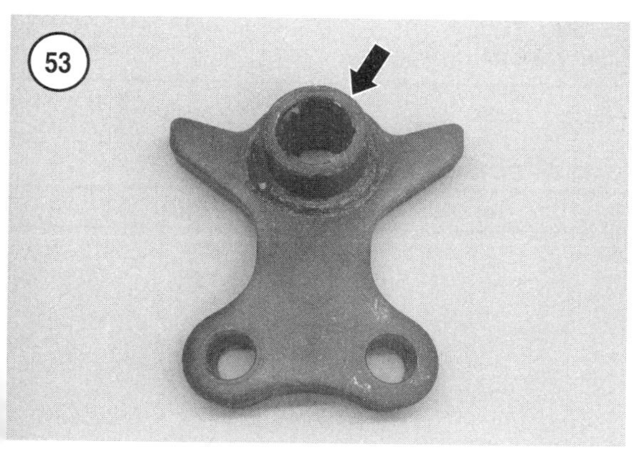
53

54

Inspection

1. Wipe the steering shaft clean.
2. Inspect the steering shaft (**Figure 55**) for the following:
   a. Distortion or damage.
   b. Enlarged tie rod holes in the pitman arm, if removed.
   c. Cracked cotter pin hole.
   d. Damaged threads.
3. Inspect the steering shaft holders and seals for wear or damage.

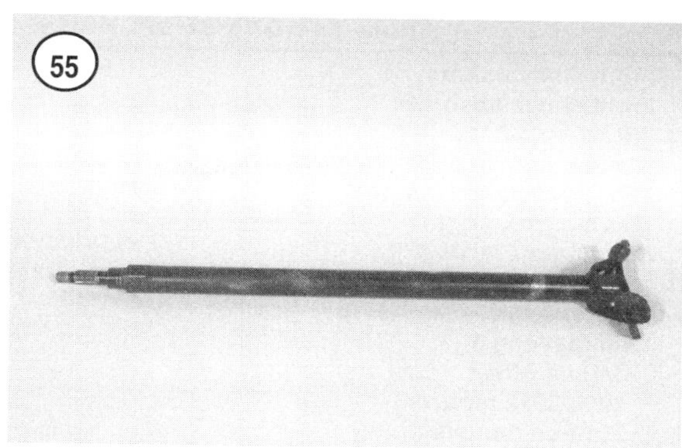
55

56

4. Inspect the pitman arm (**Figure 53**) for wear or damage.
5. Inspect the bearing by turning the inner race. The bearing should turn smoothly and have minimal, if any play.
6. If necessary, replace the bearing and seals as described in this section.

Steering Shaft Bearing and Seals Replacement

Refer to **Figure 24**.

1. Pry the upper and lower seals out of the bearing holder.
2. Remove the bearing retainer from the bearing holder in the frame using a 30-mm hex tool (K&L part No. 35-8576 [**Figure 56**]), or an equivalent.
3. Drive the bearing out the top of the holder.
4. Clean the retainer and the bearing holder bore.
5. Apply waterproof grease to the new bearing and seals.
6. Insert the bearing into the bearing holder. Install the bearing so the manufacturer's marks face up.
7. Install and tighten the bearing retainer to 65 N•m (48 ft.-lb.).
8. Place the seals squarely over the bores in the bearing holder, and seat the seals into the bore. When driving the seals, use a driver or socket that fits against the outer edge of the seals.

Table 1 FRONT SUSPENSION AND STEERING SPECIFICATIONS

Front suspension type	Double wishbone
Front shock absorber	
Type	Oil or gas/oil dampened
Travel	115 mm (4.53 in.)
Spring installed length	260.5 mm (10.26 in.)
Spring free length	269 mm (10.59 in.)
Steering	
Camber angle	–1.0°
Caster angle	5°
Kingpin angle	14.8°
Kingpin offset	
2006-2012 models	2.8 mm (0.11 in.)
2013-on models	5.2 mm (0.20 in.)
Toe-in	2-12 mm (0.08-0.47 in.)
Trail length	21 mm (0.83 in.)
Tire inflation pressure (front and rear)	
Maximum	27.5 kPa 4.0 psi
Minimum	24.5 kPa 3.6 psi

Table 2 TIGHTENING TORQUE SPECIFICATIONS

Item	N•m	in.-lb.	ft.-lb.
Axle nut	70	–	52
Ball joint nuts	25	–	18
Handlebar holder bolts	23	–	17
Lower control arm bolts	55	–	40
Shock absorber retaining bolts	48	–	35
Steering shaft bearing retainer	65	–	48
Steering shaft holder nuts	23	–	17
Steering shaft nut	180	–	132
Tie rod end locknut	18	–	13
Tie rod end ball joint nut	25	–	18.5
Upper control arm bolt			
2006-2012 models	38	–	28
2013-on models	40	–	29

CHAPTER THIRTEEN

REAR AXLE AND SUSPENSION

This chapter contains repair and replacement procedures for the rear axle and suspension assemblies.

Rear suspension specifications are listed in **Table 1** and **Table 2**, located at the end of this chapter.

Refer to Chapter Eleven for wheel, tire and drive chain service information.

WARNING
Self-locking nuts are used to retain several suspension components. Replace any nut that does not resist turning during installation.

WHEEL HUB

Removal/Installation

1. Remove the rear wheels as described in Chapter Eleven.
2. Remove the cotter pin and nut from the axle (**Figure 1**).

NOTE
*If the hub is stuck to the splines, use penetrating oil and a hub puller (**Figure 3**) to slide the hub off the axle. Do not strike the hub.*

3. Pull the wheel hub (**Figure 2**) from the axle splines. If the other hub will be removed, mark the hubs so they can be reinstalled in the same position on the axle.
4. Inspect the hub for cracks, damaged splines and other damage. Replace broken studs.
5. Reverse the removal procedure to install the hub while noting the following:
   a. Apply grease to the hub splines and to the threads and seating surface before tightening the nut.
   b. Tighten the wheel hub nut to 200 N•m (148 ft.-lb.). After tightening the nut, continue turning it until the cotter pin hole is aligned. Do not loosen the nut to align the cotter pin hole.
   c. Install a new cotter pin.

REAR AXLE

Removal

This section describes the removal, inspection and installation of the rear axle. The rear brake caliper and driven sprocket can be removed with the axle installed. Before beginning removal, read the removal and installation procedures and have the required special tools on hand. Refer to **Figure 4**.

1. Park the ATV on level ground and block the front wheels.
2. Obtain maximum chain slack using the chain adjustment procedure in Chapter Three.
3. Remove both setscrews (A, **Figure 5**) in the axle nut.
4. Push down on the brake pedal to lock the rear brake.

NOTE
*A suitable axle nut removal tool may be fabricated by grinding the opening of a 1 3/4-inch crows-foot wrench (**Figure 6**) to fit the 46-mm axle nut.*

5. Using an axle nut wrench (Yamaha part No. YM-37134/90890-01498, or an equivalent), loosen the axle nut (B, **Figure 5**).
6. If sprocket or brake disc replacement is necessary, loosen the nuts or bolts while holding down the brake pedal.
7. Remove the rear wheel hubs as described in this chapter.
8. Remove the rear brake caliper as described in Chapter Fourteen.
9. Remove the axle nut (A, **Figure 7**) and conical washer (B).

NOTE
*It is not necessary to remove the brake disc prior to removing the hub as shown in **Figure 7**.*

10. Remove the brake disc hub (C, **Figure 7**).
11. Before removing the axle, check the condition of the axle bearings. Grasp the end of the axle and move it in all directions. If excessive play is detected, replace the axle bearings as described in this chapter.
12. Reinstall the right side wheel hub (A, **Figure 8**).

WARNING
Wear safety glasses when driving out the axle.

CAUTION
*Do not use excessive force against the hub when driving out the axle. If the axle is frozen in the bearings or spacer due to rust, refer to **Frozen Axle Removal** in this section.*

13. Place a piece of pipe (B, **Figure 8**) against the wheel hub. Do not allow the pipe to contact the axle threads. Tap against the pipe to force out the axle from the left side of the swing arm.

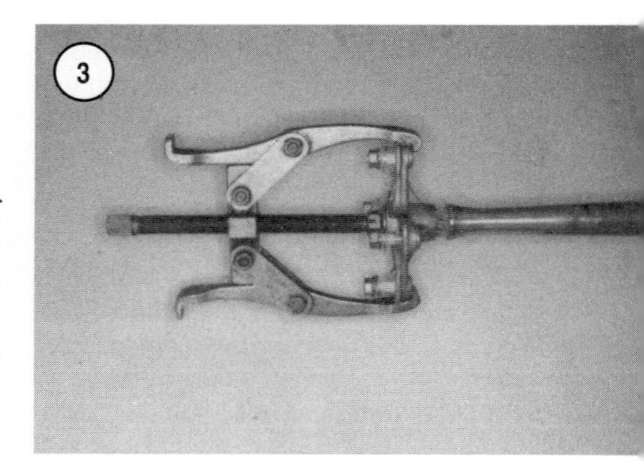

14. If necessary, remove the circlip (A, **Figure 9**) and then remove the sprocket hub (B) from the rear axle.
15. Inspect the rear axle as described in this section.
16. Inspect the seals and bearings as described in *Rear Axle Hub* (this chapter).

Inspection

1. Clean the axle. All splines must be clean for inspection. Prevent any damage to the axle bearing surfaces during the inspection procedure.

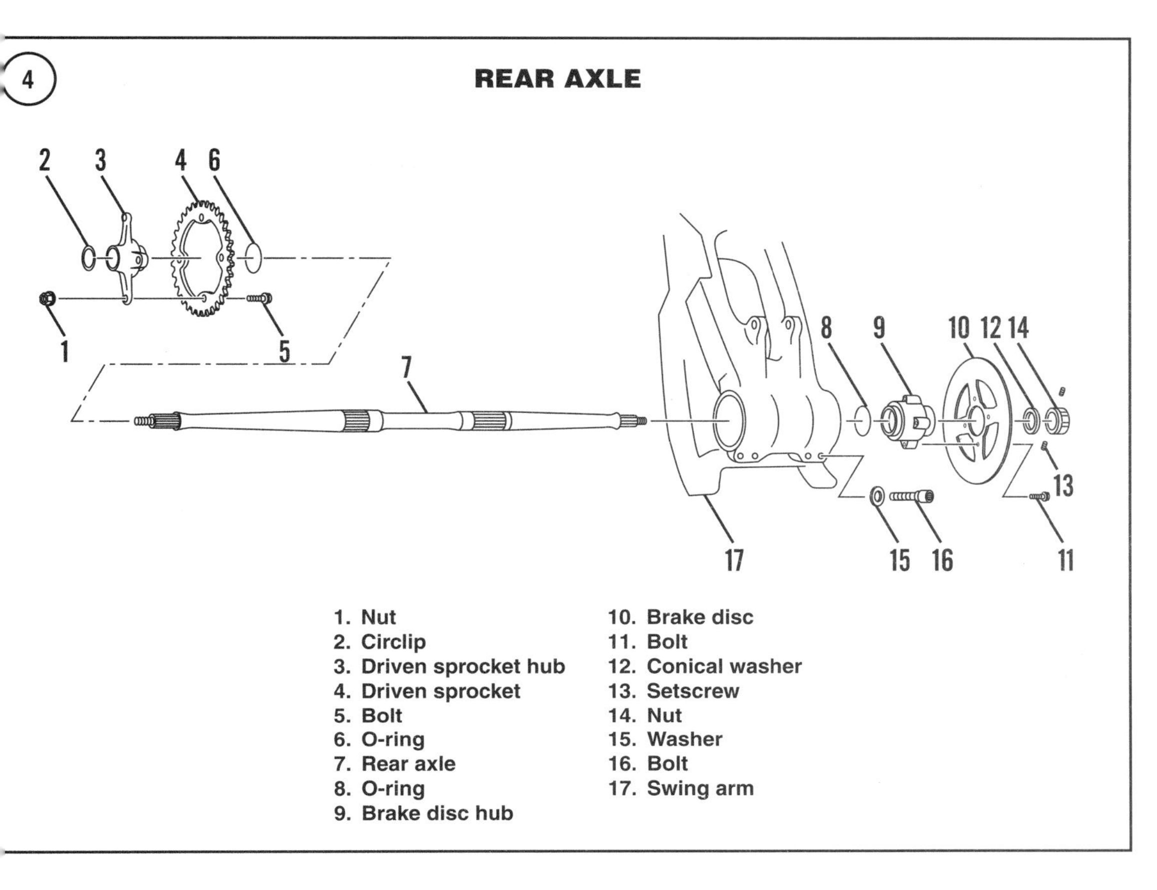
4
REAR AXLE
2
3
4
6
1
5
7
8
9
10
12
14
13
11
17
15
16
1. Nut
2. Circlip
3. Driven sprocket hub
4. Driven sprocket
5. Bolt
6. O-ring
7. Rear axle
8. O-ring
9. Brake disc hub
10. Brake disc
11. Bolt
12. Conical washer
13. Setscrew
14. Nut
15. Washer
16. Bolt
17. Swing arm

5
A
B

7
B
C
A

13

6

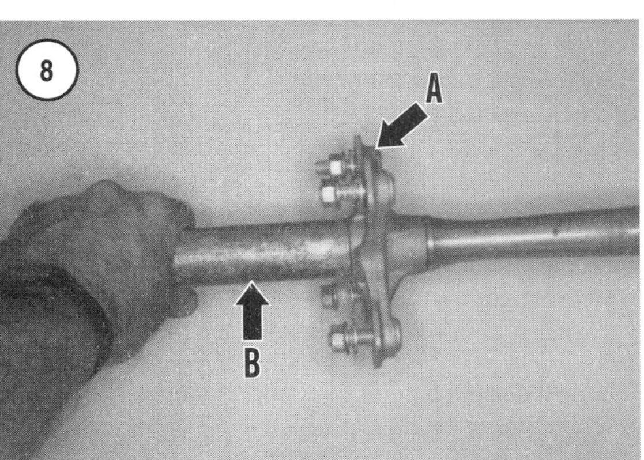
8
A
B

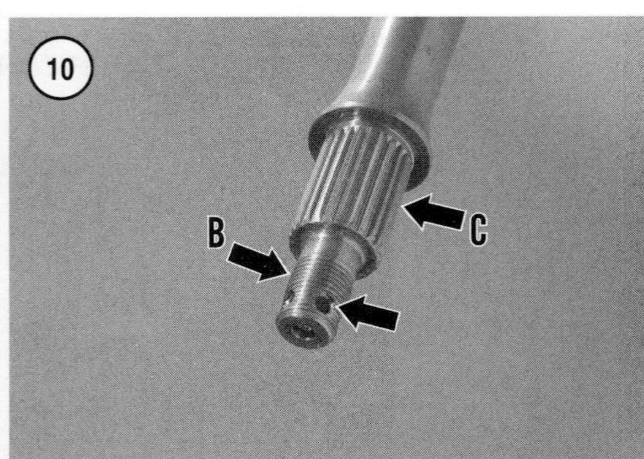

2. At each end of the axle, inspect the following:
   a. Cotter pin holes (A, **Figure 10**). Check for cracks or fractures around the holes. Replace the axle if it is damaged.
   b. Axle nut threads (B, **Figure 10**). Check for uniform and symmetrical threads. Screw the axle nut onto the threads and check for roughness and play. If damage is detected, try restoring the threads with a thread die.
   c. Wheel hub splines (C, **Figure 10**). Check for worn, distorted and broken splines. Inspect the splines in each wheel hub for damage. Fit each hub onto its respective end of the axle and feel for play. If play or wear is detected, replace the parts.
   d. Brake disc hub splines (A, **Figure 11**). Check for worn, distorted and broken splines. Inspect the fit of the brake hub on the splines. Check for looseness between the parts. If play or wear is detected, replace the parts.
   e. Driven sprocket hub splines (B, **Figure 11**). Check for worn, distorted and broken splines. Inspect the fit of the sprocket hub on the splines. Check for looseness between the parts. If play or wear is detected, replace the parts.
3. Inspect the axle where it contacts the bearings (C, **Figure 11**) in the axle hub. Check for scoring, galling and other damage. If damage is evident, inspect the bearings in the axle hub, as described in this chapter. Replace any damaged parts.
4. Inspect the driven sprocket hub and brake disc hub as follows:
   a. Remove the O-rings from the axle.
   b. Check for cracks or fractures at the hub, between the mounting ears and at the bolt holes.
   c. Inspect the condition of the hub splines.

NOTE

When measuring runout, the actual amount of runout is one-half the reading of the dial indicator.

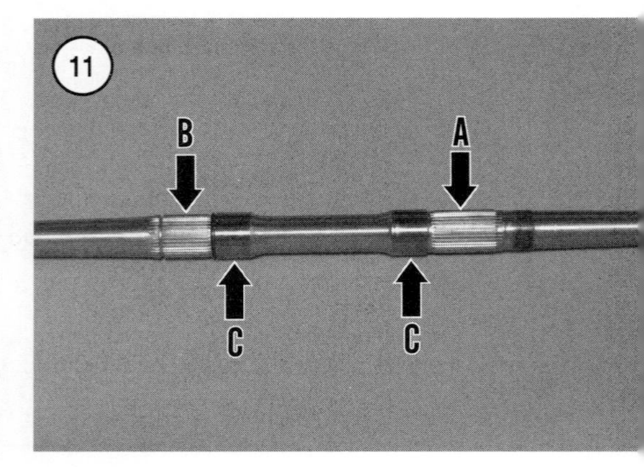

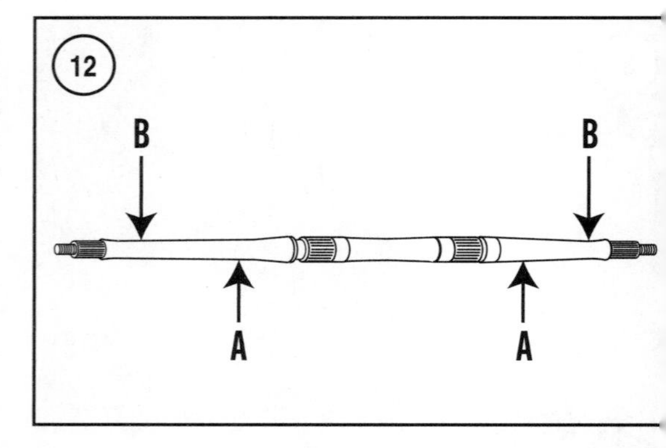

5. Check the axle for straightness using a dial indicato (A, **Figure 12**) and V-blocks (B). Replace the axle runout exceeds the service limit specified in **Table 1**.

Installation

Refer to **Figure 4**.

1. Apply grease to the lips of the seals in both side of the axle bearing holder.
2. Apply grease to the axle splines and axle bearin surfaces.
3. If removed, install a new, lubricated O-rin (**Figure 13**) onto the axle. Then, install the driv sprocket hub (B, **Figure 9**) and the circlip (A).

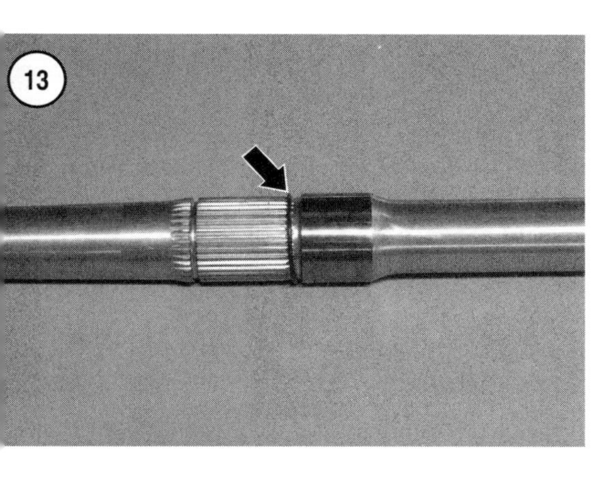

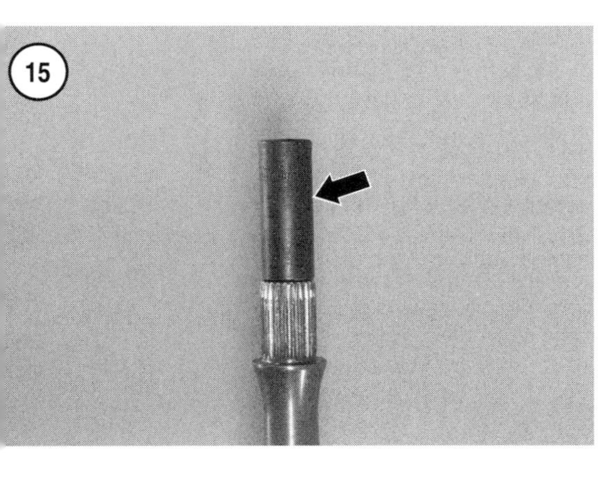

NOTE
Insert the axle through the drive chain in Step 4 while installing the axle.

. Install the axle into the rear axle hub.
. Install a new, lubricated O-ring onto the axle **Figure 14**)
. Install the rear brake hub and disc, if not removed rom the hub.
. Install the conical washer so the concave side is oward the brake disc hub.
. Apply threadlock to the axle nut threads, and install it on the axle.

NOTE
Temporarily install a wheel hub. Hold the wheel hub to prevent axle rotation while tightening the axle nut.

9. Tighten the axle nut (**Figure 6**) to 240 N•m (176 ft.-lb.).
10. Apply threadlock to the setscrew threads. Install the setscrews in the axle nut and tighten to 7 N•m (62 in.-lb.).
11. Install the rear brake caliper as described in Chapter Fourteen.
12. Install the drive chain as described in Chapter Eleven.
13. Install the rear wheel hubs as described in this chapter.
14. Install the rear wheels as described in Chapter Eleven.

Frozen Axle Removal

WARNING
Wear safety glasses when driving against the axle.

The following procedure describes removal of an axle that is frozen in the axle bearings and cannot be removed using the standard removal procedure. This procedure describes axle and axle hub removal as an assembly, rather than separation of the axle from the hub.

1. Perform Steps 1-10 under *Rear Axle Removal* (this section).
2. Perform Steps 2-6 under *Rear Axle Hub Removal* (this chapter).
3. Reinstall the right side wheel hub (A, **Figure 8**).
4. Place a piece of pipe (B, **Figure 8**) against the wheel hub. Do not allow the pipe to contact the axle threads. Tap against the pipe to force out the axle and axle hub from the left side of the swing arm.
5. Secure the axle hub in a vise at the mid-section of the hub. Do not grip the axle hub seating surface.

WARNING
Use an impact socket rather than an ordinary socket in Step 6. An ordinary socket may shatter.

6. Place a suitable impact socket (**Figure 15**) on the right end of the axle. Make sure the impact socket seats against the axle shoulder, but will not damage the axle threads when struck.

NOTE
Applying heat to the left end of the rear axle hub will assist in axle movement.

7. Drive against the axle end sufficiently to expose the circlip next to the driven sprocket hub (**Figure 16**).

NOTE
Sprocket removal is necessary for access to the axle hub end surface.

8. Remove the circlip and sprocket hub.
9. Remove the axle assembly from the vise.

CAUTION
Make sure the rear axle hub is adequately supported to prevent hub damage.

10. Place the axle assembly in a vertical position so the left end of the rear axle hub is supported and the right axle end is up. The axle and left end bearings will be driven out of the rear axle hub.
11. Repeat Step 6.
12. Heat the left end of the rear axle hub around the bearing compartment.

NOTE
Do not apply force that may damage the axle or rear axle hub. If necessary, take the axle assembly to a dealership.

13. Using a suitable hammer, drive the axle (A, **Figure 17**) with the left end bearings (B) and spacer (C) out of the rear axle hub (D).
14. Remove the spacer, and then press the old bearings off the axle.
15. Remove the bearings from the rear axle hub.

CAUTION
Do not mar the bearing contact surfaces on the axle when cleaning corrosion from the axle.

16. Remove corrosion from the bearing surfaces (A, **Figure 18**) and splines (B).
17. Carefully inspect the axle and rear axle hub for damage incurred during axle removal.

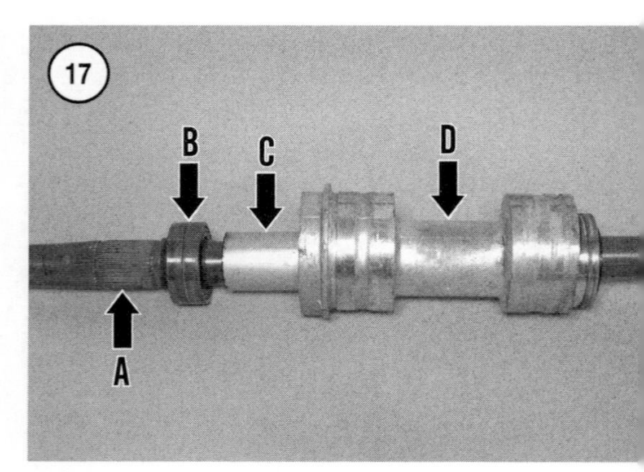

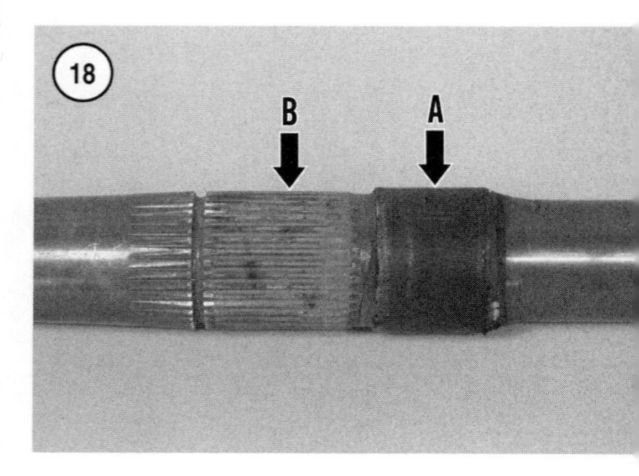

REAR AXLE HUB

Removal/Installation

The swing arm contains the rear axle hub (**Figure 19**). The hub contains the axle bearings and seals.
1. Remove the rear axle as described in this chapter.
2. Remove the snap ring (A, **Figure 20**).
3. Remove the caliper mounting bracket (B, **Figure 20**).
4. Loosen the two pairs of pinch bolts (C, **Figure 20**) at the back end of the swing arm.
5. Remove the brake caliper bracket locating coll (A, **Figure 21**).
6. Remove the O-rings (**Figure 22**) from the hub.
7. Lightly tap the axle hub (B, **Figure 21**) out th left side of the swing arm using a soft mallet.
8. Inspect the axle hub as described in this section.

Disassembly/Inspection

1. Wipe the axle hub and swing arm clean. Do n immerse the axle hub in solvent unless the bearing and seals require replacement.

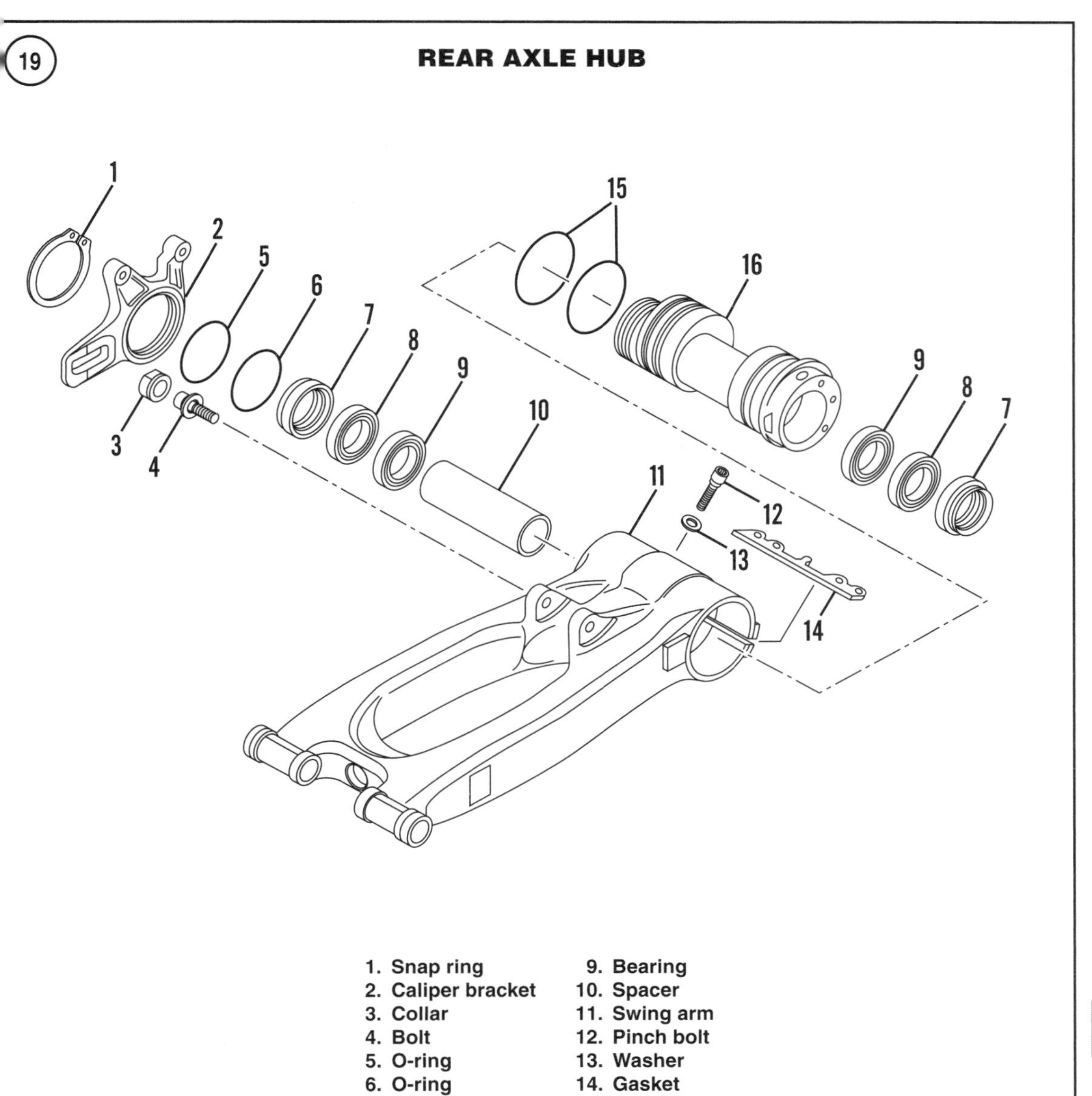

1. Snap ring
2. Caliper bracket
3. Collar
4. Bolt
5. O-ring
6. O-ring
7. Oil seal
8. Bearing
9. Bearing
10. Spacer
11. Swing arm
12. Pinch bolt
13. Washer
14. Gasket
15. O-ring
16. Axle hub

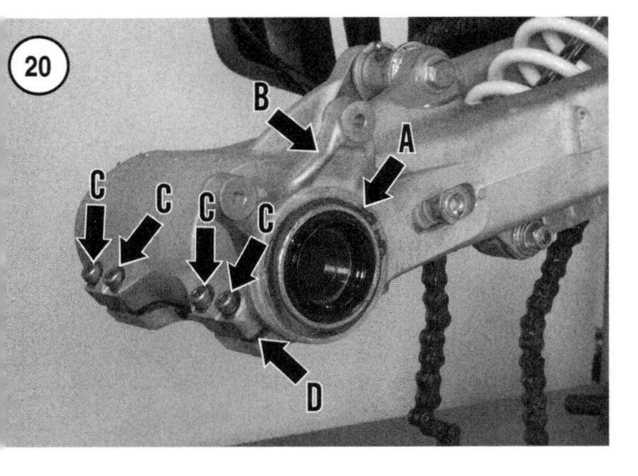

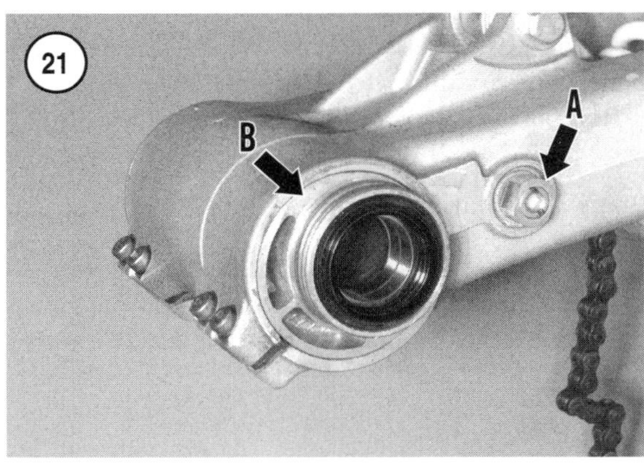

2. Inspect the caliper mounting bracket for damage.
3. Inspect the dust seals (A, **Figure 23**) for tears, distortion or other damage. If rust or moisture is evident on the inner bearing races or bearing spacer, a leak is occurring at the seals. Inspect the bearings and replace the seals as described in this section.
4. Inspect the bearings as follows:
   a. Turn each bearing inner race (B, **Figure 23**). Feel for roughness, noise or binding. The bearings should turn smoothly and quietly.

NOTE
Always replace bearings as a pair.

   b. Check for axial and radial (**Figure 24**) play. Replace the bearings if worn or damaged. Remove and install the bearings as described in this section.
5. After the bearings and seals have been inspected or replaced, prepare the axle hub for installation as follows:
   a. Install new, lubricated O-rings (**Figure 25**) onto the axle hub.
   b. Coat the exterior surface of the axle hub (that fits inside the swing arm) with waterproof grease.

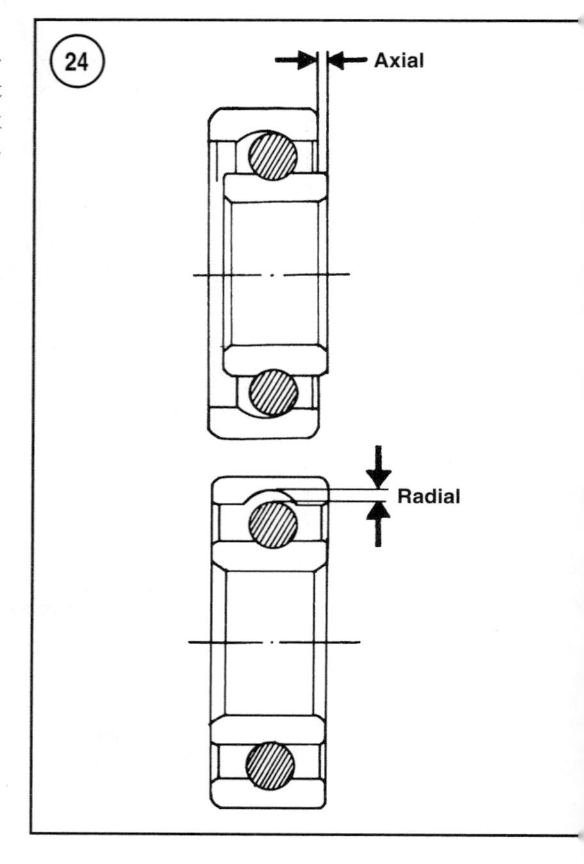

Seal Replacement

Seals are used to prevent the entry of moisture and dirt into the hub and bearings. Always install new seals whenever the axle hub is being reconditioned.

Refer to *Seal Replacement* in Chapter One.

Bearing Replacement

1. Remove the seals as described in this section.
2. Insert a drift into one end of the axle hub and push the spacer between the bearings (**Figure 26**) to one side.
3. Refer to *Bearings* (Chapter One), and then remove and install the bearings. The inner bearing in

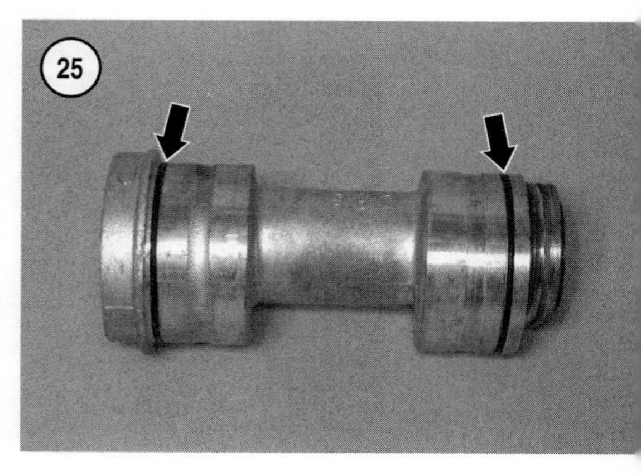

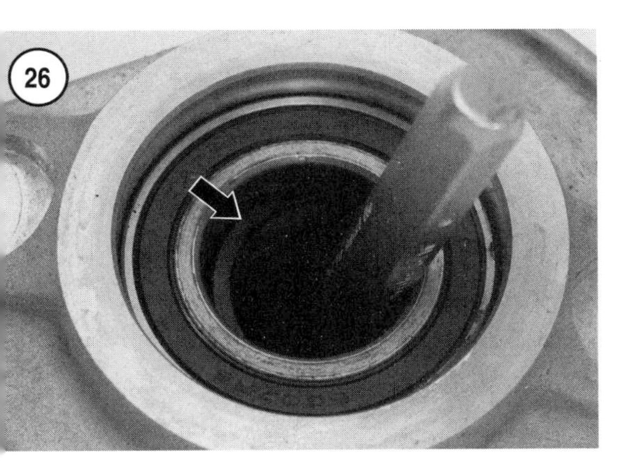

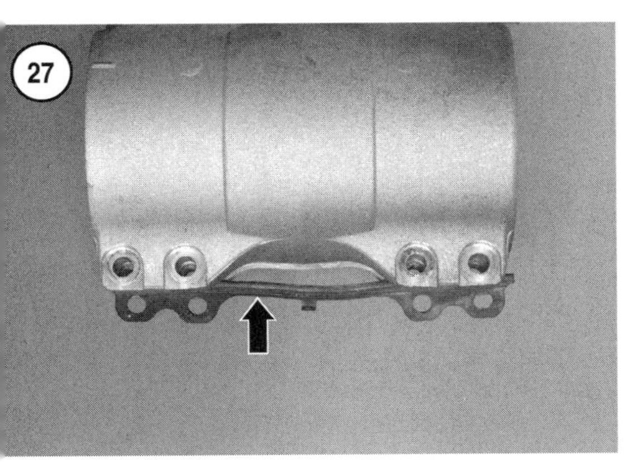

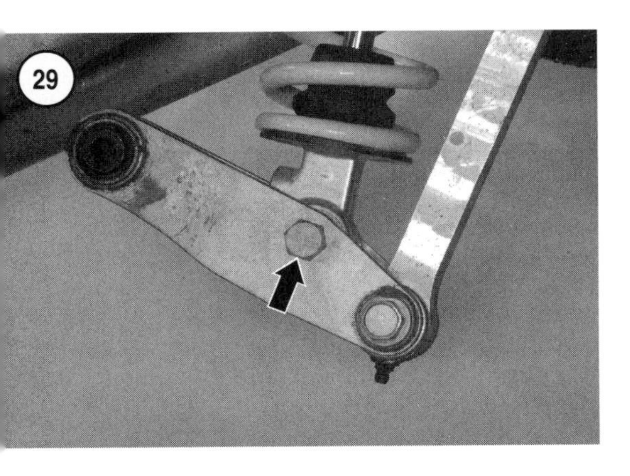

each end is sealed on both sides. Install the outer bearing in each end so the open side is toward the inner bearing.

Installation

1. Install a new gasket (**Figure 27**) and the pinch bolts. Do not tighten the bolts.
2. Install and seat the axle hub (B, **Figure 21**) into the swing arm from the left side. Work slowly to prevent damaging the O-rings on the hub.

NOTE
The inner O-ring has a larger circumference than the outer O-ring.

3. Install new, lubricated O-rings (**Figure 22**). The inner O-ring sits in the crevice between the face of the hub and the hub outer diameter. The outer O-ring sits in the inner groove. The outer groove accepts the snap ring.
4. Install the caliper bracket locating collar (A, **Figure 21**).
5. Apply grease to the inner contact surface of the caliper bracket.

NOTE
Rotate the axle hub as needed to prevent contact between the swing arm and caliper bracket during bracket installation.

6. Fit the caliper bracket onto the axle hub and engage it with the collar.
7. Install a new snap ring (A, **Figure 20**).
8. Tighten the pinch bolts to 21 N•m (15.5 ft.-lb.).
9. Install the rear axle as described in this chapter.
10. Adjust the chain as described in Chapter Three.

SHOCK ABSORBER

The single shock absorber is a spring-loaded, hydraulically-damped unit with an integral oil/nitrogen reservoir. To adjust the shock absorber, refer to Chapter Three.

Removal/Installation

1. Remove the seat as described in Chapter Fifteen.
2. Support the ATV so the rear wheels are off the ground.
3. Place a jack or other support under the swing arm so it cannot fall.
4. Remove the upper relay arm bolt (**Figure 28**).
5. Remove the lower shock absorber mounting bolt (**Figure 29**).

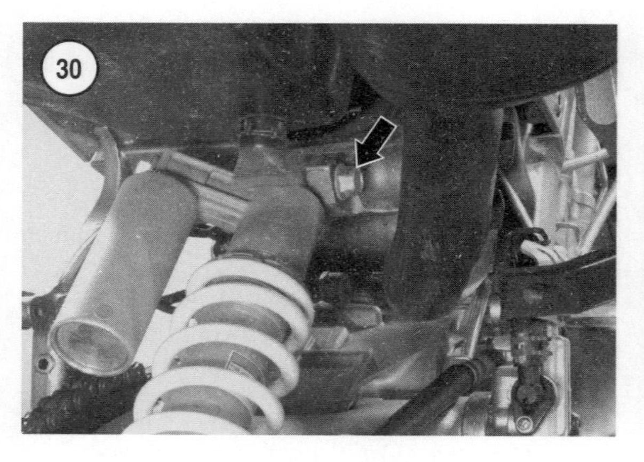

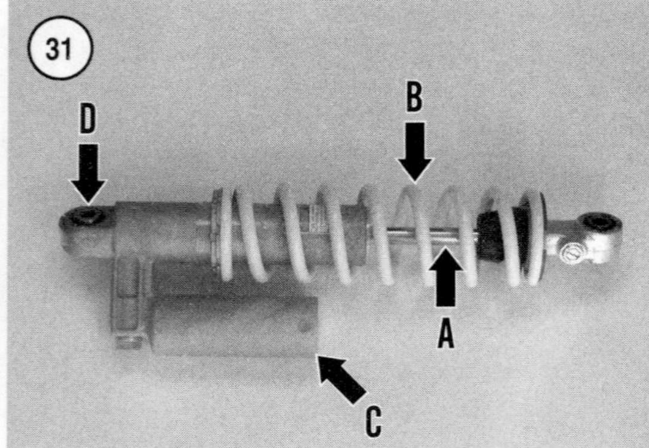

6. Remove the upper mounting bolt from the shock absorber and frame (**Figure 30**).
7. Remove the shock absorber. Service the unit as described in this section.
8. Reverse the removal procedure to install the shock absorber while noting the following:
   a. Lubricate all bearings, seals and pivot bolts with lithium grease.
   b. Install the washers on the upper and lower shock absorber bolts so the flat side of the washer contacts the bolt head or the nut.
   c. Tighten the upper shock absorber bolt to 55 N•m (40.5 ft.-lb.).
   d. Tighten the lower shock absorber bolt to 43 N•m (32 ft.-lb.).
   e. Tighten the upper relay arm bolt to 43 N•m (32 ft.-lb.).

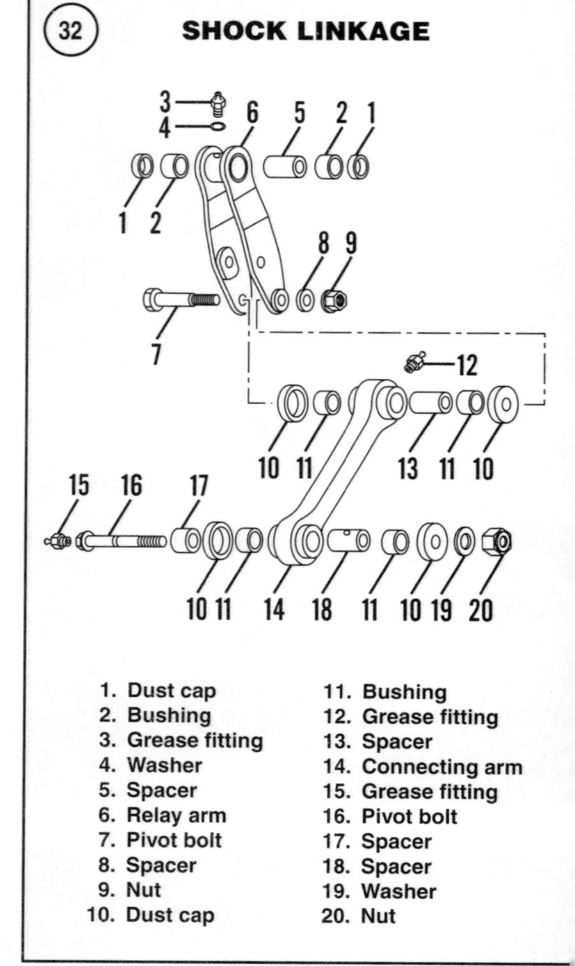

Inspection

Individual parts are not available for the rear shock absorber.

1. Inspect the shock absorber for gas or oil leaks.
2. Check the damper rod (A, **Figure 31**) for bending, rust or other damage.
3. Inspect the spring (B, **Figure 31**) as described in this chapter.
4. Inspect the reservoir (C, **Figure 31**) for leaks or damage.
5. Inspect the bearing, spacer and seals in the upper end (D, **Figure 31**) of the shock absorber as follows:
   a. Check the seals for cracks, wear or other damage.
   b. Check the spacer for cracks, scoring, wear or other damage.
   c. Check the needle bearing for wear, play, flat spots, rust or bluish discoloration (overheating).
   d. Lubricate the spacer with grease and insert it into the bearing. The spacer should turn freely and smoothly with no play.
6. Inspect the lower mounting hole for damage and excessive wear.
7. If the shock is leaking, or if it is time to replace the shock oil, refer all service to a dealership or suspension specialist.

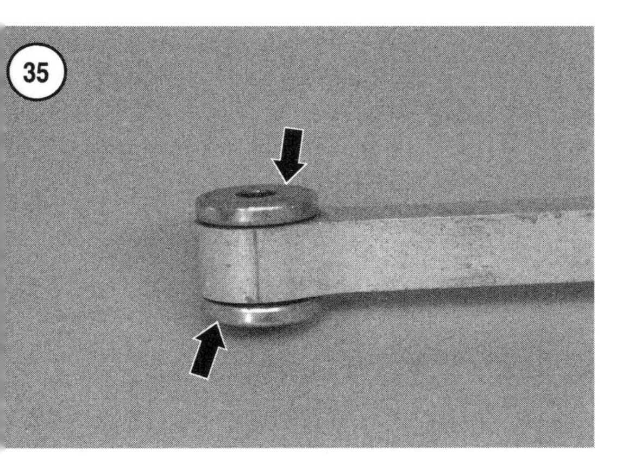

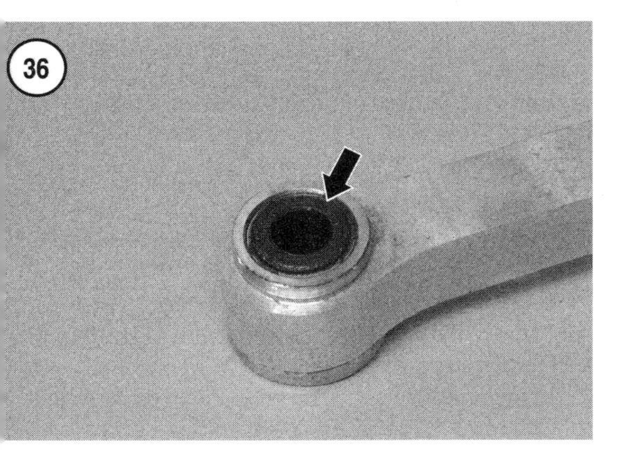

SHOCK LINKAGE

The shock linkage consists of the relay arm, connecting arm, pivot bolts, seals, spacers, bushings and needle bearings. The linkage operates in a harsh environment; follow the service interval recommendations in Chapter Three.

NOTE
Motion Pro part No. 08-0213 may be used to remove and install the bearings in the shock linkage.

Removal/Installation

This procedure details the removal and separation of the connecting arm and relay arm assemblies. Refer to **Figure 32**.

NOTE
The connecting arm and relay arm may be removed for service without removing the swing arm.

1. Clean the shock linkage components to prevent dirt from contaminating the bearings during removal.
2. Remove the shock absorber as described in this chapter.

CAUTION
Do not damage the grease fitting during removal of the connecting arm pivot bolt.

3. Remove the pivot bolt (**Figure 33**) from the connecting arm. Then, remove the connecting arm and relay arm (**Figure 34**).
4. Remove the pivot bolt and separate the relay arm and connecting arm.
5. Inspect and service the connecting arm and relay arm as described in this section.
6. Reverse the removal steps to install the parts. Note the following:
   a. Lubricate all bushings, seals and spacers with lithium grease.
   b. Insert all bolts from the right side of the ATV.
   c. Tighten the lower connecting arm-to-relay arm bolt to 43 N•m (32 ft.-lb.).
   d. Tighten the upper connecting arm-to-frame bolt to 55 N•m (40.5 ft.-lb.).

Inspection/Repair

1. Remove the dust caps (**Figure 35**) from the connecting arm.
2. Remove the spacer (**Figure 36**) from the connecting arm.
3. Remove the spacers from the relay arm.

4. Carefully pry the seals (A, **Figure 37**) from the bushing bores.
5. Clean and dry the relay arm, connecting arm, seals, spacers and bushings.
6. Inspect the following:
   a. Inspect the relay arm and connecting arm for cracks or bends. Check the pivot bolt holes for scoring, wear and elongation.
   b. Lay the relay arm on a flat surface and check that both arms are parallel and the pivot bolt passes straight from one bore to the other.
   c. Check the pivot bolts for scoring, wear and other damage.
   d. Check the seals for cracks, wear or other damage.
   e. Check the spacers for cracks, scoring, wear or other damage.
   f. Check the bushings (B, **Figure 37**) for wear, play, flat spots, rust or blue discoloration (overheating). Lubricate the spacers with lithium grease and insert them into their respective bushings. The parts should turn freely and smoothly with no play. If play or roughness exists, replace the bushing as described in this section. Replace the bushings and spacers as a set.
6. Replace bushings in the relay arm or the connecting arm as follows:
   a. Support the part in a press or service tool.
   b. Place a driver against the bushing and force the bushing out of the part.
   c. Clean and inspect the mounting bore.
   d. Lubricate the new bushing with lithium grease.
   e. Refer to **Table 1** for the required depth to insert the bushing(s). The depth is required so the seals can be seated in both sides of the bore.
   f. Place the new bushing squarely into the bore and force it into place.
   g. Measure the bushing depth and force in the bushing(s) as required.
7. Lubricate the bushings, seals and spacers with lithium grease.
8. Install the seals and spacers. Install the seals with the manufacturer's marks facing out.
9. Install the relay arm and connecting arm as described in this section.

SWING ARM

Bearing Inspection

The general condition of the swing arm bearings can be determined with the swing arm mounted on the ATV. Periodically check the bearings for play, roughness or damage. If the swing arm will be removed from the frame, make the check prior to removing the swing arm pivot bolt. If the swing arm

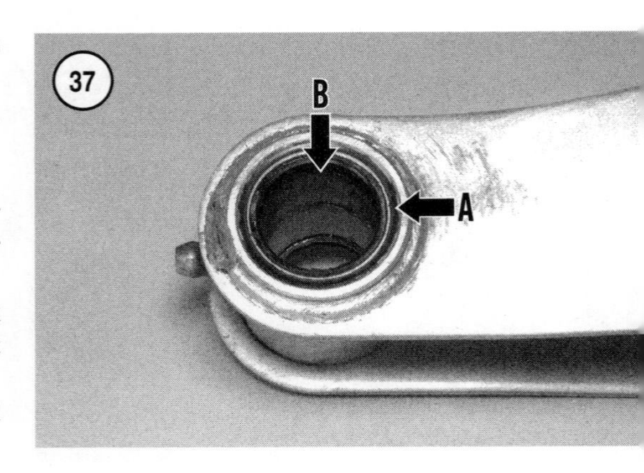

will not be removed from the frame, perform the following steps before making the inspection.
1. Remove the rear wheels as described in Chapter Eleven.
2. Remove the shock absorber as described in this chapter.
3. Refer to Chapter Three and adjust the drive chain to obtain maximum slack. Lift the chain off the driven sprocket.
4. Check the bearings as follows:
   a. Grasp the ends of the swing arm and leverage it from side to side horizontally. There should be no detectable play in the bearings.
   b. Pivot the swing arm up and down. The bearings must pivot smoothly.
   c. If there is play or roughness in the bearings, remove the swing arm and inspect the bearing and pivot assembly for wear.
5. Install the shock absorber as described in this chapter.
6. Install the rear wheels as described in Chapter Eleven.
7. Adjust the chain (Chapter Three).

Removal/Installation

This procedure assumes the swing arm is being removed for service or replacement. Therefore, major assemblies attached to the swing arm are completely removed.

Refer to **Figure 38**.
1. Remove the swing arm skidplate as described in Chapter Fifteen.
2. Remove the axle, axle hub and shock absorber as described in this chapter.
3. Remove the parking brake cable (A, **Figure 39**) and brake hose guides (B) from the swing arm.
4. Remove the nut and washer (**Figure 40**).
5. Remove the swing arm pivot bolt (**Figure 41**).
6. Remove the swing arm.
7. Inspect and service the swing arm as described in this section.

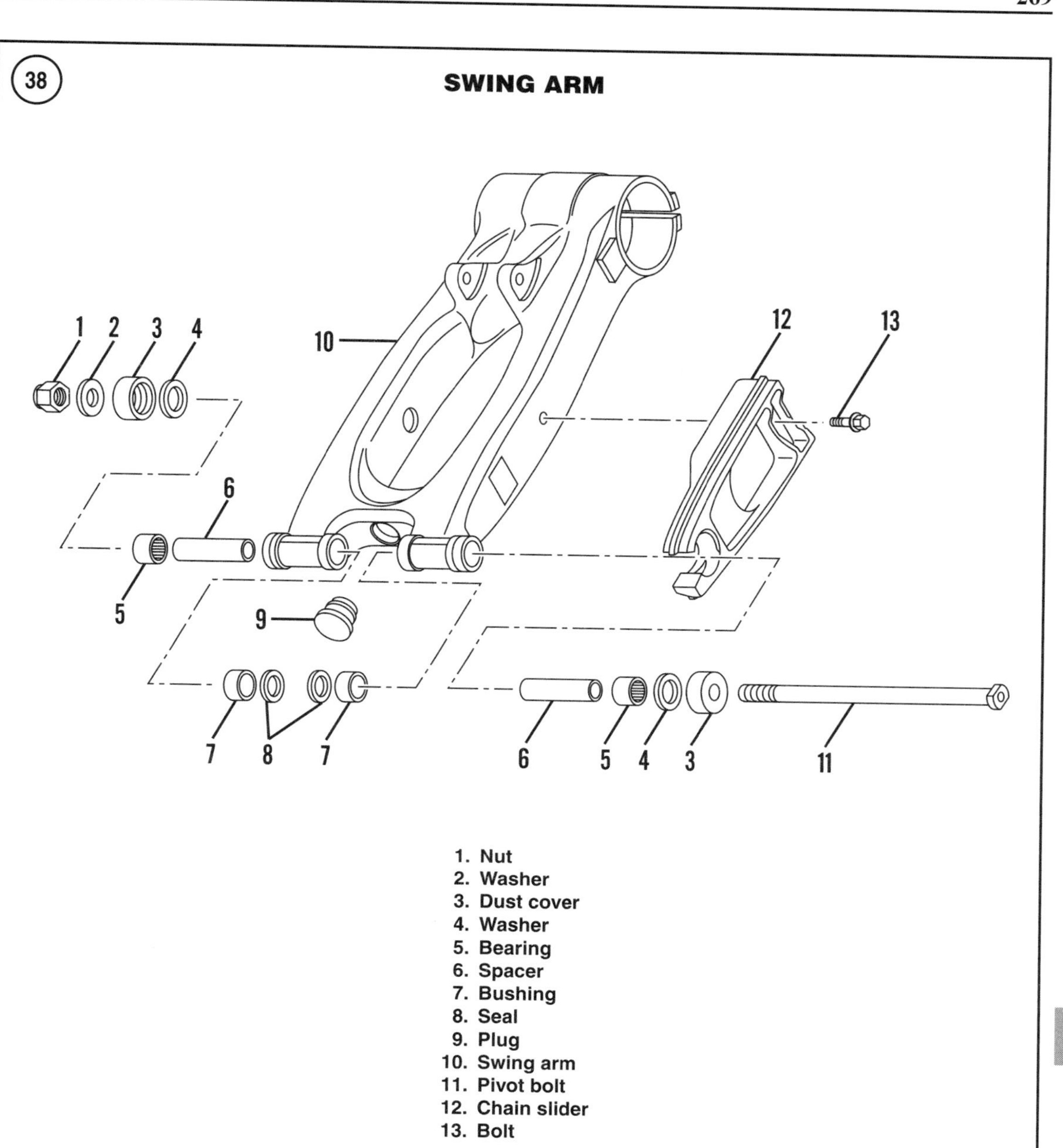
38
SWING ARM
1
2
3
4
5
6
7
8
9
10
11
12
13
1. Nut
2. Washer
3. Dust cover
4. Washer
5. Bearing
6. Spacer
7. Bushing
8. Seal
9. Plug
10. Swing arm
11. Pivot bolt
12. Chain slider
13. Bolt

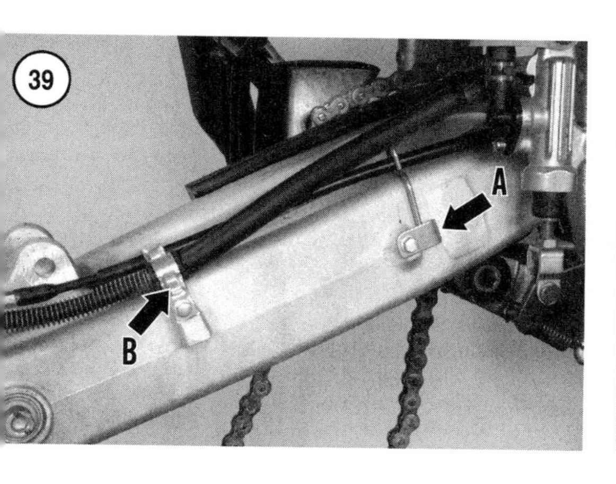
39
A
B

40

41

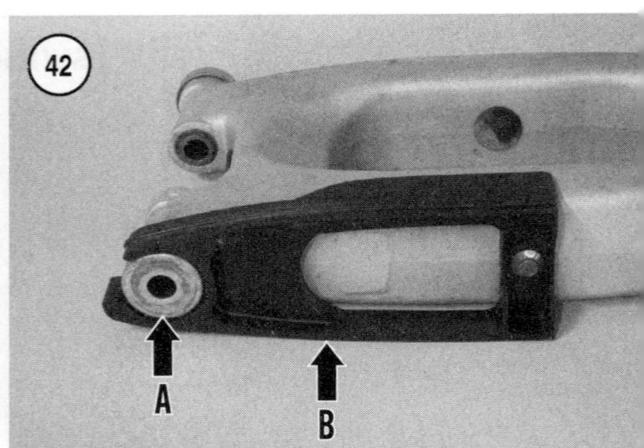

42

8. Reverse the removal steps to install the swing arm assembly while noting the following:
   a. Check that the chain is routed above and below the swing arm before inserting and tightening the swing arm pivot bolt.
   b. Tighten the swing arm pivot bolt to 100 N•m (74 ft.-lb.).
   c. Adjust the chain (Chapter Three).

43

Disassembly/Inspection/Assembly

During disassembly, identify the parts so they may be inspected and reinstalled in their original locations. Refer to **Figure 38**.

1. On the left side, remove the dust cap (A, **Figure 42**) and chain slider (B).
2. If necessary, remove the washer (**Figure 43**) inside the dust cap.
3. Remove the spacer (**Figure 44**).
4. If necessary, extract the inner seal (A, **Figure 45**).
5. Repeat Steps 1-4 for remaining swing arm leg.
6. Clean the parts. Inspect the swing arm casting. Check for fractures and other damage. If damage is detected, replace the swing arm, or have a dealership or machine shop determine if it can be repaired.
7. Inspect the needle bearings (**Figure 46**) for wear, play, flat spots, rust or discoloration.
   a. If the rollers are a bluish color, overheating has occurred.
   b. Inspect the bearing cages for cracks, rust or other damage.
   c. Lubricate the bearing and pivot collar, and then insert the spacer into the bearing (**Figure 47**). The spacer should turn freely and smoothly with no play. If play or roughness exists, replace the bearing as described in this section.
8. Inspect the bushings (B, **Figure 45**) for wear, play and deterioration. The bushings are a synthetic material and may not show obvious wear.
   a. Lubricate the pivot spacer and insert it into the bushing. The spacer should turn freely and smoothly with no play.

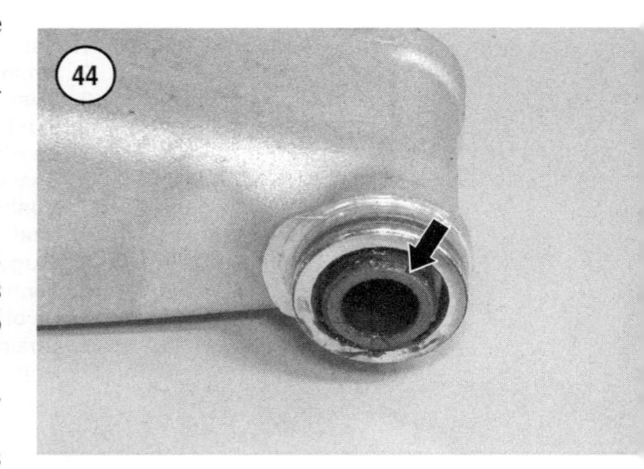
44

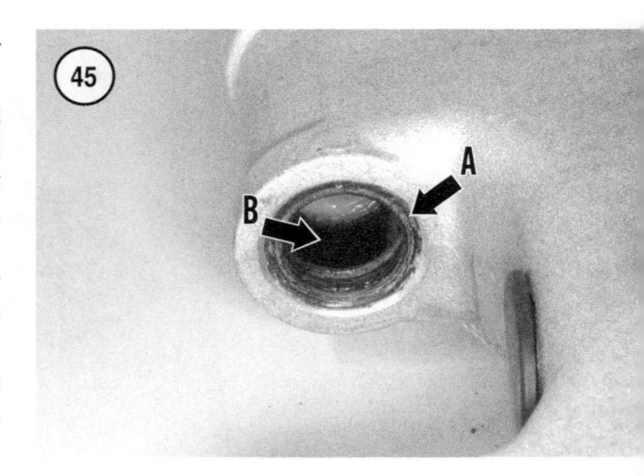

45

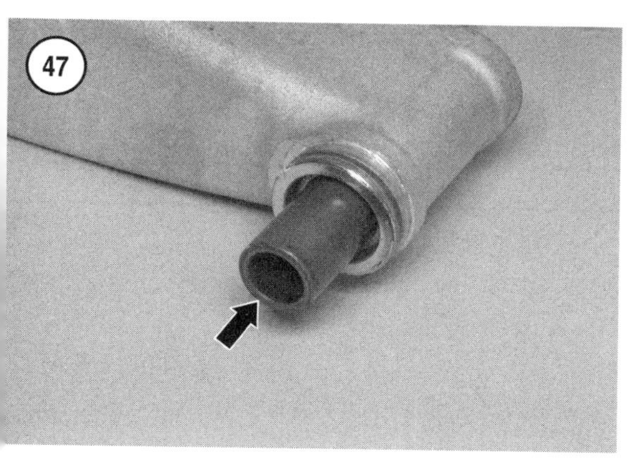

   b. If play or roughness exists, replace the bushing as described in this section.

9. Inspect the dust cap assembly, seals, spacer and pivot bolt assembly.
   a. Inspect the seals for cracks, wear or deterioration.
   b. The dust cap assembly should seal firmly over the bearing bore.
   c. Inspect the pivot bolt for straightness. Replace the bolt if bent.

10. Inspect the chain slider. Replace the slider if it is worn. Severe damage can occur to the swing arm if the chain wears through the slider.

11. Clean and inspect the chain roller (**Figure 48**) attached to the frame. Replace the roller if worn or seized.

12. Clean and inspect the pivot boss (**Figure 49**) at the rear of the engine. Lubricate the pivot boss with lithium grease.

13. Reverse the disassembly steps to assemble the swing arm. Note the following:
   a. If necessary, replace the bearings and bushings as described in this section.
   b. Apply lithium grease to the parts as they are assembled.
   c. Install the inner seals so the manufacturer's marks face out.

Bearing and Bushing Replacement

NOTE
Motion Pro part No. 08-0213 may be used to remove and install the bearings in the swing arm.

Replace the bearings and bushings after disassembling, cleaning and inspecting the parts as described in this section. Replace bearings and bushings as a set.

Refer to Chapter One for bearing removal and installation techniques while noting the following:

CAUTION
The swing arm casting is brittle and must be supported properly. Failure to provide adequate support around the bearing bore can result in cracking of the casting. If in doubt, have a dealership remove and replace the parts. If the parts are severely seized in the bore, apply penetrating oil and work slowly.

1. Install the bushings first, then install the bearings.
2. Install bushings to a depth of 9 mm (0.35 in.) from the bore opening.
3. Install bearings to a depth of 5 mm (0.20 in.) from the bore opening.
4. After bushing and bearing installation, insert the spacers and check for fit and smooth operation.

Table 1 REAR SUSPENSION SPECIFICATIONS

Rear shock absorber	
Type	Coil spring/gas-oil damper
Travel	110 mm (4.33 in.)
Spring free length	
2006-2014 models	255 mm (10.04 in.)
2015-on models	252 mm (9.92 in.)
Spring rate	46 N/mm (263 lb./in.)
Stroke	0-110 mm (0-4.33 in.)
Connecting arm bushing depth	1 mm (0.04 in.)
Relay arm bushing depth	6.5 mm (0.26 in.)
Swing arm pivot	
End play service limit	1.0 mm (0.04 in.)
Side clearance service limit	1.0 mm (0.04 in.)
Rear wheel travel	256 mm (10.08 in.)
Swing arm bushing depth	9 mm (0.35 in.)
Swing arm bearing depth	5 mm (0.20 in.)

Table 2 REAR SUSPENSION TORQUE SPECIFICATIONS

Item	N•m	in. lb.	ft-lb.
Axle hub pinch bolts	21	–	15.5
Axle nut	240	–	177
Axle nut setscrews	7	62	–
Connecting arm bolts			
Upper	55	–	40.5
Lower	43	–	32
Rear shock absorber			
Upper bolt	55	–	40.5
Lower bolt	43	–	32
Swing arm pivot bolt	100	–	74
Swing arm-to-upper relay arm pivot bolt	43	–	32
Wheel hub nut	200	–	148

CHAPTER FOURTEEN

BRAKES

This chapter covers service, repair and replacement procedures for the front and rear disc brake systems. Brake specifications are located in **Table 1** and **Table 2** at the end of this chapter.

BRAKE FLUID SELECTION

WARNING
Do not intermix silicone based (DOT 5) brake fluid with glycol-based (DOT 4) brake fluid as it can cause brake system failure.

When adding brake fluid, use DOT 4 brake fluid from a sealed container. DOT 4 brake fluid is glycol-based and draws moisture, which greatly reduces its ability to perform correctly. Purchase brake fluid in small containers and discard small leftover quantities. Do not store a container of brake fluid with less than 1/4 of the fluid remaining.

Do not reuse drained fluid. Discard old fluid properly.

BRAKE SERVICE

The brake system transmits hydraulic pressure from the master cylinder to the brake caliper. This pressure is transmitted from the caliper to the brake pads, which grip both sides of the brake disc and slow the ATV. As the pads wear, the caliper piston moves out of the caliper bore to automatically compensate for pad wear. As this occurs, the fluid level in the reservoir goes down, which must be raised with additional fluid.

Proper service includes carefully-performed procedures and a clean work environment. Debris that enters the system can damage the components and cause poor brake performance. Do not use sharp tools while servicing the master cylinder, caliper or piston. Any damage to these components could cause a loss of hydraulic pressure in the system. If there is any doubt about having the ability to correctly and safely service the brake system, have a professional technician perform the task.

Consider the following when servicing the brake system:

WARNING
Whenever working on the brake system, do not inhale brake dust. It may contain asbestos, which can cause lung injury and cancer. Wear a face mask that meets OSHA requirements for trapping asbestos particles, and wash hands and forearms thoroughly after completing the work.

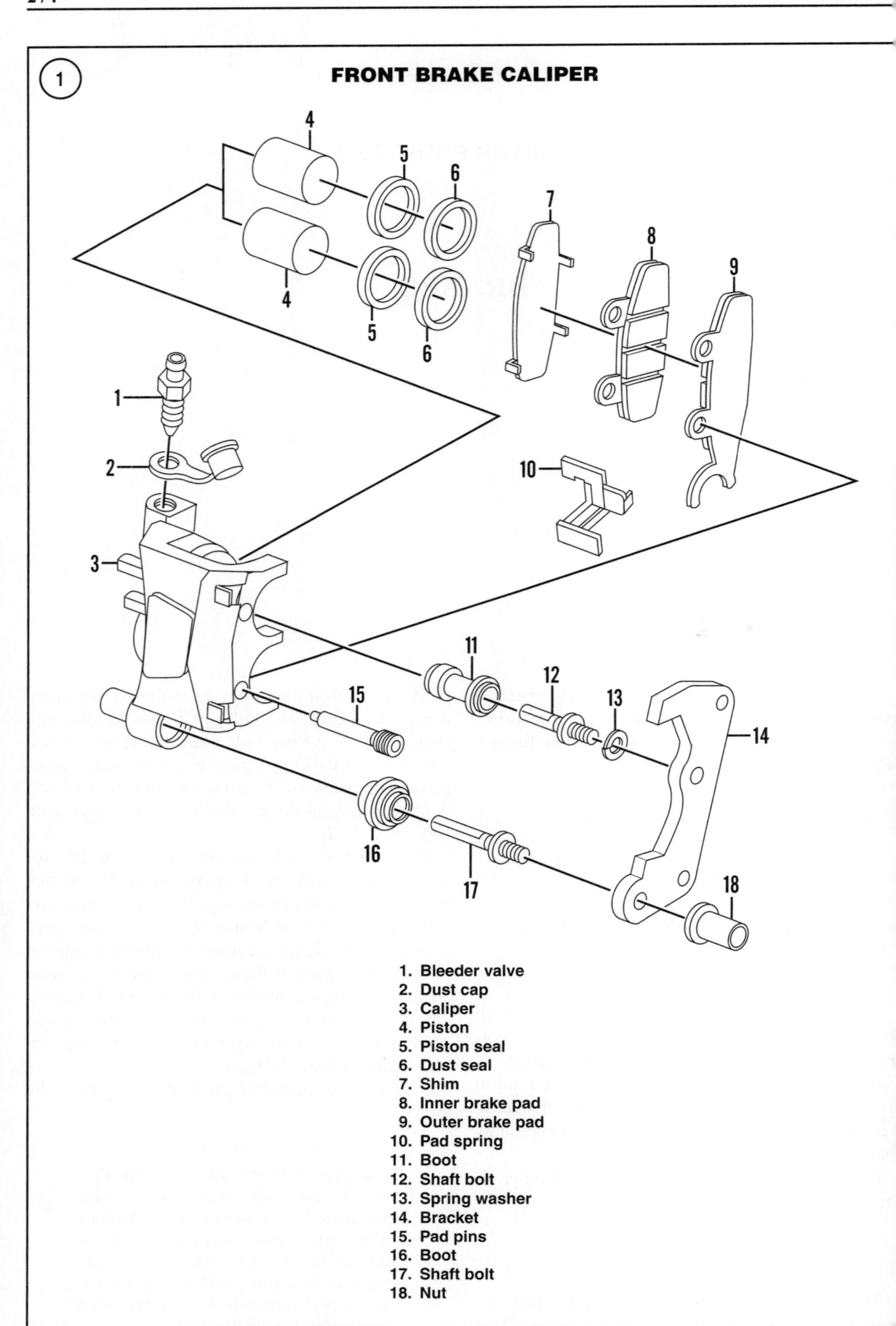
1
FRONT BRAKE CALIPER
4
5
6
7
8
9
4
5
6
1
2
10
3
11
12
13
14
15
16
17
18
1. Bleeder valve
2. Dust cap
3. Caliper
4. Piston
5. Piston seal
6. Dust seal
7. Shim
8. Inner brake pad
9. Outer brake pad
10. Pad spring
11. Boot
12. Shaft bolt
13. Spring washer
14. Bracket
15. Pad pins
16. Boot
17. Shaft bolt
18. Nut

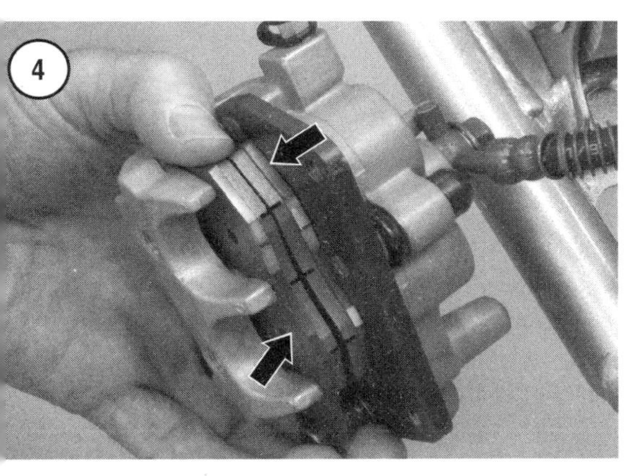

. When properly maintained, hydraulic compo-
ents rarely require disassembly. Make sure it is nec-
ssary.
. Keep the reservoir covers in place to prevent the
ntry of moisture and debris.

WARNING
NEVER use compressed air to clean any part of the brake system. This releases the harmful brake pad dust. Use an aerosol brake cleaner to clean parts when servicing any component still installed on the ATV.

WARNING
Do not add to or replace the brake fluid with silicone (DOT 5) brake fluid. It is not compatible with the system and may cause brake failure.

3. Clean parts with DOT 4 brake fluid, an aerosol brake parts cleaner or denatured alcohol. Never use petroleum-based solvents on internal brake system components. They cause seals to swell and distort.
4. Do not allow brake fluid to contact plastic, painted or plated parts. It will damage the surface.
5. Dispose of brake fluid properly.
6. If the hydraulic system has been opened (not including the reservoir cover), the system must be bled to remove air from the system. Refer to *Brake Bleeding* in this chapter.

FRONT BRAKE PADS

Brake pad life depends on the riding habits of the rider and the type of material used to manufacture the brake pads. Replace the front pads when they are worn to within 1 mm (0.040 in.) of the backing plate, or if the pads have been contaminated with oil or other chemicals.

Removal/Installation

The brake pads can only be replaced by removing the caliper from the steering knuckle. Brake hose disconnection is not necessary. Keep the caliper supported and do not allow it to hang from the brake hose. When replacing brake pads, replace both pads as a set.

If the caliper will be rebuilt, or, if other damage is detected during this procedure, the pads can be removed when the caliper is at the workbench. Refer to *Front Brake Caliper* in this chapter for complete removal, repair and installation. Refer to **Figure 1**.

1. Remove the front wheel as described in Chapter Eleven.
2. Loosen the pad pins (**Figure 2**).
3. Remove the caliper mounting bolts (**Figure 3**), and lift the caliper from the disc. Avoid kinking the brake hose.

NOTE
Do not operate the brake lever with the pads removed. Doing so may force the caliper piston out of the bore.

4. Remove the pad pins. Then, remove the pads (**Figure 4**).
5. Remove the pad spring (**Figure 5**).
6. Push in the caliper pistons to create room for the new pads.

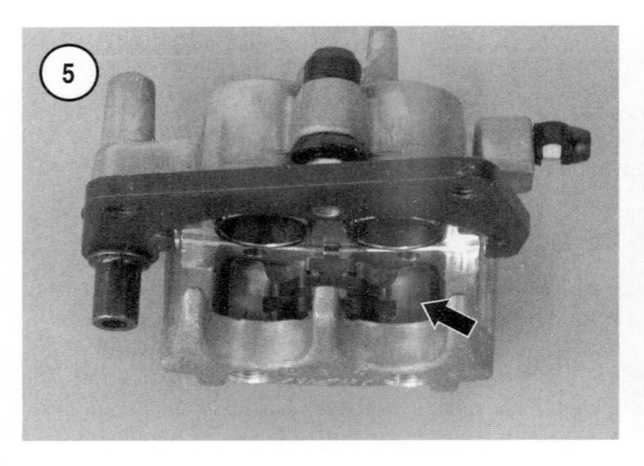

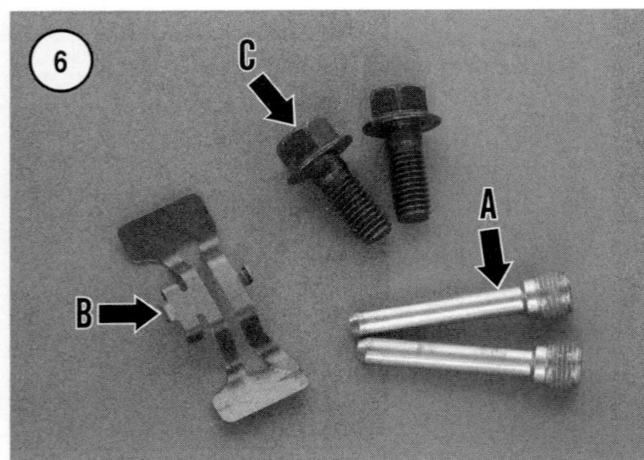

CAUTION
Monitor the level of fluid in the master cylinder reservoir. Brake fluid will back flow to the reservoir when the caliper piston is pressed into the bore. Do not allow brake fluid to spill from the reservoir, or damage can occur to painted and plastic surfaces. Immediately clean up any spills, flooding the area with water.

7. Clean the interior of the caliper and inspect for the following:
   a. Leaking or damage around the piston, bleeder valve and hose connection.
   b. Damaged or missing boots.
   c. Excessive drag of the caliper bracket when it is moved in and out of the caliper. If corrosion or water is detected around the rubber boots, clean the shaft bolts and lubricate them with lithium-base grease.
8. Inspect the pad pins (A, **Figure 6**), pad spring (B) and mounting bolts (C). The pins and spring must be in good condition to allow the inner pad to move slightly when installed. Check that both small tabs on the spring are not corroded or missing.
9. Inspect the front brake pads (**Figure 7**) for wear and damage.
   a. Replace the front pads when they are worn to within 1 mm (0.040 in.) of the backing plate, as shown by the wear indicator (**Figure 8**). Always replace pads that have become contaminated with oil or other chemicals.
   b. If the pads are worn unevenly, the caliper is probably not sliding correctly on the caliper bracket. The caliper must be free to float on the pad pins and shaft bolts. Buildup or corrosion on the parts can hold the caliper in one position, causing brake drag and excessive pad wear.
10. Install the shim (**Figure 9**) onto the back of the brake pad.
11. Install the pad spring with the small tabs pointing out.

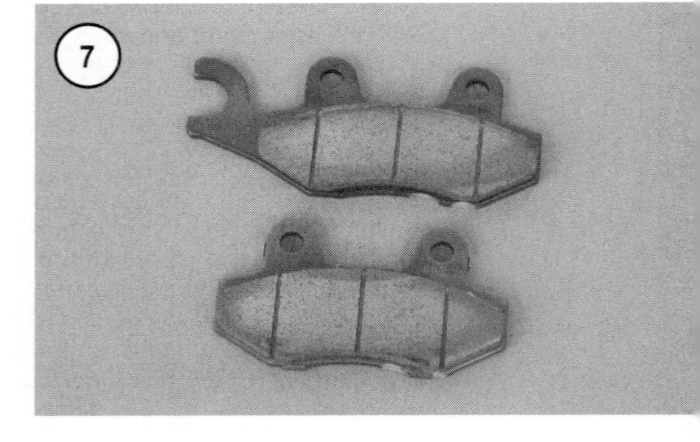

12. Install the inner pad, seating the pad under th caliper bracket and against the piston.
13. Install the outer pad.
14. Align and install the pad pins. Tighten the pin after the caliper is installed.
15. Spread the pads so there is clearance to fit th caliper over the brake disc.
16. Position the caliper over the brake disc and hu assembly, and slide the caliper down around th brake disc.
17. Install and tighten the front caliper mountin bolts to 28 N•m (21 ft.-lb.).
18. Apply threadlock to the pad pins and tighten t 17 N•m (12.5 ft.-lb.).
19. Operate the brake lever several times to seat th pads.
20. Check the brake fluid reservoir and replenish c remove fluid as necessary.
21. With the front hub raised, check that the hu spins freely and the brake operates properly.
22. Install the front wheel as described in Chapte Eleven.

FRONT BRAKE CALIPER

Removal/Installation

Use the following procedure to remove the calipe from the steering knuckle:

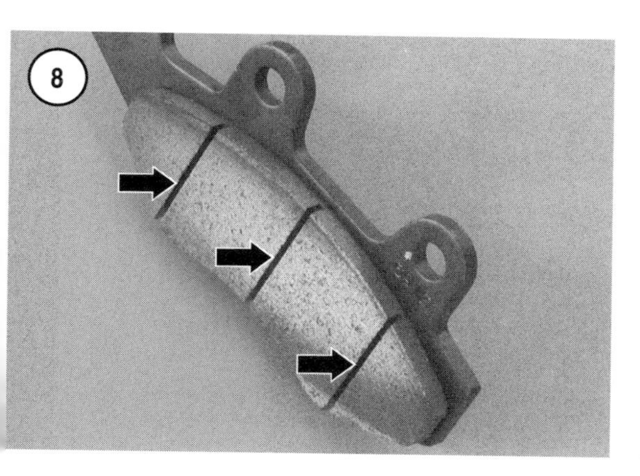

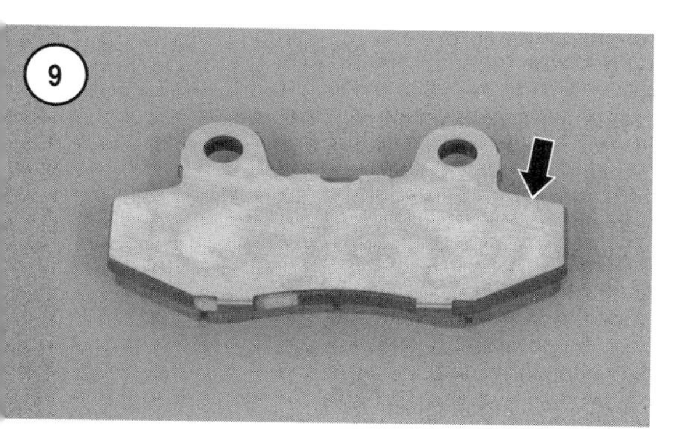

1. Remove the front wheel as described in Chapter Eleven.
2. If the caliper will be disconnected from the brake hose, drain the brake system as described in this chapter. After draining, remove the brake hose union bolt (A, **Figure 10**) and both washers. Tie a plastic bag around the end of the hose to catch any leaks or drips.
3A. If the caliper will be removed from the ATV, remove the caliper mounting bolts (B, **Figure 10**).
3B. If the caliper will be left attached to the brake hose:
   a. Remove the caliper mounting bolts (B, **Figure 10**) and secure the caliper with a length of wire. Do not allow the caliper to hang by the brake hose.

NOTE
Use of a spacer block will prevent the pistons from being forced out of the caliper if the front brake lever is applied with the brake caliper removed.

   b. Insert a spacer block between the brake pads.
4. Inspect and service the caliper as described in this chapter.
5. Reverse the removal procedure to install the caliper while noting the following:
   a. Install and tighten the front caliper mounting bolts to 28 N•m (21 ft.-lb.).

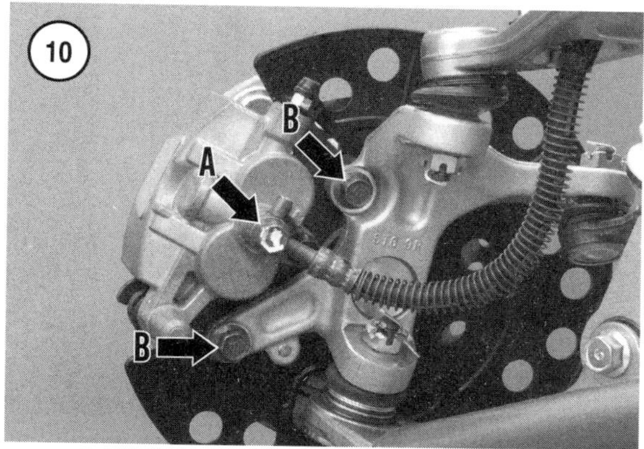

   b. Install new seal washers on the union bolt. Position the pin on the brake hose end against the boss on the front caliper, and tighten the union bolt to 27 N•m (20 ft.-lb.).
   c. If the caliper was rebuilt, or the brake hose disconnected from the caliper, fill and bleed the brake system as described in this chapter.
   d. Operate the brake lever several times to seat the pads.
   e. Check the brake fluid reservoir and replenish or remove fluid, as necessary.
   f. With the front hub raised, check that the hub spins freely and the brake operates properly.
   g. Install the front wheel as described in Chapter Eleven.

Disassembly

Refer to **Figure 1**.

Removing the pistons hydraulically

If the piston and dust seals are in good condition and there are no signs of brake fluid leaking from the bores, it may be possible to remove the pistons hydraulically. However, note that brake fluid will spill from the caliper once the pistons are free.

Read this procedure through to understand the steps and tools required.

1. Remove the front brake caliper as described in this section. Do not loosen or remove the brake hose.
2. Remove the pads and caliper bracket from the caliper.
3. Remove the pad spring from the caliper.

NOTE
Have a supply of paper towels and a pan available to catch and wipe up any spilled brake fluid.

4. Hold the caliper with the pistons facing down and slowly operate the brake lever to push the pistons out

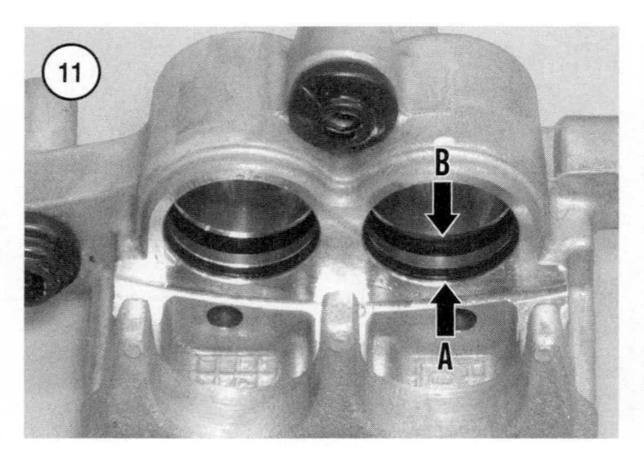

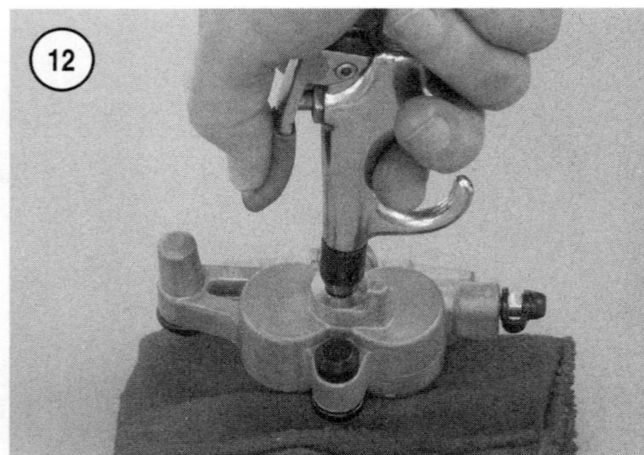

of their bores. If both pistons move evenly, continue until they extend far enough to be removed by hand.

5. If the pistons do not move evenly, perform the following:
   a. Stop and push the extended piston back into its bore by hand, so that both pistons are even.
   b. Operate the brake lever again. If the results are the same, reposition the extended piston again, and operate the brake lever while preventing the moving piston from extending. Install a strip of wood across the caliper to block the moving piston.
   c. If the other piston now starts to move, continue with this technique until both pistons move evenly and can be gripped and removed by hand.
   d. After removing the pistons, hold the caliper over the drain pan to catch the brake fluid draining through the caliper.

6. Remove the banjo bolt with an impact gun (air or electric), if available. Otherwise, hold the caliper in a secure manner and remove the banjo bolt with hand tools. If the caliper cannot be held securely to remove the bolt, stuff paper towels into the caliper bores to absorb brake fluid leaking from the hose and reservoir. Temporarily reinstall the caliper bracket and mount the caliper onto the slider with its mounting bolts to hold it in place. Then, remove the banjo bolt and both washers.

7. Use a small wooden or plastic tool and remove the dust seals (A, **Figure 11**) and piston seals (B) from the caliper bore grooves and discard them.

8. Remove the bleeder valve and dust cap from the caliper.

9. Clean and inspect the brake caliper assembly as described in this section.

Removing the pistons with compressed air

1. Remove the front brake caliper as described in this section.

2. Remove the pads and the caliper bracket from the caliper.

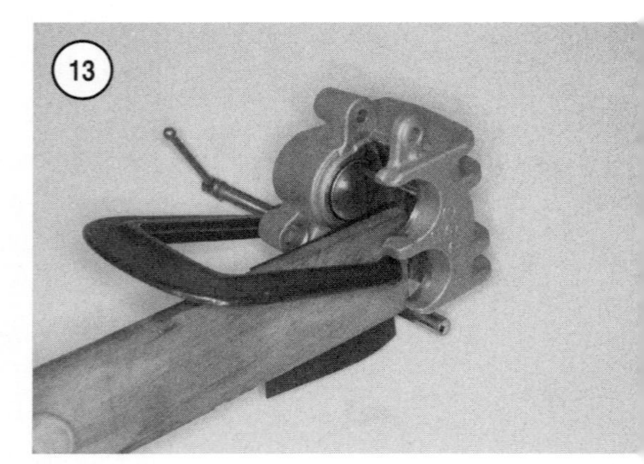

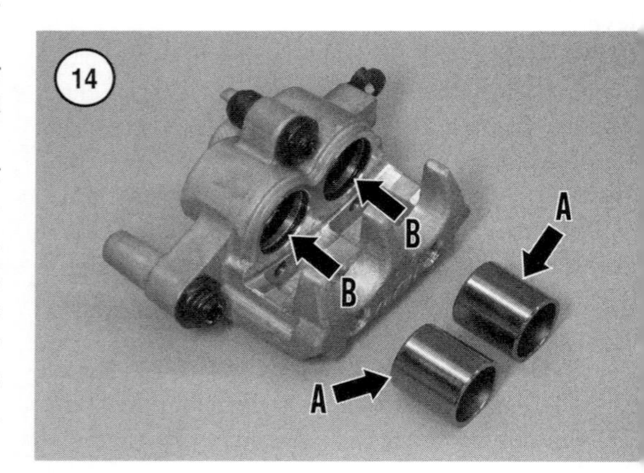

3. Remove the pad spring from the caliper.

4. Make sure the bleeder valve is closed so air ca not escape.

WARNING
Wear eye protection when using compressed air to remove the pistons, and keep your fingers away from the piston.

5. Cushion the caliper pistons with a shop rag an position the caliper with the piston bores facin down. Apply compressed air through the brake hos port (**Figure 12**) to pop the pistons out. If only on

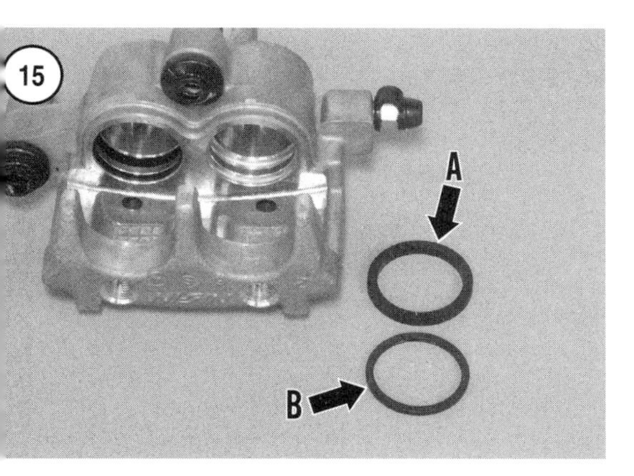

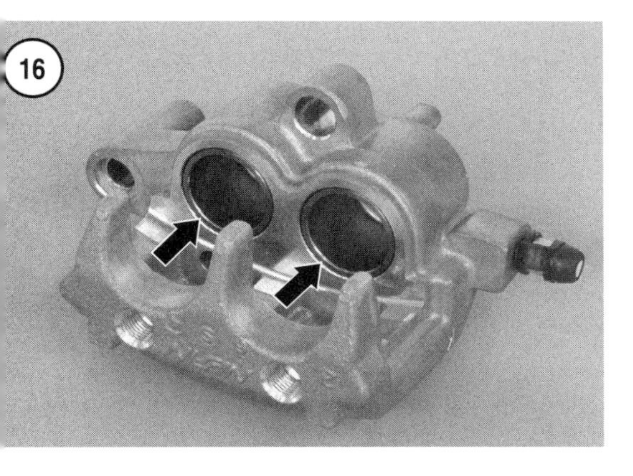

iston came out, block its bore opening with a piece f thick rubber (old inner tube), a wooden block and clamp as shown in **Figure 13**. Apply compressed ir again and remove the remaining piston.

CAUTION
*Do not try to pry out the piston (A, **Figure 14**). This will damage the piston and caliper bore (B, **Figure 14**).*

. Use a small wooden or plastic tool and remove e dust (A, **Figure 11**) and piston seals (B) from the aliper bore grooves and discard them.

7. Remove the bleeder valve and dust cap from the caliper.
8. Clean and inspect the brake caliper assembly as described in this section.

Assembly

NOTE
Use new DOT 4 brake fluid when lubricating the piston seals, pistons and caliper bores in the following steps.

1. Install the bleeder valve and dust cap. Tighten the valve to 6 N•m (53 in.-lb.).
2. Soak the new piston seals and dust seals in brake fluid.
3. Lubricate the cylinder bores with brake fluid.

NOTE
*The piston seals (A, **Figure 15**) are thicker than the dust seals (B).*

NOTE
Make sure each seal fits squarely inside its bore groove.

4. Install a new piston seal (B, **Figure 11**) into each rear bore groove.
5. Install a new dust seal (A, **Figure 11**) into each front bore groove.
6. Lubricate the pistons with brake fluid.

CAUTION
The tight piston-to-seal fit can make piston installation difficult. Do not install the pistons by pushing them straight in as they may bind in their bores and tear the seals.

7. With the open side facing out, align a piston with the caliper bore. Rock the piston slightly to center it in the bore while at the same time pushing the lower end past the seals. When the lower end of the piston passes through both seals, push and bottom the piston in the bore (**Figure 16**). After installing the other piston, clean any spilled brake fluid from the area in front of the pistons to prevent brake pad contamination.

CAUTION
Use only lithium-base grease specified for brake use. Do not use brake fluid to lubricate the rubber boots or fixed shafts.

8. Pinch the open end of the large rubber boot (A, **Figure 17**) and push this end through the mounting hole in the caliper until its outer shoulder bottoms.

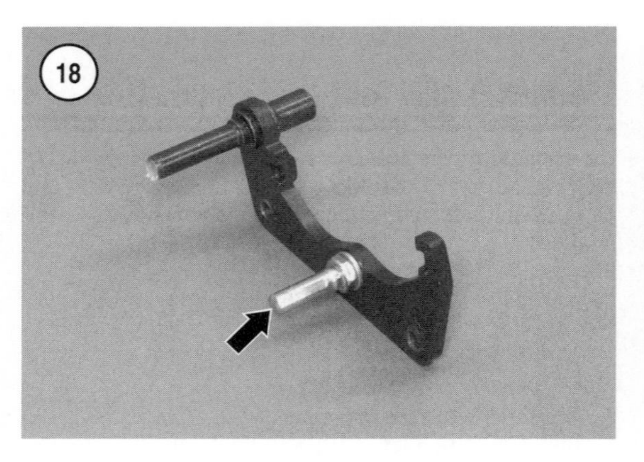

Make sure the boot opening faces toward the inside of the caliper. Partially fill the boot with lithium-base grease.

9. Install the small boot (B, **Figure 17**) into the groove in the caliper. Partially fill the boot with lithium-base grease.
10. If removed, install the shaft bolts into the caliper bracket. Note the location of the short shaft bolt and lockwasher (**Figure 18**). Tighten the shaft bolts securely.
11. Lubricate the caliper bracket shaft bolts with lithium-base grease.
12. Align and slide the mounting bracket into the caliper body (**Figure 19**). Hold the caliper and slide the caliper bracket in and out by hand. Make sure there is no roughness or binding.
13. Install the brake caliper assembly and brake pads as described in this chapter.

Inspection

All models use a floating caliper design, in which the caliper slides or floats on threaded shaft bolts mounted parallel with each other on the caliper and caliper bracket. Rubber boots around each shaft bolt prevent dirt from damaging the shafts. If the shaft bolts are worn or damaged, the caliper can move out of alignment on the caliper bracket. This will cause brake drag, uneven pad wear and overheating. Inspect the rubber boots and shaft bolts during caliper inspection as they play a vital role in brake performance.

Refer to **Figure 1** when servicing the front brake caliper assembly. Replace any parts that are out of specification (**Table 1**) or damaged as described in this section.

WARNING
Do not allow oil or grease on the brake components. Do not clean the parts with kerosene or other petroleum products. These chemicals cause the rubber brake system components to swell, which may cause brake failure.

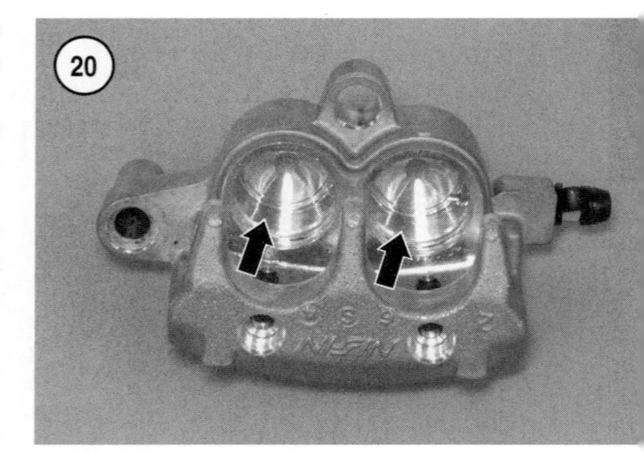

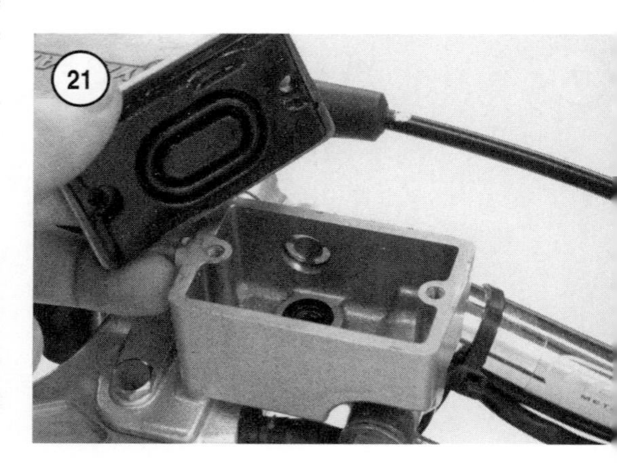

CAUTION
The caliper bore and seal grooves can be difficult to clean, especially if brake fluid was leaking past the seals. Clean the grooves carefully to avoid damaging the grooves and bore surfaces.

1. Clean and dry the caliper and the other meta parts. Clean the seal grooves carefully. If the con tamination is difficult to remove, soak the calipe

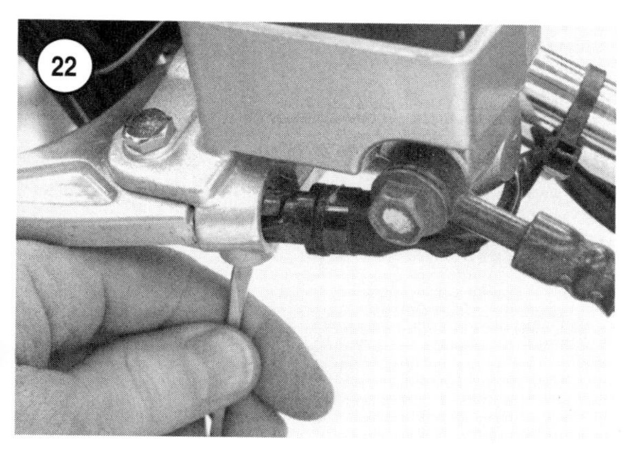

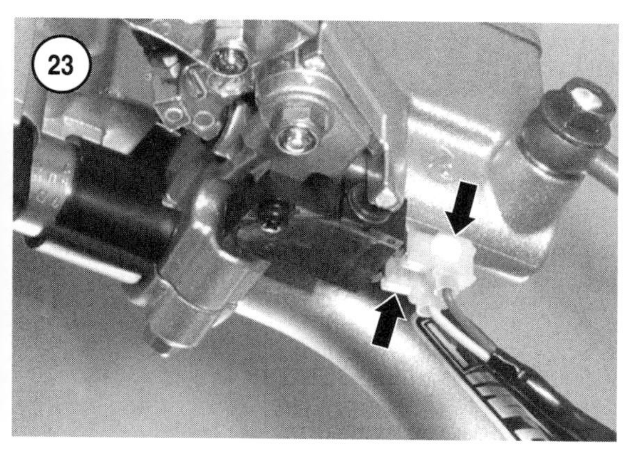

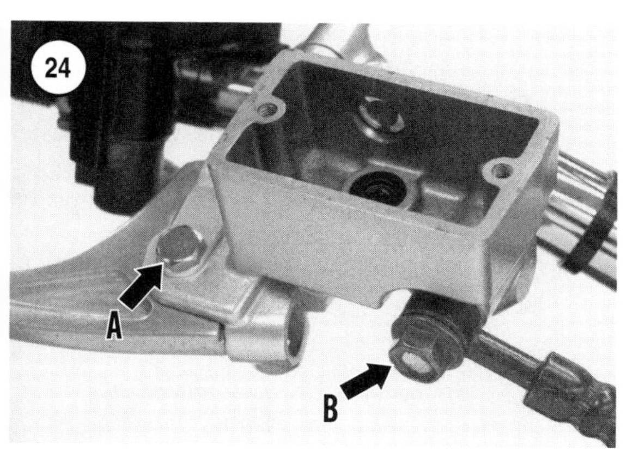

in a suitable solvent, and then reclean. If any of the rubber parts are to be reused, clean them with denatured alcohol or new DOT 4 brake fluid. Do not use a petroleum-based solvent.

2. Inspect the caliper bracket, shafts and rubber boots as follows:
   a. Inspect the rubber boots for cracks, tearing, weakness or other damage.
   b. Inspect the shaft bolts (**Figure 18**) on the caliper bracket for excessive or uneven wear. If the shaft bolt is damaged, replace it.
3. Check each cylinder bore for corrosion, pitting, deep scratches or other wear.
4. Measure the inside diameter of the front caliper bores (**Figure 20**). Compare the measurement with the specification in **Table 1**.
5. Check the pistons for wear marks, scoring, cracks or other damage.
6. Check the bleeder valve and dust cap for wear or damage. Make sure air can pass through the bleeder valve.
7. Check the union bolt for wear or damage. Discard the washers.
8. Inspect the brake pads and pad spring as described in *Front Brake Pads* (this chapter).

FRONT MASTER CYLINDER

Removal/Installation

Use the following procedure to remove the front master cylinder/brake fluid reservoir.

CAUTION
Do not allow brake fluid to splash from the reservoir or hose. Brake fluid can damage painted and plastic surfaces. Immediately clean up any spills, flooding the area with water.

1. Cover and protect the bodywork and area surrounding the master cylinder.
2. Drain the brake system as described in this chapter.
3. Remove the cap and diaphragm and verify that the master cylinder reservoir (**Figure 21**) is empty. Wipe the interior of the reservoir to absorb all remaining fluid.

4A. On 2006 models, remove the brake light switch. Use a small tool (**Figure 22**) to press on the barb that locks the switch into the master cylinder.

4B. On 2007-on models, disconnect the two electrical connectors (**Figure 23**) from the front brake light switch.

5. If the master cylinder will be rebuilt, remove the brake lever pivot bolt (A, **Figure 24**) while the master cylinder remains stable.
6. Remove the brake hose union bolt (B, **Figure 24**) from the master cylinder as follows:
   a. Remove the union bolt and seal washers from the brake hose. Have a shop cloth ready to absorb excess brake fluid that drips from the hose.
   b. Tie a plastic bag around the end of the hose.
7. Remove the bolts (A, **Figure 25**) securing the master cylinder to the handlebar, and remove the master cylinder.
8. Repair the master cylinder as described in this section.

9. Reverse the removal procedure to install the master cylinder. Note the following:
   a. Check that the indentations on the handlebar collar are engaged with the throttle assembly and master cylinder.
   b. The mounting bracket (B, **Figure 25**) must be installed so the UP and arrow marks are facing up. Tighten the upper bolt first, and then the bottom bolt. Tighten the bracket bolts to 7 N•m (62 in.-lb.).
   c. Position the brake hose fitting so it is slightly angled downward, keeping the hose straight.
   d. Install new seal washers on the union bolt. Tighten the union bolt to 27 N•m (20 ft.-lb.).
   e. Check that the brake light operates when the lever is operated.

10. Fill the brake fluid reservoir and bleed the brake system as described in this chapter.

Disassembly/Reassembly/Inspection

Refer to **Figure 26**. Use the following procedure to disassemble, inspect and assemble the master cylinder. The piston, seals and spring are only available as a complete assembly.

1. Remove the master cylinder as described in this section.
2. On 2007-on models, remove the mounting screw and brake switch.
3. Remove the boot from the piston. The boot is a friction fit. To avoid damaging the boot on removal, apply penetrating lubricant around the perimeter of the boot. Carefully pull the bottom edge back so the lubricant can loosen the boot.
4. Remove the snap ring (**Figure 27**) from the master cylinder as follows:
   a. Press down on the piston to relieve pressure on the snap ring. Then, remove the snap ring.
   b. Slowly relieve the pressure on the piston.
5. Remove the piston assembly (**Figure 28**) from the bore.
6. Clean all parts that will be reused with fresh brake fluid or isopropyl (rubbing) alcohol.
7. Inspect the master cylinder bore for wear, pitting or corrosion.
8. Measure the inside diameter (**Figure 29**) of the master cylinder bore. Refer to **Table 1** for specifications.
9. Inspect and clean the threads and orifices in the reservoir. Clean with compressed air.
10. Inspect the brake lever bore and pivot bolt for wear.
11. Inspect the diaphragm and reservoir cap for damage.
12. Inspect the mounting hardware and union bolt for corrosion and damage. Install new seal washers on the union bolt.

13. Assemble the piston, seals and spring (**Figure 30**) as follows:
    a. Soak the seals in fresh DOT 4 brake fluid for 15 minutes. This will soften and lubricate the seals.
    b. Apply brake fluid to the piston so the seals can slide over the ends.
    c. Mount the seals on the piston. Identify the wide (open) side of both seals. When installed, the wide side of the seals must face in the direction of the arrow (**Figure 30**). Mount the seals with the small hole closest to the spring end of the piston.
    d. Install and seat the spring onto the piston.
14. Install the piston and snap ring into the master cylinder as follows:
    a. Place the master cylinder in a vise with soft jaws. Do not overtighten the vise or master cylinder damage could occur.
    b. Lubricate the master cylinder bore and piston assembly with brake fluid.
    c. Insert the piston assembly into the master cylinder.

NOTE

After the piston seals have entered the master cylinder, the piston should be held in place until the snap ring is installed. Anytime the seals come out of the master cylinder, there is a chance of damaging the seal lips during the reinsertion process. This should be avoided.

    d. While holding the piston in the master cylinder, install the snap ring (**Figure 27**) so the flat side faces out.
15. Apply lithium-base grease to the inside of the boot. Seat the boot into the master cylinder.
16. Install the lever and pivot bolt. Apply waterproof grease to the pivot bolt and lever contact point.
17. Loosely attach the diaphragm and cap to the reservoir.

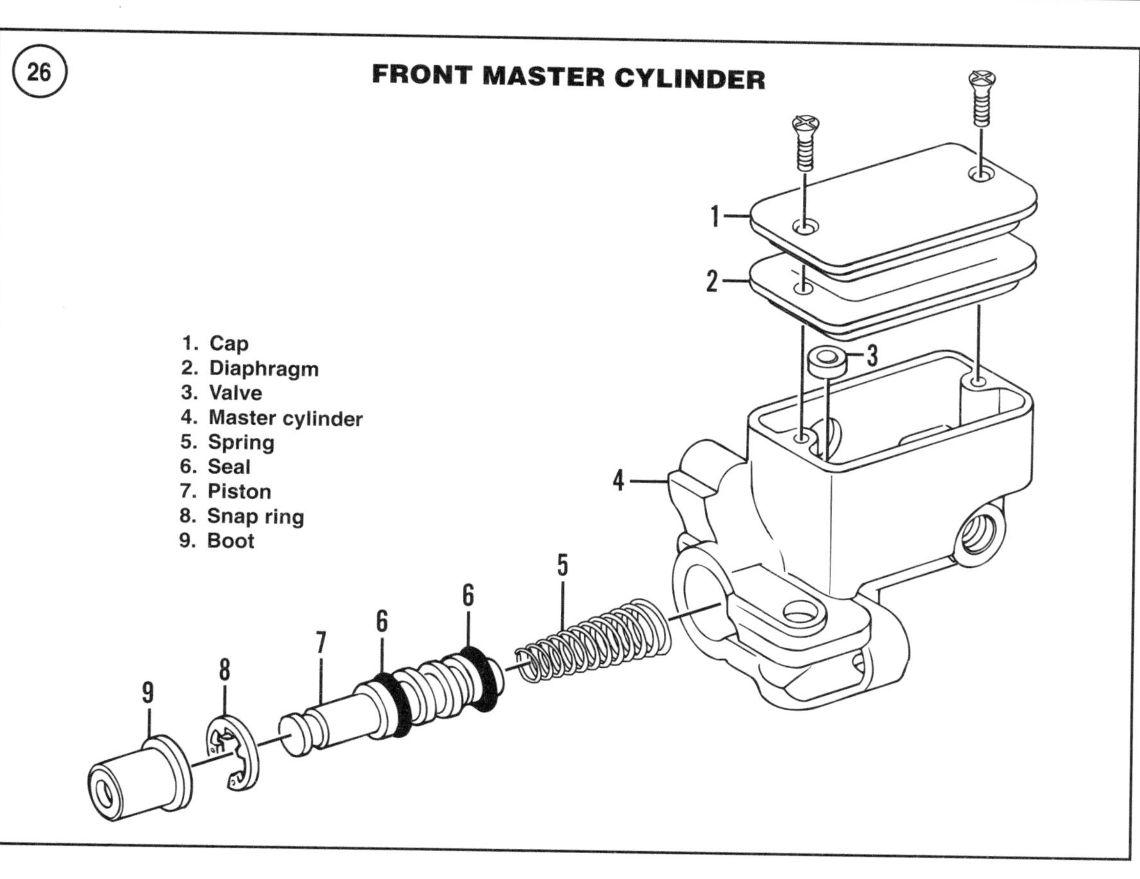
26
FRONT MASTER CYLINDER
1. Cap
2. Diaphragm
3. Valve
4. Master cylinder
5. Spring
6. Seal
7. Piston
8. Snap ring
9. Boot
1
2
3
4
5
6
6
7
8
9

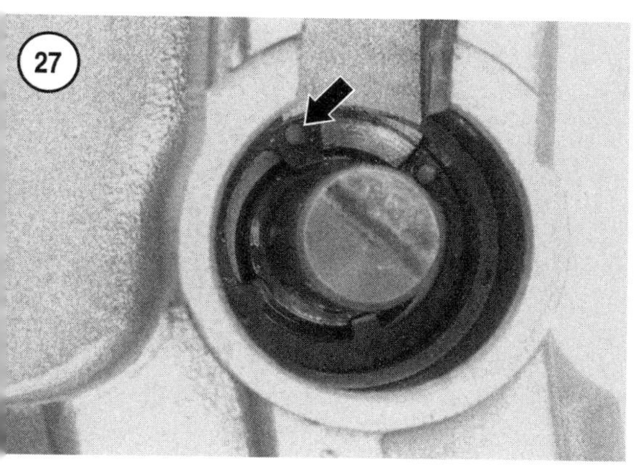
27

29

28

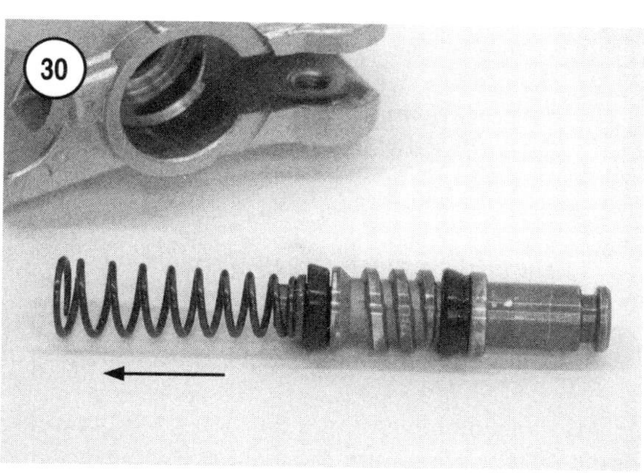
30

18. On 2007-on models, install the brake switch and mounting screw.
19. Install the master cylinder as described in this section.

REAR BRAKE PADS

Brake pad life depends on the riding habits of the rider and the type of material used to manufacture the brake pads. Replace the rear pads when they are worn to within 1 mm (0.040 in.) of the backing plate, or if they have been contaminated with oil or other chemicals.

Brake pad replacement requires caliper removal from the swing arm. Brake hose disconnection from the caliper is not necessary. Keep the caliper supported and do not allow it to hang from the brake hose.

If the caliper will be rebuilt, or, if other damage is detected during this procedure, the pads can be removed when the caliper is on the workbench. Refer to *Rear Brake Caliper* in this chapter for complete caliper removal, repair and installation procedures.

Replacement (2006-2012 Models)

1. Loosen, but do not remove, the pad pins (**Figure 31**).
2. Remove the caliper mounting bolts (**Figure 32**). Avoid kinking the brake hose.
3. Press down on the pads to relieve the pressure on the pad pins, and then remove the pins from the caliper (A, **Figure 33**).
4. Remove the pads, shim and insulator.

CAUTION
Monitor the level of fluid in the master cylinder reservoir. Brake fluid will back flow to the reservoir when the caliper piston is moved back into the bore. Do not allow brake fluid to spill from the reservoir, or damage can occur to painted and plastic surfaces. Immediately clean up any spills, flooding the area with water.

NOTE
Do not operate the brake pedal with the pads removed. Doing so may force the caliper piston out of the bore.

NOTE
The brake piston is threaded on the internal parking brake adjustment bolt. The piston must be turned to manually move the piston in or out of the caliper bore.

5. Insert a suitable tool into the slots (A, **Figure 34**) in the piston. Then, turn the piston clockwise so the piston retracts into the bore to create room for th new pads. Turn the piston in far enough so the pis ton face is flush with the caliper surface (B, **Figu 34**).
6. Remove the inner pad spring (A, **Figure 35**).
7. Clean the interior of the caliper and inspect f the following:
   a. Leaking or damage around the pistons, bleed valve and hose connection.
   b. Damaged or missing boots.
   c. Excessive drag of the caliper bracket when is moved in and out of the caliper. If corrosic or water is detected around the rubber boot

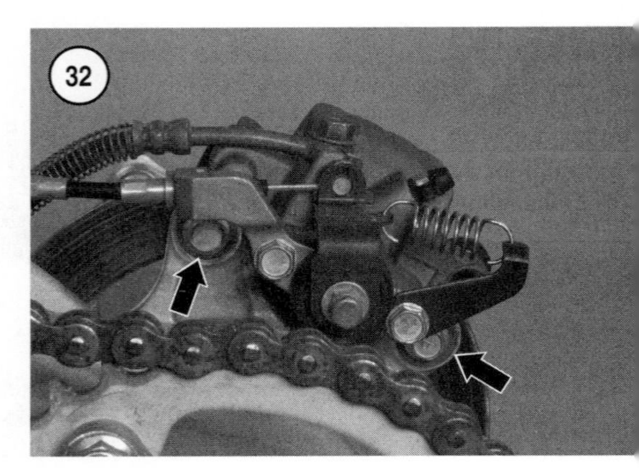

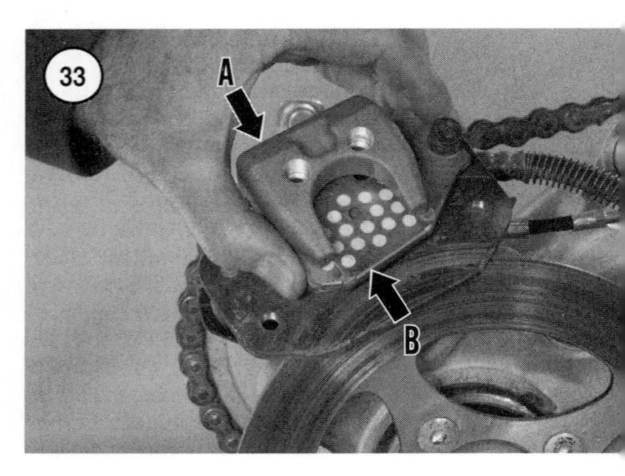

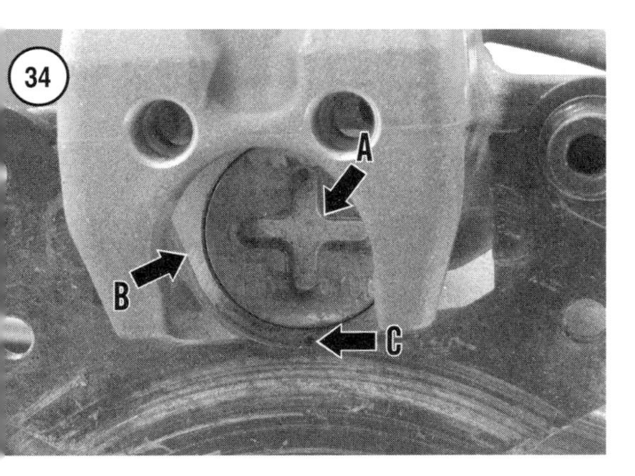

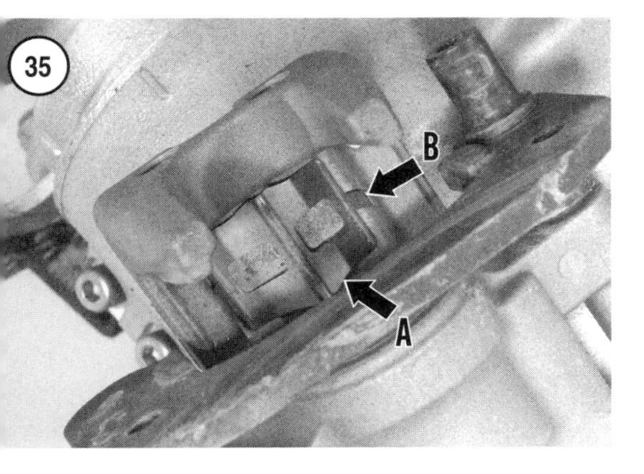

36

clean the shaft bolts and lubricate them with lithium-base grease.

. Inspect the pad pins (A, **Figure 36**), pad spring nd mounting bolts. The pins and spring must be in ;ood condition to allow the inner pad to move slighty when installed.

. Inspect the rear brake pads (B, **Figure 36**) for vear and damage.

a. Replace the rear pads when they are worn to within 1 mm (0.040 in.) of the backing plate, as shown by the wear indicator grooves (C, **Figure 36**). Always replace pads that have been contaminated with oil or other chemicals.

b. If the pads are worn unevenly, the caliper is probably not sliding correctly on the caliper bracket. The caliper must be free to float on the shaft bolts. Buildup or corrosion on the shaft bolts can hold the caliper in one position, causing brake drag and excessive pad wear.

10. Install the pad spring with the small tabs pointing out and the clip (B, **Figure 35**) near the piston.

11. Note the orientation of the slots (A, **Figure 34**) in the brake piston face. One of the slots must point toward the punch mark (C, **Figure 34**) on the caliper centerline. Rotate the piston as needed while also positioning the piston flush with the caliper surface (B, **Figure 34**).

12. Install the pads. Make sure the pin (A, **Figure 37**) on the backside of the inner pad fits into the slot (B) on the piston. Make sure the shim is installed on the back of the outer brake pad (B, **Figure 33**).

13. Press down on the pads. Then, align and install the pad pins. Tighten the pins after caliper installation.

14. Spread the pads so there is clearance to fit the caliper around the brake disc.

15. Position the caliper over the brake disc, and slide the caliper down around the brake disc.

16. Install and tighten the rear caliper mounting bolts to 34 N•m (25 ft.-lb.).

17. Tighten the pad pins to 17 N•m (12.5 ft.-lb.).

18. Operate the brake lever several times to seat the pads.

19. Check the brake fluid reservoir and replenish or remove fluid, as necessary.

20. With the rear axle raised, check that the axle spins freely and the brake operates properly.

Replacement (2013-on Models)

1. Loosen but do not remove the pad pins (**Figure 38**).

2. Remove the caliper mounting bolts (**Figure 39**). Avoid kinking the brake hose.

3. Press down on the pads to relieve the pressure on the pad pins, then remove the pins (**Figure 40**).
4. Remove the pads.

CAUTION

In the following step, monitor the level of fluid in the master cylinder reservoir. Brake fluid will back flow to the reservoir when the caliper piston is pressed into the bore. Do not allow brake fluid to spill from the reservoir, or damage can occur to painted and plastic surfaces. Immediately clean up any spills, flooding the area with water.

NOTE

Do not operate the brake pedal with the pads removed. Doing so may force the caliper pistons out of the bore.

5. Push the caliper pistons into the bore to create room for the new pads.
6. Remove the inner pad spring (A, **Figure 41**).
7. Clean the interior of the caliper and inspect for the following:
   a. Leakage or damage around the pistons, bleeder valve and hose connection.
   b. Damaged or missing boots.
   c. Excessive drag of the caliper bracket when it is moved in and out of the caliper. If corrosion or water is detected around the rubber boots, clean the parts and lubricate with lithium-base grease.
8. Inspect the pad pins (A, **Figure 42**), pad spring and mounting bolts. The pins and spring must be in good condition to allow the inner pad to slightly move when installed.
9. Inspect the pads (B, **Figure 42**) for wear and damage.
   a. Replace the pads when they are worn to within 1 mm (0.040 in.) of the backing plate, as shown by the wear indicator grooves (C, **Figure 42**). Always replace pads that have been contaminated with oil or other chemicals.
   b. If the pads are worn unevenly, the caliper is probably not sliding correctly on the caliper bracket. The caliper must be free to float on the slide shafts. Buildup or corrosion on the shafts can hold the caliper in one position, causing brake drag and excessive pad wear.
10. Install the pad spring with the small tabs pointing out and the clip (B, **Figure 41**) near the pistons.
11. Install the pads.
12. Press down on the pads, then align and install the pad pins. Tighten the pins after the caliper is installed.

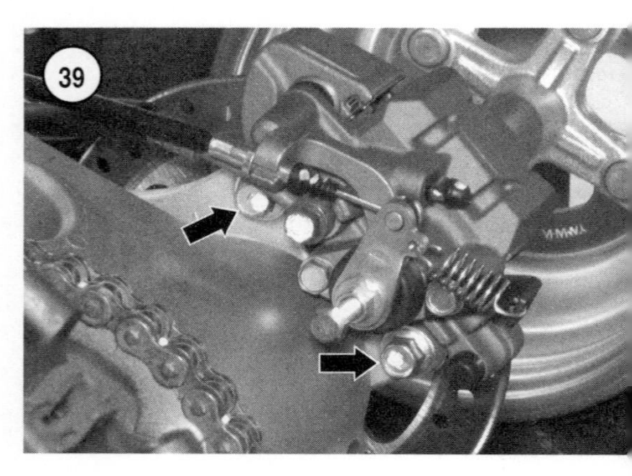

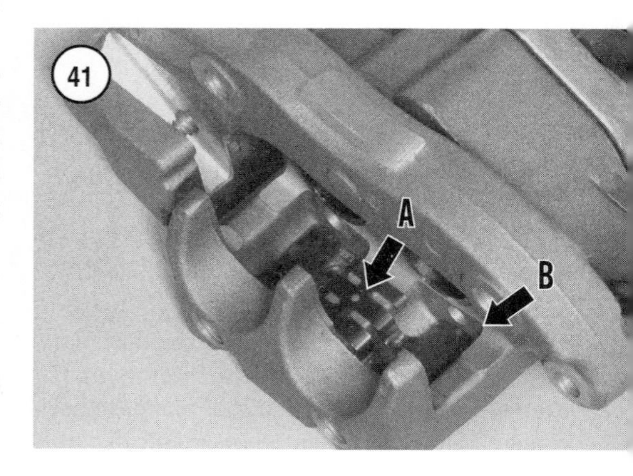

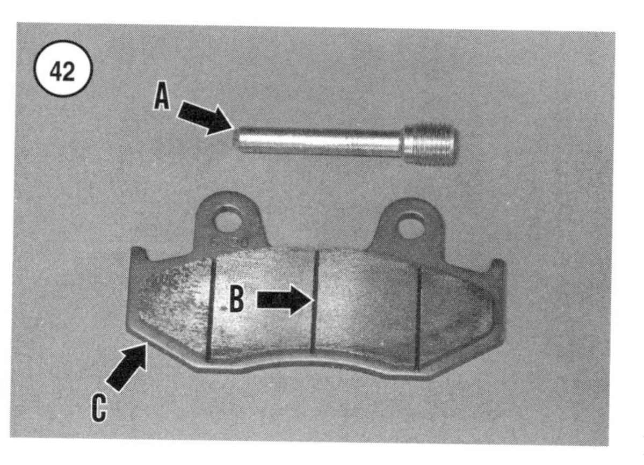

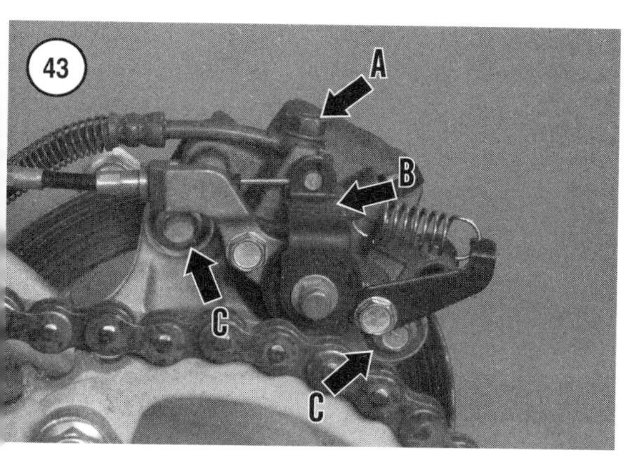

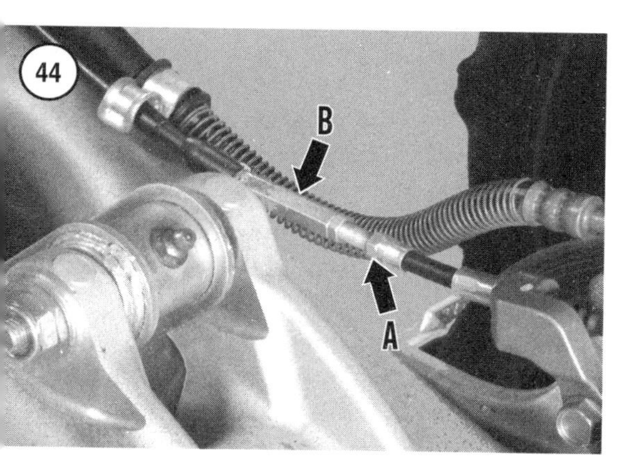

3. Spread the pads so there is clearance to fit the aliper around the brake disc.
4. Position the caliper onto the brake disc, then nstall and tighten the caliper mounting bolts to 43 N•m (32 ft.-lb.).
5. Tighten the pad pins to 17 N•m (150 in.-lb.).
6. Operate the brake lever several times to seat the ads.
7. Check the brake fluid reservoir and replenish or emove fluid, as necessary.
8. With the rear axle raised, check that the axle pins freely and the brake operates properly.

REAR BRAKE CALIPER (2006-2012 MODELS)

The rear brake caliper is equipped with a self-adjusting parking brake. A threaded sleeve inside the piston fits on a threaded stud inside the caliper. When hydraulic pressure forces the piston outward, the piston sleeve rotates the stud. Stud rotation reduces internal clearance in the parking brake mechanism resulting from brake pad wear. No parking brake components in the piston or brake caliper are available separately.

Removal/Installation

Use the following procedure to remove the caliper from the swing arm.

1. If the caliper will be disassembled, do the following:
   a. Drain the brake system as described in this chapter. After draining, loosen the brake hose union bolt (A, **Figure 43**) while the caliper is mounted. Leave the bolt finger-tight.

   NOTE

   If necessary, disengage the upper end of the parking brake cable from the handlebar lever to obtain sufficient cable slack.

   b. On the parking brake cable, loosen the locknut (A, **Figure 44**) and turn the cable adjuster (B) until there is enough slack in the cable to remove it from the parking brake lever (B, **Figure 43**).
2. Remove the caliper mounting bolts (C, **Figure 43**). Remove the caliper from the disc. Avoid kinking the brake hose.

3A. If the caliper will be left attached to the brake hose, but not disassembled and serviced, do the following:
   a. Suspend the caliper with a length of wire. Do not let the caliper hang from the brake hose.
   b. Insert a small wood block between the brake pads. This will prevent the caliper piston from extending out of the caliper if the brake lever is operated.

3B. If the caliper will be disassembled, do the following:
   a. Remove the union bolt and seal washers from the brake hose. Have a shop cloth ready to absorb excess brake fluid that drips from the hose.
   b. Tie a plastic bag around the end of the hose to prevent brake fluid from damaging other surfaces.
   c. Drain excess brake fluid from the caliper.
   d. Remove the rear brake pads as described in this chapter.
   e. Repair the rear caliper as described in this section.

4. Reverse the removal procedure to install the caliper while noting the following:
   a. Install and tighten the rear caliper mounting bolts to 34 N•m (25 ft.-lb.).
   b. If removed, install new seal washers on the union bolt. Position the brake hose fitting so the pin contacts the boss (**Figure 45**) on the rear caliper. Then, tighten the union bolt to 30 N•m (22 ft.-lb.).
   c. If the caliper was rebuilt, or the brake hose disconnected from the caliper, fill and bleed the brake system as described in this chapter.
5. Operate the brake lever several times to seat the pads.
6. Check the brake fluid reservoir and replenish or remove fluid as necessary.
7. If necessary, adjust the parking brake (Chapter Three).
8. With the rear wheels raised, check that the disc spins freely and the brake operates properly.

Disassembly

Refer to **Figure 46**.
1. Remove the rear brake caliper as described in this section.
2. Remove the rear brake pads as described in this chapter.
3. Slide the caliper bracket (**Figure 47**) out of the caliper.
4. Unscrew the piston from the caliper using the slots (A, **Figure 48**) in the piston face.
5. Remove the dust seal (A, **Figure 49**) from the front bore groove.
6. Remove the piston seal (B, **Figure 49**) from the rear bore groove.
7. If necessary, remove the pad spring (A, **Figure 50**) in the caliper bracket.
8. If necessary, remove the boots (B, **Figure 50**) from the brake caliper.
9. To remove the rear parking brake assembly, perform the following:
   a. Remove the return spring (A, **Figure 51**).
   b. Loosen the locknut (B, **Figure 51**) and remove the adjust bolt (C).
   c. Remove the parking brake lever (D, **Figure 51**).
   d. Remove the actuator cover (A, **Figure 52**).
   e. Loosen and remove the actuator (B, **Figure 52**).
   f. Remove the two bolts (A, **Figure 53**) that hold the parking brake housing to the rear brake caliper. Remove the spring arm (B, **Figure 53**), and then remove the parking brake housing (C).
   g. Remove the gasket (**Figure 54**).
10. Remove the bleeder valve and its cover from the caliper.

11. Further disassembly is not recommended. Parts inside the caliper and piston are not available separately.

Brake Caliper Inspection

All models use a floating caliper design, in which the caliper slides or floats on threaded shaft bolts mounted parallel with each other on the caliper and caliper bracket. Rubber boots around each shaft bolt prevent dirt from damaging the shafts. If the shaft bolts are worn or damaged the caliper can move out of alignment on the caliper bracket. This will cause brake drag, uneven pad wear and overheating. Inspect the rubber boots and shaft bolts during caliper inspection as they play a vital role in brake performance.

Refer to **Figure 46** when servicing the rear brake caliper assembly. Replace parts that are out of specification (**Table 1**) or damaged as described in this section.

WARNING
Do not allow oil or grease on the brake components. Do not clean the parts with kerosene or other petroleum products. These chemicals cause the rubber brake system components to swell, which may cause brake failure.

CAUTION
The caliper bore and seal grooves can be difficult to clean, especially if brake fluid was leaking past the seals. Clean the grooves carefully to avoid damaging the grooves and bore surfaces.

1. Clean and dry the caliper and all of the other metal parts. Clean the seal grooves carefully. If the contamination is difficult to remove, soak the caliper in a suitable solvent and then reclean. If any of the rubber parts are to be reused, clean them with dena

46

REAR BRAKE CALIPER (2006-2012 MODELS)

1. Boot
2. Bracket
3. Washer
4. Shaft bolt
5. Pad pins
6. Boot
7. Shaft bolt
8. Boot
9. Brake caliper
10. Bleeder valve
11. Dust cap
12. Gasket
13. Parking brake housing
14. Bolt
15. Bracket
16. Boot
17. Actuator
18. Spring
19. Parking brake lever
20. Nut
21. Bolt
22. Insulator
23. Shim
24. Pad spring
25. Outer brake pad
26. Inner brake pad
27. Dust seal
28. Piston seal
29. Piston

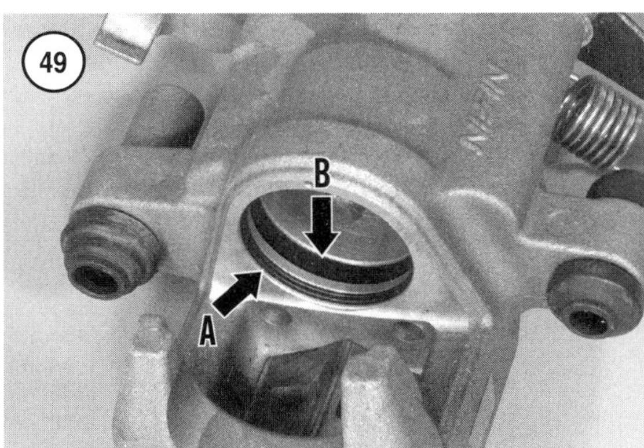

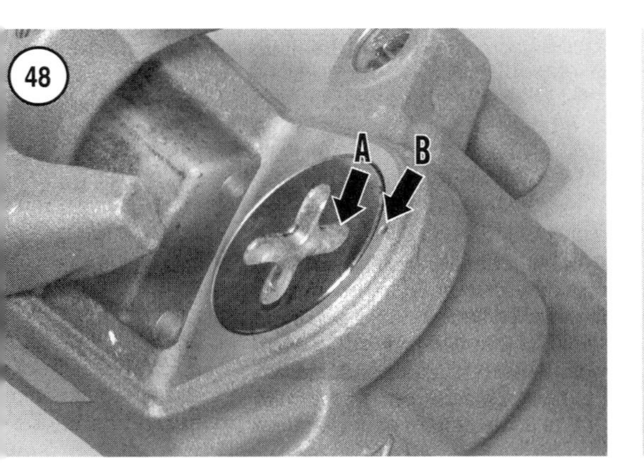

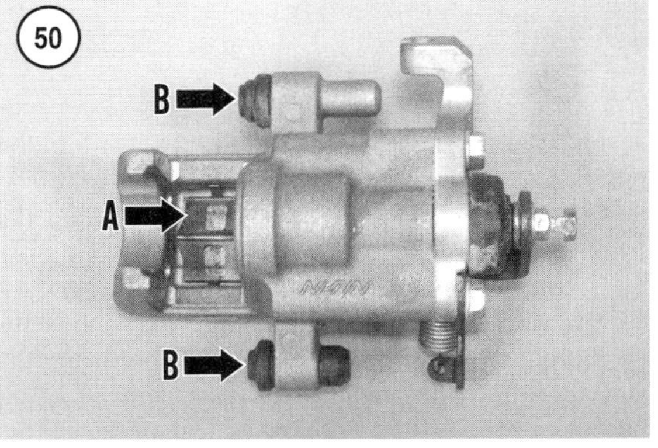

tured alcohol or new DOT 4 brake fluid. Do not use a petroleum-based solvent.

2. Inspect the caliper bracket, shafts and rubber boots as follows:
   a. Inspect the rubber boots for cracks, tearing, weakness or other damage.
   b. Inspect the shaft bolts (A, **Figure 55**) on the caliper bracket (B) for excessive or uneven wear. If the shaft bolt is damaged, replace it.
3. Check the caliper bore for corrosion, pitting, deep scratches or other wear.
4. Measure the inside diameter (**Figure 56**) of the rear caliper bore.
5. Check the piston for wear marks, scoring, cracks or other damage.
6. Check the bleeder valve and dust cap for wear or damage. Make sure air can pass through the bleeder valve.
7. Check the union bolt for wear or damage. Discard the washers.
8. Inspect the brake pads and pad spring as described in *Rear Brake Pads* (this chapter).
9. Inspect the actuator and parking brake housing for damaged threads, or other damage.
10. Inspect the parking brake actuator cover. Replace it if damaged.

Assembly

NOTE
Use new DOT 4 brake fluid when lubricating parts in the following steps.

1. Install the bleeder valve and dust cap into the caliper.
2. Soak the new piston seals and dust seals in brake fluid.
3. Lubricate the cylinder bores with brake fluid.

NOTE
*The piston seals (B, **Figure 49**) are thicker than the dust seals (A).*

NOTE
Make sure each seal fits squarely inside its bore groove.

4. Install a new piston seal (B, **Figure 49**) into the rear bore groove.
5. Install a new dust seal (A, **Figure 49**) into the front bore groove.
6. Lubricate the piston with brake fluid.
7. Thread the piston sleeve onto the stud in the caliper bore. Screw the piston into the caliper using the slots (A, **Figure 48**) in the piston face. Turn the piston until the piston is flush with the surface of the caliper

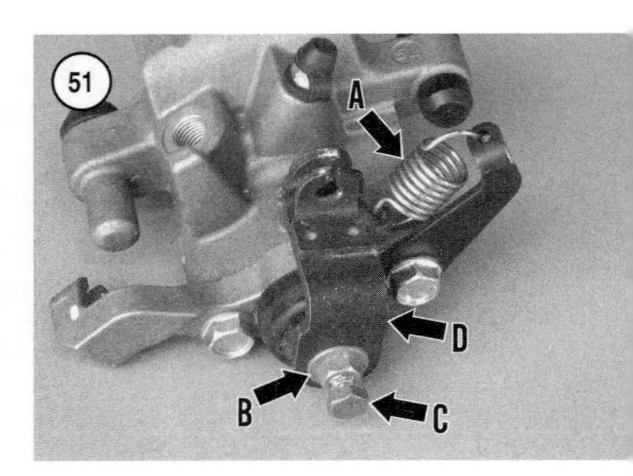

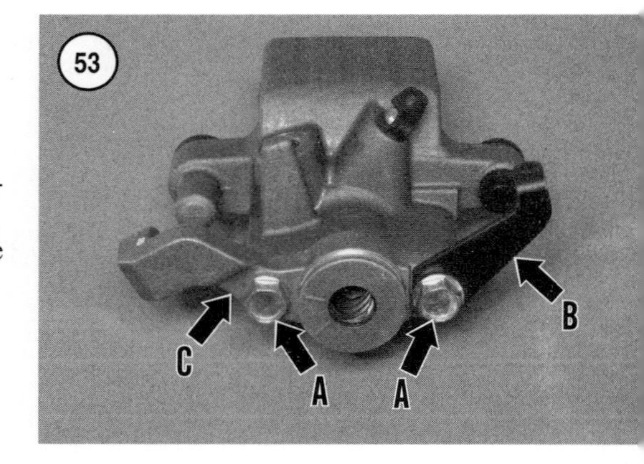

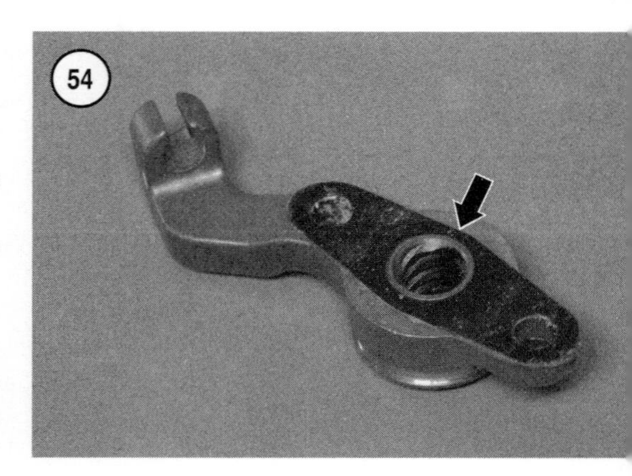

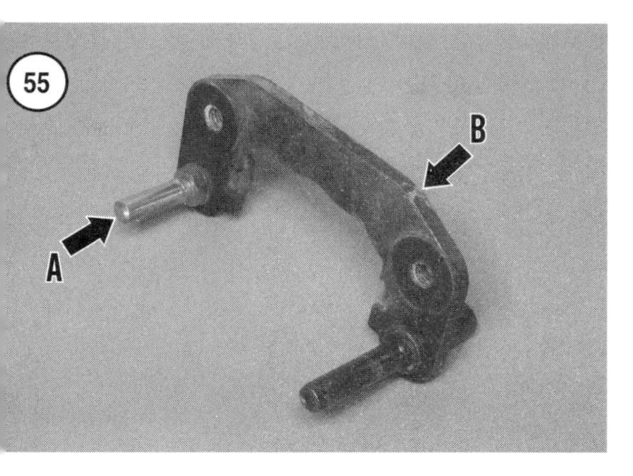

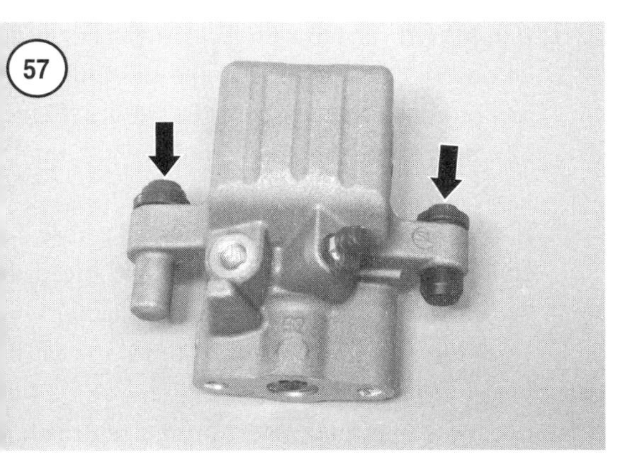

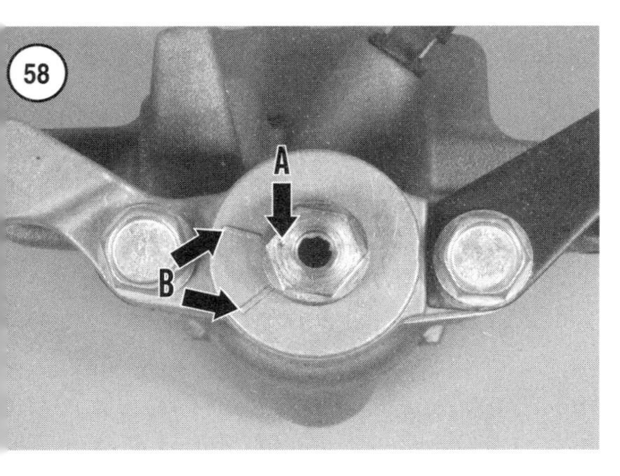

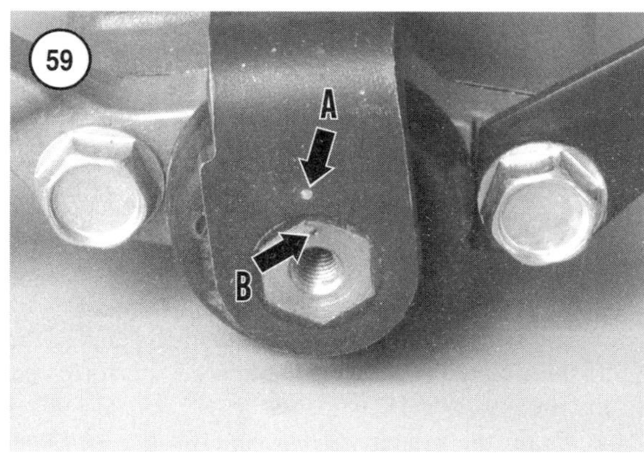

and a slot on the piston aligns with the punch mark (B, **Figure 48**) on the caliper. After installing the piston, clean spilled brake fluid from the area in front of the piston to prevent brake pad contamination.

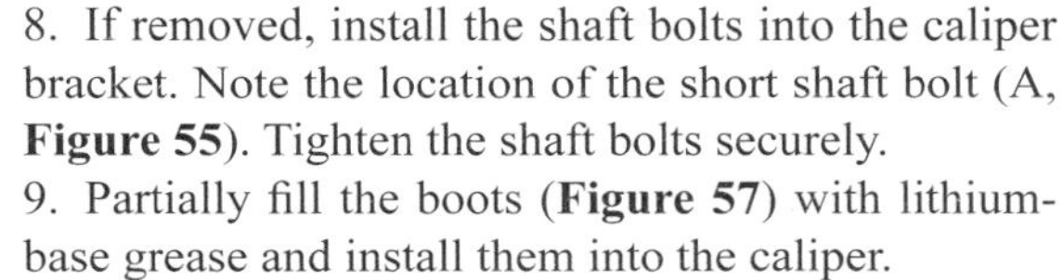

CAUTION

Use only lithium-base grease specified for brake use. Do not use brake fluid to lubricate the rubber boots or fixed shafts.

8. If removed, install the shaft bolts into the caliper bracket. Note the location of the short shaft bolt (A, **Figure 55**). Tighten the shaft bolts securely.
9. Partially fill the boots (**Figure 57**) with lithium-base grease and install them into the caliper.
10. Lubricate the caliper bracket shaft bolts with lithium-base grease.
11. Align and slide the mounting bracket (**Figure 47**) into the caliper body. Hold the caliper and slide the caliper bracket in and out by hand. Make sure there is no roughness or binding.
12. If removed, install the parking brake housing as follows:
    a. Install the gasket onto the brake housing.
    b. Place the parking brake housing (C, **Figure 53**) onto the brake caliper, aligning the mounting holes and gasket.
    c. Apply threadlock onto the parking brake housing mounting bolts prior to installation. Install the bolts (A, **Figure 53**), including the spring arm (B). Tighten the bolts to 22 N•m (16 ft.-lb.).
    d. Install and tighten the actuator until it stops. The mark (A, **Figure 58**) on the actuator must be located between the marks (B) on the housing. If not, check for damage or incorrect assembly.
    e. Install the actuator cover (A, **Figure 52**).
    f. Install the parking brake lever and spring. The punch mark (A, **Figure 59**) on the lever must align with the punch mark (B) on the actuator.

g. Install the adjust bolt (C, **Figure 51**) and locknut (B).

13. Install the rear brake caliper assembly and rear brake pads as described in this chapter.

REAR BRAKE CALIPER (2013-ON MODELS)

Removal/Installation

1. If the caliper will be disassembled, perform the following:
   a. Drain the system as described in this chapter. After draining, loosen the brake hose union bolt (A, **Figure 60**) while the caliper is mounted. Leave the bolt finger-tight. It will be removed in a later step.
   b. On the parking brake cable, loosen the locknut (A, **Figure 61**) and turn the cable adjuster (B) until there is enough slack in the cable to remove it from the parking brake lever (B).

NOTE
If necessary, disengage the upper end of the parking brake cable from the handlebar lever to obtain sufficient cable slack.

2. Remove the caliper mounting bolts (C, **Figure 60**). Remove the caliper from the disc. Avoid kinking the brake hose.

3A. If the caliper will be left attached to the brake hose, but not disassembled and serviced perform the following:
   a. Suspend the caliper with a length of wire. Do not let the caliper hang from the brake hose.
   b. Insert a small wood block between the brake pads. This will prevent the caliper piston from extending out of the caliper if the brake lever is operated.

3B. If the caliper will be disassembled, perform the following:
   a. Remove the union bolt and seal washers from the brake hose. Have a shop cloth ready to absorb excess brake fluid that drips from the hose.
   b. Tie a plastic bag around the end of the hose to prevent brake fluid from damaging other surfaces.
   c. Drain excess brake fluid from the caliper.
   d. Remove the brake pads as described in this chapter.
   e. Repair the caliper as described in this section.

4. Reverse this procedure to install the caliper while noting the following:
   a. Install and tighten the caliper mounting bolts to 43 N•m (32 ft.-lb.).

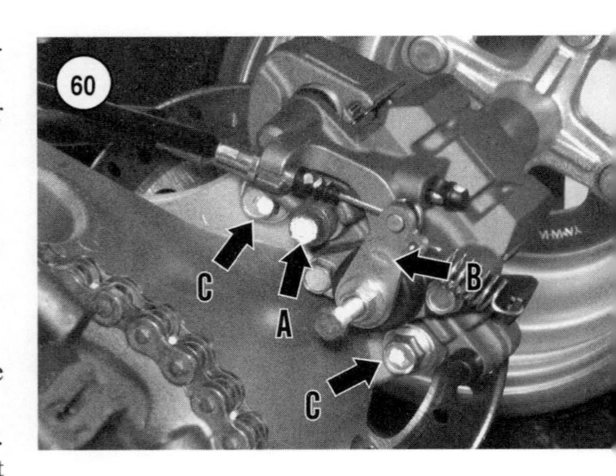

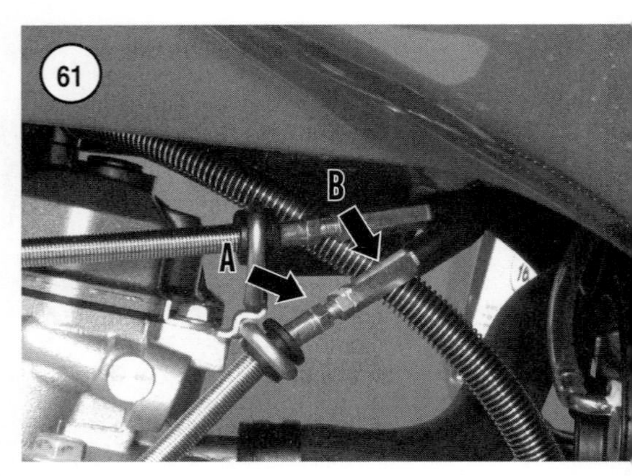

   b. If removed, install new seal washers on th union bolt. Position the brake hose fitting s the pin contacts the boss on the caliper (**Figu 62**), then tighten the union bolt to 30 N•m (2 ft.-lb.).
   c. If the caliper was rebuilt, or the brake hose di connected from the caliper, fill and bleed th brake system as described in this chapter.

5. Operate the brake lever several times to seat th pads.

6. Check the brake fluid reservoir and replenish remove fluid as necessary.

7. If necessary, adjust the parking brake (Chapt Three).

8. With the rear wheels raised, check that the di spins freely and the brake operates properly.

Disassembly

Refer to **Figure 63**.

CAUTION
Do not pry out the pistons. This will damage the pistons and caliper bore.

Removing the piston hydraulically

If the piston and dust seals are in good condition and there are no signs of brake fluid leaking from the bore, it may be possible to remove the pistons hydraulically. However, note that brake fluid will spill from the caliper once the pistons become free.

1. Remove the rear brake caliper as described in this chapter. Do not loosen or remove the brake hose.
2. Remove the rear brake caliper pads as described in this chapter.
3. Remove the caliper bracket from the caliper. Have a supply of paper towels and a pan available to catch and wipe up spilled brake fluid.
4. Hold the caliper with the pistons facing out and operate the brake pedal to push the pistons out of the caliper bores.
5. Remove the union bolt with an impact gun (air or electric), if available. Otherwise, hold the caliper and caliper bracket against the swing arm with an adjustable wrench and remove the union bolt with hand tools.
6. Perform the relevant steps in the following section to complete caliper disassembly.

Removing the piston with compressed air

1. Remove the brake caliper as described in this chapter.
2. Remove the rear brake caliper pads as described in this chapter.
3. Slide the caliper bracket out of the caliper.

WARNING
Wear eye protection when using compressed air to remove the piston. Keep your fingers away from the piston.

4. Cushion the piston with a shop rag and position the caliper with the piston bore facing down. Apply compressed air through the brake hose port (**Figure 64**) to force out the pistons.

CAUTION
Do not try to pry out the pistons. This will damage the piston and caliper bore.

5. Remove the dust (A, **Figure 65**) and piston seal (B) from the caliper bore grooves and discard them.
6. Remove the small O-ring (**Figure 66**) from the inside of the parking brake housing.
7. To remove the rear parking brake assembly, perform the following:
   a. Remove the return spring (A, **Figure 67**).
   b. Loosen the locknut (B, **Figure 67**) and remove the adjust bolt (C).
   c. Remove the parking brake lever (**Figure 68**).
   d. Remove the actuator cover (**Figure 69**).
   e. Turn out and remove the actuator (**Figure 70**).
   f. Remove the two bolts (A, **Figure 71**) that hold the parking brake housing to the rear brake caliper. Remove the spring arm (B, **Figure 71**), then remove the parking brake housing (C).
   g. Remove the gasket (**Figure 72**).
8. If necessary, remove the boots (A, **Figure 73**) from the brake caliper.
9. If necessary, remove the pad spring on the caliper bracket (A, **Figure 74**).
10. If necessary, remove the shafts (B, **Figure 74**) from the caliper bracket.
11. Remove the bleeder valve and its cover from the caliper.
12. Remove the pad spring from the caliper (B, **Figure 73**).

Brake Caliper Inspection

All models use a floating caliper design, in which the caliper slides or floats on threaded shafts mounted parallel with each other on the caliper and caliper bracket. Rubber boots around each shaft prevent dirt from damaging the shafts. If the shafts are worn or damaged the caliper may move out of alignment on the caliper bracket. This will cause brake drag, uneven pad wear and overheating. Inspect the rubber boots and shafts during caliper inspection as they play a vital role in brake performance.

Refer to **Figure 63** when servicing the rear brake caliper assembly. Replace parts that are out of specification listed in **Table 1**, or damaged as described in this section.

WARNING
Do not allow oil or grease on the brake components. Do not clean the parts with kerosene or other petroleum products. These chemicals cause the rubber brake system components to swell, which may cause brake failure.

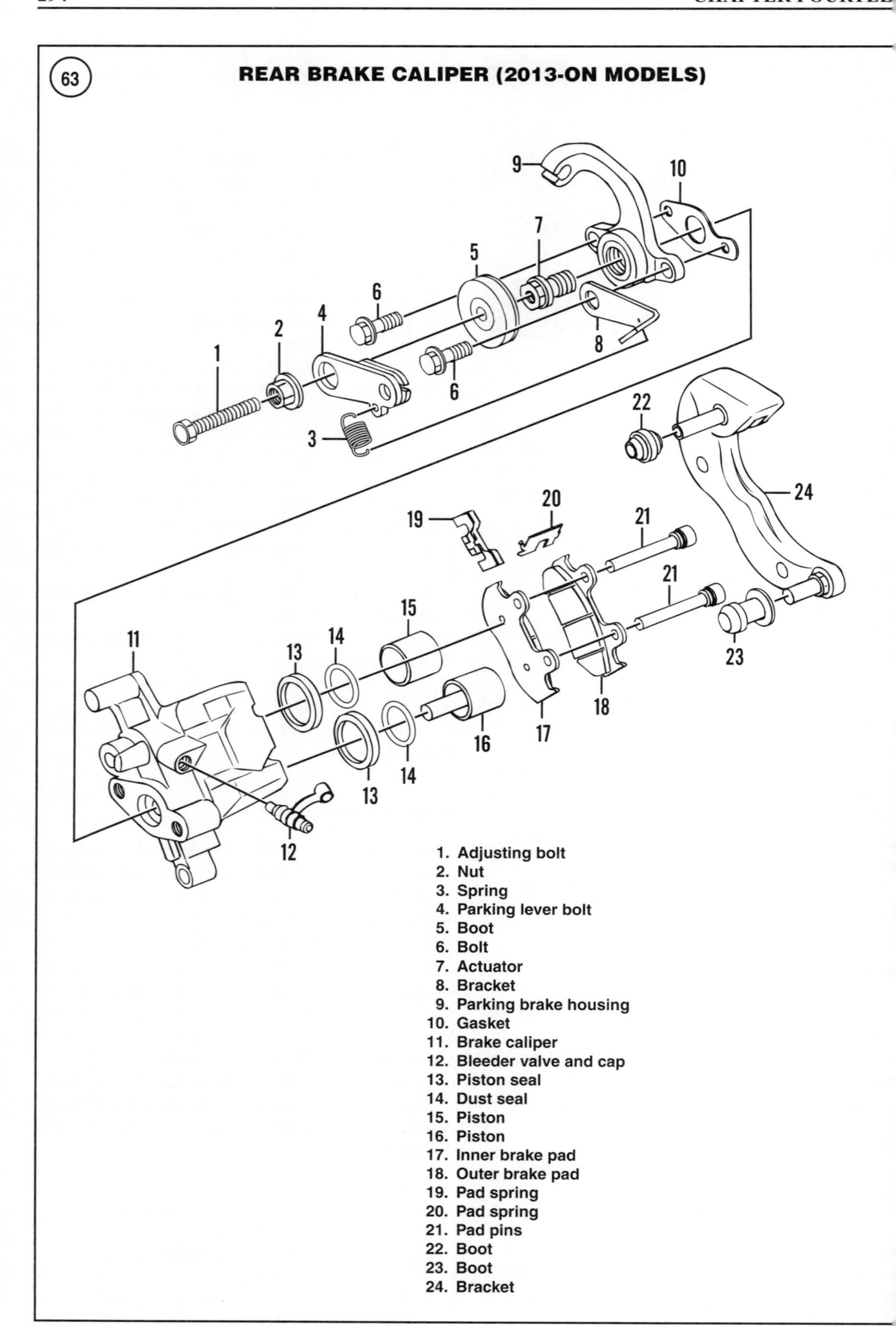
63
REAR BRAKE CALIPER (2013-ON MODELS)
1
2
3
4
5
6
6
7
8
9
10
11
12
13
13
14
14
15
16
17
18
19
20
21
21
22
23
24
1. Adjusting bolt
2. Nut
3. Spring
4. Parking lever bolt
5. Boot
6. Bolt
7. Actuator
8. Bracket
9. Parking brake housing
10. Gasket
11. Brake caliper
12. Bleeder valve and cap
13. Piston seal
14. Dust seal
15. Piston
16. Piston
17. Inner brake pad
18. Outer brake pad
19. Pad spring
20. Pad spring
21. Pad pins
22. Boot
23. Boot
24. Bracket

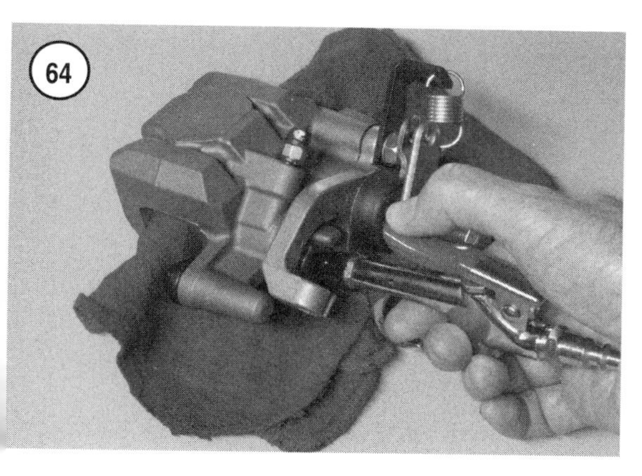

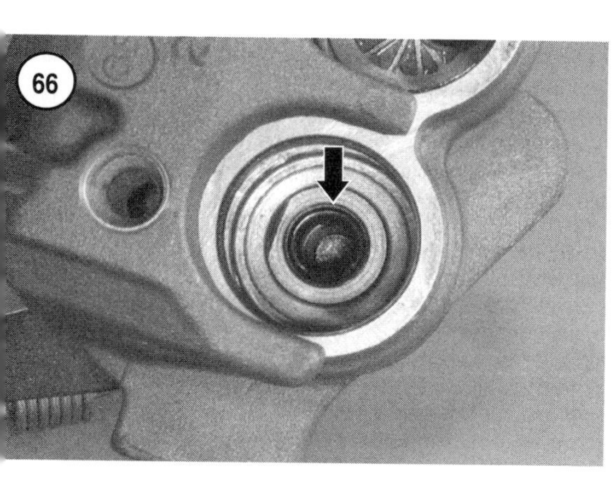

67
B
A
C

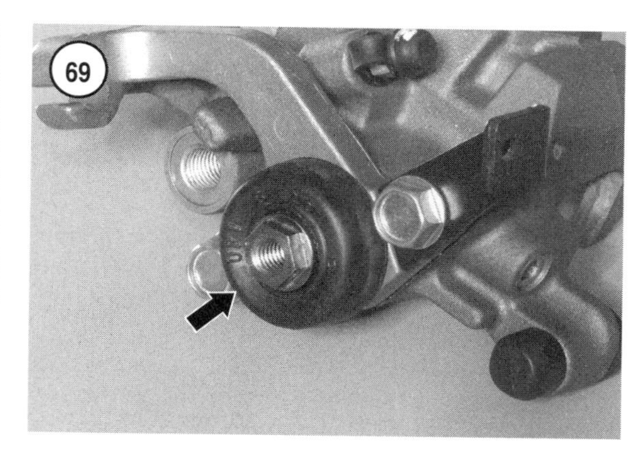

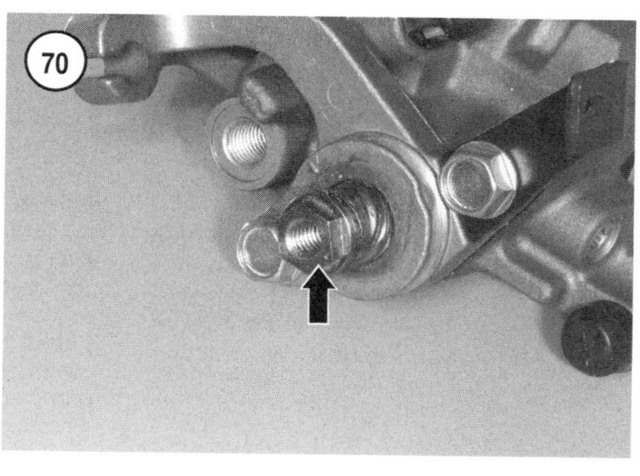

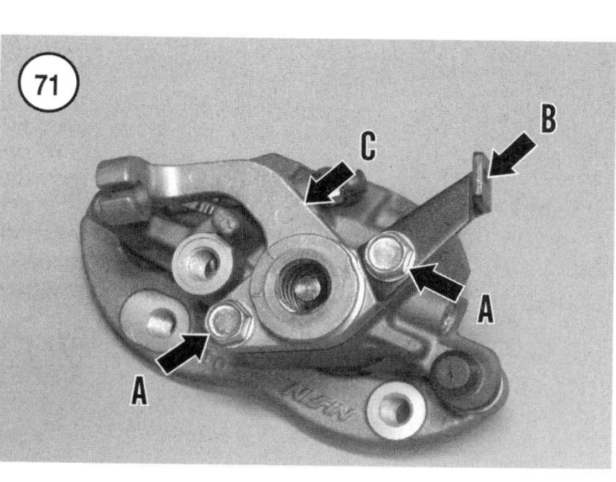

CAUTION
The caliper bore and seal grooves can be difficult to clean, especially if brake fluid was leaking past the seals. Clean the grooves carefully to avoid damaging the grooves and bore surfaces.

1 Clean and dry the caliper and the other metal parts. Clean the seal grooves carefully. If the contamination is difficult to remove, soak the caliper in a suitable solvent and then reclean. If any of the rubber parts are to be reused, clean them with denatured alcohol or new DOT 4 brake fluid. Do not use a petroleum-based solvent.
2. Inspect the caliper bracket, shafts and rubber boots as follows:
   a. Inspect the rubber boots for cracks, tearing, weakness or other damage.
   b. Inspect the shafts on the caliper bracket (B, Figure 74) for excessive or uneven wear. If the shaft is damaged, replace the shaft.
3. Check each cylinder bore for corrosion, pitting, deep scratches or other wear.
4. Measure the inside diameter of the caliper bore (Figure 75).
5. Check the piston for wear marks, scoring, cracks or other damage.
6. Check the bleeder valve and cap for wear or damage. Make sure air can pass through the bleeder valve.
7. Check the union bolt for wear or damage. Discard the washers.
8. Inspect the brake pads and pad spring as described under *Front Brake Pads* in this chapter.
9. Inspect the actuator and parking brake housing (**Figure 76**) for damaged threads, or other damage.
10. Inspect the parking brake actuator cover. Replace if damaged.

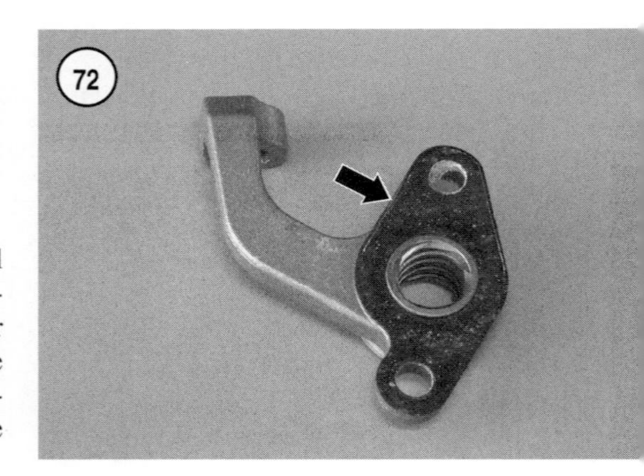

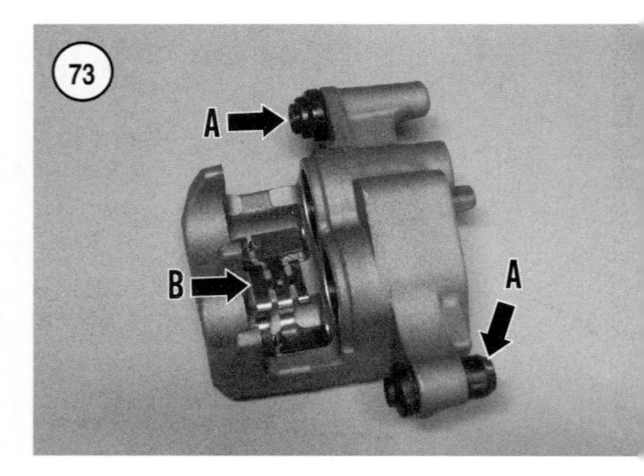

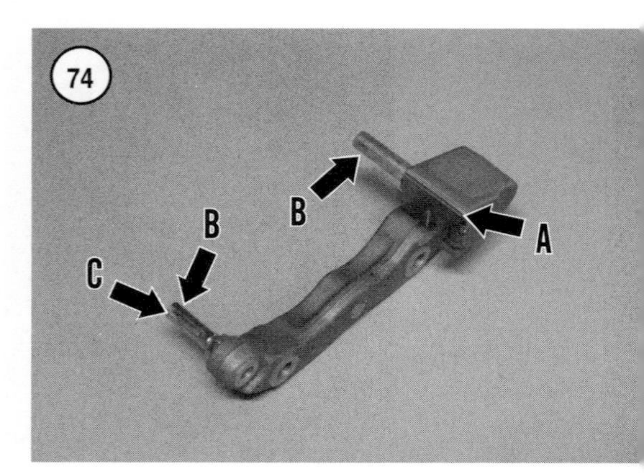

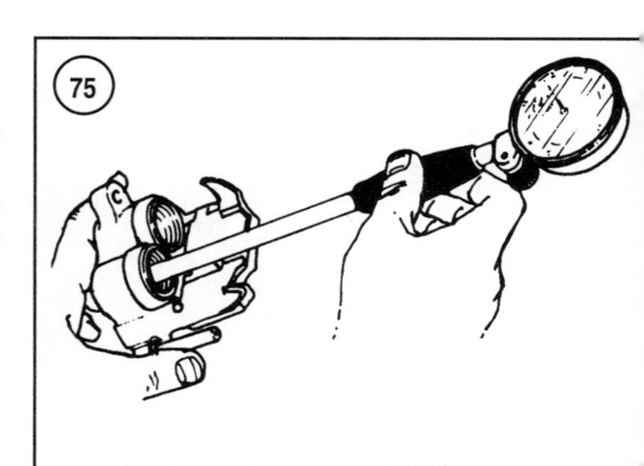

Assembly

NOTE
Use new DOT 4 brake fluid when lubricating parts in the following steps.

1. Install the bleeder valve and its cover into the caliper.
2. Install the new parking brake O-ring into the groove in the back of the caliper. Refer to **Figure 66**.
3. Soak the new piston and dust seals in brake fluid.
4. Lubricate the cylinder bores with brake fluid.

NOTE
The piston seals are thicker than the dust seals.

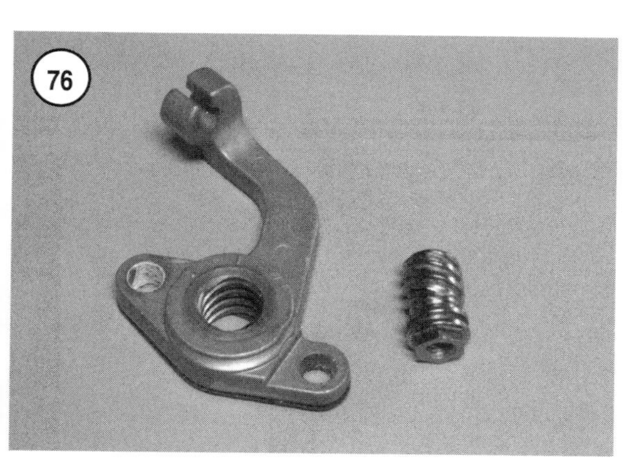

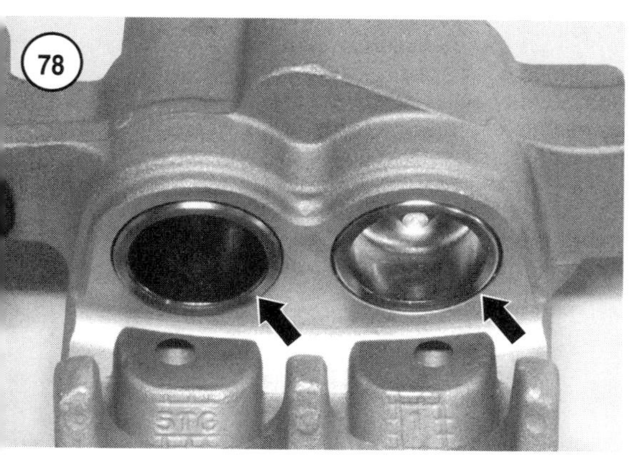

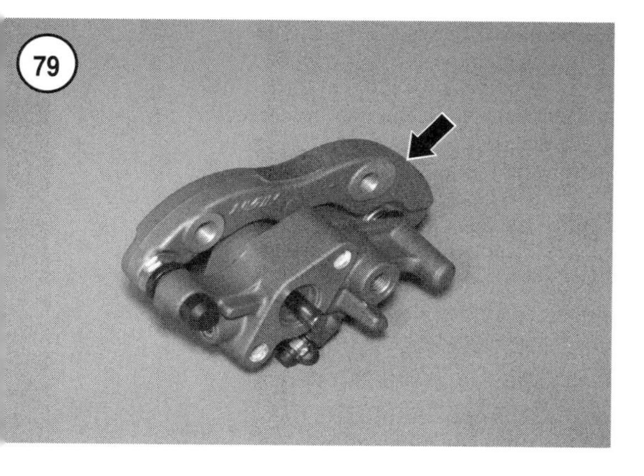

5. Install a new piston seal (A, **Figure 77**) into each rear bore groove.
6. Install a new dust seal (B, **Figure 77**) into each front bore groove.

NOTE
Make sure each seal fits squarely inside its bore groove.

7. Lubricate the pistons with brake fluid.

CAUTION
The tight piston-to-seal fit can make piston installation difficult. Do not install the pistons by pushing them straight in as they may bind in their bores and tear the seals.

8. With the open side facing out, align a piston with the caliper bore. Rock the piston slightly to center it in the bore while at the same time pushing the lower end past the seals. When the lower end of the piston passes through both of the seals, push and bottom the piston in the bore (**Figure 78**). After installing the other piston, clean spilled brake fluid from the area in front of the pistons to prevent brake pad contamination.

CAUTION
In the following steps, use only lithium-base grease specified for brake use. Do not use brake fluid to lubricate the rubber boots or fixed shafts.

9. If removed, install the shafts into the caliper bracket. Note the location of the short shaft (C, **Figure 74**). Tighten the shafts securely.
10. Partially fill the boots with lithium-base grease and install them (A, **Figure 79**) into the caliper.
11. Lubricate the caliper bracket shafts with lithium-base grease.
12. Align and slide the mounting bracket onto the caliper body (**Figure 76**). Hold the caliper and slide the caliper bracket in and out by hand. Make sure there is no roughness or binding.
13. If removed, install the parking brake housing as follows:
   a. Install the gasket (**Figure 72**) onto the brake housing.
   b. Place the parking brake housing (C, **Figure 71**) onto the brake caliper, aligning the mounting holes and gasket.
   c. Apply threadlocking compound onto the parking brake housing mounting bolts prior to installation. Install the bolts (A, **Figure 71**), including the spring arm (B). Tighten the bolts to 23 N•m (17 ft.-lb.).

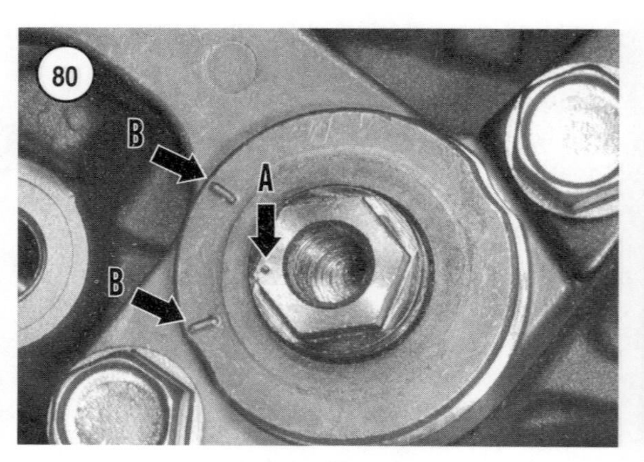

d. Turn in the actuator until it stops. The mark on the actuator (A, **Figure 80**) must be located between the marks (B) on the housing. If not, check for damage or incorrect assembly.
e. Install the actuator cover (**Figure 69**).
f. Install the parking brake lever and spring. The lever centerline must align with the punch mark on the actuator **(Figure 81**).
g. Install the adjust bolt (C, **Figure 70**) and locknut (B).

14. Install the brake caliper assembly and brake pads as described in this chapter.

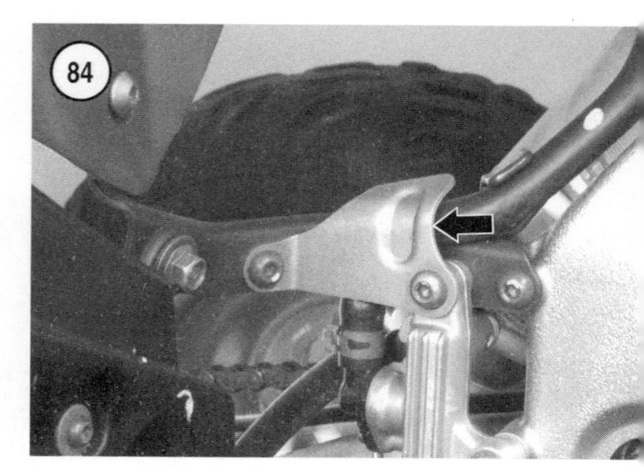

REAR MASTER CYLINDER

Removal/Installation

Use the following procedure to remove the rear master cylinder from the ATV. Refer to *Inspection* in this section to make internal repairs to the master cylinder.

1. Drain the brake system as described in this chapter.
2. Remove the cap and diaphragm and verify that the reservoir is empty.
3. Remove the cotter pin, washer and clevis pin (**Figure 82**), that secure the master cylinder clevis to the brake pedal.

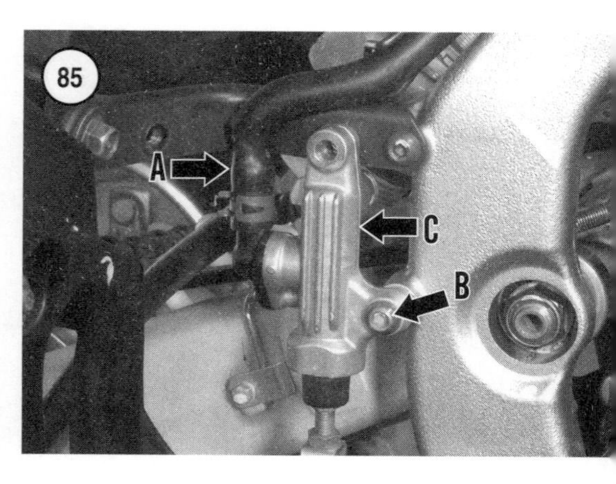

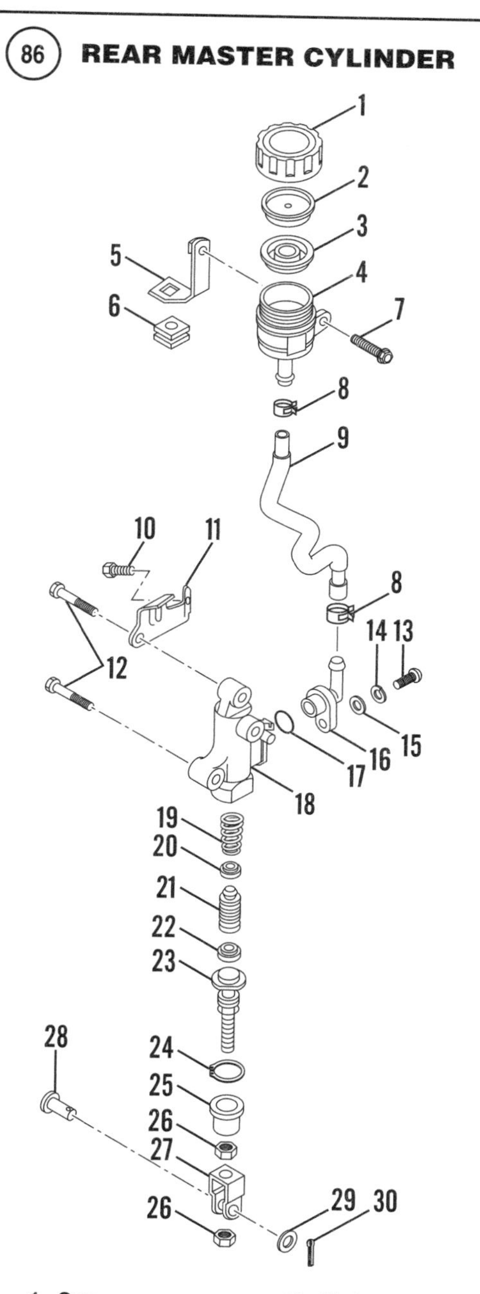

86 REAR MASTER CYLINDER

1. Cap
2. Diaphragm holder
3. Diaphragm
4. Reservoir
5. Bracket
6. Grommet
7. Bolt
8. Clamp
9. Hose
10. Screw
11. Bracket
12. Bolt
13. Screw
14. Lockwasher
15. Washer
16. Fitting
17. O-ring
18. Master cylinder
19. Spring
20. Primary seal
21. Piston
22. Secondary seal
23. Push rod
24. Snap ring
25. Boot
26. Nut
27. Clevis
28. Clevis pin
29. Washer
30. Cotter pin

NOTE

Have shop cloths ready to absorb excess brake fluid that drips from disconnected hoses. Wrap the hose ends in plastic bags to prevent brake fluid from damaging other surfaces.

4. Remove the union bolt (A, **Figure 83**) and seal washers from the brake hose end.
5. Remove the cover (**Figure 84**). Note that one cover bolt also serves as a master cylinder mounting bolt.
6. Detach the reservoir hose (A, **Figure 85**) from the master cylinder.
7. Remove the master cylinder mounting bolt (B, **Figure 85**), and remove the master cylinder (C).
8. Disassemble and inspect the master cylinder as described in this section.
9. Reverse the removal procedure to install the master cylinder. Note the following:
   a. Tighten the master cylinder and cover mounting bolts to 20 N•m (15 ft.-lb.).
   b. Install new seal washers on the union bolt. Position the brake hose fitting so the pin contacts the boss (B, **Figure 83**) on the rear master cylinder. Then, tighten the union bolt to 30 N•m (22 ft.-lb.).
   c. Install a new cotter pin on the clevis pin.
   d. Fill the brake fluid reservoir and bleed the brake system as described in this chapter.

Disassembly/Inspection/Reassembly

Use the following procedure to disassemble, inspect and assemble the master cylinder using new parts. The piston, seals and spring are only available as a complete assembly. Refer to **Figure 86**.

1. Remove the master cylinder as described in this section.
2. Remove the clamp and reservoir hose from the hose fitting.
3. Remove the mounting screw (A, **Figure 87**). Then, remove the fitting (B, **Figure 87**) and O-ring.
4. Remove the lower snap ring from the master cylinder as follows:
   a. Unseat the boot from the master cylinder bore and fold it toward the clevis. The boot is a friction fit. To avoid damaging the boot on removal, apply penetrating lubricant around the perimeter of the boot. Carefully pull the bottom edge back so the lubricant can loosen the boot.
   b. If desired, lock the master cylinder in a vise with soft jaws.

c. Press and tilt the pushrod to relieve pressure on the snap ring (**Figure 88**). Then, remove the snap ring with snap ring pliers.
d. Slowly relieve the pressure on the piston.

5. Remove the piston (A, **Figure 89**) and pushrod (B) assemblies from the bore
6. Inspect the master cylinder assembly.
   a. Clean all parts with fresh brake fluid or isopropyi (rubbing) alcohol.
   b. Inspect the master cylinder bore for wear, pitting or corrosion.
   c. Measure the inside diameter (**Figure 90**) of the rear master cylinder bore. Refer to **Table 1** for specifications.
   d. Inspect and clean the threads and orifices (**Figure 91**) in the master cylinder. Clean with compressed air.
   e. Inspect the pushrod assembly. Check the parts for corrosion and wear. Install a new snap ring on the pushrod, with the sharp edge of the snap ring facing the rubber boot. Do not expand the new snap ring when installing it on the pushrod.
   f. Inspect the clevis pin, union bolt and mounting hardware for wear or damage.
   g. Inspect the reservoir, diaphragm, diaphragm holder and reservoir cap for damage.
7. Assemble the piston, seals and spring (A, **Figure 89**) as follows:
   a. Soak the seals in fresh DOT 4 brake fluid for 15 minutes. This will soften and lubricate the seals.
   b. Apply brake fluid to the piston so the seals can slide over the ends.
   c. Mount the seals on the piston. Identify the wide (open) side of both seals. When installed, the wide side of the seals must face in the direction of the arrow (**Figure 92**). Mount the seals with the small hole closest to the spring end of the piston.
   d. Install and seat the spring onto the piston. Attach the small spring end to the piston.
8. Install the piston and pushrod assembly into the master cylinder as follows:
   a. Lubricate the master cylinder bore and piston assembly with brake fluid.
   b. Apply a small amount of lithium-base brake grease to the contact area of the pushrod.
   c. Insert the piston into the master cylinder.
   d. If desired, lock the master cylinder in a vise with soft jaws. Do not overtighten the vise or master cylinder damage could occur.
   e. Compress the snap ring with snap ring pliers.
   f. Press and tilt the pushrod in the master cylinder while guiding the snap ring into position. If the snap ring does not easily seat, release the

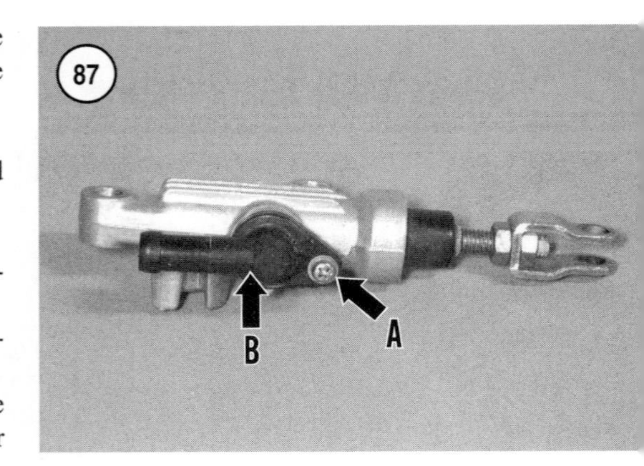

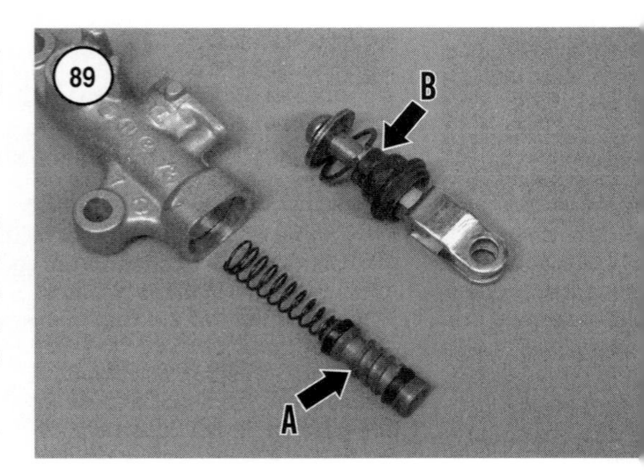

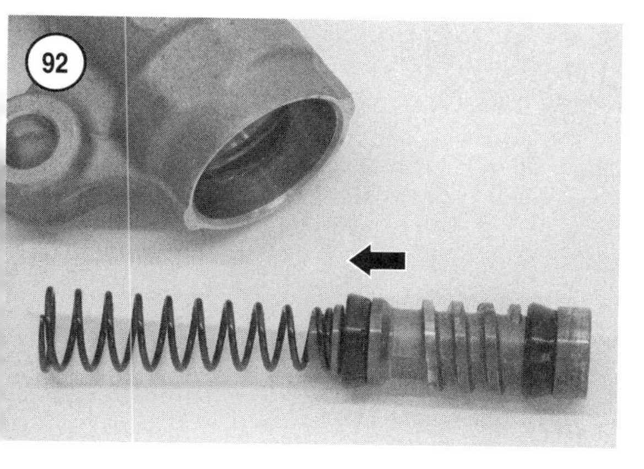

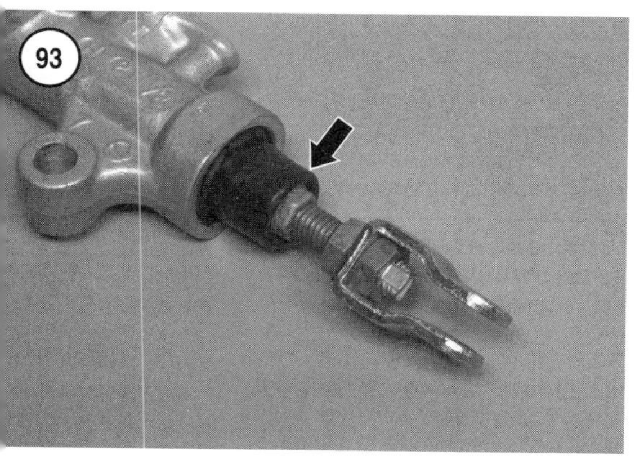

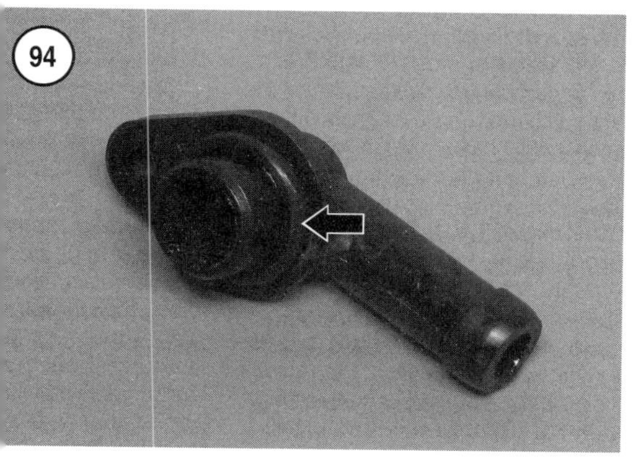

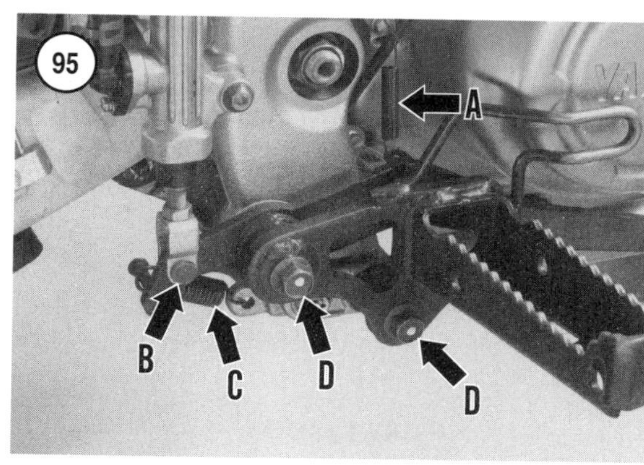

snap ring and use the tip of the pliers to press it into the groove. Keep the pushrod compressed until the snap ring is seated.

9. Apply lithium-base brake grease to the inside of the boot. Seat the boot (**Figure 93**) in the master cylinder.
10. Install a new, lubricated O-ring (**Figure 94**) onto the hose fitting. Then, install the hose fitting into the master cylinder. Install the mounting screw (A, **Figure 87**) and tighten securely.
11. Attach the reservoir and hose to the fitting, and clamp into place.
12. Install the diaphragm, diaphragm holder and cap onto the reservoir.
13. Install the master cylinder as described in this section.

REAR BRAKE PEDAL

The rear brake pedal rides on a boss located on the right footrest flange.

Removal/Installation

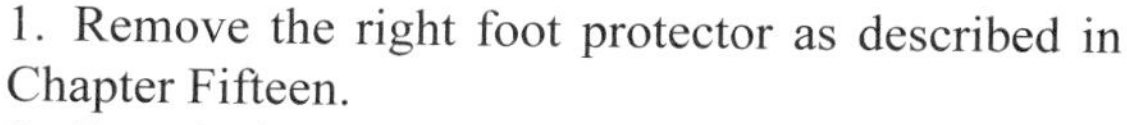

1. Remove the right foot protector as described in Chapter Fifteen.
2. Detach the brake light switch spring (A, **Figure 95**) from the brake pedal.
3. Remove the master cylinder clevis pin (B, **Figure 95**).
4. Detach the brake return spring (C, **Figure 95**).
5. Remove the right footrest retaining bolts (D, **Figure 95**). Then, remove the footrest.
6. Remove the e-clip (**Figure 96**) and washer. Then, separate the brake pedal from the footrest.
7. Remove the brake pedal while also detaching the pedal return spring.
8. Clean and inspect the parts for wear and damage in the areas shown (**Figure 97**).
9. Reverse the removal steps to install the rear brake pedal while noting the following:

a. Apply waterproof grease to the pedal bore and pedal shaft.
b. Tighten the footrest bolts to 78 N•m (57 ft.-lb.).
c. Install a new cotter pin in the clevis pin.
d. Check brake operation.
e. Check pedal height. If necessary, adjust the pedal (Chapter Three).
f. Check brake light operation. If necessary, adjust the rear brake switch (Chapter Three).

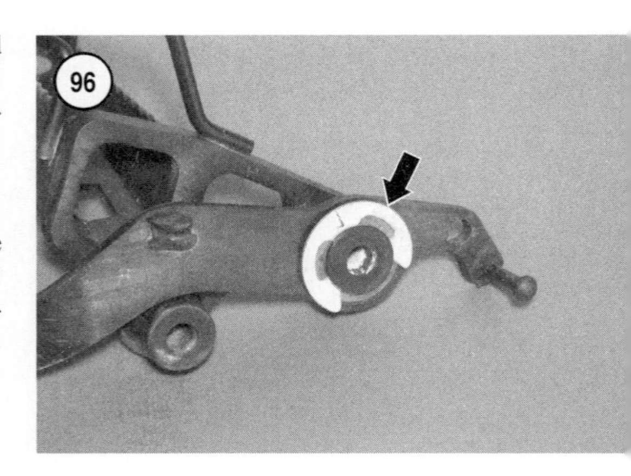

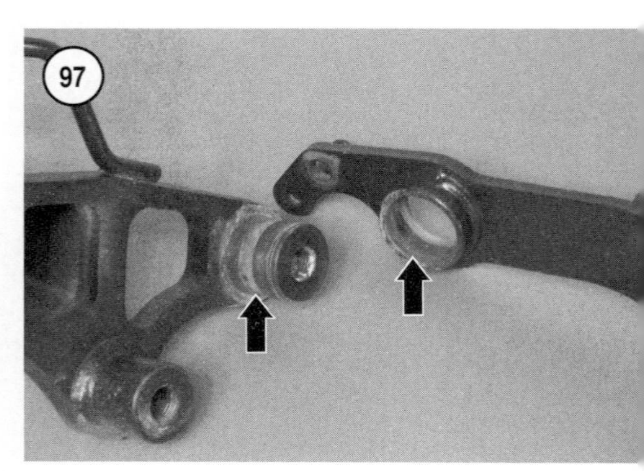

BRAKE DISC

The front brake discs are mounted on the front wheel hubs. The rear brake disc is mounted a splined hub that is driven by the rear axle.

Inspection

The brake disc can be inspected while mounted on the ATV. Small marks on the disc are not important, but radial scratches that run all the way around the disc surface and are deep enough to snag a fingernail can reduce braking effectiveness and increase brake pad wear. If these grooves are evident, and the brake pads are wearing rapidly, replace the brake disc.

Do not machine a deeply scored or warped disc. Removing disc material causes the disc to overheat rapidly and warp. Maintain the discs by keeping them clean and corrosion-free. Clean the discs with a non-petroleum solvent.

Refer to **Table 1** for brake disc specifications. Replace an excessively worn or damaged brake disc.

1. If checking the front brake discs, remove the front wheel (Chapter 11).
2. Measure the thickness (**Figure 98**) at several locations around the disc with a micrometer. Replace the disc if its thickness at any point is less than the service limit in **Table 1**.

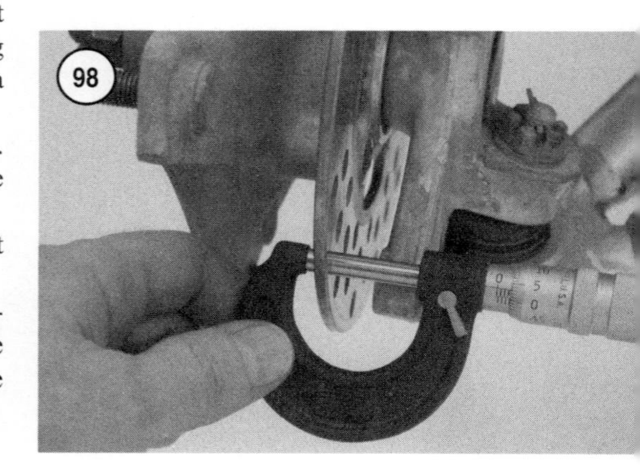

NOTE
If the disc thickness is within specifications, also check the disc parallelism to locate differences in disc thickness. Excessive parallelism will cause brake grab and a pulsating brake lever or pedal when the brakes are applied.

3. Check disc parallelism as follows:
   a. Divide the disc into six different points equally spaced 60° apart.
   b. Measure the disc thickness with a micrometer at each of these six points. If there is a noticeable variation in disc thickness, replace the disc.

NOTE
Before checking front brake disc runout, make sure the wheel bearings are in good condition and the wheel is running true as described in Chapter Twelve.

NOTE
Excessive brake disc runout causes the disc to push against the pistons, which pushes the brake pads back into the caliper. This condition causes brake chatter and increased brake le-

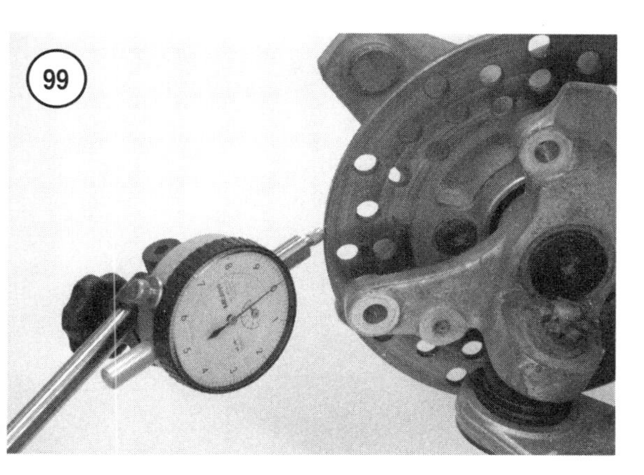
99

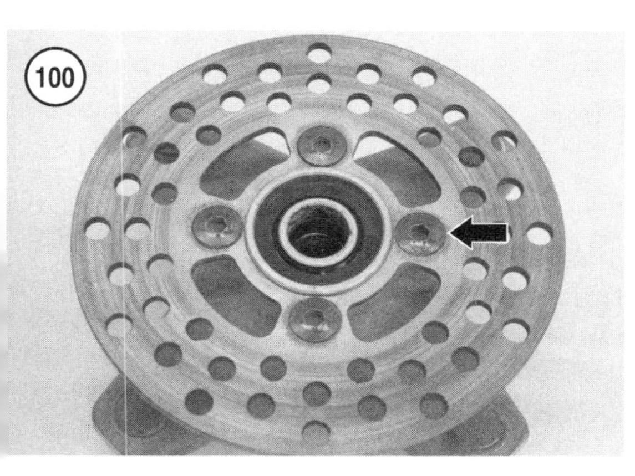
100

101

102

ver or pedal travel when applying the brakes.

4. Measure disc runout (**Figure 99**) with a dial indicator. Replace the disc if the runout exceeds the service limit in **Table 1**.

Removal/Installation

1A. To remove the front brake disc:
   a. Remove the front wheel hub as described in Chapter Twelve.
   b. Remove the bolts (**Figure 100**) securing the brake disc to the front wheel hub.

1B. To remove the rear brake disc:
   a. Apply the rear wheel brake.
   b. Loosen, but do not remove, the rear brake disc mounting bolts (**Figure 101**).
   c. Remove the right, rear wheel hub as described in Chapter Thirteen.
   d. Remove the rear brake caliper as described in this chapter.
   e. Remove the brake disc bolts and remove the brake disc.

2. Reverse the removal steps to install the brake disc while noting the following:
   a. Apply threadlock to the brake disc mounting bolt threads.
   b. Tighten the brake disc mounting bolts to the specification in **Table 2**.

FRONT BRAKE HOSE/LINE REPLACEMENT

The upper brake hose and center brake line can be replaced separately. The lower brake hoses must be replaced as an assembly with the tee fitting (A, **Figure 102**).

NOTE
Some residual brake fluid will remain in the lines. Have a supply of paper towels and a pan available to catch and wipe up spilled brake fluid.

1. Drain the front brake system as described in this chapter. Because air has entered the brake lines, not all of the brake fluid will drain out.
2. To remove the lower brake hoses, perform the following:
   a. Remove the brake hose guard (A, **Figure 103**) on each upper control arm.
   b. Remove the union bolt (B, **Figure 103**) and sealing washers on each front brake caliper. Hold the open hose end in a container to catch any residual brake fluid.

c. Unscrew the nut (B, **Figure 102**) securing the center brake line in the tee fitting.
d. Remove the tee fitting mounting bolt (C, **Figure 102**).
e. Note the routing of the brake hose through the frame and the front suspension arms, and remove the hose. Reinstall the hose through the same path to avoid damage to the hose during suspension arm movement when riding.

3. To remove the upper brake hose, perform the following:
   a. Remove the front fender as described in Chapter Fifteen.
   b. Remove the union bolt (**Figure 104**) and sealing washers from the master cylinder.
   c. Remove any clamps securing the brake hose.
   d. Unscrew the nut (**Figure 105**) securing the center brake line to the hose fitting.
   e. Detach the clip that secures the hose fitting in the bracket. Remove the brake hose.
4. To remove the center brake line, perform the following:
   a. Remove the front fender as described in Chapter Fifteen.
   b. Unscrew the nut (B, **Figure 103**) securing the center brake line in the tee fitting.
   c. Unscrew the nut (**Figure 105**) securing the center brake line to the upper hose fitting.
   d. Note the routing of the brake line, and remove it.
5. Note the following during installation:
   a. Install new sealing washers.
   b. Position the pin on the lower brake hose end against the boss on the caliper.
   c. Tighten the union bolts to 27 N•m (20 ft.-lb.).
   d. Tighten the brake line nuts to 19 N•m (14 ft.-lb.).
   e. Tighten the tee fitting mounting bolt to 10 N•m (89 in.-lb.).
   f. Refill the master cylinder with fresh DOT 4 brake fluid. Bleed both front brakes as described in this chapter.

REAR BRAKE HOSE REPLACEMENT

NOTE
Some residual brake fluid will remain in the lines. Have a supply of paper towels and a pan available to catch and wipe up spilled brake fluid.

1. Drain the rear brake system as described in this chapter. Because air has entered the brake lines, not all of the brake fluid will drain out.

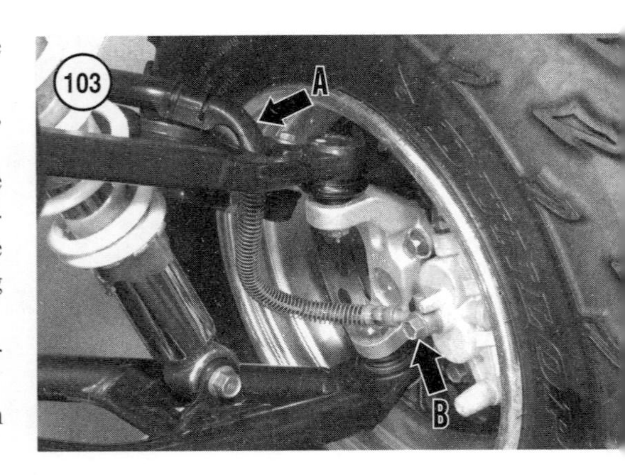

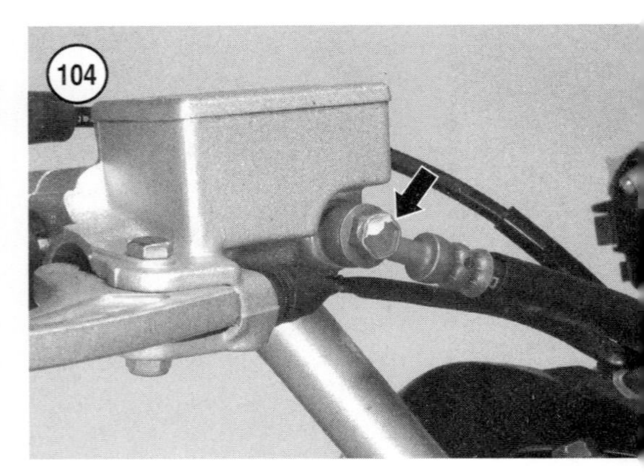

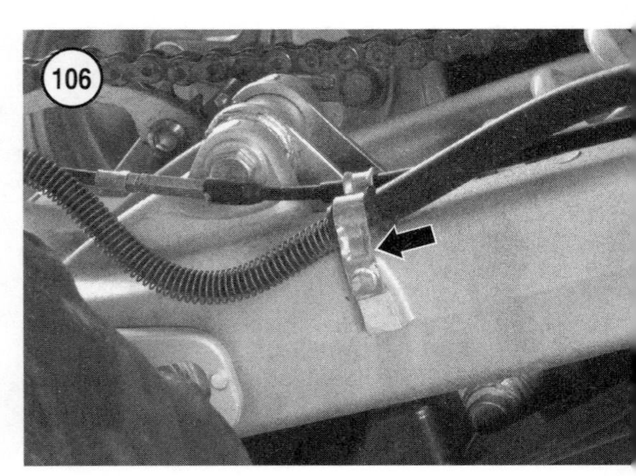

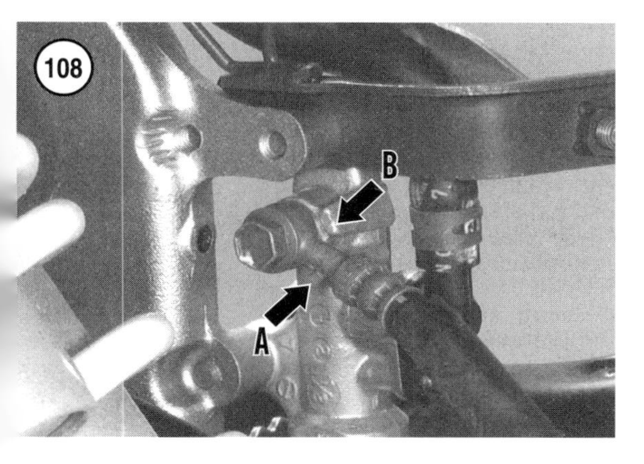

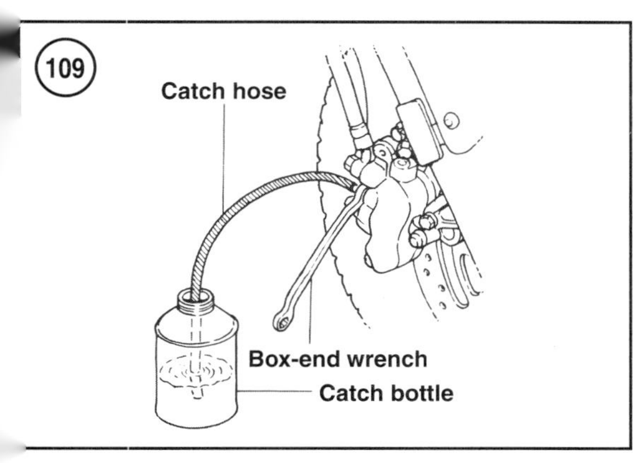

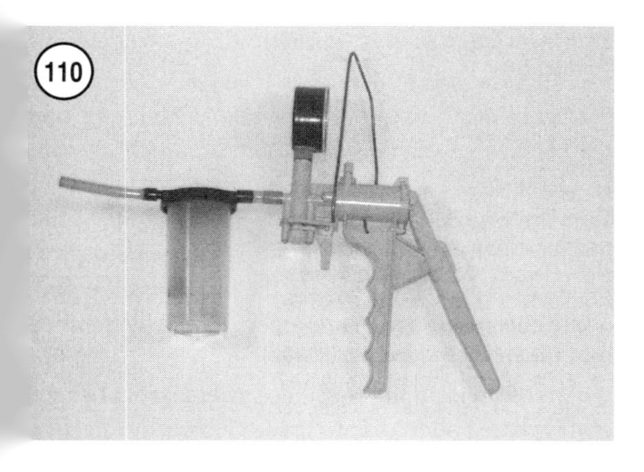

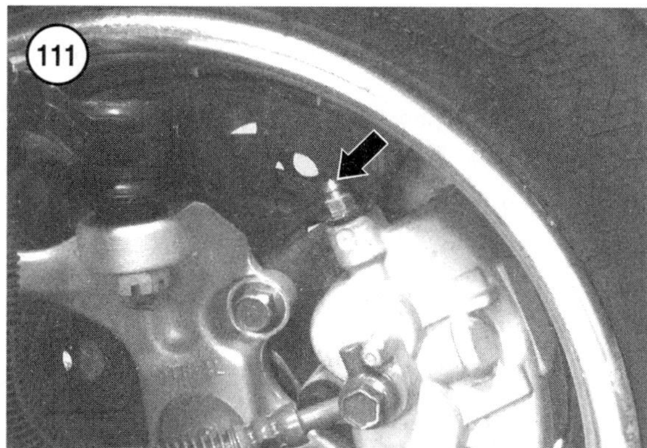

2. Remove the clamps (**Figure 106**) securing the brake hose.
3. Remove the union bolt and sealing washers on the rear brake caliper and the rear master cylinder. Hold the open hose end in a container to catch any residual brake fluid.
4. Note the routing of the brake hose, and remove it.
5. When installing the brake hose, note the following:
   a. Install new sealing washers.
   b. Position the brake hose end so the pin (**Figure 107**) contacts the boss on the caliper.
   c. Position the brake hose fitting so the pin (A, **Figure 108**) contacts the boss (B) on the master cylinder.
   d. Tighten the union bolts to 30 N•m (22 ft.-lb.).

BRAKE SYSTEM DRAINING

Before disconnecting a brake hose when servicing the brake system, pump as much brake fluid from the system as possible. This prevents brake fluid from leaking from the open lines.

The brake system can be drained either manually or with a vacuum pump. When draining the system manually, the master cylinder is used as a pump to expel brake fluid from the system. An empty bottle, a length of clear hose that fits tightly onto the caliper bleeder valve and a wrench are required (**Figure 109**). When using vacuum to drain the system, a hand-operated vacuum pump like the Mityvac (**Figure 110**) is required.

1. Remove the cover and diaphragm from the reservoir.

2A. When draining the system manually, perform the following:
   a. Lift off the dust cap from the caliper bleeder valve (**Figure 111**), and connect the hose to the bleeder valve. Insert the other end of the hose into a clean bottle.

b. Apply (do not pump) the brake lever or brake pedal until it stops, and then hold it in this position.
c. Open the bleeder valve with a wrench, and apply the brake lever or brake pedal until it reaches the end of its travel. This expels some of the brake fluid from the system.
d. Hold the lever or pedal in this position and close the bleeder valve. Then, slowly release the lever or pedal.
e. Repeat this sequence to remove as much brake fluid as possible.

2B. When using a vacuum pump, perform the following:
a. Assemble the vacuum pump and connect it to the caliper bleeder valve (**Figure 111**) following the manufacturer's instructions.
b. Operate the pump lever five to ten times to create a vacuum in the line. Then, open the bleeder valve with a wrench. Brake fluid will begin to flow into the bottle connected to the vacuum pump.
c. When the fluid draining from the system begins to slow down and before the gauge on the pump (if so equipped) reads zero, close the bleeder valve.
d. Repeat this sequence to remove as much brake fluid as possible.

3. Close the bleeder valve and disconnect the hose or vacuum pump.
4. If necessary, use a syringe to remove any brake fluid remaining in the bottom of the master cylinder reservoir.
5. Reinstall the diaphragm and cover.
6. Discard the brake fluid removed from the system.

BRAKE BLEEDING

Whenever air enters the brake system, bleed the system to remove the air. Air can enter the system when the brake fluid level drops too low, after flushing the system or when a union bolt or brake hose is loosened or removed. Air in the brake system will increase lever or pedal travel while causing it to feel spongy and less responsive. Under excessive conditions, it can cause complete loss of the brake pressure.

NOTE
When bleeding the brakes, check the fluid level in the master cylinder frequently. If the reservoir runs dry, air will enter the system.

Bleed the brakes manually or with a vacuum pump. Both methods are described in this section.

When adding brake fluid during the bleeding process, use new DOT 4 brake fluid. Do not reuse brake fluid drained from the system or use a silicone based DOT 5 brake fluid. Because brake fluid is very harmful to most surfaces, wipe up any spills immediately with soapy water.

Manual Bleeding

This procedure describes how to bleed the brake system manually by using the master cylinder as a pump. An empty bottle, length of clear hose and a wrench are required (**Figure 109**).

1. Make sure the brake system union bolts are tight.

CAUTION
Dirt that is left inside the bleeder valve opening can enter the brake system. This could plug the brake hose and contaminate the brake fluid.

2. Remove the dust cap from the brake bleeder valve and clean the valve and its opening of all dirt and debris. If a dust cap was not used, use a thin screwdriver or similar tool and compressed air to remove all dirt from inside the bleeder valve opening.
3. Connect the clear hose to the bleeder valve (**Figure 111**) on the caliper. Place the other end of the hose into a container filled with enough new brake fluid to keep the hose end submerged. Loop the hose higher than the bleeder valve to prevent air from being drawn into the caliper during bleeding.

CAUTION
Cover all parts that could become damaged by brake fluid. Wash spilled brake fluid from any surface immediately, as it will damage the finish. Use soapy water and rinse completely.

4. Remove the master cylinder cover and diaphragm. Fill the reservoir to the upper level.
5. Apply the brake lever or brake pedal, and open the bleeder valve. This will force air and brake fluid from the brake system. Close the bleeder valve before the brake lever or pedal reaches its maximum limit or before brake fluid stops flowing from the bleeder valve. Do not release the brake lever or pedal while the bleeder valve is open. If the system was previously drained or new parts installed, brake fluid will not start draining from the system until after several repeated attempts are made. This is normal.

NOTE

As the brake fluid enters the system, the level will drop in the master cylinder reservoir. Maintain the level at the upper level of the reservoir to prevent air from being drawn into the system.

Repeat the process until the brake fluid exiting the stem is clear, with no air bubbles. If the system is fficult to bleed, tap the master cylinder and caliper ousing with a soft-faced mallet to dislodge internal r bubbles so they can be released.

NOTE

If the brake lever or pedal feel firm, indicating that air has been bled from the system, yet air bubbles are still visible in the hose connected to the bleeder valve, air may be entering the hose from its connection around the bleeder valve.

The system is bled when the brake lever or pedal els firm, and there are no air bubbles exiting the stem. Close the bleeder valve and remove the eed hose.

WARNING

Do not ride the vehicle until both brakes operate correctly. Make sure the brake lever and pedal travel is not excessive and they do not feel spongy. If either condition exists, repeat the bleeding procedure.

If necessary, add brake fluid to correct the level the master cylinder reservoir. It must be above the w level line.

acuum Bleeding

This procedure describes how to bleed the brake stem with a vacuum pump like the Mityvac pump **igure 110**).

Make sure the brake system union bolts are tight.

CAUTION

Dirt left inside the bleeder valve opening can enter the brake system. This could plug the brake hose and contaminate the brake fluid.

Remove the dust cap from the bleeder valve and ean the valve and its opening of all dirt and other bris. If a dust cap was not used, use a thin screwiver or similar tool and compressed air to remove l dirt from inside the bleeder valve opening.

CAUTION

Cover all parts that could be damaged by brake fluid. Wash any spilled brake fluid from any surface immediately, as it will damage the finish. Use soapy water and rinse completely.

3. Remove the master cylinder cover and diaphragm. Fill the reservoir to the upper level.
4. Assemble the vacuum tool according to the manufacturer's instructions.
5. Attach the pump hose to the bleeder valve (**Figure 111**).

NOTE

When bleeding the system with a vacuum pump, the brake fluid level in the master cylinder will drop rapidly. This is especially true for the rear reservoir because it contains a small amount of brake fluid. Stop often and check the brake fluid level. Maintain the level at the upper level to prevent air from being drawn into the system.

6. Operate the pump handle five to ten times to create a vacuum in the line between the pump and caliper. Then, open the bleeder valve with a wrench. Doing so forces air and brake fluid from the system. Close the bleeder valve before the brake fluid stops flowing from the valve or before the master cylinder reservoir runs empty. If the vacuum pump is equipped with a vacuum gauge, close the bleeder valve before the vacuum reading on the gauge reaches 0 HG of vacuum.
7. Repeat the process until the brake fluid exiting the system is clear, with no air bubbles. If the system is difficult to bleed, tap the master cylinder and caliper housing with a soft-faced mallet to dislodge the internal air bubbles so they can be released.
8. The system is bled when the brake lever or pedal feels firm, and there are no air bubbles exiting the system. Tighten the bleeder valve and disconnect the pump hose.

WARNING

Do not ride the vehicle until both brakes operate correctly. Make sure brake lever and pedal travel is not excessive and they do not feel spongy. If either condition exists, repeat the bleeding procedure.

9. If necessary, add fluid to correct the level in the master cylinder reservoir. It must be above the low level line.

Table 1 BRAKE SERVICE SPECIFICATIONS

	New mm (in.)	Service limit mm (in.)
Brake disc thickness		
Front	3.5 (0.138)	3.0 (0.12)
Rear		
2006 models	3.6 (0.142)	3.0 (0.12)
2007-2012 models	4.0 (0.16)	3.0 (0.12)
2013-on models	4.0 (0.16)	3.5 (0.14)
Brake disc runout	–	0.15 (0.006)
Brake pad thickness		
Front	4.3 (0.17)	1.0 (0.039)
Rear		
2006-2012 models	5.6 (0.22)	1.0 (0.039)
2013-on models	5.4 (0.21)	1.0 (0.039)
Caliper bore inside diameter		
Front	25.4 (1.000)	–
Rear		
2006-2012 models	32.03 (1.26)	–
2013-on models	25.40 (1.00)	–
Master cylinder bore inside diameter		
Front and rear	12.7 (0.500)	–

Table 2 BRAKE TORQUE SPECIFICATIONS

	N•m	in.-lb.	ft.-lb.
Bleeder valve	6	53	–
Brake tee fitting mounting bolt	10	88	–
Brake line nuts	19	168	–
Caliper pad pins	17	–	12.5
Footrest bolts	78	–	57
Front brake disc mounting bolts	28	–	21
Front caliper mounting bolts	28	–	21
Front caliper pad pins	17	150	–
Front caliper union bolt	27	–	20
Front master cylinder bracket bolts	7	62	–
Front master cylinder union bolt	27	–	20
Parking brake housing mounting bolts	22	195	--
Rear brake disc mounting bolts	33	–	24
Rear caliper mounting bolts			
2006-2012 models	34	–	25
2013-on models	43	–	31
Rear caliper pad pins	17	150	–
Rear caliper union bolt	30	–	22
Rear master cylinder mounting bolts	20	177	–
Rear master cylinder union bolt	30	–	22

CHAPTER FIFTEEN

BODY

This chapter contains removal and installation procedures for body and frame components.

PLASTIC SCREW FASTENERS

The ATV is equipped with plastic screw assemblies (**Figure 1**) to secure many body components to
the frame or other parts. The center screw (A, **Figure**
1) forces a set of fingers (B) to expand which secures
the adjacent parts together.

To remove the fastener, fully back out the screw.
If necessary, hold the fastener body while backing
out the screw. Pull the fastener assembly out of the
secured parts.

To install the fastener, make sure the screw is
backed out so the fingers are closed. Push the fastener into the holes in the parts to be secured. Turn
the screw in until it bottoms. Make sure the parts are
secure. If not, it may be necessary to install a new
fastener.

RETAINING TABS

Some panels are equipped with directional tabs
(**Figure 2**). The tab fits into a slot in the adjoining
panel. Be sure to move the panel properly to disengage or engage the tab in the slot.

SEAT

Removal/Installation

The seat latch (**Figure 3**) is located forward of the
taillight.

1. Pull rearward the bottom of the seat latch and
raise the rear of the seat.
2. Pull back on the seat to disengage the prongs from
the front mount.
3. To install the seat, align the front pocket (A,
Figure 4) and prong (B) on the seat with the post and
opening on the ATV.
4. Slide the seat forward and lock the rear of the seat
into place.
5. Lightly lift the rear of the seat to ensure it is
locked into place.

FRONT FENDER PANEL

Removal/Installation

1. Unscrew the front fender panel retaining screws
(A, **Figure 5**).

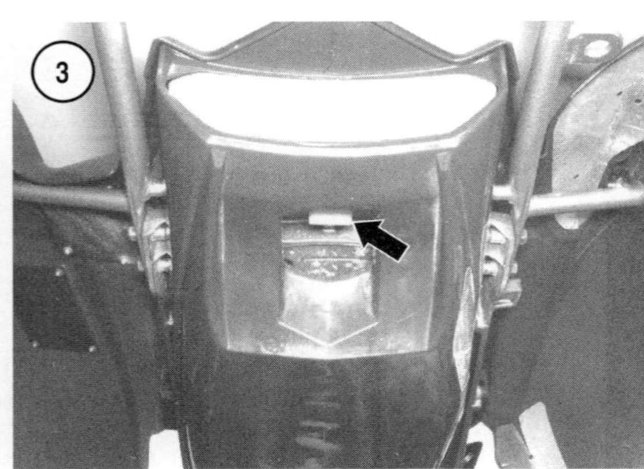

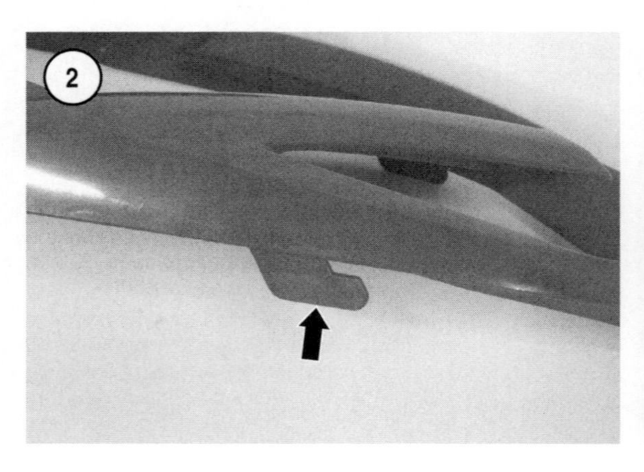

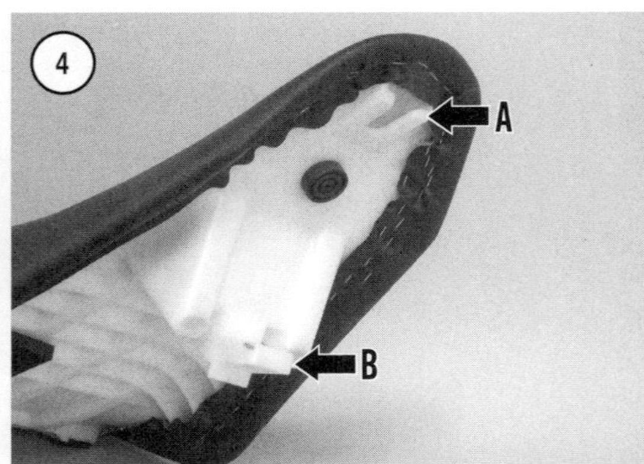

2. Disengage the panel hooks from the slots in the front fender and remove the front fender panel (B, **Figure 5**).
3. Reverse the removal steps to install the front fender panel.

FUEL TANK COVER

Removal/Installation

1. Remove the seat as described in this chapter.
2. Remove the front fender panel as described in this chapter.
3. Remove the fuel tank gas cap (A, **Figure 6**).
4. Remove the plastic screw fasteners (B, **Figure 6**).
5. Disengage the cover retaining tabs by moving the cover (C, **Figure 6**) up and to the rear.
6. Remove the fuel tank cover.
7. Reverse the removal steps to install the fuel tank cover.

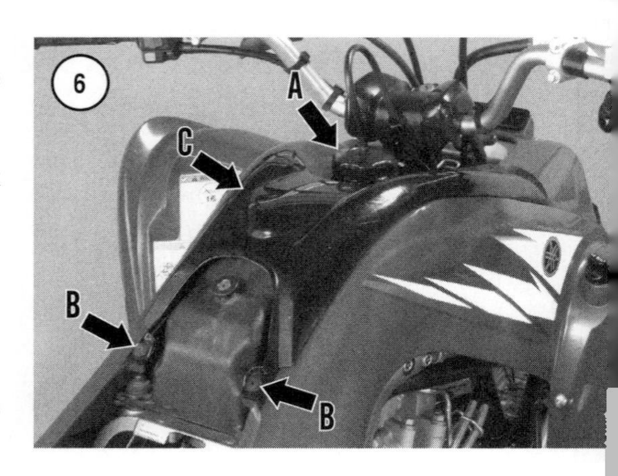

FRONT FENDER

Removal/Installation

1. Remove the fuel tank cover as described in this chapter.

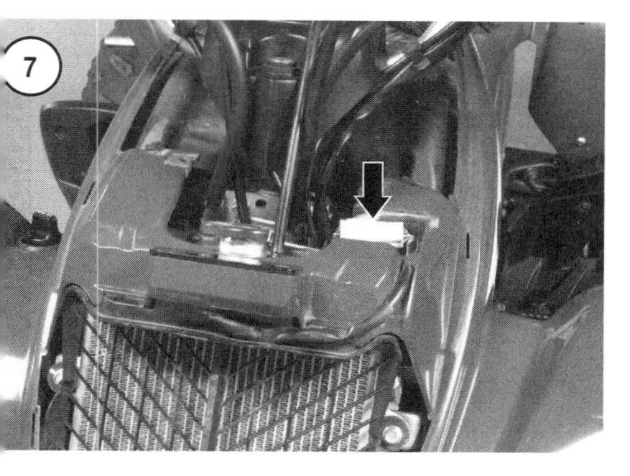

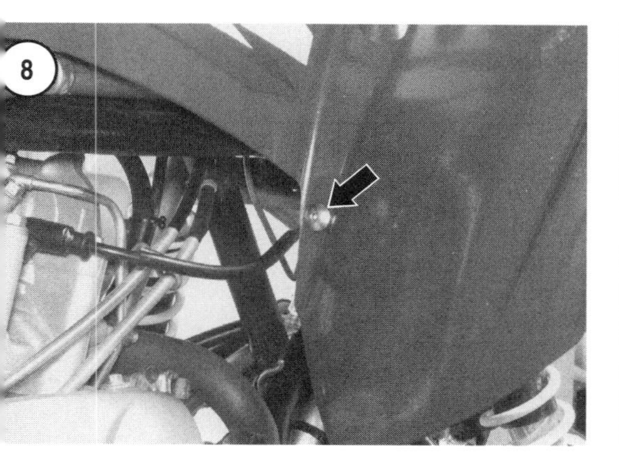

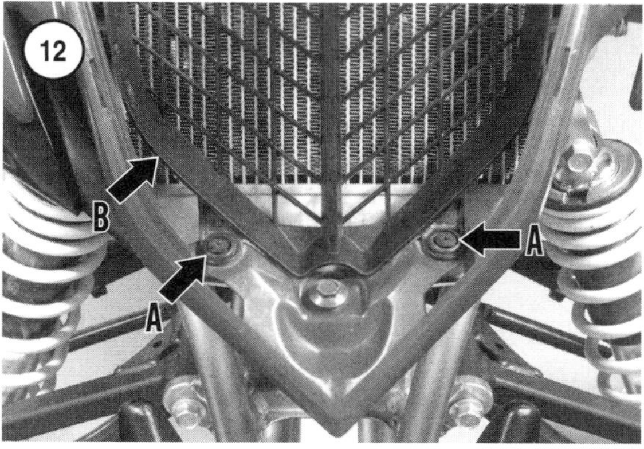

2. Remove the front fender panel as described in this chapter.
3. Remove the headlights as described in Chapter Nine.
4. Disconnect the indicator light panel connector (**Figure 7**).
5. Remove the fender backsplash panel bolt (**Figure 8**) on both sides.
6. Remove the mounting bolts (**Figure 9**) and flanged collars that secure the front fender and rear fender to the frame.
7. Remove the inner fender mounting bolt (**Figure 10**) and flanged collar on each side.
8. Remove the front fender mounting bolt (**Figure 11**).
9. Remove the front fender.
10. Reverse the removal steps to install the front fender while noting the following:
    a. Tighten the inner bolts (**Figure 10**) to 10 N•m (89 in.-lb.).
    b. Tighten the remaining fender mounting bolts to 7 N•m (62 in.-lb.).

FRONT GRILLE

Removal/Installation

1. Remove the plastic screw fasteners (A, **Figure 12**).

2. Remove the grille by pulling out the lower portion of the front grille (B, **Figure 12**) and releasing the locating tabs at the top of the grille.
3. Reverse the removal steps to install the front grille.

HANDLEBAR COVER

Removal/Installation

1. Pull the fuel tank cap vent hose (**Figure 13**) out of the handlebar cover.
2. Pull up the handlebar cover (**Figure 14**) to dislodge it from the handlebar.
3. If necessary, remove the ignition switch as described in Chapter Nine.
4. Reverse the removal steps to install the handlebar cover.

13

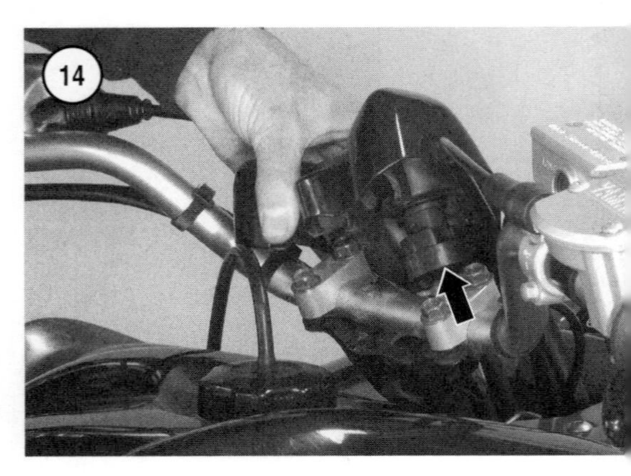
14

REAR LOWER COVER

Removal/Installation

1. Remove the front bolt (**Figure 15**) and flanged collar on each side.
2. Push the cover rearward so it disengages from the rubber mount.
3. Disconnect the taillight connector (**Figure 16**) and remove the cover.
4. Reverse the removal steps to install the rear lower cover. Make sure the rubber mount (**Figure 17**) is in good condition.

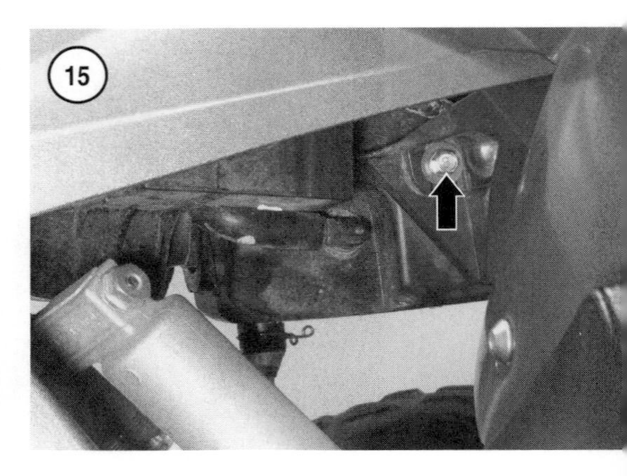
15

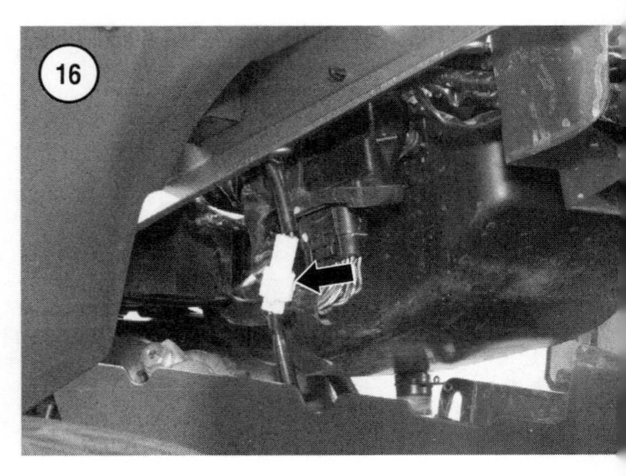
16

REAR FENDER

Removal/Installation

1. Remove the seat as described in this chapter.
2. Remove the mounting bolts (**Figure 9**) and flanged collars that secure the front fender and rear fender to the frame.
3. Disengage the front fender from the rear fender so the rear fender can be removed.
4. Remove the rear lower cover as described in this chapter.

NOTE
It is not necessary to disconnect the relays. Dismount the relays from their mounting brackets.

5. Remove the radiator fan relay (A, **Figure 18**), starting circuit cutoff relay (B), headlight relay (C) and fuse box (D) as described in Chapter Nine.
6. Remove the upper rear fender mounting bolt (E, **Figure 18**).

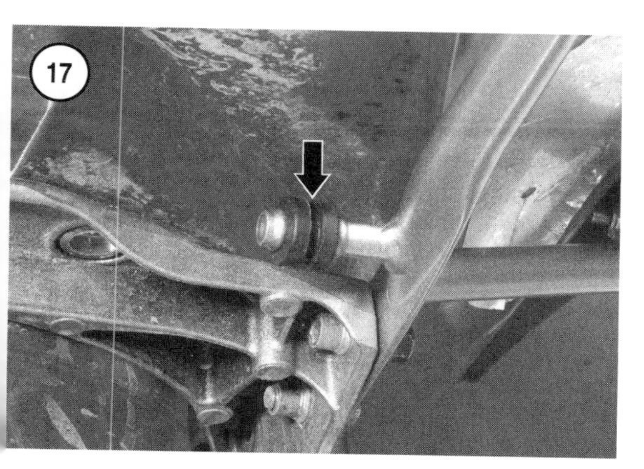

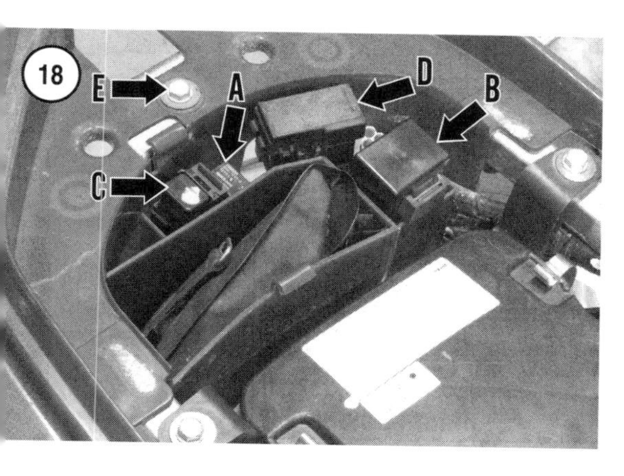

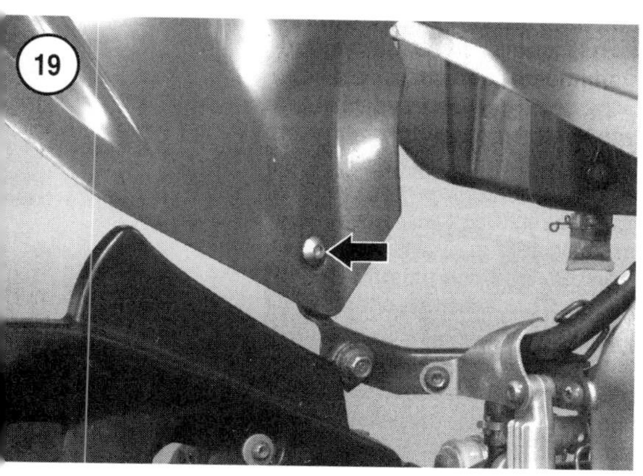

7. Remove the lower rear fender mounting bolt (**Figure 19**) on each side.
8. Remove the bolt (A, **Figure 20**) securing the fender to the bracket on each side.
9. While routing the wiring through the rear fender, remove the rear fender.
10. Reverse the removal steps to install the rear fender while noting the following:
   a. Tighten the upper rear fender mounting bolt (E, **Figure 18**) to 7 N•m (62 in.-lb.).
   b. Tighten the lower rear fender mounting bolts (**Figure 19**) to 7 N•m (62 in.-lb.)
   c. Tighten the rear fender-to-bracket mounting bolts (A, **Figure 20**) to 9 N•m (80 in.-lb.).

REAR GUARD

Removal/Installation

1. Remove the rear lower cover as described in this chapter.
2. Remove the rear fender-to-bracket mounting bolt (A, **Figure 20**) on both sides.
3. Remove the rear guard mounting bolts (B, **Figure 20**) on both sides.
4. Remove the rear guard.
5. Reverse the removal steps to install the rear guard while noting the following:
   a. Tighten the rear guard mounting bolts to 32 N•m (23 ft.-lb.).
   b. Tighten the rear fender-to-bracket mounting bolts to 7 N•m (62 in.-lb.).

OIL TANK

NOTE

Removal of the left exhaust pipe is necessary to provide clearance for oil tank removal. In some instances, removal of just the left exhaust pipe may be possible. But, rust or damage may require complete exhaust system removal.

Removal/Installation With Oil Hoses

1. Drain the engine oil as described in Chapter Three.
2. Disassemble the exhaust system as described in Chapter Four to remove the left exhaust pipe.
3. Detach the oil tank breather hose (A, **Figure 21**) from the oil tank.
4. Remove the retaining bolt (A, **Figure 22**), and detach the oil tank inlet hose fitting (B) from the engine. Account for the hollow dowel (A, **Figure 23**)

and O-ring (B) which may remain in the fitting or engine.

5. Unscrew the oil tank outlet hose fitting (C, **Figure 23**) from the engine.
6. Remove the oil tank mounting bolt (**Figure 24**) on each side.
7. Detach any clamps or holders securing the oil hoses.
8. Remove the oil tank and oil hoses.
9. If necessary to remove the oil outlet hose, remove the bolts securing the fitting to the bottom of the oil tank and separate the fitting from the tank.
10. If necessary to remove the oil inlet hose, remove the retaining bolt (B, **Figure 21**), and detach the fitting (C) from the oil tank. Account for the hollow dowel (A, **Figure 25**) and O-ring (B) which may remain in the fitting or tank.
11. If necessary, clean and inspect the oil tank.
12. Inspect and, if necessary, clean the screen (A, **Figure 26**) on the outlet fitting.
13. Reverse the removal steps to install the oil tank while noting the following:
    a. Install new O-rings (B, **Figure 23** and B, **Figure 26**).
    b. Tighten the bolts securing the outlet hose fitting to the oil tank to 10 N•m (89 in.-lb.).
    c. Tighten the oil outlet hose fitting at the engine to 35 N•m (26 ft.-lb.).
    d. Tighten the bolts securing the oil inlet hose fittings at the oil tank or engine to 10 N•m (89 in.-lb.).
    e. Fill the engine and oil tank with oil as described in Chapter Three.

Removal/Installation Without Oil Hoses

1. Drain the engine oil as described in Chapter Three.
2. Disassemble the exhaust system as described in Chapter Four to remove the left exhaust pipe.
3. Detach the oil tank breather hose (A, **Figure 21**) from the oil tank.

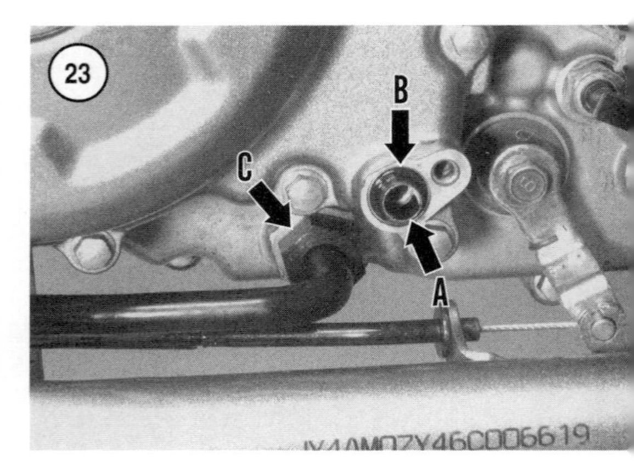

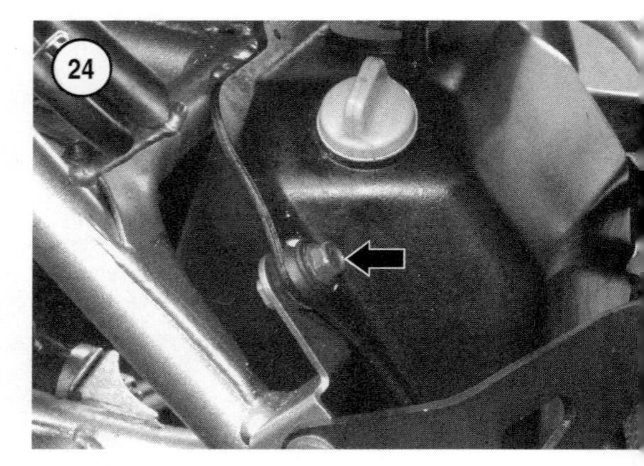

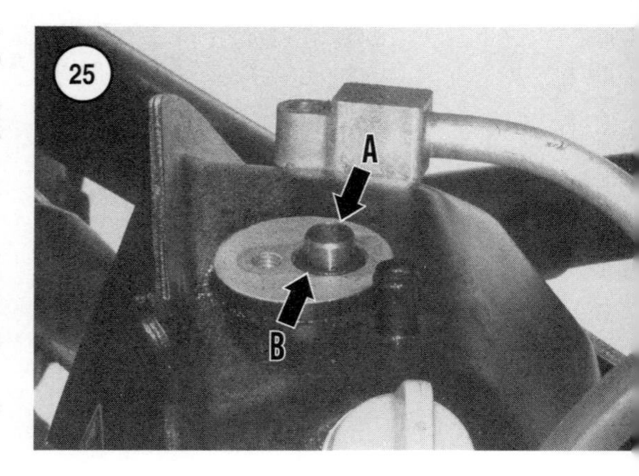

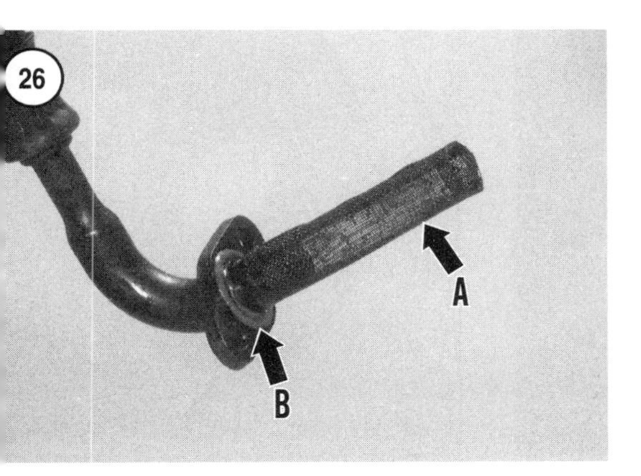

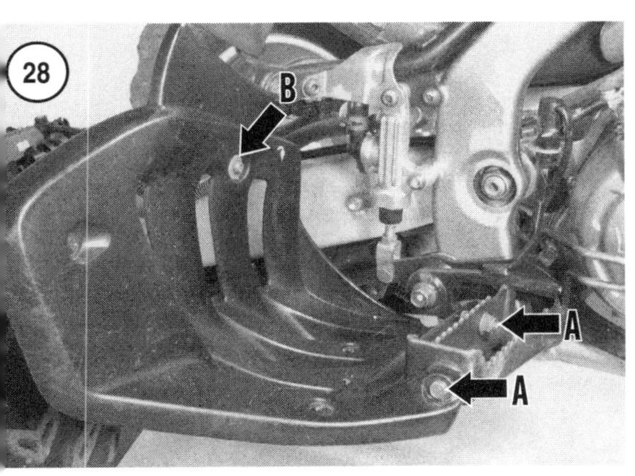

4. Remove the retaining bolt (B, **Figure 21**), and detach the oil tank inlet hose fitting (C) from the oil tank. Account for the hollow dowel (A, **Figure 25**) and O-ring (B) which may remain in the fitting or tank.
5. Remove the oil tank mounting bolt **(Figure 24)** on each side.

NOTE
The oil tank must be raised for access to the oil outlet hose fitting bolts.

6. Raise the oil tank and remove the bolts (**Figure 27**) securing the oil outlet hose fitting to the bottom of the oil tank and separate the fitting from the tank.
7. Remove the oil tank.
8. Clean and inspect the oil tank.
9. Inspect and, if necessary, clean the screen (A, **Figure 26**) on the outlet fitting.
10. Reverse the removal steps to install the oil tank while noting the following:
   a. Install new O-rings (B, **Figure 23** and B, **Figure 26**).
   b. Tighten the bolts securing the outlet hose fitting at the oil tank to 10 N•m (89 in.-lb.).
   c. Tighten the bolt securing the inlet hose fitting at the oil tank to 10 N•m (89 in.-lb.).
   d. Fill the engine and oil tank with oil as described in Chapter Three.

FOOT PROTECTORS

Removal/Installation

1. Remove the bolts securing the foot protector to the footrest (A, **Figure 28**).
2. Remove the rear retaining bolt (B, **Figure 28**).
3. Remove the foot protector.
4. Reverse the removal steps to install the foot protector while noting the following:
   a. Tighten the 6-mm mounting bolt to 13 N•m (115 in.-lb.).
   b. Tighten the 8-mm mounting bolts to 16 N•m (12 ft.-lb.).

RIGHT FOOTREST

The right footrest holds the rear brake pedal in place. Refer to rear brake pedal service in Chapter Fourteen.

LEFT FOOTREST

Removal/Installation

1. Remove the foot protector as described in this chapter.
2. Remove the footrest retaining bolts (**Figure 29**).

3. Remove the footrest.
4. Reverse the removal steps to install the footrest. Tighten the footrest bolts to 78 N•m (58 ft.-lb.).

ENGINE SKIDPLATE

Removal/Installation

1. Detach the plastic straps (A, **Figure 30**) securing the rear of the skidplate to the frame.
2. Remove the four bolts securing the skidplate (B, **Figure 30**) to the frame.
3. Remove the skidplate.
4. Reverse the removal steps to install the skidplate. Apply threadlock to the bolt threads. Tighten the bolts to 7 N•m (62 in.-lb.).

SWING ARM SKIDPLATE

Removal/Installation

1. Remove the four bolts securing the skidplate (**Figure 31**) to the swing arm.
2. Remove the skidplate.
3. Reverse the removal steps to install the swing arm skidplate. Tighten the bolts to 7 N•m (62 in.-lb.).

Table 1 BODY TORQUE SPECIFICATIONS

	N•m	in.-lb.	ft.-lb.
Engine skidplate	7	62	–
Footrest bolts	78	–	58
Foot protector mounting bolts			
6-mm	13	115	–
8-mm	16	–	12
Front bumper bolts	12	106	–
Front fender	See text		
Oil inlet hose fitting on engine	10	89	–
Oil inlet hose fitting on oil tank	10	89	–
Oil outlet hose fitting on engine	35	–	26
Oil tank outlet hose fitting	10	89	
Rear fender mounting bolts	7	62	–
Rear fender-to-bracket bolts	9	80	–
Rear guard mounting bolts	32	–	24
Swing arm skidplate	7	62	–

INDEX

A

Air induction system, 2015-on models 89
Alternator 201
  specifications 219
Axle, rear 257
  hub 262

B

Battery 198
  maintenance 75
  negative terminal 198
  specifications 219
Body
cover, rear, lower 312
  engine, skidplate 316
  fasteners, plastic screw 309
  fender
    front 310
      panel 309
    rear 312
  foot protectors 315
  footrest
    left 315
    right 315
  fuel, tank, cover 310
  grille, front 311
  guard, rear 313
  handlebar, cover 312
  oil tank 313
  retaining tabs 309
  seat 309
  skidplate
    engine 316
    swing arm 316
  swing arm, skidplate 316
  torque 316
Brakes
  bleeding 306
  caliper
    front 276
    rear
      2006-2012 models 287
      2013-on models 292
  disc 302
  draining 305
  fluid selection 273
  front
    caliper 276
    hose, line replacement 303
    master cylinder 281
    pads, ... 275
  hose
    replacement, rear 304
    line replacement, front 303
  maintenance 63
  master cylinder
    front 281
    rear 298
  pads
    front 275
    rear 284
  pedal, rear 301

Brakes (continued)
rear
caliper
2006-2012 models . . . 287
2013-on models . . . 292
hose replacement . . . 304
master cylinder . . . 298
pads . . . 284
pedal . . . 301
service . . . 273
specifications . . . 308
torque . . . 308
troubleshooting . . . 40

C

Camshaft
cam chain and guide . . . 106, 131
rocker arms . . . 100
Charging system . . . 201
specifications . . . 219
Clutch . . . 149
cable . . . 162
reverse . . . 162
Clutch, lever . . . 61
release lever assembly . . . 157
shift
external mechanism . . . 158
reverse lever . . . 161
specifications . . . 163
torque . . . 163
troubleshooting . . . 37
Control cable, inspection and lubrication . . . 60
Cooling
coolant
reservoir . . . 225
temperature sensor . . . 226
cooling system . . . 212
hoses, clams . . . 222
maintenance . . . 76
precautions/inspection . . . 221
pressure test . . . 222
radiator . . . 224
fan . . . 226
sensor, coolant temperature . . . 226
specifications . . . 229
thermostat . . . 223
torque . . . 230
water pump . . . 226
Cover, rear, lower . . . 312
Crankcase . . . 139
breather hoses, maintenance . . . 78
cover
left . . . 126
right . . . 132
position sensor . . . 191
seal and bearing replacement . . . 144
Crankshaft . . . 146
balancer drive gears . . . 137
position sensor . . . 214
Cylinder . . . 111

D

Diagnostic codes . . . 44
Drive chain . . . 237
maintenance . . . 67
specifications . . . 239
torque . . . 239

E

Electrical
alternator . . . 201
battery . . . 198
negative terminal . . . 198
charging system . . . 201
component replacement . . . 197
connectors . . . 198
continuity testing . . . 197
cooling system . . . 212
electronic diagnostic system . . . 33
fundamentals . . . 18
fuses . . . 217
fuse box . . . 218
ignition . . . 202
specifications, starter system . . . 219
lights . . . 210
sensor, crankshaft position, . . . 214
specifications
alternator and charging system . . . 219
battery . . . 219
bulb . . . 219
fuse . . . 220
ignition system . . . 219
starter system . . . 219
test . . . 220
starter . . . 203
relay . . . 209
starting circuit cutoff system . . . 208
switches . . . 214
torque . . . 220
troubleshooting
electronic diagnostic system . . . 33
engine, starting system . . . 40
testing . . . 40
wiring diagrams . . . 323
Engine
leakdown test . . . 37
lower end . . . 122
break-in . . . 147
camshaft, chain and guides . . . 131

crankcase 139
cover
left 126
right. 132
seal and bearing replacement 144
crankshaft 146
balancer drive gears 137
flywheel (alternator rotor) and starter clutch. 128
oil, pump 133
servicing engine in frame 122
specifications, service 148
starter idle gear. 128
torque. 148
limiter 127
noise 36
oil 55
performance 32
skidplate 316
starting 29
troubleshooting. 40
does not 30
Engine, top end
air induction system, 2015-on models 89
camshaft
cam chain and guide 106
rocker arms 100
cylinder. 111
cylinder head 95, 119
exhaust 89
piston, rings 114
specifications. 119
camshaft 120
cylinder and piston 120
torque 121
valves 106
troubleshooting
leakdown test. 37
noise 36
performance 32
starting 29
does not 30
Exhaust 89
maintenance 83

F

Fasteners 4
plastic screw 309
Fender
front 310
panel 309
rear. 312
Footrest
left 315
right 315
Fuel
air box 192
delivery system, tests 180
ECU 188
fuel injection (FI) 178
injection, maintenance. 77
injector. 187
pump. 182
relay 184
sensor
coolant temperature 191
crankshaft position. 191
intake
air pressure. 190
air temperature. 191
lean-angle 191
speed 191
throttle position 189
specifications 196
electrical 196
tank 181
capacity 25
cover 310
plate 182
throttle
body 185
cable, replacement. 194
torque 196
Fuses 217
fusebox 218
specifications 220

G

General information
conversion formulas. 26
dimensions and weight 25
electrical, fundamentals 18
fasteners 4
manual organization 1
metric tap drill sizes 27
safety. 1
serial numbers and information labels. 3
service methods 18
shop supplies 6
storage 24
tools 8
measuring tools 14
warnings, cautions and notes 1
Grille, front 311

H

Handlebar 240
cover. 312

Hoses, clamps 222

I

Ignition system 202
specifications 219
starter 203
relay 209
specifications 219
starting circuit cutoff system 208
timing 80

L

Lights 210
Lubrication
control cable, inspection and lubrication 60
engine, oil 55
oil pump 133
recommended lubricants, fluids and capacities . 86
throttle cable, speed limiter adjustment 60

M

Maintenance
battery 75
brakes 63
clutch, lever 61
cooling 76
crankcase, breather hoses 78
drive chain 67
exhaust 83
fuel, injection 77
pre-ride inspection 54
reverse cable 62
schedule 84
specifications 85
steering 70
suspension
front 71
rear 74
tires, and wheels 69
torque 88
wheel, front, bearing inspection 70
fasteners 84

O

Oil
pump 133
tank 313

P

Piston, rings 114

R

Radiator 22
fan 22

S

Seat 30
Sensor
coolant temperature 19
coolant temperature 22
crankcase position 19
crankshaft, postion 21
intake
air pressure 19
air temperature 19
lean-angle 19
speed 19
throttle position 18
Serial numbers and information labels . . . . .
Shift, internal mechanism 16
Shock absorber 242, 26
Shock linkage 26
Skidplate, swing arm 31
Spark plug 7
Specifications
alternator 21
battery 21
brakes 30
charging system 21
clutch 16
cooling 22
drive chain 23
electrical
battery 21
bulb 21
fuse 22
ignition system 21
est 22
engine
lower end
service 14
top end 11
camshaft 12
cylinder and piston 12
cylinder head 11
fuel 19
electrical 19
ignition system 21
maintenance 8
steering 25
suspension
front 25
SE and all 2009-on models 8
rear 27
except SE and all 2009 models 8
SE and all 2009-on models 8

tires . . . 238
transmission . . . 177
shaft . . . 177
tune-up . . . 85
wheels . . . 238
teering
knuckle . . . 250
maintenance . . . 70
shaft . . . 254
specifications . . . 256
troubleshooting . . . 42
uspension
front
control arms . . . 251
handlebar . . . 240
maintenance . . . 71
shock absorbers . . . 242
specifications . . . 256
SE and all 2009-on models . . . 85
steering
knuckle . . . 250
shaft . . . 254
tie rods . . . 246
torque . . . 256
wheel hub, front . . . 243
rear
axle . . . 257
hub . . . 262
maintenance . . . 74
shock absorber . . . 265
shock linkage . . . 267
specifications . . . 272
except SE and all 2009 models . . .
SE and all 2009-on models . . . 87
swing arm . . . 268
torque . . . 272
wheel hub . . . 257
wing arm . . . 268
witches . . . 214

T

hermostat . . . 223
hrottle cable
replacement . . . 194
speed limiter adjustment . . . 60
ires . . . 232
inflation pressure . . . 239
maintenance . . . 69
specifications . . . 238
ools . . . 8
measuring tools . . . 14
orque
body . . . 316
brakes . . . 308
clutch . . . 163
cooling . . . 230
drive chain . . . 239
electrical . . . 220
engine
lower . . . 148
top end . . . 121
fuel . . . 196
general . . . 26
maintenance . . . 88
suspension
front . . . 256
rear . . . 272
wheel . . . 239
Transimission
countershaft . . . 171
reverse . . . 174
inspection . . . 174
mainshaft . . . 168
service . . . 164
shift
external mechanism, troubleshooting . . . 39
internal mechanism . . . 164
shift drum and forks . . . 176
specifications . . . 177
shaft . . . 177
troubleshooting . . . 39
shift, external mechanism . . . 39
Trouble code . . . 43
12 . . . 46
13 . . . 47
14 . . . 47
15 . . . 48
16 . . . 48
21 . . . 49
22 . . . 49
30 . . . 50
33 . . . 50
41 . . . 51
42 . . . 51
43 . . . 52
44 . . . 53
46 . . . 53
50 . . . 53
Troubleshooting
brakes . . . 40
clutch . . . 37
diagnostic codes . . . 44
electrical
electronic diagnostic system . . . 33
engine, starting system . . . 40
testing . . . 40
engine
leakdown test . . . 37
noise . . . 36
performance . . . 32

16

Troubleshooting (continued)
engine (continued)
starting 29
does not 30
steering and handling 42
transmission 39
shift, external mechanism 39
trouble codes. 43
troublecodes (continued)
12. 46
13. 47
14. 47
15. 48
16. 48
21. 49
22. 49
30. 50
33. 50
41. 51
42. 51
43. 52
44. 53
46. 53
50. 53
Tune-up 54
air filter 58
compression test 8
ignition, timing 8
spark plug 7
specifications 8
valve, clearance adjustment 8

V

Valves . . . . . 1(
clearance adjustment 8

W

Wheels. 23
bearing inspection 7
hub
front 24
rear 25
maintenance 6
specifications 23
sprockets. 23
torque 23
Wiring diagrams. 32

2006-2008 RAPTOR 700R MODELS

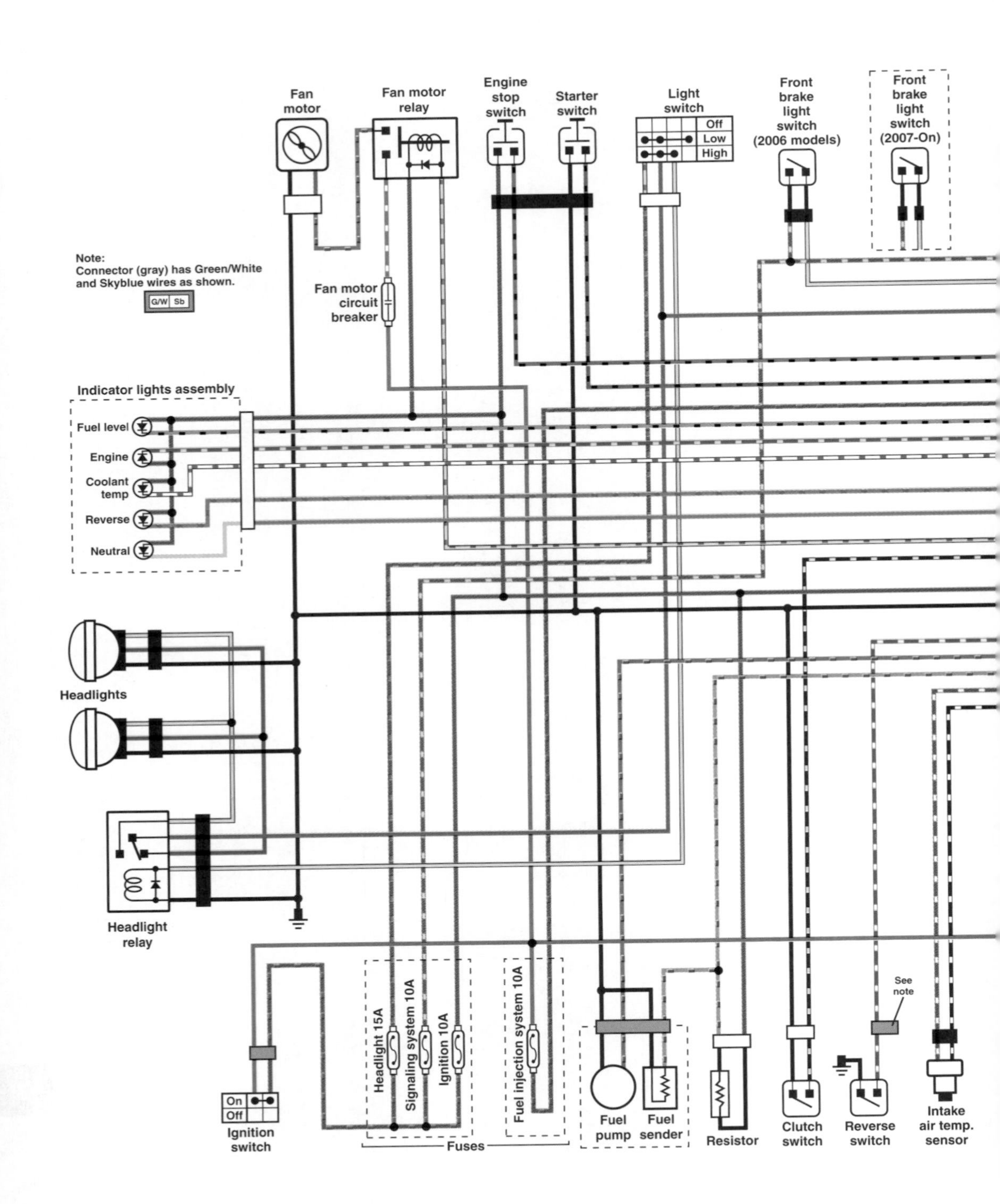

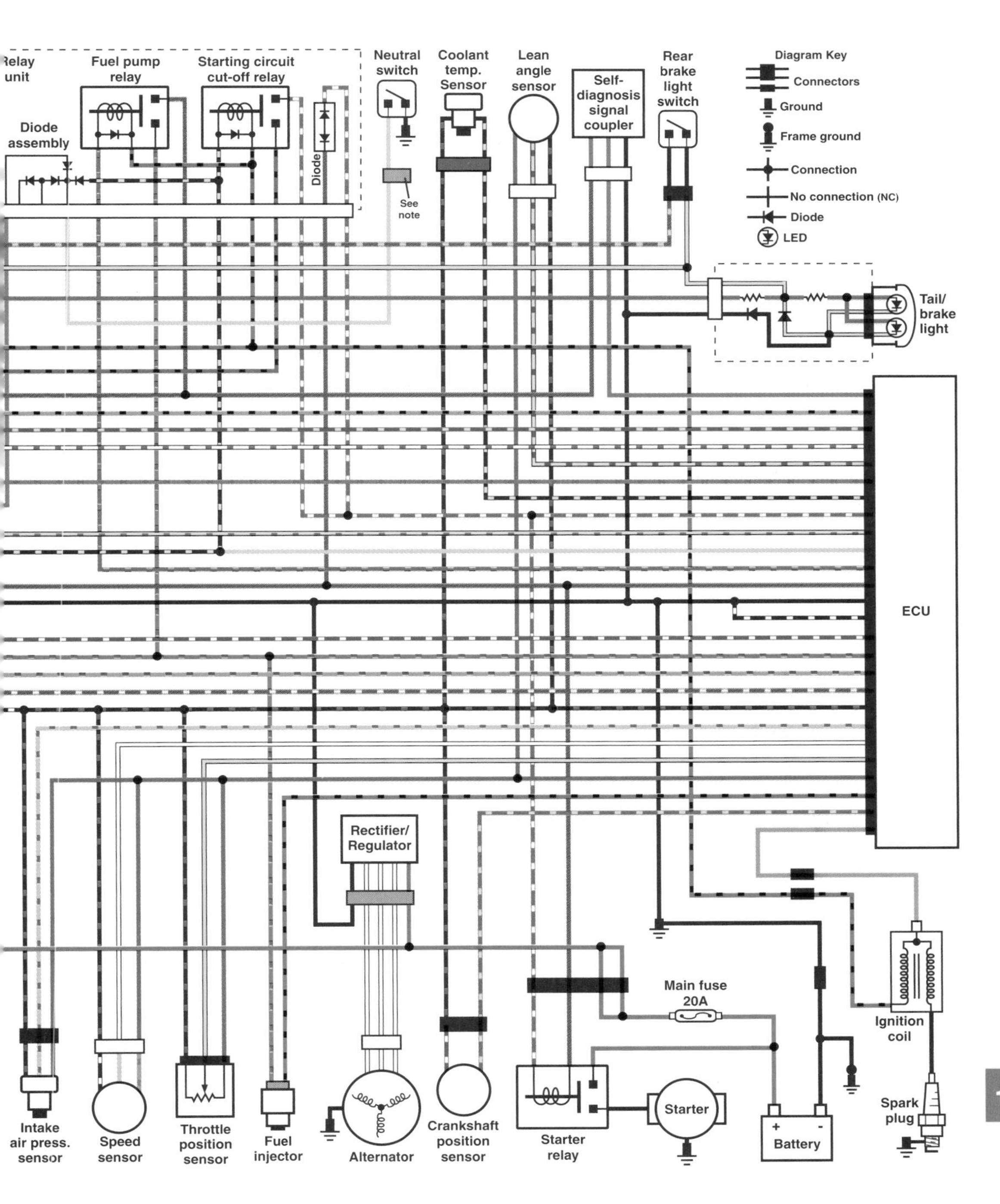
Relay unit
Fuel pump relay
Starting circuit cut-off relay
Diode assembly
Diode
Neutral switch
See note
Coolant temp. Sensor
Lean angle sensor
Self-diagnosis signal coupler
Rear brake light switch
Diagram Key
Connectors
Ground
Frame ground
Connection
No connection (NC)
Diode
LED
Tail/ brake light
ECU
Rectifier/ Regulator
Main fuse 20A
Ignition coil
Spark plug
Intake air press. sensor
Speed sensor
Throttle position sensor
Fuel injector
Alternator
Crankshaft position sensor
Starter relay
Starter
Battery

2009-2012 RAPTOR 700R MODELS

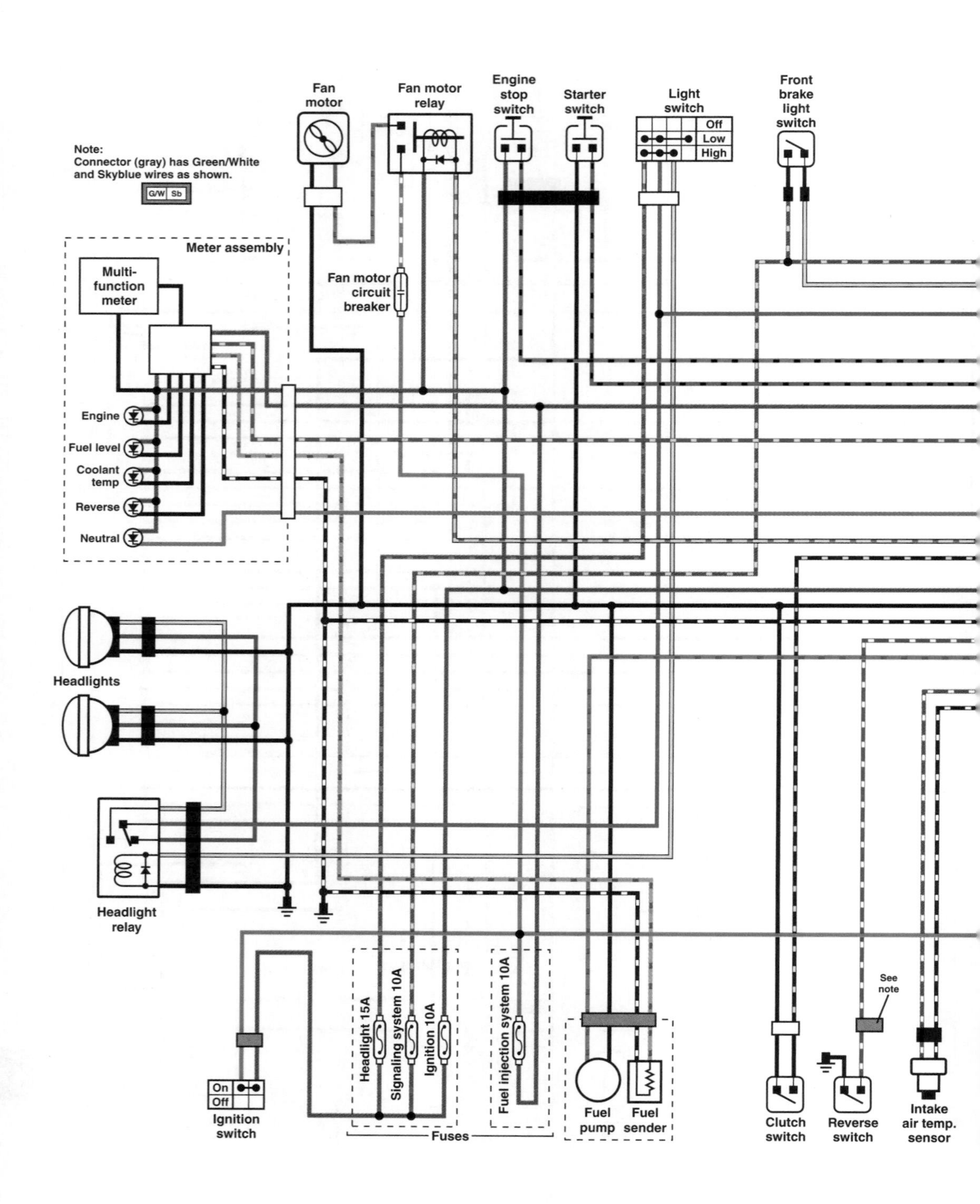

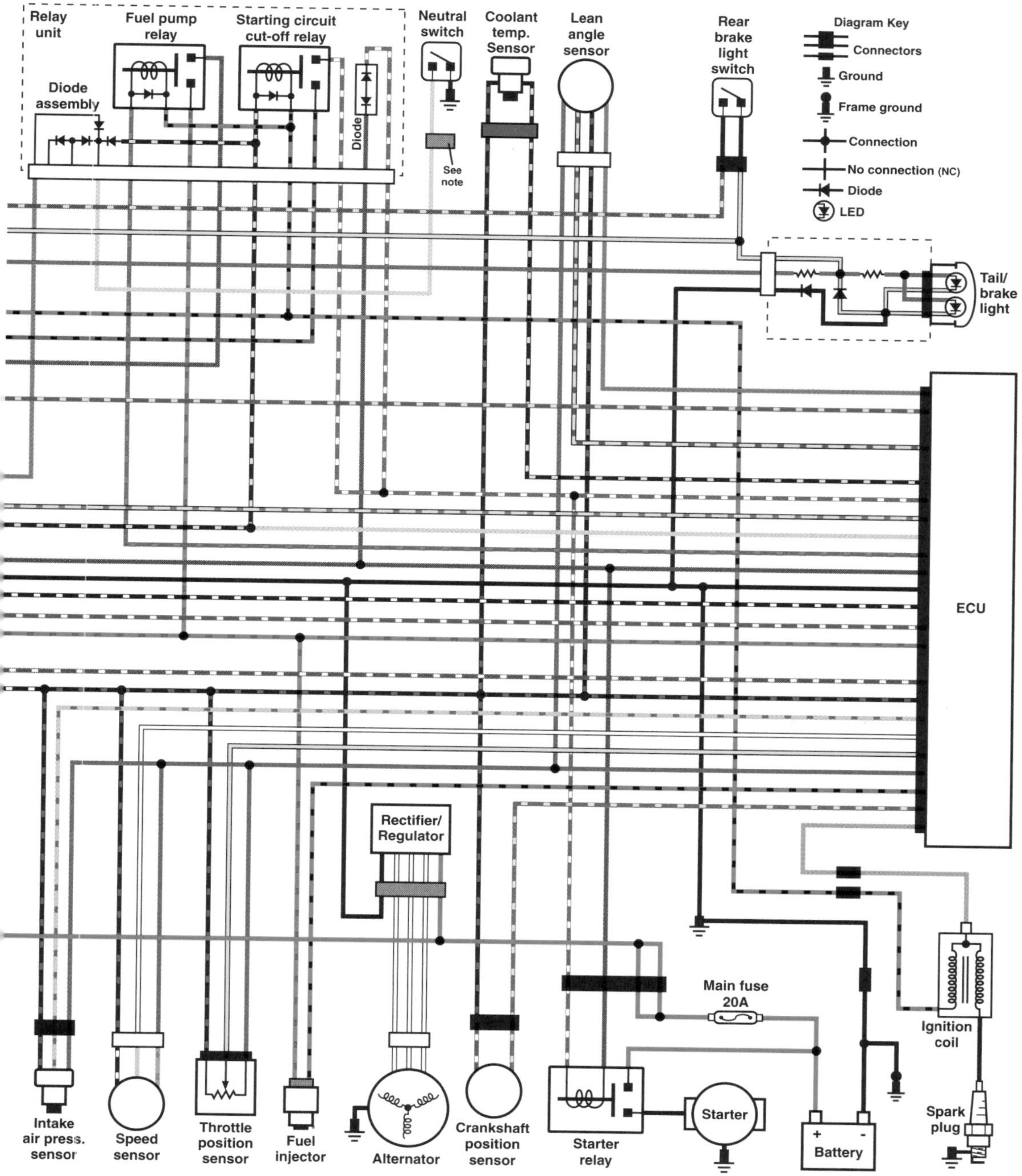

Relay unit
Fuel pump relay
Starting circuit cut-off relay
Diode assembly
Diode
Neutral switch
See note
Coolant temp. Sensor
Lean angle sensor
Rear brake light switch
Diagram Key
Connectors
Ground
Frame ground
Connection
No connection (NC)
Diode
LED
Tail/ brake light
ECU
Rectifier/ Regulator
Main fuse 20A
Ignition coil
Intake air press. sensor
Speed sensor
Throttle position sensor
Fuel injector
Alternator
Crankshaft position sensor
Starter relay
Starter
Battery
Spark plug

17

2013-2014 RAPTOR 700R MODELS

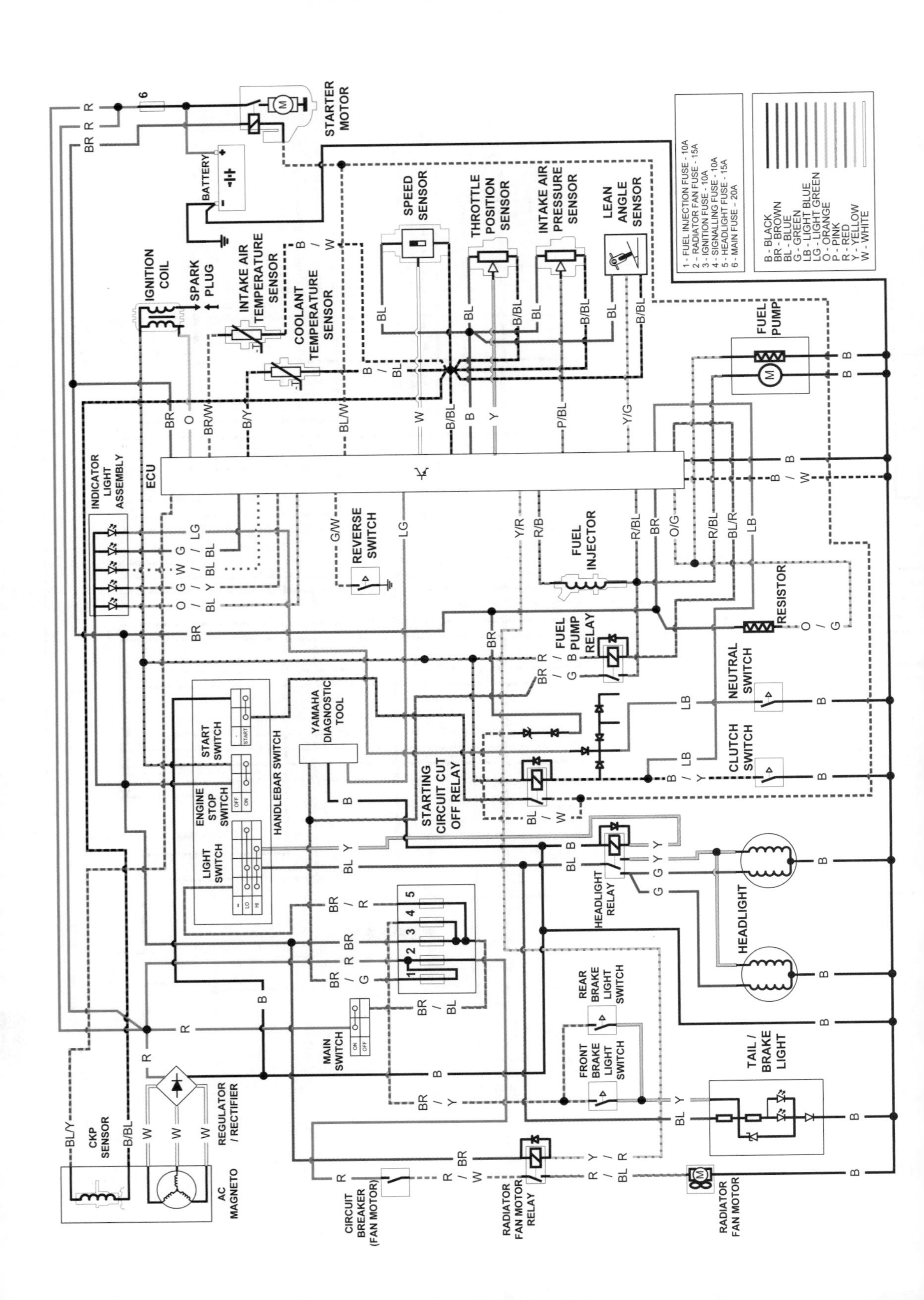

2015-2016 RAPTOR 700R MODELS

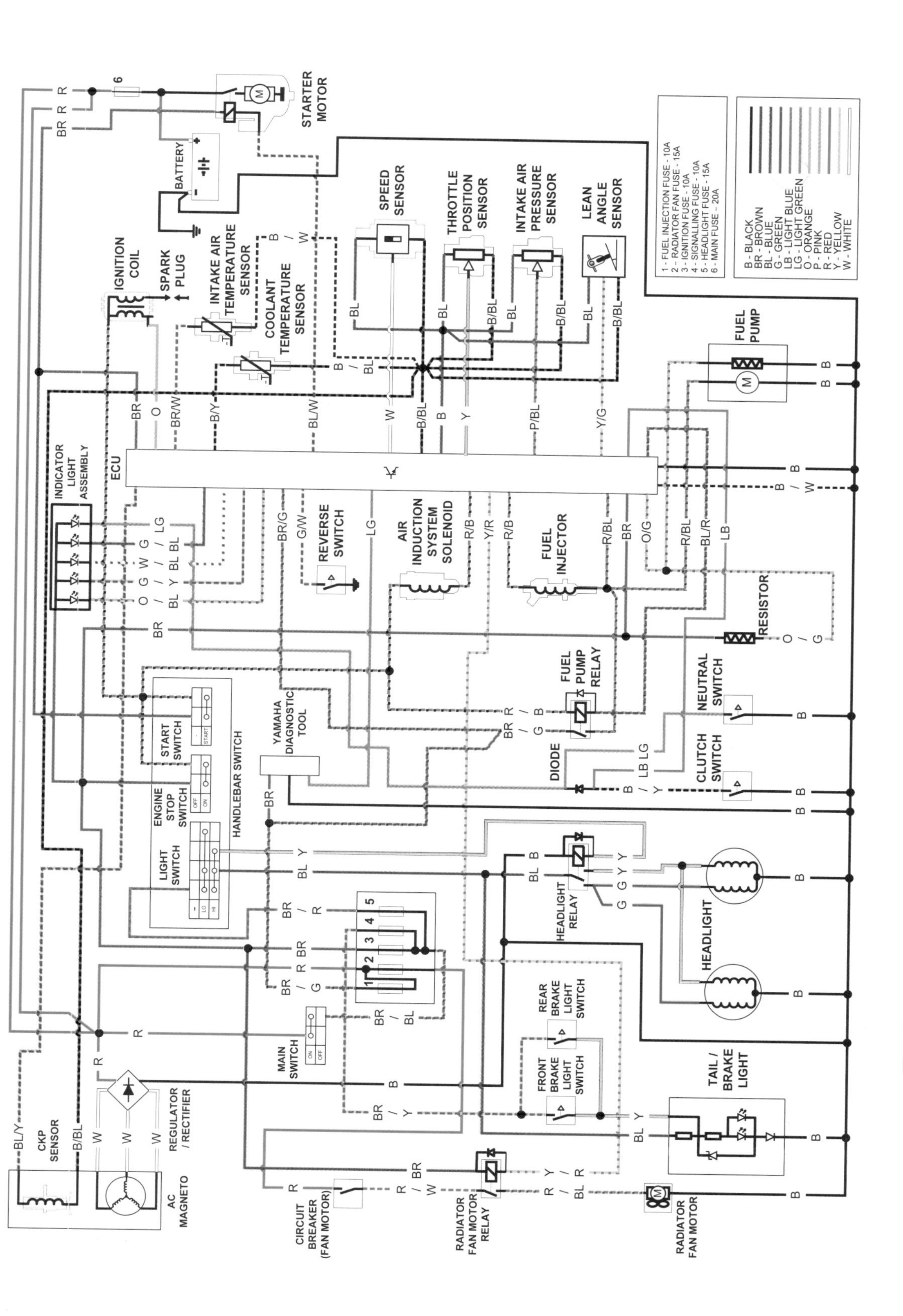